ABOUT THE EDITOR

☆☆☆☆☆☆☆☆☆☆☆☆☆☆☆☆☆☆☆☆☆☆☆☆☆☆☆☆☆☆☆☆☆☆

John Anthony Scott is a distinguished historian
and teacher. He holds a B.A. and M.A. from
Oxford University and a M.A. and Ph.D. from
Columbia University. He is currently Chairman
of the History Department, Fieldston School,
Riverdale, New York. He was coeditor of INTRO-
DUCTION TO CONTEMPORARY CIVILIZATION IN
THE WEST, and is the author of REPUBLICAN
IDEAS AND THE DEMOCRATIC TRADITION IN
FRANCE as well as other books and numerous
popular and scholarly articles.

In his own classes, Mr. Scott supplies students
with mimeographed copies of original documents
so that they can grapple firsthand with the issues
and ideas of history. All the materials in this book
have been so used. They were selected because
they have most excited student enthusiasm and
thought.

"Scott is the leading practitioner of the most
exciting new art in U.S. high school history
teaching—throwing away textbooks and going
to original sources."   —*Time Magazine*

☆☆☆☆☆☆☆☆☆☆☆☆☆☆☆☆☆☆☆☆☆☆☆☆☆☆☆☆☆☆☆☆☆☆

Living
Documents
in
American
History

☆☆☆☆☆☆☆☆☆☆☆☆☆☆☆☆☆☆☆☆☆☆☆☆☆☆☆☆☆☆

Edited and
with Introductions by
JOHN A. SCOTT

WASHINGTON SQUARE PRESS, INC. • NEW YORK

LIVING DOCUMENTS IN AMERICAN HISTORY

A *Washington Square Press* edition published 1964
1st printing....................November, 1963

"The Crossing to Pennsylvania" from "Journey to Pennsylvania" by Gottlieb Mittleberger, edited and translated by Oscar Handlin and John Clive is reprinted by permission of The John Harvard Library of the Belknap Press of Harvard University Press. Copyright, 1960, by The President and Fellows of Harvard College.

Selections from "Journal of a Residence on a Georgia Plantation" by Frances Anne Kemble as edited by John Anthony Scott is reprinted by permission of Alfred A. Knopf, Inc. Copyright, 1961, by Alfred A. Knopf, Inc.

L

Published by
Washington Square Press, Inc., 630 Fifth Avenue, New York, N.Y.

WASHINGTON SQUARE PRESS editions are distributed in the U.S. by Affiliated Publishers, a division of Pocket Books, Inc., 630 Fifth Avenue, New York 20, N.Y.

Contents

THE AMERICAN REVOLUTION

THE EARLY NATIONAL PERIOD
1783–1814

JACKSONIAN AMERICA
1814–1848

UNION AND SECESSION
1849–1863

APPENDIX

PREFACE

This book is issued following the hundredth anniversary of the Emancipation Proclamation of 1863, in commemoration of the central achievement of the Civil War: the liberation of the slaves. It is dedicated to all who would study America's past in order to gain inspiration and insight from the thoughts and deeds of men and women in days gone by; and in order to understand more clearly their country's destiny as an interracial democracy with full and equal rights for all.

One hundred years after the Emancipation Proclamation the United States finds itself in the throes of a tremendous struggle for the achievement of complete equality for its Negro citizens, and for the final elimination of helotry, or second-class citizenship. Racial prejudice and enforced segregation are vestiges of slavery that survive into our own times as the odious legacy of an earlier day; they still exert a baneful influence upon American thought and conduct. The struggle to eradicate this evil imparts a deep meaning to the life of our times. It arouses in the American people a dedicated idealism and an heroic energy; for it sets forth, as its objective, fulfillment of the great promise of the Declaration of Independence —equal rights for all—which neither the Revolution itself nor the Civil War was capable of carrying through to its appointed end. The struggle for equal rights is an unfinished task: generations now alive are called upon to complete it.

It is the function of historical science to illuminate this objective which lies before us all, to explain its nature and how it came to be, to win youth to the ideal that it exemplifies, and to help provide the inspiration necessary if difficult things are to be accomplished fully, completely, finally and well.

Where possible I have selected for inclusion in this book documents that deal vividly and clearly with the great theme of human rights in a democratic Republic, and with the specific historical experiences that have shaped American thought on this question. There is a wealth of available material. In the actual choice of what to print I was guided by a number of criteria: I have sought documents that exemplify high standards of literary excellence and craftsmanship; that illustrate and exalt the power of human reason as an instru-

ment to illuminate the unknown and to aid in the solution
of human problems; and that are imbued throughout with a
deep sense of the dignity of human life and the meaning of
human struggle.

Some editors who prepare literary and historical materials
for public use follow a practice of deleting from the documents
they reproduce passages which, in their opinion, are immaterial
or irrelevant. Not infrequently the result is a series of sentences
or paragraphs strung together with lines of dots indicating
an incessant tampering with the original source. This is a
practice which I am radically opposed to, and have not followed in this book. Documents here submitted are printed
in their entirety. It is the editor's function, in my view, to
submit the evidence whole and unabridged. The final judgment of what is material or immaterial must be left to the
reader. In certain cases, it is true, I have found it necessary
to reproduce a portion only of a larger work. But invariably
the portion reproduced has its own inner unity as a specific
topic; in no case has material been eliminated from within
the body of writing thus selected.

In preparing this modern edition of the original sources
I have, where possible, gone back to the original manuscripts;
or, where those manuscripts have not survived or were unavailable, to the original pamphlets or other publications in
which the writings were first issued. In a few instances I
have relied upon versions given in later secondary works, but
only when I had satisfied myself that these represented an
improved edition of an earlier and less perfect original.
Much of the material reproduced herein has been uti-
lized by specialists, but it has been unavailable to the general reading public for a hundred years or more. This book
represents the beginning of an effort to make generally and
cheaply available to Americans the brilliant historical writings
that are obscurely preserved in our great libraries and re-
positories, and which constitute no small part of the cultural
and intellectual heritage of the United States.

It is not surprising that little-known and rare sources, however excellent, are not generally and cheaply available. But
it is strange that even such fundamental historical records
as the Massachusetts Body of Liberties and the Articles of
Confederation are not easily and inexpensively available, with-

out abridgement, to the vast numbers of our high school students and to their teachers. For this reason a number of these fundamental documents have been included in their entirety in the Appendix to this volume.

No effort has been made to present a "complete" coverage of American history in the first two or more centuries of its development: this selection can make absolutely no claim to be representative or all-inclusive. Insofar as intellectual and academic training are concerned, documentary study illustrates a method of approach to history and affords opportunity for critical analysis: this is the important thing. I have tried to cover a number of problems and struggles that were of decisive significance in the American past; emphatically, I have not tried to cover everything in the history of the period under consideration. The effort to cover everything often leads historians and historical editors to give everything equal weight. It may lead the student to the conclusion that since everything is important, nothing is important. And it may also leave him with the unfortunate impression that history is a sea strewn only with flotsam, that it possesses neither order, coherence, nor progression. Such a conclusion is untrue: it does disservice alike to history and to mankind.

The underlying principle of scientific education in history, from the elementary to the post-graduate level, in my view, is this: the student must be encouraged to examine for himself or for herself the direct, immediate and living evidence of the past. This is communicated to us in human utterance as recorded in writing and song, in art, architecture and artifact. The present work is designed for high school and college students and their teachers, and for the general public, as a modest introduction to America's magnificent written record in the modern epoch.

Many teachers have written to me in recent months, asking what materials I use in teaching American history and how these might be obtained. This book is a first answer to their question. All the materials I have included have been examined in mimeographed form by many hundreds of high school students as part of their work in American history. The nature of their response—the proven value of these documents in the classroom—was the final factor determining their inclusion here. The favorable reception of these particular pieces in my own classes and those of my closest colleagues encourages me to publish them in the belief that what has been helpful to us may prove of value to others.

A special word must be said about the inclusion of folk songs. The great struggles and experiences of the American people throughout their history have found expression in song. These songs are historical documents in their own right. They speak to us in a direct, dramatic and personal way, and I believe that they possess immeasurable value to the student of our history. They enable us to identify emotionally and imaginatively with men and women in times gone by, and have a unique dimension in the communication of national traditions and of human values.[1] Tens of thousands of our young people are rediscovering the folk heritage of America in the folk-song renaissance that has been gathering momentum over the past ten years. As historians we have the opportunity to widen and deepen the student's appreciation of folk music as an important aspect of national history, and to utilize both music and lyrics to raise the literary and artistic standards of our people. Such an opportunity should not be neglected.

*   *   *   *   *

In the editorial work I have received valuable help from many sources. My thanks go to a number of great libraries— in particular, the Library of Congress, Columbia and Brown University libraries and the American Antiquarian Society— for the facilities they accorded me for the use and reproduction of rare materials. Margaret C. Blaker, Archivist of the Bureau of American Ethnology, provided references on Frank Hamilton Cushing, and W. Edwin Hemphill, editor of the Papers of John C. Calhoun, now in course of publication, gave me useful information concerning the manuscript of Calhoun's speech of March 4, 1850. Mrs. Louisa Barlow Jay spent many hours with me discussing her uncle, Robert Gould Shaw, and other members of her distinguished family, and kindly permitted me to utilize unpublished correspondence in her possession. Arthur Kinoy freely made available to me his researches on George Ripley and his pene-

---

[1] For a fuller development of this thesis, see my "Folklore and Folksong in Education," *New York Folklore Quarterly*, XVIII (Winter 1962), pp. 294–302.

trating commentaries on the Federal Constitution, some of these in the form of briefs prepared for the Federal Courts. I am indebted to Phillip Flayderman of Washington Square Press for the encouragement that he gave to this project and the care with which he supervised its execution; to Mrs. Eve Lederman for the scrupulous typing of many drafts, and to my wife, Maria Scott, for assistance with proof. Last but not least I must acknowledge with gratitude the work of innumerable students who have read these documents and have given me the benefit of their thinking about them.

JOHN ANTHONY SCOTT
May 17, 1963

Pre-
Columbian

Outlines of
═Zuñi Creation Myths═

BY FRANK HAMILTON CUSHING
(TÉNATSALI)

Introduction

The Indians who trod this continent for thousands of years before the Scands came to Vinland or Columbus to the Caribbean were the first American patriots. They crossed the land on moccasined feet, and worshiped it as the mother and giver of life. The splendor of America found expression in the poetic names which the people gave to its rivers, lakes, mountains and forests.

We must not idealize the Indians, but we must also not underrate them. Living under primitive conditions they struggled against a harsh and often dangerous environment with primitive tools and primitive concepts. Like people everywhere they held beliefs about the origin and meaning of life, about the nature of man and of the hereafter. To understand the Indians fully, we must approach them through a sympathetic study of their beliefs, their customs and their ideas.

The Indians were great storytellers. This is true, indeed, of most so-called "primitive" peoples. Before men discovered the use of writing and developed the alphabet, history had to be transmitted by memory, by word of mouth. It was in a thousand memorized tales, in a body of mythology, that the traditions, the customs and the philosophy of a people would become enshrined.

The Indians of the United States possessed a rich mythology. The latter achieved its most elaborate and developed form in the legends of the pueblo, or village, dwellers of Arizona and New Mexico. The almost infinite legends of the Zuñi people in particular have been woven together and interpreted for us by Frank Hamilton Cushing in a primitive epic that must be considered a minor masterpiece of American literature.

F. H. Cushing (1857-1900) was a genius endowed with a profound and brilliant imagination. He grew up in central New York, leading a solitary outdoor life, poring over Indian flints and shards, dreaming himself back into the prehistoric past. His deep love of Indian ways was matched by a handicraft skill of a high order, which enabled him to reproduce Indian pottery, basket work and weaving. At the age of seventeen he prepared a report on the antiquities of Orleans County, which was published in Washington in 1874. This work attracted the attention of Major John Wesley Powell, great explorer of the West and pioneer American ethnologist. When the United States Bureau of Ethnology was formed in 1879 under Powell's leadership, in order to study and conserve American Indian culture, Cushing became a member of its staff. That same year he left for Zuñiland, where it was his purpose to remain indefinitely, studying the life and culture of the Zuñis. Actually this sojourn occupied nearly five years, from August, 1879, to March, 1884.

Once with the Zuñis, Cushing became a member of the tribe, wore Indian dress, and participated in Indian occupations and pastimes. He acquired a knowledge of the Zuñi language, made voluminous sketches and notes, attended meetings of the clan and sacred societies. He examined Indian ruins in the deserts for miles around and conducted excavations that unearthed a mass of data concerning Zuñi ceremonial life. He was taken into the priesthood of the Bow and was appointed head War Chief. He was adopted into the Macaw clan with the name Ténatsali, or medicine flower.

Cushing's hosts revealed to him a sacred epic which he described as "of great length, metrical, rhythmical even, in parts, and filled with archaic expressions nowhere to be found in the modern Zuñi." This epic, part of which Cushing was allowed to listen to in 1881, represented the story of the Zuñi, the origin of their ceremonials and way of life, the statement of their view of God and the universe. As aboriginal unwritten history and literature, it had been jealously guarded by the priests and transmitted by word of mouth from generation to generation from the remotest past. Its discovery and translation (albeit from memory, for Cushing was not permitted to record anything during the sacred recitations) must be regarded as a major achievement of American ethnology.

Cushing was recalled from the Zuñis in 1884 after helping

the Indians to resist the encroachment of white men upon their ancestral lands. Serious illness followed, in the intervals of which he prepared his translations of the creation myths and other Zuñi folk tales. His renderings are interpretations, both poetic and original, of a folkway with which he had become deeply familiar. He died in 1900, his work unfinished, an American worthy to be remembered, who approached the Indians with love and humility, with pen in hand, not gun.

The creation myths were first published in the Annual Report of the United States Bureau of American Ethnology. Cushing prefaced his work with a long and brilliant article on Zuñi history and culture. His version of the myths might be called a symphonic poem, composed of separate but related themes and episodes, skillfully interwoven. The story tells eloquently of the diverse origins of the Zuñi peoples, of their desert wanderings, of their weary search for a "promised land," or "middle" where the earth's crust would not seethe and quake, of the key role in their culture of corn, of the arts of hybridization, of rain.

The version of the myths here reproduced follows the original faithfully in relating the main themes of the Zuñi story; but not all the diverse episodes relating to the origin of the priesthood and sacred ceremonials have been included.

OUTLINES OF
ZUÑI CREATION MYTHS*

The Genesis of the Worlds

Before the beginning of the new-making, Awonawílona— the Maker and Container of all, the All-father Father— solely had being. There was nothing else whatsoever throughout the great space of the ages save everywhere black darkness in it, and everywhere void desolation.

In the beginning of the new-made, Awonawílona conceived within himself and thought outward in space, whereby mists of increase, steams potent of growth, were evolved and uplifted. Thus, by means of his innate knowledge, the All-

Source: Frank Hamilton Cushing, "Outline of Zuñi Creation Myths," United States Bureau of American Ethnology: *13th Annual* Report, 1891–2 (Washington, D.C., 1896), pp. 325–447.

container made himself in person and form of the sun whom we hold to be our father and who thus came to exist and appear. With his appearance came the brightening of the spaces with light, and with the brightening of the spaces the great mist-clouds were thickened together and fell, whereby was evolved water in water; yea, and the world-holding sea.

With his substance of flesh outdrawn from the surface of his person, the Sun-father formed the seed-stuff of twin worlds, impregnating therewith the great waters, and lo! in the heat of his light these waters of the sea grew green and scums rose upon them, waxing wide and weighty until, behold! they became Awitelin Tsíta, the "four-fold containing Mother-earth," and Apoyan Tä'chu, the "all-covering Father-sky."

The Genesis of Men and the Creatures

From the lying together of these two upon the great world waters, so vitalizing, terrestrial life was conceived; whence began all beings of earth, men and the creatures, in the four-fold womb of the world.

Thereupon the Earth-mother repulsed the Sky-father, growing big and sinking deep into the embrace of the waters below, thus separating from the Sky-father in the embrace of the waters above. As a woman forebodes evil for her first-born ere born, even so did the Earth-mother forebode, long withholding from birth her myriad progeny and meantime seeking counsel with the Sky-father. "How," said they to one another, "shall our children, when brought forth, know one place from another, even by the white light of the Sun-father?"

Now, like all the surpassing beings, the Earth-mother and the Sky-father were changeable, even as smoke in the wind; transmutable as thought, manifesting themselves in any form at will, like as dancers may by mask-making.

Thus, as a man and woman, spoke they, one to the other. "Behold!" said the Earth-mother as a great terraced bowl appeared at hand and within it water, "this is as upon me the homes of my tiny children shall be. On the rim of each world-country they wander in, terraced mountains shall stand, making in one region many, whereby country shall be known from country, and within each, place from place. Behold again!" said she as she spat on the water and rapidly smote and stirred it with her fingers. Foam formed, gathering about the terraced rim, mounting higher and higher. "Yea," said she, "and from my bosom they shall draw nourishment, for in such as this shall they find the substance of life whence we were ourselves sustained, for see!"

Then with her warm breath she blew across the terraces; white flecks of the foam broke away, and, floating over above the water, were shattered by the cold breath of the Sky-father attending, and forthwith shed downward abundantly fine mist and spray! "Even so, shall white clouds float up from the great waters at the borders of the world, and clustering about the mountain terraces of the horizons, be borne aloft and abroad by the breaths of the surpassing of soul-beings, and of the children, and shall be hardened and broken by thy cold, shedding downward, in rain-spray, the water of life, even into the hollow places of my lap! For therein chiefly shall nestle our children, mankind and creature-kind, for warmth in thy coldness."

Lo! even the trees on high mountains near the clouds and the Sky-father crouch low toward the Earth-mother for warmth and protection! Warm is the Earth-mother, cold the Sky-father, even as woman is warm, man the cold being!

"Even so!" said the Sky-father; "Yet not alone shalt *thou* be helpful unto our children, for behold!" and he spread his hand abroad with the palm downward, and into all the wrinkles and crevices thereof he set the semblance of shining yellow corn-grains; in the dark of the early world-dawn they gleamed like sparks of fire, and moved as his hand was moved over the bowl, shining up from and also moving in the depth of the waters therein. "See!" said he, pointing to the seven grains clasped by his thumb and four fingers, "by such shall our children be guided; for behold, when the Sun-father is not nigh, and thy terraces are as the dark itself (being all hidden therein), then shall our children be guided by lights, like to these lights of all the six regions turning around the midmost one; as in and around the midmost place, where these our children shall abide, lie all the other regions of space! Yea! and even as these grains gleam up from the water, so shall seed-grains like them, yet numberless, spring up from thy bosom when touched by my waters, to nourish our children."

The Gestation of Men and the Creatures

Anon in the nethermost of the four cave-wombs of the world, the seed of men and the creatures took form and increased. Even as within eggs in warm places worms speedily appear, which growing, presently burst their shells and become as may happen, birds, tadpoles, or serpents, so did men and all creatures grow and multiply in many kinds. Thus the lowermost womb or cave-world, which was the place of first formation and black as a chimney at night time, foul too as the internals of the belly, became overfilled with being. Everywhere were unfinished creatures, crawling like reptiles one over another in filth and black darkness, crowding thickly together and treading each other, one spitting on another or doing other indecency, insomuch that loud became their murmurings and lamentations, until many among them sought to escape, growing wiser and more manlike.

The Forthcoming from Earth of the Foremost of Men

Then came among men and the beings, it is said, the wisest of wise men and the foremost, the all-sacred master, Póshaiyank'ya, he who appeared in the waters below, even as did the Sun-father in the wastes above, and who arose from the nethermost sea, and pitying men still, won upward, gaining by virtue of his wisdom issuance from that first world-womb through ways so dark and narrow that those who, seeing a little, crowded after, could not follow, so eager were they and so mightily did they strive with one another. Alone, then, he fared upward from one cave to another, out into the great breadth of daylight. There, the earth lay, like a vast island in the midst of the great waters, wet and unstable. And alone fared he forth dayward, seeking the Sun-father and supplicating him to deliver mankind and the creatures there below.

The Birth from the Sea of the Twin Deliverers of Men

Then did the Sun-father take counsel within himself, and casting his glance downward spied, on the great waters, a foam-cap near to the Earth-mother. With his beam he impregnated and with his heat incubated the foam-cap, whereupon she gave birth to Uanam Achi Píahkoa, the Beloved Twins, who descended. To them the Sun-father imparted, still retaining, control-thought and his own wisdom, even as to the offspring of wise parents their knowingness is imparted, and as to his right hand and his left hand a skillful man gives craft freely, surrendering not his knowledge. He gave them, of himself and their mother the foam-cap, the great cloud-bow, and for arrows the thunderbolts of the four quarters, and for buckler the fog-making shield, which—spun of the floating clouds and spray and woven, as of cotton we spin and weave—supports as on wind, yet hides (as a shadow hides) its bearer, defending also.

And of men and all creatures he gave them the fathership and dominion, also as a man gives over the control of his work to the management of his hands. Well instructed of the Sun-father, they lifted the Sky-father with their great cloud-bow into the vault of the high zenith, that the earth might become warm and thus fitter for their children, men and the creatures. Then along the trail of the sun-seeking Póshaiyank'ya, they sped backward swiftly on their floating fog-shield, westward to the Mountain of Generation. With their magic knives of the thunderbolt they spread open the uncleft depths of the mountain, and still on their cloud-shield—even as a spider in her web descendeth—so descended they unerringly, into the dark of the underworld. There they abode with men and the creatures, attending them, coming to know them, and becoming known of them as masters and fathers, thus seeking the ways for leading them forth.

The Birth and Delivery of Men and the Creatures

Now there were growing things in the depths, like grasses and crawling vines. So now the Beloved Twins breathed on the stems of these grasses growing tall, as grass is wont to do toward the light, under the opening they had cleft and whereby they had descended; causing them to increase vastly and rapidly by grasping and walking round and round them, twisting them upward until lo! they reached forth even into the light. And where successively they grasped the stems ridges were formed and thumb-marks whence sprang branching leaf-stems. Therewith the two formed a great ladder whereon men and the creatures might ascend to the second cave-floor, and thus not be violently ejected in aftertime by the throes of the Earth-mother, and thereby be made demoniac and deformed.

Up this ladder, into the second cave-world, men and the beings crowded, following closely the Two Little but Mighty Ones. Yet many fell back and, lost in the darkness, peopled the underworld, whence they were delivered in aftertime amid terrible earth shakings, becoming the monsters and fearfully strange beings of olden time. Lo! in this second womb it was dark as is the night of a stormy season, but larger of space and higher than had been the first, because it was nearer the navel of the Earth-mother, hence named K'ólin tehuli, the place of gestation. Here again men and the beings increased and the clamor of their complainings grew loud and beseeching. Again the Two, augmenting the growth of the great ladder, guided them upward, this time not all at once, but in successive bands to become in time the fathers of the six kinds of men—the yellow, the tawny gray, the red, the white, the mingled, and the black races—and with them the gods and creatures of them all. Yet this time also, as before, multitudes were lost or left behind.

The third great cave-world, whereunto men and the creatures had now ascended, being larger than the second and higher, was lighter, like a valley in starlight, and named Awisho tehuli, the vaginal-womb. Here the various peoples and beings began to multiply apart in kind one from another; and as the nations and tribes of men and the creatures thus waxed numerous as before, here, too, it became overfilled. As before, generations of nations now were led out successively—yet many lost, also as hitherto—into the next and last world-cave, Tépahaian tehuli, the womb of parturition.

Here it was light like the dawning, and men began to perceive and to learn variously according to their natures, wherefore the Twins taught them to seek first of all our Sun-father, who would, they said, reveal to them wisdom and knowledge of the ways of life—wherein also they were instructing them as we do little children. Yet like the other cave-worlds, this too became, after long time, filled with progeny; and finally, at periods, the Two led forth the nations of men and the kinds of being, into this great upper world, which is called Ték'-ohaian úlahnane, or the world of disseminated light.

Men and the creatures were nearer alike then than now: black were our fathers the late born of creation, like the caves from which they came forth; cold and scaly their skins like those of mud-creatures; goggled their eyes like those of an owl; membranous their ears like those cave-bats; webbed their feet like those of walkers in wet and soft places; and according as they were elder or younger, they had tails, longer or shorter. They crouched when they walked, often indeed, crawling along the ground like toads, lizards and newts; like infants who still fear to walk straight, they crouched, as beforetime they had in their cave-worlds, that they might not stumble and fall, or come to hurt in the uncertain light thereof.

And when the morning star rose they blinked excessively as they beheld its brightness and cried out with many mouth-motionings that surely now the Father was coming; but it was only the elder of the Bright Ones, gone before with elder nations and with his shield of flame, heralding from afar—as we herald with wet shell scales or crystals—the approach of the Sun-father! And when, low down in the east the Sun-father himself appeared, what though shrouded in the midst of the great world waters, they were so blinded and heated by his light and glory that they cried out to one another in anguish and fell down wallowing and covering their eyes with their bare hands and arms. Yet ever anew they looked afresh to the light, and anew struggled toward the sun as moths and other night creatures seek the light of a camp fire; yea, and what though burned, seek ever anew that light!

Thus ere long they became used to the light, and to this world they had entered. Wherefore, when they arose and no longer walked bended, lo! it was then that they first looked full upon one another and in horror of their filthier parts, strove to hide these, even from one another, with girdles of bark and rushes; and when by thus walking only upon their hinder feet the same became bruised and sore, they sought to protect them with plaited sandals of yucca fiber.

The Origin of Priests

It was thus, by much devising of ways, that men began to grow knowing in many things, and were instructed by what they saw, and so became wiser and better able to receive the words and gifts of their fathers and elder brothers, the gods and priests. For already masters-to-be were amongst them. Even in the dark of the underworlds such had come to be; as had, indeed, the various kinds of creatures-to-be, so these. And according to their natures they had found and cherished things and had been granted gifts by the gods; but as yet they knew not the meaning of their own powers and possessions, even as children know not the meanings and right uses of the precious or needful things given them; nay, nor yet the functions of their very parts! Now in the light of the Sun-father, persons became known from persons, and these things from other things; and thus the people came to know their many fathers among men, to know them by themselves or by the possessions they had.

The Unripeness of the World, and the Search for the Middle

As it was with men and the creatures, so with the world; it was young and unripe. Unstable its surface was, like that of a marsh; dank, even the high places, like the floor of a cavern, so that seeds dropped on it sprang forth, and even the substance of offal became growing things.

Earthquakes shook the world and rent it. Beings of sorcery, demons and monsters of the underworld fled forth. Creatures turned fierce, becoming beasts of prey, wherefore others turned timid, becoming their quarry. Wretchedness and hunger abounded; black magic, war, and contention entered when fear did into the hearts of men and the creatures. Yea, fear was everywhere among them, wherefore, everywhere the people, hugging in dread their precious possessions, became wanderers they, living on the seeds of grasses, eaters of dead and slain things! Yet still, they were guided by the Two Beloved, ever in the direction of the east, told and taught that they must seek, in the light and under the pathway of the sun, the middle of the world, over which alone they could find the earth stable, or rest them and bide them in peace.

When the tremblings grew stilled for a time, the people were bidden to gather and pause at the first of sitting-places, which was named the place of elevation. Yet still poor and defenseless and unskilled were the children of men, still moist and from time to time unstable the world they abode in. Still also, great demons and monsters of prey fled violently forth in times of earthquake and menaced all wanderers and timid creatures. Therefore the Beloved Twins took counsel one with the other and with the Sun-father, and instructed by him, the elder said to the younger, "Brother, behold!

That the earth be made safer for men, and more stable,
Let us shelter the land where our children be resting,
Yea! the depths and the valleys beyond shall be sheltered
By the shade of our cloud-shield! Let us lay to its circle
Our firebolts of thunder, aimed to all the four regions,
Then smite with our arrows of lightning from under.
Lo! the earth shall heave upward and downward with thunder!
Lo! fire shall belch outward and burn the world over,
And floods of hot water shall seethe swift before it!
Lo! smoke of earth-stenches shall blacken the daylight
And deaden the senses of them else escaping
And lessen the number of fierce preying monsters!
That the earth be made safer for men, and more stable."

"It were well," said the younger, ever eager, and forthwith they made ready as they had between themselves devised. Then said the elder to the younger,

"Wilt thou stand to the right, or shall I, younger brother?"
"I will stand to the right," said the younger, and stood there.
To the left stood the elder, and when all was ready,
'Hluáa they let fly at the firebolts, their arrows!
Deep bellowed the earth, heaving upward and downward.
"It is done," said the elder. "It is well," said the younger.

Dread was the din and stir. The heights staggered and the

mountains reeled, the plains boomed and crackled under the floods and fires, and the high hollow-places, hugged of men and the creatures, were black and awful, so that these grew crazed with panic and strove alike to escape or to hide more deeply. But erewhile they grew deafened and deadened, forgetful and asleep! A tree lighted of lightning burns not long! Presently thick rain fell, quenching the fires; and waters washed the face of the world, cutting deep trails from the heights downward, and scattering abroad the wrecks and corpses of stricken things and beings, or burying them deeply. Lo! they are seen in the mountains to this day; and in the trails of those fierce waters cool rivers now run, and where monsters perished lime of their bones we find, and use in food stuff! Gigantic were they, for their forms little and great were often burned or shriveled and contorted into stone. Seen are these, also, along the depths of the world.

Where they huddled together and were blasted thus, their blood gushed forth and flowed deeply, here in rivers, there in floods; but it was charred and blistered and blackened by the fires, into the black rocks of the lower mesas. There were vast plains of dust, ashes and cinders, reddened as is the mud of a hearth-place. There were great banks of clay and soil burned to hardness—as clay is when baked in the kiln-mound—blackened, bleached or stained yellow, gray, red, or white, streaked and banded, bended or twisted. Worn and broken by the heavings of the underworld and by the waters and breaths of the ages, they are the mountain-terraces of the Earth-mother, dividing country from country. Yet many were the places behind and between these—dark cañons, deep valleys, sunken plains—unharmed by the fires, where they swerved or rolled higher; as, close to the track of a forest fire, green grow trees and grasses, and even flowers continue to bloom.

Therein, and in the land sheltered by the shield, tarried the people, awakened, as from fearful dreams. Dry and more stable was the world now, less fearsome its lone places, since changed to rock were so many monsters of prey.

But ever and anon the earth trembled anew in that time, and the people were troubled. "Thus being, it is not well," said the Two. "Let us again seek the Middle." So they led their myriads far eastward and tarried them at Tésak'ya Yäla (place of bare mountains).

Yet soon again the world rumbled, and again they led the

way into a country and place called Támëlan K'yaíyawan
(where tree boles stand in the midst of the waters). There the
people abode for long, saying (poor people!) "this is the Middle!" Therefore they built homes. At times they met people
who had gone before, thus learning much of ways in war, for
in the fierceness that had entered their hearts with fear, they
deemed it not well, neither liked they to look upon strangers
peacefully. And many strange things also were learned and
happened there, that are told in other speeches of the ancient
talk.

Having fought and grown strong, lo! when at last the earth
groaned and the conches sounded warning, and the Twins
bade them forth, forsooth! they murmured much, and many
(foredoomed!), turned headstrong and were left to perish
miserably in their own houses as do rats in falling trees, or
flies in forbidden food!

But the greater company went obediently forward, until at
last they neared Shípololon K'yaía (steam mist in the midst of
the waters). Behold! they saw as they journeyed, the smoke of
men's hearth-fires and a great assemblage of houses scattered
over the hills before them! And when they came closer they
met dwellers in those places, nor looked peacefully upon them
—having erstwhile in their last standing-place, had touch of
war—but challenged them rudely, to know, forsooth, who
they were and why there.

The Origin of Corn

"We are the People of Seed," said these strangers, replying
to our fathers of old, "born elder brothers of ye, and led of
the gods!"

"Nay," contended our fathers, "verily, we are led of the
gods and of us are the Seed people and the substance of seed
whereof our wise elders carry the potencies." Whereupon
they grew yet more angry, so dark were they of understanding!

The people who called themselves "of the Seed" bade them
pause. "Behold," said they, "we have powers above yours, yet
without your aid we cannot exert them; even as the mothers
of men may not be fertile save of the fathers. You are our
younger brothers, for verily so are *your* People of Seed, and
more precious than they know are they and their sacred keep-

ings ye—unwittingly alack!—so boast of; even as we are more wise than you are and in ourselves quickening withal, for you are like virgins, unthinking, yet fertile. Let us look peacefully upon one another. Do you therefore, try first your powers with the sacred things you carry according as you have been instructed or may best devise; then will we according to our knowledge of these things and our own practices try our powers with them also, showing forth our customs unto you."

At last, after much wrangling and council, the people agreed to this. And they set apart the time, eight days (as now days are numbered) wherein to make their preparations, which was well; for therefrom resulted to them great gain, yea, and the winning of these stranger villagers, and by wise and peaceful acts rather than by war and the impetuosity of right hands.

In the borders of the plain in the midst of cedars (fuel furnishers of the food-maturing fire, these), and under the shade of hemlocks (tree goddesses of the food-growing water, these), they encamped. And at the foot of the hemlocks, facing the sunlight, they builded them of cedar boughs a great bower: like to it, only lesser, are those whence we watch and foster the ripening of our corn; for from their bower thus fashioned, our fathers and mothers, the priests and priest-matrons of old, watched and labored for the first birth of corn, and in this wondrous wise, as young parents watch for the birth of their children, though not knowing of what kind or favor they will be, nevertheless expectantly of heart; and as we now watch the fulfillment of our harvests.

So, the seed-priests and master-keepers of the possessions, and their fathers, fasted and intently contemplated their sacred substances to divine the means thereof. And it seemed good to them to cut wands of the spaces, painting them significantly and pluming them in various ways with the feathers of the cloud and summer sun-loving birds; thinking thereby to waft the breath of their prayers and incantations (taught by the Surpassing Ones all in the new time of the world), and to show forth their meanings even so far as unto the ancient sitting spaces of those who first taught them.

When all else was prepared, they made a shrine around their *múetone* (or medicine seed of hail and soil), their *k'yáetone* (or medicine seed of the water and rain), and their *chúetone* (or medicine seed of grains). And around these, and reaching out toward the sun before them, they set their plumed wands of message. For the plain was dry and barren, and they wanted fresh soil by the hail torrents, moisture by the rain, and growth of seed-substance, that they might the better exhibit their powers to these strangers; if perchance, in response to their labors and beseechings, these things would be granted to them.

Therefore, that the meaning of their beseechings might be the more plain and sure of favor, certain ones of the sage priests sought out and placed the largest and most beautifully colored grass seeds they could find among the stores of their wayfarings, in the gourd with the *chúetone;* and then cut from branches of the easy growing cottonwood and willow, gleaned from the ways of water, goodly wands which they plumed and planted, like in color to each kind of seed they had selected; yellow, green, red, white, black, speckled, and mottled; one for each side of the sacred gourd, one to be laid upon it, one to be laid under it, and one to be placed within it; and as soon as finished, thus they disposed the wands.

Now when night came, these master-priests took the *chúetone*—all secretly, whilst the others were drowsy—and carried it, with the plumed wands they had made, out into the plain, in front of the bower. There they breathed into these things the prayers and over them softly intoned the incantations which had been taught them in the new time of the world. Then they placed the *chúetone* on the ground of the plain and on each side of it, by the light of the seven great stars which were at that time rising bright above them, they planted one of the plumed wands with the seeds of its color; first, the brightest, yellow with the yellow grass seeds, on the north; then the blue with the green grass seeds, on the west; then the red with the red grass seeds, to the south; and the white with the white seeds, to the east. But the other three plumed wands they could not plant, one above, the other below, and the last within the gourd; so looking at the stars they saw how they were set, four of them as though around a gourd like their own, and three others as though along its handle!

"*Ha! Chukwe!*" said they. "'Tis a sign, maybe, of the Sky-father!" Whereupon they set each of the others in a line, the black one with its seeds of black, nearest to the sacred gourd below the handle; the speckled one with its spotted seeds next, on the other side of the handle; and the mottled one with its dappled seeds far out at the end of the handle, that it might (being of the colors of all the others) point out each of them, as it were, and lead them all!

And when, on the morrow, the watchers saw the plumes standing there all beautiful in the plain, and asked who planted them, and for what, the priests replied, "Verily they were planted in the night, while you heedlessly drowsed, by the seven stars."

Thereat the people, mistaking their meaning, exclaimed, "Behold! the seed wands of the stars themselves!" And they rejoiced in the omen that their prayers had been heard so far. And lo! during the eight days and nights there arose thick mists; hail and rain descended until torrents poured down from the mountains, bringing new soil and spreading it evenly over the plain. And when on the morning of the ninth day the clouds rolled away, "*eluu!*" shouted our fathers of the Seed kin to the stranger people:

"Water and new soil bring we, where erst was barren hardness; yea, even grasses, tall and plumed as were our wands, and spiked with seed"—for the grass seed had sprouted and the new wands taken root and grown, and now had long feathery blades and tall, tasseled stems, waving in the wind. "Yea, verily!" cried the People of the First-growing-grass kin, chief of the clans of Seed, "we *are* the People of the Seed!"

But the strangers, heeding not their boastings, replied, "Yea, verily, enough! It is well. Truly, water and new soil you have brought, and grasses growing great therefrom, yet you have not brought forth new life therefor of the flesh of men or the seed of seeds! Come now, let us labor together, in order that what you have begun may be perfected. New soil and the seed of its production, the seed of water, yea even the substance of seed itself we had not; yet of the seed of seed we are verily the people, and our maidens are the mothers thereof, as you shall see."

Then they, too, set apart eight days, during which to prepare for their custom, and they further said:

"That we may be perfect in the plenishing and generation of the seed of seeds, send us forth, O ye comers, a youth of the kin of Water and of those who hold possession of the precious *k'yáetone*, which give unto us likewise, that we join it to the *chúetone* ye have placed in the midst of the growing plants, according to our understanding of its meaning and relation. And let the youth be goodly and perfect and whole of seed."

Therefore the fathers of the people chose forth, it is said, Yápotuluha, of the clans of Water, foster child of the great Sun-priest Yanáuluha, and named of him. And into his hand they gave the *k'yáetone* and certain of their wands of worship, and sent him to the strangers, glorious to look upon. Now there were in the village of the stranger Seed people seven maidens, sisters of one another, virgins of one house, and foster children of Paíyatuma, the God of Dew, himself. And they were surpassingly beautiful, insomuch so that they were likened to the seven bright stars and are sung of in the songs of the Seed people and told of in their stories.

They, too, were chosen and breathed upon by all the fathers and matrons of the Seed, and with the youth Yápotuluha, instructed in the precious rites and incantations of their custom. And during all the time of preparation rain fell as before, only gently and warm, and on the eighth day the matrons and fathers led the maidens and youth, all beautifully arrayed, down into the plain before the bower where watched the people and grew the grasses. And there they danced and were breathed of the sacred medicine seeds.

All through the night backward and forward danced they to the song line of the elders, and in accordance therewith by the side of the growing plants, motioning them upward with their magic wands and plumes, as we, with implements of husbandry, encourage the growth upward of the corn plants today. As time went on, the matron of the dance led the youth and the first maiden apart, and they grasped, one on either side, the first plants, dancing around them, gently drawing them upward as they went, even as the Two Beloved had caused to grow the canes of the underworld.

So also did the youth and each maiden in turn grasp the other plants in their turn, until all had grown to the tallness of themselves and were jointed where they had grasped them; yea, and leaved as with waving plumes of the macaw himself. And now, in the night, the keepers of the great shells, of the Badger kin, brought forth fire with their hands from roots, and kindled it in front of the bower toward the east, that its heat might take the place of the sun and its light shine brightly on the dancers, making their acts verily alive; and, as the dawn approached, the youth and first maiden were led apart as before by the Mother-making matron, and together embraced the first of the full-grown plants; and so, in turn, the youth and each of the other maidens embraced the other plants.

And as they embraced the first plant, the fire flamed brightly, with the first catching and flush of the wood, and yellow was its light; and as they embraced the second plant, the flames were burning smokily with the fuller grasping of the wood, and blue was the light; and as they were embracing the third plant, the fire reached its fullness of mastery over the wood, and red was its light; and as they were embracing the fourth plant, the fire was fumeless and triumphant over the wood, and white was its light; and as they were embracing the fifth plant, the fire gave up its breath in clouds of sparks, and streaked, of many colors, was its light; and as they were embracing the sixth plant, the fire swooned and slept, giving more heat, as it were, than light, thus somber was the light; yet, as they were embracing the seventh plant, it wakened afresh, did the fire, in the wind of the morning, and glowed as does the late fire of the wanderer, with a light of *all* the colors.

Now when the day dawned, lo! where the mid-persons of the youth and maidens had touched most unitedly and warmly the plants, new parts appeared to the beholders, showing through their coverings many colors, soft hair shrouding them, as if to make precious their beauty.

Whilst the people still gazed at these, wondering, out from the Eastland came Paíyatuma and Ténatsali of the All-colored flowers, God of the Seasons, followed by Kwélele with his flame-potent fire wand. Paíyatuma touched the plants with the refreshing breath of his flute; Ténatsali with the flesh-renewing breath of his flowers; Kwélele, with the ripening breath of his torch. Thereby the new parts were hardened, some to fruitfulness. Others, being too closely touched, burned to the very heat of generative warmth, unfruitful in itself, but fruitful making!

Then, as Paíyatuma waved his flute, lo! following Ténatsali the maidens and the attendant Kwélele went forth and disappeared in the mists of the morning.

The Renewal of the Search for the Middle

Thus, happily, were our fathers joined to the People of the Dew, and the many houses on the hills were now builded together in the plain where first grew the corn plants abundantly; being prepared year after year by the beautiful custom of the ever young maidens, and attended faithfully by the labors of the people and the vigils of their fathers.

When men had almost forgotten the seeking of the Middle, the earth trembled anew, and the shells sounded warning. Murmuring sore when the Beloved Twins came and called them again, yet carrying whatsoever they could with them— more preciously than all else save their little ones, the seed of corn!—they and the people they had dwelt with, journeyed on, seeking safety. For now, their kin were mingled; thus, their children were one people. Wheresoever they rested, they builded them great houses of stone, all together, as may still be seen. And in the plains ever they built them bowers for the watching of the renewal and growth of the seeds of the corn. Therefore, they never hungered, whether journeying anon or sitting still.

Now with much of journeying the people came to grow weary with ever seeking for the Middle all together, along a single way, insomuch that increasingly they murmured whenever they were summoned, and must needs be leaving their homes and accustomed ranging-places. And so they fell to devising among themselves, until at last it seemed good to them to be sending messengers forth in one direction and another, the sooner to feel out the better way, and find signs of the Middle; as, by dividing, a company of hunters the sooner find trace of their quarry.

Now there was a priest of the people, named Ka'wimosa, thus named because he it was who was to establish, all unwittingly, the most potent and good sacred dance as happened after this wise:

He had four sons (some say more) and a daughter. And his eldest son was named K'yäklu, which signifies, it is said, "Whensoever"; for he was wiser of words and the understanding thereof than all others, having listened to the councils of men with all beings, since ever the inner beginning! So, when it was asked who of the precious ones (children of priest-fathers and priest-mothers) should journey northward, seeking to learn the distance thitherward to the great embracing waters, that the Middle might be the better surmised; nor said the Twins aught, as we say naught, to little children weary of a way that must, weary or nay, be accomplished!

When this was asked, Ka'wimosa, the priest, bethought himself of his wise eldest son and said, "Here is he!" Thus K'yäklu was summoned, and made ready with sacrifice presentations from all the priests to all the Surpassing Ones for the great journey; and he departed.

Long the people waited. But at last it was said, "Lost is our K'yäklu! For wise of words was he, but not wise of ways."

And the fathers, mourning, again called a council. Again, when it was inquired, Ka'wimosa the priest bethought him, and cried, "Here!" And again were made ready duly and sent forth messengers, this time southward, the next younger brothers of K'yäklu; for, said the father, they will guide one another if you send two. And of these, also, much is told in other talks of our ancient speech; but then, they too, lingered by the way.

Once more a council was called, and again, when it was inquired, Ka'wimosa cried "Here!" and this time the youngest son, who was named Síweluhsiwa, because he was a long-haired youth of great beauty; and the daughter, who was named Síwiluhsitsa, because she was a long-tressed maiden of beautiful person; they also were summoned, and made ready duly and sent eastward.

There came a time when the people for whom Síweluhsiwa and Síwiluhsitsa[1] had gone forth to seek the way, could tarry no longer awaiting them; for, hearing the earth rumble, the Twin Beloved and their Warrior-leaders of the Knife summoned the tribes forth to journey again. Now in these days the people had grown so vast that no longer could they journey together; but in great companies they traveled, like herds of bison severed when too numerous for the grass of a single plain. The Bearers of the Ice-wands and the Ancient Brotherhood of the Knife led the clans of the Bear, the Crane, the Grouse and others of the people of Winter, through the northernmost valleys, carrying ever in their midst the precious *múetone*. The Fathers of the People, Keepers of the Seed, and the Ancient Brotherhood of Priests led the clans of the Macaw and other Summer people through the middle valleys, carrying ever in their midst the precious *k'yáetone*. They, being de-

---

[1] Other Zuñi tales tell of the wanderings of the children of the priest Ka'wimosa, who were sent out as scouts to seek the promised land. One of the most tragic and beautiful of these sagas deals with Síweluhsiwa and Síwiluhsitsa, brother and sister, and parents of a misbegotten race of oracles, the Ka'yemäshi.

liberate and wise, sought rather in the pathway between the northward and the southward for the place of the Middle.

The Seed-fathers of the Seed-kin, the Keepers of Fire, and the Ancient Brotherhood of Paíyatuma led the All-seed clans, the Sun, Badger and other Summer people, through the southern valleys, carrying ever in their midst the precious *chúetone*.

Leading them all, whether through the northern ways, through the middle ways, or through the southern ways, now here, now there, were the Two Beloved ones, and with them their Warriors of the Knife.

Now although those who went by the northern way were called the Bear and Crane father-people, yet with them went some of all the clans, as the Parrot-macaws of the middle, and the Yellow-corn ones of the southern people.

And although the People of the middle way were called the Macaw father-people, yet with them went Bear and Crane people of the north, nevertheless, and Seed people of the south, also (a few) those of the White Corn.

And although the People of the southern way were called the All-seed father-people, yet with them went a few of both the northern and the middle ways. And this was well! That even though any one of these bands might hap to be divided through wildness of the way or stress of war, they nevertheless might retain, each of them, the seed of all the kin-lines. Moreover, this of itself speedily came to be, through the mingling of the clans from one to another in the strands of marriage.

And although thus apart the peoples journeyed, descending from the westward the valleys toward north and toward south, like gathering streams from a wide rain-storm; yet also like rain-streams gathering in some great river or lagoon, so they came together and thus abode in seasons of rest. Strong and impetuous, the Bear kindred on the one hand were the first to move and farthest to journey; on the other hand the Seed kindred led the way; whereas the heart of them all of the Macaw kindred, deliberately (as was their custom) pursued the middle-course of the Sun-father.

In such order, then, they came, in time, within sight of the great divided mountain of the *Ka'yemäshi*. Seeing smoke and mist rising therefrom, they all, one after another, hastened thither. The Bear people were the first to approach, and great was their dismay when, on descending into the plain, they beheld a broad river, flowing, not as other waters were wont to flow in that land, from east to west, but straight across their pathway, from toward the south, northward. And lo! on the farther side were the mysterious mountains they sought, but between them rolled swiftly these wide turbid waters, red with the soil of those plains.

The Origin of Death by Dying, and the Abode of Souls

Not for long did the impetuous fathers of the Bear and Crane deliberate. No! Straightway they strode into the stream and feeling forth with their feet that it even might be forded —for so red were its waters that no footing could be seen through them—they led the way across. Yet great was their fearfulness; for, full soon, as they watched the water moving under their very eyes, strange chills did pervade them, as though they were themselves changing in being to creatures moving and having being in the waters; even as still may be felt in the giddiness which besets those who, in the midst of troubled or passing waters, gaze long into them. Nevertheless, they won their way steadfastly to the farther shore.

But the poor women who, following closely with the little children on their backs, were more tender, became crazed with these dread fear-feelings of the waters, wherefore, the little ones to whom they clung but the more closely, were instantly changed by the terror. They turned cold, then colder; they grew scaly, fuller webbed and sharp clawed of hand and feet, longer of tail too, as if for swimming and guidance in unquiet waters. Lo! they felt of a sudden to the mothers that bore them, as the feel of dead things; and, wriggling, scratched their bare shoulders until, shrieking wildly, these mothers let go all hold of them and were even fain to shake them off—fleeing from them in terror.

Thus multitudes of them fell into the swift waters, wailing shrilly and plaintively, as even still it may be said they are heard to cry at night time in those lone waters. For, no sooner did they fall below the surges than they floated and swam away, still crying—changed verily, now, even in bodily form; for, according to their several totems, some became like to the lizard, chameleon, and newt; others like to the frog, toad, and turtle. But their souls, what with the sense of falling, still falling, sank down through the waters, as water itself, being started, sinks down through the sands into the depths below. There, under the lagoon of the hollow mountain where it was once split in two by the angry maiden-sister Síwiluhsitsa as told in other tales, dwelt, in their seasons, the soul-beings of ancient men of war and violent death. There were the towns for the "finished" or dead, Hápanawan or the Abode of Ghosts; there also the great pueblo of the Ka'ka, the town of many towns wherein stood forever the great assembly house of ghosts; the kiva which contains the six great chambers in the midst of which sit, at times of gathering in council, the god-priests of all the Ka'ka exercising the newly dead in the Ka'k'okshi or dance of good, and receiving from them the offerings and messages of mortal men to the immortal ones.

Now, when the little ones sank, still sank, seeing naught, the lights of the spirit dancers began to break upon them, and they became, as be the ancients, changeable, and were numbered with them. And so, being received into the midst of the undying ancients, lo! these little ones thus made the way of dying and the path of the dead; for whither they led, in that olden time, others, fain to seek them (insomuch that they died), followed; and yet others followed these; and so it has continued to be even unto this day.

But the mothers, still crying, knew not this—knew not that their children had returned unharmed into the world whence even themselves had come and whither they too needs now must go, constrained thither by the yearnings of their own hearts in the time of mourning. Loudly, still, they wailed, on the farther shore of the river.

The Great Council of Men and the Beings for the Determination of the True Middle

But the warnings yet still sounded anon and the gods and master-priests of the people could not rest.

No, they called a great council of men and the beings, beasts, birds and insects of all kinds changeable; these were gathered in the council.

After long deliberation it was said:

"Where is K'yanästipe, the water-skate? Lo! legs has he of great extension, six in number. Maybe he can feel forth with them to the uttermost of all the six regions, thereby pointing out the very Middle." And K'yanästipe, being summoned, appeared in his own shape and form, but greater, for lo! it was the Sun-father himself. And he answered their questions before he was asked, saying, "Yes, that can I do." And he lifted himself to the zenith, and extended his finger-feet six to all of the six regions, so that they touched to the north, the great waters; and to the west, and the south, and the east, the great waters; and to the northeast, the waters above; and to the southwest, the waters below.

But to the north, his finger-foot grew cold, so he drew it in; and to the west, the waters being nearer, touched his finger-foot thither extended, so he drew that in also. But to the south and east far reached his other finger-feet. Then gradually he settled downward and called out: 'Where my heart and navel rest, beneath them mark ye the spot and there build ye a town of the midmost, for there shall be the midmost place of the earth-mother, even the navel; albeit not the center, because of the nearness of cold in the north and the nearness of waters in the west." And when he descended (squatting), his belly rested over the middle of the plain and valley of Zuñi; and when he drew in his finger-legs, lo! there were the trail-roads leading out and in like stays of a spider's net, into and forth from the place he had covered.

Then the fathers of the people built in that spot, and rested upon it their tabernacle of sacred treasures. But K'yanästipe had swerved in lowering, and their town was reared a little south of the very midmost place. Nevertheless, no longer in aftertime sounded the warnings. Hence, because of their great good fortune (*hálowilin*) in thus finding the stable middle of the world, the priest-fathers of the people called this midmost town the Abiding place of Happy Fortune (*Hálonawan*).

The Flooding of the Towns, and the Staying of the Flood

Yet, because they had erred even so little, and because the first priest of after times did evil, lo! the river to the southward ran full, and breaking from its pathway cut in two the great town, burying houses and men in the mud of its impetuosity. Whence, those who perished not and those of the flooded towns round about fled to the top of the Mountain of Thunder, they with all their seed people and things, whence the villages they built there were named the seed towns of the mountain.

But when by the sacrifice of the youth priest and maiden priestess—as told in other speech—the waters had been made to abate and the land became good to walk upon, all the people descended, calling that high mountain place, which ever after hath echoed thunder, Tâaiyálane, or the Mountain of Thunder. When all the towns were rebuilt, then on the northern side of the river they built anew the Town of the Middle, calling it Hálona Itíwana, Halona the Midmost.

Now at last never more did the world rumble.

The
Colonial
Period

The colonial period of American history, taken as the span of time from the founding of Virginia in 1607 up to the outbreak of the American Revolution, covers nearly one half of the total history of the American people. One writer has dubbed this period "the neglected first half" of our history—a label whose accuracy, unfortunately, cannot easily be denied. Anyone who wants to convince himself of the degree of neglect accorded to the study of American colonial origins has only to pick up a history text at random.[1]

Yet the colonial period constitutes the formative period of American nationality; only in the light of what was going on in this first, perhaps crucial, one hundred and seventy years of colonial development can we hope to understand not only why the American Revolution occurred but the even more puzzling question, why it was successful. The embattled colonists, a poor, ill-equipped and thinly scattered population, were in arms against the world's largest, most powerful and wealthiest empire. The bonds that united them and that made possible both the struggle and the victory were not lightly nor casually achieved; and the story of colonial times is the story of how those bonds came to be forged. This story is not only of the first order of importance for the understanding of America's revolutionary heritage and revolutionary origins. It is interwoven with the present and the future; it has much to contribute to an understanding of our contemporary society and of the people whose destiny we are called upon to grasp and to become a part of.

A nation is a type of human association, but of a very special kind. It has a high degree of stability; it may exist for centuries, even for millennia. Nations claim and exact the supreme loyalty of the individuals composing them. The story of the modern world is the story of how it has come to be populated by such nations, and how it has come to be ruled by the governments, or states, which are their political expression and the instruments of their sovereign will. Though the American nation was thrust together with great speed—in the first in-

---

[1] One excellently written and popular reference work for college students, Henry Bamford Parkes, *The United States of America* (New York, 1953), devotes 90 out of 733 pages to the colonial period, from the first beginnings to the outbreak of the Revolution.

stance over the course of only a couple of hundred years—
while its European counterparts evolved far more gradually,
yet in all cases the same fundamental operative factors had to
be present.

A people, in the first instance, cannot become a nation unless they have a common land, unless they live permanently in
each other's presence, in the same place. A common territory
is the physical basis or condition of communication between
people; it is a permanent common bond, the object of people's
loyalty and devotion as their home, the source of their bread,
their place in the sun.

In the colonial period the settlers who came to the New
World achieved, in a century and a half, the creation of the
first American national domain. They carved out, cleared and
settled the coastal plain lying between the Atlantic Ocean
and the mountain barrier of the Appalachians, between the
wilds of Maine and the forests of Georgia. This was a historic
achievement of the first magnitude; and it was carried out
lowly, painfully, with enormous human sacrifice. It provided
the physical basis of American national life, a land to be the
object of an overriding loyalty, and a place where English
settlers, faced with a new environment, new problems, and
new conditions of life, would insensibly grow away from
the mother country in terms of thought and speech, aspirations, traditions, way of life.

From the very start America was the promised land. Puritan
settlers came with the vision of a land set aside by God, to be
inhabited and cultivated by them and their descendants until
the end of time. This dream of America became the embodiment of a new life and a new future. The will to struggle
and die for it is evidenced in the earliest writings of the English pioneers—notably in the letter of Thomas Dudley to the
Countess of Lincoln, the first of the documents reproduced
below.

American colonization was one phase in the discovery and
exploitation of the world by the European powers in the
modern era. But the colonies of the New World were unique
in that they had of necessity to be peopled from abroad before
they could yield one iota of profit to the planters, merchants,
and speculators who were the empire builders of those days.
The process of transplanting people was promoted by these
same commercial and landed interests in search of crude

labor for their enterprises and profitable freights for their ocean-going ships. The peopling of the mainland colonies in the seventeenth and eighteenth centuries is a sad story. Tens of thousands of Africans were enslaved and carried in by force; white slaves and semi-slaves were dragged in as prisoners of war, deportees and bonded servants. The sufferings that these people underwent in coming to the New World are told in the eloquent words of Gottfried Mittelberger and Alexander Falconbridge under the heading "White Servants and Negro Slaves" (p. 68).

Most of the white immigrants during the colonial period came from the British Isles; and they brought with them a common language, a common literary, legal, and cultural heritage. All these things are indispensable to a common national life. The American people found these materials readily available. They did not have to create them afresh; they only had to utilize, adapt, and apply them in the task of creating a new tradition and a new community.

In the pages that follow, we have singled out two of these cultural factors for illustration. The first of them is religion. Most of the free white immigrants were of Protestant stock; for them law, literacy, education, the sense of history and of the future all found their focus in the Bible. From the viewpoint of the development of national unity and national identity, we cannot overestimate the significance of the great eighteenth-century religious movements that spread with rapidity throughout the colonial area. Beginning with scenes of great enthusiasm and even hysteria, these ended with the spread of literacy, education and organized religious life throughout the country. Here we find the rooting of the spiritual unity of Protestant believers, transcending the petty divisions of provincial boundary and interest. Protestantism, as a national faith, inculcated a democratic and a revolutionary lesson as well as a purely religious one. Both the theory and the practice of religion in colonial America had a deep significance in the achievement of national unity; this is illustrated (p. 112) under the heading "The Great Awakening," which includes, especially, contributions from the pen of that titan among American religious leaders and thinkers, Jonathan Edwards.

Historically, nothing has more served to unite people and to prepare them for the struggles of life than their music. How

the Americans took their marvelously varied and beautiful
musical heritage, using it to develop a new tradition, is illustrated throughout this book.

It would be wrong to give the impression that by 1776 the
Americans had achieved nationhood in the modern, highly
integrated sense of that word, or that they needed only an
independent government and the creation of a separate national state to complete the job. Opposite forces were also at
work—forces of separatism and of provincial isolation. These
derived their strength from the fact that the colonies were
originally launched haphazardly as distinct and even competing ventures, and that they were forced together, into mutual
cooperation, by accident and necessity, rather than by design.
The goal of national unity was pursued always in a relentless
struggle against strong centrifugal forces; against local sovereignties and local interests that refused to subordinate themselves to the national interest, and that guarded jealously
against the least infringement of their rights or powers. This
struggle is not yet over. The pages of this book will bear eloquent witness to its historical significance and reality.

First
═Settlements═

LETTER TO BRIDGET,
COUNTESS OF LINCOLN
(1631)

BY THOMAS DUDLEY

Introduction

Thomas Dudley's letter to the Countess of Lincoln, reproduced in full below, is one of the first writings that we have
from the pen of a settler in New England. Actual firsthand
testimony to pioneer life on the frontier, it was written before
the Massachusetts Bay Colony was one year old, and by a man
who was one of the top leaders and organizers of the venture.
Other considerations aside, its qualities as an eyewitness ac-

count, its vivid description of death and hardship among the settlers on a bleak and forlorn coast, render it noteworthy.

But Dudley's letter has a much wider significance as well, for it reflects an event of utmost importance in the seventeenth-century history of the English-speaking world. The Puritan colonization of America grew directly out of the Reformation that began to sweep Europe in the early sixteenth century, and that was still gathering momentum in the seventeenth. This titanic religious movement may be considered the starting point of American intellectual and cultural life: he who would understand modern America can no more avoid the study of the Reformation than a physicist can bypass the study of mathematics. And, for the same reason, it is inappropriate to labor here for a definition of "Puritan." Puritanism cannot be shortly and simply defined; not only was it a many-sided social and religious movement embodying profound, complex and often conflicting ideas, it was also a political and revolutionary movement that shook the very structure of English society, and, for that matter, French and Dutch as well.

The Puritans, setting aside the traditional organization and structure of the Catholic Church, evolved, during the late sixteenth and early seventeenth centuries, an elaborate theological system of their own. It was in this intellectual and philosophic framework, in a context of Christian thought and morality, that American culture was to develop. Puritanism, indeed, has had a deep influence on the fabric of American thought and society ever since. In terms both of world outlook and of political philosophy it may be considered central to the understanding of the American intellectual and revolutionary heritage.

This fact may be illustrated by the extraordinary emphasis which Americans, from the very start, have placed upon written law, upon government by the book rather than by the man. Not only has the Puritan tradition placed its peculiar stamp upon American legal institutions, it has caused the lawyer to be thrust forward, and to play a role of unusual importance in the unfolding of American political and social struggles.

There were a number of reasons why the Puritan immigrants laid special emphasis on written law. They were, in the first place, part of the wider Protestant movement that had jettisoned the total authority and pretensions of the Catholic

Church that had ruled its faithful not mainly through the written, or canon, law, but through the power of precedent, custom and ritual, and through the very real personal influence of bishop and priest. Protestantism rejected all such authority and was obliged to fall back upon the authority of the Bible as the written word of God, as a divine revelation to the faithful. For this reason the promotion of literacy and biblical instruction played a central role in the Puritan concept of education. The Bible, in translation, was enshrined in the center of the meeting house; the latter, as a place of exposition and instruction, became spiritually more akin to the Jewish synagogue than to the Catholic sanctuary. The Puritan child learned, as he grew older, to respect and to revere the "higher law" of God, a law that was written down and could easily be looked up. The minister himself was a kind of spiritual lawyer, whose function was to translate and expound the law to his flock.

In the second place, the Puritan settlers of Massachusetts Bay derived their very right to exist in the New World from the express written authorization granted to them by Charles I, King of England. It was customary in those days for an explorer to take possession of new lands in the name of the king or state to whom he owed allegiance; and the English kings, along with the French and the Spanish, claimed a goodly portion of the New World by right of prior discovery. Charters issued by the Crown were legal documents authorizing individuals, groups or trading ventures to own, develop and govern colonial territories for their personal advancement and profit in compliance with the stipulated conditions set down in the document itself. The Massachusetts Bay Colony was in the almost unique position of being able to transport its charter and the headquarters of its government to the actual site of colonization. This defined for a half century the political and legal framework within which the colonizing experiment was to develop.

Traditional concepts of the rights of Englishmen, in the third place, stemmed from the Magna Carta: a code of human rights and a guarantee against royal infringement of these that had been extracted from John I in 1215. The Bay authorities soon came under pressure to write down, or codify, the fundamental man-made laws and guarantees which, in conformity to the law of God, should guide the administration of the Commonwealth. Hence the enactment of the famous Body of Liberties in 1641 (see Appendix p. 589) completed in 1648 by the promulgation of a penal code defining specific crimes and their prescribed penalties.

New England's Puritan origins explain the special nature of the contribution that it was to make to American civilization. Most of the settlements in the New World were born from economic and, to a lesser extent, strategic considerations. They were expressions of and episodes in the epochal expansion of western Europe at the dawn of the modern period in which Europeans, conducting for over four centuries a bitter struggle for power and wealth that had as its stage the entire world, achieved dominion over most of the inhabited globe. Any one of the American mainland settlements could be used as a focus for the study of British expansion in the seventeenth and eighteenth centuries. Such colonies were launched for gain. Virginia began with freebooters who came to look for gold; in the course of time it attracted planters seeking fortunes from the export of tobacco. New York developed as a center for the profitable export of furs; South Carolina reared its elegance on slaves and rice. And as for the common people who came to these colonies, they were largely driven there by necessity, or dragged there by force.

Almost alone of the British colonial settlements, New England was founded for ideological reasons, out of a human conviction that death and struggle in the New World was preferable to ecclesiastical despotism in the Old. This motivation for emigration was far different from that which is implied in the phrase "the desire for freedom of religion." The effort to found a godly kingdom in the promised land of America sprang from philosophic and theological conviction, from a burning desire to fulfill the pure, original precepts of Christian morality, from principle, not from a desire for earthly profit. This made the New England commonwealth unique. He who wishes to understand America must study first of all the Old England, and then the New. Many of the greatest social and moral aspirations of American man received for more than two centuries their first impulse, and their principal development, upon New England soil.

The Massachusetts Bay Colony was the foundation of the State of Massachusetts, and from it sprang in time all the other important New England settlements. In the late 1620's

Puritan dissenters from the West of England, East Anglia—Norfolk, Suffolk and Essex counties—and Lincolnshire came together and in 1629 secured from the Crown a charter for a trading venture to be called the Massachusetts Bay Company. The charter invested this Company with the right to trade and colonize in New England, with ownership of the soil, and with powers of government. The Company soon came under the domination of a group led by John Winthrop and Thomas Dudley, who sought to remove the whole enterprise—themselves, the Company, the charter—to New England. Under these circumstances there came about the large-scale migration of 1630 described in Dudley's letter. This precipitated the flight of many Puritans to New England in the 1630's and marked the start of the effective colonization of that area.

Dudley (1576-1653) was himself a nobleman who spent much of his adult life as a steward to the Earl of Lincoln; his letter conveys news of his situation to an old friend, the wife of his previous employer. While quite a young man he had come under Puritan influence, and the intensity of his religious convictions may be measured by the fact that at the age of fifty-four—when most men are looking forward to retirement—he left his native land to found a new commonwealth on a strange and unknown shore. Not only did he survive the ordeal of colonization that he so vividly describes, but he lived on for a quarter of a century in the Bay Colony, serving four terms as governor and thirteen as deputy-governor. Clearly he was a man of great will power, who battled through to his godly ends undaunted by setbacks, suffering and everpresent death. All the more moving is this iron man's quiet and unadorned account of the simple human sacrifice upon which the Bay Colony was built.

LETTER*

From Governour Thomas Dudley,
to Bridget, Countess of Lincoln,
written nine months after the arrival of the emigrants
in the Massachusetts Bay.

"To the right honourable, my very good Lady, the
Lady Bridget, Countess of Lincoln.

Madam,

Your letters (which are not common or cheap), following me hither into New England, and bringing with them renewed testimonies of the accustomed favours you honoured me with in the old, have drawn from me this narrative retribution (which in respect of your proper interest in some persons of great note amongst us), were the thankfullest present I had to send over the seas. Therefore I humbly intreat your honour this be accepted as payment from him, who neither hath, nor is any more, than your honour's old thankful servant,

"Boston in New England,   Thomas Dudley."
March 12, 1631."

For the satisfaction of your honour and some friends, and for use of such as shall hereafter intend to increase our planta-

---

Source: This document has been termed "the most interesting as well as authentic document in our early annals"—that is, in the annals of New England. The fate of the original manuscript remains a mystery, but a shortened version of the letter, evidently made from a manuscript copy of the original, was published in Boston in 1696. John Farmer of Concord, New Hampshire, discovered this manuscript copy and printed it in full in 1834 in the *Collections* of the New Hampshire Historical Society. Two years later it was reissued by Peter Force, a Washington, D.C., printer and editor, in his *Tracts and Other Papers Relating Principally to the Origin, Settlement, and Progress of the Colonies in North America from the Discovery of the Country to the Year 1776,* Vol. II. In 1846 Alexander Young of Boston published a modern version in his *Chronicles of the First Planters of the Colony of Massachusetts Bay.* Since that time, until our own days, it has been largely inaccessible to the public.

The edition of the "Letter" printed here is based upon Force, but the spelling and punctuation have been modernized.

tion in New England, I have in the throng of domestic, and not altogether free from public business, thought fit to commit to memory our present condition, and what hath befallen us since our arrival here; which I will do shortly, after my usual manner, and must do rudely, having yet no table, nor other room to write in, than by the fireside upon my knee, in this sharp winter; to which my family must have leave to resort, though they break good manners, and make me many times forget what I would say, and say what I would not.

Now concerning the English that are planted here, I find that about the year 1620 certain English set out from Leyden in Holland intending their course for Hudson's river the mouth whereof lieth south of the river of the Pecoates, but ariseth as I am informed northwards in about 43°, and so a good part or it within the compass of our patent. These being much weather beaten and wearied with seeking the river, after a most tedious voyage arrived at length in a small Bay lying north east from Cape Cod, where, landing about the month of December, by the favour of a calm winter such as was never seen here since, began to build their dwellings in that place which is now called New Plymouth, where, after much sickness, famine, poverty and great mortality (through all which God by an unwonted Providence carried them), they are now grown up to a people, healthful, wealthy, politic and religious. Such things doth the Lord for those that wait for his mercies. These of Plymouth came with patents from King James and have since obtained others from our sovereign King Charles, having a Governour and Council of their own. There was about the same time one Mr. Weston, an English merchant, who sent divers men to plant and trade who sat down by the river of Wesaguscus [Weymouth], but these coming not for so good ends as those of Plymouth sped not so well, for the most of them dying and languishing away, they who survived were rescued by those of Plymouth out of the hands of Chickatalbott and his Indians, who oppressed these weak English, and intended to have destroyed them, and the Plymotheans also, as is set down in a tract written by Mr. Winslow of Plymouth. Also since one Capt. Wollaston with some thirty with him, came near to the same place and built on a hill which he named Mount Wollaston, but being not supplied with renewed provisions they vanished away as the former did. Also divers merchants of Bristol, and some other places have yearly for these eight years or thereabouts sent ships hither at the fishing times to trade for beaver where their factors, dishonestly for their gains, have furnished the Indians with guns, swords, powder and shot.

Touching the plantation which we here have begun, it fell out thus about the year 1627 some friends being together in Lincolnshire, fell into some discourse about New England and the planting of the gospel there; and after some deliberation, we imparted our reasons by letters and messages to some in London and the west country where it was likewise deliberately thought upon, and at length with often negotiation so ripened that in the year 1628 we procured a patent from his Majesty for our planting between the Massachusetts Bay, and Charles River on the south; and the river of Merrimac on the north and three miles on either side of those rivers and bay, as also for the government of those who did or should inhabit within that compass; and the same year we sent Mr. John Endicott and some with him to begin a plantation and to strengthen such as he should find there, which we sent thither from Dorchester and some places adjoining; from whom the same year receiving hopeful news. The next year 1629 we sent divers ships over with about three hundred people, and some cows, goats and horses, many of which arrived safely. These by their too large commendations of the country, and the commodities thereof, invited us so strongly to go on, that Mr. Winthrop of Suffolk (who was well known in his own country and well approved here for his piety, liberality, wisdom and gravity) coming in to us, we came to such resolution that in April 1630 we set sail from Old England with four good ships [Arbella, Jewell, Ambrose and Talbot]. And in May following eight more followed, two having gone before in February and March, and two more following in June and August, besides another sent out by a private merchant. These seventeen ships arrived all safe in New England, for the increase of the plantation here, this year 1630; but made a long, a troublesome, and a costly voyage being all wind bound long in England, and hindered with contrary winds after they set sail and so scattered with mists and tempests that few of them arrived together. Our four ships which set out in April arrived here in June and July, where we found the colony in a sad and unexpected condition, about eight of them being dead the winter before and many of those alive, weak and sick: all the corn and bread amongst them all hardly sufficient to feed them for a fortnight, insomuch that the remainder of one hundred and eighty servants we had the two years before sent over, coming to us for victuals to sustain them, we found ourselves wholly unable to feed them by reason that the provisions shipped for them were taken out of the ship they were put in, and they who were trusted to ship them in another failed us, and left them behind; whereupon necessity forced us to our extreme loss to give them all liberty; who had cost us about sixteen or twenty £s a person furnishing and sending over.

But bearing these things as we might, we began to consult of the place of our sitting down: for Salem where we landed, pleased us not. And to that purpose some were sent to the Bay to search up the rivers for a convenient place; who upon their return reported to have found a good place upon Mystic; but some other of us seconding these to approve or dislike of their judgment, we found a place liked us better three leagues up Charles River. And thereupon unshipped our goods into other vessels and with much cost and labour brought them in July to Charles Town; but there receiving advertisements by some of the late arrived ships from London and Amsterdam of some French preparations against us (many of our people brought with us being sick of fevers and the scurvy and we thereby unable to carry up our ordinance and baggage so far) we were forced to change counsel and for our present shelter to plant dispersedly, some at Charles Town which standeth on the north side of the mouth of Charles River; some on the south side thereof, which place we named Boston (as we intended to have done the place we first resolved on), some of us upon Mystic, which we named Medford; some of us westwards on Charles River, four miles from Charles Town, which place we named Watertown; others of us two miles from Boston in a place we named Rocksbury, others upon the river of Saugus between Salem and Charles Town. And the western men four miles south from Boston at a place we named Dorchester.

This dispersion troubled some of us, but help it we could not, wanting ability to remove to any place fit to build a town upon, and the time too short to deliberate any longer lest the winter should surprise us before we had builded our houses. The best counsel we could find out was to build a fort to retire to, in some convenient place if any enemy pressed thereunto, after we should have fortified ourselves against the injuries of wet and cold. So ceasing to consult further for that time they who had health to labour fell to building, wherein many were interrupted with sickness and many died weekly, yea almost daily. Amongst whom were Mrs. Pynchon, Mrs. Coddington, Mrs. Phillips, and Mrs. Alcock, a sister of Mr. Hooker's. Insomuch that the ships being now upon their return, some for England some for Ireland, there was as I take it not much less than an hundred (some think many more), partly out of dislike of our government which restrained and punished their excesses, and partly through fear of famine (not seeing other means than by their labour to feed themselves), which returned back again. And glad were we so to be rid of them. Others also afterwards hearing of men of their own disposition, which were planted at Piscataqua went from us to them, whereby though our numbers were lessened yet we accounted ourselves nothing weakened by their removal. Before the departure of the ships we contracted with Mr. Peirce, master of the Lyon of Bristol, to return to us with all speed with fresh supplies of victuals, and gave him directions accordingly. With this ship returned Mr. Revell, one of the five undertakers here, for the joint stock of the company, and Mr. Vassall one of the assistants, and his family; and also Mr. Bright, a minister sent hither the year before.

The ships being gone, victuals wasting and mortality increasing, we held divers fasts in our several congregations, but the Lord would not yet be deprecated; for about the beginning of September died Mr. Gager, a right godly man, a skillful surgeon and one of the deacons of our congregation. And Mr. Higginson, one of the ministers of Salem, a zealous and a profitable preacher; this of a consumption, that of a fever; and on the 30th of September died Mr. Johnson, another of the five undertakers (the lady Arbella his wife being dead a month before). This gentleman was a prime man amongst us having the best estate of any, zealous for religion and the greatest furtherer of this plantation. He made a most godly end, dying willingly, professing his life better spent in promoting this plantation than it would have been in any other way. He left to us a loss greater than the most conceived. Within a month after died Mr. Rossiter, another of our assistants, a godly man and of a good estate which still weakened us more, so that there now were left of the five undertakers but the

Governour, Sir Richard Saltonstall, and myself, and seven other of the assistants. And of the people who came over with us from the time of their setting sail from England in April 1630 until December following there died by estimation about two hundred at the least. So low hath the Lord brought us!

Well, yet they who survived were not discouraged, but bearing God's corrections with humility and trusting in his mercies, and considering how after a great ebb he had raised up our neighbours at Plymouth, we began again in December to consult about a fit place to build a town upon, leaving all thoughts of a fort, because upon any invasion we were necessarily to lose our houses when we should retire thereinto; so after divers meetings at Boston, Rocksbury and Watertown, on the 28th December we grew to this resolution to bind all the assistants (Mr. Endicott and Mr. Sharpe excepted, which last purposeth to return by the next ships into England) to build houses at a place, a mile east from Watertown near Charles River, the next spring, and to winter there the next year, that so by our examples and by removing the ordinance and munition thither, all who were able, might be drawn thither, and such as shall come to us hereafter to their advantage be compelled so to do; and so if God would, a fortified town might there grow up, the place fitting reasonably well thereto.

I should before have mentioned how both the English and the Indian corn being at ten shillings a strike, and beaver being valued at six shillings a pound, we made laws to restrain the selling of corn to the Indians, and to leave the price of beaver at liberty, which was presently sold for ten and twenty shillings a pound. I should also have remembered how the half of our cows and almost all our mares and goats sent us out of England, died at sea in their passage hither, and that those intended to be sent us out of Ireland were not sent at all; all which together with the loss of our six months building, occasioned by our intended removal to a town to be fortified, weakened our estates, especially the estates of the undertakers who were three or four thousand £ s engaged in the joint stock which was now not above so many hundred; yet many of us laboured to bear it as comfortably as we could, remembering the end of our coming hither and knowing the power of God who can support and raise us again, and useth to bring his servants low, that the meek may be made glorious by deliverance, Psal. 112.

In the end of this December, departed from us the ship Handmaid of London, by which we sent away one Thomas Morton, a proud insolent man who had lived here divers years and had been an attorney in the west country while he lived in England. Multitude of complaints we received against him for injuries done by him both to the English and Indians, for not bringing a canoe unto him to cross a river withal, whereby he hurt one, and shot through the garments of another; for the satisfaction of the Indians wherein, and that it might appear to them and to the English that we meant to do justice impartially, we caused his hands to be bound behind him and set his feet in the bilbows, and burned his house to the ground, all in the sight of the Indians, and so kept him prisoner til we sent him for England, whither we sent him, for that my Lord Chief Justice there so required that he might punish him capitally for fouler misdemeanours there perpetrated, as we were informed.

I have no leisure to review and insert things forgotten, but out of due time and order must set them down as they come to memory. About the end of October, this year 1630, I joined with the Governour and Mr. Mavereck in sending out our pinnace to the Narragansetts to trade for corn and to supply our wants, but after the pinnace had doubled Cape Cod, she put into the next harbour she found, and there meeting with Indians who showed their willingness to truck, she made her voyage there and brought us one hundred bushels of corn at about four shillings a bushel, which helped us somewhat. From the coast where they traded they saw a very large island four leagues to the east, which the Indians commended as a fruitful place full of good vines and free from sharp frosts having only one entrance into it, by a navigable river inhabited by a few Indians, which for a trifle would leave the island, if the English would set them upon the main; but the pinnace having no direction for discovery, returned without sailing to it, which in two hours they might have done. Upon this coast they found store of vines full of grapes dead ripe, the season being past; whither we purpose to send the next year sooner, to make some small quantity of wine if God enable us, the vines growing thin with us and we not having any leisure yet to plant vineyards.

But now having some leisure to discourse of the motives for other men's coming to this place or their abstaining from it, after my brief manner I say this: that if any come hither to plant for worldly ends that can live well at home he commits an error of which he will soon repent him. But if for spiritual and that no particular obstacle hinder his removal, he may find here what may well content him: vizt: materials to build, fuel to burn, ground to plant, seas and rivers to fish in, a pure air to breathe in, good water to drink til wine or beer can be made, which together with the cows, hogs and goats brought hither already may suffice for food, for as for fowl and venison, they are dainties here as well as in England. For clothes and bedding they must bring them with them til time and industry produce them here. In a word, we yet enjoy little to be envied but endure much to be pitied in the sickness and mortality of our people. And I do the more willingly use this open and plain dealing lest other men should fall short of their expectations when they come hither as we to our great prejudice did, by means of letters sent us from hence into England, wherein honest men out of a desire to draw over others to them wrote somewhat hyperbolically of many things here. If any godly men out of religious ends will come over to help u. in the good work we are about, I think they cannot dispose of themselves nor of their estates more to God's glory and the furtherance of their own reckoning, but they must not be of the poorer sort yet for divers years. For we have found by experience that they have hindered, not furthered the work. And for profane and debauched persons their oversight in coming here is wondered at, where they shall find nothing to content them. If there be any endued with grace and furnished with means to feed themselves and theirs for eighteen months, and to build and plant, let them come into our Macedonia and help us, and not spend themselves and their estates in a less profitable employment. For others I conceive they are not yet fitted for this business.

Touching the discouragement which the sickness and mortality which every first year hath seized upon us, and those of Plymouth, as appeareth before, may give to such who have cast any thoughts this way (of which mortality it may be said of us almost as of the Egyptians, that there is not a house where there is not one dead, and in some houses many), the natural causes seem to be in the want of warm lodging and good diet to which Englishmen are habituated at home; and in the sudden increase of heat which they endure that are landed here in summer, the salt meats at sea having prepared their bodies thereto, for those only these last two years died of fevers who landed in June and July; as those of Plymouth who landed in winter died of the scurvy, as did our poorer sort whose houses and bedding kept them not sufficiently warm, nor their diet sufficiently in heart. Other causes God may have as our faithful minister Mr. Wilson (lately handling that point) showed unto us, which I forbear to mention, leaving this matter to the further dispute of physicians and divines. Wherefore to return, upon the third of January died the daughter of Mr. Sharpe, a godly virgin making a comfortable end, after a long sickness. The plantation here received not the like loss of any woman since we came hither, and therefore she well deserves to be remembered in this place; and to add to our sorrows upon the fifth day came letters to us from Plymouth advertising us of this sad accident following.

About a fortnight before there went from us in a shallop to Plymouth six men and a girl, who in an hour or two before night, on the same day they went forth, came near to the mouth of Plymouth Bay, but the wind then coming strongly from the shore, kept them from entering and drove them to seawards, and they having no better means to help themselves let down their killick that so they might drive the more slowly, and be nearer land when the storm should cease. But the stone slipping out of the killick and thereby they driving faster than they thought all the night, to the morning when they looked out, they found themselves out of sight of land, which so astonished them, the frost being extreme and their hands so benumbed with cold that they could not handle their oars, neither had any compass to steer by, that they gave themselves for lost and lay down to die quietly; only one man who had more natural heat and courage remaining than the rest, continued so long looking for land, that the morning waxing clearer, he discovered land and with much difficulty hoisted the sail, and so the wind a little turning two days after, they were driven from Plymouth Bay; they arrived at a shore unknown unto them.

The stronger helped the weaker out of the boat and taking

their sail on shore made a shelter thereof, and made a fire, but the frost had so pierced their bodies that one of them died about three days after their landing, and most of the others grew worse, both in body and courage, no hopes of relief being within their view. Well, yet the Lord pitying them and two of them who only could use their legs going abroad, rather to seek than to hope to find help, they met first with two Indian women, who sent unto them an Indian man who informed that Plymouth was within fifty miles and offered together to procure relief for them, which they gladly accepting he performed, and brought them three men from Plymouth (the Governour and council of Plymouth liberally rewarding the Indian and took care for the safety of our people) who brought them all alive in their boat thither, save one man who with a guide chose rather to go over land but quickly fell lame by the way, and getting harbour at a trucking house the Plymotheans had in those parts, there he yet abides. At the others landing at Plymouth, one of them died as he was taken out of the boat, another (and he the worst in the company) rotted from the feet upwards where the frost had gotten most hold, and so died within a few days. The other three after God had blessed the surgeons' skill, used toward them, returned safe to us.

I set down this the more largely, partly because the first man that died was a godly man of our congregation, one Richard Garrad, a shoemaker, who at the time of his death more feared he should dishonour God than cared for his own life, as also because divers boats have been in manifest peril this year, yet the Lord preserved them all, this only excepted. Amongst those who died about the end of this January, there was a girl of eleven years old the daughter of one John Ruggles, of whose family and kindred died so many, that for some reason it was a matter of observation amongst us; who in the time of her sickness expressed to the minister and to those about her, so much faith and assurance of salvation, as is rarely found in any of that age, which I thought not unworthy here to commit to memory. And if any tax me for wasting paper with recording these small matters, such may consider that little mothers bring forth little children small commonwealths; matters of small moment the reading whereof yet is not to be despised by the judicious because small things in the beginning of natural or politic bodies are as remarkable as greater in bodies full grown.

Upon the fifth of February arrived here Mr. Peirce with the ship Lyon of Bristol with supplies of victuals from England who had set forth from Bristol the first of December before. He had a stormy passage hither, and lost one of his sailors not far from our shore, who in a tempest having helped to take in the spritsail lost his hold as he was coming down and fell into the sea, where after long swimming he was drowned, to the great dolour of those in the ship, who beheld so lamentable a spectacle, without being able to minister help to him. The sea was so high and the ship drove so fast before the wind, though her sails were taken down. By this ship we understood of the fight of three of our ships and two English men-of-war coming out of the straits with fourteen Dunkirks, upon the coast of England, as they returned from us in the end of the last summer, who through God's goodness with the loss of some thirteen or fourteen men out of our three ships, and I know not how many out of the two men-of-war, got at length clear of them. The Charles, one of our three, a stout ship of three hundred ton being so torn that she had not much of her left whole above water. By this ship we also understood the death of many of those who went from us the last year to old England as likewise of the mortality there, whereby we see there are ⸺ us in other places as well as with us.

Also to increase the heap of our sorrows we received advertisement by letters from our friends in England and by the reports of those who came hither in this ship to abide with us (which were about twenty-six), that those who went discontentedly from us the last year, out of their evil affections towards us, have raised many false and scandalous reports against us, affirming us to be Brownists in religion and ill affected to our state at home; and that these vile reports have won credit with some who formerly wished us well. But we do desire, and cannot but hope, that wise and impartial men will at length consider that such malcontents have ever pursued this manner of casting dirt to make others to seem as foul as themselves, and that our godly friends to whom we have been known will not easily believe that we are not so soon turned from the profession we so long have made in our native country. And for our further clearing I truly affirm that I know no one person who came over with us the last year to be altered in his judgement and affection either in ecclesiastical or civil respects since our coming hither, but we do continue to pray daily for our sovereign lord the king, the queen, the prince, the royal blood, the council and whole state as duty binds us to do and reason persuades others to believe, for how ungodly and unthankful should we be if we should not thus do, who come hither by virtue of his Majesty's letters patents, and under his gracious protection under which shelter we hope to live safely and from whom kingdom and subjects, we now have received and hereafter expect relief. Let our friends therefore give no credit to such malicious aspersions, but be more ready to answer for us, than we hear they have been: we are not like those which have dispensations to lie, but as we were free enough in Old England, to turn our insides outwards sometimes to our disadvantage very unlike is it that now (being *procul a bulmine*) we should be so unlike ourselves; let therefore this be sufficient for us to say, and others to hear in this matter.

Amongst others who died about this time was Mr. Robert Welden, whom in the time of his sickness we had chosen to be Captain of a Hundred Foot, but before he took possession of his place he died the 16th of this February, and was buried as a soldier with three volleys of shot. Upon the 22nd of February we held a general day of thanksgiving throughout the whole Colony for the safe arrival of the ship which came last with our provisions.

About this time we apprehended one Robert Wright who had been sometimes a linen draper in Newgate market and after that a brewer on the bank side and on Thames Street. This man we lately understood had made an escape in London from those who came to his house to apprehend him for clipping the king's coin. Upon his examination he confessed the fact and his escape, but affirmed he had the king's pardon for it under the broad seal which he yet not being able to prove, and one to whom he was known charging him with untruth in some of his answers, we therefore committed him to prison to be sent by the next ship to England.

Likewise we were lately informed that one Mr. Gardiner, who arrived here a month before us (and who passed here for a knight by the name of Sir Christopher Gardiner all this while), was no knight, but instead thereof, had two wives, now living in a house at London, one of which came about September last from Paris in France (where her husband had left her four years before) to London, where she had heard her husband had married a second wife, and whom by enquiry she found out, and they both condoling each other's estate wrote both their letters to the Governour (by Mr. Peirce who had conference with both the women in the presence of Mr. Allerton of Plymouth), his first wife desiring his return and conversion; his second his destruction for his foul abuse, and for robbing her of her estate of a part whereof she sent an inventory hither comprising therein many rich jewels, much plate and costly linen. This man had in his family (and yet hath) a gentlewoman whom he called his kinswoman and whom one of his wives in her letter names Mary Grove, affirming her to be a known harlot, whose sending back into Old England she also desired together with her husband.

Shortly after this intelligence we sent to the house of the said Gardiner (which was seven miles from us) to apprehend him and his woman with a purpose to send them both to London to his wives there, but the man, who having heard some rumour from some who came in the ship that letters were come to the Governour requiring justice against him, was readily prepared for flight so soon as he should see any crossing the river likely to apprehend him which he accordingly performed; for he dwelling alone easily discerned such who were sent to take him, half a mile before they approached his house, and with his piece on his neck went his way as most men think northwards, hoping to find some English there like to himself but likely enough it is which way soever he went, he will lose himself in the woods and be stopped with some rivers in his passing, notwithstanding his compass in his pocket, and so with hunger and cold will perish, before he find the place he seeks.

His woman was brought unto us and confessed her name, and that her mother dwells eight miles from Boirdly in Shropshire, and that Gardiner's father dwells in or near Gloucester and was (as she said) brother to Stephen Gardiner Bishop of Winchester, and did disinherit his son for his twenty-six years' absence in his travels in France, Italy, Germany, and Turkey; that he had (as he told her) married a wife in his travels, from whom he was divorced and the woman long since dead—that both herself and Gardiner were both Catholics, til of late, but were now Protestants, that she takes him to be a knight, but never heard where he was knighted. The woman was impenitent and close, confessing no more than was wrested from her by her own contradictions, so we have taken order to send her to the two wives in Old England to search her farther.

Upon the 8th of March, from after it was fair day light until about 8 of the clock in the forenoon, there flew over all the towns in our plantations so many flocks of doves, each flock containing many thousands and some so many that they obscured the light, that it passeth credit, if but the truth should be written, and the thing was the more strange, because I scarce remember to have seen ten doves since I came into the country. They were all turtles as appeared by divers of them we killed, flying somewhat bigger than those of Europe, and they flew from the north east to the south west; but what it portends I know not.

The ship now waits but for wind, which when it blows there are ready to go aboard therein for England Sir Richard Saltonstall, Mr. Sharpe, Mr. Coddington, and many others, the most whereof purpose to return to us again, if God will. In the meantime we are left a people poor and contemptible ~~~ ~~~h as trust in God, and are contented with our condition, being well assured that he will not fail nor forsake us.

I had almost forgotten to add this, that the wheat we received by this last ship stand us in thirteen or fourteen shillings a strike, and the peas about eleven shillings a strike beside the adventure, which is worth three or four shillings a strike, which is an higher price than I ever tasted bread before.

Thus Madam, I have as I can, told your honour all our matters, knowing your wisdom can make good use thereof. If I live not to perform the like office of my duty hereafter, likely it is some other will do it better.

Before the departure of the ship (which yet was wind bound) there came unto us Sagamore John and one of his subjects requiring satisfaction for the burning of two wigwams by some of the English, which wigwams were not inhabited but stood in a place convenient for their shelter, when upon occasion they should travel that ways. By examination we found that some English fowlers having retired into that which belonged to the subject and leaving a fire therein carelessly, which they had kindled to warm them, were the cause of burning thereof; for that which was the Sagamore's we could find no certain proof how it was fired, yet lest he should think us not sedulous enough to find it out and so should depart discontentedly from us, we gave both him and his subjects satisfaction for them both.

The like accident of fire also befell Mr. Sharpe and Mr. Colborne upon the 17th of this March both whose houses, which were as good, and as well furnished as the most in the plantation were, in two hours space burned to the ground together with much of their household stuff, apparel, and other things as also some goods of others who sojourned with them in their houses; God so pleasing to exercise us with corrections of this kind, as he hath done with others, for the prevention whereof in our new town intended this summer to be builded, we have ordered that no man there shall build his chimney with wood, nor cover his house with thatch, which was readily assented unto, for that divers other houses have been burned since our arrival (the fire always beginning in the wooden chimneys), and some English wigwams which have taken fire in the roofs covered with thatch or boughs.

And that this ship might return into Old England with heavy news, upon the 18th day of March, came one from Salem and told us that upon the 15th thereof, there died Mrs. Skelton, the wife of the other minister there, who about eighteen or twenty days before handling cold things in a sharp morning, put herself into a most violent fit of the wind colic and of vomiting, which continuing, she at length fell into a fever and so died as before. She was a godly and an helpful woman, and indeed the main pillar of her family, having left behind her an husband and four children weak and helpless, who can scarce tell how to live without her. She lived desired and died lamented and well deserves to be honourably remembered.

Upon the 25th of this March, one of Watertown having lost a calf, and about 10 of the clock at night hearing the howling of some wolves not far off, raised many of his neighbours out of their beds, that by discharging their muskets near about the place, where he heard the wolves, he might so put the wolves to flight, and save his calf; the wind serving fit to carry the report of the muskets to Rocksbury, three miles off at such a time, the inhabitants there took an alarm, beat up their drum, armed themselves, and sent in post to us to Boston to raise us also. So in the morning the calf being found safe, the wolves affrighted, and our danger past, we went merrily to breakfast.

I thought to have ended before, but the stay of the ship, and my desire to inform your honour of all I can, hath caused this addition; and every one having warning to prepare for the ship's departure tomorrow, I am now this 28th of March 1631, sealing my letters.

Song, Ballad, ===and Psalm====

SCARBOROUGH FAIR
WESTERN WIND
THE TWO SISTERS
THE CHERRY TREE CAROL
OLD HUNDRED

Introduction

The American musical heritage is a vast and complex treasury. Much of it yet remains to be assimilated into American culture and to be made available to large numbers of American people. In this treasury, and in the study of our history, folk music has a special place. Folk music and song have embodied the historical experiences of our people in a direct and vivid way, and have transmitted these experiences orally from generation to generation. Folk song embodies the living memory, the national identity and the moral conscience of a nation.

Among the many strands that go into the composition of

American folk song—American Indian, African and the successive waves of immigrant contributions from Europe, the near East and the Caribbean—the heritage from the British Isles has a special place. The songs brought by British and Irish immigrants in colonial times constituted the original foundation from which American musical expression was to grow. These ballads and lyrics were in many cases a heritage from medieval times. They would be carried by pioneers into the depths of the new continent; they would be sung wherever the English language was spoken.

I have selected four examples from hundreds that might have been given. Brought to this country in the earliest days, they have proved very popular with westward-moving people, and have provided the basic themes for endless musical and thematic variations. Scarborough Fair—2-G in Francis J. Child's great canon, English and Scottish Popular Ballads—is a riddle song of a type widely prevalent in medieval Europe. The melody comes from northern England, and this song is still sung to this very day by English children in the form known as "Strawberry Lane." American versions have been traced from New England, through the South and the Midwest, all the way to California and British Columbia.

Western Wind is a song that has been sung in endless variations by the British people and their American cousins. Parts of it are extremely old and may be traced back, at the very least, to the early sixteenth century. The following version, both melody and lyric, was published in 1788 in a collection of Scottish songs, the Scots Musical Museum, m̃ade notable by contributions from the pen of Robert Burns. In Child's collection the text is entitled Jamie Douglas. Slight modifications in it have been made for the convenience of English, as opposed to Scottish, singers.

The Two Sisters is an ancient ballad of love and jealousy that has been sung for centuries and is still sung to this day on both sides of the Atlantic with innumerable variations of story and melody. The variant given below comes from Virginia. Also from the South is the version here given of the Cherry Tree Carol, a religious ballad that took its form from medieval European legend and that was widely used in the New World by Christian people, slave and free alike. The melody is played upon a scale of five notes only, the so-called pentatonic scale.

The Psalms of David possessed, from the very beginning of our history, an extraordinary importance for American popular music. The Puritans considered the singing of psalms, or "spiritual songs," a holy duty in accordance with biblical injunction. These psalms had been penned "by an extraordinary gift of the Spirit, for the sake especially of God's spiritual Israel . . . we under the new Testament are bound to sing them as well as they under the old." [1]

Dissatisfied with existing English versions of the psalms, which they felt were too far from the spirit of the original, the Bay Colony ministers made their own translation from the original Hebrew. This book is known to us as the Bay Psalm Book. Published at Boston in 1640, it was the first work ever to be printed in the mainland colonies.

Later American critics have attacked the language of the Bay Psalm Book for its clumsiness, comparing it unfavorably to the earlier Ainsworth and King James versions. This criticism is wide of the mark. The Bay Colony translation was done into meter appropriate for singing to simple tunes; the question of prose balance and structure was irrelevant. "If," wrote John Cotton in the preface to the Bay Psalm Book, "in our English tongue we are to sing them, then as all our English songs (according to the course of our English poetry) do run in metre, so ought David's psalms to be translated into metre."

As for melodies, Puritan psalmists borrowed much from both French and English popular tradition, following, as they put it, "the graver sort of tunes of [our] own country songs." The psalms so set were put to a diversity of uses. In meeting on Sunday the congregation sang them in unison, though in the course of time the different groups developed their own special style of singing and harmonization. Of an evening they might be sung to the charming settings of Thomas Ravenscroft and other leading English composers. They might, too, be sung at work in the field, or on the road to battle, or in other time of trial.

Old Hundred, or the Hundredth Psalm, was one of the most popular and beloved of these old devotional songs. Below (p. 66) is the version of this psalm from the Bay Psalm Book, with the melodic line (long meter) as given in Ravenscroft's Psalter of 1621.

[1] *Bay Psalm Book,* preface.

SCARBOROUGH FAIR

I am a-go-ing to Scar-bor-ough Fair,

Par-sley, sage, rose-ma-ry and thyme; Re-

mem-ber me to one that lives there;

Once she was a true love of mine.

1. I am a-going to Scarborough Fair,
    Parsley, sage, rosemary, and thyme.
   Remember me to one who lives there;
    Once she was a true love of mine.

2. Tell her to make me a cambric shirt,
    Parsley, sage, rosemary, and thyme.
   Without a stitch of needlework,
    And then she'll be a true love of mine.

3. Tell her to wash it in yonder dry well,
    Parsley, sage, rosemary, and thyme.
   Where water ne'er sprang nor drop of rain fell,
    And then she'll be a true love of mine.

4. Tell her to dry it on yonder hawthorn,
      Parsley, sage, rosemary, and thyme.
   Which has not seen blossom since Adam was born,
      And then she'll be a true love of mine.

5. Now you have asked me questions three,
      Parsley, sage, rosemary, and thyme.
   I hope you'll answer as many for me,
      And then you'll be a true love of mine.

6. You must find me an acre of land,
      Parsley, sage, rosemary, and thyme.
   Between the ocean and the sea sand,
      And then you'll be a true love of mine.

7. You must plow it with one ram's horn,
      Parsley, sage, rosemary, and thyme.
   And sow it all over with one peppercorn,
      And then you'll be a true love of mine.

8. You must reap it with a strap of leather,
      Parsley, sage, rosemary, and thyme.
   And bind it all up with one peacock feather,
      And then you'll be a true love of mine.

9. And when you have done and finished this work,
      Parsley, sage, rosemary, and thyme.
   Come to me for your cambric shirt,
      And then you'll be a true love of mine.

WESTERN WIND

O wa - ly, wa - ly, up yon bank, And
wa - ly, wa - ly, down yon brae; And
wa - ly by yon ri - ver-side, Where
I and my true love wont to— gae! O
wa - ly, wa - ly, love is bon - ny, A
lit - tle while when it is— new; But
when 'tis old, it wax- es cold, And
wears a - way like morn - ing— dew!

O waly, waly, up yon bank,
And waly, waly, down yon brae;
And waly by yon riverside,
Where I and my true love wont to gae!
O waly, waly, love is bonny,
A little while when it is new;
But when 'tis old, it waxes cold,
And wears away like morning dew!

I leant my back unto an oak,
I thought it was a trusty tree;
But first it bowed and then it broke,
And so did my false love to me.
When cockle shells turn silver bells,
And mussels grow on every tree;
When frost and snow shall warm us all,
Then shall my love prove true to me.

'Tis not the frost that freezes fell
Nor blowing snow's inclemency;
'Tis not such cold that makes me cry,
But my love's heart grown cold to me.
O western wind, when wilt thou blow,
And shake the green leaves off the tree?
O gentle death, when wilt thou come,
And take a life that wearies me?

But had I wist before I kissed
That love had been so ill to win,
I'd locked my heart in a case of gold,
And pinned it with a silver pin.
O! O! if my young babe were born,
And set upon the nurse's knee;
And I myself were dead and gone;
For maid again I'll never be.

THE TWO SISTERS

There lived an old lord by the north-ern sea,

Bow down; There lived an old lord by the

north-ern sea, The boughs they bend to me.— There

lived an old lord by the north-ern sea, And

he had daugh-ters one, two, three;

I will be true, true to my love, Love, and my

love will be true to me. ___

1. There lived an old lord by the northern sea,
     Bow down;
   There lived an old lord by the northern sea,
     The boughs they bend to me.
   There lived an old lord by the northern sea,
   And he had daughters one, two, three;
       I will be true, true to my love,
       Love, and my love will be true to me.

2. A young man came a-courting there,
     Bow down;
   A young man came a-courting there,
     The boughs they bend to me.
   A young man came a-courting there,
   He found the youngest very fair;
       I will be true, true to my love,
       Love, and my love will be true to me.

3. He gave this girl a beaver hat,
   The eldest she thought ill of that.

4. He gave the youngest a gay gold ring,
   But to the eldest not a thing.

5. "Sister, oh sister, let us walk out
   To see the ships go sailing about."

6. As they went a-walking at the sea's brim,
   The eldest shoved the youngest in.

7. "Sister, oh sister, lend me your hand,
   And you shall have my house and land."

8. "I'll give you neither hand nor glove,
   But I will have your own true love."

9. Down she sank and away she swam
   Until she came to the old mill dam.

10. The miller came out with his fish hook,
    And he fished that fair maid out of the brook.

11. He robbed her of her gay gold ring,
    And into the brook he pushed her again.

12. The miller was hanged at his own mill gate,
    The eldest sister she shared his fate.

THE CHERRY TREE CAROL

When Joseph was an old man,
An old man was he,
He married Virgin Mary,
The Queen of Galilee,
He married Virgin Mary
The Queen of Galilee.

When Joseph and Mary
Walked through the orchard green,
There were apples and cherries
So many to be seen.
There were apples and cherries
So many to be seen.

Now Mary said to Joseph,
So meek and so mild,
"Joseph, gather me some cherries,
For I am with child.
Joseph, gather me some cherries
For I am with child."

Then Joseph flew in anger,
In anger flew he.
"Let the father of thy baby
Gather cherries for thee.
Let the father of thy baby
Gather cherries for thee."

Then the tree spoke unto Mary,
And it began to bow,
"Mary, gather some cherries,
From the uttermost bough.
Mary, gather some cherries
From the uttermost bough."

Psalm 100

A Psalm of Praise

Make ye a joy-ful sound-ing noise
Un - to Je - ho - vah, all the earth:
Serve ye Je -ho - vah with glad - ness:
Be - fore his pres-ence come with mirth.

Make ye a joyful sounding noise
Unto Jehovah, all the earth:
Serve ye Jehovah with gladness:
Before his presence come with mirth.

Know that Jehovah he is God,
Who hath us formed it is he,
And not ourselves: his own people
And sheep of his pasture are we.

Enter into his gates with praise,
Into his courts with thankfulness:
Make ye confession unto him,
And his name reverently bless.

Because Jehovah he is good
For evermore is his mercy:
And unto generations all
Continue doth his verity.

White Servants and
Negro Slaves

JOURNEY TO PENNSYLVANIA (1756)

BY GOTTFRIED MITTELBERGER

Introduction

The Puritan commonwealth was an exception in the story of American settlement. Most colonies were promoted, not for religious purposes, but to serve the interests of empire. This was in accordance with the mercantile theories of the seventeenth and eighteenth centuries, which taught that colonies were an absolute advantage to their mother country: for they fostered trade, promoted shipping and the merchant marine, bolstered the political and economic power of the colonizing state, and profited individual investors, planters and commercial interests.

The acquisition of New York and the launching of Pennsylvania, Maryland, Virginia and the Carolinas was entirely in accordance with such mercantile doctrine. But the development of these plantations faced a major and continually recurring problem: the shortage of labor by means of which to settle the new land and to raise profitable crops for overseas export.

Indian slaves could in no way satisfy the seemingly bottomless demand for labor as the development of the mainland and West Indian colonies proceeded in the seventeenth and eighteenth centuries. The Indian population on the eastern seaboard had never been very great; and it declined after the arrival of the whites as a result of war, enslavement and epidemic disease. Another possible solution was the importation of white workers from the British Isles, Ireland and Europe. One authority has estimated that in the colonial period more than one half of all immigrants to the colonies south of New England came as contract laborers. These were the poor, landless and oppressed of western Europe. Their chronic yearning for escape was a spark easy to fan into a flame, channeled and directed into emigration if the opportunity should arise. From the need of such people, and from the need of American planters for labor, arose a formidable "interest" of sea captains, shippers and traders whose business it was to collect cargoes of laborers, transport them to the New World, and sell them into temporary servitude.

The search for profitable cargoes, for a money profit to be made from this trade, produced a shameless scouring of the British Isles and western Germany. Magistrates emptied the jails and turned their inhabitants over to shippers, who whisked them off to colonial servitude. Handbills were broadcast advertising colonial opportunity in glowing terms and stimulating a passion among the poor to abandon the homeland and to emigrate. Emigrant agents collected children and paupers off the streets and cajoled them on board ship by trickery or carried them there by force. Prisoners of war garnered in punitive expeditions against the Irish and the Scots were shipped wholesale to the West Indian and mainland colonies.

Many of these people, but by no means all, signed contracts—"indentures"—specifying the length of service to be performed in the New World in return for transportation and freedom dues. Profits accrued when the middleman, or supplier of immigrant labor, sold these contracts to bidders in the colonies. The indentured servant was, in effect, a temporary slave. After his period of compulsory service he had a right to freedom and to dues of land, clothing, etc., that were customarily granted to the emancipated serf.

During the eighteenth century the stream of immigrant traffic switched from the British Isles to southwest Germany. German immigrants of this period are known as "redemptioners." They differed from the British immigrants in that they had no written contract and were sold off to purchasers at whatever terms the latter were able to exact. These people came mainly from Baden, Württemberg and the Palatinate. They provided a rich harvest for Dutch shippers and sea captains seeking principally to satisfy the demand for labor consequent upon the founding of Pennsylvania and its development in the period following 1681.

Pennsylvania, Maryland, Virginia and South Carolina constituted the main market for contract servants and redemptioners. The trade was terrible for the sufferings that it inflicted during the sea passage upon thousands of people, for the exploitation of the survivors during their period of servitude in the New World, for the separation of families, and for the harsh treatment meted out. On completion of their term of labor the servants vanished into the back country to become pioneers and small farmers, to join the ranks of the anonymous poor, and to accentuate the bitterness existing between the coastal rich and the underprivileged of the Piedmont.

The story of white servant immigration to America finds expression in the writings of Gottfried Mittelberger. A native of Württemberg, he arrived in Philadelphia in 1750 and remained in Pennsylvania for four years, returning to his native land to publish, in 1756, the indictment of the white slave trade which is his enduring contribution to the American story. His book is divided into two parts, the first of which deals with the recruiting, transportation and sale of labor; the second is devoted to a description of Pennsylvania. The first part of the book is reproduced below.

JOURNEY TO PENNSYLVANIA*
[THE CROSSING]

In the month of May 1750 I left my birthplace Enzweihingen in the district of Vaihingen for Heilbronn, where an organ was waiting for me, ready to be shipped to Pennsylvania. With this organ I took the usual route down the Neckar and the Rhine to Rotterdam in Holland. From Rotterdam I sailed with a transport of approximately 400 souls —Württemberger, Durlacher, Palatines, and Swiss, etc.— across the North Sea to Cowes in England; and, after a nine-day stopover there, across the Atlantic, until at last on the tenth of October 1750 I landed in Philadelphia, the capital of Pennsylvania.

The trip from home to Rotterdam including the sojourn

---

*Source: Reprinted by permission of the publishers from Gottfried Mittelberger, edited and translated by Oscar Handlin and John Clive, Journey to Pennsylvania. The John Harvard Library of the Belknap Press of Cambridge, Mass.: Harvard University Press, copyright, 1960, by the President and Fellows of Harvard College.

there, took fully seven weeks because of the many delays encountered both in going down the Rhine and in Holland. Without these one could have completed the journey more quickly. The voyage from Rotterdam to Philadelphia took fifteen weeks. I spent nearly four years in America and, as my testimonials show, held the post of organist and school-teacher in the German St. Augustine's Church in Providence. Besides that I gave private music and German lessons in the house of Captain von Diemer, as attested by the following certificate:

> Whereas the bearer Mr. Mittelberger, music master, has re-solved to return from this province to his native land, which is in the Duchy of Württemberg in Germany, I have at his re-quest granted these lines to certify that the above named Mr. Mittelberger has behaved himself honestly, diligently, and faithfully in the offices of schoolmaster and organist during the space of three years in the Township of New-Providence, County of Philadelphia and Province of Pennsylvania, &c. So that I and all his employers were entirely satisfied, and would willingly have him to remain with us. But as his call obliges him to proceed on his long journey, we would recommend the said Mr. Mittelberger to all persons of dignity and character; and beg their assistance, so that he may pass and repass until he arrives at his respective abode; which may God grant, and may the benediction of Heaven accompany him in his journey. Deus benedicat susceptis ejus ferat eum ad amicos suos maxi-ma prosperitate. [1]

Dabam, Providentiae Philadelphiae
    Comitatu Pennsylvania in America,
    die 25. Apr. A. D. 1754

                John Diemer, Cap.
                Sam. Kennedy, M.D.
                Henry Pawling, Esqr.

[Witnesses]
Henry Marsteller
Matthias Gmelin.

I made careful inquiries into the conditions of the coun-try. And what I am going to describe in this book I partly found out for myself, and partly heard from reliable people who know what they were talking about. I should no doubt have been able to report and to recount more if, at the time, I had ever considered publishing anything about Pennsyl-

---

[1] May God bless his undertaking and bring him to his friends with the greatest dispatch.

vania. But I always thought myself far too feeble to do that sort of thing. It was only the misfortunes I encountered on my voyage to and fro (for in the country itself things went well with me, because I was able to earn a living right away, and could easily support myself well), and the nasty tricks the Newlanders wanted to play on me and my family, as I shall relate further on, that first gave me the idea not to keep what I knew to myself.

But what really drove me to write this little book was the sad and miserable condition of those traveling from Germany to the New World, and the irresponsible and merciless proceedings of the Dutch traders in human beings and their man-stealing emissaries—I mean the so-called Newlanders. For these at one and the same time steal German people under all sorts of fine pretexts, and deliver them into the hands of the great Dutch traffickers in human souls. From this business the latter make a huge profit, and the Newlanders a smaller one.

This, as I say, is the principal reason for my publishing this little book. In fact I had to take a solemn oath to write it. For before I left Pennsylvania, when it became known that I wanted to return to Württemberg, numerous Württemberger, Durlacher, and Palatines (a great many of whom live there and spend their days moaning and groaning about ever having left their native country) begged me with tears and uplifted hands, and even in the name of God, to publicize their misery and sorrow in Germany. So that not only the common people but even princes and lords might be able to hear about what happened to them; and so that innocent souls would no longer leave their native country, persuaded to do so by the Newlanders, and dragged by them into a similar kind of slavery. And so I vowed to the great God, and promised those people to reveal the entire truth about it to people in Germany, according to the best of my knowledge and ability.

I hope, therefore, that my dear countrymen and indeed all of Germany will be no less concerned to get news and factual information about how far it is to Pennsylvania and how long it takes to get there; about what the journey costs, and what discomforts and dangers one has to undergo in the bargain; about what happens when the people arrive in America well or ill; about how they are sold and scattered around; and, finally, about what conditions in general are like. I conceal neither good nor bad aspects; and thus I hope that the world, liking an honest man, will look on me as impartial and truthful. Once people have read all this, I have no doubt that those who might still have some desire to go over there will stay at home and will carefully avoid this long and difficult voyage and the misfortunes connected with it; since such a journey will mean for most who undertake it the loss of all they possess, of freedom and peace, and for some the loss of their very lives and, I can even go so far as to say, of the salvation of their souls.

To travel from Durlach or Württemberg as far as Holland and the open sea one must reckon on a trip of 200 hours.[2] From there across the sea to England as far as Cowes, where all ships drop anchor before they finally begin the great ocean crossing, another 150 hours. From there over 100 hours until one completely loses sight of England. Then across the Atlantic, that is from land to land, as the sailors put it, 1,200 hours. Finally from the first sight of land in Pennsylvania to Philadelphia, over 40 hours. Altogether such a journey adds up to 1,700 hours or 1,700 French miles.

This journey lasts from the beginning of May until the end of October, that is, a whole six months, and involves such hardships that it is really impossible for any description to do justice to them. The reason for this is that the Rhine boats must pass by thirty-six different customs houses between Heilbronn and Holland. At each of these all the ships must be examined, and these examinations take place at the convenience of the customs officials. Meanwhile, the ships with the people in them are held up for a long time. This involves a great deal of expense for the passengers; and it also means that the trip down the Rhine alone takes from four to six weeks.

When the ships with their passengers arrive in Holland they are there held up once again for from five to six weeks. Because everything is very expensive in Holland the poor people must spend nearly all they own during this period. In addition various sad accidents are likely to occur here. I have, for instance, seen with my own eyes two of the chil-

---

[2] Mittelberger, as was contemporary German practice, uses *Stunden* or hours as a measure of distance, conventionally equal to 3.75 to 4 kilometers, or about 2.4 miles.

dren of a man trying to board ship near Rotterdam meet sudden death by drowning.

In Rotterdam, and to some extent also in Amsterdam, the people are packed into the big boats as closely as herring, so to speak. The bedstead of one person is hardly two feet across and six feet long, since many of the boats carry from four to six hundred passengers, not counting the immense amount of equipment, tools, provisions, barrels of fresh water, and other things that also occupy a great deal of space.

Because of contrary winds it sometimes takes the boats from two to four weeks to make the trip from Holland to Cowes. But, given favorable winds, that voyage can be completed in eight days or less. On arrival everything is examined once more and customs duties paid. It can happen that ships have to ride at anchor there from eight to fourteen days, or until they have taken on full cargoes. During this time everyone has to spend his last remaining money and to consume the provisions that he meant to save for the ocean voyage, so that most people must suffer tremendous hunger and want at sea where they really feel the greatest need. Many thus already begin their sufferings on the voyage between Holland and England.

When the ships have weighed anchor for the last time, usually off Cowes in Old England, then both the long sea voyage and misery begin in earnest. For from there the ships often take eight, nine, ten, or twelve weeks sailing to Philadelphia, if the wind is unfavorable. But even given the most favorable winds, the voyage takes seven weeks.

During the journey the ship is full of pitiful signs of distress—smells, fumes, horrors, vomiting, various kinds of sea sickness, fever, dysentery, headaches, heat, constipation, boils, scurvy, cancer, mouth-rot, and similar afflictions, all of them caused by the age and the highly-salted state of the food, especially of the meat, as well as by the very bad and filthy water, which brings about the miserable destruction and death of many. Add to all that shortage of food, hunger, thirst, frost, heat, dampness, fear, misery, vexation, and lamentation as well as other troubles. Thus, for example, there are so many lice, especially on the sick people, that they have to be scraped off the bodies. All this misery reaches its climax when in addition to everything else one must also suffer through two to three days and nights of storm, with everyone convinced that the ship with all aboard is bound to sink. In such misery all the people on board pray and cry pitifully together.

In the course of such a storm the sea begins to surge and rage so that the waves often seem to rise up like high mountains, sometimes sweeping over the ship; and one thinks that he is going to sink along with the ship. All the while the ship, tossed by storm and waves, moves constantly from one side to the other, so that nobody aboard can either walk, sit, or lie down; and the tightly-packed people on their cots, the sick as well as the healthy, are thrown every which way. One can easily imagine that these hardships necessarily affect many people so severely that they cannot survive them.

I myself was afflicted by severe illness at sea, and know very well how I felt. These people in their misery are many times very much in want of solace, and I often entertained and comforted them with singing, praying, and encouragement. Also, when possible, and when wind and waves permitted it, I held daily prayer meetings with them on deck, and, since we had no ordained clergyman on board, was forced to administer baptism to five children. I also held services, including a sermon, every Sunday, and when the dead were buried at sea, commended them and our souls to the mercy of God.

Among those who are in good health impatience sometimes grows so great and bitter that one person begins to curse the other, or himself and the day of his birth, and people sometimes come close to murdering one another. Misery and malice are readily associated, so that people begin to cheat and steal from one another. And then one always blames the other for having undertaken the voyage. Often the children cry out against their parents, husbands against wives and wives against husbands, brothers against their sisters, friends and acquaintances against one another.

But most of all they cry out against the thieves of human beings! Many groan and exclaim: "Oh! If only I were back at home, even lying in my pig-sty!" Or they call out: "Ah, dear God, if I only once again had a piece of good bread or a good fresh drop of water." Many people whimper, sigh, and cry out pitifully for home. Most of them become homesick at the thought that many hundreds of people must necessarily perish, die, and be thrown into the ocean in such misery. And this in turn makes their families, or those who were responsible for their undertaking the journey, oftentimes fall almost into despair—so that it soon becomes practically impossible to rouse them from their depression. In a word, groaning, crying, and lamentation go on aboard day and night; so that even the hearts of the most hardened, hearing all this, begin to bleed.

One can scarcely conceive what happens at sea to women in childbirth and to their innocent offspring. Very few escape with their lives; and mother and child, as soon as they have died, are thrown into the water. On board our ship, on a day on which we had a great storm, a woman about to give birth and unable to deliver under the circumstances, was pushed through one of the portholes into the sea because her corpse was far back in the stern and could not be brought forward to the deck.

Children between the ages of one and seven seldom survive the sea voyage; and parents must often watch their offspring suffer miserably, die, and be thrown into the ocean, from want, hunger, thirst, and the like. I myself, alas, saw such a pitiful fate overtake thirty-two children on board our vessel, all of whom were finally thrown into the sea. Their parents grieve all the more, since their children do not find repose in the earth, but are devoured by the predatory fish of the ocean. It is also worth noting that children who have not had either measles or smallpox usually get them on board the ship and for the most part perish as a result.

On one of these voyages a father often becomes infected by his wife and children, or a mother by her small children, or even both parents by their children, or sometimes whole families one by the other, so that many times numerous corpses lie on the cots next to those who are still alive, especially when contagious diseases rage on board.

Many other accidents also occur on these ships, especially falls in which people become totally crippled and can never be completely made whole again. Many also tumble into the sea.

It is not surprising that many passengers fall ill, because in addition to all the other troubles and miseries, warm food is served only three times a week, and at that is very bad, very small in quantity, and so dirty as to be hardly palatable at all. And the water distributed in these ships is often very black, thick with dirt, and full of worms. Even when very thirsty, one is almost unable to drink it without loathing. It is certainly true that at sea one would often spend a great deal of money just for one good piece of bread, or one good drink of water—not even to speak of a good glass of wine— if one could only obtain them. I have, alas, had to experience that myself. For toward the end of the voyage we had to eat the ship's biscuit, which had already been spoiled for a long time, even though in no single piece was there more than the size of a thaler that was not full of red worms and spiders' nests. True, great hunger and thirst teach one to eat and drink everything—but many must forfeit their lives in the process. It is impossible to drink sea water, since it is salty and bitter as gall. If this were not the case, one could undertake such an ocean voyage with far less expense and without so many hardships.

When at last after the long and difficult voyage the ships finally approach land, when one gets to see the headlands for the sight of which the people on board had longed so passionately, then everyone crawls from below to the deck, in order to look at the land from afar. And people cry for joy, pray, and sing praises and thanks to God. The glimpse of land revives the passengers, especially those who are half-dead of illness. Their spirits, however weak they had become, leap up, triumph, and rejoice within them. Such people are now willing to bear all ills patiently, if only they can disembark soon and step on land. But, alas, alas!

When the ships finally arrive in Philadelphia after the long voyage only those are let off who can pay their sea freight or can give good security. The others, who lack the money to pay, have to remain on board until they are purchased and until their purchasers can thus pry them loose from the ship. In this whole process the sick are the worst off, for the healthy are preferred and are more readily paid for. The miserable people who are ill must often still remain at sea and in sight of the city for another two or three weeks —which in many cases means death. Yet many of them, were they able to pay their debts and to leave the ships at once, might escape with their lives.

Before I begin to describe how this commerce in human beings takes place I must report what the voyage to Philadelphia or Pennsylvania costs. Any one older than ten years has to pay £10, or 60 florins, for the passage from Rotterdam to Philadelphia. Children between five and ten pay half fare, that is to say £5, or 30 florins. All children under the age of five get free passage. In return the passengers are transported across the ocean; and as long as they are at sea, they get their board, however bad it is (as I reported above).

All this covers only the sea voyage; the cost of land transportation from home to Rotterdam, including the Rhine passage, comes to at least 40 florins no matter how economically one tries to live on the way. This does not include the expenses of any extraordinary contingencies. I can assure readers of this much—that many travelers on the journey from their homes to Philadelphia spent 200 florins, even with all possible thrift.

This is how the commerce in human beings on board ship takes place. Every day Englishmen, Dutchmen, and High Germans come from Philadelphia and other places, some of them very far away, sometime twenty or thirty or forty hours' journey, and go on board the newly arrived vessel that has brought people from Europe and offers them for sale. From among the healthy they pick out those suitable for the purposes for which they require them. Then they negotiate with them as to the length of the period for which they will go into service in order to pay off their passage, the whole amount of which they generally still owe. When an agreement has been reached, adult persons by written contract bind themselves to serve for three, four, five, or six years, according to their health and age. The very young, between the ages of ten and fifteen, have to serve until they are twenty-one, however.

Many parents in order to pay their fares in this way and get off the ship must barter and sell their children as if they were cattle. Since the fathers and mothers often do not know where or to what masters their children are to be sent, it frequently happens that after leaving the vessel, parents and children do not see each other for years on end, or even for the rest of their lives.

People who arrive without the funds to pay their way and who have children under the age of five, cannot settle their debts by selling them. They must give away these children for nothing to be brought up by strangers; and in return these children must stay in service until they are twenty-one years old. Children between five and ten who owe half-fare, that is, thirty florins, must also go into service in return until they are twenty-one years old, and can neither set free their parents nor take their debts upon themselves. On the other hand, the sale of children older than ten can help to settle a part of their parents' passage charges.

A wife must be responsible for her sick husband and a husband for his sick wife, and pay his or her fare respectively, and must thus serve five to six years not only for herself or himself, but also for the spouse, as the case may be. If both should be ill on arrival, then such persons are brought directly from the ship into a hospital, but not until it is clear that no purchaser for them is to be found. As soon as they have recovered, they must serve to pay off their fare, unless they have the means immediately to discharge the debt.

It often happens that whole families—husband, wife, and children—being sold to different purchasers, become separated, especially when they cannot pay any part of the passage money. When either the husband or the wife has died at sea, having come more than halfway, then the surviving spouse must pay not only his or her fare, but must also pay for or serve out the fare of the deceased.

When both parents have died at sea, having come more than halfway, then their children, especially when they are still young and have nothing to pawn or cannot pay, must be responsible for their own fares as well as those of their parents, and must serve until they are twenty-one years old. Once free of service, they receive a suit of clothing as a parting gift, and if it has been so stipulated the men get a horse and the women a cow.

When a servant in this country has the opportunity to get married he has to pay £5 to £6, that is, 30 to 36 florins for every year that he would still have had to serve. But many who must purchase and pay for their brides in this manner come to regret their purchases later. They would just as soon surrender their damnably expensive wares again and lose their money into the bargain.

No one in this country can run away from a master who has treated him harshly and get far. For there are regulations and laws that ensure that runaways are certainly and quickly recaptured. Those who arrest or return a fugitive get a good reward. For every day that someone who runs away is absent from his master he must as a punishment do service an extra week, for every week an extra month, and for every month a half year. But if the master does not want to take back the recaptured runaway, he is entitled to sell him to someone else for the period of as many years as he would still have had to serve.

Occupations vary, but work is strenuous in this new land; and many who have just come into the country at an advanced age must labor hard for their bread until they die. I will not even speak of the young people. Most jobs involve cutting timber, felling oak trees, and levelling, or as one says there, clearing, great tracts of forest, roots and all. Such forest land, having been cleared in this way, is then laid out in fields and meadows. From the best wood that has been felled people construct railings or fences around the new fields. Inside these, all meadows, all lawns, gardens, and orchards, and all arable land are surrounded and enclosed by thickly cut wood planks set in zigzag fashion one above the other. And thus cattle, horses, and sheep are confined to pasture land.

Our Europeans who have been purchased must work hard all the time. For new fields are constantly being laid out; and thus they learn from experience that oak tree stumps are just as hard in America as they are in Germany. In these hot regions there is particularly fulfilled in them that with which the Lord God afflicted man in the first book of Moses, on account of his sin and disobedience, namely: "Thou shalt eat thy bread in the sweat of thy brow." Thus let him who wants to earn his piece of bread honestly and in a Christian manner and who can only do this by manual labor in his native country stay *there* rather than come to America.

For, in the first place, things are no better in Pennsylvania. However hard one may have had to work in his native land, conditions are bound to be equally tough or even tougher in the new country. Furthermore the emigrant has to undertake the arduous voyage, which means not only that he must suffer more misery for half a year than he would have to suffer doing the hardest labor, but also that he must spend approximately two hundred florins which no one will refund to him. If he has that much money, he loses it; if he does not have it, he must work off his debt as a slave or as a miserable servant. So let people stay in their own country and earn their keep honestly for themselves and their families. Furthermore, I want to say that those people who may let themselves be talked into something and seduced into the voyage by the thieves of human beings are the biggest fools if they really believe that in America or Pennsylvania roasted pigeons are going to fly into their mouths without their having to work for them.

How sad and miserable is the fate of so many thousand German families who lost all the money they ever owned in the course of the long and difficult voyage, many of whom perished wretchedly and had to be buried at sea and who, once they have arrived in the new country, saw their old and young separated and sold away into places far removed one from the other! The saddest aspect of all this is that in most instances parents must give away their young children getting nothing in return. For such children are destined never to see or recognize parents, brothers, and sisters again, and, after they have been sold to strangers, are not brought up in any sort of Christian faith.

In Pennsylvania there exist so many varieties of doctrines and sects that it is impossible to name them all. Many people do not reveal their own particular beliefs to anyone. Furthermore there are many hundreds of adults who not only are unbaptized, but who do not even want baptism. Many others pay no attention to the sacraments and to the Holy Bible, or even to God and His Word. Some do not even believe in the existence of a true God or Devil, heaven or hell, salvation or damnation, the resurrection of the dead, the last judgment and eternal life, but think that everything visible is of merely natural origin. For in Pennsylvania not only is everyone allowed to believe what he wishes; he is also at liberty to express these beliefs publicly and freely.

Thus when young people not raised in the fundamentals of religion must go into service for many years with such freethinkers and unbelievers and are not permitted by these people to attend any church or school, especially when they live far away from them, then such innocent souls do not reach a true knowledge of the Divine and are brought up like heathen or Indians.

The ocean voyage is sometimes dangerous for those people who bring money and effects with them from home, because at sea much is often spoiled by inrushing water. And sometimes they are robbed on board by dishonest people. Thus such once-wealthy folk are to have really unhappy experiences.

As an example, let me tell the sad story of a man from Württemberg. Late in the year 1753 Bailiff Daser, well known to us at home, arrived in Philadelphia in a miserable and unhappy state, having come from Nagold with his wife and eight children. Not only had he been robbed on sea to the tune of 1,800 florins, but on account of these thefts he and the English ship's captain got involved in a great lawsuit at Philadelphia. Litigation brought him no gain. On the contrary, he had to pay costs and thus lost a great deal more. Mr. Daser had to pay 600 florins to cover the passage for himself and his family. Since, however, he had been robbed of his money, all his effects, including his boxes, were publicly auctioned off for a trifling sum at a *vendue*, or public auction. Thus he and his family found themselves in even more miserable circumstances.

When at this point he wanted to borrow some money in order to buy a plantation, he was shamefully cheated by his creditor. He had made an agreement with this man, to pay him back the borrowed sum within two years. But the person who drew up the *obligation*, or bond, as it is known there, wrote, as the result of an intentional slip of the tongue by the unscrupulous creditor, "two days" instead of "two years." Mr. Daser signed the agreement not realizing that he was signing his own doom, since he knew no English. The game was played in such a way that since he did not repay the money within two days, all he owned was sold, even the shirt from his very back. Actually he had not even received the money in the first place thanks to the creditor's negligence and his various subterfuges.

Indeed, he would probably have ended up in prison, or been forced to sell his children, if, through my intercession, he had not been saved by Captain von Diemer, who always showed great and laudable concern for Germans. The same Captain von Diemer out of charity then supplied Daser and his family with food, money, beds, and living quarters until the end of the trial. He also gave security for him, so that Mr. Daser did not have to go to debtors' prison. When I departed Captain von Diemer promised Mr. Daser and me, with hand and mouth, to help take care of the Daser family and their needs as long as he lived. During a period of eight weeks, Mr. Daser took his meals in our house, and slept there, too. But, in truth, because of the many sad misfortunes he had suffered, he became very despondent and half lost his mind. His two oldest unmarried daughters and his oldest son were forced to go into service shortly before my departure, each bound by written contract for three years.

I want to take this opportunity to relate some curious and most unfortunate instances of shipwreck. On St. James's Day in 1754, a ship with some 360 souls on board, mainly Württemberger, Durlacher, and Palatines, was driven onto a rock at night by a storm between Holland and Old England. It received three shocks, each time accompanied by loud crashes. Finally it came apart lengthwise underneath. So much water rushed in that the ship started to sink early the next morning.

When the peril was at its greatest and people tried to save themselves, sixty-three persons jumped into one boat. Since this boat was already overloaded, and since yet another person swam to it and held on, it was impossible to drive him off in any other way than by chopping off his hands; so that he had to drown. Another person is supposed to have jumped onto a barrel which had fallen out of the great ship, in order to save himself in that way. But the barrel capsized at once and sank with him.

The people who remained on board the great ship, however, held on some to the rigging, some to the masts. Many stood deep in water, clapping their hands together over their heads, and crying together in an indescribably piteous manner. From the boat one could eventually see the great ship sink with three hundred souls aboard before one's very eyes. However, merciful God sent help, in the form of an English ship in the vicinity, to the rest who had saved themselves in the boat. This took them aboard in their great peril after their shipwreck, and brought them back to land. This great misfortune would not even have become known in Germany, had the ship perished during the night with all aboard.

The following unfortunate sea voyage involving many Germans has hardly or not at all become known in Germany. In 1752 a ship arrived in Philadelphia from Holland which had taken an entire half year to make the crossing. This ship had been battered by many storms during the entire winter and was unable to land, until at last another better ship came to

help it in its miserable, starved-out, and half-wrecked state.
This ship was able to bring 21 out of approximately 340 persons to Philadelphia. Not only had these been at sea for a full
half year, and driven by the storm onto the coast of Ireland,
but most people aboard had died of starvation. They had lost
mast and sails, captain and mates. And the rest would never
have reached land, if God had not come to their aid with another ship and had thus guided them here.

Another unfortunate sea voyage has probably also not become known in Germany. Some years ago an entire ship full
of Germans is supposed to have been lost at sea. These people,
too, were reported to have come to Philadelphia. But no one
ever heard anything about them except that a description of
this same ship was sent from Holland to the merchants of
Philadelphia. News of such totally lost and wrecked ships is
not publicized in Germany lest people be frightened away
from the voyage, and prevented from making it.

I find it impossible to hold back what I heard from a reliable
source in Pennsylvania by means of a bundle of letters posted
at sea on the tenth of December 1754 that reached me on the
first of September 1755. In these letters I am told in piteous
fashion that in the autumn of the year just past (1754), once
again more than 22,000 souls arrived in Philadelphia alone, a
great burden to the country. Most of them were Württemberger, for at that time there took place a big emigration from
Württemberg. The rest were Palatines, Durlacher, and Swiss.
They were so miserably sick and wretched that once again
most people had to sell their children on account of great
poverty. Such a great mass of people imposed a great burden
on the land, especially the multitude of the sick, of whom
many daily continue to fill the graves.

While I was in the country, twenty to twenty-four ships full
of people arrived in Philadelphia alone during the autumn of
every year. Within the space of four years the city was invaded by more than 25,000 souls. This figure is in addition to
those who died at sea or during the voyage, and does not
count those ships full of people that sailed to other English
colonies, that is, to New York, Boston, Maryland, Nova Scotia,
and Carolina. Thus these colonies were filled up and people
as people in the city of Philadelphia became worthless.

But the fact that so many still go to America and especially
to Pennsylvania is to be blamed on the swindles and persua-

sions practiced by so-called Newlanders. These thieves of human beings tell their lies to people of various classes and professions, among whom may be found many soldiers, scholars, artists, and artisans. They abduct people from their princes and lords and ship them to Rotterdam or Amsterdam for sale. There they get three florins, or one ducat, from the merchant, for each person ten years or older. On the other hand the merchants get from sixty to seventy or eight florins for such a person in Philadelphia, depending on the debts that said person has incurred on the voyage.

If such a Newlander has gathered together a transport and does not want to go to America himself, he stays behind, and spends the winter in Holland or elsewhere. In the spring he once more collects money in advance from his merchants, for the purchase of human beings. Then he begins to travel again, pretending to have come from Pennsylvania in order to buy all kinds of merchandise and to export it back there.

Often the Newlanders claim to have the authorization of the American government and of their fellow-countrymen in America to collect legacies belonging to these people. They also say that they want to take this certain and good opportunity to invite the friends, brothers and sisters, and even the fathers and mothers of those in America to join them. And it frequently happens that such old people follow their relatives, persuaded into the hope of finding better living conditions.

The Newlanders try to make these old people leave the country so that they can lure other people to go along with them. And so they pull the wool over the eyes of many who say that if such and such relatives would only come along, then they would be willing to risk the trip. This sort of enticement takes various forms. A favorite method is for these thieves of human beings to show the poor people money that, however, turns out to be nothing more than bait from Holland for human beings, and thus accursed blood-money.

Sometimes these thieves of human beings are able to talk persons of special rank, such as nobles or skilled or learned people, into making the trip. If these folk are able neither to pay their passage nor to give security, then they, just like the common poor folk, are not allowed to leave the ship, and must stay aboard until somebody comes and buys them from the ship's captain. And when they are finally let off, then they have to serve the lords and masters who purchased them, just as if they were common wage-laborers.

Their rank, skill and learning does not help them at all. For in America only workmen and artisans are needed. And the worst of it is that such people, not used to this kind of work, are beaten like cattle until they have learned hard labor. For this reason several people, finding themselves so wretchedly cheated by the Newlanders, have committed suicide. Others have fallen into such a state of despair that no one could any longer be of help to them. Still others have run away and have subsequently fared even worse than before.

It often happens that the merchants in Holland make a secret agreement with the captain and the Newlanders. This stipulates that the latter sail the fully-loaded ships not to Pennsylvania where these people want to go but to another place in America where they calculate they can sell their human cargo for a better price. In this way many who already have acquaintances or even perhaps friends, brothers, and sisters in Pennsylvania, to whose help and care they had been looking forward, are painfully hurt by being separated from their families and friends whom because of such godless misrouting they will never get to see again, either in this or that country. Thus both in Holland and at sea one has to put oneself into the hands of the wind and the captain; since at sea no one knows for certain just where the ship is proceeding. The blame for this rests with the Newlanders, and with a few unscrupulous dealers in human flesh in Holland.

Many people going to Philadelphia entrust the remains of the money they are able to bring away from home to these Newlanders. These thieves, however, often remain in Holland along with the money. Or they proceed from Holland on board another ship to a different English colony; so that the poor defrauded people, when they get to America, have no other recourse but to go into service, or to sell their children, if they have any, in order to get away from the ship.

Let me illustrate this by a curious example. In 1753 a noble lady, N.N., arrived in Philadelphia with two half-grown daughters and a young son. In the course of the Rhine journey this lady had made a loan of more than 1,000 reichsthaler to a Newlander otherwise well known to her. This villain remained in Holland along with the money after the departure of the lady's ship. Thus she was put into a position of such great want and need that her two daughters were forced to go into service. The same poor lady sent her son back across the ocean in the spring of the following year in order to locate the man who had stolen her money. But by the time of my departure in 1754 no one had heard anything of this man. Indeed, it was said that the young man looking for him had lost his life in the course of his search.

It is, by the way, impossible to touch on all the circumstances here. Besides, I am absolutely certain that those Newlanders or thieves of human beings who return never tell others the whole story and the real truth about such a miserable, difficult, and in the bargain highly dangerous voyage. When the Newlanders leave Pennsylvania or one of the other English colonies they are often given many letters to take along. When they get to Holland with these letters they have them broken open, or break them open themselves. And if someone has written in lamentation and told the truth, then such a letter is either rewritten or even thrown away.

In Pennsylvania I heard from the very lips of such thieves of human beings that in Holland there are many Jews who for a small fee are able to reproduce all seals and who can perfectly imitate all handwritings on demand. They are able to reproduce all strokes and letters, all signs and special features so faithfully that the person whose handwriting they have imitated must himself admit that it is indeed his own hand. Using such tricks they are able to cheat even people who are not gullible; and on those they practice their evil tricks all the more covertly. They themselves tell their intimates that this sort of thing is the best way of easily persuading people to leave for America.

They almost succeeded in deceiving me. For in Holland they tried to see to it that I should not leave America for good; and they attempted to use trickery and force in order to talk me into returning to England and America. These same merchants tried to convince me verbally in Rotterdam, as well as in writing from Amsterdam, that my wife and child with my sister-in-law and many of my countrymen had embarked for Philadelphia last summer with the year's final transport. In the course of this attempt they told me in great detail the names of my wife, my child and myself, as well as their height and their age. They also said that my wife had stated that her husband had been an organist in Pennsylvania for four years. They also showed me my wife's name in a letter and told me with what ship and captain they had sailed from Amsterdam; and how my wife had been accommodated in berth Number Twenty-Two with four other women.

All of this made me extraordinarily confused and irresolute. I showed them my wife's letters in which she clearly indicated that she would never go to America without me; that on the contrary she was expecting me with longing; and that she had once again received news from me to the effect that I had decided, God willing, to return to Germany during the next year. For all those reasons I could not possibly believe what they were telling me. This put me into such a state of consternation that I did not know what I ought to believe or do. At last, after mature deliberation, and without a doubt of the intent of Divine direction, I decided to complete my journey, in God's name, especially since I had already carried out the major part of it, that is, 1,400 hours, and had reached Germany.

In this I succeeded, and thus, thanks be to God, I escaped this great temptation. For I found that what these people had tried to tell and show me about my family in Holland was not true, since I encountered my wife and child happily at home. Had I believed these seducers of the people and returned by sea to England and America instead of coming home, this news might perhaps not have become so quickly known. In fact, my family and I would hardly or not at all have met again in this world.

The above mentioned thieves of human beings, as I found out afterwards, had described me and my wife completely and by name to the merchants in Holland. And the Newlanders for the second time tried to wheedle my wife into going to America. They doubtless thought that once I had left America I would reveal their whole bag of tricks as well as the miserable condition of the great mass of unfortunate families who had gone out there, and would in this way do great harm to their transports and their trafficking in human flesh.

At this point I must mention something that I forgot to relate before. As soon as the ships transporting people from Europe have anchored at Philadelphia, that is, the following morning, all male persons fifteen years or older are unloaded from the ship and put on to a boat. Then they are conducted two by two into town to the courthouse or city hall. There they must take the oath of allegiance to the Crown of Great Britain. When they have done this, they are taken back to the ships. Only then does the commerce in human beings begin, as I described it earlier.

I want to add only one other thing, namely, that when persons are purchased they are asked for neither discharge papers nor references. If someone has escaped the hangman and has the rope still dangling around his neck or left both his ears in Europe, there would not on that account exist any obstacles for him in Pennsylvania. If, however, he indulges in wrongdoing once again, there is no hope for him. Thus Pennsylvania is an ideal country for gallows-and-wheel customers.

AN ACCOUNT OF THE SLAVE TRADE ON THE COAST OF AFRICA (1788)

BY ALEXANDER FALCONBRIDGE

Introduction

Indentured servitude, a form of chattel slavery, was in vogue in the American mainland colonies until the middle of the eighteenth century. From the point of view of planters and employers it had a number of disadvantages, the most serious of which were its temporary nature, the relative scarcity of the supply of workers, the consequent high cost of purchase, and the ease with which such white servants might escape.

All these reasons help to explain why, in the eighteenth century, the permanent servitude of the black man replaced the temporary service of the white on American tobacco, rice, indigo and sugar plantations. How rapid and extensive this changeover was is illustrated by the figures. In 1700 there were not more than 25,000 Negro slaves, or less than one-tenth of all the inhabitants, in the mainland colonies. Ninety years later the number of Negro slaves had risen to nearly 800,-000; and they constituted one-fifth of the total population.

These Negro slaves were human beings captured in Africa, torn forcibly from their homeland, and sold into bondage in the New World. The first Europeans in modern times to explore the west coast of Africa were the Portuguese; and from their first probings in the fifteenth century until the abolition of the slave trade in the nineteenth, uncounted numbers of Africans were transported across the Atlantic and landed in the Americas. The most conservative estimate sets the figure of those so transported at fifteen million souls. It is possible that the actual figure might be double that number. As for the tally of those who were enslaved but did not survive embarkation or passage, we cannot even hazard a guess.

By 1700 Britain had wrested from France control of a major portion of the slave trade. During the eighteenth century she became the foremost slave-trading power in the world. In the course of this century Britain and her colonies transported an estimated two million people from their African homeland to the West Indian and mainland colonies. The center of this trade was at Liverpool; but ships were also fitted out from West Indian ports, from New York, and from New England. The ships proceeded to the Gulf of Guinea, dropped anchor at one of a number of slaving stations —such as Bonny or Calabar—gathered a shipload of slaves, often by purchase from local chieftains, and made the return trip to a New World port.

Slavery, to be sure, had its disadvantages for the planter. Men without hope of emancipation, and compelled to sow and reap a harvest that they may not enjoy, prove both dangerous people and inefficient tools: Southern planters lived in terror of their slaves. Yet Negro slavery had its attractions, and these proved decisive. Many more workers could be secured for the same price; their labor and that of their children became the property of the owner not for a limited period of years merely but in perpetuity; they were easily available; and, perhaps most significant of all, the African was branded with a black skin. He could be easily identified, segregated, and brought back if he ran away.

The history of the slave trade has been abundantly documented, but the account of it that is published below is probably unique. It is an eyewitness account of the Atlantic crossing as recorded by an actual participant. Alexander Falconbridge was an English surgeon driven by poverty to take employment with slave ships plying between the African coast and the West Indies. He made a number of trips in the late 1770's and early '80's before his marriage to a woman of means permitted him to leave the sea.

Falconbridge's experience with the slave trade coincided with a rising indignation in Britain at the moral enormities of this business, and a rising determination that an end must be put to it. Thus the publication of his testimony in the form of a pamphlet in 1788 was something of an event in the history of the antislavery movement, and it marked Falconbridge as in some sense a leader of the antislavery cause. In 1787 British humanitarian initiative had resulted in the founding of the St. George's Bay Company to promote the settlement on the west coast of Africa of free Negroes and runaway slaves who could find no other permanent home in the British Empire. Falconbridge became governor of this new colony for a short time in 1791; he founded Granville Town with the help of survivors of an earlier effort of settlement. Such was the origin of Sierra Leone, which became an independent African state in 1961.

The truth of the facts attested by Falconbridge have been corroborated from numerous sources. An Account of the Slave Trade is the only known published work from his pen. The pamphlet is divided into two parts, one of which deals with the sufferings of the white seamen involved in the slave trade, and the other with those of the slaves themselves. This second part of the work is reproduced below.

AN ACCOUNT OF THE SLAVE TRADE*

The Manner in Which the Slaves are Procured

After permission has been obtained for *breaking trade,* as it is termed, the captains go ashore, from time to time, to examine the Negroes that are exposed to sale, and to make their purchases. The unhappy wretches thus disposed of, are bought by the black traders at fairs, which are held for that purpose, at the distance of upwards of two hundred miles from the sea coast; and these fairs are said to be supplied from an interior part of the country. Many Negroes, upon being questioned relative to the places of their nativity, have asserted, that they have travelled during the revolution of several moons (their usual method of calculating time), before they have reached

*Source: Alexander Falconbridge, *An Account of the Slave Trade on the Coast of Africa* (London, 1788).

the places they were purchased by the black traders. At these fairs, which are held at uncertain periods, but generally every six weeks, several thousands are frequently exposed to sale, who had been collected from all parts of the country for a very considerable distance round. While I was upon the coast, during one of the voyages I made, the black traders brought down, in different canoes, from twelve to fifteen hundred Negroes, which had been purchased at one fair. They consisted chiefly of men and boys, the women seldom exceeding a third of the whole number. From forty to two hundred Negroes are generally purchased at a time by the black traders, according to the opulence of the buyer; and consist of those of all ages, from a month to sixty years and upwards. Scarce any age or situation is deemed an exception, the price being proportionable. Women sometimes form a part of them, who happen to be so far advanced in their pregnancy, as to be delivered during their journey from the fairs to the coast; and I have frequently seen instances of deliveries on board ship. The slaves purchased at these fairs are only for the supply of the markets at P———, and Old and New Calabar.

There is great reason to believe, that most of the Negroes shipped off from the coast of Africa, are *kidnapped*. But the extreme care taken by the black traders to prevent the Europeans from gaining any intelligence of their modes of proceeding; the great distance inland from whence the Negroes are brought; and our ignorance of their language (with which, very frequently, the black traders themselves are equally unacquainted), prevent our obtaining such information on this head as we could wish. I have, however, by means of occasional inquiries, made through interpreters, procured some intelligence relative to the point, and such, as I think, puts the matter beyond a doubt.

From these I shall select the following striking instances: While I was in employ on board one of the slave ships, a Negro informed me that being one evening invited to drink with some of the black traders, upon his going away, they attempted to seize him. As he was very active, he evaded their design, and got out of their hands. He was, however, prevented from effecting his escape by a large dog, which laid hold of him, and compelled him to submit. These creatures are kept by many of the traders for that purpose; and being trained to the inhuman sport, they appear to be much pleased with it.

I was likewise told by a Negro woman that as she was on her return home, one evening, from some neighbours, to whom she had been making a visit by invitation, she was kidnapped; and, notwithstanding she was big with child, sold for a slave. This transaction happened a considerable way up the country, and she had passed through the hands of several purchasers before she reached the ship. A man and his son, according to their own information, were seized by professed kidnappers, while they were planting yams, and sold for slaves. This likewise happened in the interior parts of the country, and after passing through several hands, they were purchased for the ship to which I belonged.

It frequently happens that those who kidnap others are themselves, in their turns, seized and sold. A Negro in the West Indies informed me that after having been employed in kidnapping others, he had experienced this reverse. And he assured me that it was a common incident among his countrymen.

Continual enmity is thus fostered among the Negroes of Africa, and all social intercourse between them destroyed; which most assuredly would not be the case, had they not these opportunities of finding a ready sale for each other.

During my stay on the coast of Africa, I was an eye-witness of the following transaction: a black trader invited a Negro, who resided a little way up the country, to come and see him. After the entertainment was over, the trader proposed to his guest, to treat him with a sight of one of the ships lying in the river. The unsuspicious countryman readily consented, and accompanied the trader in a canoe to the side of the ship, which he viewed with pleasure and astonishment. While he was thus employed, some black traders on board, who appeared to be in the secret, leaped into the canoe, seized the unfortunate man, and dragging him into the ship, immediately sold him.

Previous to my being in this employ, I entertained a belief, as many others have done, that the kings and principal men *breed* Negroes for sale, as we do cattle. During the different times I was in the country, I took no little pains to satisfy myself in this particular; but notwithstanding I made many inquiries, I was not able to obtain the least intelligence of this being the case, which it is more than probable I should have done, had such a practise prevailed. All the information I could procure, confirms me in the belief, that to *kidnapping*, and to crimes (and many of these fabricated as a pretext), the slave trade owes its chief support.

The following instance tends to prove that the last mentioned artifice is often made use of. Several black traders, one of whom was a person of consequence, and exercised an authority somewhat similar to that of our magistrates, being in want of some particular kind of merchandise, and not having a slave to barter for it, they accused a fisherman, at the river Ambris, with extortion in the sale of his fish; and as they were interested in the decision, they immediately adjudged the poor fellow guilty, and condemned him to be sold. He was accordingly purchased by the ship to which I belonged, and brought on board.

As an additional proof that kidnapping is not only the general, but almost the sole mode, by which slaves are procured, the black traders, in purchasing them, choose those which are the roughest and most hardy; alleging that the smooth Negroes have been *gentlemen*. By this observation we may conclude they mean that nothing but fraud or force could have reduced these smooth-skinned gentlemen to a state of slavery.

It may not be here unworthy of remark, in order to prove that the wars among the Africans do not furnish the number of slaves they are supposed to do, that I never saw any Negroes with recent wounds; which must have been the consequence, at least with some of them, had they been taken in battle. And it being the particular province of the surgeon to examine the slaves when they are purchased, such a circumstance could not have escaped my observation. As a farther corroboration, it might be remarked, that on the Gold and Windward Coasts, where fairs are not held, the number of slaves procured at a time are usually very small.

The preparations made at Bonny by the black traders, upon setting out for the fairs which are held up the country, are very considerable. From twenty to thirty canoes, capable of containing thirty or forty Negroes each, are assembled for this purpose; and such goods put on board them as they expect will be wanted for the purchase of the number of slaves they intend to buy. When their loading is completed, they commence their voyage, with colours flying, and music playing; and in about ten or eleven days, they generally return to Bonny with full cargoes. As soon as the canoes arrive at the trader's landing-place, the purchased Negroes are cleaned, and oiled with palm-oil; and on the following day they are exposed to sale for the captains.

The black traders do not always purchase their slaves at the same rate. The speed with which the information of the arrival of ships upon the coast is conveyed to the fairs, considering it is in the interest of the traders to keep them ignorant, is really surprising. In a short time after the ships arrive upon the coast, especially if several make their appearance together, those who dispose of the Negroes at the fairs are frequently known to increase the price of them.

These fairs are not the only means, though they are the chief, by which the black traders on the coast are supplied with Negroes. Small parties of them, from five to ten, are frequently brought to the houses of the traders, by those who make a practise of kidnapping; and who are constantly employed in procuring a supply, while purchasers are to be found.

When the Negroes, whom the black traders have to dispose of, are shown to the European purchasers, they first examine them relative to their age. They then minutely inspect their persons, and inquire into the state of their health; if they are afflicted with any infirmity, or are deformed, or have bad eyes or teeth; if they are lame, or weak in their joints, or distorted in the back, or of a slender make, or are narrow in the chest; in short, if they have been, or are afflicted in any manner, so as to render them incapable of much labour; if any of the foregoing defects are discovered in them, they are rejected. But if approved of, they are generally taken on board the ship the same evening. The purchaser has liberty to return on the following morning, but not afterwards, such as upon re-examination are found exceptionable.

The traders frequently beat those Negroes which are objected to by the captains, and use them with great severity. It matters not whether they are refused on account of age, illness, deformity, or for any other reason. At New Calabar, in particular, the traders have frequently been known to put them to death. Instances have happened at that place that the traders, when any of their Negroes have been objected to, have dropped their canoes under the stern of the vessel, and instantly beheaded them, in sight of the captain.

Upon the Windward Coast, another mode of procuring slaves is pursued; which is, by what they term *boating;* a mode that is very pernicious and destructive to the crews of the ships. The sailors, who are employed in this trade, go in boats up the rivers, seeking for Negroes among the villages situated on the banks of them. But this method is very slow, and not always effectual. For, after being absent from the ship during a fortnight or three weeks, they sometimes return with only from eight to twelve Negroes. Numbers of these are procured in consequence of alleged crimes, which, as before observed, whenever any ships are upon the coast, are more productive than at any other period. Kidnapping, however, prevails here.

I have good reason to believe that of one hundred and twenty Negroes, which were purchased for the ship to which I then belonged, then lying at the river Ambris, by far the greater part, if not the whole, were kidnapped. This, with various other instances, confirms me in the belief that kidnapping is the fund which supplies the thousands of Negroes annually sold off these extensive Windward and other coasts, where boating prevails.

Treatment of the Slaves

As soon as the wretched Africans, purchased at the fairs, fall into the hands of the black traders, they experience an earnest of those dreadful sufferings which they are doomed in future to undergo. And there is not the least room to doubt, but that even before they can reach the fairs, great numbers perish from cruel usage, want of food, travelling through inhospitable deserts, etc. They are brought from the places where they are purchased to Bonny, etc. in canoes; at the bottom of which they lie, having their hands tied with a kind of willow twigs, and a strict watch is kept over them. Their usage in other respects, during the time of the passage, which generally lasts several days, is equally cruel. Their allowance of food is so scanty, that it is barely sufficient to support nature. They are, besides, much exposed to the violent rains which frequently fall here, being covered only with mats that afford but a slight defence; and as there is usually water at the bottom of the canoes, from their leaking, they are scarcely ever dry.

Nor do these unhappy beings, after they become the property of the Europeans (from whom, as a more civilised people, more humanity might naturally be expected), find their situation in the least amended. Their treatment is no less rigorous. The men Negroes, on being brought aboard the ship, are immediately fastened together, two and two, by handcuffs on their wrists, and by irons rivetted on their legs. They are then sent down between the decks, and placed in an apartment partitioned off for that purpose. The women likewise are placed in a separate apartment between decks, but without being ironed. And an adjoining room, on the same deck, is besides appointed for the boys. Thus are they all placed in different apartments.

But at the same time, they are frequently stowed so close, as to admit of no other posture than lying on their sides. Neither will the height between decks, unless directly under the grating, permit them the indulgence of an erect posture; especially where there are platforms, which is generally the case. These platforms are a kind of shelf, about eight or nine feet in breadth, extending from the side of the ship towards the centre. They are placed nearly midway between the decks, at the distance of two or three feet from each deck. Upon these the Negroes are stowed in the same manner as they are on the deck underneath.

In each of the apartments are placed three or four large buckets, of a conical form, being near two feet in diameter at the bottom, and only one foot at the top, and in depth about twenty-eight inches; to which, when necessary, the Negroes have recourse. It often happens that those who are placed at a distance from the buckets, in endeavouring to get to them, tumble over their companions, in consequence of their being shackled. These accidents, although unavoidable, are productive of continual quarrels, in which some of them are always bruised. In this distressed situation, unable to proceed, and prevented from getting to the tubs, they desist from the attempt; and, as the necessities of nature are not to be repelled, ease themselves as they lie. This becomes a fresh source of broils and disturbances, and tends to render the condition of the poor captive wretches still more uncomfortable. The nuisance arising from these circumstances, is not unfrequently increased by the tubs being much too small for the purpose intended, and their being usually emptied but once every day. The rule for doing this, however, varies in different ships, according to the attention paid to the health and convenience of the slaves by the captain.

About eight o'clock in the morning the Negroes are generally brought upon deck. Their irons being examined, a long chain, which is locked to a ring-bolt, fixed in the deck, is run through the rings of the shackles of the men, and then locked to another ring-bolt, fixed also in the deck. By this means fifty or sixty, and sometimes more, are fastened to one chain, in order to prevent them from rising, or endeavouring to escape. If the weather proves favourable, they are permitted to remain in that situation till four or five in the afternoon, when they are disengaged from the chain, and sent down.

The diet of the Negroes, while on board, consists chiefly of horse beans, boiled to the consistence of a pulp; of boiled yams and rice, and sometimes a small quantity of beef or pork. The latter are frequently taken from the provisions laid in for the sailors. They sometimes make use of a sauce, composed of palm oil, mixed with flour, water, and pepper, which the sailors call *slabber sauce*. Yams are the favourite food of the Eboe, or Bight Negroes, and rice or corn, of those from the Gold and Windward Coasts; each preferring the produce of their native soil.

In their own country, the Negroes in general live on animal food and fish, with roots, yams, and Indian corn. The horse beans and rice, with which they are fed aboard ship, are chiefly taken from Europe. The latter, indeed, is sometimes purchased on the coast, being far superior to any other.

The Gold Coast Negroes scarcely ever refuse any food that is offered them, and they generally eat larger quantities of whatever is placed before them, than any other species of Negroes, whom they likewise excel in strength of body and mind. Most of the slaves have such an aversion to the horse beans, that unless they are narrowly watched, when fed upon deck, they will throw them overboard, or in each other's faces when they quarrel.

They are commonly fed twice a day, about eight o'clock in the morning, and four in the afternoon. In most ships they are only fed with their *own food* once a day. Their food is served up to them in tubs, about the size of a small water bucket.

They are placed round these tubs in companies of ten to each tub, out of which they feed themselves with wooden spoons. These they soon lose, and when they are not allowed others, they feed themselves with their hands. In favourable weather they are fed upon deck, but in bad weather their food is given them below. Numberless quarrels take place among them during their meals; more especially when they are put upon short allowance, which frequently happens, if the passage from the coast of Guinea to the West India islands, proves of usual length. In that case, the weak are obliged to be content with a very scanty portion. Their allowance of water is about half a pint each at every meal. It is handed round in a bucket, and given to each Negro in a pannekin, a small utensil with a straight handle, somewhat similar to a sauce-boat. However, when the ships approach the islands with a favourable breeze, they are no longer restricted.

Upon the Negroes refusing to take sustenance, I have seen coals of fire, glowing hot, put on a shovel, and placed so near their lips, as to scorch and burn them. And this has been accompanied with threats, of forcing them to swallow the coals, if they any longer persisted in refusing to eat. These means have generally had the desired effect. I have also been credibly informed that a certain captain in the slave trade poured melted lead on such of the Negroes as obstinately refused their food.

Exercise being deemed necessary for the preservation of their health, they are sometimes obliged to dance, when the weather will permit their coming on deck. If they go about it reluctantly, or do not move with agility, they are flogged; a person standing by them all the time with a cat-o'-nine-tails in his hand for that purpose. Their music, upon these occasions, consists of a drum, sometimes with only one head; and when that is worn out, they do not scruple to make use of the bottom of one of the tubs before described. The poor wretches are frequently compelled to sing also; but when they do so, their songs are generally, as may naturally be expected, melancholy lamentations of their exile from their native country.

The women are furnished with beads for the purpose of affording them some diversion. But this end is generally defeated by the squabbles which are occasioned, in consequence of their stealing them from each another.

On board some ships, the common sailors are allowed to

have intercourse with such of the black women whose consent they can procure. And some of them have been known to take the inconstancy of their paramours so much to heart, as to leap overboard and drown themselves. The officers are permitted to indulge their passions among them at pleasure, and sometimes are guilty of such brutal excesses as disgrace human nature.

The hardships and inconveniences suffered by the Negroes during the passage are scarcely to be enumerated or conceived. They are far more violently affected by the seasickness than the Europeans. It frequently terminates in death, especially among the women. But the exclusion of the fresh air is among the most intolerable. For the purpose of admitting this needful refreshment, most of the ships in the slave trade are provided, between the decks, with five or six air-ports on each side of the ship, of about six inches in length, and four in breadth; in addition to which, some few ships, but not one in twenty, have what they denominate *wind-sails*. But whenever the sea is rough and the rain heavy, it becomes necessary to shut these, and every other conveyance by which the air is admitted. The fresh air being thus excluded, the Negroes' rooms very soon grow intolerably hot. The confined air, rendered noxious by the effluvia exhaled from their bodies, and by being repeatedly breathed, soon produces fevers and fluxes, which generally carries off great numbers of them.

During the voyages I made, I was frequently a witness to the fatal effects of this exclusion of the fresh air. I will give one instance, as it serves to convey some idea, though a very faint one, of the sufferings of those unhappy beings whom we wantonly drag from their native country, and doom to perpetual labour and captivity. Some wet and blowing weather having occasioned the port-holes to be shut, and the grating to be covered, fluxes and fevers among the Negroes ensued. While they were in this situation, my profession requiring it, I frequently went down among them, till at length their apartments became so extremely hot, as to be only sufferable for a very short time. But the excessive heat was not the only thing that rendered their situation intolerable. The deck, that is, the floor of their rooms, was so covered with the blood and mucus which had proceeded from them in consequence of the flux, that it resembled a slaughter-house. It is not in the power of the human imagination to picture to itself a situation more dreadful or disgusting. Numbers of the slaves having fainted, they were carried upon deck, where several of them died, and the rest were, with great difficulty, restored. It had nearly proved fatal to me also. The climate was too warm to admit the wearing of any clothing but a shirt, and that I had pulled off before I went down; notwithstanding which, by only continuing among them for about a quarter of an hour, I was so overcome with the heat, stench, and foul air, that I had nearly fainted; and it was not without assistance that I could get upon deck. The consequence was that I soon after fell sick of the same disorder, from which I did not recover for several months.

A circumstance of this kind sometimes repeatedly happens in the course of a voyage; and often to a greater degree than what has just been described; particularly when the slaves are much crowded, which was not the case at that time, the ship having more than a hundred short of the number she was to have taken in.

This devastation, great as it was, some few years ago was greatly exceeded on board a Liverpool ship. I shall particularise the circumstances of it, as a more glaring instance of an insatiable thirst for gain, or of less attention to the lives and happiness, even of that despised and oppressed race of mortals, the sable inhabitants of Africa, perhaps was never exceeded; though indeed several similar instances have been known.

This ship, though a much smaller ship than that in which the event I have just mentioned happened, took on board at Bonny, at least six hundred Negroes; but according to the information of the black traders, from whom I received the intelligence immediately after the ship sailed, they amounted to near *seven hundred*. By purchasing so great a number, the slaves were so crowded, that they were even obliged to lie one upon another. This occasioned such a mortality among them, that, without meeting with unusual bad weather, or having a longer voyage than common, nearly one half of them died before the ship arrived in the West Indies.

That the public may be able to form some idea of the almost incredible small space into which so large a number of Negroes were crammed, the following particulars of this ship are given. According to Liverpool custom she measured 235 tons. Her width across the beam, 25 feet. Length between the decks, 92 feet, which was divided into four rooms, thus:

Store room, in which there were not any Negroes
placed   15 feet

Negroes' rooms—men's room   about   45 feet
                women's ditto   about   10 feet
                boys' ditto   about   22 feet

        Total room for Negroes   77 feet*

*Exclusive of the platform before described, from 8 to 9 feet
in breadth, and equal in length to that of the rooms.

It may be worthy of remark, that the ships in this trade are
usually fitted out to receive only one-third women Negroes, or
perhaps a smaller number, which the dimension of the room
allotted for them, above given, plainly show, but in a greater
disproportion.

One would naturally suppose that an attention to their own
interest would prompt the owners of the Guinea ships not to
suffer the captains to take on board a greater number of
Negroes than the ship would allow room sufficient for them
to lie with ease to themselves, or, at least, without rubbing
against each other. However that may be, a more striking instance than the above, of avarice, completely and deservedly
disappointed, was surely never displayed: for there is little
room to doubt, but that in consequence of the expected premium usually allowed to the captains, of £6 per cent. sterling
on the produce of the Negroes, this vessel was so thronged as
to occasion such a heavy loss.

The place allotted for the sick Negroes is under the
half deck, where they lie on the bare planks. By this means,
those who are emaciated, frequently have their skin, and even
their flesh, entirely rubbed off, by the motion of the ship, from
the prominent parts of the shoulders, elbows, and hips, so as
to render the bones in those parts quite bare. And some of
them, by constantly lying in the blood and mucus that had
flowed from those afflicted with the flux, and which, as before
observed, is generally so violent as to prevent their being kept
clean, have their flesh much sooner rubbed off than those who
have only to contend with the mere friction of the ship. The
excruciating pain which the poor sufferers feel from being
obliged to continue in such a dreadful situation, frequently

English slave vessel, we determined to leave the place. The night before our departure the tent was struck; which was no sooner perceived by some of the Negro women on board, than it was considered as a prelude to our sailing, and about eighteen of them, when they were sent between decks, threw themselves into the sea through one of the gun ports, the ship carrying guns between decks. They were all of them, however, excepting one, soon picked up; and that which was missing was, not long after, taken about a mile from the shore.

. I once knew a Negro woman, too sensible of her woes, who pined for a considerable time, and was taken ill of a fever and dysentery; when, declaring it to be her determination to die, she refused all food and medical aid, and in about a fortnight after, expired. On being thrown overboard, her body was instantly torn to pieces by the sharks.

The following circumstances also came within my knowledge. A young female Negro, falling into a desponding way, it was judged necessary, in order to attempt her recovery, to send her on shore, to the hut of one of the black traders. Elevated with the prospect of regaining her liberty by this unexpected step, she soon recovered her usual cheerfulness; but hearing, by accident, that it was intended to take her on board the ship again, the poor young creature hung herself.

It frequently happens that the Negroes, on being purchased by the Europeans, become raving mad, and many of them die in that state, particularly the women. While I was one day ashore at Bonny, I saw a middle-aged stout woman, who had been brought down from a fair the preceding day, chained to the post of a black trader's door, in a state of furious insanity. On board a ship in Bonny River, I saw a young Negro woman chained to the deck, who had lost her senses, soon after she was purchased and taken on board. In a former voyage, on board a ship to which I belonged, we were obliged to confine a female Negro, of about twenty-three years of age, on her becoming a lunatic. She was afterwards sold during one of her lucid intervals.

One morning, upon examining the place allotted for the sick Negroes, I perceived that one of them, who was so emaciated as scarcely to be able to walk, was missing, and was convinced that he must have gone overboard in the night, probably to put a more expeditious period to his sufferings. And, to conclude on this subject, I could not help being sensibly affected, on a former voyage, at observing with what apparent eagerness a black woman seized some dirt from off an African yam, and put it into her mouth, seeming to rejoice at the opportunity of possessing some of her native earth.

From these instances I think it may be clearly deduced that the unhappy Africans are not bereft of the finer feelings, but have a strong attachment to their native country, together with a just sense of the value of liberty. And the situation of the miserable beings above described, more forcibly urges the necessity of abolishing a trade which is the source of such evils, than the most eloquent harangue, or persuasive arguments could do.

Laments and
Lullabies

KATIE CRUEL
DEÍRIN DÉ

Introduction

The refrain of the beautiful love lament Katie Cruel is Elizabethan, but the words were probably composed in this country. Found principally in New England, it has been used as a lament, as a children's ditty and—during the Revolutionary War—as a marching song.

Though the main flood was not to be until the nineteenth century, the colonial period witnessed the first immigration to the New World of Catholic Irish. With them came their heritage of exquisite Gaelic songs. These are now part of the American heritage simply because they are here. Deírin dé, one version of which we reproduce below with a modern translation, began life as a lullaby. Sung in the hold of an immigrant ship by some maidservant recalling the warmth of childhood in a time of trouble, it was transformed into a whisper of anguish.

KATIE CRUEL

When I first came to town, They called me the
ro - ving jew - el; Now they've changed their
tune, And call me Ka - tie Cru - el.
O lit - tle lol - ly day, O the
lit - tle li - o - day.
O that I were where I would be, Then would I
be where I am not; But I am where I
must be, Where I would be I can - not;

O lit - tle lol - ly day, O the lit - tle li - o - day.

When I first came to town
They called me the roving jewel;
Now they've changed their tune
And call me Katie Cruel.
   O little lolly day,
   O the little lioday.
O that I were where I would be,
Then would I be where I am not;
But I am where I must be,
Where I would be I cannot.
   O little lolly day,
   O the little lioday.

I know who I love,
And I know who does love me;
I know where I'll go,
And I know who'll go with me.
   O little lolly day,
   O the little lioday.
O that I were where I would be,
Then would I be where I am not;
But I am where I must be,
Where I would be I cannot.
   O little lolly day,
   O the little lioday.

Through the woods I'll go,
And through the bog and mire;
Straightway down the road
Till I come to my heart's desire.
  O little lolly day,
  O the little lioday.
O that I were where I would be,
Then would I be where I am not;
But I am where I must be,
Where I would be I cannot.
  O little lolly day,
  O the little lioday.

Deírin dé

Deír - in dé,— deír - in dé, The
night - jar calls from the grass- y moor.
Deír - in dé,— deír - in dé, The
bit - tern booms from the reed-bound shore.
Deír - in dé,— deír - in dé,— On the
west - ward hill the sheep will stray.
Deír - in dé,— deír - in dé, — My
child will watch them from break of day.

Deírin dé, deírin dé,
The nightjar calls from the grassy moor.
Deírin dé, deírin dé,
The bittern booms from the reed-bound shore.
Deírin dé, deírin dé,
On the westward hill the sheep will stray.
Deírin dé, deírin dé,
My child will watch them from break of day.

Deírin dé, deírin dé,
Berry picking shall be his play.
Deírin dé, deírin dé,
Sleep now, my darling, 'til break of day.

Deírin dé, deírin dé,
Tá'n gabhairin oíche amuh san bhfraoch.
Deírin dé, deírin dé,
Tá'n bunán donn a' labhairt san bhfeith.
Deírin dé, deírin dé,
Geóidh ba siar le h'-éirghe an lae.
Deírin dé, deírin dé,
Is raghaidh mo leanbh 'a bhfeighilt ar feár.

Deírin dé, deírin dé,
Leogfad mo leanbh a pioca sméar.
Deírin dé, deírin dé,
Ach codail go sámh go fáinne an lae.

The Great
══Awakening══

"In the morning they arise like grass which groweth up.
In the morning it florisheth and groweth up, in the evening it is cut down and withereth."

> William Tennent at the funeral of
> his son Gilbert, March, 13, 1731.

─────── **INTRODUCTORY REMARKS** ───────

As the colonial settlements became established, preoccupa-
tion with the life of religion was rarely uppermost. In New
England Puritanism's original and passionate impulse waned;
the churches lost contact with the people, fell victim to a
narrow complacency, and too often catered only to a segment
of the community. Everywhere, in the mainland colonies, the
demands of a hard, practical world crowded in upon men—
the ordeal of labor on farm and frontier, the ever-recurring
strife with the Indians and the French, the lure of wealth
through planting, commerce, or speculation.

These problems were exemplified with special force on
the frontier. As the frontier moved westward, settlers found
themselves isolated from the centers of civilization and of
religious life. The people lacked trained ministers to nourish
a community existence, to foster education, and to give attention to spiritual needs. But in colonial days the majority of
Americans lived a frontier existence. Death was omnipresent;
it could strike in a dozen different forms, through plague,
malaria, disease, through war or frontier ambush, through
snakebite, or fire or accident. Here man lived always on the
edge of the eternal, and here his need of spiritual consolation
and peace of mind was great.

From this situation of frontier isolation, and the decay of religious life in the more settled areas, sprang a series of religious revivals or awakenings, giving expression to the ever-present human desire for a truly shared life, with mercy and brotherhood among men; for a religion that was more than formal ceremony and memorized creed, that, in a sense, arose out of popular need and reflected popular experience. Many such awakenings occurred locally, sporadically, during the eighteenth century. But the first truly national revival that appealed to people up and down the colonies, overriding local distinctions of class or birth, that had its impact in the towns and villages as well as on the frontier, occurred in the 1740's. The Great Awakening, as it was called, was an outburst of fiery evangelism that swept the American mainland colonies from Georgia to Maine. And it was carried forward, not only by great and able itinerant ministers, but by lay preachers who spoke to the people wherever they could gather an audience—in meeting houses, in the streets, on the commons, in the open fields, and even in the forests.

The itinerant preacher spoke to people who had either fallen away from established churches or who, by virtue of their remote and isolated life, had never been reached by them. From this came the direct and popular type of sermon which these men preached. Formalism and pedantry were cast to the winds; they talked in blunt and vivid terms readily comprehensible to the ordinary, poverty-stricken, often ignorant and unlettered settler or villager. The audiences that gathered to listen to these missionaries accounted also for the extemporaneous nature of the revivalist sermon. Itinerants were not infrequently masters of oratory, skilled in divining a people's mood, playing upon it, fanning it into a passion, and directing it. There was no place in this type of human and religious appeal for the prepared script. A man might prepare in a general way what he had to say, but he must search his own heart for the words that he would use when actually facing his listeners; those words must come forth as utterance inspired by God. In no other way could the revivalist sermon have the power to move the indifferent or to arouse the slumbering desire for a godly life and for salvation.

The great itinerants felt their vocation as prophets sent to awaken a sinning people to a sense of their fall from grace, and to the imperative need to seek a rebirth in Christ. To achieve this end they unlimbered, in their preachments, the heaviest and sublimest artillery of medieval theology, holding up to their horrified audience a picture of hell-fire and eternal damnation as the wages of sin and as a sanction to spur the search for righteousness and for repentance.

To this end, eighteenth-century American Protestantism —and the majority of British settlers were of Protestant background—turned the traditional Puritan concept of election upon its head, and, as it were, democratized it. Seventeenth-century Calvinism had taught that the majority of men were doomed and damned from eternity for their evil nature and for the evil acts that flowed of necessity from that nature. God, said they, had chosen, in his inscrutable wisdom, to save only a minority of men, the elect; knowledge of election came from an inner spiritual experience. Conversion of a sinner was not something that man could achieve of his own unaided powers. The grace and the strength to achieve salvation was a free gift of God, and came from Him alone.

The eighteenth century itinerants did not formally depart from the rigors of this creed, but they cast a wider net. All men, said they, could be saved if only they would repent, throw themselves on God's mercy, and believe in Him. More often than not this message produced a highly emotional reaction; and, if in the course of time the passions thus fired died down, each outburst bore abundant fruit as new churches were founded, new congregations organized. Thus the Great Awakening fostered the practice of an independent religious life among the masses and struck a telling blow at the Old World concept that religious establishments were a necessary foundation of the social order. By the same token it contributed powerfully to America's awakening sense of nationalism, for it taught a democratic creed—the brotherhood of man in Christ—a creed that leaped over narrow provincial boundaries and brought to the people a revolutionary faith; the same faith that in Europe—and notably in Holland, England and France—had fired struggle for national independence against an oppressive, decadent, authoritarian and outmoded dynastic rule.

A host of able men led the Awakening, and among the greatest of these might be mentioned John Wesley, one of the founders of Georgia; his associate and follower, George Whitefield; and Jonathan Edwards, whose life and thought is intimately linked with the movement that swept New England in the decade 1734-44. His writings are an unrivaled source both for the study of the Awakening and for the evolution of New England Protestantism during the eighteenth century. The two examples reproduced below emphasize complementary aspects of Edwards' thinking: on the one side, the reality of hell-fire and damnation, but, on the other, his love of ordinary men and women, his deep belief in the possibility of human redemption through faith and repentance.

Other aspects of the Awakening are illustrated (p. 139) by the reproduction of religious songs of the time, and of the testimony of Charles Chauncy, leading Boston Congregationalist theologian and staunch opponent of popular religious "enthusiasm."

THE LIFE AND DEATH OF
ABIGAIL HUTCHINSON (1736)

BY JONATHAN EDWARDS

Introduction

Jonathan Edwards (1703-58) was born at East Windsor, Connecticut, the son of a Congregational minister. In 1726 he became associated with his grandfather, Solomon Stoddard, in the ministry at Northampton, Massachusetts, which charge he assumed completely with the death of Stoddard in 1729. He began to preach sermons of great simplicity and enormous power, dedicated to the proposition that the human soul must seek salvation through the agonies of a striving for inner repentance, rather than through compliance with a formalized church ritual. In 1734 the revival got under way in Northampton and the surrounding countryside—the first decisive manifestation in a frontier region of the movement that was to reach its New England climax in 1741-42 and thereafter rapidly to decline.

In 1736 Edwards prepared A Faithful Narrative of the Surprising Works of God in the Conversion of Many Hundred Souls in Northampton, and the Neighboring Towns and Villages of the County of Hampshire, in the Province of Massa-

chusetts Bay in New-England. *This work was published as a
pamphlet in 1737. It is a historical article of the first importance in which Edwards gives us a firsthand account of the
beginnings of the Great Awakening in the Connecticut
River Valley. We have selected for reproduction from the
Narrative Edwards' account of the conversion of a young
woman, Abigail Hutchinson, evidently dying from cancer of
the throat. This piece tells us much of Edwards as well as of
his people—his compassion, his psychological insight and his
artistry as writer and thinker. Abigail, in the grave for over two
hundred years, still lives in the exquisite image of her that the
writer records.*

THE LIFE AND DEATH OF
ABIGAIL HUTCHINSON

To give a clearer idea of the nature and manner of the
operations of God's Spirit, in this wonderful effusion of it, I
would give an account of two particular instances. The first
is an adult person, a young woman whose name was Abigail
Hutchinson. I pitch upon her especially, because she is now
dead, and so it may be more fit to speak freely of her than of
living instances; though I am under far greater disadvantages
on other accounts, to give a full and clear narrative of her experiences, than I might of some others, nor can any account
be given but what has been retained in the memories of
her near friends and some others, of what they have heard her
express in her lifetime.

She was of a rational, understanding family; there could be
nothing in her education that tended to enthusiasm, but rather
to the contrary extreme. It is in no wise the temper of the
family to be ostentatious of experiences, and it was far from
being her temper. She was, before her conversion, to the observation of her neighbors, of a sober and inoffensive conversation, and was a still, quiet, reserved person. She had long
been infirm of body, but her infirmity had never been observed
at all to incline her to be notional or fanciful, or to occasion
any thing of religious melancholy. She was under awakenings
scarcely a week, before there seemed to be plain evidence of
her being savingly converted.

She was first awakened in the winter season, on Monday,

by something she heard her brother say of the necessity of being in good earnest in seeking regenerating grace, together with the news of the conversion of the young woman before mentioned, whose conversion so generally affected most of the young people here. This news wrought much upon her, and stirred up a spirit of envy in her towards this young woman, whom she thought very unworthy of being distinguished from others by such a mercy, but withal it engaged her in a firm resolution to do her utmost to obtain the same blessing; and, considering with herself what course she should take, she thought that she had not a sufficient knowledge of the principles of religion to render her capable of conversion; whereupon she resolved thoroughly to search the Scriptures, and accordingly immediately began at the beginning of the Bible, intending to read it through. She continued thus till Thursday, and then there was a sudden alteration, by a great increase of her concern, in an extraordinary sense of her own sinfulness, particularly the sinfulness of her nature, and wickedness of her heart, which came upon her (as she expressed it) as a flash of lightning, and struck her into an exceeding terror. Upon which she left off reading the Bible in course as she had begun, and turned to the New Testament, to see if she could not find some relief there for her distressed soul.

Her great terror, she said, was that she had sinned against God: her distress grew more and more for three days, until (as she said) she saw nothing but blackness of darkness before her, and her very flesh trembled for fear of God's wrath; she wondered and was astonished at herself, that she had been so concerned for her body, and had applied so often to physicians to heal that, and had neglected her soul. Her sinfulness appeared with a very awful aspect to her, especially in three things, viz., her original sin, and her sin in murmuring at God's providence, in the weakness and afflictions she had been under, and in want of duty to parents, though others had looked upon her to excel in dutifulness. On Saturday she was so earnestly engaged in reading the Bible, and other books, that she continued in it, searching for something to relieve her, till her eyes were so dim, that she could not know the letters. Whilst she was thus engaged in reading, prayer, and other religious exercises, she thought of those words of Christ, wherein he warns us not to be as the heathen, that think they shall be heard for their much speaking; which, she said, led her to see that she had trusted to her own prayers and religious performances, and now she was put to a nonplus, and knew not which way to turn herself, or where to seek relief.

While her mind was in this posture, her heart, she said, seemed to fly to the minister for refuge, hoping that he could give her some relief. She came the same day, to her brother, with a countenance of a person in distress, expostulating with him, why he had not told her more of her sinfulness, and earnestly inquiring of him, what she should do. She seemed, that day, to feel in herself an enmity against the Bible, which greatly affrighted her. Her sense of her own exceeding sinfulness continued increasing from Thursday till Monday, and she gave this account of it, that it had been an opinion, which, till now she had entertained, that she was not guilty of Adam's sin, nor any way concerned in it, because she was not active in it; but that now she saw she was guilty of that sin, and all over defiled by it, and that the sin which she brought into the world with her was alone sufficient to condemn her.

On the Sabbath day she was so ill that her friends thought it not best that she should go to public worship, of which she seemed very desirous; but when she went to bed on the Sabbath day night, she took up a resolution that she would, the next morning, go to the minister, hoping to find some relief there. As she awaked on Monday morning a little before day, she wondered within herself at the easiness and calmness she felt in her mind, which was of that kind which she never felt before; as she thought of this, such words as these were in her mind; the words of the Lord are pure words, health to the soul, and marrow to the bones; and then these words came to her mind—the blood of Christ cleanses from all sin; which were accompanied with a lively sense of the excellency of Christ, and his sufficiency to satisfy for the sins of the whole world. She then thought of that expression—it is a pleasant thing for the eyes to behold the sun—which words then seemed to her to be very applicable to Jesus Christ. By these things her mind was led into such contemplations and views of Christ, as filled her exceeding full of joy. She told her brother in the morning that she had seen (i.e., in realizing views by faith) Christ the last night, and that

she had really thought that she had not knowledge enough
to be converted; but, said she, God can make it quite easy!
On Monday she felt all day a constant sweetness in her soul.
She had a repetition of the same discoveries of Christ three
mornings together, that she had on Monday morning, and
much in the same manner, at each time, waking a little before
day, but brighter and brighter every time.

At the last time, on Wednesday morning, while in the enjoyment of a spiritual view of Christ's glory and fulness, her
soul was filled with distress for Christless persons, to consider
what a miserable condition they were in; and she felt in herself a strong inclination immediately to go forth to warn
sinners, and proposed it the next day to her brother to assist
her in going from house to house, but her brother restrained
her, telling her of the unsuitableness of such a method. She
told one of her sisters that day, that she loved all mankind,
but especially the people of God. Her sister asked her why
she loved all mankind? She replied, because God had made
them. After this there happened to come into the shop where
she was at work, three persons that were thought to have
been lately converted; her seeing them as they stepped in
one after another into the door, so affected her, and so drew
forth her love to them, that it overcame her, and she almost
fainted: and when they began to talk of the things of religion,
it was more than she could bear—they were obliged to cease
on that account. It was a very frequent thing with her to be
overcome with a flow of affection to them that she thought
godly, in conversation with them, and sometimes only at the
sight of them.

She had many extraordinary discoveries of the glory of God
and Christ; sometimes in some particular attributes, and sometimes in many. She gave an account that once, as those four
words passed through her mind, WISDOM, JUSTICE,
GOODNESS, and TRUTH, her soul was filled with a sense of
the glory of each of these divine attributes, but especially the
last. Truth, she said, sunk the deepest! and, therefore, as
these words passed, this was repeated, TRUTH, TRUTH! Her
mind was so swallowed up with a sense of the glory of God's
truth and other perfections, that she said, it seemed as though
her life was going and that she saw it was easy with God to
take away her life by discoveries of himself. Soon after this
she went to a private religious meeting, and her mind was full

of a sense and view of the glory of God all the time; and when the exercise was ended, some asked her concerning what she had experienced; and she began to give them an account, but as she was relating it, it revived such a sense of the same things, that her strength failed, and they were obliged to take her and lay her upon the bed. Afterwards she was greatly affected, and rejoiced with these words: *Worthy is the Lamb that was slain.*

She had several days together a sweet sense of the excellency and loveliness of Christ in his meekness, which disposed her continually to be repeating over these words, which were sweet to her, MEEK AND LOWLY IN HEART, MEEK AND LOWLY IN HEART. She once expressed herself to one of her sisters to this purpose, that she had continued whole days and whole nights, in a constant ravishing view of the glory of God and Christ, having enjoyed as much as her life could bear. Once as her brother was speaking of the dying love of Christ, she told him that she had such a sense of it, that the mere mentioning it was ready to overcome her.

Once, when she came to me, she told how that at such and such a time she thought she saw as much of God, and had as much joy and pleasure as was possible in this life, and that yet afterwards God discovered himself yet far more abundantly, and she saw the same things that she had seen before, yet more clearly, and in another and far more excellent and delightful manner, and was filled with a more exceeding sweetness. She likewise gave me such an account of the sense she once had from day to day of the glory of Christ, and of God, in his various attributes, that it seemed to me she dwelt for days together in a kind of beatific vision of God, and seemed to have, as I thought, as immediate an intercourse with him, as a child with a father; and at the same time she appeared most remote from any high thought of herself, and of her own sufficiency, but was like a little child, and expressed a great desire to be instructed, telling me that she longed very often to come to me for instruction, and wanted to live at my house, that I might tell her her duty.

She often expressed a sense of the glory of God appearing in the trees and growth of the fields, and other works of God's hands. She told her sister that lived near the heart of the town, that she once thought it a pleasant thing to live in the middle of the town; but now, said she, I think it much more pleasant to sit and see the wind blowing the trees, and to behold in the country what God has made. She had sometimes the powerful breathings of the Spirit of God on her soul, while reading the Scripture, and would express a sense that she had of the certain truth and divinity thereof. She sometimes would appear with a pleasant smile on her countenance, and once when her sister took notice of it and asked why she smiled, she replied, I am brimful of a sweet feeling within! She often used to express how good and sweet it was to lie low before God, and the lower, said she, the better! And that it was pleasant to think of lying in the dust all the days of her life, mourning for sin. She was wont to manifest a great sense of her own meanness and dependence. She often expressed an exceeding compassion, and pitiful love, which she found in her heart towards persons in a Christless condition, which was sometimes so strong, that as she was passing by such in the streets, or those that she feared were such, she would be overcome by the sight of them. She once said, that she longed to have the whole world saved—she wanted, as it were, to pull them all to her—she could not bear to have one lost.

She had great longings to die, that she might be with Christ, which increased till she thought she did not know how to be patient to wait till God's time should come. But once, when she felt those longings, she thought, with herself, if I long to die, why do I go to physicians? Whence she concluded that her longings for death were not well regulated. After this she often put it to herself, which she should choose, whether to live or die, to be sick or to be well, and she found she could not tell, till at last she found herself disposed to say these words—I am quite willing to live, and quite willing to die—quite willing to be sick, and quite willing to be well; and quite willing for any thing that God will bring upon me! And then, said she, I felt myself perfectly easy in a full submission to the will of God. She then lamented much, that she had been so eager in her longings for death, as it argued want of such a resignation to God as ought to be. She seemed henceforward to continue in this resigned frame till death.

After this her illness increased upon her; and once, after she had before spent the greater part of the night in extreme pain, she awaked out of a little sleep with these words in her heart and mouth—I am willing to suffer for Christ's sake.—I am willing to spend and be spent for Christ's sake.—I am willing to spend my life, even my very life for Christ's sake! And though she had an extraordinary resignation, with respect to life or death, yet the thoughts of dying were exceeding sweet to her. At a time when her brother was reading in Job, concerning worms feeding on the dead body, she appeared with a pleasant smile, and being inquired of about it, she said, it was sweet to her to think of her being in such circumstances. At another time, when her brother mentioned to her the danger there seemed to be that the illness she then labored under, might be an occasion of her death, it filled her with joy that almost overcame her. At another time, when she met a company following a corpse to the grave, she said, it was sweet to her to think, that they would in a little time follow her in like manner.

Her illness, in the latter part of it, was seated much in her throat, and swelling inward filled up the pipe, so that she could swallow nothing but what was perfectly liquid, and but very little of that, and with great and long strugglings and stranglings, that which she took in flying out at her nostrils, till she at last could swallow nothing at all. She had a raging appetite to food, so that she told her sister, when talking with her about her circumstances, that the worst bit she threw to her swine would be sweet to her; but yet when she saw that she could not swallow it, she seemed to be as perfectly contented without it as if she had no appetite to it. Others were greatly moved to see what she underwent, and were filled with admiration at her unexampled patience. At a time, when she was striving in vain to get down a little food, something liquid, and was very much spent with it, she looked upon her sister with a smile, saying, O sister, this is for my good! At another time, when her sister was speaking of what she underwent, she told her, that she lived a heaven upon earth for all that. She used sometimes to say to her sister, under her extreme sufferings—It is good to be so! Her sister once asked her, why she said so? Why, says she, because God would have it so: it is best that things should be as God would have.—It looks best to me. After her confinement, as they were leading her from the bed to the door, she seemed overcome by the sight of things abroad, as showing forth the glory of the Being that had made them. As she lay on her death-bed, she would often say these words—God is my friend! And once looking upon her sister, with a smile, said, O sister! How good it is!

How sweet and comfortable it is to consider, and think of heavenly things! And used this argument to persuade her sister to be much in such meditations.

She expressed, on her death-bed, an exceeding longing, both for persons in a natural state, that they might be converted, and for the godly that they might see and know more of God. And when those that looked on themselves as in a Christless state came to see her, she would be greatly moved with compassionate affection. One, in particular, that seemed to be in great distress about the state of her soul, and had come to see her from time to time, she desired her sister to persuade not to come any more, because the sight of her so wrought on her compassions, that it overcame her nature. The same week that she died, when she was in distressing circumstances as to her body, some of the neighbors that came to see her, asked if she was willing to die? She replied, that she was quite willing either to live or die.—She was willing to be in pain.—She was willing to be so always as she was then, if that was the will of God. She willed what God willed. They asked her whether she was willing to die that night? She answered, yes, if it be God's will; and seemed to speak all with that perfect composure of spirit, and with such a cheerful and pleasant countenance, that it filled them with admiration.

She was very weak a considerable time before she died, having pined away with famine and thirst, so that her flesh seemed to be dried upon her bones, and therefore could say but little, and manifested her mind very much by signs. She said she had matter enough to fill up all her time with talk, if she had but strength. A few days before her death, some asked her whether she held her integrity still? Whether she was not afraid of death? She answered to this purpose, that she had not the least degree of fear of death. They asked her why she would be so confident? She answered, if I should say otherwise, I should speak contrary to what I know; there is, says she, indeed a dark entry, that looks something dark, but on the other side there appears such a bright shining light, that I cannot be afraid! She said, not long before she died, that she used to be afraid how she should grapple with death; but, says she, God has showed me that he can make it easy in great pain. Several days before she died, she could scarcely say anything but just yes and no, to questions that were asked her, for she seemed to be dying for three days together; but seemed to continue in an admirable sweet composure of soul, without any interruption, to the last, and died as a person that went to sleep, without any struggling, about noon, on Friday, June 27, 1735.

She had long been infirm, and often had been exercised with great pain; but she died chiefly of famine. It was, doubtless, partly owing to her bodily weakness, that her nature was so often overcome, and ready to sink with gracious affection; but yet the truth was, that she had more grace, and greater discoveries of God and Christ, than the present frail state did well consist with. She wanted to be where strong grace might have more liberty, and be without the clog of a weak body; there she longed to be, and there she doubtless now is. She was looked upon amongst us as a very eminent instance of Christian experience; but this is but a very broken and imperfect account I have given of her: her eminency would much more appear, if her experiences were fully related, as she was wont to express and manifest them while living. I once read this account to some of her pious neighbors, who were acquainted with her, who said to this purpose, that the picture fell much short of the life, and particularly that it much failed of duly representing her humility, and that admirable lowliness of heart, that all times appeared in her. But there are (blessed be God!) many living instances of much the like nature, and in some things no less extraordinary.

SINNERS IN THE HANDS
OF AN ANGRY GOD (1741)

BY JONATHAN EDWARDS

Introduction

"Sinners in the Hands of an Angry God" is Jonathan Edwards' most famous sermon, retaining to this day a many-sided value for the illumination that it casts upon its author, upon the Great Awakening, and upon the evolution of religion in the United States. It was delivered at Enfield, Connecticut, on July 8, 1741, at the very height of the New England revival, amid the groans and tears of the audience. The minister delivered his address from notes which were prepared for the printer later in the year.

SINNERS IN THE HANDS
OF AN ANGRY GOD*

*Deuteronomy 32:35.—Their foot shall slide in
due time.*

In this verse is threatened the vengeance of God on the
wicked unbelieving Israelites, that were God's visible people,
and lived under means of grace; and that notwithstanding all
God's wonderful works that he had wrought towards that people, yet remained, as is expressed verse 28, void of counsel,
having no understanding in them; and that, under all the cul-
tivations of heaven, brought forth bitter and poisonous fruit;
as in the two verses next preceding the text.

The expression that I have chosen for my text, *their foot
shall slide in due time,* seems to imply the following things relating to the punishment and destruction that these wicked
Israelites were exposed to:

1. That they were always exposed to destruction; as one
that stands or walks in slippery places is always exposed to
fall. This is implied in the manner of their destruction's coming upon them, being represented by their foot's sliding. The
same is expressed, Psalm 73:18: "Surely thou didst set them
in slippery places; thou castedst them down into destruction."

2. It implies, that they were always exposed to sudden, unexpected destruction. As he that walks in slippery places is
every moment liable to fall, he cannot foresee one moment
whether he shall stand or fall the next; and when he does fall,
he falls at once, without warning, which is also expressed in
that Psalm 73:18, 19: "Surely thou didst set them in slippery
places; thou castedst them down into destruction: how are
they brought into desolation as in a moment."

3. Another thing implied is, that they are liable to fall of
themselves, without being thrown down by the hand of another; as he that stands or walks on slippery ground needs
nothing but his own weight to throw him down.

4. That the reason why they are not fallen already, and do

---

*Source: The 1843 edition of *The Works of Jonathan Edwards.*

not fall now, is only that God's appointed time is not come. For it is said that when that due time, or appointed time comes, *their feet shall slide*. Then they shall be left to fall, as they are inclined by their own weight. God will not hold them up in these slippery places any longer, but will let them go; and then, at that very instant, they shall fall into destruction; as he that stands in such slippery declining ground on the edge of a pit that he cannot stand alone, when he is let go he immediately falls and is lost.

The observation from the words that I would now insist upon is this.

There is nothing that keeps wicked men at any one moment out of hell, but the mere pleasure of God.

By the mere pleasure of God, I mean his sovereign pleasure, his arbitrary will, restrained by no obligation, hindered by no manner of difficulty, any more than if nothing else but God's mere will had in the least degree or in any respect whatsoever, any hand in the preservation of wicked men one moment.

The truth of this observation may appear by the following considerations:

1. There is no want of power in God to cast wicked men into hell at any moment. Men's hands cannot be strong when God rises up: the strongest have no power to resist him, nor can any deliver out of his hands.

He is not only able to cast wicked men into hell, but he can most easily do it. Sometimes an earthly prince meets with a great deal of difficulty to subdue a rebel, that has found means to fortify himself, and has made himself strong by the number of his followers. But it is not so with God. There is no fortress that is any defence against the power of God. Though hand join in hand, and vast multitudes of God's enemies combine and associate themselves, they are easily broken in pieces: they are as great heaps of light chaff before the whirlwind; or large quantities of dry stubble before devouring flames. We find it easy to tread on and crush a worm that we see crawling on the earth; so it is easy for us to cut or singe a slender thread that any thing hangs by; thus easy it is for God, when he pleases, to cast his enemies down to hell. What are we, that we should think to stand before him, at whose rebuke the earth trembles, and before whom the rocks are thrown down!

2. They deserve to be cast into hell; so that divine justice never stands in the way, it makes no objection against God's using his power at any moment to destroy them. Yea, on the contrary, justice calls aloud for an infinite punishment of their sins. Divine justice says of the tree that brings forth such grapes of Sodom, "Cut it down, why cumbereth it the ground?" Luke 13:7. The sword of divine justice is every moment brandished over their heads and it is nothing but the hand of arbitrary mercy, and God's mere will, that holds it back.

3. They are already under a sentence of condemnation to hell. They do not only justly deserve to be cast down thither, but the sentence of the law of God, that eternal and immutable rule of righteousness that God has fixed between him and mankind, is gone out against them; and stands against them; so that they are bound over already to hell: John 3:18, "He that believeth not is condemned already." So that every unconverted man properly belongs to hell; that is his place; from thence he is: John 8:23, "Ye are from beneath": and thither he is bound; it is the place that justice, and God's word, and the sentence of his unchangeable law, assign to him.

4. They are now the objects of that very same anger and wrath of God, that is expressed in the torments of hell: and the reason why they do not go down to hell at each moment, is not because God, in whose power they are, is not then very angry with them; as angry, as he is with many of those miserable creatures that he is now tormenting in hell, and do there feel and bear the fierceness of his wrath. Yea, God is a great deal more angry with great numbers that are now on earth; yea, doubtless, with many that are now in this congregation, that, it may be, are at ease and quiet, than he is with many of those that are now in the flames of hell.

So that it is not because God is unmindful of their wickedness, and does not resent it, that he does not let loose his hand and cut them off. God is not altogether such a one as themselves, though they may imagine him to be so. The wrath of God burns against them; their damnation does not slumber; the pit is prepared; the fire is made ready; the furnace is now hot; ready to receive them; the flames do now rage and glow.

The glittering sword is whet, and held over them, and the pit hath opened her mouth under them.

5. The devil stands ready to fall upon them, and seize them as his own, at what moment God shall permit him. They belong to him; he has their soul in his possession, and under his dominion. The Scripture represents them as his goods, Luke 11:21. The devils watch them, like greedy hungry lions that see their prey, and expect to have it, but are for the present kept back; if God should withdraw his hand by which they are restrained, they would in one moment fly upon their poor souls. The old serpent is gaping for them; hell opens its mouth wide to receive them; and if God should permit it, they would be hastily swallowed up and lost.

6. There are in the souls of wicked men those hellish principles reigning, that would presently kindle and flame out into hell-fire, if it were not for God's restraints. There is laid in the very nature of carnal men, a foundation for the torments of hell: there are those corrupt principles, in reigning power in them, and in full possession of them, that are the beginnings of hell-fire. These principles are active and powerful, exceeding violent in their nature, and if it were not for the restraining hand of God upon them, they would soon break out, they would flame out after the same manner as the same corruptions, the same enmity lies in the hearts of damned souls, and would beget the same torments in them as they do in them. The souls of the wicked are in Scripture compared to the troubled sea, Isaiah 57:20. For the present God restrains their wickedness by his mighty power, as he does the raging waves of the troubled sea, saying, "Hitherto shalt thou come, and no further"; but if God should withdraw that restraining power, it would soon carry all before it. Sin is the ruin and misery of the soul; it is destructive in its nature; and if God should leave it without restraint, there would need nothing else to make the soul perfectly miserable. The corruption of the heart of man is a thing that is immoderate and boundless in its fury; and while wicked men live here, it is like fire pent up by God's restraints, whereas if it were let loose, it would set on fire the course of nature; and as the heart is now a sink of sin, so, if sin was not restrained, it would immediately turn the soul into a fiery oven, or a furnace of fire and brimstone.

7. It is no security to wicked men for one moment, that there are no visible means of death at hand. It is no security to a natural man, that he is now in health, and that he does not see which way he should now immediately go out of the world by any accident, and that there is no visible danger in any respect in his circumstances. The manifold and continual experience of the world in all ages, shows that this is no evidence that a man is not on the very brink of eternity, and that the next step will not be into another world. The unseen, unthought of ways and means of persons going suddenly out of the world are innumerable and inconceivable. Unconverted men walk over the pit of hell on rotten covering, and there are innumerable places in this covering so weak that they will not bear their weight, and these places are not seen. The arrows of death fly unseen at noonday; the sharpest sight cannot discern them. God has so many different, unsearchable ways of taking wicked men out of the world and sending them to hell, that there is nothing to make it appear, that God had need to be at the expense of a miracle, or go out of the ordinary course of his providence, to destroy any wicked man, at any moment. All the means that there are of sinners going out of the world, are so in God's hands, and so absolutely subject to his power and determination, that it does not depend at all less on the mere will of God, whether sinners shall at any moment go to hell, than if means were never made use of, or at all concerned in the case.

8. Natural men's prudence and care to preserve their own lives, or the care of others to preserve them, do not secure them a moment. This, divine providence and universal experience do also bear testimony to. There is this clear evidence that men's own wisdom is no security to them from death; that if it were otherwise we should see some difference between the wise and politic men of the world, and others, with regard to their liableness to early and unexpected death; but how is it in fact? Eccles. 2:16, "How dieth the wise man? As the fool."

9. All wicked men's pains and contrivance they use to escape hell, while they continue to reject Christ, and so remain wicked men, do not secure them from hell one moment. Almost every natural man that hears of hell, flatters himself that

he shall escape it; he depends upon himself for his own security, he flatters himself in what he has done, in what he is now doing, or what he intends to do; every one lays out matters in his own mind how he shall avoid damnation, and flatters himself that he contrives well for himself, and that his schemes will not fail. They hear indeed that there are but few saved, and that the bigger part of men that have died heretofore are gone to hell; but each one imagines that he lays out matters better for his own escape than others have done: he does not intend to come to that place of torment; he says within himself, that he intends to take care that shall be effectual, and to order matters so for himself as not to fail.

But the foolish children of men do miserably delude themselves in their own schemes, and in their confidence in their own strength and wisdom, they trust to nothing but a shadow. The bigger part of those that heretofore have lived under the same means of grace, and are now dead, are undoubtedly gone to hell; and it was not because they were not as wise as those that are now alive, it was not because they did not lay out matters as well for themselves to secure their own escape. If it were so that we could come to speak with them, and could inquire of them, one by one, whether they expected, when alive, and when they used to hear about hell, ever to be subjects of that misery, we, doubtless, should hear one and another reply, "No, I never intended to come here: I had laid out matters otherwise in my mind; I thought I should contrive well for myself: I thought my scheme good. I intended to take effectual care; but it came upon me unexpectedly; I did not look for it at that time, and in that manner; it came as a thief: death outwitted me: God's wrath was too quick for me: O my cursed foolishness! I was flattering myself, and pleasing myself with vain dreams of what I would do hereafter; and when I was saying peace and safety, then sudden destruction came upon me."

10. God has laid himself under no obligation, by any promise, to keep any natural man out of hell one moment: God certainly has made no promises either of eternal life, or of any deliverance or preservation from eternal death, but what are contained in the covenant of grace, the promises that are given in Christ, in whom all the promises are yea and amen. But surely they have no interest in the promises of the covenant

of grace that are not the children of the covenant, and that do not believe in any of the promises of the covenant, and have no interest in the Mediator of the covenant.

So that, whatever some have imagined and pretended about promises made to natural men's earnest seeking and knocking, it is plain and manifest, that whatever pains a natural man takes in religion, whatever prayers he makes, that he believes in Christ, God is under no manner of obligation to keep him a moment from eternal destruction.

So that thus it is, that natural men are held in the hand of God over the pit of hell; they have deserved the fiery pit, and are already sentenced to it; and God is dreadfully provoked, his anger is as great towards them as to those that are actually suffering the executions of the fierceness of his wrath in hell, and they have done nothing in the least, to appease or abate that anger, neither is God in the least bound by any promise to hold them up one moment; the devil is waiting for them, hell is gaping for them, the flames gather and flash about them, and would fain lay hold on them and swallow them up; the fire pent up in their own hearts is struggling to break out; and they have no interest in any Mediator, there are no means within reach that can be any security to them. In short, they have no refuge, nothing to take hold of; all that preserves them every moment is the mere arbitrary will, and uncovenanted, unobliged forbearance of an incensed God.

Application

The use may be of awakening to unconverted persons in this congregation. This that you have heard is the case of every one of you that are out of Christ. That world of misery, that lake of burning brimstone, is extended abroad under you. There is the dreadful pit of the glowing flames of the wrath of God; there is hell's wide gaping mouth open; and you have nothing to stand upon, nor any thing to take hold of. There is nothing between you and hell but the air; it is only the power and mere pleasure of God that holds you up.

You probably are not sensible of this; you find you are kept out of hell, but do not see the hand of God in it; but look at other things, as the good state of your bodily constitution, your care of your own life, and the means you use for your own preservation. But indeed these things are nothing; if God should withdraw his hand, they would avail no more to keep you from falling, than the thin air to hold up a person that is suspended in it.

Your wickedness makes you as it were heavy as lead, and to tend downwards with great weight and pressure towards hell; and if God should let you go, you would immediately sink and swiftly descend and plunge into the bottomless gulf, and your healthy constitution, and your own care and prudence, and best contrivance, and all your righteousness, would have no more influence to uphold you and keep you out of hell, than a spider's web would have to stop a falling rock. Were it not that so is the sovereign pleasure of God, the earth would not bear you one moment; for you are a burden to it; the creation groans with you; the creature is made subject to the bondage of your corruption, not willingly; the sun does not willingly shine upon you to give you light to serve sin and Satan; the earth does not willingly yield her increase to satisfy your lusts; nor is it willingly a stage for your wickedness to be acted upon; the air does not willingly serve you for breath to maintain the flame of life in your vitals, while you spend your life in the service of God's enemies. God's creatures are good, and were made for men to serve God with, and do not willingly subserve to any other purpose, and groan when they are abused to purposes so directly contrary to their nature and end. And the world would spew you out, were it not for the sovereign hand of him who hath subjected it in hope. There are the black clouds of God's wrath now hanging directly over your heads, full of the dreadful storm, and big with thunder; and were it not for the restraining hand of God, it would immediately burst forth upon you. The sovereign pleasure of God, for the present, stays his rough wind; otherwise it would come with fury, and your destruction would come like a whirlwind, and you would be like the chaff of the summer threshing floor.

The wrath of God is like great waters that are damned for the present; they increase more and more, and rise higher and higher, till an outlet is given; and the longer the stream is stopped, the more rapid and mighty is its course, when once it is let loose. It is true, that judgment against your evil work has not been executed hitherto; the floods of God's vengeance have been withheld; but your guilt in the mean time is constantly increasing, and you are every day treasuring up more wrath; the waters are continually rising, and waxing more and more mighty; and there is nothing but the mere pleasure of God, that holds the waters back, that are unwilling to be stopped, and press hard to go forward. If God should only withdraw his hand from the floodgate, it would immediately fly open, and the fiery floods of the fierceness and wrath of God, would rush forth with inconceivable fury, and would come upon you with omnipotent power; and if your strength were ten thousand times greater than it is, yea, ten thousand times greater than the strength of the stoutest, sturdiest devil in hell, it would be nothing to withstand or endure it.

The bow of God's wrath is bent, and the arrow made ready on the string, and justice bends the arrow at your heart, and strains the bow, and it is nothing but the mere pleasure of God, and that of an angry God, without any promise or obligation at all, that keeps the arrow one moment from being made drunk with your blood.

Thus are all you that never passed under a great change of heart, by the mighty power of the Spirit of God upon your souls; all that were never born again, and made new creatures, and raised from being dead in sin, to a state of new, and before altogether unexperienced light and life (however you may have reformed your life in many things, and may have had religious affections and may keep up a form of religion in your families and closets, and in the houses of God, and may be strict in it) you are thus in the hands of an angry God; it is nothing but his mere pleasure that keeps you from being this moment swallowed up in everlasting destruction.

However unconvinced you may now be of the truth of what you hear, by and by you will be fully convinced of it. Those that are gone from being in the like circumstances with you, see that it was so with them; for destruction came suddenly upon most of them; when they expected nothing of it, and while they were saying, Peace and safety: now they see, that those things that they depended on for peace and safety were nothing but thin air and empty shadows.

The God that holds you over the pit of hell, much as one holds a spider, or some loathsome insect, over the fire, abhors you, and is dreadfully provoked; his wrath towards you burns like fire; he looks upon you as worthy of nothing else, but to be cast into the fire; he is of purer eyes than to bear to have you in his sight; you are ten thousand times so abominable in his eyes, as the most hateful and venomous serpent is in ours. You have offended him infinitely more than ever a stubborn rebel did his prince: and yet it is nothing but his hand that holds you from falling into the fire every moment: it is ascribed to nothing else, that you did not go to hell the last night; that you were suffered to awake again in this world, after you closed your eyes to sleep; and there is no other reason to be given, why you have not dropped into hell since you arose in the morning, but that God's hand has held you up: there is no other reason to be given why you have not gone to hell, since you have sat here in the house of God, provoking his pure eyes by your sinful wicked manner of attending his solemn worship: yea, there is nothing else that is to be given as a reason why you do not this very moment drop down into hell.

O sinner! consider the fearful danger you are in: it is a great furnace of wrath, a wide and bottomless pit, full of the fire of wrath, that you are held over in the hand of that God, whose wrath is provoked and incensed as much against you, as against many of the damned in hell: you hang by a slender thread, with the flames of divine wrath flashing about it, and ready every moment to singe it, and burn it asunder; and you have no interest in any Mediator, and nothing to lay hold of to save yourself, nothing to keep off the flames of wrath, nothing of your own, nothing that you ever have done, nothing that you can do, to induce God to spare you one moment.

And consider here more particularly several things concerning that wrath that you are in such danger of:

1. Whose wrath it is. It is the wrath of the infinite God. If it were only the wrath of man, though it were of the most potent prince, it would be comparatively little to be regarded. The wrath of kings is very much dreaded, especially of absolute monarchs, that have the possessions and lives of their subjects wholly in their power, to be disposed of at their mere will. Prov. 20:2, "The fear of a king is as the roaring of a lion: whoso provoketh him to anger, sinneth against his own soul." The subject that very much enrages an arbitrary prince, is liable to suffer the most extreme torments that human art can invent, or human power can inflict. But the greatest earthly potentates, in their greatest majesty and strength, and when

clothed in their greatest terrors, are but feeble, despicable worms of the dust, in comparison of the great and almighty Creator and King of heaven and earth: it is but little that they can do, when most enraged, and when they have exerted the utmost of their fury. All the kings of the earth before God, are as grasshoppers; they are nothing, and less than nothing: both their love and their hatred is to be despised. The wrath of the great King of kings, is as much more terrible than theirs, as his majesty is greater. Luke 12:4, 5, "And I say unto you, my friends, be not afraid of them that kill the body, and after that have no more that they can do. But I will forewarn you whom you shall fear: fear him, which after he hath killed, hath power to cast into hell; yea, I say unto you, fear him."

2. It is the fierceness of his wrath that you are exposed to. We often read of the fury of God; as in Isaiah 59:18: "According to their deeds, accordingly he will repay fury to his adversaries." So Isaiah 66:15, "For behold, the Lord will come with fire and with his chariots like a whirlwind, to render his anger with fury, and his rebuke with flames of fire." And so in many other places. So we read of God's fierceness, Rev. 19:15. There we read of "the wine-press of the fierceness and wrath of Almighty God." The words are exceedingly terrible: if it had only been said, "the wrath of God," the words would have implied that which is infinitely dreadful: but it is not only said so, but "the fierceness and wrath of God": the fury of God! the fierceness of Jehovah! Oh how dreadful must that be! Who can utter or conceive what such expressions carry in them! But it is not only said so, but "the fierceness and wrath of Almighty God." As though there would be a very great manifestation of his almighty power in what the fierceness of his wrath should inflict, as though omnipotence should be as it were enraged, and exerted, as men are wont to exert their strength in the fierceness of their wrath. Oh! then, what will be the consequence! What will become of the poor worm that shall suffer it! Whose hands can be strong! And whose heart endure! To what a dreadful, inexpressible, inconceivable depth of misery must the poor creature be sunk who shall be the subject of this!

Consider this, you that are here present, that yet remain in an unregenerate state. That God will execute the fierceness of his anger, implies, that he will inflict wrath without any pity:

when God beholds the ineffable extremity of your case, and sees your torment so vastly disproportioned to your strength, and sees how your poor soul is crushed, and sinks down, as it were, into an infinite gloom; he will have no compassion upon you, he will not forbear the executions of his wrath, or in the least lighten his hand; there shall be no moderation or mercy, nor will God then at all stay his rough wind; he will have no regard to your welfare, nor be at all careful lest you should suffer too much in any other sense, than only that you should not suffer beyond what strict justice requires: nothing shall be withheld, because it is so hard for you to bear. Ezek. 8:18, "Therefore will I also deal in fury; mine eye shall not spare, neither will I have pity; and though they cry in mine ears with a loud voice, yet will I not hear them." Now God stands ready to pity you; this is a day of mercy; you may cry now with some encouragement of obtaining mercy: but when once the day of mercy is past, your most lamentable and dolorous cries and shrieks will be in vain; you will be wholly lost and thrown away of God, as to any regard to your welfare; God will have no other use to put you to, but only to suffer misery; you shall be continued in being to no other end; for you will be a vessel of wrath fitted to destruction; and there will be no other use of this vessel, but only to be filled full of wrath: God will be so far from pitying you when you cry to him, that it is said he will only "laugh and mock," Prov. 1:25, 26, etc.

How awful are those words, Isaiah 63:3, which are the words of the great God: "I will tread them in mine anger, and trample them in my fury, and their blood shall be sprinkled upon my garments, and I will stain all my raiment." It is perhaps impossible to conceive of words that carry in them greater manifestations of these three things, viz., contempt and hatred, and fierceness of indignation. If you cry to God to pity you, he will be so far from pitying you in your doleful case, or showing you the least regard or favor, that instead of that he will only tread you under foot: and though he will know that you cannot bear the weight of omnipotence treading upon you, yet he will not regard that, but he will crush you under his feet without mercy; he will crush out your blood, and make it fly, and it shall be sprinkled on his garments, so as to stain all his raiment. He will not only hate you, but he will have you in the utmost contempt; no place shall be thought fit for you but under his feet, to be trodden down as the mire in the streets.

3. The misery you are exposed to is that which God will inflict to that end, that he might show what that wrath of Jehovah is. God hath had it on his heart to show to angels and men, both how excellent his love is and also how terrible his wrath is. Sometimes earthly kings have a mind to show how terrible their wrath is, by the extreme punishments they would execute on those that provoke them. Nebuchadnezzar, that mighty and haughty monarch of the Chaldean empire, was willing to show his wrath when enraged with Shadrach, Meshech, and Abednego; and accordingly gave order that the burning fiery furnace should be heated seven times hotter than it was before; doubtless it was raised to the utmost degree of fierceness that human art could raise it; but the great God is also willing to show his wrath, and magnify his awful Majesty and mighty power in the extreme sufferings of his enemies. Rom. 9:22, "What if God, willing to show his wrath, and to make his power known endured with much long-suffering, the vessels of wrath fitted to destruction?" And seeing this is his design and what he has determined, to show how terrible the unmixed, unrestrained wrath, the fury, and fierceness of Jehovah is, he will do it to effect. There will be something accomplished and brought to pass that will be dreaded with a witness. When the great and angry God hath risen up and executed his awful vengeance on the poor sinner, and the wretch is actually suffering the infinite weight and power of his indignation, then will God call upon the whole universe to behold that awful majesty and mighty power that is to be seen in Isa. 33:12, 13, 14, "And the people shall be as the burning of lime, as thorns cut up shall they be burnt in the fire. Hear, ye that are afar off, what I have done; and ye that are near acknowledge my might. The sinners in Zion are afraid; fearfulness hath surprised the hypocrites," etc.

Thus it will be with you that are in an unconverted state, if you continue in it; the infinite might, and majesty, and terribleness, of the omnipotent God shall be magnified upon you in the ineffable strength of your torments: you shall be tormented in the presence of the holy angels, and in the presence of the Lamb; and when you shall be in this state of suffering, the glorious inhabitants of heaven shall go forth and look on the awful spectacle, that they may see what the wrath and fierceness of the Almighty is; and when they have seen it, they will fall down and adore that great power and majesty. Isa. 66:23, 24, "And it shall come to pass, that from one moon to another, and from one Sabbath to another, shall all flesh come to worship before me, saith the Lord. And they shall go forth and look upon the carcasses of the men that have transgressed against me; for their worm shall not die, neither shall their fire be quenched, and they shall be abhorring unto all flesh."

4. It is everlasting wrath. It would be dreadful to suffer this fierceness and wrath of Almighty God one moment; but you must suffer it to all eternity: there will be no end to this exquisite, horrible misery: when you look forward, you shall see a long forever, a boundless duration before you, which will swallow up your thoughts, and amaze your soul; and you will absolutely despair of ever having any deliverance, any end, any mitigation, any rest at all; you will know certainly that you must wear out long ages, millions of millions of ages, in wrestling and conflicting with this Almighty merciless vengeance; and then when you have so done, when so many ages have actually been spent by you in this manner, you will know that all is but a point to what remains. So that your punishment will indeed be infinite. Oh, who can express what the state of a soul in such circumstances is! All that we can possibly say about it, gives but a very feeble, faint representation of it; it is inexpressible and inconceivable: for "who knows the power of God's anger?"

How dreadful is the state of those that are daily and hourly in danger of this great wrath and infinite misery! But this is the dismal case of every soul in this congregation that has not been born again, however moral and strict, sober and religious, they may otherwise be. Oh that you would consider it, whether you be young or old! There is reason to think, that there are many in this congregation now hearing this discourse, that will actually be the subjects of this very misery to all eternity. We know not who they are, or in what seats they sit, or what thoughts they now have. It may be they are now at ease, and hear all these things without much disturbance, and are now flattering themselves that they are not the persons; promising themselves that they shall escape. If we knew that there was one person, and but one, in the whole congregation, that was to be the subject of this misery, what an awful thing it would be to think of! If we knew who it was, what an awful sight would it be to see such a person! How might all the rest of the congregation lift up a lamentable and bitter cry over him! But alas! Instead of one, how many is it likely will remember this discourse in hell! And it would be a wonder, if some that are now present should not be in hell in a very short time, before this year is out. And it would be no wonder if some persons, that now sit here in some seats of this meeting-house in health, and quiet and secure, should be there before tomorrow morning.

Revivalist
=Song=

SINNER MAN
SPRINGFIELD MOUNTAIN

Introduction

The mood of religious life, especially on the frontier, may be grasped most vividly from its music. News of the coming of an itinerant minister, or circuit rider, would be sent ahead of him. At the appointed time and place, perhaps in some great clearing, hundreds or thousands of settlers would assemble to hear the Word, to worship, to sing, and to exhort each other. From the experiences of such revival meetings, in which people came together to rededicate themselves to the service of God and man, grew a new type of devotional music —the white spiritual.

These songs were a peculiarly original and popular modification of traditional hymns that had usually been imported from England. A favorite theme was the need for swift repentance among frontier sinners in a world where life was precarious and man, woman or child might be summoned before nightfall or daybreak to face his Maker. "How will you stand on the Day of Judgment?" was the question posed. Such singing continued, and even popularized, an entirely medieval European tradition. The most magnificent music of the old Catholic Church had centered around the dies irae, the Day of Judgment when, amid the crash of thunder and the sounding of trumpets, God would call all mankind to fiery punishment or everlasting reward.

Sinner Man is a song of this type, unusual even among the spirituals for the brilliance of its imaginative sweep and its cumulative emotional effect. We have no way of knowing precisely how long people have been singing it, but the unusual hexatonic mode—i.e., six tones to the scale instead of seven—indicates its colonial origins. The following version was recorded by the English song collector, Cecil J. Sharp, during a visit to the southern Appalachians in 1917. The mountaineers who sang it for him were direct descendants of the original settlers; they have been handing down such songs directly from father to son from the days of emigration and settlement in the eighteenth century.

Springfield Mountain, in one form or another, has been found in practically every state in the Union, thus attesting to the universality of the experience which it expresses. No more apt illustration could be given of the basic, pressing theme of revivalism: repent today while there is time, for tomorrow will be too late. The Springfield Mountain of the song is near Wilbraham, Massachusetts, only a few miles from the town of Springfield which, in the 1760's, was still a frontier region, and, in the 1730's, a storm center of the New England Awakening. Many of the later versions of this song poke fun at the victim. This is natural enough; situations that are serious when we actually face them often look ridiculous in retrospect. When the rattlesnake vanished along with the frontier, who could blame later generations for not taking its fangs too seriously?

SINNER MAN

O sin-ner man, where are you going to run to?

O sin-ner man, where are you going to run to?

O sin-ner man, where are you going to run to,

All —— on that day?

Run to the moon: O moon, won't you hide me?

Run to the moon: O moon, won't you hide me?

Run to the moon: O moon won't you hide me,

All —— on that day? The

Lord said: O sin - ner man, the
moon'll be a - bleed - ing. The
Lord said: O sin - ner man, the
moon'll be a - bleed - ing. The
Lord said: O sin - ner man, the
moon'll be a -bleed-ing, All — on that day.

O sinner man, where are you going to run to?
O sinner man, where are you going to run to?
O sinner man, where are you going to run to,
All on that day?

Run to the moon: O moon, won't you hide me?
Run to the moon: O moon, won't you hide me?
Run to the moon: O moon, won't you hide me,
All on that day?
The Lord said: O sinner man, the moon'll be a-bleeding,
   etc.
    O sinner man, where are you going to run to?, *etc.*

Run to the stars: O stars, won't you hide me? *etc.*
The Lord said: O sinner man, the stars'll be a-falling, *etc.*
    O sinner man, where are you going to run to?, *etc.*

Run to the sea: O sea, won't you hide me? *etc.*
The Lord said: O sinner man, the sea'll be a-sinking, *etc.*
    O sinner man, where are you going to run to?, *etc.*

Run to the rocks: O rocks, won't you hide me? *etc.*
The Lord said: O sinner man, the rocks'll be a-rolling, *etc.*
    O sinner man, where are you going to run to?, *etc.*

Run to the Lord: O Lord, won't you hide me? *etc.*
The Lord said: O sinner man, you ought to been a-praying,
    etc.
    O sinner man, where are you going to run to?, *etc.*

Run to Satan: O Satan, won't you hide me, *etc.*
Satan said: O sinner man, step right in, *etc.*
    O sinner man, where are you going to run to?, *etc.*

SPRINGFIELD MOUNTAIN

On Springfield Mountain there did dwell,
A likely youth was known full well;
Timothy Myrick was his name,
Lieutenant Myrick's only son.

On Friday morning he did go,
Down to the meadow, for to mow,
He mowed and mowed around the field,
'Til a poisonous serpent bit his heel.

When he received his deathly wound,
He laid his scythe down on the ground,
For to return was his intent,
Crying out loud long as he went.

His cries were heard both far and near,
But no friend to him did appear,
They thought he did some workman call,
And so poor boy alone did fall.

Day being done, now, and night coming on,
The father went to seek his son,
And soon his only son he found,
Cold as a stone, dead on the ground.

'Twas the seventh of August in seventeen sixty-one,
That this sad accident was done;
Let this a warning be to all,
To be prepared when God doth call.

The Great
═Awakening (cont.)═══

A LETTER FROM A GENTLEMAN IN BOSTON
TO MR. GEORGE WISHART, ONE OF THE
MINISTERS IN EDINBURGH, CONCERNING

THE STATE OF RELIGION IN NEW ENGLAND. (1742)

BY CHARLES CHAUNCY

Introduction

The New England Awakening began in Northampton, Massachusetts, in 1734, and spread in the following year throughout the lower valley of the Connecticut River. This was a frontier revival, and only a foretaste of greater things to come. The movement got into full swing when New England was hit by the great itinerants who began to work the area over in the year 1740. Chief of these itinerants were George Whitefield, the great Methodist missionary from England, Gilbert Tennent, main architect of the revival in New Jersey, and James Davenport, an enthusiastic but rash and indiscreet preacher from Southold, Long Island.

In the wake of these trail-blazers a host of local New England itinerants followed; foremost among these was the redoubtable Edwards himself. With the help of these exhortations, revivalism reached its New England climax in the year 1741-42, and thereafter fell into decline.

To the enthusiasts the Awakening, with its mass audiences, its tears, groans, footstamping, handclapping, swooning, fits, shrieks of joy and agony, was surely the work of God. What else was all this but the visible manifestation that many, hitherto dead or indifferent to the salvation of their eternal souls, had been brought to repentance and had shown a personal witness of conversion?

Ministers in old-established New England congregations viewed the matter differently. The revival was an undeniably plebeian movement, and it manifested boisterous and popular passions that were unwelcome to New England's aristocratic leadership. Prominent among the revival's leadership were frontier preachers with dubious ministerial training and qualifications, or even none at all. This, to the minister trained at Harvard or Yale, smacked of outright demagoguery.

The revival, furthermore, challenged the theology which had become acceptable in the fashionable New England centers of learning. By the middle of the eighteenth century an enlightened rationalism was rapidly the stark doctrines of medieval damnation with which the Puritan fathers had arrived upon these shores. Revivalism challenged directly the liberal heresies of Bostonian respectability.

Charles Chauncy (1705-87), the outstanding exponent of Harvard theological liberalism in his day, locked horns with Jonathan Edwards in one of the most famous controversies in the history of American theology. His letter to George Wishart, a Scots minister, written at the height of the revival, gives us an interesting eyewitness account of itineracy and its impact upon the people as recorded by a hostile observer. Published as a pamphlet in Boston in 1742, it is here reproduced in full, but with a number of stylistic modifications.

A LETTER FROM A
GENTLEMAN IN BOSTON*

Boston, August 4, 1742

Reverend Sir,

I perceive by a printed letter from a friend in Edinburgh, containing excerpts of letters concerning the success of the Gospel in these parts, that marvellous accounts have been sent abroad of a most glorious work of grace going on in America, begun by Mr. Whitefield, and helpt forward by those in his way of preaching and acting. I should be glad there had been more truth in those accounts. Some of the things related are known falsehoods, others strangely enlarged upon; and the representations, in general, such, as exhibit a wrong idea of the religious state of affairs among us. I had thoughts of sending you the needful corrections of that pamphlet; but my circumstances being such, at present, as not to allow of this, must content myself with giving you the following summary narration of things as they have appeared among us.

The minds of people in this part of the world, had been greatly prepossest in favour of Mr. Whitefield, from the accounts transmitted of him, from time to time, as a wonder of piety, a man of God, so as no one was like him. Accordingly, when he came to town, about two years since, he was received

---

*Source: This letter was printed as a pamphlet for the Clarendon Historical Society (Edinburgh: 1883), from the original Scottish version published by George Wishart in 1742.

as though he had been an angel of God; yea, a God come down in the likeness of man. He was strangely flocked after by all sorts of persons, and much admired by the vulgar, both great and small. The ministers had him in veneration, at least in appearance, as much as the people; encouraged his preaching, attended it themselves every day in the week, and mostly twice a day. The grand subject of conversation was Mr. Whitefield, and the whole business of the town to run, from place to place, to hear him preach: and, as he preach'd under such uncommon advantages, being high in the opinion of the people, and having the body of the ministers hanging on his lips, he soon insinuated himself still further into the affections of multitudes, in so much that it became dangerous to mention his name, without saying something in commendation of him.

His reception as he past through this and the neighbouring governments of Connecticut and New York, till he came to Philadelphia, was after much the same manner; save only, that he met with no admirers among the clergy, unless here and there one, any where but in Boston: and, whether the ministers here in general, really thought better of him than they did elsewhere, I will not be too positive to affirm. 'Tis possible, they might act as tho' they had a great veneration for him, and so as to lead people into such an apprehension, from *cowardice, affectation of popularity*, or *a rigid attachment to some sentiments in divinity* they might imagine there was now an advantage to establish and propagate: and I would not undertake to prove, that they might none of them be under an undue influence from some or other of these motives.

Much began to be now said of a glorious work of God going on in the land. Evening lectures were set up in one place and another; no less than six in this town, four weekly, and two monthly ones, tho' the town does not consist of above 5000 families at the largest computation. At some of these lectures, it was common to mention Mr. Whitefield by name, both in the prayers and sermons; giving God thanks for sending such an extraordinary man among us, and making him the instrument of such extraordinary good to so many souls. He was indeed spoken of, as the angel flying through Heaven with the everlasting Gospel, and such honours sacrificed to him as were due to no mere man. Nay, to such a height did this spirit rise, that all who did not express a very high thought of Mr. Whitefield, were looked upon with an evil eye; and as to those who declared their dislike of what they judged amiss of the times, they were stigmatised as enemies of God and true religion. Yea, they were openly represented, both from the pulpit and the press, as in danger of committing the sin against the Holy Ghost, if not actually guilty even of this unpardonable sin.

And here you will doubtless be disposed to enquire, what was the great good this gentleman was the instrument of.

In answer whereto, I freely acknowledge, wherever he went he generally moved the passions, especially of the younger people, and the females among them; the effect whereof was, a great talk about religion, together with a disposition to be perpetually hearing sermons, to neglect of all other business; especially, as preach'd by those who were sticklers for the new way, as it was called. And in these things chiefly consisted the goodness so much spoken of.

I deny not, but there might be here and there a person stopp'd from going on in a course of sin; and some might be made really better. But so far as I could judge upon the nicest observation, the town, in general, was not much mended in those things wherein a reformation was greatly needed. I could not discern myself, nor many others whom I have talked with, and challenged on this head, but that there was the same pride and vanity, the same luxury and intemperance, the same lying and tricking and cheating, as before this gentleman came among us.

There was certainly no remarkable difference as to these things, and 'tis vain in any to pretend there was. This I am sure of, there was raised such a spirit of bitter, censorious, uncharitable judging, as was not known before; and is, wherever it reigns, a scandal to all who call themselves Christians: nor was it ever evident to me, but that the greatest friends to Mr. Whitefield were as much puffed up with conceit and pride as any of their neighbours; and as to some of them, and the more eminent too, I verily believe they possess a worse spirit than before they heard of his name, and it had been as well for them if they had never seen his face.

But I have only entered as yet upon that scene of things, which has made so much noise in the country. A number of ministers in one place and another, were by this time formed into Mr. Whitefield's temper, and began to appear and go about preaching, with a zeal more flaming, if possible, than his. One of the most famous among these was Mr. Gilbert

Tennent, a man of no great parts or learning; his preaching was in the extemporaneous way, with much noise and little connection. If he had taken suitable care to prepare his sermons, and followed nature in the delivery of them, he might have acquitted himself as a middling preacher; but as he preached, he was an awkward imitator of Mr. Whitefield, and too often turned off his hearers with mere stuff, which he uttered with a spirit more bitter and uncharitable than you can easily imagine. All were Pharisees, hypocrites, carnal unregenerate wretches, both ministers and people, who did not think just as he did, particularly as to the doctrines of Calvinism; and those who opposed him, and the work of God he was sure he was carrying on, would have opposed Christ Jesus himself and his apostles, had they lived in their day.

This gentleman came from New Brunswick in the Jersies to Boston, in the middle of winter (a journey of more than 300 miles), to water the good seed sown by Mr. Whitefield in this place. It was indeed at Mr. Whitefield's desire, and in consequence of a day of fasting and prayer, kept on purpose to know the mind of God as to this matter, that he came among us; the ministers in the town, though fourteen in number, being thought insufficient to carry on the good work he had begun here in the hearts of people. And though the design this gentleman professedly came upon, was a barefaced affront to the body of the ministers, yet not only the people (which is not to be wondered at), but some of the ministers themselves, admired and followed him, as much as they had done Mr. Whitefield before him; and here he was, by their encouragement, a great part of the winter, preaching every day in the week, to the taking people off from their callings, and the introducing a neglect of all business but that of hearing him preach. He went from Boston to the eastward, to visit the places where Mr. Whitefield had been; and on his return home passed through the country, preaching everywhere as he went along, in the same manner, and with the same spirit he did here in Boston.

And now it was, that Mr. Whitefield's doctrine of inward feelings began to discover itself in multitudes, whose sensible perceptions arose to such a height, as that they cried out, fell down, swooned away, and, to all appearance, were like persons in fits; and this, when the preaching (if it may be so called) had in it as little well digested and connected good sense, as you can well suppose. Scores in a congregation would be in such circumstances at a time; nay some hundreds in some places, to the filling the houses of worship with confusion not to be expressed in words, nor indeed conceived of by the most lively imagination, unless where persons have been eye and ear witnesses to these things. Though I may add here, that to a person in possession of himself, and capable of observation, this surprising scene of things may be accounted for. The speaker delivers himself, with the greatest vehemence both of voice and gesture, and in the most frightful language his genius will allow of. If this has its intended effect upon one or two weak women, the shrieks catch from one to another, till a great part of the congregation is affected; and some are in the thought, that it may be too common for those zealous in the new way to cry out themselves, on purpose to move others, and bring forward a general scream. Visions now became common, and trances also, the subjects of which were in their own conceit transported from earth to heaven, where they saw and heard most glorious things; conversed with Christ and holy angels, had opened to them the Book of Life, and were permitted to read the names of persons there, and the like. And what is a singular instance (so far as I remember) of the working of enthusiasm, laughing, loud hearty laughing, was one of the ways in which our new converts, almost everywhere, were wont to join together in expressing their joy at the conversion of others.

'Tis scarce imaginable what excesses and extravagancies people were running into, and even encouraged in; being told such things were arguments of the extraordinary presence of the Holy Ghost with them. The same houses of worship were scarce emptied night nor day for a week together, and unheard of instances of supposed religion were carried on in them. Some would be praying, some exhorting, some singing, some clapping their hands, some laughing, some crying, some shrieking and roaring out; and so invincibly set were they in these ways, especially when encouraged by any ministers (as was too often the case), that it was a vain thing to argue with them, to show them the indecency of such behaviour; and whoever indeed made an attempt this way, might be sure aforehand of being called an opposer of the spirit, and a child of the Devil.

At these times there were among the people what we call

here *exhorters;* these are such as are esteemed to be converts in the new way. Sometimes they are children, boys and girls, sometimes women; but most commonly raw, illiterate, weak, and conceited young men, or lads. They pray with the people, call upon them to come to Christ, tell them they are dropping into Hell, and take upon them what they imagine is the business of preaching. They are generally much better thought of than any ministers, except those in the new way, I mean by the friends to the extraordinaries prevalent in the land; and they are the greatest promoters of them. 'Tis indeed at the exhortations of these poor ignorant creatures, that there is ordinarily the most noise and confusion: and what may be worth a particular remark, 'tis seldom there are any great effects wrought, till the gloominess of the night comes on. It is in the evening, or more late in the night, with only a few candles in a meeting-house, that there is the screaming and shrieking to the greatest degree; and the persons thus affected are generally children, young people, and women. Other instances there may have been, but they are more rare; these bear the chief part.

I shall here insert a paragraph of a letter sent me by a friend living at New Haven, the seat of one of our colleges, a gentleman of known integrity and veracity, giving an account of the managements of one of the preachers of Mr. Whitefield's making, with the appearance following thereupon. Says he:

"After the conclusion of the exercises usual in our religious assemblies, he came down from the pulpit into the deacon's seat. His exercises were, (1) Short Prayers: wherein he used very uncommon expressions, and such as had no tendency, at least in my mind, to excite devotion; which he delivered with a boisterous voice, and in a manner to me very disagreeable. (2) Singing Psalms and Hymns: which he himself repeated with an awful tone and frightful gestures. (3) Exhorting, as they called it: to which many laymen were admitted as assistants.

"In performing these exercises they observed no stated method, but proceeded as their present thought or fancy led them. And by this means the meeting house would be filled with what I could not but judge great confusion and disorder; for the whole house would many times seem to be in a perfect hubbub, and people filled with consternation. These meetings they would continue til ten, eleven, twelve o'clock at night; in the midst of them sometimes ten, twenty, thirty, and sometimes many more would scream and cry out, or send forth the most lamentable groans, whilst others made great manifestations of joy, by clapping their hands, uttering ecstatic expressions, singing psalms, and inviting and exhorting others. Some would swoon away under the influence of distressing fears, and others swallowed up with insupportable joy. While some were fainting, others laboured under convulsive twitches of body, which they said were involuntary. But in vain shall I pretend to describe all the proceedings at those meetings. But what appeared to me most dangerous and hurtful was, that very much stress was laid on these extraordinaries, as tho' they were sure marks, or, at least sufficient evidences of a just conviction of sin on the one hand; or, on the other, of that joy which there is in believing, and so of an interest in the favour of God."

You may be ready perhaps to think I have here given you a romantic representation of things; but it is the real truth of the case without a figure. Yea, this has been the appearance in all parts of the land more or less, and so known to have been so, that there is no room for debate upon the matter: nay, those who are friends to the new way were once so far from being ashamed of these things, that they boasted of them, and entertained an ill opinion of all who did not speak of them as evidences of the wonderful power of the spirit of God. I say, they at first boasted of these things, and some of them do so still; though the generality have begun, for some time, to speak publicly of the subtility of Satan, to tell people he may appear as an angel of light, and to warn them against being carried away by his devices. Nay, Mr. Tennent himself, one of the main instruments of all our disorders, has, in a couple of letters to some of his friends, published in the prints, expressed his fears lest the churches should be undone with a spirit of enthusiasm, and these exhorters which have risen up everywhere in the land. He seems indeed to have quite turned about: the reason whereof may be this: the Moravians who came to Philadelphia with Count Zinzendorf, have been among his people, and managed with them as he did elsewhere, and brought the like confusion among them. And now he cries out of danger, and expresses himself much as those did, whom before he had sent to the Devil by wholesale.

Various are the sentiments of persons about this unusual appearance among us. Some think it to be a most wonderful work of God's grace; others a most wonderful spirit of enthusiasm; some think there is a great deal of religion, with some small mixture of extravagance; others a great deal of extravagance with some small mixture of that which may be called good; some think the country was never in such a happy state on a religious account, others that it was never in a worse.

For myself, I am among those who are clearly in the opinion, that there never was such a spirit of superstition and enthusiasm reigning in the land before; never such gross disorders and barefaced affronts to common decency; never such scandalous reproaches on the blessed spirit, making him the author of the greatest irregularities and confusions. Yet, I am of opinion also, that the appearances among us (so much out of the ordinary way, and so unaccountable to persons not acquainted with the history of the world) have been the means of awakening the attention of many; and a good number, I hope, have settled into a truly Christian temper. Tho' I must add, at the same time, that I am far from thinking, that the appearance, in general, is any other than the effect of enthusiastic heat. The goodness that has been so much talked of, 'tis plain to me, is nothing more, in general, than a commotion in the passions. I can't see that men have been made better, if hereby be meant, their being formed to a nearer resemblance to the divine being in moral holiness. 'Tis not evident to me, that persons, generally, have a better understanding of religion, a better government of their passions, a more Christian love to their neighbour, or that they are more decent and regular in their devotions towards God. I am clearly of the mind, they are worse in all these regards. They place their religion so much in the heat and fervour of their passions, that they too much neglect their reason and judgement: and instead of being more kind and gentle, more full of mercy and good fruits, they are more bitter, fierce, and implacable. And what is a grand discriminating mark of this work, wherever it takes place, is, that it makes men spiritually proud and conceited beyond measure, infinitely censorious and uncharitable to neighbours, to relations, even the nearest and dearest; to ministers in an especial manner; yea, to all mankind, who are not as they are, and don't think and act as they do. And there are few places where this work has been in any remarkable manner, but they have been filled with faction and contention; yea, in some, they have divided into parties, and openly and scandalously separated from one another.

Truly the accounts sent abroad, were sent too soon; too soon, I am satisfied, to reflect honour upon the persons who wrote them. They betray such a want of judgement, as I was really sorry to see them falling into. There are few persons now, perhaps none but such as are evidently overheated, but begin to see that things have been carried too far, and that the hazard is great, unless God mercifully interpose, lest we should be overrun with enthusiasm. And to speak the plain truth, my fear is, lest the end of these things should be Quakerism and infidelity. These we have now chiefly to guard against.

A particular account of one Mr. James Davenport, with his strange conduct in town and elsewhere, I doubt not would have been agreeable: but I have exceeded already. He is the wildest enthusiast I ever saw, and acts in the wildest manner; and yet, he is vindicated by some in all his extravagancies.

I now beg pardon, sir, for thus trespassing upon your patience. As Mr. Whitefield has been in Scotland, and human nature is the same everywhere; this narration of the effects he has been the instrument of producing here, may excite your zeal to guard the people in time against any such extravagancies, if there should be danger of them where you may be concerned.

Post-Script

I break open the letter myself to add my thoughts about some extraordinary things in Mr. Davenport's conduct.

As to his making his judgement about the internal state of persons, or their experience, a term of church-fellowship, I believe it is unscriptural, and of awful tendency to rend and tear the church: It is bottomed upon a false base, viz., that a certain and infallible knowledge of the good estate of men, from their experience, is attainable in this life. The practice is schismatical, in as much as it sets up a new term of communion which Christ has not fixed.

The late method of setting up separate meetings, upon the supposed unregeneracy of pastors of places, is enthusiastical, proud, and schismatical. All that fear God ought to oppose it as a most dangerous engine to bring the churches into the most damnable errors and confusions. The practice is built upon a twofold false hypothesis, viz., infallibility of knowledge; and that unconverted ministers will be used as instruments of no good to the church.

The practice of openly exposing ministers, who are supposed to be unconverted in public discourse, by particular application of such times and places, serves only to provoke them (instead of doing them any good), and to declare our own arrogance. It is an unprecedented, divisial, and pernicious practice; it is a lording it over our brethren, a degree superior to what any prelate has pretended since the coming of Christ (so far as I know), the Pope only excepted; though I really do not remember to have read that the Pope went on at this rate.

The sending out of unlearned men to teach others, upon the supposition of their piety, in ordinary cases, seems to bring the ministry into contempt; to cherish enthusiasm, and bring all into confusion. Whatever fair face it may have, it is a most perverse practice.

The practice of singing in the streets is a piece of weakness, and enthusiastical ostentation.

I wish you success, dear sir, in your journey: my soul is grieved for such enthusiastical fooleries, they portend much mischief to the poor church of God, if they be not seasonably checked. May your labours be blessed for that end.

I must also declare my abhorrence of all pretence to immediate inspiration, or following immediate impulses, as an enthusiastical perilous *ignis fatuus*.

The French and ══Indian Wars══════════

THE DEATH OF GENERAL WOLFE

Introduction

While the British colonists moved painfully inland from their colonial beachheads toward the great mountain barrier of the Appalachians, they had been outflanked by the French in their race for the interior of the continent. A series of brilliant explorations, from the time of Champlain in the early seventeenth century to that of Montcalm in the middle of the eighteenth, had brought the entire Mississippi Valley and its rich fur trade under French control.

Thus Britain's mainland colonies grew up in the shadow of French power and with an acute awareness of French rivalry. The military conflict between French and English erupted time and again and was fought out along the frontier, in Nova Scotia, and in the valleys of the Hudson and St. Lawrence. In the wider view it was one aspect of a world-wide struggle for imperial supremacy. So long as New France remained intact, and so long as France remained Britain's primary enemy, just so long would the colonists be involved in that struggle and would stand in need of Britain's military assistance.

The climax of the American battle for dominion came with the French and Indian wars that began in 1754 in the Ohio Valley and culminated with the British siege of Quebec in the summer of 1759. British and colonial victory in this war obliterated French power in the New World and opened a new chapter in the history of the North American continent.

General James Wolfe was a young British commander who became an American national hero when he stormed the heights of Abraham on September 13, 1759, and thus made possible the occupation of the French capital of Quebec. The ballad of his death on the field of battle is a historical song of unusual importance; and it is also one of the first American broadside ballads of which we have a record. Broadside ballads were songs that told a newsworthy story and that were printed on single sheets, or broadsides, and hawked around town and countryside. This form of "singing news" was to be immensely important during the Revolutionary War and in later times.

The following version of the ballad is a composite of two versions in the great Harris Collection of the University of Rhode Island, which houses many thousands of such broadsides, and of a version in the Isaiah Thomas Collection of the American Antiquarian Society at Worcester, Massachusetts, which also contains many early American songs. The extraordinarily beautiful Dorian melody comes from Newfoundland.

The Death of General Wolfe

1. Come all ye young men all, let this delight you;
   Cheer up, you young men all, let nothing fright you.
   Never let your courage fail when you're brought to trial,
   Nor let your fancy move at the first denial.

2. Bad news is come to town, bad news is carried,
   Bad news is whispered round, my love is married.
   Bad news is come to town, I fell a-weeping,
   They stole my love away when I was sleeping.

3. I sat down by my love thinking to enjoy her,
   I took her by the hand not to delude her,
   Whene'er I spoke a word my tongue did quiver,
   I could not speak my mind, while I was with her.

4. Love, here's a diamond ring, long time I've kept it,
   'Tis for your sake alone if you'll accept it;
   When you this posy read, think on the giver,
   Madam, remember me, or I'm undone for ever.

5. Brave Wolfe then took his leave of his dear jewel,
   Most sorely did she grieve, saying don't be cruel;
   Said he, 'tis for a space that I must leave you,
   Yet love, where'er I go, I'll not forget you.

6. So then this gallent youth did cross the ocean,
   To free America from her invasion;
   He landed at Quebec with all his party,
   The city to attack, being brave and hearty.

7. Brave Wolfe drew up his men in a line so pretty,
   On the plains of Abraham, before the city;
   A distance from the town, the French did meet him,
   With a double number they resolve to beat him.

8. The French drew up their men, for death prepared,
   In one another's face they stood and stared,
   While Wolfe and Montcalm together walked,
   Between their armies they like brothers talked.

9. Each man then took his post at their retire,
   So then these numerous hosts began to fire—
   The cannon on each side did roar like thunder,
   And youths in all their pride were torn asunder.

10. The drums did loudly beat, colors were flying,
    The purple gore did stream, and men lay dying,
    When shot off from his horse fell this brave hero,
    And we lament his loss in weeds of sorrow.

11. The French began to break, their ranks were flying,
    Wolfe seemed to revive while he lay dying.
    He lifted up his head while guns did rattle,
    And to his army said, How goes the battle?

12. His aide-de-camp replied, 'tis in our favor,
    Quebec with all her pride, nothing can save her;
    She falls into our hand with all her treasure,
    O then, brave Wolfe replied, I die with pleasure.

The American Revolution

Thomas Jefferson and the Declaration =of Independence=

The decade stretching from the conclusion of peace with France at the Treaty of Paris in 1763 to the convening of the first Continental Congress in September, 1774, was characterized by a series of collisions between the colonies and the mother country, and by a debate of mounting intensity as to the nature of the association between the two. The Declaration of Independence is an unrivaled focus for the events of these years, which it aptly summarizes and whose meaning it illuminates with matchless clarity. In his masterpiece Jefferson not only explains the past and gives the reasons for revolutionary action, he also defines the objectives of the struggle in the freedom and independence of the American nation. Because the Declaration is the key to understanding the meaning of the entire revolutionary epoch, we have chosen to concentrate upon it at this place.

I

The Declaration of Independence is composed of three parts: a statement of the principles and circumstances giving sanction and moral validity to revolutionary action; a listing of the grievances and wrongs under which the colonists suffered, and which, grouped into more general categories, provide the underlying political, social and economic causes of the American Revolution; and a formal announcement of the coming into being of a new nation that would take its place among the community of nations, and by a struggle with Great Britain would defend and achieve its right to freedom and independence.

In his opening paragraphs Jefferson set forth the reasons that justify the revolt of a people against its duly constituted government. Much of this was familiar ground to the average eighteenth-century American; it echoed the sanction for revolution arising from the experience of the English Puritans in the seventeenth century, the rationalization of that experience as given in the writings of John Locke and American political thinkers, and, perhaps most of all, it echoed the political teaching of American ministerial leadership in the years subsequent to the Great Awakening.

This section of the Declaration of Independence is the one that has been most profusely commented upon; indeed, it sets forth a profound and enduring truth of democratic philosophy. Governments must be considered as instruments for the protection and advancement of a people's welfare. Where governments cannot or will not serve popular ends, and where they exist without popular sanction or against popular consent, they are void of ethical basis or meaning. In such cases the people have a duty, and sooner or later may exercise their sovereign right, to overthrow such governments and to institute others better suited to their needs and aspirations.

Clear enough then and to us today is the third or concluding paragraph of the Declaration. It announces the rise of a new nation, gives notice of the dissolution of all political ties with the English Crown, and declares the erection of a new sovereignty—the United States of America. This was a huge step forward. Though American national feeling had been developing throughout the colonial period, even as late as 1774 few foresaw, or would have dared to advocate openly, total dissolution of the connection with England. But Bunker Hill in April, 1775, brought about a change in the public mood, and the historic inevitability of independence had been brilliantly demonstrated in Thomas Paine's pamphlet, Common Sense, which appeared in January, 1776.

The second and longest part of the Declaration, the detailed listing of the grievances which the colonists entertained, and their specific indictment of the wrongs inflicted upon them by the British government, merits more attention than it usually receives. The well-known historian Carl Becker, for example, devoted an entire book, The Declaration of Independence, to the political philosophy contained in the document; but he dismissed the list of colonial grievances in a mere half-page. Few indeed are the history texts that comment upon Jefferson's indictment of Parliament and Crown, or that explain precisely what, in each particular case, Jefferson was referring to, or what he had in mind.

Yet failure to examine carefully this second part of the

Declaration robs it of much of its value as historic testimony explaining to us the actual causes of the Revolution as seen by its leaders, by those who made it and carried it through to completion. Jefferson believed that the indictment of Parliament and Crown, the "bill of particulars," or listing of specific acts of wrongdoing committed by the British government, constituted precisely the "long train of abuses and usurpations" alleged in the opening paragraph; and proved the statement that there was a British design to reduce the colonists to slavery, to abolish their fundamental right to self-government, and to destroy their livelihood. This provided, in the last resort, the moral basis and the justification for the Revolution. The question persists: how seriously must we regard the indictment of Britain that Jefferson presents in the second part of his Declaration? Were the grievances real? If real, were they exaggerated? Were they sufficient to validate Jefferson's conclusion that revolution was justified?

Even if we give a negative answer to all of these questions, Jefferson's "bill of particulars" still requires careful examination. This list of grievances represents the reasons for the Revolution as seen, not only through the eyes of those who led it, but those who supported it as well. For this reason the modern student needs to pay careful attention to the second section of the Declaration.

But if we wish to ascertain precisely what Jefferson was referring to in his various accusations against England, we must go beyond the Declaration itself. He was, in the latter, merely restating in a condensed form what he had written out much more fully, proved and documented, in a pamphlet that was published in September, 1774, and widely read through the colonies—his Summary View of the Rights of British America. It was the Summary View that established Jefferson's reputation as a popular writer and pamphleteer; and it was because of the understanding of the subject that he had demonstrated in this earlier document that Congress chose him to draft the Declaration itself. Indeed, the Declaration of Independence was designed as nothing more than a shorter version of the Summary View brought up to date, written in popular form, and taking account of the new conditions that had come into being since the issue of the original pamphlet.

Thus the Summary View is indispensable to an understanding of the immortal paper that was to follow from Jefferson's pen. And this is the first of the documents on the American Revolution that we reproduce in full (p. 170).

According to Jefferson in the Summary View, America rightfully belonged to the settlers who conquered it and peopled it, and to their descendants. But over the years the colonists had fallen victim to a dual tyranny: the tyranny of an English Parliament that claimed the right to pass laws binding Britain's overseas dominions, and the tyranny of an executive—the Crown—that planned after 1763 to destroy colonial self-government by the deliberate substitution of despotic rule.

In this document Jefferson's central indictment of English authority focused upon the limitation of the right to free trade, upon the suppression of American manufacturing industry, upon the arrogation by Britain of title to sovereignty over the entire North American continent, and upon the suppression of basic rights of self-rule. The callous destruction of American economic interests, he argued, and the abolition of political rights, evinced a design to place the colonies in a role of permanent subordination; thus they faced the stark alternatives of resisting or becoming slaves.[1]

This thesis was buttressed by the copious citation of specific legislative measures passed by Parliament and of specific acts of the royal executive. Thereby Jefferson produced a historical analysis of the main factors precipitating the Revolution; an analysis so penetrating that the modern student may read it again and again with profit, and still derive enlightenment from it. As for his conclusion, it was clear enough. Resistance was necessary to protect America's basic national interests—in international trade, in land ownership, in political independence—against a determined and formidable attempt to impose an imperial tyranny, to subvert the rights of British America, and to wrest control of the North American continent from its rightful owners and possessors.

II

On June 11, 1776, Congress appointed a Committee of Five to draft a Declaration of Independence—Thomas Jefferson, John Adams, Benjamin Franklin, Robert R. Livingston and

---

[1] The history of Ireland under British rule proves quite clearly that this formulation of the matter was far from fanciful.

Thomas Sherman. The actual work of drafting fell to Jefferson; the final document as revised by the Committee was reported back to Congress on June 28th.

The draft thus submitted to Congress differed in one significant respect from the Declaration as amended by Congress and adopted on July 4. It included a flaming attack upon the slave trade and the institution of slavery, and it laid the blame for these evils at the door of the English king. Congress made a number of stylistic corrections, and it struck out the clause referring to the slave trade. Jefferson wrote, at the time, that this was done in deference to the wishes of the slaveowners of Georgia and South Carolina, and also because it touched Northern merchants in a tender spot. "Though," he wrote, "their people have very few slaves themselves, yet they have been pretty considerable carriers of them to others."

Jefferson's effort to write a condemnation of slavery into his Declaration has an important bearing on an aspect of the document that has given rise to endless subsequent debates. What did he mean by the statement that "all men are created equal, that they are endowed by their Creator with certain inalienable rights. . . ."? Logically, if we look only at the version of the Declaration made public on July 4, Jefferson was on the horns of a dilemma: if he accepted slavery and its gross inequalities, his statement of equal and inalienable rights for all men was insincere; or, if Jefferson was sincere and did believe in equal rights for all, then he was guilty of a palpable inconsistency, since he owned slaves until the end of his life and profited personally from their labor.

The issue thus raised is not academic. In subsequent years slaveholders and their Northern spokesmen would argue that the extension of slavery throughout the Union was permissible. They would claim that this might rightfully be done because the Negro was in no way included in the concept of human equality as stated by Jefferson in the old Declaration, that "inalienable rights" applied to white men only. At the time of the Civil War no less a person than Abraham Lincoln himself was called upon, as we shall see (below, p. 519), to set the record straight.

Discussion of this question is made simpler if we bear in mind, not what Congress adopted, but what Jefferson actually wrote and his own Committee endorsed.

What Jefferson wrote, and what Congress deleted in the

helium-preserved version known to history was the literal truth. Throughout the eighteenth century the Virginia Assembly had carried on a running battle with the Crown to pass, and to have sustained, laws to impose duties on the importation of Negro slaves into Virginia. In this way Virginians hoped to curb the growth of a population whose increase gave concern to the tideland planters. Fresh importations of slaves gave a competitive advantage to inland tobacco growers, made possible further increases in the production of tobacco and further depressed its price when it was already a glut on the market. This, in turn, increased the indebtedness of Virginia and North Carolina planters to the London merchants and aggravated the financial crisis in which many planters already found themselves.

Such efforts to halt the importation of slaves flouted the interests of slave traders, whose aim it was to sell as many slaves as possible in the New World. These interests, notably the Royal Africa Company, had a powerful voice in London. Thus Virginia laws aiming to curb the slave trade were invariably vetoed by the Crown.[2]

The antislavery clause of the Declaration of Independence was struck out of Jefferson's draft in deference to the wishes of South Carolina and Georgia rice and indigo growers, who were developing thriving plantations and whose demand for slaves, at the time of the Revolution, remained unabated. But Jefferson's antislavery statement must be marked and underscored as a historic utterance. It was the first public expression of the moral evil of the institution of slavery and of the slave trade by an American political leader of the first rank. At the very outset of Jefferson's career it underlined the centrality of the slavery question in his thinking. The important thing for us to note is not that Jefferson owned slaves, but that he struggled throughout his life to extricate himself from the evil that he inherited; and that he understood and recorded the fact that slavery in a free country was a gross and dangerous anomaly.

For these reasons we reproduce (p. 188), as the second of our documents from Jefferson's pen, the Declaration of Independence as he drafted it, not as it was amended by Congress on July 4.

---

[2] For Jefferson's own elaboration of this point in the *Summary View*, see p. 180.

A Summary View of the
Rights of British America (1774)

BY THOMAS JEFFERSON

Introduction

Thomas Jefferson (1743-1826) was the son of Peter Jefferson and Jane Randolph. From his father he inherited a princely estate in Albemarle County, Virginia, and from his mother the social status that came from membership in one of the colony's leading families. He was reared as a member of the Virginia aristocracy. The onset of the Revolution found him a lord of land and slaves; a highly educated intellectual with a background of training in Latin and Greek, and the sciences; and a practicing lawyer and a member of the Virginia Assembly.

On May 22, 1774, news of the Boston Port Bill reached Virginia. This bill enacted the closing of the port of Boston, effective June 1, until that city had apologized for the tea party of the previous December, had punished its perpetrators, and had paid damages for the property losses then inflicted. A number of the younger members of the Virginia House, of whom Jefferson was one, agreed that prompt action must be taken. On May 24, a resolution was submitted in the Assembly, and passed, calling for June 1 to be set aside as a day of fasting and humiliation in which the people might join together and pray "to give us one Heart and one Mind firmly to oppose, by all just and proper Means, every injury to American Rights, . . ."

Lord Dunmore, governor of Virginia, responded by dissolving the Assembly. Its members at once adjourned to the Raleigh Tavern (Williamsburg), and called for the convening of a General Congress of the colonies in order to deliberate upon "those general measures which the united interests of America may from time to time require." A little later it was also decided to summon a special Virginia revolutionary convention on August 1—prior, that is, to the meeting of the general, or Continental Congress—in order to discuss what, immediately and concretely, Virginians could do to aid the embattled people of Boston. This convention, also, would have the task of electing Virginian delegates to the Continental Congress that would meet in Philadelphia in September.

Jefferson's Albemarle constituents elected him to represent them at the Virginia convention to be held in August. In July, as preparation for this August meeting, he drew up a "draft of instructions," which he planned to lay before the convention and which he thought might serve as a guide to the delegates who would represent Virginia at Philadelphia. But illness prevented him from attending the August meeting. His draft was printed and laid before the delegates under the title of A Summary View of the Rights of British America Set Forth in Some Resolutions Intended for the Inspection of the Present Delegates of the People of Virginia Now in Convention.

This document established Jefferson's reputation as revolutionary and pamphleteer. Its study is indispensable to a full understanding of the Declaration of Independence that was to follow from his pen. It is here reprinted in full from an original manuscript and a copy of the printed pamphlet, both in the Library of Congress. Jefferson's citation of English laws has been included in square brackets at the appropriate place, or in footnotes.

A SUMMARY VIEW OF THE RIGHTS OF BRITISH AMERICA

Resolved that it be an instruction to the said deputies when assembled in General Congress with the deputies from the other states of British America to propose to the said Congress that a humble and dutiful address be presented to his majesty begging leave to lay before him as chief magistrate of the British empire the united complaints of his majesty's subjects in America; complaints which are excited by many unwarrantable incroachments and usurpations, attempted to be made by the legislature of one part of the empire, upon those rights which God and the laws have given equally and independently to all. To represent to his majesty that these his states have often individually made humble application to his imperial throne, to obtain thro' its intervention some redress of their injured rights; to none of which was ever even an answer condescended. Humbly to hope that this their joint address, penned in the language of truth, and divested of those expressions of servility which would persuade his majesty that we are asking favors and not rights, shall obtain from his majesty a more respectful acceptance. And this his majesty will think we have reason to expect when he reflects that he is no more than the chief officer of the people, appointed by the laws, and circumscribed with definite powers, to assist in working the great machine of government erected for their use, and consequently subject to their superintendance. And in order that these our rights, as well as the invasions of them, may be laid more fully before his majesty, to take a view of them from the origin and first settlement of these countries.

Origin of the American Settlements

To remind him that our ancestors, before their emigration to America, were the free inhabitants of the British dominions in Europe, and possessed a right, which nature has given to all men, of departing from the country in which chance, not choice has placed them; of going in quest of new habitations, and of there establishing new societies, under such laws and regulations as to them shall seem most likely to promote happiness. That their Saxon ancestors had under this universal law, in like manner, left their native wilds and woods in the north of Europe, had possessed themselves of the island of Britain then less charged with inhabitants, and had established there that system of laws which has so long been the glory and protection of that country. Nor was ever any claim of superiority or dependance asserted over them by that mother country from which they had migrated: and were such a claim made it is believed his majesty's subjects in Great Britain have too firm a feeling of the rights derived to them from their ancestors to bow down the sovereignty of their state before such visionary pretensions. And it is thought that no circumstance has occurred to distinguish materially the British from the Saxon emigration. America was conquered, and her settlements made and firmly established, at the expence of individuals, and not of the British public. Their own blood was spilt in acquiring lands for their settlement, their own fortunes expended in making that settlement effectual. For themselves they fought, for themselves they conquered, and for themselves alone they have right to hold. No shilling was ever issued from the public treasures of his majesty or his ancestors for their assistance, till of very late times, after the colonies had become established on a firm and permanent footing. That then indeed, having become invaluable to Great Britain for her commercial purposes, his parliament was pleased to lend them assistance against an enemy who would fain have drawn to herself the benefits of their commerce to the great aggrandisement of herself and danger of Great Britain. Such assistance, and in such circumstances, they had often before given to Portugal and other allied states, with whom they carry on a commercial intercourse. Yet these states never supposed that, by calling in her aid, they thereby submitted themselves to her sovereignty. Had such terms been proposed, they would have rejected them with disdain, and trusted for better to the moderation of their enemies, or to a vigorous exertion of their own force. We do not however mean to underrate those aids, which to us were doubtless valuable, on whatever principles granted: but we would show that they cannot give a title to that authority which the British parliament would arrogate over us; and that they may amply be repaid, by our giving to the inhabitants of Great Britain such exclusive privileges in trade as may be advantageous to them, and at the same time not too restrictive to ourselves. That settlements having been thus effected in the wilds of America, the emigrants thought proper to adopt that system of laws under which they had hitherto lived in the mother country, and to continue their union with her by submitting themselves to the same common sovereign, who was thereby made the central link connecting the several parts of the empire thus newly multiplied.

Division of the Colonies

But that not long were they permitted, however far they thought themselves removed from the hand of oppression, to hold undisturbed the rights thus acquired at the hazard of their lives and loss of their fortunes. A family of princes was then on the British throne, whose treasonable crimes against their people brought on them afterwards the exertion of those sacred and sovereign rights of punishment, reserved in the hands of the people for cases of extreme necessity, and judged by the constitution unsafe to be delegated to any other judicature. While every day brought forth some new and unjustifiable exertion of power over their subjects on that side of the water, it was not to be expected that those here, much less able at that time to oppose the designs of despotism, should be exempted from injury. Accordingly that country which had been acquired by the lives, the labors and the fortunes of individual adventures, was by these princes at several times parted out and distributed among favorites and followers of their fortunes;* and by an assumed right of the crown alone were erected into distinct and independent governments; a measure which it is believed his majesty's prudence and understanding would prevent him from imitating at this day; as no exercise of such a power of dividing and dismembering a country has ever occurred in his majesty's realm of England, tho' now of very ancient standing; nor could it be justified or acquiesced under there or in any other part of his majesty's empire.

Parliamentary Restrictions on Our Trade

That the exercise of a free trade with all parts of the world, possessed by the American colonists as of natural right, and which no law of their own had taken away or abridged, was next the object of unjust incroachment. Some of the colonies having thought proper to continue the administration of their government in the name and under the authority of his majesty King Charles the first, whom notwithstanding his late deposition by the Commonwealth of England, they continued in the sovereignty of their state, the parliament for the Commonwealth took the same in high offence, and assumed upon themselves the power of prohibiting their trade with all other parts of the world except the island of Great Britain. This arbitrary act however they soon recalled, and by solemn treaty entered into on the 12th day of March 1651, between the said Commonwealth by their commissioners and the colony of Virginia by their house of Burgesses, it was expressly stipulated

---

* In 1621 Nova Scotia was granted by James I to Sir William Alexander. In 1632 Maryland was granted by Charles I to Lord Baltimore. In 1664 New York was granted by Charles II to the Duke of York: so also was New Jersey, which the Duke of York conveyed again to Lord Berkeley and Sir George Carteret. So also were the Delaware counties, which the same Duke conveyed again to William Penn. In 1665 the country including North and South Carolina, Georgia and the Floridas was granted by Charles II to the Earl of Clarendon, Duke of Albemarle, Earl of Craven, Lord Berkeley, Lord Ashley, Sir George Carteret, Sir John Coleton and Sir William Berkeley. In 1681 Pennsylvania was granted by Charles II to William Penn.

by the 8th article of the said treaty that they should have "free trade as the people of England do enjoy to all places and with all nations according to the laws of that Commonwealth." But that, upon the restoration of his majesty King Charles the second, their rights of free commerce fell once more a victim to arbitrary power: and by several acts of his reign as well as of some of his successors the trade of the colonies was laid under such restrictions as show what hopes they might form from the justice of a British parliament were its uncontrolled power admitted over these states.

*History has informed us that bodies of men as well as individuals are susceptible of the spirit of tyranny. A view of these acts of parliament for regulation, as it has been affectedly called, of the American trade, if all other evidence were removed out of the case, would undeniably evince the truth of this observation. Besides the duties they impose on our markets of export and import, they prohibit our going to any markets northward of cape Finesterra in the kingdom of Spain for the sale of commodities which Great Britain will not take from us, and for the purchase of others with which she cannot supply us; and that for no other than the arbitrary purpose of purchasing for themselves by a sacrifice of our rights and interests, certain privileges in their commerce with an allied state, who, in confidence that their exclusive trade with America will be continued while the principles and power of the British parliament be the same, have indulged themselves in every exorbitance which their avarice could dictate, or our necessities extort: have raised their commodities called for in America to the double and treble of what they sold for before such exclusive privileges were given them, and of what better commodities of the same kind would cost us elsewhere; and at the same time give us much less for what we carry thither, than might be had at more convenient ports. That these acts prohibit us from carrying in quest of other purchasers the surplus of our tobaccoes remaining after the consumption of Great Britain is supplied: so that we must leave them with the British merchant for whatever he will please to allow us, to be by him reshipped to foreign markets, where he will reap the benefits of making sale of them for full value.

*12. C. 2. c. 18; 14. C. 2. c. 11; 25. C. 2. c. 7; 7, 8, W. M. c. 22; 11. W.; 3, 4, Anne; 6. G. 2. c. 13.

That to heighten still the idea of parliamentary justice, and to show with what moderation they are like to exercise power, where themselves are to feel no part of it's weight, we take leave to mention to his majesty certain other acts of British parliament, by which they would prohibit us from manufacturing for our own use the articles we raise on our own lands with our own labor. By an act passed in the fifth year of the reign of his late majesty King George the second an American subject is forbidden to make a hat for himself of the fur which he has taken perhaps on his own soil. An instance of despotism to which no parallel can be produced in the most arbitrary ages of British history. By one other act passed in the 23rd year of the same reign [23. G. 2. c. 29.], the iron which we make we are forbidden to manufacture; and, heavy as that article is, and necessary in every branch of husbandry, besides commission and insurance, we are to pay freight for it to Great Britain, and freight for it back again, for the purpose of supporting, not men, but machines, in the island of Great Britain.

In the same spirit of equal and impartial legislation is to be viewed the act of parliament passed in the fifth year of the same reign [5. G. 2. c. 7.], by which American lands are made subject to the demands of British creditors, while their own lands were still continued unanswerable for their debts; from which one of these conclusions must necessarily follow, either that justice is not the same thing in America as in Britain, or else that the British parliament pay less regard to it here than there. But that we do not point out to his majesty the injustice of these acts with intent to rest on that principle the cause of their nullity, but to show that experience confirms the propriety of those political principles which exempt us from the jurisdiction of the British parliament. The true ground on which we declare these acts void is that the British parliament has no right to exercise authority over us.

That these exercises of usurped power have not been confined to instances alone in which themselves were interested; but they have also intermeddled with the regulation of the internal affairs of the colonies. The act of the 9th of Anne for establishing a post office in America seems to have had little connection with British convenience, except that of accomodating his majesty's ministers and favorites with the sale of a lucrative and easy office.

Recent Measures of Parliamentary Oppression

That thus have we hastened thro' the reigns which preceded his majesty's, during which the violation of our rights were less alarming, because repeated at more distant intervals, than that rapid and bold succession of injuries which is likely to distinguish the present from all other periods of American story. Scarcely have our minds been able to emerge from the astonishment into which one stroke of parliamentary thunder has involved us, before another more heavy and more alarming is fallen on us. Single acts of tyranny may be ascribed to the accidental opinion of a day; but a series of oppressions, begun at a distinguished period, and pursued unalterably thro' every change of ministers, too plainly prove a deliberate, systematical plan of reducing us to slavery.

That the act passed in the fourth year of his majesty's reign intitled "An act for granting certain duties in the British colonies and plantations in America, etc."; one other act passed in the fifth year of his reign intitled "An act for granting and applying certain stamp duties and other duties in the British colonies and plantations in America, etc."; one other act passed in the sixth year of his reign intitled "An act for the better securing the dependency of his majesty's dominions in America upon the crown and parliament of Great Britain"; and one other act passed in the seventh year of his reign intitled "Ant act for granting duties on paper, tea, etc."; form that connected chain of parliamentary usurpation which has already been the subject of frequent applications to his majesty and the houses of Lords and Commons of Great Britain; and, no answers having yet been condescended to any of these, we shall not trouble his majesty with a repetition of the matters they contained.

But that one other act passed in the same seventh year of his reign, having been a peculiar attempt, must ever require peculiar mention. It is intitled "an act for suspending the legislature of New York." One free and independent legislature hereby takes upon itself to suspend the powers of another, free and independent as itself, thus exhibiting a phenomenon, unknown in nature, the creator and creature of its own power. Not only the principles of common sense, but the common feelings of human nature must be surrendered up, before his majesty's subjects here can be persuaded to believe that they hold their political existence at the will of a British parliament. Shall these governments be dissolved, their property annihilated, and their people reduced to a state of nature, at the imperious breath of a body of men whom they never saw, in whom they never confided, and over whom they have no powers of punishment or removal, let their crimes against the American public be ever so great? Can any one reason be assigned why 160,000 electors in the island of Great Britain should give law to four millions in the states of America, every individual of whom is equal to every individual of them in virtue, in understanding, and in bodily strength? Were this to be admitted, instead of being a free people, as we have hitherto supposed, and mean to continue, ourselves, we should suddenly be found the slaves, not of one, but of 160,000 tyrants, distinguished too from all others by this singular circumstance that they are removed from the reach of fear, the only restraining motive which may hold the hand of a tyrant.

That by "an act to discontinue in such manner and for such time as are therein mentioned the landing and discharging lading or shipping of goods, wares and merchandize at the town and within the harbor of Boston in the province of Massachusett's bay in North America" which was passed at the last session of British parliament [14. G. 3.], a large and populous town, whose trade was their sole subsistence, was deprived of that trade, and involved in utter ruin. Let us for a while suppose the question of right suspended, in order to examine this act on principles of justice. An act of parliament had been passed imposing duties on teas to be paid in America, against which act the Americans had protested as inauthoritative. The East India Company, who till that time had never sent a pound of tea to America on their own account, step forth on that occasion the asserters of parliamentary right, and send hither many ship loads of that obnoxious commodity. The masters of their several vessels however, on their arrival in America, wisely attended to admonition, and returned with their cargoes.

In the province of New England alone the remonstrances of the people were disregarded, and a compliance, after being many days waited for, was flatly refused. Whether in this the master of the vessel was governed by his obstinacy or his instructions, let those who know, say. There are extraordinary situations which require extraordinary interposition. An exasperated people, who feel that they possess power, are not easily restrained within limits strictly regular. A number of them assembled in the town of Boston, threw the tea into the ocean and dispersed without doing any other act of violence.

If in this they did wrong, they were known, and were amenable to the laws of the land, against which it could not be objected that they had ever in any instance been obstructed or diverted from their regular course in favor of popular offenders. They should therefore not have been distrusted on this occasion. But that ill-fated colony had formerly been bold in their enmities against the house of Stuart, and were now devoted to ruin by that unseen hand which governs the momentous affairs of this great empire. On the partial representations of a few worthless ministerial dependants, whose constant office it has been to keep that government embroiled, and who by their treacheries hope to obtain the dignity of the British knighthood, without calling for a party accused, without asking a proof, without attempting a distinction between the guilty and the innocent, the whole of that ancient and wealthy town is in a moment reduced from opulence to beggary. Men who had spent their lives in extending the British commerce, who had invested in that place the wealth their honest endeavors had merited, found themselves and their families thrown at once on the world for subsistence by it's charities. Not the hundredth part of the inhabitants of that town had been concerned in the act complained of; many of them were in Great Britain and in other parts beyond sea; yet all were involved in one indiscriminate ruin, by a new executive power unheard of till then, that of a British parliament. A property of the value of many millions of money was sacrificed to revenge, not repay, the loss of a few thousands.

This is administering justice with a heavy hand indeed! And when is this tempest to be arrested in it's course. Two wharfs are to be opened again when his majesty shall think proper: the residue which lined the extensive shores of the bay of Boston are forever interdicted the exercise of commerce. This little exception seem to have been thrown in for no other purpose than that of setting a precedent for investing his majesty with legislative powers. If the pulse of his people shall beat calmly under this experiment, another and another will be tried till the measure of despotism be filled up. It would be an insult on common sense to pretend that this exception was made in order to restore it's commerce to that great town. The trade which cannot be received at two wharfs alone, must of necessity be transferred to some other place; to which it will soon be followed by that of the two wharfs. Considered in this light it would be an insolent and cruel mockery at the annihilation of the town of Boston.

By the act for the suppression of riots and tumults in the town of Boston, passed also in the last session of parliament, a murder committed there is, if the governor pleases, to be tried in the court of king's bench in the island of Great Britain, by a jury of Middlesex. The witnesses too, on receipt of such a sum as the governor shall think it reasonable for them to expend, are to enter into recognisance to appear at the trial. This is in other words taxing them to the amount of their recognisance; and that amount may be whatever a governor pleases. For who does his majesty think can be prevailed on to cross the Atlantic for the sole purpose of bearing evidence to a fact? His expenses are to be borne indeed as they shall be estimated by a governor; but who are to feed the wife and children whom he leaves behind, and who have had no other subsistence but his daily labor? Those epidemical disorders too, so terrible in a foreign climate, is the cure of them to be estimated among the articles of expence, and their danger to be warded off by the almighty power of a parliament? And the wretched criminal, if he happen to have offended on the American side, stripped of his privilege of trial by peers, of his vicinage, removed from the place where alone full evidence could be obtained, without money, without counsel, without friends, without exculpatory proof, is tried before judges predetermined to condemn. The cowards who would suffer a countryman to be torn from the bowels of their society in order to be thus offered a sacrifice to parliamentary tyranny, would merit that everlasting infamy now fixed on the authors of the act! A clause for a similar purpose had been introduced into an act passed in the 12th year of his majesty's reign entitled "an act for the better securing and preserving his majesty's dock-yards, magazines, ships, ammunition and stores" [12 G. 3. c. 24.], against which as meriting the same censures the several colonies have already protested.

That these are the acts of power assumed by a body of men foreign to our constitutions, and unacknowledged by our laws; against which we do, on behalf of the inhabitants of British

America, enter this our solemn and determined protest. And
we do earnestly intreat his majesty, as yet the only mediatory
power between the several states of the British empire, to recommend to his parliament of Great Britain the total revocation
of these acts, which however nugatory they be, may yet prove
the cause of further discontents and jealousies among us.

Refusing Assent to Laws for Trifling Reasons

That we next proceed to consider the conduct of his majesty, as holding the executive powers of the laws of these
states, and mark out his deviations from the line of duty. By
the constitution of Great Britain as well as of the several
American states, his majesty possesses the power of refusing to
pass into a law any bill which has already passed the other two
branches of legislature. His majesty however and his ancestors,
conscious of the impropriety of opposing their single opinion
to the united wisdom of two houses of parliament, while their
proceedings were unbiased by interested principles, for several ages past have modestly declined the exercise of this
power in that part of his empire called Great Britain. But by
change of circumstances, other principles than those of justice
simply have obtained an influence on their determinations.
The addition of new states to the British empire has produced
an addition of new, and sometimes opposite interests. It is now
therefore the great office of his majesty to resume the exercise
of his negative power, and to prevent the passage of laws by
any one legislature of the empire which might bear injuriously on the rights and interests of another.

Yet this will not excuse the wanton exercise of this power
which we have seen his majesty practice on the laws of the
American legislatures. For the most trifling reasons, and sometimes for no conceivable reason at all, his majesty has rejected
laws of the most salutary tendency. The abolition of domestic
slavery is the great object of desire in those colonies where it
was unhappily introduced in their infant state. But previous
to the infranchisement of the slaves we have, it is necessary to
exclude all further importations from Africa. Yet our repeated
attempts to effect this by prohibitions, and by imposing duties
which might amount to a prohibition, have been hitherto defeated by his majesty's negative: thus preferring the immediate
advantages of a few British corsairs to the lasting interests of

the American states, and to the rights of human nature deeply wounded by this infamous practice. Nay the single interposition of an interested individual against a law was scarcely ever known to fail of success, tho' in the opposite scale were placed the interests of a whole country. That this is so shameful an abuse of a power trusted with his majesty for those purposes, as if not reformed would call for some legal restrictions.

Delaying the Consideration of Our Laws

With equal inattention to the necessities of his people here, has his majesty permitted our laws to lie neglected in England for years, neither confirming them by his assent, nor annulling them by his negative: so that such of them as have no suspending clause, we hold on the most precarious of all tenures, his majesty's will, and such of them as suspend themselves till his majesty's assent be obtained we have feared might be called into existence at some future and distant period, when time and change of circumstances shall have rendered them destructive to his people here.

Requiring Suspending Clause to Almost Every Act

And to render this grievance still more oppressive, his majesty by his instructions has laid his governors under such restrictions that they can pass no law of any moment unless it has such suspending clause: so that, however immediate may be the call for legislative interposition, the law cannot be executed till it has twice crossed the Atlantic, by which time the evil may have spent its whole force.

Endeavoring to Take from the People the Right of Représentation

But in what terms reconcilable to majesty and at the same time to truth, shall we speak of a late instruction to his majesty's governor of the colony of Virginia, by which he is forbidden to assent to any law for the division of a county, unless the new county will consent to have no representative in assembly? That colony has as yet affixed no boundary to the Westward. Their western counties therefore are of indefinite extent. Some of them are actually seated many hundred miles from their eastern limits. Is it possible then that his majesty can have bestowed a single thought on the situation of those people, who, in order to obtain justice for injuries however great or small, must, by the laws of that colony, attend their county court at such a distance, with all their witnesses, monthly, till their litigation be determined? Or does his majesty seriously wish, and publish it to the world, that his subjects should give up the glorious right of representation, with all the benefits derived from that, and submit themselves the absolute slaves of his sovereign will? Or is it rather meant to confine the legislative body to their present numbers, that they may be the cheaper bargain whenever they shall become worth a purchase?

Dissolution of Representative Bodies

One of the articles of impeachment against Tresilian and the other judges of Westminster Hall in the reign of Richard II, for which they suffered death as traitors to their country, was that they had advised the king that he might dissolve his parliament at any time; and succeeding kings have adopted the opinion of these unjust judges. Since the establishment however of the British constitution at the glorious revolution on its free and ancient principles, neither his majesty nor his ancestors have exercised such a power of dissolution in the island of Great Britain; and when his majesty was petitioned by the united voice of his people there to dissolve the present parliament, who had become obnoxious to them, his ministers were heard to declare in open parliament that his majesty possessed no such power by the constitution. But how different their language and his practice here! To declare as their duty required the known rights of their country, to oppose the usurpation of every foreign judicature, to disregard the imperious mandates of a minister or governor, have been the avowed causes of dissolving houses of representatives in America. But if such powers be really vested in his majesty, can he suppose they are there placed to awe the members from such purposes as these? When the representative body have lost the confidence of their constituents, when they have notoriously made sale of their most valuable rights, when they have assumed to themselves powers which the people never put into their hands, then indeed their continuing in office becomes dangerous to the state, and calls for an exercise of the power of dissolution. Such being the causes for which the representative body should and should not be dissolved, will it not appear strange to an unbiased observer that that of Great Britain was not dissolved, while those of the colonies have repeatedly incurred that sentence?

Delaying to Issue Writs for Choice of New Representatives

But your majesty or your governors have carried this power beyond every limit known or provided for by the laws. After dissolving one house of representatives, they have refused to call another, so that for a great length of time the legislature provided by the laws has been out of existence. From this nature of things, every society must at all times possess within itself the sovereign powers of legislation. The feelings of human nature revolt against the supposition of a state so situated as that it may not in any emergency provide against dangers which perhaps threaten immediate ruin. While those bodies are in existence to whom the people have delegated the powers of legislation, they alone possess and may exercise those powers. But when they are dissolved by the lopping off one or more of their branches, the power reverts to the people, who may use it to unlimited extent, either assembling together in person, sending deputies, or in any other way they may think proper. We forbear to trace consequences further; the dangers are conspicuous with which this practice is replete.

Undertaking to Grant Lands on Advanced Terms

That we shall at this time also take notice of an error in the nature of our landholdings, which crept in at a very early period of our settlement. The introduction of the feudal tenures into the kingdom of England, though ancient, is well enough understood to set this matter in a proper light. In the earlier ages of the Saxon settlement feudal holdings were certainly altogether unknown, and very few, if any, had been introduced at the time of the Norman conquest. Our Saxon ancestors held their lands, as they did their personal property, in absolute dominion, disencumbered with any superior, answering nearly to the nature of those possessions which the feudalists term allodial: William the Norman first introduced that system generally. The lands which had belonged to those who fell in the battle of Hastings, and in the subsequent insurrections of his reign, formed a considerable proportion of the lands of the whole kingdom. These he granted out, subject to feudal duties, as did he also those of a great number of his new subjects, who by persuasions or threats were induced to surrender them for that purpose. But still much was left in the hands of his Saxon subjects, held of no superior, and not subject to feudal conditions. These therefore by express laws, enacted to render uniform the system of military defense, were made liable to the same military duties as if they had been feuds: and the Norman lawyers soon found means to saddle them also with all the other feudal burthens. But still they had not been surrendered to the king, they were not derived from his grant, and therefore they wer not holden of him. A general principle indeed was introduced that "all lands in England were held either mediately or immediately by the crown": but this was borrowed from those holdings which were truly feudal, and only applied to others for the purposes of illustration.

Feudal holdings were therefore but exceptions out of the Saxon laws of possession, under which all lands were held in absolute right. These therefore still form the basis or groundwork of the common law, to prevail wheresoever the exceptions have not taken place. America was not conquered by William the Norman, nor its lands surrendered to him or any of his successors. Possessions there are undoubtedly of the allodial nature. Our ancestors however, who migrated hither, were laborers, not lawyers. The fictitious principle that all lands belong originally to the king, they were early persuaded to believe real, and accordingly took grants of their own lands from the crown. And while the crown continued to grant for small sums and on reasonable rents, there was no inducement to arrest the error and lay it open to public view. But his majesty has lately taken on him to advance the terms of purchase and of holding to the double of what they were, by which means the acquisition of lands being rendered difficult, the population of our country is likely to be checked. It is time therefore for us to lay this matter before his majesty, and to declare that he has no right to grant lands of himself. From the nature and purpose of civil institutions, all the lands within the limits which any particular society has circumscribed around itself, are assumed by that society, and subject to their allotment only. This may be done by themselves assembled collectively, or by their legislature to whom they may have delegated sovereign authority: and, if they are allotted in neither of these ways, each individual of the society may appropriate to himself such lands as he finds vacant, and occupancy will give him title.

Sending Armed Troops Among Us

That, in order to inforce the arbitrary measures before complained of, his majesty has from time to time sent among us large bodies of armed forces, not made up of the people here, nor raised by the authority of our laws. Did his majesty possess such a right as this, it might swallow up all our other rights whenever he should think proper. But his majesty has no right to land a single armed man on our shores; and those whom he sends here are liable to our laws for the suppression and punishment of riots, routs, and unlawful assemblies, or are hostile bodies invading us in defiance of law. When in the course of the late war it became expedient that a body of Hanoverian troops should be brought over for the defence of Great Britain, his majesty's grandfather, our late sovereign, did not pretend to introduce them under any authority he possessed. Such a measure would have given just alarm to his subjects in Great Britain, whose liberties would not be safe if armed men of another country, and of another spirit, might be brought into the realm at any time without the consent of their legislature. He therefore applied to parliament who passed an act for that purpose, limiting the number to be brought in and the time they were to continue. In like manner is his majesty restrained in every part of the empire. He possesses indeed the executive power of the laws in every state; but they are the laws of the particular state which he is to administer within that state, and not those of any one within the limits of another. Every state must judge for itself the number of armed men which they may safely trust among them, of whom they are to consist, and under what restrictions they are to be laid.

Making Military Superior to Civil Power

To render these proceedings still more criminal against our laws, instead of subjecting the military to the civil power, his majesty has expressly made the civil subordinate to the military. But can his majesty thus put down all law under his feet? Can he erect a power superior to that which erected himself? He has done it indeed by force; but let him remember that force cannot give right.

That these are our grievances which we have thus laid before his majesty with that freedom of language and sentiment which becomes a free people, claiming their rights as derived from the laws of nature, and not as the gift of their chief magistrate. Let those flatter, who fear: it is not an American art. To give praise where it is not due, might be well from the venal, but would ill beseem those who are asserting the rights of human nature. They know, and will therefore say, that kings are the servants, not the proprietors of the people. Open your breast, sire, to liberal and expanded thought. Let not the name of George the third be a blot in the page of history. You are surrounded by British counsellors, but remember that they are parties. You have no ministers for American affairs, because you have none taken from among us, nor amenable to the laws on which they are to give you advice. It behooves you therefore to think and to act for yourself and your people. The great principles of right and wrong are legible to every reader: to pursue them requires not the aid of many counsellors. The whole art of government consists in the art of being honest. Only aim to do your duty, and mankind will give credit where you fail. No longer persevere in sacrificing the rights of one part of the empire to the inordinate desires of another: but deal out to all equal and impartial right. Let no act be passed by any one legislature which may infringe on the rights and liberties of another. This is the important post in which fortune has placed you, holding the balance of a great, if a well poised empire. This, sire, is the advice of your great American council, on the observance of which may perhaps depend your felicity and future fame, and the preservation of that harmony which alone can continue both to Great Britain and America the reciprocal advantages of their connection. It is neither our wish nor our interest to separate from her. We are willing on our part to sacrifice every thing which reason can ask to the restoration of that tranquility for which all must wish. On their part let them be ready to establish union on a generous plan. Let them name their terms, but let them be just. Accept of every commercial preference it is in our power to give for such things as we can raise for their use, or they make for ours. But let them not think to exclude us from going to other markets, to dispose of those commodities which they cannot use, nor to supply those wants which they cannot supply. Still less let it be proposed that our properties within our own territories shall be taxed or regulated by any power on earth but our own. The God who gave us life, gave us liberty at the same time: the hand of force may destroy, but cannot disjoin them.

This, sire, is our last, our determined resolution: and that you will be pleased to interpose with that efficacy which your earnest endeavors may insure to procure redress of these our great grievances, to quiet the minds of your subjects in British America against any apprehensions of future incroachment, to establish fraternal love and harmony thro' the whole empire, and that they may continue to the latest ages of time, is the fervent prayer of all British America.

THE DECLARATION OF INDEPENDENCE AS SUBMITTED TO THE CONTINENTAL CONGRESS (JUNE 28, 1776)

BY THOMAS JEFFERSON

Introduction

The Declaration of Independence, as submitted to Congress on June 28, 1776, is printed below. It has been prepared from Jefferson's own text, and from the so-called "Lee copy," which he sent to his close friend, Richard Henry Lee. These two texts are identical save for the most trifling variations. Comparison of this document with the Declaration as promulgated on July 4, 1776, will show how the Committee's draft differed from the version known to history.

A DECLARATION BY THE REPRESENTATIVES OF THE UNITED STATES OF AMERICA IN GENERAL CONGRESS ASSEMBLED*

When in the course of human events it becomes necessary for one people to dissolve the political bonds which have connected them with another, and to assume among the powers of the earth the separate and equal station to which the laws of nature and of nature's god entitle them, a decent respect to the opinions of mankind requires that they should declare the causes which impel them to the separation.

We hold these truths to be self-evident; that all men are created equal; that they are endowed by their Creator with inherent and inalienable rights; that among these are life, liberty, and the pursuit of happiness; that to secure these rights, governments are instituted among men, deriving their just powers from the consent of the governed; that whenever any form of government becomes destructive of these ends, it is the right of the people to alter or to abolish it, and to institute new government, laying its foundation on such principles, and organizing its powers in such form as to them shall seem most likely to effect their safety and happiness. Prudence indeed will dictate that governments long established should not be changed for light and transient causes. And accordingly all experience hath shown that mankind are more disposed to suffer, while evils are sufferable, than to right themselves by abolishing the forms to which they are accustomed. But when a long train of abuses and usurpations, begun at a distinguished period and pursuing invariably the same object, evinces a design to reduce them under absolute despotism, it is their right, it is their duty, to throw off such government, and to provide new guards for their future security. Such has been the patient sufferance of these colonies, and such is now the necessity which constrains them to expunge their former systems of government. The history of the present king of Great Britain is a history of unremitting injuries and usurpations, among which appears no

*Sources: Carl Becker, The Declaration of Independence (New York, 1922), pp. 174–84; and The Papers of Thomas Jefferson, edited by Julian P. Boyd (Princeton University Press, 1950), I, pp. 315–19.

solitary fact to contradict the uniform tenor of the rest, but all have in direct object the establishment of an absolute tyranny over these states. To prove this let facts be submitted to a candid world, for the truth of which we pledge a faith yet unsullied by falsehood.

He has refused his assent to laws the most wholesome and necessary for the public good.

He has forbidden his governors to pass laws of immediate and pressing importance, unless suspended in their operation till his assent should be obtained; and when so suspended, he has neglected utterly to attend to them.

He has refused to pass other laws for the accommodation of large districts of people, unless those people would relinquish the right of representation in the legislature; a right inestimable to them, and formidable to tyrants only.

He has called together legislative bodies at places unusual, uncomfortable, and distant from the depository of their public records, for the sole purpose of fatiguing them into compliance with his measures.

He has dissolved Representative houses repeatedly and continually, for opposing with manly firmness his invasions on the rights of the people.

He has refused for a long time after such dissolutions to cause others to be elected whereby the legislative powers, incapable of annihilation, have returned to the people at large for their exercise, the state remaining in the meantime exposed to all the dangers of invasion from without, and convulsions within.

He has endeavored to prevent the population of these states; for that purpose obstructing the laws for naturalization of foreigners; refusing to pass others to encourage their migrations hither; and raising the conditions of new appropriations of lands.

He has suffered the administration of justice totally to cease in some of these states, refusing his assent to laws for establishing judiciary powers.

He has made our judges dependent on his will alone, for the tenure of their offices, and the amount and payment of their salaries.

He has erected a multitude of new offices by a self-assumed power, and sent hither swarms of officers to harass our people, and eat out their substance.

He has kept among us, in times of peace, standing armies and ships of war, without the consent of our legislatures.

He has affected to render the military independent of, and superior to, the civil power.

He has combined with others to subject us to a jurisdiction foreign to our constitutions and unacknowledged by our laws; giving his assent to their acts of pretended legislation for quartering large bodies of armed troops among us;

For protecting them by a mock-trial from punishment for any murders which they should commit on the inhabitants of these states;

For cutting off our trade with all parts of the world;

For imposing taxes on us without our consent;

For depriving us of the benefits of trial by jury;

For transporting us beyond seas to be tried for pretended offenses;

For abolishing the free system of English laws in a neighboring province, establishing therein an arbitrary government, and enlarging its boundaries so as to render it at once an example and fit instrument for introducing the same absolute rule into these states;

For taking away our charters, abolishing our most valuable laws, and altering fundamentally the forms of our governments;

For suspending our own legislatures, and declaring themselves to be invested with power to legislate for us in all cases whatsoever.

He has abdicated government here, withdrawing his governors, and declaring us out of his allegiance and protection.

He has plundered our seas, ravaged our coasts, burnt our towns, and destroyed the lives of our people.

He is at this time transporting large armies of foreign mercenaries, to complete the works of death, desolation, and tyranny, already begun with circumstances of cruelty and perfidy unworthy the head of a civilized nation.

He has endeavored to bring on the inhabitants of our frontiers the merciless Indian savages, whose known rule of warfare is an undistinguished destruction of all ages, sexes, and conditions of existence.

He has incited treasonable insurrections of our fellow citizens, with the allurements of forfeiture and confiscation of property.

He has constrained others, taken captives on the high seas, to bear arms against their country, to become the executioners of their friends and brethren, or to fall themselves by their hands.

He has waged cruel war against human nature itself, violating its most sacred rights of life and liberty in the persons of a distant people, who never offended him, captivating and carrying them into slavery in another hemisphere, or to incur miserable death in their transportation thither. This piratical warfare, the opprobrium of *infidel* powers, is the warfare of the *Christian* king of Great Britain. Determined to keep open a market where MEN should be bought and sold, he has prostituted his negative for suppressing every legislative attempt to prohibit or restrain this execrable commerce; and that this assemblage of horrors might want no fact of distinguished die, he is now exciting those very people to rise in arms among us, and to purchase that liberty of which *he* has deprived them, by murdering the people upon whom *he* also obtruded them: thus paying off former crimes committed against the liberties of one people, with crimes which he urges them to commit against the *lives* of another.

In every stage of these oppressions we have petitioned for redress in the most humble terms; our repeated petitions have been answered only by repeated injury. A prince whose character is thus marked by every act which may define a tyrant, is unfit to be the ruler of a people who mean to be free. Future ages will scarce believe that the hardiness of one man adventured, within the short compass of twelve years only, to lay a foundation, so broad and undisguised, for tyranny over a people fostered and fixed in principles of freedom.

Nor have we been wanting in attentions to our British brethren. We have warned them from time to time of attempts by their legislature to extend a jurisdiction over these our states. We have reminded them of the circumstances of our emigration and settlement here, no one of which could warrant so strange a pretension: that these were affected at the expence of our own blood and treasure, unassisted by the wealth or the strength of Great Britain: that in constituting indeed our several forms of government, we had adopted one common king, thereby laying a foundation for perpetual league and amity with them: but that submission to their parliament was no part of our constitution, nor ever in idea, if history may be credited: and we appealed to their native justice and magnanimity, as well as to the ties of our common kindred, to disavow these usurpations, which were likely to interrupt our condition and correspondence. They too have been deaf to the voice of justice and of consanguinity; and when occasions have been given them, by the regular course of their laws, of removing from their councils the disturbers of our harmony, they have by their free election re-established them in power. At this very time, too, they are permitting their chief magistrate to send over not only soldiers of our common blood, but Scotch and foreign mercenaries to invade and destroy us. These facts have given the last stab to agonizing affection; and manly spirit bids us to renounce forever these unfeeling brethren. We must therefore endeavor to forget our former love for them, and to hold them as we hold the rest of mankind, enemies in war, in peace friends. We might have been a great and free people together; but a communication of grandeur and of freedom, it seems, is below their dignity. Be it so, since they will have it. The road to happiness and to glory is open to us too; we will climb it apart from them, and acquiesce in the necessity which denounces our eternal separation!

We therefore the Representatives of the United States of America in General Congress assembled, do, in the name and by the authority of the good people of these states, reject and renounce all allegiance and subjection to the kings of Great Britain, and all others who may hereafter claim by, through, or under them; we utterly dissolve all political connection which may heretofore have subsisted between us and the people or parliament of Great Britain; and finally we do assert and declare these colonies to be free and independent states, and that as free and independent states, they have full power to levy war, conclude peace, contract alliances, establish commerce, and to do all other acts and things which independent states may of right to. And for the support of this declaration, we mutually pledge to each other our lives, our fortunes, and our sacred honor.

Broadside Songs
═══and Ballads═══════════════════

YOUNG LADIES IN TOWN

THE RICH LADY OVER THE SEA

THE FOLKS ON T'OTHER SIDE THE WAVE

BRITISH LAMENTATION

Introduction

If we wish to understand the Revolution as a human experience, one of the best ways to approach it is through its songs. These played a not unimportant part in the struggle, helping to spread news, ridiculing the enemy, summoning courage from the bottom of men's souls for the ordeal that was upon them.

Most of the revolutionary songs were broadside ballads. When printing was first invented in the sixteenth century, English balladeers began to print ballads on single sheets, or broadsides. This tradition was readily transplanted to the colonies. The Revolutionary War witnessed a blossoming of broadsides, as songs about battles and naval encounters multiplied and were sung by soldier and civilian alike.

The Revolution, furthermore, witnessed a step forward in the evolution of American song. Americans created many new lyrics in the heat of a new and revolutionary experience. From the fusion of this utterance with traditional melody was born a uniquely American type of song.

Young Ladies in Town was first published in the Boston News Letter in 1769. Evidently it was a product of the boycott of British goods that followed the passage of the Townshend Laws of 1767. This boycott was very effective in New

England, and, during the two years that it was operative, inflicted staggering losses upon English trade. The song is notable not only for its propaganda message, but for the appeal to women to place love of country above love of finery.

The Rich Lady over the Sea has been chosen for inclusion because it is perhaps the most telling of the many songs written about the Boston Tea Party of December 16, 1773. It underlines in an unmistakable way the growing colonial conviction that the American people had come of age.

The secret of colonial strength, in the apparently unevenly matched struggle with Britain, lay in the wide popular appeal of the American cause and in the readiness of thousands of ordinary folk to give their lives in defense of their homes and their land. The enormous strength of the American will to resist was clearly understood at the time, at least by some Englishmen. The oft-repeated assertion of modern historians, based upon a very dubious statement by John Adams—that only a minority of the American people was involved in the Revolution—does not find support in the testimony of the contemporary songs.

The Folks on t'Other Side of the Wave was first published in England in 1776 and reappeared the following year in the form of a broadside, To the Commons. It is marked by a shrewd understanding of the kind of war that colonists would wage, and it warns the English House of Commons to reconsider its punitive policies. The melody is taken from an old English sea song.

British Lamentation makes the same point as the previous song, but couches it in the words of a British redcoat. It tells the story of the British war effort from the end of 1774, when the government in London dispatched reinforcements to Boston, through the stirring events of the New England campaign in 1775, right up to September 15, 1776, when British troops first landed on Manhattan Island. The version of the ballad given below is taken from a broadside in the Harris Collection of the University of Rhode Island. The melody, possessed of a haunting sadness, was recorded by Frank Warner from the singing of a New York lumberjack, John Galusha, who died in 1950. Still another version of this song was taught to Helen Hartness Flanders by Mrs. Ellen Nye Lawrence of Vermont in 1931. That it has remained in oral tradition until our own day, and that it has been found both in New England and New York, testifies to the deep roots which revolutionary broadsides struck among the common people.

YOUNG LADIES IN TOWN

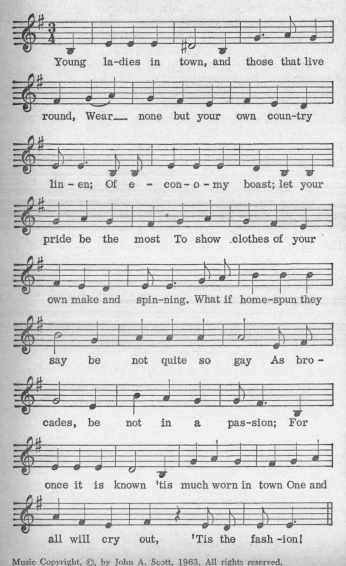

Young la-dies in town, and those that live

round, Wear— none but your own coun-try

lin-en; Of e - con-o-my boast; let your

pride be the most To show clothes of your

own make and spin-ning. What if home-spun they

say be not quite so gay As bro-

cades, be not in a pas-sion; For

once it is known 'tis much worn in town One and

all will cry out, 'Tis the fash-ion!

Young ladies in town, and those that live round,
   Wear none but your own country linen;
Of economy boast; let your pride be the most
   To show clothes of your own make and spinning.
What if homespun they say be not quite so gay
   As brocades, be not in a passion;
For once it is known 'tis much worn in town
   One and all will cry out, 'Tis the fashion!

And as one all agree that you'll not married be
   To such as will wear London factory;
But at first sight refuse, tell 'em you will choose
   As encourage our own manufactory.
No more ribbons wear, nor in rich silks appear,
   Love your country much better than fine things;
Begin without passion, 'twill soon be the fashion
   To grace your smooth locks with a twine string.

Throw away your bohea and your green hyson tea
   And all things of a new-fashioned duty;
Get in a good store of the choice Labrador
   There'll soon be enough here to suit ye.
These do without fear, and to all you'll appear
   Fair, charming, true, lovely and clever;
Though the times remain darkish, young men will be sparkish
   And love you much stronger than ever.

The Rich Lady Over The Sea

There was a rich lady lived over the sea, And she was an island queen; Her daughter lived off in the new country With an ocean of water be - tween; with an o- cean of water be - tween.

1. There was a rich lady lived over the sea,
   And she was an island queen;
   Her daughter lived off in the new country
   With an ocean of water between,
   With an ocean of water between.

2. The old lady's pockets were fillèd with gold,
   But never contented was she;
   So she ordered her daughter to pay her a tax
   Of thruppence a pound on the tea,
   Of thruppence a pound on the tea.

3. "O mother, dear mother," the daughter replied,
    "I'll not do the thing that you ax;
"I'm willing to pay a fair price on the tea,
    "But never the thruppenny tax,
        "But never the thruppenny tax."

4. "You shall!" cried the mother, and reddened with rage,
    "For you're my own daughter, you see;
"And its only proper that daughter should pay
    "Her mother a tax on the tea,
        "Her mother a tax on the tea."

5. She ordered her servant to be callèd up
    To wrap up a package of tea;
And eager for three pence a pound, she put in
    Enough for a large family,
        Enough for a large family.

6. She ordered her servant to bring home the tax,
    Declaring her child must obey;
Or, old as she was, and woman most grown,
    She'd half whip her life away,
        She'd half whip her life away.

7. The tea was conveyed to her daughter's own door,
    All down by the oceanside;
But the bouncing girl poured out every pound
    In the dark and boiling tide,
        In the dark and boiling tide.

8. And then she called out to the island queen,
    "O mother, dear mother," called she,
"Your tea you may have when 'tis steepèd enough
    "But never a tax from me,
        "But never a tax from me."

THE FOLKS ON T'OTHER SIDE THE WAVE

The folks on t'other side the wave,
  Have beef as well as you, sirs;
Some chines, and turkeys too, they have,
  And as they bake they brew, sirs.
    Blow ye winds of morning,
    Blow ye winds ay-o;
    Blow ye winds of morning,
    Blow, blow, blow.

What tho' your cannon raze their towns,
   And tumble down their houses,
They'll fight like devils, blood and bones,
   For children and for spouses.
     Blow ye winds of morning, etc.

Another truth, nay, tis no boast,
   Nor yet the lie o' the day, sirs;
The saints on Massachusetts coast
   Gain if they run away, sirs.
     Blow ye winds of morning, etc.

For further than your bullets fly
   A common man may run, sirs;
And wheat will grow beneath a sky
   Where cannot reach a gun, sirs.
     Blow ye winds of morning, etc.

BRITISH LAMENTATION

'Twas on De-cem-ber's fif-teenth day, when we set sail for A-mer-i-ca; 'Twas on that dark and dis-mal day, When we set sail for A-mer-i-ca. 'Twas in that dark and ___ dis-mal time, ___ when we set sail for the Nor-thern clime, where drums do beat and trum-pets sound, and un-to Bos-ton ___ we were bound.

'Twas on December's fifteenth day,
When we set sail for America;
'Twas on that dark and dismal day,
When we set sail for America.
'Twas in that dark and dismal time,
When we set sail for the northern clime,
Where drums do beat and trumpets sound,
And unto Boston we were bound.

And when to Boston we did come,
We thought by the aid of our British guns,
To drive the rebels from that place,
And fill their hearts with sore disgrace.
But to our sorrow and surprise,
We saw men like grasshoppers rise;
They fought like heroes much enraged,
Which did affright old General Gage.

Like lions roaring for their prey,
They feared no danger or dismay;
Bold British blood runs through their veins,
And still with courage they sustain.
We saw those bold Columbia sons
Spread death and slaughter from their guns:
Freedom or death! these heroes cry,
They did not seem afraid to die.

We sailed to York, as you've been told,
With the loss of many a Briton bold,
For to make those rebels own our king,
And daily tribute to him bring.
They said it was a garden place,
And that our armies could with ease,
Pull down their town, lay waste their lands,
In spite of all their boasted bands.

A garden place it was indeed,
And in it grew many a bitter weed,
Which will pull down our highest hopes,
And sorely wound our British troops.

'Tis now September the seventeenth day,
I wish I'd never come to America:
Full fifteen thousand has been slain,
Bold British heroes every one.

Now I've received my mortal wound,
I bid farewell to Old England's ground;
My wife and children will mourn for me,
Whilst I lie cold in America,
Fight on America's noble sons,
Fear not Britannia's thundering guns,
Maintain your cause from year to year,
God's on your side, you need not fear.

The
Early
National
Period
=1783-1814=

Federalists and
Jeffersonians

The outbreak of the Revolutionary War brought about the collapse of the British colonial administration in America and saw the emergence of thirteen sovereign states, each with its own revolutionary government. Military necessity forced these states to draw together for the conduct of a common defense and a common foreign policy. But each was jealous of its newly established sovereignty and surrendered none of it to the Confederation which was set up as the instrument to make possible cooperation and victory. This Confederation, given formal, constitutional existence by the Articles of Confederation which were ratified by all the states during the war, was essentially a military and political alliance of sovereign and independent states. A rough modern analogy would be the United Nations: it came into being during wartime and originated in the United Nations Declaration of January 1, 1942. Its immediate purpose, as a wartime alliance of twenty-six sovereign States, was to bring about the defeat of Hitler, Tojo and Mussolini. But when peace came it remained in being, armed with minimal powers in the field of world government and conciliation.

The end of the war and the achievement of independence witnessed the development of a crisis concerning the nature of the Union and its government. The new Constitution drawn up in 1787 proposed to limit the sovereignty of the states and to endow the central government with permanent and sovereign powers. The submission of this controversial document to the people of the United States for ratification touched off a major political debate, which raged throughout the country from the fall of 1787 to the spring of 1789. This war of words brought to the fore many different aspects of the problem confronting the American people: how to create a continental government that would ensure peace, security and national development without riding roughshod over state authority and while continuing to remain in some measure responsive to the popular will.

The *Federalist*, or pro-Constitution, viewpoint was expressed in the Federalist Papers. These eighty-five essays appeared more or less continuously in the New York press from October, 1787 until August, 1788. They were published at the same time in book form. The majority came from the pen of Alexander Hamilton, and a lesser number were written by James Madison and John Jay. They remain to this day a fundamental commentary upon the American Constitution, in which Hamilton and his collaborators undertook to prove to the American people the vital necessity for a closer form of union, and in which they developed the theory of a national government of the United States.

The Federalist Papers may be divided into two parts. The first (nos. 1-29) is an analysis of the problems and weaknesses besetting the Confederation; the second (nos. 30-85) deals with the powers to be assigned to the Federal government, and the organization of those powers in the separate departments of administration. It is with the first only of these topics that we shall be concerned.

In Papers nos. 1-29—as might be expected of three authors writing in haste and without the possibility of a very close collaboration—the exposition of the crisis facing the people and the states is developed in a clumsy and erratic way.[1] But from these essays taken as a whole, the following pattern emerges:

1. The authors subjected the Confederation to a searching critique. They demonstrated its essential weakness, even impotence, as an organ of government, and argued that it was inadequate to provide for the political needs of the country and to guarantee its development (nos. 15-22).

2. The weakness of the central government, taken by itself, would not have been of much concern to most of Hamilton's contemporaries. On the contrary, such weakness, in their eyes, was a positive merit. They had had bitter experience with central governments and their oppressive powers; and it made, to them, little sense to substitute one potentially oppressive central government for another. People in those days placed their main reliance upon the states governments which had emerged during the course of the Revolution itself. These were

---

[1] Hamilton himself, in the first edition of the *Papers* published in 1788, pointed out the "violations of method and repetitions of ideas which cannot but displease a critical reader."

close at hand, subject to popular pressure, and to some extent under popular control, depending on the individual state.

For this reason the authors of the Federalist Papers had to show that weakness in the central government constituted a danger to the American people and to their national interest. Weakness, they argued, invites intervention in one form or another by the country's foreign enemies; it invites mutual dissent and competition among the states; it brings on the risk of both civil and international war. Such fragmentation of power—we might call it, in modern terminology, the balkanization of America—will in turn jeopardize the existence of the national government and place in question the very survival of the United States as a single nation (nos. 2-8).

3. The Federalist showed to their satisfaction that weakness in the central government would prove a danger. But this was not the same as showing that a strong central government would eliminate the dangers described: might it not even intensify the problems which the country faced? The authors of the Papers, consequently, had to prove the corollary of the proposition that weakness in the central government was dangerous; namely, that strong central government would in fact eliminate such dangers, would promote freedom, civil liberties and independence, and would not undermine them, as critics of the Federalist position most feared (nos. 9-13).

But the authors of the Papers could not provide the proof needed without turning their attention to foreign affairs. The demonstration here fell to Alexander Hamilton.

Anti-Federalists had made the objection that a strong central government in possession of powerful military forces would constitute a bulwark of tyranny and a menace to the Republican liberties of a free country. In answer to this Hamilton drew attention to the situation of Great Britain, which for centuries had enjoyed parliamentary institutions and a degree of civic freedom which were the wonder of all Europe. He pointed out that this phenomenon was connected with Britain's "insular situation," and the fact that Britain, being cut off by a sea barrier from Europe and from the danger of invasion, had been able to preserve her freedom primarily through the militia, or people in arms, coupled with a powerful navy. Insularity had saved Britain from the institution of a standing army and from the evils of militarism inseparable from this. Insularity was directly connected with

Britain's favorable position in Europe, where endemic war and the fear of invasion had engendered militarism and the destruction of liberty that American patriots so rightly feared.

4. It was clear to Hamilton that the United States enjoyed an insular position to a far greater degree than Britain. All that the country had to do was to exploit the natural advantages of its insular situation; then, like Britain, it could enjoy peace and security without the burdens and the dangers of a standing army. It could do this precisely as Britain had done —by a defense that relied primarily upon a militia under the leadership of a small professional force of trained soldiers,[2] and by developing a strong navy. If this policy were adopted, that same military force, which in the hands of individual states would endanger the Union, would, under Federal control, become a guarantor of liberty and independence (nos. 23-29).

Hamilton thus established the defense and maintenance of America's insular position—and its corollary in the freedom of the seas—as the basis for American foreign policy. This concept had nothing whatever in common with the doctrinaire isolationism so industriously propagated in the twentieth century. Insularity meant isolation from the military affairs of Europe; it neither stated nor implied any isolation from the cultural life of Europe, nor indeed, of the world. On the contrary, Hamilton, as a spokesman for America's commercial and manufacturing classes, was a champion of international trade and, inseparable from this, of the fullest cultural contact among nations. It was precisely this policy that proved to be the key to American greatness in the nineteenth century— in the fullest sense an internationalist and not an isolationist foreign policy; one that followed peaceful relations with all peoples, the abrogation of militarism both at home and abroad, and participation to the fullest extent in the cultural life of Europe and of the world, involving the free flow of people, of ideas and of goods.

Two essays that focus on the dangers of a weak government and the advantages of insularity are nos. 7 and 8. They are reproduced below because they are among the most brilliant

---

[2] The germ of Hamilton's idea of the relationship of professional force to militia—even if the latter were under the control of the states—was developed in his "Report on a Military Peace Establishment" made to the Continental Congress in September, 1783. *The Papers of Alexander Hamilton* (New York, 1962), III, pp. 378–97.

contributions to the entire series as well as being a fitting introduction to the subject.

Federalism possessed in the person of Alexander Hamilton a political theorist of the first rank. The anti-Federalists possessed no spokesman of equivalent stature. A body of opinion rather than a political party, anti-Federalism was a label which in 1787 covered the vast majority of Americans whose views spanned a wide political spectrum, and who were united only by a common suspicion, ranging anywhere from mild disagreement to outspoken hostility, of the new Constitution and its supporters.

The anti-Federalists were weakened not only by lack of theoretical unity and coherence, but by the fact that many of them were obliged to admit the justice of much Federalist criticism of the Confederation. Conceding the need for at least some measure of stronger government, anti-Federalist thought focused upon the issue of precisely what powers such government should have; what safeguards should be provided against abuses inherent in governmental process; and how to prevent the new governmental machine from becoming, in the hands of the rich, an instrument for the oppression of the poor.

Anti-Federalist opposition here found a coherent focus around the absence in the new Constitution of a Bill of Rights.

By the end of the eighteenth century the concept of written and immutable guarantees against governmental abuses had become deeply ingrained in American thinking. This tradition had been established as early as 1641 by the enactment of the Massachusetts Body of Liberties.[3] It received an immense impetus from the struggle against arbitrary British rule which resulted in the overthrow of the old colonial administrations and the establishment, during the revolutionary years, of new regimes governed by constitutional rules that the states had themselves enacted. The drafters of these new state constitutions had to reckon with the fact that the people would not ratify such instruments without the inclusion of a Bill of Rights; and by 1787 it was a fixed pole of American popular thought that government was a dangerous instrument which might easily be abused by unscrupulous men for their own ends. It was clear that government might promote not the

---

[3] See Appendix, p. 589-606.

welfare of the people, but private purposes, unless strict barriers were erected to prohibit the invasion or the destruction of human rights. Power must be limited in its exercise, or it must not be exercised at all.

The Constitution of 1787 was charged with many shortcomings. But the criticism that it failed to include a clear and systematic statement of the rights of man, both in his civil capacity and when accused of crime, proved the most damaging and politically the most decisive. An explicit commitment to provide amendments guaranteeing the rights of man, by Federalist leaders in key states, such as Massachusetts, New York and Virginia, was necessary before the people in these states would permit the Constitution to be ratified.

The second of the documents reproduced below is from the pen of the influential anti-Federalist Richard Henry Lee. It deals with this aspect of anti-Federalist criticism of the Constitution.

The American Constitution finally emerged as a synthesis of Federalist and anti-Federalist intentions. The Bill of Rights was written into the instrument at the insistence of the people. It is the anti-Federalists' enduring contribution to the national document.

THE FEDERALIST, NOS. 7 AND 8 (1787)

BY ALEXANDER HAMILTON

Introduction

Alexander Hamilton (ca. 1757-1804), the son of Rachel Fawcett and an immigrant Scotsman, James Hamilton, was born on the island of St. Christopher in the British West Indies. Hamilton and his younger brother James were left orphans by their father's desertion in 1763 and by the death of their mother five years later. Thus when Hamilton was about eleven years old his formal schooling came to an end. Apprenticed to a merchant on the island of St. Croix he demonstrated a brightness that caught the attention of island leaders, and was packed off to the mainland for an education. He landed at Boston in October, 1772, in his sixteenth year.

In 1773 Hamilton was admitted to King's College in New York City. Identifying himself with America's rising revolutionary mood, he plunged into political agitation and pamphleteering; at the same time he did not neglect his studies, particularly in ancient and European history, and in political philosophy. In 1776 he received a commission as a captain of militia and was given command of a company of artillery. By the end of that same year he had come to General Washington's attention for his coolness in action and the skill with which he handled his men and his guns. The following year Washington took Hamilton on to his staff, and the young man served for the rest of the war first in this capacity and later with Lafayette at Yorktown.

After the war Hamilton took up his pen again to criticize the Continental Congress—of which he was a member for a while—for its ineptness. The convocation of the Constitutional Convention at Philadelphia in 1787 was due to his initiative, and crowned years of unremitting agitation that he had undertaken on behalf of governmental reform. Hamilton was originally sent to the Convention as a delegate from New York, but he left the assemblage in disgust, since it was not prepared to go as far down the road of national consolidation as he wished. Yet he recognized in the results of the Convention a huge step forward from the Articles of Confederation; and he threw himself into the battle for constitutional ratification with characteristic energy.

The *Federalist* nos. 7 and 8* illuminate Hamilton's approach to foreign policy. He must, indeed, be considered as a principal architect of the guiding principles in this field established during the early national period. His ideas find further amplification in Washington's Farewell Address of 1796 of which he was one of the principal authors.

THE DANGERS OF DISUNION THAT ARISE FROM INTERNAL RIVALRIES, STANDING ARMIES, AND WAR (HAMILTON)

FEDERALIST NO. 7

It is sometimes asked, with an air of seeming triumph, what inducements the states could have, if disunited, to make war upon each other? It would be a full answer to this question to

---

Source: These two articles were published in the New York press in November, 1787. They are reprinted, with minor corrections, from the edition of the *Federalist* published by George F. Hopkins (New York, 1802).

say—precisely the same inducements which have, at different times, deluged in blood all the nations in the world. But unfortunately for us, the question admits of a more particular answer. There are causes of difference within our immediate contemplation, of the tendency of which, even under the restraints of a federal constitution, we have had sufficient experience to enable us to form a judgment of what might be expected, if those restraints were removed.

Territorial disputes have at all times been found one of the most fertile sources of hostility among nations. Perhaps the greatest proportion of the wars that have desolated the earth have sprung from this origin. This cause would exist, among us, in full force. We have a vast tract of unsettled territory within the boundaries of the United States. There still are discordant and undecided claims between several of them; and the dissolution of the union would lay a foundation for similar claims between them all. It is well known that they have heretofore had serious and animated discussions concerning the right to the lands which were ungranted at the time of the revolution, and which usually went under the name of crown lands. The states within the limits of whose colonial governments they were comprised have claimed them as their property; the others have contended that the rights of the crown in this article devolved upon the Union; especially as to all that part of the western territory which, either by actual possession, or through the submission of the Indian proprietors, was subject to the jurisdiction of the King of Great Britain, till it was relinquished by the treaty of peace. This, it has been said, was at all events an acquisition to the confederacy by compact with a foreign power. It has been the prudent policy of Congress to appease this controversy, by prevailing upon the states to make cessions to the United States for the benefit of the whole. This has been so far accomplished, as under a continuation of the Union, to afford a decided prospect of an amicable termination of the dispute. A dismemberment of the confederacy, however, would revive this dispute, and would create others on the same subject. At present, a large part of the vacant western territory is by cession at least, if not by any anterior right, the common property of the Union. If that were at an end, the states which have made cessions, on a principle of federal compromise, would be apt, when the motive of the grant had ceased, to reclaim the lands as a reversion. The other states would no doubt insist on a proportion, by right of representation. Their argument would be, that a grant once made could not be revoked; and that the justice of their participating in territory acquired or secured, by the joint efforts of the confederacy, remained undiminished. If, contrary to probability, it should be admitted by all the states, that each had a right to a share of this common stock, there would still be a difficulty to be surmounted, as to a proper rule of apportionment. Different principles would be set up by different states for this purpose; and as they would affect the opposite interests of the parties, they might not easily be susceptible of a pacific adjustment.

In the wide field of western territory, therefore, we perceive an ample theatre for hostile pretensions, without any umpire or common judge to interpose between the contending parties. To reason from the past to the future, we shall have good ground to apprehend, that the sword would sometimes be appealed to as the arbiter of their differences. The circumstances of the dispute between Connecticut and Pennsylvania, respecting the lands at Wyoming, admonish us not to be sanguine in expecting an easy accommodation of such differences. The Articles of Confederation obliged the parties to submit the matter to the decision of a federal court. The submission was made, and the court decided in favour of Pennsylvania. But Connecticut gave strong indications of dissatisfaction with that determination; nor did she appear to be entirely resigned to it, till by negotiation and management something like an equivalent was found for the loss she supposed herself to have sustained. Nothing here said is intended to convey the slightest censure on the conduct of that state. She no doubt sincerely believed herself to have been injured by the decision; and states, like individuals, acquiesce with great reluctance in determinations to their disadvantage.

Those who had an opportunity of seeing the inside of the transactions, which attended the progress of the controversy between this state and the district of Vermont, can vouch the opposition we experienced, as well from states not interested as from those which were interested in the claim; and can attest the danger, to which the peace of the confederacy might have been exposed, had this state attempted to assert its rights by force. Two motives preponderated in that opposition; one, a jealousy entertained of our future power; another, the interest of certain individuals of influence in the neighbouring states, who had obtained grants of lands under the actual government of that district. Even the states which brought forward claims, in contradiction to ours, seemed more solicitous to dismember this state, than to establish their own pretensions. These were New Hampshire, Massachusetts, and Connecticut. New Jersey and Rhode Island upon all occasions discovered a warm zeal for the independence of Vermont; and Maryland, until alarmed by the appearance of a connection between Canada and that place, entered deeply into the same views. These being small states, saw with an unfriendly eye the perspective of our growing greatness. In a review of these transactions we may trace some of the causes which would be likely to embroil the states with each other, if it should be their unpropitious destiny to become disunited.

The competitions of commerce would be another fruitful source of contention. The states less favourably circumstanced, would be desirous of escaping from the disadvantages of local situation, and of sharing in the advantages of their more fortunate neighbours. Each state, or separate confederacy, would pursue a system of commercial polity peculiar to itself. This would occasion distinctions, preferences, and exclusions, which would beget discontent. The habits of intercourse, on the basis of equal privileges, to which we have been accustomed from the earliest settlement of the country, would give a keener edge to those causes of discontent, than they would naturally have, independent of this circumstance. *We should be ready to denominate injuries, those things which were in reality the justifiable acts of independent sovereignties consulting a distinct interest.* The spirit of enterprise, which characterizes the commercial part of America, has left no occasion of displaying itself unimproved. It is not at all probable, that this unbridled spirit would pay much respect to those regulations of trade, by which particular states might endeavour to secure exclusive benefits to their own citizens. The infractions of these regulations on one side, the efforts to prevent and repel them on the other, would naturally lead to outrages, and these to reprisals and wars.

The opportunities, which some states would have of rendering others tributary to them, by commercial regulations, would be impatiently submitted to by the tributary states. The relative situation of New York, Connecticut, and New Jersey, would afford an example of this kind. New York, from the necessities of revenue, must lay duties on her importations. A great part of these duties must be paid by the inhabitants of the two other states, in the capacity of consumers of what we import. New York would neither be willing nor able to forego this advantage. Her citizens would not consent that a duty paid by them should be remitted in favour of the citizens of her neighbours; nor would it be practicable, if there were not this impediment in the way, to distinguish the customers in our own markets.

Would Connecticut and New Jersey long submit to be taxed by New York for her exclusive benefit? Should we be long permitted to remain in the quiet and undisturbed enjoyment of a metropolis, from the possession of which we derived an advantage so odious to our neighbours, and, in their opinion, so oppressive? Should we be able to preserve it against the incumbent weight of Connecticut on the one side, and the co-operating pressure of New Jersey on the other? These are questions that temerity alone will answer in the affirmative.

The public debt of the Union would be a further cause of collision between the separate states or confederacies. The apportionment, in the first instance, and the progressive extinguishment, afterwards, would be alike productive of ill humour and animosity. How would it be possible to agree upon a rule of apportionment, satisfactory to all? There is scarcely any that can be proposed, which is entirely free from real objections. These, as usual, would be exaggerated by the adverse interest of the parties. There are even dissimilar views among the states, as to the general principle of discharging the public debt. Some of them, either less impressed with the importance of national credit, or because their citizens have little, if any, immediate interest in the question, feel an indifference, if not a repugnance, to the payment of the domestic debt, at any rate. These would be inclined to magnify the difficulties of a distribution. Others of them, a numerous body of whose citizens are creditors of the public, beyond the proportion of the state in the total amount of the national debt, would be strenuous for some equitable and effectual provision. The procrastinations of the former, would excite the resentments of the latter. The settlement of a rule would in the meantime be postponed, by real differences of opinion, and affected delays. The citizens of the states interested, would clamour; foreign powers would urge, for the satisfaction of their just demands; and the peace of the states would be exposed to the double contingency of external invasion and internal contention.

But suppose the difficulties of agreeing upon a rule surmounted, and the apportionment made. Still there is great room to suppose, that the rule agreed upon would, in the experiment, be found to bear harder upon some states than upon others. Those which were sufferers by it, would naturally seek for a mitigation of the burthen. The others would as naturally be disinclined to a revision, which was likely to end in an increase of their own incumbrances. Their refusal would afford to the complaining states a pretext for withholding their contributions, too plausible not to be embraced with avidity; and the non-compliance of these states with their engagements, would be a ground of bitter dissention and altercation. If even the rule adopted should in practice justify the equality of its principle, still delinquencies in payment, on the part of some of the states, would result from a diversity of other causes— the real deficiency of resources; the mismanagement of their finances; accidental disorders in the administration of the government; and in addition to the rest, the reluctance with which men commonly part with money for purposes that have outlived the exigencies which produced them, and interfere with the supply of immediate wants. Delinquencies from whatever causes would be productive of complaints, recriminations, and quarrels. There is, perhaps, nothing more likely to disturb the tranquillity of nations than their being bound to mutual contributions for any common object, which does not yield an equal and coincident benefit. For it is an observation as true as it is trite, that there is nothing men differ so readily about as the payment of money.

Laws in violation of private contracts, as they amount to aggressions on the rights of those states, whose citizens are injured by them, may be considered as another probable source of hostility. We are not authorized to expect, that a more liberal, or more equitable spirit would preside over the legislations of the individual states hereafter, if unrestrained by any additional checks, than we have heretofore seen, in too many instances, disgracing their several codes. We have observed the disposition to retaliation excited in Connecticut, in consequence of the enormities perpetrated by the legislature of Rhode Island; and we may reasonably infer, that in similar cases, under other circumstances, a war, not of *parchment*, but of the sword, would chastise such atrocious breaches of moral obligation and social justice.

The probability of incompatible alliances between the different states or confederacies, and different foreign nations, and the effects of this situation upon the peace of the whole, have been sufficiently unfolded in some preceding papers. From the view they have exhibited of this part of the subject, this conclusion is to be drawn, that America, if not connected at all, or only by the feeble tie of a simple league offensive and defensive, would, by the operation of such opposite and jarring alliances, be gradually entangled in all the pernicious labyrinths of European politics and wars; and by the destructive contentions of the parts into which she was divided, would be likely to become a prey to the artifices and machinations of powers equally the enemies of them all. *Divide et impera* must be the motto of every nation that either hates or fears us.

Federalist No. 8

Assuming it therefore as an established truth, that, in case of disunion, the several states, or such combinations of them as might happen to be formed out of the wreck of the general confederacy, would be subject to those vicissitudes of peace and war, of friendship and enmity with each other, which have fallen to the lot of all neighbouring nations not united under one government, let us enter into a concise detail of some of the consequences that would attend such a situation.

War between the states, in the first periods of their separate existence, would be accompanied with much greater distresses than it commonly is in those countries, where regular military establishments have long obtained. The disciplined armies always kept on foot on the continent of Europe, though they bear a malignant aspect to liberty and economy, have, notwithstanding, been productive of the signal advantage of rendering sudden conquests impracticable, and of preventing that rapid desolation, which used to mark the progress of war, prior to their introduction. The art of fortification has contributed to the same ends. The nations of Europe are encircled with chains of fortified places, which mutually obstruct invasion. Campaigns are wasted in reducing two or three frontier garrisons, to gain admittance into an enemy's country. Similar impediments occur at every step, to exhaust the strength, and delay the progress of an invader. Formerly an invading army would penetrate into the heart of a neighbouring country, almost as soon as intelligence of its approach could be received; but now, a comparatively small force of disciplined troops acting on the defensive, with the aid of posts, is able to impede, and finally to frustrate, the enterprises of one much more considerable. The history of war, in that quarter of the globe, is no longer a history of nations subdued, and empires overturned, but of towns taken and retaken, of battles that decide nothing, of retreats more beneficial than victories, of much effort and little acquisition.

In this country, the scene would be altogether reversed. The jealousy of military establishments would postpone them as long as possible. The want of fortifications, leaving the frontiers of one state open to another, would facilitate inroads. The populous states would with little difficulty over-run their less populous neighbours. Conquests would be as easy to be made, as difficult to be retained. War, therefore, would be desultory and predatory. *Plunder* and devastation ever march in the train of irregulars. The calamities of individuals would make the principal figure in the events, which would characterize our military exploits.

This picture is not too highly wrought; though, I confess, it would not long remain a just one. Safety from external danger is the most powerful director of national conduct. Even the ardent love of liberty will, after a time, give way to its dictates. The violent destruction of life and property incident to war; the continual effort and alarm attendant on a state of continual danger, will compel nations the most attached to liberty, to resort for repose and security to institutions which have a tendency to destroy their civil and political rights. To be more safe, they, at length, become willing to run the risk of being less free.

The institutions chiefly alluded to are *standing armies*, and the correspondent appendages of military establishments. Standing armies, it is said, are not provided against in the new constitution; and it is thence inferred that they would exist under it. This inference, from the very form of the proposition, is, at best, problematical and uncertain. But standing armies, it may be replied, must inevitably result from a dissolution of the confederacy. Frequent war, and constant apprehension, which require a state of as constant preparation, will infallibly produce them. The weaker states, or confederacies, would first have recourse to them, to put themselves upon an equality with their more potent neighbours. They would endeavour to supply the inferiority of population and resources, by a more regular and effective system of defence, by disciplined troops, and by fortifications. They would, at the same time, be obliged to strengthen the executive arm of government; in doing which, their constitutions would acquire a progressive direction towards monarchy. It is of the nature of war to increase the executive, at the expense of the legislative authority.

The expedients which have been mentioned would soon give the states, or confederacies, that made use of them, a superiority over their neighbours. Small states, or states of less natural strength, under vigorous governments, and with the assistance of disciplined armies, have often triumphed over large states, or states of greater natural strength, which have been destitute of these advantages. Neither the pride, nor the safety, of the more important states, or confederacies, would permit them long to submit to this mortifying and adventitious superiority. They would quickly resort to means similar to those by which it had been effected, to reinstate themselves in their lost pre-eminence. Thus we should in a little time see established in every part of this country, the same engines of despotism which have been the scourge of the old world. This, at least, would be the natural course of things; and our reasonings will be likely to be just, in proportion as they are accommodated to this standard.

These are not vague inferences deduced from speculative defects in a constitution, the whole power of which is lodged in the hands of the people, or their representatives and delegates; they are solid conclusions, drawn from the natural and necessary progress of human affairs.

It may perhaps be asked, by way of objection, why did not standing armies spring up out of the contentions which so often distracted the ancient republics of Greece? Different answers equally satisfactory may be given to this question. The industrious habits of the people of the present day, absorbed in the pursuits of gain, and devoted to the improvements of agriculture and commerce, are incompatible with the condition of a nation of soldiers, which was the true condition of the people of those republics. The means of revenue, which have been so greatly multiplied by the increase of gold and silver, and of the arts of industry, and the science of finance, which is the offspring of modern times, concurring with the habits of nations, have produced an entire revolution in the system of war, and have rendered disciplined armies, distinct from the body of the citizens, the inseparable companion of frequent hostility.

There is a wide difference also, between military establishments in a country which, by its situation, is seldom exposed to invasions, and in one which is often subject to them, and always apprehensive of them. The rulers of the former can have no good pretext, if they are even so inclined, to keep on foot armies so numerous as must of necessity be maintained in the latter. These armies being, in the first case, rarely, if at all, called into activity for interior defence, the people are in no danger of being broken to military subordination. The laws are not accustomed to relaxations in favour of military exigencies; the civil state remains in full vigour, neither corrupted nor confounded with the principles or propensities of the other state. The smallness of the army forbids competition with the natural strength of the community, and the citizens, not habituated to look up to the military power for protection, or to submit to its oppressions, neither love nor fear the soldiery: they view them with a spirit of jealous acquiescence in a necessary evil, and stand ready to resist a power which they suppose may be exerted to the prejudice of their rights.

The army under such circumstances, though it may usefully aid the magistrate to suppress a small faction, or an occasional mob, or insurrection, will be utterly incompetent to the purpose of enforcing encroachments against the united efforts of the great body of the people.

But in a country where the perpetual menacings of danger oblige the government to be always prepared to repel it, her armies must be numerous enough for instant defence. The continual necessity for his services enhances the importance of the soldier, and proportionably degrades the condition of the citizen. The military state becomes elevated above the civil. The inhabitants of territories often the theatre of war, are unavoidably subjected to frequent infringements on their rights, which serve to weaken their sense of those rights; and by degrees, the people are brought to consider the soldiery not only as their protectors, but as their superiors. The transition from this disposition to that of considering them as masters, is neither remote nor difficult: but it is very difficult to prevail upon a people under such impressions, to make a bold, or effectual resistance, to usurpations, supported by the military power.

The kingdom of Great Britain falls within the first description. An insular situation, and a powerful marine, guarding it in a great measure against the possibility of foreign invasion, supersede the necessity of a numerous army within the kingdom. A sufficient force to make head against a sudden descent till the militia could have time to rally and embody, is all that has been deemed requisite. No motive of national policy has demanded, nor would public opinion have tolerated a larger number of troops upon its domestic establishment. This peculiar felicity of situation has, in a great degree, contributed to preserve the liberty, which that country to this day enjoys, in spite of the prevalent venality and corruption. If Britain had been situated on the continent, and had been compelled, as she would have been, by that situation, to make her military establishments at home co-extensive with those of the other great powers of Europe, she, like them, would in all probability at this day be a victim to the absolute power of a single man. It is possible, though not easy, for the people of that island to be enslaved from other causes; but it cannot be by the prowess of an army so inconsiderable as that which has been usually kept up within the kingdom.

If we are wise enough to preserve the Union, we may for ages enjoy an advantage similar to that of an insulated situation. Europe is at a great distance from us. Her colonies in our vicinity will be likely to continue too much disproportioned in strength to be able to give us any dangerous annoyance. Extensive military establishments cannot, in this position, be necessary to our security. But if we should be disunited, and the integral parts should either remain separated, or which is most probable, should be thrown together into two or three confederacies, we should be in a short course of time in the predicament of the continental powers of Europe. Our liberties would be a prey to the means of defending ourselves against the ambition and jealousy of each other.

This is an idea not superficial nor futile, but solid and weighty. It deserves the most serious and mature consideration of every prudent and honest man of whatever party. If such men will make a firm and solemn pause, and meditate dispassionately on its vast importance; if they will contemplate it in all its attitudes, and trace it to all its consequences, they will not hesitate to part with trivial objections to a constitution, the rejection of which would in all probability put a final period to the Union. The airy phantoms that now flit before the distempered imaginations of some of its adversaries, would then quickly give place to the more substantial prospects of dangers, real, certain, and extremely formidable.

LETTERS FROM THE FEDERAL FARMER TO THE REPUBLICAN, No. 4

BY RICHARD HENRY LEE

Introduction

Richard Henry Lee (1732-94) was among the best known and most influential critics of the Constitution of 1787. Lee entered the Virginia House of Burgesses in 1758, and came to the forefront as a revolutionary leader when he took the initiative in organizing a county boycott—the Westmoreland Association—of British goods in protest against the Stamp Tax of 1765. In the following years the triumvirate of Lee, Jefferson and Patrick Henry exerted a deep influence over Virginia politics. In 1774 Lee was elected a delegate to the Continental Congress, and for much of the remainder of his life served in this capacity or as a member of the House of Delegates of his own state.

The Continental Congress appointed Lee as a delegate to the Constitutional Convention in 1787, but he declined to serve. His opposition to the new form of government was expressed in a series of five letters dated October 8 to 15, 1787, and published as a forty-page pamphlet in New York that same year under the title Letters from the Federal Farmer to the Republican.* Letter No. 4, which deals with the question of a Bill of Rights, is reproduced below. The opening portion of this letter deals with matters that have no relationship to the main topic, and is therefore omitted.

---

* The full title is: Observation leading to a fair examination of the system of government, proposed by the late Convention; and to several essential and necessary alterations in it. In a number of Letters from the Federal Farmer to the Republican. New York, 1787.

Letters from the Federal Farmer to the Republican, No. 4

October 12th, 1787

There are certain rights which we have always held sacred in the United States, and recognized in all our constitutions, and which, by the adoption of the new Constitution in its present form, will be left unsecured. By Article VI of the proposed Constitution,

> This Constitution, and the laws of the United States which shall be made in pursuance thereof; and all treaties made, or which shall be made, under the authority of the United States, shall be the supreme law of the land; and the Judges in every State shall be bound thereby, anything in the Constitution or laws of any State to the contrary notwithstanding.

It is to be observed that when the people shall adopt the proposed Constitution, it will be their last and supreme act; it will be adopted, not by the people of New Hampshire, Massachusetts, etc., but by the people of the United States; and wherever this Constitution, or any part of it, shall be incompatible with their ancient customs, rights, the laws or the constitutions heretofore established in the United States, it will entirely abolish them and do them away. And not only this, but the laws of the United States which shall be made in pursuance of the federal Constitution, will be also supreme laws, and wherever they shall be incompatible with those customs, rights, laws or constitutions heretofore established, they will also entirely abolish them and do them away.

By the article before recited, treaties also made under the authority of the United States, shall be the supreme law. It is not said that these treaties shall be made in pursuance of the Constitution, nor are there any constitutional bounds set to those who shall make them. The President and two-thirds of the Senate will be empowered to make treaties indefinitely, and when these treaties shall be made, they will also abolish all laws and state constitutions incompatible with them. This power in the President and Senate is absolute, and the Judges will be bound to allow full force to whatever rule, article, or thing the President and Senate shall establish by treaty. Whether it be practicable to set any bounds to those who make treaties, I am not able to say; if not, it proves that this power ought to be more safely lodged.

The federal Constitution, the laws of Congress made in pursuance of the Constitution, and all treaties, must have full force and effect in all parts of the United States; and all other laws, rights, and constitutions which stand in their way must yield. It is proper the national laws should be supreme, and superior to state or district laws; but then the national laws ought to yield to unalienable or fundamental rights, and national laws, made by a few men, should extend only to a few national objects.

This will not be the case with the laws of Congress. To have any proper idea of their extent, we must carefully examine the legislative, executive, and judicial powers proposed to be lodged in the general government, and consider them in connection with a general clause in Article I, section 8, in these words (after enumerating a number of powers):

> To make all laws which shall be necessary and proper for carrying into execution the foregoing powers, and all other powers vested by this Constitution in the government of the United States, or in any department or officer thereof.

The powers of this government, as has been observed, extend to internal as well as external objects, and to those objects to which all others are subordinate. It is almost impossible to have a just conception of their powers, or of the extent and number of the laws which may be deemed necessary and proper to carry them into effect, till we shall come to exercise those powers and make the laws. In making laws to carry those powers into effect, it is to be expected, that a wise and prudent Congress will pay respect to the opinions of a free people, and bottom their laws on those principles which have been considered as essential and fundamental in the British, and in our government. But a Congress of a different character will not be bound by the Constitution to pay respect to those principles.

It is said that when a people make a Constitution and delegate powers, that all powers not delegated by them to those who govern, are reserved in the people; and that the people, in the present case, have reserved in themselves, and in their state governments, every right and power not expressly given by the federal Constitution to those who shall administer the national government. It is said, on the other hand, that the people, when they make a constitution, yield all power not expressly reserved to themselves. The truth is, in either case, a mere matter of opinion, and men usually take either side of the argument, as will best answer their purposes. But the general presumption being, that men who govern will in doubtful cases construe laws and constitutions most favourably for increasing their own powers, all wise and prudent people, in forming constitutions, have drawn the line, and carefully described the powers parted with and the powers preserved. By the state constitutions, certain rights have been reserved in the people; or rather, they have been recognized and established in such a manner, that state legislatures are bound to respect them, and to make no laws infringing upon them. The state legislatures are obliged to take notice of the bills of rights of their respective states. The bills of rights, and the state constitutions, are fundamental compacts only between those who govern, and the people of the same state.

In the year 1788 the people of the United States made a federal Constitution, which is a fundamental compact between them and their federal rulers. These rulers, in the nature of things, cannot be bound to take notice of any other compact. It would be absurd for them, in making laws, to look over thirteen, fifteen, or twenty state constitutions, to see what rights are established as fundamental, and must not be infringed upon in making laws in the society. It is true, they would be bound to do it if the people, in their federal compact, should refer to the state constitutions, recognize all parts not consistent with the federal Constitution, and direct their federal rulers to take notice of them accordingly; but this is not the case as the plan stands proposed at present, and it is absurd to think so unnatural an idea is intended or implied.

I think my opinion is not only founded in reason, but I think it is supported by the report of the convention itself. If there are a number of rights established by the state constitutions, and which will remain sacred, and the general government is bound to take notice of them, it must take notice of one as well as another. And if [it were] unnecessary to recognize or establish one by the federal Constitution, it would be unnecessary to recognize or establish another by it. If the federal government is to be construed so far in connection with the state constitutions as to leave the trial by jury in civil causes, for instance, secured; on the same principles it would have left the trial by jury in criminal causes, the benefits of the writ of *habeas corpus*, etc., secured. They all stand on the same footing: they are the common rights of Americans, and have been recognized by the state constitutions. But the convention found it necessary to recognize or re-establish the benefits of that writ, and the jury trial in criminal cases.

As to *ex post facto* laws, the convention has done the same in one case and gone further in another. It is part of the compact between the people of each state and their rulers, that no *ex post facto* laws shall be made. But the convention, by Article I, section 10, have put a sanction upon this part even of the state compacts. In fact, the 9th and 10th sections in Article I, in the proposed Constitution, are no more nor less than a partial Bill of Rights; they establish certain principles as part of the compact upon which the federal legislators and officers can never infringe. It is here wisely stipulated, that the federal legislature shall never pass a bill of attainder, or *ex post facto* law; that no tax shall be laid on articles exported, etc. The establishing of one right implies the necessity of establishing another and similar one.

On the whole, the position appears to me to be undeniable, that this Bill of Rights ought to be carried further, and some other principles established, as a part of this fundamental compact between the people of the United States and their federal rulers.

It is true, we are not disposed to differ much at present about religion; but when we are making a Constitution, it is to be hoped for ages and millions yet unborn, why not establish the free exercise of religion as a part of the national compact?

There are other essential rights which we have justly understood to be the rights of freemen: as freedom from hasty and unreasonable search warrants, warrants not founded on oath and not issued with due caution, for searching and seizing men's papers, property, and persons.

The trial by jury in civil causes, it is said, varies so much in the several states, that no words could be found for the uniform establishment of it. If so, the federal legislation will not be able to establish it by any general laws. I confess I am of opinion it may be established, but not in that beneficial manner in which we may enjoy it, for the reasons before mentioned. When I speak of the jury trial of the vicinage, or the trial of the fact in the neighborhood, I do not lay so much stress upon the circumstance of our being tried by our neighbors. In this enlightened country men may be probably impartially tried by those who do not live very near them; but the trial of facts in the neighborhood is of great importance in other respects. Nothing can be more essential than the cross-examining witnesses, and generally before the triers of the facts in question. The common people can establish facts with much more ease with oral than written evidence; when trials of facts are removed to a distance from the homes of the parties and witnesses, oral evidence becomes intolerably expensive, and the parties must depend on written evidence, which to the common people is expensive and almost useless; it must be frequently taken *ex parte,* and but very seldom leads to the proper discovery of truth.

The trial by jury is very important in another point of view. It is essential in every free country, that common people should have a part and share of influence in the judicial as well as in the legislative department. To hold open to them the offices of senators, judges, and offices to fill which an expensive education is required, cannot answer any valuable purposes for them. They are not in a situation to be brought forward and to fill those offices; these, and most other offices of any considerable importance, will be occupied by the few. The few, the well born, etc., as Mr. Adams calls them, in judicial decisions as well as in legislation, are generally disposed, and very naturally too, to favor those of their own description.

The trial by jury in the judicial department, and the collection of the people by their representatives in the legislature, are those fortunate inventions which have procured for them, in this country, their true proportion of influence, and the wisest and most fit means of protecting themselves in the community. Their situation, as jurors and representatives, enables them to acquire information and knowledge in the affairs and government of the society; and to come forward, in turn, as the centinels and guardians of each other. I am very sorry that a few of our countrymen should consider jurors and representatives in a different point of view, as ignorant, troublesome bodies, which ought not to have any share in the concerns of government.

I confess I do not see in what cases the Congress can, with any pretence of right, make a law to suppress the freedom of the press; though I am not clear, that Congress is restrained from laying any duties whatever on printing, and from laying duties particularly heavy on certain pieces printed, and perhaps Congress may require large bonds for the payment of these duties. Should the printer say, the freedom of the press was secured by the constitution of the state in which he lived, Congress might, and perhaps, with great propriety, answer, that the federal Constitution is the only compact existing between them and the people; in this compact the people have named no others, and therefore Congress, in exercising the powers assigned them, and in making laws to carry them into execution, are restrained by nothing beside the federal Constitution, any more than a state legislature is restrained by a compact between the magistrates and people of a county, city, or town of which the people, in forming the state constitution, have taken no notice.

It is not my object to enumerate rights of inconsiderable importance; but there are others, no doubt, which ought to be established as a fundamental part of the national system.

It is worthy of observation, that all treaties are made by foreign nations with a confederacy of thirteen states; that the western country is joined to thirteen states; thirteen states have jointly and severally engaged to pay the public debts. Should a new government be formed of nine, ten, eleven, or twelve states, those treaties could not be considered as binding on the foreign nations who made them. However, I believe the probability will be, that if nine states adopt the Constitution, the others will.

It may also be worthy our examination, how far the provision for amending this plan, when it shall be adopted, is of any importance. No measures can be taken towards amendments, unless two-thirds of the Congress, or two-thirds of the legislature of the several states shall agree.

While power is in the hands of the people, or democratic part of the community, more especially as at present, it is easy, according to the general course of human affairs, for the few influential men in the community to obtain conventions, alterations in government, and to persuade the common people that they may change for the better, and to get from them a part of the power. But when power is once transferred from the many to the few, all changes become extremely difficult. The government, in this case, being beneficial to the few, they will be exceedingly artful and adroit in preventing any measures which may lead to a change; and nothing will produce it, but great exertions and severe struggles on the part of the common people.

Every man of reflection must see, that the change now proposed is a transfer of power from the many to the few, and the probability is, the artful and ever active aristocracy will prevent all peaceful measures for changes, unless when they shall discover some favourable moment to increase their own influence.

I am sensible, thousands of men in the United States are disposed to adopt the proposed Constitution, though they perceive it to be essentially defective, under an idea that amendments of it may be obtained when necessary. This is a pernicious idea. It argues a servility of character totally unfit for the support of free government; it is very repugnant to t'... perpetual jealousy respecting liberty, so absolutely necessary in all free states, spoken of by Mr. Dickinson. However, if our countrymen are so soon changed, and the language of 1774 is become odious to them, it will be in vain to use the language of freedom, or to attempt to rouse them to free enquiries. But I shall never believe this is the case with them, whatever present appearances may be, till I shall have very strong evidence indeed of it.

THE FEDERAL FARMER

Broadside
Ballads,
==1800-14=========================

Introduction

By 1800 the Federalists, as a political party, had played out their role. They had made notable contributions to the theory and organization of the new national government under the Constitution; but they had alienated large numbers of people who considered that too many of their policies were actuated by narrow and selfishly exclusive class interest. The imposition of an unpopular excise tax and the suppression of the rebellion against it in 1794; Alexander Hamilton's bitterly controverted measures for funding the national debt; the establishment of a National Bank under private direction and control; the Jay treaty with England and the pursuit of a foreign policy openly hostile to France and only avoiding war with that country by the smallest of margins; and the Alien and Sedition Laws of 1798, one at least of which was clearly unconstitutional and an obvious flouting of the Bill of Rights—these and other examples gave point to the anti-Federalist argument that the ratification of the Constitution had brought upon the heads of the American people those dire evils of oligarchical and tyrannical rule which the opponents of the Constitution had predicted in the great debate of 1787-89.

The election of Thomas Jefferson to the presidency in 1800 and the passing of the Federalists from the political stage marked the triumph of a new popular mood. National feeling had begun to flower with a new ebullience, and it found a focus and a symbol in the Constitution and the Union as the expression of American unity and strength. These feelings were heightened by the War of 1812 against England. Whether it was a justifiable struggle or a tragic blunder—depending upon one's point of view—it showed that American fighters could beat Britain's best both on land and sea, and it fanned the fires of national pride to new heights.

The War of 1812 was, in an extremely practical way, a watershed in American history. It projected the United States into an era of rapid sectional development. Speeding up the breaking of Indian power in the lands between the Appalachians and the Mississippi, it accelerated the race for the settlement of the West that was before long to pit the slave system against the free. The last major international conflict in which the United States was involved prior to the outbreak of the Civil War, it inaugurated a period of nearly half a century of peacetime development.

The four songs chosen from the many created at this time illustrate the new mood of what might be termed American romantic nationalism. Jefferson and Liberty is a campaign song written for the election of 1800, expressing the thought that Jeffersonian America would be the best and freest land in the world and definitely the country of the future. The beautiful rousing melody is an Irish jig.

The Constitution and the Guerrière is a broadside set to the charming tune of an old English drinking song. It celebrates the famous encounter between the man-o'-war Constitution (Captain Isaac Hull) and the Guerrière (Captain James Dacres) on August 9, 1812. The Hunters of Kentucky tells the story of the greatest land victory of the war—Andrew Jackson's defeat of hardened British veterans at the battle of New Orleans on January 8, 1815. Written by Samuel Woodworth (1785-1842), this song became immensely popular during Andrew Jackson's presidency.

Johnny Bull my jo John is a swift recapitulation of the main events of the war. The melody, perhaps one of the loveliest that has come down to us from the olden days, is probably more than four hundred years old. Robert Burns composed a lyric which he set to this tune, and this appeared in the Scots Musical Museum in 1790, under the title John

Anderson my jo John. An earlier version of the song was in circulation in the colonies. It began:

> John Anderson my jo John
> I wonder what you mean,
> To lie so long in the morning
> And sit so long at e'en?
> You'll blear all your eye, John,
> And why should you do so?
> Come sooner to your bed at e'en,
> John Anderson, my jo.

This most likely furnished the inspiration for the song that was sung in the War of 1812.

JEFFERSON AND LIBERTY

The— gloom-y night be-fore us flies, The
reign of ter-ror now is o'er; Its gags, in-qui-si-
tors and spies, Its herds of harpies are no more.
Re-joice, Co-lum-bia's sons, re-joice; To
ty-rants ney-er bend the knee, But join with heart and
soul and voice For Jef-fer-son and lib-er-ty.

The gloomy night before us flies,
The reign of terror now is o'er;
Its gags, inquisitors and spies,
Its herds of harpies are no more.
  Rejoice, Columbia's sons, rejoice;
  To tyrants never bend the knee,
  But join with heart and soul and voice
  For Jefferson and liberty.

No lordling here with gorging jaws
Shall wring from industry the food;
Nor fiery bigots' holy laws
Lay waste our fields and streets in blood!
    Rejoice, Columbia's sons, rejoice; etc.

Here strangers from a thousand shores,
Compelled by tyranny to roam,
Shall find, amidst abundant stores,
A nobler and happier home.
    Rejoice, Columbia's sons, rejoice; etc.

Here art shall lift her laurel'd head,
Wealth, industry and peace divine;
And where dark, pathless forest spread,
Rich fields and lofty cities shine.
    Rejoice, Columbia's sons, rejoice; etc.

CONSTITUTION AND GUERRIÈRE

It oft-times has been told That the Brit-ish sea-men bold Could flog the tars of France so neat and han-dy O! But they nev-er met their match, 'Til the Yan-kees did them catch, O the Yan-kee boys for fight-ing Are the dan-dy O! O the Yan-kee boys for fight-ing Are the dan-dy O!

It ofttimes has been told
That the British seamen bold
Could flog the tars of France
        So neat and handy O!
But they never met their match
'Til the Yankees did them catch,
O the Yankee boys for fighting
        Are the dandy O!

The *Guerrière,* a frigate bold
On the foaming ocean rolled,
Commanded by Dacres
        The grandee O!
With as proud a British crew
As a rammer ever drew,
He could flog the Frenchmen two to one
        So handy O!

Then Dacres loudly cries
"Make this Yankee ship your prize,
You can do it in thirty minutes
        So neat and handy O!
Twenty-five's enough I'm sure
And if you'll do it in a score,
I'll treat you to a double share
        Of brandy O!"

The British shot flew hot,
Which the Yankees answered not,
'Till they got within a space they thought
        Was handy O!
"Now," Hull says to his crew,
"Boys lets see what you can do.
If we take this boasting Briton
        We're the dandy O!"

Then the first broadside we poured
Swept her mainmast by the board
Which made this lofty frigate look
        Abandoned O!

Then Dacres he did sigh,
And to his officers did cry
"Lord, I didn't think these Yankees
    Were so handy O!"

Our second told so well,
That their fore and mizzen fell
Which doused the royal ensign
    So neat and handy O!
"By George," says he, "we're done!"
And they fired a lee gun,
While the Yankees struck up Yankee
    Doodle Dandy O!

Now fill your glasses full,
And we'll drink a toast to Captain Hull,
And merrily we'll push around
    The brandy O!
John Bull may toast his fill,
Let the world say what it will,
But the Yankee boys for fighting
    Are the dandy O!

HUNTERS OF KENTUCKY

Ye gen-tle-men and la-dies fair who grace this fa-mous cit - y, Just lis-ten if you've time to spare, while I re-hearse a dit - ty; And for an op-por-tu-ni-ty, con- ceive your-selves quite luck - y, For 'tis not oft-en here you see a hun-ter from Ken-tuck-y.

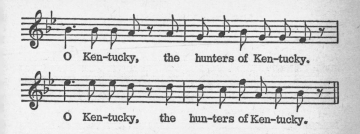

O Ken-tucky, the hunters of Ken-tucky.

O Ken-tucky, the hun-ters of Ken-tucky.

1

Ye gentlemen and ladies fair who grace this famous city,
Just listen if you've time to spare, while I rehearse a ditty;
And for an opportunity, conceive yourselves quite lucky,
For 'tis not often here you see a hunter from Kentucky.
    O Kentucky, the hunters of Kentucky.
    O Kentucky, the hunters of Kentucky.

2

We are a hardy freeborn race, each man to fear a stranger,
Whate'er the game, we join in chase, despising toil and danger;
And if a daring foe annoys, whate'er his strength and forces,
We'll show him that Kentucky boys are "alligator horses."
    O Kentucky, etc.

3

I s'pose you've read it in the prints how Packenham attempted
To make old hickory Jackson wince, but soon his schemes
    repented;
For we with rifles ready cock'd, thought such occasion lucky,
And soon around the hero flock'd the hunters of Kentucky.
    O Kentucky, etc.

4

You've heard I s'pose how New Orleans is fam'd for wealth
    and beauty,
There's girls of ev'ry hue it seems, from snowy white to sooty,
So Packenham he made his brags, if he in fight was lucky,
He'd have their girls and cotton bags, in spite of old Kentucky.
    O Kentucky, etc.

5

But Jackson he was wide awake, and wasn't scar'd at trifles,
For well he knew what aim we take with our Kentucky rifles;
So he led us down to Cypress swamp, the ground was low
and mucky,
There stood John Bull in martial pomp, and here was old
Kentucky.
O Kentucky, etc.

6

A bank was rais'd to hide our breast not that we thought of
dying,
But that we always like to rest, unless the game is flying:
Behind it stood our little force—none wish'd it to be greater,
For ev'ry man was half a horse, and half an alligator.
O Kentucky, etc.

7

They did not let our patience tire, before they show'd their
faces—
We did not choose to waste our fire, so snugly kept our places;
And when so near to see them wink, we thought it time to
stop 'em;
And 'twould have done you good I think, to see Kentuckians
drop 'em.
O Kentucky, etc.

8

They found at last 'twas vain to fight, where lead was all their
booty;
And so they wisely took to flight, and left us all our beauty,
And now if danger e'er annoys, remember what our trade is
Just send for us Kentucky boys, and we'll protect you, ladies.
O Kentucky, etc.

Johnny Bull, my jo John

O Johnny Bull, my jo John, I wonder what you mean;
Are you on foreign conquest bent, or what ambitious scheme?
Now list to brother Jonathan, your fruitless plans forego;
Remain on your fast-anchored isle, O Johnny Bull my jo.

O Johnny Bull, my jo John, don't come across the main;
Our fathers bled and suffered, John, our freedom to maintain,
And him who in the cradle, John, repelled the ruthless foe,
Provoke not when to manhood grown, O Johnny Bull my jo.

O Johnny Bull, my jo John, on Erie's distant shores,
See how the battle rages, and loud the cannon roars;
But Perry taught our seamen to crush the assailing foe,
He met and made them ours, O Johnny Bull my jo.

What though at Washington, a base marauding band,
Our monuments of art, John, destroyed with ruthless hand?
It was a savage warfare, beneath a generous foe,
And brings the more disgrace on you, O Johnny Bull my jo.

O Johnny Bull, my jo John, when all your schemes have failed,
To wipe away the stigmas, John, for New Orleans you sailed;
Far heavier woes await thee John, for Jackson meets the foe,
Whose name and fame's immortal, O Johnny Bull my jo.

Your schemes to gather laurels here I guess were badly
   planned;
We have whipped you on the ocean, jo, we have bothered you
   on land:
Then hie thee to Old England, John, thy fruitless plans forego,
And haste to thy fast-anchored isle, O Johnny Bull my jo.

Jacksonian America
=1814-1848=

The Jacksonian era, narrowly considered, is the period between 1829 and 1840 when Jackson, and after him Martin van Buren, were in the White House. But in the broader sense the period from 1814 to 1848—from the end of the War of 1812 to the end of the war with Mexico—has a unity that enables us to treat it as a whole and to give it the label "Jacksonian."

The conclusion of peace with Britain in 1814 released the huge energy of the American people and permitted it to be turned to peacetime pursuits: to the building of the nation, the development of its economy, and the settlement of its vast lands. Military and constitutional problems, dominant in the public mind for nearly half a century, became subordinate to the tasks of peace.

But in this new period national development assumed a sectional form. In three principal divisions of the United States—South and Southwest, Northwest, and Northeast—social advance assumed a form unique to that particular area, or section. The basis was laid for the conflict of sectional interest that erupted into repeated national and political crises.

In the Northeast the industrial revolution began to take hold, laying the foundations for the titanic technological advances of the Civil War and later days. If the economic changes occurring principally in New York, New Jersey, Pennsylvania and New England were on a small scale in comparison to what was to come, they were nonetheless of the first order of significance for that day, and had a deep impact upon the social order. Factories were built to produce guns, clocks, hardware and textiles for the expanding western market; a vast new communication network of roads, railroads and canals was laid; water- and then steampower was harnessed to drive machines; cities sprang up as swarms of starving immigrants came from across the Atlantic to provide the crude labor for the whole process.

Industrialization involved not only economic advances but moral and social problems. This was a period of rapid social change, when old landmarks were being swept away and traditional morality undermined. Slum housing, drunkenness, prostitution, long hours of grueling work, unemployment, starvation and crime, all followed in the wake of industry and urbanization. A new greed of gain was abroad in the land, clearly sacrificing human life, liberty and happiness to the pursuit of Mammon. Economic advances were being made in seeming disregard of the cost in terms of the human wastage and degradation, the human sickness and suffering that was involved.

Hence the appearance, in literature and in life, of a new and critical concern with the evils of the social order; and hence the rise of speculation concerning the nature of a just society and the means to be taken to achieve it. This aspect of Jacksonian America is introduced below under the heading "The Transcendental Revolt."

In the South events were taking place that would cut short the generalized Northern concern for social justice, and would channel that concern into one specific, all-absorbing direction. As we have seen (pp. 167-8), the Revolutionary period had witnessed a certain division of opinion among slaveholders. Whereas rice and cotton planters on the Georgia and Carolina coasts were driving a thriving business, tobacco planters in Virginia were facing an economic crisis compounded by an overextension of tobacco production, exhaustion of tobacco-growing lands, and a chronic collapse of tobacco prices on the international market. This crisis was aptly expressed by Jefferson when he wrote:

> "The value of the slave is every day lessening; his burthen on his master daily increasing. Interest is therefore preparing the disposition to be just; and this will be goaded from time to time by the insurrectionary spirit of the slaves." [1]

Jefferson himself believed that the slavery question would ultimately be resolved throughout the South in the same manner that it was then being resolved in the North: namely, by gradual manumission of the slaves and a gradual fading away of the institution of slavery. Unhappily the sharp rise in the demand for raw cotton, generated by the development of industrialism in Britain, provided a solution of a different sort for the South's economic crisis and for its superfluity of slaves. Cotton became a Southern crop, and the production of sugar, rice and tobacco took an entirely

[1] To William A. Burwell: Washington, D.C., Jan. 28, 1805. *Thomas Jefferson's Farm Book* (Princeton, 1953), p. 20.

secondary place. The end of the War of 1812, and the simultaneous destruction of Indian power in the Southwest, witnessed a vast and rapid extension of cotton acreage in the deep South, and a huge increase in the number of slaves employed in the planting of cotton. The Jacksonian era, therefore, was characterized, not by the gradual eradication of slavery as a major American problem, but by its extension throughout a cotton kingdom of vast dimensions that stretched from South Carolina to Texas.

Utimately this formidable and expanding slave power was to lay claim not merely to United States territories, but to control of the Union itself. Thereby it would pose a moral crisis for the American people and their democracy—a crisis of survival in the most fundamental sense as it contradicted the political assumptions of the Declaration of Independence, the Constitution, the Bill of Rights and the basic traditions of American law and of Christian morality.

If this fact only became clear to large numbers of people over a period of years, the significance of the regeneration of slavery and its political implications for the entire American people were grasped quickly by a minority. From this comprehension, and the sense of urgency and national danger which it generated, arose the antislavery movement. The latter gave rise, in the Jacksonian period, to an enormous literature designed to educate and alert the American people with respect to the moral evil and the political peril which the new, hydra-headed monster in the South presented.

Antislavery agitation was shaped in part by the requirements of a running battle that had to be waged with its proslavery antagonists. By the mid '30's Southern proslavery spokesmen were aware that their peculiar institution was under formidable attack. Not only was slavery coming under the hostile scrutiny of both Northern and Southern critics, but in the international arena the tide was moving strongly against the system of bondage and the infamous traffic in slaves. In Haiti the French slave empire had collapsed under the blows of the slave insurrection in 1790. As for Britain, she had outlawed the slave trade in 1807, and declared the emancipation of her West Indian slaves in 1833. Slavery, thought Southerners, must be defended as aggressively as it was being attacked if it were to survive.

This aspect of Jacksonian life is dealt with (p. 305), under the heading "Slavery and Civil Rights." This was the struggle that, in the fullness of time, would absorb the energies and the very lives of the North's most dedicated leaders and intellectuals.

The advance of slavery into the West raised a question which as time went by Northerners posed ever more insistently. By what right, they asked, did slaveowners take their human chattels into United States territory which had been acquired by war or purchase? By 1848 this had become the central question of American political life. The answer to it involved the nature of the Union itself. It was debated in a number of political crises throughout the Jacksonian period and did not receive its final settlement until the conclusion of the Civil War.

The first of these successive crises broke in 1819 when Missouri applied for admission to the Union. The acquisition of the vast Louisiana Territory from France in 1803, and the establishment of definite boundaries to the area acquired as a result of treaties with Spain and England in 1818-19, raised a new issue: How was Louisiana to be organized? Was slavery to be permitted in the newly acquired territory or was it to be banned? Missouri's application for statehood posed such questions, and it took two years' debate to effectuate a compromise. The disputed territory was divided into free and slave, and, more important, the principle was established that such a division of newly acquired territory was a proper procedure.

But the North-South conflict was too deep-seated to be laid to rest for very long. It broke out again in the late '20's, this time over the tariff question. Ostensibly the issue involved was clear and limited: Did the Federal government have the right to impose a protective tariff giving Northern industry and commerce economic advantages at the expense of consumers in general and specifically of Southerners? And did the Federal government have the right to allocate the revenue so collected to "internal improvements"—to the building of roads and canals that might further benefit one section at the expense of another? But underlying such questions were even more fundamental issues: Who, in the last resort, was to control the Federal Government? A Northern free-state majority, already rapidly outstripping the South in wealth and population? Or a Southern slaveowning minority, concerned above all else either to control Federal policies or to establish safeguards for its "minority rights" against the encroachments of the majority? In the struggle over the tariff, which came to a head in 1832-33, proslavery interests were sharpening the weapons of nullification and secession against the day when the Union would no longer permit itself to be used as an instrument for the advancement of proslavery policies. The great constitutional issues thus raised are dealt with below in the section headed "Nature of the Union."

Jacksonian America was an era of vast energy, rapid expansion, rapid change and colorful movement. The great westward thrust of that time began with emigrants from western Europe and ended in California. The mood of the period and the experience of the ordinary man may be fathomed in the songs that people composed and sang to tell of the days that they lived through and the deeds they did. Representative lyrics and ballads of the period are included in the group entitled "Westward by Land and by Sea."

The Transcendental Revolt

SERMON DELIVERED AT THE ORDINATION OF THE REV. JARED SPARKS TO THE PASTORAL CARE OF THE FIRST INDEPENDENT CHURCH IN BALTIMORE, MAY 5, 1819

BY WILLIAM ELLERY CHANNING

Introduction

Far into the nineteenth century religious awakenings continued to blaze a path through rural, westward-moving America. They fulfilled the traditional function of bringing the unchurched—particularly in pioneer settlements—into the church, and organizing its administration. Through these revival meetings the traditional Puritan doctrine of the innate depravity of man continued to be preached. The sermons warned of the vengefulness of a righteous God, and the imminence of the fires of hell as the wages of an unrepentant sinner.

Such doctrines, as time went by, became increasingly repugnant to Bostonians. From the very beginning Boston had developed as an urban civilization. Its sophistication was enhanced by its growing wealth and prosperity, by the breadth of its international contacts, both commercial and cultural, and by the application of a calculating, scientific and rationalist approach to the affairs of life. Bold new speculation over the course of years, from the time of the Great Awakening and even earlier, began to sap the intellectual pillars of Puritan orthodoxy. Original sin, man's innate depravity, freedom of the human will, the improvability of human nature and the concept of God himself as a vengeful rather than a benevolent being—all these ideas were re-examined. Step by step the outlines of a humane, liberal and, from the Puritan viewpoint, quite heretical theology, began to emerge.

The demolition of orthodox Calvinism, long in preparation, was formally accomplished in the early years of the nineteenth century under the auspices of William Ellery Channing (1780-1842). Channing, one of the intellectual giants of his day, was the pastor of the Federal Street Church in Boston since 1803; he was also—with the delivery of the Baltimore sermon of 1819 reproduced in full below—the recognized leader of New England liberalism and its humanitarian creed.

This sermon was an event of epoch-making significance in American intellectual history. A declaration of war upon traditionalist doctrine and the age-old tenets of Calvinist religion, it marked the advance and accelerated the triumph of liberal and humanist religious thought among the Bostonian elite. It was important not so much because it shattered the old faith—already, as we have pointed out, undermined by nearly a century of rationalist criticism—as because it opened the way to new and impressive perspectives of social thought. "His clear and comprehensive statement of faith in human power and dignity," writes one of Channing's biographers, "and his brilliant defense of human reason and rectitude, gave strength to the principles of a moral Christianity that was congenial to the interests and the ideals of a new age." [1]

The teaching of Calvinism centered around the doctrines of the Trinity, the total depravity of human nature, predestination, and the infallibility of the Bible. It was against these four basic points that Channing directed his onslaught.

Calvinists had never challenged the traditional Catholic belief that the divinity consisted of three persons in one— Father, Son and the Holy Ghost. The implication of this belief was that God, in interceding with himself on behalf of man, had been crucified upon the Roman cross. But if Christ was God, and therefore not human, this underlined the imperfectibility of man. If, on the other hand, Christ was human—partaking of the divine spirit only in the same way that other men do—then his sacrifice exalted the possibility of human choice, human growth and human perfection. For Channing, therefore, casting out Trinitarian doctrine was a central necessity in terms of his affirmation of a liberal and humane view of man.

Calvinists taught—and here again, they were in agreement with the Catholics—that human nature was essentially weak, sinful and depraved. According to this doctrine the evil in man stemmed from the original Promethean act of eating the forbidden apple from the Tree of Knowledge. As a result of this sin man lost his virtue and was doomed forever to labor in the sweat of his brow and to suffer torments of divine punishment in retribution for his evil nature and for the evil acts that followed necessarily from that nature.

Was salvation possible for man, inheriting such an evil nature and the predisposition to sin? Here the Calvinists had departed radically from the teachings of Catholicism. The Catholic Church had worked out, over the centuries, the doctrine that salvation was possible for all men so long as they were received into the Church, accepted its sacraments, and strove for a penitential life on earth and for the intercession of the saints in Heaven. Calvinism dourly rejected this perspective; had it not, for centuries, provided a harvest of gold and power for the Catholic priesthood, the self-constituted guardians of the gates of Heaven?

But, rejecting the Catholic solution, they were driven back logically to an acceptance of the iron necessities flowing from

[1] Arthur W. Brown, *Always Young for Liberty* (Syracuse, N.Y., 1956), p. 134.

the premise of original sin. Man, they taught, could not receive grace, achieve repentance, or set about spiritual regeneration without outside help, without the intervention of God. But whom would God decide to save? If all, then there was no sense in striving for morality or salvation; but if only some, how was such an essentially arbitrary act to be rationalized or explained? The acceptance of predestination logically involved an impossible dilemma. Liberal theology found it both more rational and more realistic to teach that man is endowed with freedom of will: that he may by his own choice avail himself of God's grace, by his own efforts redeem himself from sin and perfect the fallible nature with which he is endowed.

The authority of the Catholic Church had been based, not so much upon the Scriptures, but upon centuries of tradition and the steady accumulation of ecclesiastical law and doctrine. When the Protestants broke loose from the Church they jettisoned its vast authority along with the institution itself. They were driven, out of necessity, to base their new teachings and institutions, not upon the force of historical law and precedent, but upon the single authority of the Bible. The Bible at once assumed in Protestant eyes a supernatural significance and a central role entirely foreign to Catholic practice. The Bible, said the Protestants, revealed the meaning of history and the destiny of man. It was the sole repository of revealed truth. It was the word of God himself.

Nowhere is the advance of rationalism seen so clearly as in the approach of the liberal theologians, and in particular of Channing, to the study of the Bible. Channing stated boldly that not all the parts of the Bible were of equal merit; and he characterized "the dispensation of Moses" as "imperfect, earthly, obscure, adapted to the childhood of the human race. . . ." As for the New Testament, which he considered to be the foundation of the Christian religion, he insisted that the same standards of textual criticism be applied to it as to other texts whose meaning one wished to analyze and establish. "We profess," said he, "not to know a book, which demands a more frequent exercise of reason than the Bible . . . its style nowhere affects the precision of science, or the accuracy of definition."

SERMON DELIVERED AT THE ORDINATION
OF THE REV. JARED SPARKS*

The peculiar circumstances of this occasion not only justify, but seem to demand a departure from the course generally followed by preachers at the introduction of a brother into the sacred office. It is usual to speak of the nature, design, duties and advantages of the Christian ministry; and on these topics I should now be happy to insist, did I not remember that a minister is to be given this day to a religious society, whose peculiarities of opinion have drawn upon them much remark, and may I not add, much reproach. Many good minds, many sincere Christians, I am aware, are apprehensive that the solemnities of this day are to give a degree of influence to principles which they deem false and injurious. The fears and anxieties of such men I respect; and, believing that they are grounded in part on mistake, I have thought it my duty to lay before you as clearly as I can, some of the distinguishing opinions of that class of Christians in our country, who are known to sympathize with this religious society. I must ask your patience, for such a subject is not to be despatched in a narrow compass. I must also ask you to remember, that it is impossible to exhibit, in a single discourse, our views of every doctrine of revelation, much less the differences of opinion which are known to subsist among ourselves. I shall confine myself to topics on which our sentiments have been misrepresented, or which distinguish us most widely from others. May I not hope to be heard with candour? God deliver us all from prejudice, and unkindness, and fill us with the love of truth and virtue.

*Source: Channing's sermon was first published as a pamphlet in Baltimore in 1819. In this form it enjoyed a wide circulation. In revising this edition for later publication in Boston, Channing softened some of the polemical asperities, and also greatly expanded a number of important passages. The Baltimore version of the sermon is reproduced here, but significant additions or changes made in the Boston edition are given in appropriate footnotes. Passages omitted from the Boston edition are marked with square brackets.

The sources used for this purpose were:

(1) *A Sermon Delivered at the Ordination of the Rev. Jared Sparks to the Pastoral Care of the First Independent Church in Baltimore, May 5, 1819* (Baltimore, 1819).

(2) *Collected Works of William Ellery Channing* (Boston, 1841), Vol. III.

There are two natural divisions under which my thoughts will be arranged. I shall endeavour to unfold, first, the principles which we adopt in interpreting the Scriptures. And second, some of the doctrines which the Scriptures, so interpreted, seem to us clearly to express.

I

We regard the Scriptures as the records of God's successive revelations to mankind, and particularly of the last and most perfect revelations of his will by Jesus Christ. Whatever doctrines seem to us to be clearly taught in the Scriptures, we receive without reserve or exception. We do not, however, attach equal importance to all the books in this collection. Our religion, we believe, lies chiefly in the New Testament. The dispensation of Moses, compared with that of Jesus, we consider as imperfect, earthly, obscure, adapted to the childhood of the human race, a preparation for a nobler system, and chiefly useful now as serving to confirm and illustrate the Christian Scriptures. Jesus Christ is the only master of Christians, and whatever he taught, either during his personal ministry, or by his inspired apostles, we regard as of divine authority, and profess to make the rule of our lives.

This authority, which we give to the Scriptures, is a reason, we conceive, for studying them with peculiar care, and for inquiring anxiously into the principles of interpretation, by which their true meaning may be ascertained. The principles adopted by the class of Christians in whose name I speak, need to be explained, because they are often misunderstood. We are particularly accused of making an unwarrantable use of reason in the interpretation of Scripture. We are said to exalt reason above revelation, to prefer our own wisdom to God's. Loose and undefined charges of this kind are circulated so freely, and with such injurious intentions, that we think it due to ourselves, and to the cause of truth, to express our views with some particularity.

Our leading principle in interpreting Scripture is this, that the Bible is a book written for men, in the language of men, and that its meaning is to be sought in the same manner as that of other books. We believe that God, when he condescends to speak and write, submits, if we may so say, to the established rules of speaking and writing. How else would the

Scriptures avail us more than if communicated in an unknown tongue?

Now all books, and all conversation, require in the reader or hearer the constant exercise of reason; or their true import is only to be obtained by continual comparison and inference. Human language, you well know, admits various interpretations, and every word and every sentence must be modified and explained according to the subject which is discussed, according to the purposes, feelings, circumstances and principles of the writer, and according to the genius and idioms of the language which he uses. These are acknowledged principles in the interpretation of human writings; and a man, whose words we should explain without reference to these principles, would reproach us justly with a criminal want of candour, and an intention of obscuring or distorting his meaning.

Were the Bible written in a language and style of its own, did it consist of words, which admit but a single sense, and of sentences wholly detached from each other, there would be no place for the principles now laid down. We could not reason about it, as about other writings. But such a book would be of little worth; and perhaps, of all books, the Scriptures correspond least to this description. The word of God bears the stamp of the same hand, which we see in his works. It has infinite connections and dependencies. Every proposition is linked with others, and is to be compared with others, that its full and precise import may be understood. Nothing stands alone. The New Testament is built on the Old. The Christian dispensation is a continuation of the Jewish, the completion of a vast scheme of providence, requiring great extent of view in the reader. Still more, the Bible treats of subjects on which we receive ideas from other sources besides itself; such subjects as the nature, passions, relations, and duties of man; and it expects us to restrain and modify its language by the known truths which observation and experience furnish on these topics.

We profess not to know a book, which demands a more frequent exercise of reason than the Bible. In addition to the remarks now made on its infinite connections, we may observe, that its style nowhere affects the precision of science, or the accuracy of definition. Its language is singularly glowing, bold, and figurative, demanding more frequent departures from the literal sense, than that of our own age and country, and consequently demands more continual exercise of judgment. We find too, that the different portions of this book, instead of being confined to general truths, refer perpetually to the times when they were written, to states of society, to modes of thinking, to controversies in the church, to feelings and usages which have passed away, and without the knowledge of which we are constantly in danger of extending to all times, and places, what was of temporary and local application. We find, too, that some of these books are strongly marked by the genius and character of their respective writers, that the Holy Spirit did not so guide the apostles as to suspend the peculiarities of their minds, and that a knowledge of their feelings, and of the influences under which they were placed, is one of the preparations for understanding their writings. With these views of the Bible, we feel it our bounden duty to exercise our reason upon it perpetually, to compare, to infer, to look beyond the letter to the spirit, to seek in the nature of the subject, and the aim of the writer, his true meaning; and, in general, to make use of what is known, for explaining what is difficult, and for discovering new truths.

Need I descend to particulars to prove that the Scriptures demand the exercise of reason? Take, for example, the style in which they generally speak of God, and observe how habitually they apply to him human passions and organs. Recollect the declarations of Christ, that he came not to send peace, but a sword; that unless we eat his flesh, and drink his blood, we have no life in us; that we must hate father and mother, pluck out the right eye; and a vast number of passages equally bold and unlimited. Recollect the unqualified manner in which it is said of Christians, that they possess all things, know all things, and can do all things. Recollect the verbal contradiction between Paul and James, and the apparent clashing of some parts of Paul's writings with the general doctrines and end of Christianity. I might extend the enumeration indefinitely, and who does not see, that we must limit all these passages by the known attributes of God, of Jesus Christ, and of human nature, and by the circumstances under which they were written, so as to give the language a quite different import from what it would require, had it been applied to different beings, or used in different connections.

Enough has been said to show in what sense we make use of reason in interpreting Scripture. From a variety of possible interpretations, we select that which accords with the nature of the subject, and the state of the writer, with the connection of the passage, with the general strain of Scripture, with the known character and will of God, and with the obvious and acknowledged laws of nature. In other words, we believe that God never contradicts, in one part of Scripture, what he teaches in another; and never contradicts, in revelation, what he teaches in his works and providence. And we, therefore, distrust every interpretation, which, after deliberate attention, seems repugnant to any established truth. We reason about the Bible precisely as civilians do about the Constitution under which we live; who, you know, are accustomed to limit one provision of that venerable instrument by others, and to fix the precise import of its parts by inquiring into its general spirit, into the intentions of its authors, and into the prevalent feelings, impressions, and circumstances of the time when it was framed. Without these principles of interpretation, we frankly acknowledge, that we cannot defend the divine authority of the Scriptures. Deny us this latitude, and we must abandon this book to its enemies.

We do not announce these principles as original, or peculiar to ourselves; all Christians occasionally adopt them, not excepting those, who most vehemently decry them, when they happen to menace some favourite article of their creed. All Christians are compelled to use them in their controversies with infidels. All sects employ them in their warfare with one another. All willingly avail themselves of reason, when it can be pressed into the service of their own party, and only complain of it, when its weapons wound themselves. None reason more frequently than our adversaries. It is astonishing what a fabric they rear from a few slight hints about the fall of our first parents; and how ingeniously they extract from detached passages mysterious doctrines about the divine nature. We do not blame them for reasoning so abundantly, but for violating the fundamental rules of reasoning, for sacrificing the plain to the obscure, and the general strain of Scripture to a scanty number of insulated texts.

We object strongly to the contemptuous manner in which human reason is often spoken of by our adversaries, because it leads, we believe, to universal scepticism. If reason be so dreadfully darkened by the fall, that its most decisive judgments on religion are unworthy of trust, then Christianity, and even natural theology, must be abandoned; for the existence and veracity of God, and the divine original of Christianity, are conclusions of reason, and must stand or fall with it. If revelation be at war with this faculty, it subverts itself, for the great question of its truth is left by God to be decided at the bar of reason. It is worthy of remark, how nearly the bigot and the sceptic approach. Both would annihilate our confidence in our faculties, and both throw doubt and confusion over every truth. We honour revelation too highly to make it the antagonist of reason, or to believe that it calls us to renounce our highest powers.

We indeed grant, that the use of reason in religion, is accompanied with danger. But we ask any honest man to look back on the history of the church, and say, whether the renunciation of it be not still more dangerous. Besides, it is a plain fact, that men reason as erroneously on all subjects, as on religion. Who does not know the wild and groundless theories, which have been framed in physical and political science? But who ever supposed, that we must cease to exercise reason on nature and society, because men have erred for ages in explaining them? We grant, that the passions continually, and sometimes fatally, disturb the rational faculty in its inquiries into revelation. The ambitious contrive to find doctrines in the Bible, which favour their love of dominion. The timid and dejected discover there a gloomy system, and the mystical and fanatical, a visionary theology. The vicious can find examples or assertions on which to build the hope of a late repentance, or of acceptance on easy terms; the falsely refined contrive to light on doctrines which have not been soiled by vulgar handling. But the passions do not distract the reason in religious, any more than in other inquiries, which excite strong and general interest; and this faculty, of consequence, is not to be renounced in religion, unless we are prepared to discard it universally. The true inference from the almost endless errors, which have darkened theology, is not that we are to neglect and disparage our powers, but to exert them more patiently, circumspectly, uprightly. The worst errors, after all, have sprung up in that church which proscribes reason, and demands from its members implicit faith. The most pernicious doctrines have been the growth of the darkest times, when the general credulity encouraged bad men and enthusiasts to broach their dreams and inventions, and to stifle the faint remonstrances of reason, by the menaces of everlasting perdition. Say what we may, God has given us a rational nature, and will call us to account for it. We may let it sleep, but we do so at our peril. Revelation is addressed to us as rational beings. We may wish, in our sloth, that God had given us a system, demanding no labour of comparing, limiting and inferring. But such a system would be at variance with the whole character of our present existence; and it is the part of wisdom to take revelation, as it is given to us, and to interpret it by the help of the faculties, which it everywhere supposes, and on which it is founded.

To the views now given, an objection is commonly urged from the character of God. We are told, that God being infinitely wiser than men, his discoveries will surpass human reason. In a revelation from such a teacher, we ought to expect propositions, which we cannot reconcile with one another, and which may seem to contradict established truths; and it becomes us not to question or explain them away, but to believe, and adore, and to submit our weak and carnal reason to the divine word. To this objection, we have two short answers. We say, first, that it is impossible that a teacher of infinite wisdom should expose those, whom he would teach, to infinite error. But if once we admit, that propositions, which in their literal sense appear plainly repugnant to one another, or to any known truth, are still to be literally understood and received, what possible limit can we set to the belief of contradictions? What shelter have we from the wildest fanaticism, which can always quote passages that in their literal and obvious sense give support to its extravagancies? How can the Protestant escape from transubstantiation, a doctrine most clearly taught us, if the submission of reason, now contended for, be a duty? How can we ever hold fast the truth of revelation, for if one apparent contradiction may be true, so may another, and the proposition, that Christianity is false, though involving inconsistency, may still be a verity.

We answer again, that, if God be infinitely wise, he cannot sport with the understandings of his creatures. A wise teacher discovers his wisdom in adapting himself to the capacities of his pupils, not in perplexing them with what is unintelligible, not in distressing them with apparent contradiction, not in filling them with a sceptical distrust of their powers. An infinitely wise teacher, who knows the precise extent of our

minds, and the best method of enlightening them, will surpass
all other instructors in bringing down truth to our apprehension, and in showing its loveliness and harmony. We ought,
indeed, to expect occasional obscurity in such a book as the
Bible, which was written for past and future ages, as well
as for the present. But God's wisdom is a pledge, that whatever is necessary for *us*, and necessary for salvation, is revealed too plainly to be mistaken, and too consistently, to be
questioned by sound and upright mind. It is not the mark of
wisdom, to use an unintelligible phraseology, to communicate
what is above our capacities, to confuse and unsettle the intellect, by appearances of contradiction. We honour our
heavenly Teacher too much to ascribe to him such a revelation. A revelation is a gift of light. It cannot thicken our darkness and multiply our perplexities.

II

Having thus stated the principles according to which we
interpret Scriptures, I now proceed to the second great head
of this discourse, which is, to state some of the views which
we derive from that sacred book, particularly those which distinguish us from other Christians.

First: We believe in the doctrine of God's unity, or that
there is one God, and one only. To this truth we give infinite
importance, and we feel ourselves bound to take heed, lest any
man spoil us of it by vain philosophy. The proposition, *that
there is one God*, seems to us exceedingly plain. We understand by it, that there is one being, one mind, one person,
one intelligent agent, and one only, to whom underived and
infinite perfection and dominion belong. We conceive, that
these words could have conveyed no other meaning to the
simple and uncultivated people, who were set apart to be
the depositaries of this great truth, and who were utterly
incapable of understanding those hair-breadth distinctions
between *being* and *person*, which the sagacity of latter ages
has discovered. We find no intimation, that this language
was to be taken in an unusual sense, or that God's unity
was a quite different thing from the oneness of other intelligent beings.

We object to the doctrine of the Trinity, that it subverts the
unity of God.[1] According to this doctrine, there are three in-

---

[1] "That, whilst acknowledging in words, it subverts in effect the unity of
God."—Boston authorized edition.

finite and equal persons, possessing supreme divinity, called the Father, Son, and Holy Ghost. Each of these persons, as described by theologians, has his own particular consciousness, will, and perceptions. They love each other, converse with each other, and delight in each other's society. They perform different parts in man's redemption, each having his appropriate office, and neither doing the work of the other. The Son is mediator, and not the Father. The Father sends the Son, and is not himself sent; nor is he conscious, like the Son, of taking flesh. Here then, we have three intelligent agents, possessed of different consciousnesses, different wills, and different perceptions, performing different acts, and sustaining different relations; and if these things do not imply and constitute three minds or beings, we are utterly at a loss to know how three minds or beings are to be formed. It is difference of properties, and acts, and consciousness, which leads us to the belief of different intelligent beings, and if this mark fail us, our whole knowledge falls; we have no proof, that all the agents and persons in the universe are not one and the same mind. When we attempt to conceive of three Gods, we can do nothing more, than represent to ourselves three agents, distinguished from each other by similar marks and peculiarities to those, which separate the persons of the Trinity; and when common Christians hear these persons spoken of as conversing with each other, loving each other, and performing different acts, how can they help regarding them as different beings, different minds?

We do then, with all earnestness, though without reproaching our brethren, protest against the irrational and unscriptural doctrine of the Trinity. "To us," as to the apostle and the primitive Christians, "there is one God, even the Father." With Jesus, we worship the Father, as the only living and true God. We are astonished, that any man can read the New Testament, and avoid the conviction, that the Father alone is God. We hear our Saviour continually appropriating this character to the Father. We find the Father continually distinguished from Jesus by this title. "God sent his Son." "God anointed Jesus." Now, how singular and inexplicable is this phraseology, which fills the New Testament, if this title belong equally to Jesus, and if a principal object of this book is to reveal him as God, as partaking equally with the Father in supreme divinity. We challenge our opponents to adduce one passage in the New

Testament, where the word God means three persons, where it is not limited to one person, and where, unless turned from its usual sense by the connection, it does not mean the Father. Can stronger proof be given, that the doctrine of three persons in the Godhead, is not a fundamental doctrine of Christianity?

This doctrine, were it true, must, from its difficulty, singularity, and importance, have been laid down with great clearness, guarded with great care, and stated with all possible precision. But where does this statement appear? From the many passages, which treat of God, we ask for one, one only, in which we are told, that he is a three-fold being, or, that he is three persons, or, that he is Father, Son, and Holy Ghost. On the contrary, in the New Testament, where, at least, we might expect many express assertions of this nature, God is declared to be one, without the least attempt to prevent the acceptation of the words in their common sense; and he is always spoken of and addressed in the singular number, that is, in language which was universally understood to intend a single person, and to which no other idea could have been attached, without an express admonition. So entirely do the Scriptures abstain from stating the Trinity, that when our opponents would insert it into their creeds and doxologies, they are compelled to leave the Bible, and to invent forms of words altogether unsanctioned by scriptural phraseology. That a doctrine so strange, so liable to misapprehension, so fundamental as this is said to be, and requiring such careful exposition, should be left so undefined and unprotected, to be made out by inference, and to be hunted through distant and detached parts of Scripture, this is a difficulty, which, we think, no ingenuity can explain.

We have another difficulty. Christianity, it must be remembered, was planted and grew up amidst sharp-sighted enemies, who overlooked no objectionable part of the system, and who must have fastened with great earnestness on a doctrine involving such apparent contradictions as the Trinity. We cannot conceive an opinion against which the Jews, who prided themselves on their adherence to God's unity, would have raised an equal clamour. Now, how happens it, that in the apostolic writings, which relate so much to objections against Christianity, and to the controversies, which grew out of this religion, not *one word* is said, implying that objections were brought against the gospel from the doctrine of the Trinity, not one word is uttered in its defence and explanation, not a

word to rescue it from reproach and mistake? This argument
has almost the force of demonstration. We are persuaded, that
had three divine persons been announced by the first preachers of Christianity, all equal, and all infinite, one of whom was
the very Jesus, who had lately died on a cross, this peculiarity
of Christianity would have almost absorbed every other, and
the great labour of the apostles would have been to repel the
continual assaults, which it would have awakened. But the
fact is, that not a whisper of objection to Christianity, on that
account, reaches our ears from the apostolic age. In the epistles we see not a trace of controversy called forth by the
Trinity.

We have further objections to this doctrine, drawn from its
practical influence. We regard it as unfavourable to devotion,
by dividing and distracting the mind in its communion with
God. It is a great excellence of the doctrine of God's unity,
that it offers to us *one object* of supreme homage, adoration
and love, one infinite Father, one Being of Beings, one original
and fountain, to whom we may refer all good, on whom all
our powers and affections may be concentrated, and whose
lovely and venerable nature may pervade all our thoughts.
True piety, when directed to an undivided Deity, has a chaste-
ness, a singleness, most favourable to religious awe and love.
Now the Trinity sets before us three distinct objects of supreme
adoration; three infinite persons, having equal claims on our
hearts; three divine agents, performing different offices, and to
be acknowledged and worshipped in different relations. And is
it possible, we ask, that the weak and limited mind of man
can attach itself to these with the same power and joy, as to
one infinite Father, the only first cause, in whom all the blessings of nature and redemption meet, as their centre and
source? Must not devotion be distracted by the equal and rival
claims of three equal persons, and must not the worship of
the conscientious, consistent Christian be disturbed by apprehension, lest he withhold from one or another of these, his
due proportions of homage?

We also think, that the doctrine of the Trinity injures devotion, not only by joining to the Father other objects of worship, but by taking from the Father the supreme affection,
which is his due, and transferring it to the Son. This is a most
important view. That Jesus Christ, if exalted into the infinite
Divinity, should be more interesting than the Father, is pre-

cisely what might be expected from history, and from the principles of human nature. Men want an object of worship like themselves, and the great secret of idolatry lies in this propensity. A God, clothed in our form, and feeling our wants and sorrows, speaks to our weak nature more strongly, than a Father in heaven, a pure spirit, invisible, and unapproachable, save by the reflecting and purified mind. We think too, that the peculiar office ascribed to Jesus by the popular theology, makes him the most attractive person in the Godhead. The Father is the depositary of the justice, the vindicator of the rights, the avenger of the laws of the Divinity. On the other hand, the Son, the brightness of the divine mercy, stands between the incensed deity and guilty humanity, exposes his meek head to the storms, and his compassionate breast to the sword of the divine justice, bears our whole load of punishment, and purchases with his blood every blessing which descends from heaven. Need we state the effect of these representations, especially on common minds, for whom Christianity was chiefly designed, and whom it seeks to bring to the Father, as the loveliest being? We do believe, that the worship of a bleeding, suffering God, tends strongly to absorb the mind, and to draw it from other objects, just as the human tenderness of the Virgin Mary has given her so conspicuous a place in the devotions of the church of Rome. We believe too, that this worship, though attractive, is not most fitted to spiritualize the mind, that it awakens human transport, rather than that deep veneration of the moral perfections of God, which is the essence of piety.

Second: Having thus given our views of the unity of God, I proceed to observe, that we believe in the *unity of Jesus Christ*. We believe that Jesus is one mind, one soul, one being, as truly one as we are, and equally distinct from the one God. We complain of the doctrine of the Trinity, that not satisfied with making God three beings, it makes Jesus Christ two beings, and thus introduces infinite confusion into our conceptions of his character. This corruption of Christianity, alike repugnant to common sense and to the general strain of Scripture, is a remarkable proof of the power of a false philosophy in disfiguring the simple truth of Jesus.

According to this doctrine, Jesus Christ, instead of being one mind, one conscious intelligent principle, whom we can understand, consists of two souls, two minds, the one divine, the other human; the one weak, the other almighty; the one ignorant, the other omniscient. Now we maintain, that this is to make Christ two beings. To denominate him one person, one being, and yet to suppose him made up of two minds, infinitely different from each other, is to abuse and confound language, and to throw darkness over all our conceptions of intelligent natures. According to the common doctrines, each of these two minds in Christ has its own consciousness, its own will, its own perceptions. They have in fact no common properties. The divine mind feels none of the wants and sorrows of the human, and the human is infinitely removed from the perfection and happiness of the divine. Can you conceive of two beings in the universe more distinct? We have always thought that one person was constituted and distinguished by one consciousness. The doctrine, that one and the same person should have two consciousnesses, two wills, two souls infinitely different from each other, this we think an enormous tax on human credulity.

We say, that if a doctrine, so strange, so difficult, so remote from all the previous conceptions of men, be indeed a part, and an essential part of revelation, it must be taught with great distinctness, and we ask our brethren to point to some plain, direct passage, where Christ is said to be composed of two minds infinitely different, yet constituting one person. We find none. Our opponents, indeed, tell us, that this doctrine is necessary to the harmony of the Scriptures, that some texts ascribe to Jesus Christ human, and others divine properties, and that to reconcile these, we must suppose two minds, to which these properties may be referred. In other words, for the purpose of reconciling certain difficult passages, which a just criticism can in a great degree, if not wholly, explain, we must invent an hypothesis vastly more difficult, and involving gross absurdity. We are to find our way out of a labyrinth by a clue, which conducts us into mazes infinitely more inextricable.

Surely if Jesus Christ felt that he consisted of two minds, and that this was a leading feature of his religion, his phraseology respecting himself would have been coloured by this peculiarity. The universal language of men is framed upon the idea, that one person is one mind, and one soul; and when the multitude heard this language from the lips of Jesus, they must have taken it in its usual sense, and must have referred to a single soul, all which he spoke, unless expressly instructed to interpret it differently. But where do we find this instruction? Where do you meet, in the New Testament, the phraseology which abounds in Trinitarian books, and which necessarily grew from the doctrine of two natures in Jesus? Where does this divine teacher say, This I speak as God, and this as man; this is true only of my human mind, this only of my divine? Where do we find in the epistles a trace of this strange phraseology? Nowhere. It was not needed in that day. It was demanded by the errors of a later age.

We believe then, that Christ is one mind, one being, and I add, a being distinct from the one God. That Christ is not the one God, not the same being with the Father, is a necessary inference from our former head, in which we saw that the doctrine of three persons in God is a fiction. But on so important a subject, I would add a few remarks. We wish, that our opponents would weigh one striking fact. Jesus, in his preaching, continually spoke of God. The word was always in his mouth. We ask, does he, by this word, ever mean himself? We say, *never*. On the contrary, he most plainly distinguishes between God and himself, and so do his disciples. How this is to be reconciled with the idea, that the manifestation of Christ, as God, was a primary object of Christianity, our adversaries must determine.

If we examine the passages in which Jesus is distinguished from God, we shall see, that they not only speak of him as another being, but seem to labour to express his inferiority. He is continually spoken of as the Son of God, sent of God, receiving all his powers from God, working miracles because God was with him, judging justly because God taught him, having claims on our belief, because he was anointed and sealed by God, and as able of himself to do nothing. The New Testament is *filled* with this language. Now we ask, what impression this language was fitted and intended to make? Could any, who heard it, have imagined, that Jesus was the *very God*, to whom he was so industriously declared to be inferior, the *very Being*, by whom he was sent, and from whom he professed to have received his message and power? Let it here be remembered, that the human birth, and bodily form, and humble circumstances, and mortal sufferings of Jesus, must all have prepared men to interpret, in the most unqualified manner, the language in which his inferiority to God was declared. Why then was this language used so continually, and without limitation, if Jesus were the supreme deity, and if this truth were an essential part of his religion? I repeat it, the human condition and sufferings of Christ, tended strongly to exclude from men's minds the idea of his proper Godhead; and of course, we should expect to find in the New Testament perpetual care and effort to counteract this tendency, to hold him forth as the same being with his Father, if this doctrine were, as is pretended, the soul and centre of his religion. We should expect to find the phraseology of Scripture cast into the mould of this doctrine, to hear familiarly of God the Son, of our Lord God Jesus, and to be told, that to us there is one God, even Jesus. But instead of this, the inferiority of Christ pervades the New Testament. It is not only implied in the general phraseology, but repeatedly and decidedly expressed, and unaccompanied with any admonition to prevent its application to his whole nature. Could it then have been the great design of the sacred writers, to exhibit Jesus as the supreme God?

I am aware, that these remarks will be met by two or three texts, in which Christ is called God, and by a class of passages, not very numerous, in which divine properties are said to be ascribed to him. To these we offer one plain answer. We say, that it is one of the most established and obvious principles of criticism, that language is to be explained according to the known properties of the subject to which it is applied. Every man knows, that the same words convey very different ideas, when used in relation to different beings. Thus, Solomon *built* the temple in a different manner from the architect, whom he employed; and God *repents* differently from man. Now, we maintain, that the known properties and circumstances of Christ, his birth, sufferings, and death, his constant habit of speaking of God as a distinct being from himself, his praying to God, his ascribing to God all his power and offices, these acknowledged properties of Christ, we say, oblige us to interpret the comparatively few passages, which are thought to make him the supreme God, in a manner consistent with his distinct and inferior nature. It is our duty to explain such texts by the rule, which we apply to other texts, in which human beings are called Gods, and are said to be partakers of the divine nature, to know and possess all things, and to be filled with all God's fulness. These latter passages we do not hesitate to modify, and restrain, and turn from the most obvious sense, because this sense is opposed to the known properties of the beings to whom they relate; and we maintain, that we adhere to the same principle, and use no greater latitude in explaining, as we do, the passages which are thought to support the Godhead of Christ.

Trinitarians profess to derive some important advantages from their mode of viewing Christ. It furnishes them, they tell us, with an infinite atonement, for it shows them an infinite being, suffering for their sins. The confidence with which this fallacy is repeated astonishes us. When pressed with the question, whether they really believe that the infinite and unchangeable God suffered and died on the cross, they acknowledge that this is not true, but that Christ's human mind alone sustained the pains of death. How have we then an infinite sufferer? This language seems to us an imposition on common minds, and very derogatory to God's justice, as if this attribute could be satisfied by a sophism and a fiction.

We are also told, that Christ is a more interesting object, that his love and mercy are more felt, when he is viewed as the supreme God, who left his glory to take humanity and to suffer for men. That Trinitarians are strongly moved by this representation, we do not mean to deny, but we think their emotions altogether founded on a misapprehension of their own doctrines. They talk of the second person of the Trinity leaving his glory, and his Father's bosom, to visit and save the world. But this second person, being the unchangeable and infinite God, was evidently incapable of parting with the least degree of his perfection and felicity. At the moment of his taking flesh, he was as intimately present with his Father as before, and equally with his Father filled heaven, and earth, and immensity. This, Trinitarians acknowledge, and still they profess to be touched and overwhelmed by the amazing humiliation of this immutable being! But not only does their doctrine, when fully explained, reduce Christ's humiliation to a fiction, it almost wholly destroys the impressions with which his cross ought to be viewed. According to their doctrine, Christ was, comparatively, no sufferer at all. It is true, his human mind suffered; but this, they tell us, was an infinitely small part of Jesus, bearing no more proportion to his whole nature, than a single hair of our heads to the whole body, or than a drop to the ocean. The divine mind of Christ, that which was most properly himself, was infinitely happy, at the very moment of the suffering of his humanity. Whilst hanging on the cross, he was the happiest being in the universe, as happy as the infinite Father; so that, his pains, compared with his felicity, were nothing. This Trinitarians do and must acknowledge. It follows necessarily from the immutableness of the divine nature, which they ascribe to Christ; so that their system, justly viewed, robs his death of interest, weakens our sympathy with his sufferings, and is, of all others, most unfavourable to a love of Christ, founded on a sense of his sacrifices for mankind.

We esteem our own views to be vastly more affecting [especially those of us, who believe in Christ's pre-existence]. It is our belief that Christ's humiliation was real and entire, that the whole Saviour, and not a part of him, suffered, that his crucifixion was a scene of deep and unmixed agony. As we stand round his cross, our minds are not distracted, or our sensibility weakened, by contemplating him as composed of incongruous and infinitely differing minds, and as having a balance of infinite felicity. We recognize in the dying Jesus but one mind. This, we think, renders his sufferings, and his patience and love in bearing them, incomparably more impressive and affecting than the system we oppose.

Third: Having thus given our belief on two great points, namely, that there is one God, and that Jesus Christ is a being distinct from, and inferior to God, I now proceed to another point on which we lay still greater stress. We believe in the *moral perfection of God.* We consider no part of theology so important as that which treats of God's moral character; and we value our views of Christianity chiefly as they assert his amiable and venerable attributes.

It may be said, that in regard to this subject, all Christians agree, that all ascribe to the supreme Being, infinite justice, goodness, and holiness. We reply, that it is very possible to speak of God magnificently, and to think of him meanly; to apply to his person high-sounding epithets, and to his government, principles which make him odious. The heathens called Jupiter the greatest and the best; but his history was black with cruelty and lust. We cannot judge of men's real ideas of God, by their general language, for in all ages, they have hoped to soothe the deity by adulation. We must inquire into their particular views of his purposes, of the principles of his administration, and of his disposition towards his creatures.

We conceive that Christians have generally leaned towards a very injurious view of the supreme Being. They have too often felt, as if he were raised, by his greatness and sovereignty, above the principles of morality, above those eternal laws of equity and rectitude, to which all other beings are subjected. We believe, that in no being, is the sense of right so strong, so omnipotent, as in God. We believe that his almighty power is entirely submitted to his perception of rectitude; and this is the ground of our piety. It is not because he is our Creator merely, but because he created us for good and holy purposes; it is not because his will is irresistible, but because his will is the perfection of virtue, that we pay him allegiance. We cannot bow before a being, however great and powerful, who governs tyrannically. We respect nothing but excellence, whether on earth, or in heaven. We venerate not the loftiness of God's throne, but the equity and goodness in which it is established.

We believe that God is infinitely good, kind, benevolent, in the proper sense of these words; good in disposition, as well as in act; good not to a few, but to all; good to every individual, as well as to the general system.

We believe too, that God is just; but we never forget, that his justice is the justice of a good being, dwelling in the same mind, and acting in harmony with perfect benevolence. By this attribute we understand God's infinite regard to virtue, or moral worth, expressed in a moral government; that is, in giving excellent and equitable laws, and in conferring such rewards, and inflicting such punishments, as are most fitted to secure their observance. God's justice has for its end the highest virtue of the creation, and it punishes for this end alone, and thus it coincides with benevolence; for virtue and happiness, though not the same, are inseparably conjoined.

God's justice thus viewed, appears to us to be in perfect harmony with his mercy. According to the prevalent systems of theology, these attributes are so discordant and jarring, that to reconcile them is the hardest task, and the most wonderful achievement of infinite wisdom. To us they seem to be intimate friends, always at peace, breathing the same spirit, and seeking the same end. By God's mercy, we understand not a blind instinctive compassion, which forgives without reflection, and without regard to the interests of virtue. This, we acknowledge, would be incompatible with justice, and also with enlightened benevolence. God's mercy, as we understand it, desires strongly the happiness of the guilty, but only through their penitence. It has a regard to character as truly as his justice. It defers punishment, and suffers long, that the sinner may return to his duty, but leaves the impenitent and unyielding to the fearful retribution threatened in God's word.

To give our views of God, in one word, we believe in his *parental character*. We ascribe to him, not only the name, but the dispositions and principles of a father. We believe that he has a father's concern for his creatures, a father's desire for their improvement, a father's equity in proportioning his commands to their powers, a father's joy in their progress, a father's readiness to receive the penitent, and a father's justice for the incorrigible. We look upon this world [2] as a place of education, in which he is training men by mercies and sufferings, by aids and temptations, by means and opportunities of various virtues, by trials of principle, by the conflicts of reason and passion, by a discipline suited to free and moral beings, for union with himself, and for a sublime and ever growing virtue in Heaven.

Now we object to the systems of religion, which prevail among us, that they are adverse, in a greater or less degree, to these purifying, comforting, and honourable views of God, that they take from us our Father in Heaven, and substitute for him a being, whom we cannot love if we would, and whom we ought not to love if we could. We object, particularly on this ground, to that system, which arrogates to itself the name of orthodoxy, and which is now most industriously propagated through our country. This system [3] teaches, that God brings us

---

[2] "We look upon this world as a place of education, in which he is training men by prosperity and adversity, by aids and obstructions, by conflicts of reason and passion, by motives to duty and temptations to sin, by a various discipline suited to free and moral beings for union with himself. . . ."

[3] "This system indeed takes various shapes, but in all it casts dishonor on the Creator. According to its old and genuine form, it teaches, that God brings us into life wholly depraved, so that under the innocent features of our childhood is hidden a nature averse to all good, and propense to all evil, a nature which exposes us to God's displeasure and wrath, even before we have acquired power to understand our duties, or to reflect upon our actions. According to a more modern disposition, it teaches, that we came from the hands of our Maker with such a constitution, are placed under such influences and circumstances, as to render certain and infallible the total depravity of every human being, from the first moment of his moral agency; and it also teaches, that the offence of the child, who brings into life this ceaseless tendency to unmingled crime, exposes him to the sentence of everlasting damnation. Now, according to the plainest principle of morality, we maintain, that a natural constitution of the mind, unfailingly disposing it to evil and evil alone, would

into existence wholly depraved, so that under the innocent features of our childhood, is hidden a nature averse to all good, and propense to all evil; and it teaches that God regards us with displeasure before we have acquired power to understand our duties, or reflect upon our actions. Now if there be one plain principle of morality, it is this, that we are accountable beings, only because we have conscience, a power of knowing and performing our duty, and that in as far as we want this power, we are incapable of sin, guilt, or blame. We should call a parent a monster, who should judge and treat his children in opposition to this principle, and yet this enormous immorality is charged on our Father in Heaven.

This system also teaches, that God selects from the corrupt mass of men a number to be saved, and that they are plucked, by an irresistible agency, from the common ruin, whilst the rest are commanded, under penalty of aggravated woe, to make a change in their characters, which their natural corruption places beyond their power, and are also promised pardon on conditions, which necessarily avail them nothing, unless they are favoured with a special operation of God's grace, which he is predetermined to withhold. This mockery of mercy, this insult offered to the misery of the non-elect, by hollow proffers of forgiveness, completes the dreadful system which is continually obtruded upon us as the gospel, and which strives to monopolize the reputation of sanctity.

That this religious system does not produce all the effects on character, which might be anticipated, we most joyfully admit. It is often, very often, counteracted by nature, conscience, common sense, by the general strain of Scripture, by the mild example and precepts of Christ, and by the many positive declarations of God's universal kindness, and perfect equity. But still we think that we see [occasionally] its unhappy influence. It discourages the timid, gives excuses to the bad, feeds the vanity of the fanatical, and offers shelter to the bad feelings of the malignant. By shocking, as it does, the fundamental principles of morality, and by exhibiting a severe and partial deity, it tends strongly to pervert the moral faculty, to form a gloomy, forbidding, and servile religion, and to lead men to substitute censoriousness, bitterness, and persecution,

absolve it from guilt; that to give existence under this condition would argue unspeakable cruelty; and that to punish the sin of this unhappily constituted child with endless ruin, would be a wrong unparalleled by the most merciless despotism."

for a tender and impartial charity. We think too, that this system, which begins with degrading human nature, may be expected to end in pride; for pride grows out of a consciousness of high distinctions, however obtained, and no distinction is so great as that, which is made between the elected and abandoned of God.

The false and dishonourable views of God, which have now been stated, we feel ourselves bound to resist unceasingly. Other errors we can pass over with comparative indifference. But we ask our opponents to leave to us a God, worthy of our love and trust, in whom our moral sentiments may delight, in whom our weaknesses and sorrows may find refuge. We cling to the divine perfections. We meet them everywhere in creation, we read them in the Scriptures, we see a lovely image of them in Jesus Christ; and gratitude, love, and veneration call on us to assert them. Reproached, as we often are, by men, it is our consolation and happiness, that one of our chief offences is the zeal with which we vindicate the dishonoured goodness and rectitude of God.

Fourth: Having thus spoken of the unity of God; of the unity of Jesus, and his inferiority to God; and of the perfections of the divine character; I now proceed to give our views of the *mediation of Christ* and *of the purposes of his mission*. With regard to the great object which Jesus came to accomplish, there seems to be no possibility of mistake. We believe, that he was sent by the Father to effect a moral, or spiritual deliverance of mankind; that is, to rescue men from sin and its consequences, and to bring them to a state of everlasting purity and happiness. We believe, too, that he accomplishes this sublime purpose by a variety of methods; by his instructions respecting God's unity, parental character, and moral government, which are admirably fitted to reclaim the world from idolatry and impiety, to the knowledge, love, and obedience of the Creator; by his promises of pardon to the penitent, and of divine assistance to those who labour for progress in moral excellence; by the light which he has thrown on the path of duty; by his own spotless example, in which the loveliness and sublimity of virtue shine forth to warm and quicken, as well as guide us to perfection; by his threatenings against incorrigible guilt; by his glorious discoveries of immortality; by his sufferings and death; by that signal event, the resurrection, which powerfully bore witness to his divine mission, and brought down to men's senses a future life; by his continual intercession, which obtains for us spiritual aid and blessings; and by the power with which he is invested of raising the dead, judging the world, and conferring the everlasting rewards promised to the faithful.

We have no desire to conceal the fact that a difference of opinion exists among us, in regard to an interesting part of Christ's mediation; I mean, in regard to the precise influence of his death on our forgiveness. Some suppose, that this event contributes to our pardon, as it was a principal means of confirming his religion, and of giving it a power over the mind; in other words, that it procures forgiveness by leading to that repentance and virtue, which is the great and only condition on which forgiveness is bestowed. Many of us are dissatisfied with this explanation, and think that the Scriptures ascribe the remission of sins to Christ's death, with an emphasis so peculiar, that we ought to consider this event as having a special influence in removing punishment, as a condition or method of pardon, without which, repentance would not avail us, at least to that extent, which is now promised by the gospel.

Whilst, however, we differ in explaining the connection between Christ's death and human forgiveness, a connection, which we all gratefully acknowledge, we agree in rejecting many sentiments, which prevail in regard to his mediation. The idea, which is conveyed to common minds by the popular system, that Christ's death has an influence in making God placable or merciful [in quenching his wrath], in awakening his kindness towards men, we reject with horror. We believe, that Jesus, instead of making the Father merciful, is sent by the Father's mercy to be our Saviour;[4] that he is nothing to the human race, but what he is by God's appointment; that he communicates nothing but what God empowers him to be-

---

[4] In the Boston edition, this sentence is considerably expanded and amplified. There it reads as follows:

"We are happy to find, that this very dishonorable notion is disowned by intelligent Christians of that class from which we differ. We recollect, however, that, not long ago, it was common to hear of Christ, as having died to appease God's wrath, and to pay the debt of sinners to his inflexible justice; and we have a strong persuasion, that the language of popular religious books, and the common mode of stating the doctrine of Christ's mediation, still communicate very degrading views of God's character. They give to multitudes the impression that the death of Jesus produces a change in the mind of God towards man, and that in this its efficacy chiefly consists. No error seems to us more pernicious. We can endure no shade over the pure goodness of God. We earnestly maintain, that Jesus, instead of calling forth, in any way or degree, the mercy of the Father, was sent by that mercy, to be our Saviour. . . ."

stow; that our Father in Heaven is originally, essentially and eternally placable, and disposed to forgive; and that his un-borrowed, underived, and unchangeable love, is the only foun-tain of what flows to us through his Son. We conceive, that Jesus is dishonoured, not glorified, by ascribing to him an in-fluence, which clouds the splendour of divine benevolence.

We farther agree in rejecting, as unscriptural and absurd, the explanation given by the popular system, of the manner in which Christ's death procures forgiveness for men. This sys-tem[5] teaches, that man having sinned against an infinite being, is infinitely guilty, and some even say, that a single transgres-sion, though committed in our early and inconsiderate years, merits the eternal pains of hell. Thus, an infinite penalty is due from every human being; and God's justice insists, that it shall be borne either by the offender, or a substitute. Now, from the nature of the case, no substitute is adequate to the work of sustaining the full punishment of a guilty world, save the infinite God himself; and accordingly, God took on him human nature, that he might pay to his own justice the debt of punishment incurred by men, and might enable himself to exercise mercy. Such is the prevalent system. Now, to us, this doctrine seems to carry on its front, strong marks of absurdity, and we maintain that Christianity ought not to be encumbered with it, unless it be laid down in the New Testament fully and expressly. We ask our adversaries, then, to point to some plain passages where it is taught. We ask for one text, in which we are told that God took human nature, that he might [appease his own anger towards men, or] make an infinite satisfaction to his own justice; for one text, which tells us, that human guilt

---

[5] This, and the two successive sentences, are greatly expanded in the Boston edition, which reads:

"This system used to teach as its fundamental principle, that man, having sinned against an infinite Being, has contracted infinite guilt, and is conse-quently exposed to an infinite penalty. We believe, however, that this reason-ing, if reasoning it may be called, which overlooks the obvious maxim, that the guilt of a being must be proportioned to his nature and powers, has fallen into disuse. Still the system teaches that sin, of whatever degree, exposes to endless punishment, and that the whole human race, being infallibly involved by their nature in sin, owe this awful penalty to the justice of their Creator. It teaches, that this penalty cannot be remitted, in consistency with the honor of the divine law, unless a substitute be found to endure it or to suffer an equivalent. It also teaches, that, from the nature of the case, no substitute is adequate to this work, save the infinite God himself; and accordingly God, in his second person, took on him human nature, that he might pay to his own justice the debt of punishment incurred by men, and might thus reconcile forgiveness with the claims and threatenings of his law. Such is the prevalent system."

is infinite, and requires a correspondent substitute; that Christ's sufferings owe their efficacy to their being borne by an infinite being; or that his divine nature gives infinite value to the sufferings of the human.

Not one word of this description can we find in the Scriptures; not a text, which even hints at these strange doctrines. They are altogether, we believe, the fictions of theologians. Christianity is in no degree responsible for them. We are astonished at their prevalence. What can be plainer, than that God cannot, in any sense, be a sufferer, or bear a penalty in the room of his creatures? How dishonourable to him is the supposition, that his justice is now so severe as to exact infinite punishment for the sins of frail and feeble men, and now so easy and yielding as to accept the limited pains of Christ's human soul, as a full equivalent for the infinite and endless woes due from the world? How plain is it also, according to this doctrine, that God, instead of being plenteous in forgiveness, never forgives; for it is absurd to speak of men as forgiven, when their whole punishment is borne by a substitute? A scheme more fitted to bring Christianity into contempt, and less suited to give comfort to a guilty and troubled mind, could not, we think, be easily invented.

We believe too, that this system is unfavourable to the character. It naturally leads men to think, that Christ came to change God's mind, rather than their own, that the highest object of his mission was to avert punishment, rather than to communicate holiness, and that a large part of religion consists in disparaging good works and human virtue, for the purpose of magnifying the value of Christ's vicarious sufferings. In this way, a sense of the infinite importance, and indispensable necessity of personal improvement is weakened, and high sounding praises of Christ's cross seem often to be substituted for obedience to his precepts. For ourselves, we have not so learned Jesus. Whilst we gratefully acknowledge, that he came to rescue us from punishment, we believe, that he was sent on a still nobler errand, namely, to deliver us from sin itself, and to form us to a sublime and heavenly virtue. We regard him as a Saviour, chiefly as he is the light, physician, and guide of the dark, diseased, and wandering mind. No influence in the universe seems to us so glorious, as that over the character; and no redemption so worthy of thankfulness, as the restoration of the soul to purity. Without this, pardon, were it possi-

ble, would be of little value. Why pluck the sinner from hell,
if a hell be left to burn in his own breast? Why raise him to
Heaven, if he remain a stranger to its sanctity and love? With
these impressions, we are accustomed to value the gospel
chiefly as it abounds in effectual aids, motives, excitements to
a generous and divine virtue. In this virtue, as in a common
centre, we see all its doctrines, precepts, promises meet; and
we believe that faith in this religion is of no worth, and contributes nothing to salvation, any farther than as it uses these
doctrines, precepts, promises, and the whole life, character,
sufferings, and triumphs of Jesus, as the means of purifying
the mind, of changing it into the likeness of his celestial excellence.

Fifth: Having thus stated our views of the highest object of
Christ's mission, that it is the recovery of men to virtue, or
holiness, I shall now, in the last place, give our views of the
nature of Christian virtue, or *true holiness*. We believe that all
virtue has its foundation in the moral nature of man, that is, in
conscience, or his sense of duty, and in the power of forming
his temper and life according to conscience. We believe that
these moral faculties are the grounds of responsibility, and the
highest distinctions of human nature, and that no act is praise-
worthy, any farther than it springs from their exertion. We believe, that no dispositions infused into us without our own
moral activity, are of the nature of virtue, and therefore, we
reject the doctrine of irresistible divine influence on the human
mind, moulding it into goodness, as marble is hewn into a
statue. Such goodness, if this word may be used, would not be
the object of moral approbation, any more than the instinctive
affections of inferior animals, or the constitutional amiableness
of human beings.

By these remarks, we do not mean to deny the importance
of God's aid or spirit; but by his spirit, we mean a moral, illu-
minating, and persuasive influence, not physical, not compulsory, not involving a necessity of virtue. We object, strongly, to the idea of many Christians respecting man's impotence
and God's irresistible agency on the heart, believing that they
subvert our responsibility and the laws of our moral nature,
that they make men machines, that they cast on God the blame
of all evil deeds, that they discourage good minds, and inflate
the fanatical with wild conceits of immediate and sensible inspiration.

Among the virtues, we give the first place to the *love of God*. We believe, that this principle is the true end and happiness of our being, that we were made for union with our Creator, that his infinite perfection is the only sufficient object and true resting place for the insatiable desires and unlimited capacities of the human mind, and that without him, our noblest sentiments, admiration, veneration, hope, and love, would wither and decay. We believe too, that the love of God is not only essential to happiness, but to the strength and perfection of all the virtues; that conscience, without the sanction of God's authority and retributive justice, would be a weak director; that benevolence, unless nourished by communion with his goodness, and encouraged by his smile, could not thrive amidst the selfishness and thanklessness of the world; and that self government, without a sense of the divine inspection, would hardly extend beyond an outward and partial purity. God, as he is essentially goodness, holiness, justice, and virtue, so he is the life, motive, and sustainer of virtue in the human soul.

But whilst we earnestly inculcate the love of God, we believe that great care is necessary to distinguish it from counterfeits. We think that much which is called piety is worthless. Many have fallen into the error that there can be no excess in feelings, which have God for their object; and, distrusting as coldness that self-possession, without which virtue and devotion lose all their dignity, they have abandoned themselves to extravagancies, which have brought contempt on piety. Most certainly, if the love of God be that, which often bears its name, the less we have of it, the better. If religion be the shipwreck of understanding, we cannot keep too far from it. On this subject, we always speak plainly. We cannot sacrifice our reason to the reputation of zeal. We owe it to truth and religion, to maintain, that fanaticism, partial insanity, sudden impressions, and ungovernable transports, are anything, rather than piety.

We conceive, that the true love of God, is a moral sentiment, founded on a clear perception, and consisting in a high esteem and veneration of his moral perfections. Thus, it perfectly coincides, and is in fact the same thing with the love of virtue, rectitude, and goodness. You will easily judge, then, what we esteem the surest and only decisive signs of piety. We lay no stress on strong excitements. We esteem *him,* and *him only* a pious man, who practically conforms to God's moral perfections and government, who shows his delight in God's benevolence, by loving and serving his neighbour; his delight in God's justice, by being resolutely upright; his sense of God's purity, by regulating his thoughts, imagination, and desires; and whose conversation, business, and domestic life are swayed by a regard to God's presence and authority. In all things else men may deceive themselves. Disordered nerves may give them strange sights, and sounds, and impressions. Texts of Scripture may come to them as from heaven. Their whole souls may be moved, and their confidence in God's favour be undoubting. But in all this there is no religion. The question is, do they love God's commands, in which his character is fully displayed, and give up to these their habits and passions? Without this, ecstacy is a mockery. One surrender of desire to God's will, is worth a thousand transports. We do not judge of the bent of men's minds by their raptures, any more than we judge of the natural direction of a tree during a storm. We rather suspect loud profession, for we have observed, that deep feeling is generally noiseless, and least seeks display.

We would not, by these remarks, be understood as wishing to exclude from religion warmth, and even transport. We honour, and highly value, true religious sensibility. We believe, that Christianity is intended to act powerfully on our whole nature, on the heart as well as the understanding and the conscience. We conceive of heaven as a state where the love of God will be exalted into an unbounded fervour and joy; and we desire, in our pilgrimage here, to drink into the spirit of that better world. But we think, that religious warmth is only to be valued, when it springs naturally from an improved character, when it comes unforced, when it is the recompense of obedience, when it is the warmth of a mind which understands God by being like him, and when, instead of disordering, it exalts the understanding, invigorates conscience, gives a pleasure to common duties, and is seen to exist in connection with cheerfulness, judiciousness, and a reasonable frame of mind. When we observe a fervour, called religious, in men whose general character expresses little refinement and elevation, and whose piety seems at war with reason, we pay it little respect. We honour religion too much to give its sacred name to a feverish, forced, fluctuating zeal, which has little power over the life.

Another important branch of virtue, we believe to be love of Christ. The greatness of the work of Jesus, the spirit with which he executed it, and the sufferings which he bore for our salvation, we feel to be strong claims on our gratitude and veneration. We see in nature no beauty to be compared with the loveliness of his character, nor do we find on earth a benefactor to whom we owe an equal debt. We read his history with delight, and learn from it the perfection of our nature. We are particularly touched by his death, which was endured for our redemption, and by that strength of charity, which triumphed over his pains. His resurrection is the foundation of our hope of immortality. His intercession gives us boldness to draw nigh to the throne of grace, and we look up to heaven with new desire, when we think, that if we follow him here, we shall there see his benignant countenance, and enjoy his friendship for ever.

I need not express to you our views on the subject of the *benevolent virtues*. We attach such importance to these, that we are sometimes reproached with exalting them above piety. We regard the spirit of love, charity, meekness, forgiveness, liberality, and beneficence, as the badge and distinction of Christians, as the brightest image we can bear of God, as the best proof of piety. On this subject, I need not, and cannot enlarge, but there is one branch of benevolence which I ought not to pass over in silence, because we think that we conceive of it more highly and justly, than many of our brethren. I refer to the duty of candour, charitable judgment, especially towards those who differ in religious opinion. We think, that in nothing have Christians so widely departed from their religion, as in this particular. We read with astonishment and horror, the history of the church, and sometimes when we look back on the fires of persecution, and the zeal of Christians in building up walls of separation, and in giving up one another to perdition, we feel as if we were reading the records of an infernal, rather than a heavenly kingdom. An enemy to our religion, if asked to describe a Christian, would, with some show of reason, depict him as an idolater of his own distinguishing opinions, covered with badges of party, shutting his eyes on the virtues, and his ears on the arguments of his opponents, arrogating all excellence to his own sect, and all saving power to his own creed, sheltering under the name of pious zeal the love of domination, the conceit of infallibility, and the spirit of intolerance, and trampling on men's rights under the pretence of saving their souls.

We can hardly conceive of a plainer obligation on beings of our frail and fallible nature, who are instructed in the duty of candid judgment, than to abstain from condemning men of apparent conscientiousness and sincerity, who are chargeable with no crime but that of differing from us in the interpretation of the Scriptures, and differing, too, on topics of great and acknowledged obscurity. We are astonished at the hardihood of those, who, with Christ's warnings sounding in their ears, take on them the responsibility of making creeds for his church, and cast out professors of virtuous lives for imagined errors, for the guilt of thinking for themselves. We know that zeal for truth is the cover for this usurpation of Christ's prerogative; but we think that zeal for truth, as it is called, is very suspicious, except in men, whose capacities and advantages, whose patient deliberations, and whose improvements in humility, mildness, and candour, give them a right to hope that their views are more just, than those of their neighbours. Much of what passes for a zeal for truth, we look upon with little respect, for it often appears to thrive most luxuriantly where other virtues shoot up thinly and feebly; and we have no gratitude for those reformers, who would force upon us a doctrine, which has not sweetened their own tempers, or made them better men than their neighbours.

We are accustomed to think much of the difficulties attending religious inquiries; difficulties springing from the slow development of our minds, from the power of early impressions, from the state of society, from human authority, from the general neglect of the reasoning powers, from the want of just principles of criticism, and of important helps in interpreting Scriptures, and from various other causes. We find, that on no subject have men, and even good men, engrafted so many strange conceits, wild theories, and fictions of fancy, as on religion, and remembering, as we do, that we ourselves are sharers of the common frailty, we dare not assume infallibility in the treatment of our fellow Christians, or encourage in common Christians, who have little time for investigation, the habit of denouncing and contemning other denominations, perhaps more enlightened and virtuous than their own. Charity, forbearance, a delight in the virtues of different sects, a backwardness to censure and condemn, these are virtues, which, however poorly practised by us, we admire and recommend, and we would rather join ourselves to the church in which they abound than to any other communion, however elated with the belief of its own orthodoxy, however strict in guarding its creed, however burning with zeal against imagined error.

I have thus given the distinguishing views of those Christians in whose names I have spoken. We have embraced this system, not hastily or lightly, but after much deliberation, and we hold it fast, not merely because we believe it to be true, but because we regard it as purifying truth, as a doctrine according to godliness, as able to "work mightily" and to "bring forth fruit" in them who believe. That we wish to spread it, we have no desire to conceal; but we think, that we wish its diffusion, because we regard it as more friendly to practical piety and pure morals, than the opposite doctrines, because it gives clearer and nobler views of duty, and stronger motives to its performance, because it recommends religion at once to the understanding and the heart, because it asserts the lovely and venerable attributes of God, because it tends to restore the benevolent spirit of Jesus to his divided and afflicted church, and because it cuts off every hope of God's favour, except that which springs from practical conformity to the life and precepts of Christ. We see nothing in our views to give offence, save their purity, and it is their purity, which makes us seek and hope their extension through the world.

I now turn to the usual addresses of the day.

My friend and brother—You are this day to take upon you important duties, to be clothed with an office, which the Son of God did not disdain; to devote yourself to that religion, which the most hallowed lips have preached, and the most precious blood sealed. We trust that you will bring to this work a willing mind, a firm purpose, a martyr's spirit, a readiness to toil and suffer for the truth, a devotion of your best powers to the interests of piety and virtue. I have spoken of the doctrines, which you will probably preach; but I do not mean, that you are to give yourself to controversy. You will remember, that good practice is the end of preaching, and will labour to make your people holy livers, rather than skilful disputants. Be careful, lest the desire of defending what you deem truth, and of repelling reproach and misrepresentation, turn you aside from your great business, which is to fix in men's minds a living conviction of the obligation, sublimity and happiness of Christian virtue. The best way to vindicate your sentiments, is to show, in your preaching and life, their intimate connection with Christian morals, with a high and delicate sense of duty, with candour towards your opposers, with inflexible integrity, and with an habitual reverence for God. If any light can pierce and scatter the clouds of prejudice, it is that of a pure example. You are to preach a system which has nothing to recommend it, but its fitness to make men better; which has no unintelligible doctrine for the mystical, no extravagancies for the fanatical, no dreams for the visionary, no contradictions for the credulous, which asks no sacrifice of men's understanding, but only of their passions and vices; and the best and only way to recommend such a system is, to show forth its power in purifying and exalting the character. My brother, may your life preach more loudly than your lips. Be to this people a pattern of all good works, and may your instructions derive authority from a well grounded belief in your hearers, that you speak from the heart, that you preach from experience, that the truth which you dispense has wrought powerfully in your own heart, that God, and Jesus, and Heaven are not merely words on your lips, but most affecting realities to your mind, and springs of hope and consolation, and strength, in all your trials. Thus labouring, may you reap abundantly, and have a testimony of your faithfulness, not only on your own conscience, but on the esteem, love, virtues, and improvements of your people.

Brethren of this church and society—We rejoice with you in the prospects of this day. We rejoice in the zeal, unanimity and liberality, with which you have secured to yourselves the administration of God's word and ordinances, according to your own understanding of the Scriptures. We thank God, that he has disposed you to form an association, on the true principles of Christianity and of Protestantism, that you have solemnly resolved to call no man master in religion, to take your faith from no human creed, to submit your consciences to no human authority, but to repair to the gospel, to read it with your own eyes, to exercise upon it your own understanding, to search it, as if not a sect existed around you, and to follow it wherever it may lead you. Brethren, hold fast your Christian and Protestant liberty. We wish you continued peace, and growing prosperity. We pray God, that your good works may glorify your Christian profession, that your candour, and serious attention may encourage our young brother in the arduous work to which you have called him, and that your union with him, beginning in hope, may continue in joy, and may issue in the friendship and union of heaven.

To all who hear me, I would say, with the apostle; *prove all things, hold fast that which is good.* Do not, brethren, shrink from the duty of searching God's word for yourself through fear of human censure and denunciation. Do not think that you may innocently follow the opinions, which prevail around you, without investigation, on the ground, that Christianity is now so purified from errors, as to need no laborious research. There is much reason to believe, that Christianity is at this moment dishonoured by gross and cherished corruptions. If you remember the darkness, which hung over the gospel for ages; if you consider the impure union, which still subsists in almost every Christian country between the church, and the state, and which enlists men's selfishness, and ambition, on the side of established error; if you recollect in what degree the spirit of intolerance has checked free inquiry, not only before but since the Reformation; you will see that Christianity cannot have freed itself from all the human inventions which disfigured it under the papal tyranny. No. Much stubble is yet to be burnt; much rubbish to be removed; many gaudy decorations, which a false taste has hung around Christianity, must be swept away; and the earth-born fogs, which have long shrouded it, must be scattered, before this divine fabric will rise before us in its native, and awful majesty, in its harmonious proportions, in its mild and celestial splendours. This glorious reformation in the church, we hope, under God's blessing, from the demolition of human authority in matters of religion, from the fall of these hierarchies, huge establishments, general convocations or assemblies, and other human institutions, by which the minds of individuals are oppressed under the weight of numbers, and a Papal dominion is perpetuated in the Protestant church.[6] Our earnest prayer to God is, that he will overturn, and overturn, and overturn the strongholds of spiritual usurpation, until He shall come, whose right it is to rule the minds of men; that the conspiracy of ages against the liberty of Christians may be brought to an end; that the servile assent, so long yielded to human creeds, may give place to honest and fearless inquiry into the Scriptures; and that Christianity, thus purified from error, may put forth its almighty energy, and prove itself, by its ennobling influence on the mind, to be indeed "the power of God unto salvation."

THE CLAIMS OF THE AGE ON THE WORK OF THE EVANGELIST. SERMON DELIVERED AT THE ORDINATION OF J. S. DWIGHT AS PASTOR OF THE 2ND CONGREGATIONAL CHURCH, NORTHAMPTON, MASSACHUSETTS, MAY 20, 1840

BY GEORGE RIPLEY

Introduction

The meaning of transcendentalism in American life and literature during the Jacksonian era finds one of its most far-reaching illustrations in the thought and career of George Ripley (1802-80).[1] Born in Greenfield, Massachusetts, he was raised by a mother who was a staunch champion of theological conservatism. Until the end of his life Ripley found in

---

[6] In the Boston edition this sentence reads: "This glorious Reformation in the church, we hope, under God's blessing, from the progress of the human intellect, from the moral progress of society, from the consequent decline of prejudice and bigotry, and, though last, not least, from the subversion of human authority in matters of religion, from the fall of those hierarchies, and other human institutions, by which the minds of individuals are oppressed under the weight of numbers, and a Papal dominion is perpetuated in the Protestant church."

[1] I am indebted to Arthur Kinoy for making available to me, for the purpose of writing this introductory note, his forthcoming biography of George Ripley. It is based upon the author's Harvard University Senior Thesis (Bowdoin Prizewinner, 1942), entitled "The Earthly Responsibility of the Idealist."

Jonathan Edwards a source of the deepest intellectual and emotional inspiration; from Edwards he gained a conviction of the divinity of the human soul and an abiding sense of the reality of God in every man.

In 1819, the same year that Channing delivered his historical Baltimore address, Ripley entered Harvard College, the traditional center of American Arminianism, and now the disseminator of a triumphant Arminian creed. He graduated in 1823 at the head of his class, imbued with the conviction that knowledge must be used, not for the advancement of a few, but for the benefit of mankind; that the scholar's first obligation lay with the common people, and that the most honorable and effective way of contributing to human progress lay through the vocation of the ministry.

That same year, accordingly, Ripley entered the Harvard Divinity School. On graduation he assumed charge of the Purchase Street Church in Boston, and was ordained as its pastor on November 8, 1826. This date marked the entry into the Unitarian ministry of one of its most promising and brilliant young representatives.

During the next ten years Ripley elaborated the philosophic basis of his concept of Christian religion as a moral code whose truth man recognizes directly and intuitively. Following the inspiration of European thinkers—notably Victor Cousin and Immanuel Kant—he helped to develop the American form of intuitional philosophy that has become known to history as transcendentalism. These new insights were reflected in Ripley's sermons; here he taught that the command of the divinity is intuitively perceived, that it is ascertained by the power of reason, and that morality consists in scrupulously obeying this inner voice. The purpose of life on earth is to follow this inner voice as the voice of God.

But the moral life, he insisted, was not to be led in the abstract, nor the spiritual quest pursued in isolation from the world. The minister and scholar must be concerned with the moral life of the community; he must not stand aloof from the people, but must involve himself in the life and well-being of his fellow men, and must entertain close relations with them. The minister must bring his learning to the people, must help them in their efforts to understand their destiny and to secure its accomplishment.

But by the mid '30's Ripley and those who thought like him were voices crying in the wilderness. The Unitarian ministry as a whole had turned away from the reforming ardor of its youth and had become conservative. Ripley's forward-moving position was not acceptable, and the young minister found himself under attack for his crusading views. From this polarization of Unitarian thinking stemmed one of the most famous controversies in the history of American religion—the debate in 1839 between Ripley and Andrews Norton, his onetime teacher and professor of Divinity at Harvard, over the nature of the Christian miracles as testaments to the truth of Christianity.

Ripley, as might be expected under these circumstances, had grown increasingly restive, increasingly dissatisfied with his ministry at the Purchase Street Church, increasingly anxious to find new ways to manifest his love for his fellow man and to be of service to him. In October, 1840, hard on the heels of the controversy with Andrews Norton, he handed in his resignation as pastor of Purchase Street: at the same time he was maturing plans to launch a cooperative colony in which he, and like-minded people, could live human brotherhood rather than merely preach it.

This cooperative colony, which has become famous as Brook Farm, was launched in 1841. It sprang from Ripley's desire to express and teach the inherent truths of Christian morality. Christianity, to him, was an instrument for the agitation of an unjust social order, for the moving of multitudes, for the education of the human race. Christianity had a social mission: it exemplified conduct motivated by a sublime and deeply felt ideal. Christian action was a weapon in the struggle for the emancipation of man.

This Christian social message was a response to the new conditions that, by 1840, had come to transform New England. Since the War of 1812 industrialization had been advancing with rapid strides, and it had brought with it a host of new social evils: poor living conditions, low wages, child labor, poverty, prostitution and crime; in a word, the exploitation of man by man. And the Depression of 1837, which thrust out thousands to starve upon the streets, was a stark, bitter illustration of the fact that existing society crushed idealism, made a mockery of Christianity, betrayed the high ideals of the Revolution, and exalted money and money-making at the expense of the most elementary human needs. Religion, thought Ripley, must be man's guide and sanction in the struggle to engineer a just society. To teach this message, and to follow it, was the first obligation of an Evangelist.

How was a truly just social order to be created? It must be achieved by awakening man's slumbering soul to its own inborn knowledge of the good. But this could not be done by preachment, which, under existing conditions, was in vain. It must be done by abolishing the existing social order which stood, in all its ugliness and crudity, between man and his salvation.

Such was the nature of the salvo fired in the sermon reproduced below. It was delivered by its author at the very moment when he was planning his resignation from the Purchase Street Church, and was preparing, along with Ralph Waldo Emerson, Nathaniel Hawthorne and others, to embark upon the Brook Farm experiment. It is a sermon of historic significance in the literature of Christian action and social reform. We see the similarities in spirit between Ripley and Channing, but we see also Ripley's huge advance. We see the philosophy underlying the Brook Farm experiment: a Christian teaches by example. His life is a practical demonstration to others of the Christian ideal.

"THE CLAIMS OF THE AGE ON THE WORK OF THE EVANGELIST."*

Do the Work of an Evangelist.

2 Timothy, IV. 5.

The work of an Evangelist is to preach the Gospel of Christ. He is set apart from the common pursuits of men, to explain and enforce the ideas which give dignity to every pursuit, which nourish the higher life of the soul under the pressure of everyday cares, which transform the world from a market of

---

Source: This sermon is reproduced in full from the pamphlet published in Boston in 1840.

sordid competition and grasping selfishness, to a scene of noble
endeavor and disinterested love, and which thus vivify and
strengthen the elements of character that raise man to communion with God, and connect him with eternity. The great
object of his calling is not so much speculation as exposition;
he is not so much bent on the discovery of new truth, as on
the illustration of old; the materials for his teachings are not
to be sought from afar, but are already present in the revelations of Jesus; he is not commissioned to change or to contro-
vert the opinions of a Christian community, but to point out
the significance and profoundness of those opinions, to separate their essence from their form, to redeem them from the
perversions to which they have been subjected, to exhibit
them in their true point of view, to present them in their relation to the culture of the soul and the improvement of society,
and, in this manner, to help his fellow Christians to understand
and apply the religion which they profess.

In all ages, men have been hoping for a better state of
things; a noble discontent with the present has inspired the
prophecy of a brighter future; this prophecy contains within
itself the pledge of its fulfilment; what we long for in youth,
is granted in old age; and this we believe to be no less true of
society, than of the individual. But a variety of means have
been devised for the accomplishment of this purpose; some
have rested their hopes on improved systems of legislation;
others, on the advancement of science; some have expected
the introduction of a millennium of prosperity from the general diffusion of knowledge, and others from the development
of material resources and the perfection of machinery. The
Christian, on the other hand, who comprehends his religion,
to whom its spirit is not concealed by its letter, whose faith
has not been taken on trust, nor assumed for effect, but is enlightened and sincere, looks to the cross of Christ for the salvation of the world. The idea which was realized in the life of
Jesus, must be also realized in the institutions of men, before
the kingdom of God can be established on earth. The spiritual
presence of Christ is the remedy for sin; men must be purified
from transgression by the influence of divine truth; they must
obtain a moral oneness with the Universal Father, before they
can live in the cheerful fraternity of brethren; they must be
baptized in the spirit of purity and love, before an abode in

heavenly places can be built up amidst the discord and confusion of the dwellings on earth.

In the hope of this consummation, which prophets have foretold, which the soul of man has longed for from the beginning, a new Evangelist to-day commences his stated labors in the Gospel of Christ. He is now consecrated not for a vague and indefinite work, but to give full effect, within the sphere of his ministry, to the idea with which Jesus was inspired; he is not to utter an uncertain sound on the trumpet, but to proclaim distinctly, what his Master proclaimed, at the well-side in Samaria, that the hour has come for the true worshippers to worship the Father in spirit and truth; he is not to fight as one that beateth the air, but with the weapons of Christ to attack the strongholds of sin.

This is the great purpose of the ministry of the Gospel. This has been its professed object in every period of the church; but how inadequately it has been fulfilled, let history declare; let the present state of religion and morality in the Christian world, as we courteously term it, bear testimony. Indeed, the institution of the ministry has fallen so far short of its design; so few effects, comparatively, are produced by its operations; it has proved so impotent in penetrating society with the spirit of Jesus; so many obstructions and shackles impede its vigorous action; that many thoughtful persons incline to the opinion, that it has fallen into irrecoverable decrepitude, that its day has wholly gone by, and that with the advance of civilization, with the unfolding of freer and nobler religious ideas, it must give place to other forms of instruction more in harmony with the character of the age, and the independent strivings of the human spirit.

It is certain, that the aspect of the Christian ministry has greatly changed, even within the remembrance of the younger portion of this audience; its relations with society are less distinctly defined than formerly; it is deprived of the predominant and almost exclusive influence which it once enjoyed; other powerful means of social action have sprung up by its side, and in some degree, thrown it into the shade; the freedom of opinion is not so much fettered by its authority; its incumbents are not permitted to claim a monopoly of truth, nor their decisions regarded as oracles, and their connection with the people of their charge, which was once deemed almost a freehold for life, is now among the most contingent of all contingent events.

Nor has the ministry succeeded in producing anything like a uniformity of opinion on religious subjects. This has always been a favorite purpose with the professed teachers of divine truth; they have taken their own views of revelation as the standard of infallibility; they have regarded their own interpretation of the Gospel as of equal authority with the Gospel itself; they have identified the systems of theology which they found in the church, with the inspired conceptions of the mind of Christ. At a former period—and one indeed not very remote —the views which they cherished were generally shared by their people; men looked up to them as the authorized expounders of religion; and if there was sometimes a secret dissent from their opinions, there was little open disavowal of them. Every church held fast to its own creed, either written or understood; there were few disputes in regard to its meaning; and though the great division between those who relied on authority and those who trusted to rational conviction may always be traced, there was a pervading unanimity in each respective division; every household of faith spoke in a language which all its members recognised and understood; there was a family altar around which each one felt himself at home.

A different state of things is now experienced among all the churches of the land. The unlimited freedom of thought which happily prevails in this community, produces a general fermentation; the ancient repose is disturbed; the stagnation of the past has given place to intense mental action; the doctrines of the theologians are brought before the tribunal of the people; a struggle has taken place between the old and the new; the most rigid creeds have been unable to prevent the progress of thought; so that there is scarcely a church of any communion, in which opinion is not divided, and the foundations of ages shaken to their centre.

It is natural to suppose, that these combined influences would diminish the importance of the ministry, and by changing its character, deprive it of its authority. There are some who secretly wish, and others who fear, the realization of this event. The popular lecturer, the philosopher, the educator, it is thought by many, sustain hostile relations with the evangelist; they are supposed to take the work out of his hands; to leave him nothing to do; to make his occupation a sinecure;

they must increase, while he must decrease; and the pulpit must ultimately give place to the chairs of the lyceum, the university, or the common school. But from these views I strongly dissent. I cannot recognise such an antagonism between the ministry and the prevailing tendencies of the day, as many apprehend or imagine. If the evangelist comprehends the character of his work, he will perceive that it is one which can be performed by none but himself; if it does not cover the whole ground of modern society, there is no institution which can take its place; his office may be modified, but it cannot be destroyed; he may discover new and more effective modes of discharging its duties; but the truth as it is in Jesus will still remain the instrument for the reformation of society, and the salvation of man.

Neither is there any reason to dread an unfavorable influence from the tendencies already alluded to, which are looked on by many as opposed to the ministry. It is true, that people are not content with merely the instructions of the church; they demand other teachers besides their ministers; the pulpit has ceased to be an exclusive light; religion is not the only subject on which the mind is exercised; and on this, men are becoming disposed to form their convictions from personal inquiry rather than from foreign dictation. I cannot but rejoice in this aspect of the present times. It seems to me an indication of great good. I welcome the public teacher, who gives the ripest fruits of his solitary studies to the mass of attentive hearers that throng the lecture room. He prepares the mind for pure religion, by enlarging the sphere of its interests, awakens habits of thought that are an essential condition of improvement from the pulpit, and averts the dangers of superstition, by the exhibition of enlightened views on other subjects. I welcome the philosopher, who shows the foundation of religion in the primitive elements of the soul, who demonstrates the grounds of our belief in divine things, who illustrates the harmony between the reason of man and the revelations of Christ, and identifies the disclosures of inspiration with the noblest instincts of humanity. He is a fellow-laborer with the Evangelist; they afford each other, the mutual aid which is essential to both; the services of neither can be dispensed with; and the ministry is made not less important nor less effectual, when the truths which it proclaims are shown by science to be built upon a rock.

The work of the Evangelist, therefore, may be regarded as a real work; the most sincere and living men may wish to share in its service; it presents a sphere for the highest qualities of the intellect and the heart; and could it be carried on in the true spirit of Jesus, in complete accordance with his divine idea, it would shake and agitate society, as the trees of the forest are moved by the vernal winds, before they assume the new foliage which nature prepares with every revolving season for her favorites. The work of the Evangelist, we have said, is to preach the Gospel of Christ. But the Gospel of Christ is the great antagonist principle of error and sin; it wages a deadly warfare against every form of corruption; the restoration of the soul to the image of God is the only object in which it can rest; never can it be content with any thing short of this; it moves forward with the step of fate, rather let me say, with the resistless march of divine Providence, to the regeneration of society, the complete and triumphant establishment of the kingdom of God on earth. The Gospel announces the supremacy of the spirit over the arrangements of men: "what shall it profit a man, though he gain the whole world and lose his own soul." It asserts the hope of unlimited progress: "Heaven and earth shall pass away," says Jesus, "but my word shall not pass away"; "I am the light of the world, and he that followeth me, shall not walk in darkness but shall have the light of life"; he will not only see but live; and he that both lives and sees will go on; and this holds true alike of communities and of individuals. It announces the prostration of evil in the prevalence of good. Humanity is destined to a higher condition than it has yet enjoyed: "I saw Satan falling like lightning from Heaven"; and "I, if I be lifted up, will draw all men to myself."

The Evangelist then engages in the realization of the predictions of Jesus. He surveys the world from the cross of his Master, and, in the spirit of him who died there, resolves that, God helping, he will be true to the idea which he came to announce. He commences his work with earnest faith, yet with clear insight. While he does not distrust the power of the Gospel, he perceives that its influence has never been fully exerted on society, or on the church. He knows that the name of Christ is far more prevalent than his spirit; that his religion has been crushed beneath the inventions of men; that no sect of modern times completely embodies or comprehends his sublime conception; and that men must sit long at the feet of Jesus, before they can appreciate the simplicity of truth.

The true work of the Evangelist, at the present day, therefore, is to bring the religion of society into accordance with the religion of Christ. He has nothing to do with the perpetuation of prevalent ideas; he is not to ask how far his preaching will fall in with the tone of the times; he will scorn the enjoyment of popular favor, if it be gained at the expense of his own convictions; he will love his fellow men too well ever to flatter them with smooth words; but he takes his stand on the fact which no one can deny, that the prevailing religion of Christendom is below the standard of Christ, that no community is to be found in which the spirit of the Gospel is carried into full effect; he will therefore proclaim the truth which he sees, let it cut where it will; he will never wish to blunt the edge of the sword of the spirit which is the word of God; and will announce the whole counsel of his Master, whether men will hear, or whether they will forbear.

Do you ask in what respects the prevalent religion of society is below the religion of Christ, I would ask, in return, in what respects it comes up to that standard? Where is the community, in which the order of society, the general tone of morality, the everyday dealings between man and man, are based on the new commandment which the Redeemer gave to his disciples? Where is the church which can justly be described as the communion of the faithful; which enjoys the fellowship of the Holy Ghost; and which is crowned with the love, and joy, and peace, which are the peculiar fruits of the Spirit? Where are the perfect men in Christ Jesus, who have attained to the fulness of the stature of the sons of God; whose conversation is in Heaven; and to whom we could apply without misgiving, the common apostolic description of the disciples of Jesus, "They are the temple of God, and the spirit of God dwelleth in them."

Think not, brethren, that in these remarks, I wish to condemn others and exalt ourselves. I speak not of this or that church, of this or that sect; I speak not of errors which we may see around us, and from which we are exempt; I claim no exemption for ourselves, from evils which belong to our age; I speak of the prevailing religion of society in this the nineteenth century from Him, whose garments'

hem we scarce seem as yet to have touched; and surely not
with the feeling of reproach or scorn, but in deepest grief,
do I confess, that we are all under the same condemnation;
that calling ourselves Christians, we have yet failed to embody
the idea of Jesus in our personal characters or our social institutions. We seem to have departed from Christ in the lapse of
ages; we idolize our profession of the Gospel, while we poorly
comprehend its spirit; and were the Master whose name we
bear, to appear in the midst of us to-day, I should tremble
for his reception; the Son of Man, should he come, would
he find faith on the earth; or would he not rather be, like a
root out of dry ground; without form or comeliness and no
beauty in him that we should desire him. When he departed
from his friends, he told them, that he should not leave them
alone; he promised to be present in the spirit of truth. The
influence of the Divine Comforter was the common legacy of
the church: "Lo, I am with you always, even to the end of
the world"; and "Because I live, ye shall live also."

Brethren, do we witness the fulfilment of this promise?
Do we believe in its reality? Have we any hope of its blessings
in our personal experience? Do we look for the presence
of Christ, the visible influence of that spirit which filled
and fired his soul, in our institutions, in our churches, in
society? We delight to call ourselves by that name which
is above every name. We are lavish in our cries of Lord,
Lord, to him, who was once despised and rejected of men.
Our whole land is covered with temples erected for his honor.
Every Sabbath the music of the Christian bells summons our
thronging population to the house of God; they come from
every valley and every hill-top to celebrate him who brought
glad tidings; the solemn anthem rises in his praise; holy men
utter words of supplication in his name; his sayings are repeated as though they possessed a talismanic power to expel
all evil; but is Christ present there? Does his spirit yet speak
in his churches? Do we behold his divine image in the faces
of his disciples? Are they one with him, as he was one with
God? Do they display a lofty hope, like that which irradiated
the hour of crucifixion; a generous love, which acknowledges
no limits but those of humanity; a sublime trust in God, which
casts out every unworthy fear; and a cheerful earnestness in
the discharge of duty, which finds encouragement even in the
song of birds and the bloom of spring? If we cannot give the

answer which we would to such inquiries, then has the Evangelist a work to perform, which is not likely to be soon completed; he is to enthrone Christ in the hearts of his disciples, and penetrate the church with the influence of his truth.

Christ announced the preëminence of spiritual worship over the observance of forms. He utterly repudiated the idea that any prescribed ceremony was essential to sincere homage; Jerusalem and Gerizim, in his view, were alike indifferent; he attached no importance to the gold on the altar, to the fringe on the garment; the spirit, in which the gift was brought, the purity of heart which consecrated it, were the essential conditions; the time and the place of prayer were nothing compared with the trust and love from which it flowed; many words were not required for its due performance; the "God be merciful to me a sinner," of the publican, was of more value in the sight of heaven, than the thrice-repeated "God I thank thee that I am not as other men are," of the self-complacent Pharisee.

This feature of the religion of Christ is opposed to a prominent feature in the religion of society. There are too many who make a regular observance of religious forms a substitute for the spirit of religion; they confound the means with the end; they attach a saving virtue to rites whose sole value consists in their spiritual influence; and measure the amount of their piety by the length of their prayers, the frequency with which they are offered, or the form and the place in which they are presented. We become attached to certain words, as if they possessed an inherent efficacy; our fathers worshipped in this mountain, and we would fain remain on it forever; we gather round the mossy wellside, from which they were wont to draw, and can scarce believe that other fountains also contain the waters of life; we think of the ancient Jacob, who drank thereof himself, with his children, and his cattle; and forget that greater one than Jacob, or than Moses, or than all the goodly fellowship of the prophets, who stood and cried, "if any man thirst, let him come unto me and drink; and the water that I shall give him shall be in him a well of water springing up unto everlasting life."

Again, Jesus asserted the supremacy of holiness in comparison with speculative belief. He never prescribes a definite creed, the reception of which is essential to discipleship; he makes the affections the primary seat of religion, not the understanding; and in all his teachings, throws no light on the questions which exercise philosophers; but simply announces the necessity of holiness to the salvation of the soul. According to Jesus, religion is the possession of inward life, not the belief of an abstract doctrine; when he speaks of faith, it is the faith of devout trust, not of curious research; the faith which confides in the omnipotence of truth, not that which relies on systems of speculation. He is silent on those perplexing topics which have divided opinion in all ages of the world; he attacks the prevalence of evil, but does not attempt to explain its origin; he declares the universal Providence of a benignant Father, but does not help us to comprehend the mystery of his attributes; he confirms the instinctive hope of all souls, that death is not the destruction of life, but does not enable the eye to see, nor the heart of man to imagine the precise condition of our future existence; his instructions are confined to points of greater moment; relating more directly to the present wants of man; to the universal interests of the race, not to the speculative curiosity of the few; and adapted to inspire the soul with the love of righteousness, rather than to train the intellect to accuracy of opinion. According to Jesus, he is accepted of God, who worships the Father in the beauty of holiness; goodness is the most appropriate homage to the Infinite Spirit of goodness; and he who loves his Maker with all his heart, and his neighbor as himself, has already entered into the kingdom of heaven.

This fact in the religion of Christ is opposed to the spirit of exclusiveness, in matters of speculative belief, which prevails to a greater or less extent, in all the churches of Christendom. We have not yet learned to bear with patience the honest differences of opinion, which must ever spring up among children of the same family, and disciples of the same Lord. Uniformity of faith is still desired as the condition of communion; we judge men by their speculations, not by their lives; and are reluctant to acknowledge the claims of a brother to the household of faith, if he express his allegiance to Christ in a language at variance with our own. The purity of a church is estimated by the fidelity of its adherence to fixed doctrinal standards; the words of men are elevated to a higher rank than the spirit of Christ; the beautiful arrangement of the Christian graces presented by the apostle is reversed;

while we say, that now abideth faith, hope, and charity, these three; but the least of these is charity. In this respect, the modern church exhibits a mournful contrast with the primitive model. In the days of the Apostles, no creed embodied abstract conceptions which all must receive; the Greek and the Jew brought the diverse ideas which a different culture had given them, into the common fellowship of the faithful; each enjoyed his private opinions undisturbed; no one was called to account by his neighbor, for his peculiar construction of the truth which they held together; one aspect of Christianity is exhibited by John and another by Matthew, but they do not exclude each other; and though it is true that divisions began to creep in to the disorderly church at Corinth, while one declared that he was of Paul, and another, that he was of Apollos, the spirit of sectarianism was promptly rebuked by the catholic Apostle; he would not hear to the suggestion that Christ was divided, and boldly insisted, that though there was a diversity of operations, the universal working was of God.

The restoration of the church to the original platform, will be a prominent endeavor of the Evangelist who comprehends his calling. Liberty, Holiness, Love, will be the motto under which he works. He will strive to preserve a unity of spirit, in the bond of peace; his ideal of a Christian community, will be a band of brothers emancipated by submission to Christ from all external authority; claiming no more dominion over the faith of each other, than did the Apostle over that of his proselytes; united in allegiance to Christ, disclaiming all allegiance to man; maintaining the freedom of the sons of God, and refusing to be brought into subjection for a moment.

Again, Jesus asserted the necessity of personal religious experience. His teachings always imply the existence of a religious nature in man, of the continual presence of God in his works, and of the immediate relation of the human soul with the Creator. He was conscious of the intimate connection of his own spirit with the Divine Spirit; for he dwelt as it were in the bosom of God; he never ceased to enjoy a living insight into divine things; but a similar relation he announced as the privilege of the faithful; blessed are the pure in heart, for they shall see God; and the glory which thou hast given me, I have given them; that they may all be one; even as thou, Father, art in me, and I in thee, that they also may be one in us. The establishment of this personal relation with God, is what we mean by personal religious experience; and the promise of this to every sincere believer, I regard as one of the chief distinctions of Christianity. I take the language of Jesus in its literal sense. I dare not explain it away into Jewish metaphor or oriental hyperbole. I think he meant to assert a plain matter of fact, when he declared that the spirit which dwelt in him should be given to those that believe on his name; that they also should perceive religious truth for themselves; that they should be conscious of the love of the Father, and rejoice in the freedom of the sons of God; that the anointing of the Holy Ghost would teach them, so that they should see with their own eyes, and live by a faith which needed no external authority as a prop.

The reality of personal experience, in the depth and extent with which it was set forth by Christ, is far from being admitted by the Christian church. The present tendency of thought is to keep it in the background, if not to reject it totally. We are inclined to substitute a blind reliance on tradition, for a clear insight into divine truth; to confound the passive reception of ideas on foreign authority with their vital appropriation from personal experience; and in our zeal for the supremacy of the Father, or the divinity of the Son, not to know so much as whether there be any Holy Ghost. This doctrine, it is true, has not failed to receive a cordial testimony, from believers in the church in every age. Its reality was maintained by Luther, in his conflicts with the hierarchy. Fenelon was condemned by the Pope for accepting its consequences; Sir Henry Vane, rejoiced on the scaffold in its glorious light; it opened a new world of revelation to Barclay and George Fox; it was the grand argument of Roger Williams, for the freedom of the soul; and in words that can never die, and which redeem from unmingled aversion the errors of a great man, it was nobly set forth by the former illustrious pastor of Northampton, from whom yonder church takes its name, and whom posterity will continue to revere as one of "the clearest and richest minds that ever ripened in New England."

Still, the religion now most prevalent in society, is of a different stamp. It makes less account of experience than of authority, strives to submit the soul to a foreign yoke, robs the believer of his independence as a freeman of the Lord, reduces the light of revelation to the erudition of the pedant, and changes the character of Christianity from the law of spiritual life, to the letter of the statute-book, and a system of dogmatical formulas. Let the Evangelist then proclaim the dispensation of the spirit. Let him cling to the promise with earnest faith, "Behold the days come, saith the Lord, that I will pour out my spirit on all flesh; and they shall no more teach every one his brother; for all shall be taught of God." Let him exhibit Christianity as the pledge of the blessed Comforter, the Spirit of Truth, who will abide forever with the faithful; he will thus commend himself to every man's conscience in the sight of God; many hearts will bear witness to his word; and the truths which he announces, will be sustained not by the wisdom of men, but by the demonstration of the spirit, and power from on high.

Once more, Christ announced the coming of the kingdom of God on earth. He wished to establish the divine laws in the institutions of men. By the kingdom of heaven, he represents a state of society in which human passions should be subject to celestial wisdom; in which natural order should prevail; and the principles of eternal justice bear rule over selfish policy. He claimed to fulfil the prophecies which foretold the Messiah. But the reign of the Messiah, according to the Hebrew prediction, was to consist in the prevalence of righteousness in human institutions. A purer and more happy state of society was to be realized on earth. The dominion of force was to give way to the influence of love. The cheerful worship of the Creator was to banish the abject service of superstition. Nations were to exchange the weapons of war for the utensils of industry; violence was no more to be heard in the land, nor complaining in the streets; man would cease to lift up his hand against his brother; the people were to dwell in safety; each would eat of the fruit of his own vine and fig-tree; oppressions would cease; slavery would be destroyed; ambition would have no sphere; mutual love would crown every dwelling; sorrow and sighing would flee away; Jerusalem would become gladness, and Judah a joy; the knowledge of the Lord would cover the whole earth, as the waters cover the sea; and all flesh would see it, and rejoice together.

In view of these sublime hopes, Jesus announced that the kingdom of God was at hand. Conscious of the fulness of

Divinity which possessed his spirit, he declared "I am the light of the world." He distinctly foretold, that the faith of ages would yet be realized; that the inspired visions of the ancient seers were no delusion; that a better futurity was in reserve for the race; and that human society would carry into effect the laws of God, would be converted from the disorder of centuries, into the harmony and joy of the kingdom of Heaven.

The realization of these predictions is entrusted to the fidelity of the Church. This is the primary object of its establishment. It can have no true life when it loses sight of this end. "Thy kingdom come," should be its unceasing prayer. And when the Church shall engage in the fulfilment of this mission, when the spirit of wisdom, of justice, and of a fervent love of souls shall be poured out upon it from on high, when the whole body of the faithful shall be inspired with the presence of Jesus, the work of the Evangelist will, to some degree, be accomplished; the great promise of God to man will be fulfilled; and the aged Simeons, who now wait in the temple for the dawning of a brighter day, may bow their hoary heads in peace, for their eyes will have seen the salvation of the Lord.

The prevalence of the spirit of Christ in the institutions of men is the hope of the world. On this depends the redemption of humanity. Every believing heart looks forward to the coming of a better day; it accepts the promise that Jesus shall reign till he has put all enemies under his feet; but, in our anticipation of the future, let us strive to comprehend the teachings of our Master. When the millennium dawns upon the earth, it will not be ushered in by the thunders of Sinai; no trump of archangel will proclaim it; no blazing universe will be the sign of its approach; it will not be announced by the sun turned into darkness, and the moon into blood, and the elements melting with fervent heat; but soft and gentle, as the descent of the dove on the Saviour at his baptism in the wilderness, will it appear in the heart of man; like the New Jerusalem coming down from God out of heaven, as a bride adorned for her husband, it will be borne to the world on the wings of love; and we need not inquire into the day or the hour of its advent, which no man knoweth, or can know —nor the angels in heaven, nor the Son—nor any but the Father, who has placed the times and seasons in his own power; but we shall know that it is here, even at the door, as soon as the kingdom of God is within our souls, and there is peace on earth and good will among men. This is the great consummation for which all good spirits long. Then will the sign of the Son of Man be seen not in the heavens, but on the earth; it will be displayed in every human face; strong and gentle voices will declare it; the universal heart will beat under its presence; the abodes of men will be the dwelling-place of God; and his will be done on earth as it is in heaven.

I have thus spoken of some of the aspects in which the work of the Evangelist presents itself to our regard at the present day. The accomplishment of this work depends no less on the spirit of the people than on his own fidelity. Let them receive their pastors rather in the relation of prophets than of priests; expecting from them the delivery of truth rather than the performance of a pageant; and accepting the faithful rebuke of their sins, instead of demanding of them to prophesy smooth things and to utter deceits. In these days, the minister must speak out his earnest convictions, or he had better be dumb; polished conventionalisms are worn out; and dainty phrases no longer satisfy the craving hunger of the soul. If he thinks that he must color his own views to suit the popular taste; that he must exhibit truth, not as it appears to his own mind, but as it is supposed to appear to other minds; he at once sacrifices the sincerity and independence of a man; he becomes a time-server and a slave; and of all slaves, a slave in the pulpit is the most to be pitied. A wise people will never allow this. A few individuals may now and then demand it; but in the long run, it will never meet the approval of the people of New England. They require the honest utterance of opinion in their public teachers; they will not be put off with words that have lost their meaning, instead of the living expression of divine truth; and he who acts most powerfully on their minds by the force of ideas, who arouses them from the slumber of inveterate habit, who proclaims the dawning of a better day, and who shows in every tone and look, that he is in earnest with their soul, will be their chosen guide. He will engage in the work of an Evangelist for their benefit, and they will encourage him in its performance.

Slavery
and
Civil
Rights

"THE DANGERS OF THE NATION,"
PARK STREET CHURCH, BOSTON,
JULY 4, 1829

BY WILLIAM LLOYD GARRISON

Introduction

The appearance of William Lloyd Garrison on the national scene marked the opening of a new era in American antislavery thought and agitation. Since the time of the Revolution there had been antislavery agitation, both North and South; but it had been dominated, and to a considerable extent paralyzed, by the concept of "colonization." Colonizationists might or might not concede that slavery was an evil, but they all believed and taught that the Negro slave was inherently inferior and unfit to associate with white men. The emancipation of such slaves, they believed, should be followed by immediate colonization, or settlement, on the coasts of Africa.

Colonization sentiment did not arise out of thin air, but was fed by a factual record of achievement. In the British Empire, as we have seen (p. 91), it led to the foundation of Sierra Leone in 1787. This colony had sprung from the practical necessity of finding a place to set down slaves liberated at the time of the American Revolution. A similar necessity induced the United States government to acquire its own African settlement in 1822. Manumitted slaves from the American South and Africans taken from illicit traders intercepted on the high seas were sent to this spot, which was later named Liberia. The colony was placed under the supervision of the American Colonization Society, established in 1816 under governmental auspices for that very purpose.

Colonization served the interest of the slaveholder. It provided a dumping ground for emancipated slaves, who were highly unwelcome in the South; and it funneled off the social concern and the ready cash of people of good will, in the thought that the Colonization Society would "solve" a difficult and complex question. There was no actual possibility that this could be done. In the forty-four years between its foundation and the Civil War, the Society shipped only 12,000 ex-slaves to Liberia. At that rate several thousand years would have been required to ship the total United States' Negro population back to Africa.

Garrison recognized that the colonization idea dulled the conscience of the American people and prevented them from realizing the enormity of slavery, its dangers, and the real dimensions of the problem it posed to American society. Declaring a resolute war upon colonization as a feasible program of emancipation, he captured the attention of the public with the idea that the immediate emancipation of the slaves was an absolute necessity and a practical possibility; that the Negro was an American citizen who must not only be freed, but integrated into American society with rights and privileges absolutely equal to those of the white man. This new approach, and the agitation that accompanied it and made it known, must be reckoned as a major contribution to public life and thought in the United States. Garrison's work opened a path to new perspectives of antislavery thought, action and organization throughout the Northern states.

William Lloyd Garrison was born in Newburyport, Massachusetts, in 1805, the son of a New Brunswick sea captain, and of Frances Maria Lloyd, of Deer Island, Maine. Garrison's father abandoned his family when William Lloyd was three years old, and the boy was raised by his mother as a devout Baptist. Apprenticed when still in his teens to a Newburyport printer, Garrison schooled himself in his own free time by avidly reading the English classics.

In 1828 the young man met Benjamin Lundy, a New Jersey Quaker and colonizationist, who was devoting his life to the effort to arouse antislavery sentiment among the American people, and who advocated the total but gradual abolition of slavery throughout the country. Lundy imparted to Garrison a burning interest in the slavery question; impressed with the young man's dedication and ability, he offered him the editorship of The Genius of Universal Emancipation, Lundy's own antislavery paper, published in Baltimore. This post Garrison gladly accepted.

In the spring of 1829 Garrison left Bennington, Vermont, where he was then working, to join Lundy in Baltimore. On his way South he stopped at Boston and called upon a number of ministers whom he hoped to interest in the antislavery cause. One of these offered Garrison his pulpit, thus enabling him to deliver the Fourth of July sermon that is reproduced below. It illustrates the beauty and forcefulness of his prose style and marks the opening of a career dedicated to proving to the American people that slavery was the greatest problem facing them, one which they must eradicate if the Republic were to survive.

In this early sermon—the author was but twenty-four when he composed it, and as yet barely on the threshold of his antislavery career—the sharp differentiation between Garrison's position and that of the colonizationists is clearly evident. "Our colored population," he says, "were born on our soil and are therefore entitled to all the privileges of American citizens. This is their country by birth, not by adoption." Notable, too, is his rejection of racism and the noble and entirely democratic affirmation that "education and freedom will elevate our colored population to a rank with whites —making them useful, intelligent, and peaceable citizens." In its wider sweep this address elevates slavery to the level of a national, not a sectional, problem. Its eradication, insists Garrison, is a moral imperative dictated both by the precepts of Christianity and of the Declaration of Independence. As a vision of American equality, as a cry of warning to the American people, "The Dangers of the Nation" may be said to rank with the very best of the Fourth of July addresses delivered by America's leading statesmen.

"THE DANGERS OF THE NATION"*

It is natural that the return of a day which established the liberties of a brave people should be hailed by them with more than ordinary joy; and it is their duty as Christians and patriots to celebrate it with signal tokens of thanksgiving.

Fifty-three years ago, the Fourth of July was a proud day for our country. It clearly and accurately defined the rights of man; it made no vulgar alterations in the established usages of society; it presented a revelation adapted to the common sense of mankind; it vindicated the omnipotence of public opinion over the machinery of kingly government; it shook, as with the voice of a great earthquake, thrones which were seemingly propped up with Atlantean pillars; it gave an impulse to the heart of the world, which yet thrills to its extremities.

It may be profitable to inquire, whether the piety which founded, and the patriotism which achieved our liberties, remain unimpaired in principle, undiminished in devotion. Possibly our Samson is sleeping in the lap of Delilah, with his locks shorn and his strength departed. Possibly his enemies have put out his eyes, and bound him with fetters of brass, and compelled him to grind in the prison-house; and if, in his rage and blindness, he find the pillars of the fabric, woe to those for whose sport he is led forth!

For many years, the true friends of their country have witnessed the return of this great jubilee with a terror, that no consolation could remove, and with a grief, that no flattery could assuage. They have seen, that, instead of being distinguished for rationality of feeling and purity of purpose, it has exhibited the perversion of reason and the madness of intemperance. Patriotism has degenerated into mere animal indulgence; or, rather, into the most offensive personalities. Liberty has gone hand in hand with licentiousness—her gait unsteady, her face bloated, her robe bedraggled in the dust. It seems as if men had agreed, by common consent, that an act, which, on any other day, would impeach a fair reputation, on this, should help enlarge that reputation. The love of country has been tested by the exact number of libations poured forth, the most guns fired, the greatest number of

*Source: Selections from the Writings of William Lloyd Garrison, pp. 44–61; and Old South Leaflets (Boston, 1899), VIII.

toasts swallowed, and the loudest professions of loyalty to the Union, uttered over the wine-cup.

Indeed, so dear is Liberty to many, that they cannot make too free with her charms: they owe her so much, that they owe the Most High nothing. It would shock their sensibility, and tarnish their reputation as patriots, to be caught at a religious celebration of our national anniversary. The day, they argue, should be properly appreciated; and, unless a man gets gloriously inebriated, either at home or in the streets, at his own or a public table, in digesting his own good sayings or those of others—unless he declaims roundly in praise of freedom, and drinks perdition to tyrants—it shows that he is either a monarchist or a bigot.

But it is not the direct, palpable, and widely extensive mischief to public morals, which alone makes the Fourth of July the worst and most disastrous day in the whole three hundred and sixty-five. There is, if possible, a corruption more deep—an intoxication more fascinating and deadly. It is that torrent of flattery, artfully sweetened and spiced, which is poured out for the thirsty multitude to swallow; it is that thriftless prodigality of praise, that presumptuous defiance of danger, that treacherous assurance of security, that impudent assumption of ignorance, that pompous declamation of vanity, that lying attestation of falsehood, from the lips of tumid orators, which are poisoning our life-blood.

We are a vain people, and our love of praise is inordinate. We imagine, and are annually taught to believe, that the republic is immortal; that its flight, like a strong angel's, has been perpetually upward, till it has soared above the impurities of earth, and beyond the remotest star; and, having attained perfection, is forever out of the reach of circumstance and change. An earthquake may rock all Europe, and engulf empires at a stroke; but it cannot raise an inch of republican territory, nor disturb the composure of a platter on our shelves. The ocean may gather up its forces for a second deluge, and overtop the tallest mountains; but our ark will float securely when the world is drowned. The storm may thicken around us; but a smile from the goddess of Liberty will disperse the gloom, and build a rainbow wherever she turns her eye. We shall remain "till the heavens be no more."

It is this fatal delusion, which so terrifies men of reflection and foresight; which makes the Christian shudder at the prospect before us, and the Patriot weep in despair; which, unless the mercy of God interpose, seals the doom of our country.

When a people become so infatuated as to deny the existence, and to doubt the possibility of danger; when they hear the language of reproof with angry emotions, and ridicule the remonstrances of wisdom as the croakings of imbecility; when they imagine every virtue to dwell in mere liberty, and are content to take the shadow for the substance, the name for the object, the promise for the possession, there is no extreme of folly into which they cannot be led, no vice which they will not patronize, no error which they will not adopt, no pitfall into which they will not stumble.

At such a crisis, the reason of men becomes more obtuse than animal instinct. The frugal and industrious ant does not wait till the cold winds of winter stiffen her legs, before she stores her provisions; the bird of passage migrates when autumn expires; the deer needs only to hear the bark of the hounds, and, without waiting for their approach, he tosses back his broad antlers, and dashes onward with the speed of an arrow. But a nation of infatuated freemen take no warning from history; they learn nothing from experience. To their vision, the signs of the times are always ominous of good. Like the inhabitants of Jerusalem, they must hear the avenger thundering at their gates, and see their destiny prefigured by dreadful omens in the heavens, before they will acknowledge that the judgments of God are sure. They must tread on the cinders of a national conflagration, and count the number of smoking ruins, before they will believe in the combustibleness of the republic.

"Our fate," says a distinguished essayist, "is not foretold by signs and wonders: the meteors do not indeed glare in the form of types, and print it legibly in the sky: but our warning is as distinct, and almost as awful, as if it were announced in thunder by the concussion of all the elements."

I know that this may be viewed as the phantasm of a disordered imagination. I know, too, it is easy to persuade ourselves that we shall escape those maladies, which have destroyed other nations. But, how closely soever a republic may resemble the human body in its liability to disease and death, the instance is not on record, where a people expired on account of excessive watchfulness over their own health, or of any premature apprehension of decay; and there is no national epitaph which says, "they were well, they wished to be better, they took physic, and died."

I speak not as a partisan or an opponent of any man or measures, when I say, that our politics are rotten to the core. *We* boast of our freedom, who go shackled to the polls, year after year, by tens, and hundreds, and thousands! *We* talk of free agency, who are the veriest machines—the merest automata—in the hands of unprincipled jugglers! *We* prate of integrity, and virtue, and independence, who sell our birthright for office, and who, nine times in ten, do not get Esau's bargain—no, not even a mess of pottage! Is it republicanism to say, that the majority can do no wrong? Then I am not a republican. Is it aristocracy to say, that the people sometimes shamefully abuse their high trust? Then I am an aristocrat. Rely upon it, the republic does not bear a charmed life: our prescriptions, administered through the medium of the ballot-box—the mouth of the political body —may kill or cure, according to the nature of the disease, and our wisdom in applying the remedy. It is possible that a people may bear the title of freemen, who execute the work of slaves. To the dullest observer of the signs of the times, it must be apparent, that we are rapidly approximating to this condition. Never were our boasts of liberty so inflated as at this moment—never were they greater mockeries. We are governed, not by our sober judgments, but by our passions: we are led by our ears, not by our understandings.

Wherein do we differ from the ancient Romans? What shall save us from their fate?

"It is remarkable," says a writer, to whom all history was as familiar as his alphabet, "it is remarkable that Cicero, with all his dignity and good sense, found it a popular seasoning of his harangue, six years *after* Julius Caesar had established a monarchy, and only six months *before* Octavius totally subverted the commonwealth, to say: 'It is not possible for the people of Rome to be slaves, whom the gods have destined to the command of all nations. Other nations may endure slavery, but the proper end and business of the Roman people is liberty.'"

But there is another evil, which, if we had to contend against nothing else, should make us quake for the issue. It is gangrene preying upon our vitals—an earthquake rumbling under our feet—a mine accumulating materials for a national catastrophe. It should make this a day of fasting and prayer, not of boisterous merriment and idle pageantry—a day of great lamentation, not of congratulatory joy. It should spike every cannon, and haul down every banner. Our garb should be sackcloth—our heads bowed in the dust—our supplications, for the pardon and assistance of Heaven.

Last week, this city was made breathless by a trial of considerable magnitude. The court chamber was inundated for hours, day after day, with a dense and living tide, which swept along like the rush of a mountain torrent. Tiers of human bodies were piled up to the walls, with almost miraculous condensation and ingenuity. It seemed as if men abhorred a vacuum equally with Nature; they would suspend themselves, as it were, by a nail, and stand upon air with the aid of a peg. Although it was a barren, ineloquent subject, and the crowd immense, there was no perceptible want of interest—no evidence of impatience. The cause was important, involving the reputation of a distinguished citizen. There was a struggle for mastery between two giants—a test of strength in tossing mountains of law. The excitement was natural.

I stand up here in a more solemn court, to assist in a far greater cause; not to impeach the character of one man, but of a whole people—not to recover the sum of a hundred thousand dollars, but to obtain the liberation of two millions of wretched, degraded beings, who are pining in hopeless bondage—over whose sufferings scarcely an eye weeps, or a heart melts, or a tongue pleads either to God or man. I regret that a better advocate had not been found, to enchain your attention, and to warm your blood. Whatever fallacy, however, may appear in the argument, there is no flaw in the indictment; what the speaker lacks, the cause will supply.

Sirs, I am not come to tell you that slavery is a curse, debasing in its effect, cruel in its operation, fatal in its continuance. The day and the occasion require no such revelation. I do not claim the discovery as my own, "that all men are born equal," and that among their inalienable rights are "life, liberty, and the pursuit of happiness." Were I addressing any other than a free and Christian assembly, the enforcement of this truth might be pertinent. Neither do I intend to analyze the horrors of slavery for your inspection, nor to freeze your blood with authentic recitals of savage cruelty. Nor will time allow me to explore even a furlong of that immense wilderness of suffering, which remains unsubdued in our land. I take it for granted that the existence of these evils is acknowledged, if not rightly understood. My object is to define and enforce our duty, as Christians and philanthropists.

On a subject so exhaustless, it will be impossible, in the moiety of an address, to unfold all the facts which are necessary to its full development. In view of it, my heart wells up like a living fountain, which time cannot exhaust, for it is perpetual. Let this be considered as the preface of a noble work, which your inventive sympathies must elaborate and complete.

I assume, as distinct and defensible propositions,

I   That the slaves of this country, whether we consider their moral, intellectual or social condition, are pre-eminently entitled to the prayers, and sympathies, and charities of the American people; and that their claims for redress are as strong as those of any Americans could be, in a similar condition.

II   That, as the free states—by which I mean non-slaveholding states—are constitutionally involved in the guilt of slavery, by adhering to a national compact that sanctions it; and in the danger, by liability to be called upon for aid in case of insurrection; they have the right to remonstrate against its continuance, and it is their duty to assist in its overthrow.

III   That no justificative plea for the perpetuity of slavery can be found in the condition of its victims; and no barrier against our righteous interference, in the laws which authorize the buying, selling and possessing of slaves, nor in the hazard of a collision with slaveholders.

IV   That education and freedom will elevate our colored population to a rank with the whites—making them useful, intelligent and peaceable citizens.

In the first place, it will be readily admitted, that it is the duty of every nation primarily to administer relief to its own necessities, to cure its own maladies, to instruct its own children, and to watch over its own interests. He is "worse than an infidel," who neglects his own household, and squanders his earnings upon strangers; and the policy of that nation is unwise, which seeks to proselyte other portions of the globe at the expense of its safety and happiness. Let me not be misunderstood. My benevolence is neither contracted nor selfish. I pity that man whose heart is not larger than a whole continent. I despise the littleness of that patriotism which blusters only for its own rights, and, stretched to its utmost dimensions, scarcely covers its native territory; which adopts as its creed, the right to act independently, even to the verge of licentiousness, without restraint, and to tyrannize wherever it can with impunity. This sort of patriotism is common. I suspect the reality, and deny the productiveness of that piety, which confines its operations to a particular spot—if that spot be less than the whole earth; nor scoops out, in every direction, new channels for the waters of life. Christian charity, while it "begins at home," goes abroad in search of misery. It is as copious as the sun in heaven. It does not, like the Nile, make a partial inundation, and then withdraw; but it perpetually overflows, and fertilizes every barren spot. It is restricted only by the exact number of God's suffering creatures. But I mean to say, that, while we are aiding and instructing foreigners, we ought not to forget our own degraded countrymen; that neither duty nor honesty requires us to defraud ourselves, that we may enrich others.

The condition of the slaves, in a religious point of view, is deplorable, entitling them to a higher consideration, on our part, than any other race; higher than the Turks or Chinese, for they have the privileges of instruction; higher than the Pagans, for they are not dwellers in a gospel land; higher than our red men of the forest, for we do not bind them with gyves, nor treat them as chattels.

And here let me ask, what has Christianity done, by direct effort, for our slave population? Comparatively nothing. She has explored the isles of the ocean for objects of commiseration; but, amazing stupidity! She can gaze without emotion on a multitude of miserable beings at home, large enough to constitute a nation of freemen, whom tyranny has heathenized by law. In her public services, they are seldom remembered, and in her private donations they are forgotten. From one end of the country to the other, her charitable societies form golden links of benevolence, and scatter their contributions like rain-drops over a parched heath; but they bring no sustenance to the perishing slave. The blood of souls is upon her garments, yet she heeds not the stain. The clankings of the prisoner's chains strike upon her ear, but they cannot penetrate her heart.

I have said, that the claims of the slaves for redress are as strong as those of any Americans could be, in a similar condition. Does any man deny the position? The proof, then, is found in the fact, that a very large proportion of our colored population were born on our soil, and are therefore entitled to all the privileges of American citizens. This is their country by birth, not by adoption. Their children possess the same inherent and inalienable rights as ours; and it is a crime of the blackest dye to load them with fetters.

Every Fourth of July, our Declaration of Independence is produced, with a sublime indignation, to set forth the tyranny of the mother country, and to challenge the admiration of the world. But what a pitiful detail of grievances does this document present, in comparison with the wrongs which our slaves endure! In the one case, it is hardly the plucking of a hair from the head; in the other, it is the crushing of a live body on the wheel; the stings of the wasp contrasted with the tortures of the inquisition. Before God, I must say, that such a glaring contradiction, as exists between our creed and practice, the annals of six thousand years cannot parallel. In view of it, I am ashamed of my country. I am sick of our unmeaning declamation in praise of liberty and equality; of our hypocritical cant about the unalienable rights of man. I could not, for my right hand, stand up before a European assembly, and exult that I am an American citizen, and denounce the usurpations of a kingly government as wicked and unjust; or, should I make the attempt, the recollection of my country's barbarity and despotism would blister my lips, and cover my cheeks with burning blushes of shame.

Will this be termed a rhetorical flourish? Will any man coldly accuse me of intemperate zeal? I will borrow, then, a ray of humanity from one of the brightest stars in our American galaxy, whose light will gather new effulgence to the end of time. "This, sirs, is a cause, that would be dishonored and betrayed, if I contented myself with appealing only to the understanding. It is too cold, and its processes are too slow for the occasion. I desire to thank God, that, since he has given me an intellect so fallible, he has impressed upon me an instinct that is sure. On a question of shame and honor —liberty and oppression—reasoning is sometimes useless, and worse. I feel the decision in my pulse: if it throws no light upon the brain, it kindles a fire at the heart."

Let us suppose that endurance has passed its bounds, and that the slaves, goaded to desperation by the cruelty of their oppressors, have girded on the armor of vengeance. Let us endeavor to imagine the appeal which they would publish to the world, in extenuation of their revolt. The preamble might be taken from our own Declaration of Independence, with a few slight alterations. Then what a detail of wrongs would follow! Speaking at first from the shores of Africa, and changing their situation with the course of events, they would say:

"They (the American people), arrogantly styling themselves the champions of freedom, for a long course of years have been guilty of the most cruel and protracted tyranny. They have invaded our territories, depopulated our villages, and kindled among us the flames of an exterminating war. They have wedged us into the holds of their 'floating hells,' with suffocating compactness, and without distinction of age or sex—allowing us neither to inhale the invigorating air of heaven, nor to witness the cheering light of the sun, neither wholesome food nor change of raiment—by which treatment thousands have expired under the most horrible sufferings. They have brought us to a free and Christian land (so called) and sold us in their market-places like cattle—even in the proud capital of their Union, and within sight of their legislative halls, where tyranny struts in the semblance of Liberty. They have cruelly torn the wife from her husband, the mother from her daughter, and children from their parents, and sold them into perpetual exile. They have confined us in loathsome cells and secret prisons—driven us in large droves from state to state, beneath a burning sky, half naked, and heavily manacled—nay, retaken and sold many, who had by years of toil obtained their liberation. They have compelled us 'to till their ground, to carry them, to fan them when they sleep, and tremble when they wake,' and rewarded us only with stripes, and hunger, and nakedness. They have lacerated our bodies with whips, and brands, and knives, for the most innocent and trifling offences, and often solely to gratify their malignant propensities; nor do they esteem it a crime worthy of death to murder us at will. Nor have they deprived us merely of our liberties. They would destroy our souls, by endeavoring to deprive us of the means of instruction—of a knowledge of God, and Jesus Christ, and the Holy Spirit, and a way of salvation: at the same time, they have taxed the whole country (our own labor among other things) to instruct and enlighten those who are at a great remove from them, whom they never fettered nor maimed, whose condition is not so dark or pitiable as our own. They have——"

But why need I proceed? My powers of description are inadequate to the task. A greater than Jefferson would fail. Only the pen of the recording angel can declare their manifold wrongs and sufferings; and the revelation will not be made till the day of judgment.

We say, that the disabilities imposed upon our fathers, by the mother country, furnished just cause for rebellion; that their removal was paramount to every other consideration; and that the slaughter of our oppressors was a justifiable act; for we should resist unto blood to save our liberties. Suppose that to-morrow should bring us tidings that the slaves at the South had revolted, *en masse*, and were spreading devastation and death among the white population. Should we celebrate their achievements in song, and justify their terrible excesses? And why not, if our creed be right? Their wrongs are unspeakably grievous, and liberty is the birthright of every man.

We say, that France was justified in assisting our fathers to maintain their independence; and that, as a nation, we owe her our liveliest gratitude for her timely interference. Suppose, in case of a revolt, that she, or some other European power, should furnish our slaves with guns and ammunition, and pour her troops into our land. Would it be treacherous or cruel? Why, according to our revolutionary credenda? The argument, tremendous as it is, is against us! Well, it may be done! At a fit moment, a foreign foe may stir up a rebellion, and arm every black, and take the lead in the enterprise. The attempt would not be difficult; the result can be easily imagined.

We say, that the imprisonment of an inconsiderable number of our seamen, by Great Britain, authorized the late war; and we boast of our promptitude to redress their wrongs. More than a million of native-born citizens are at this moment enduring the galling yoke of slavery. Who cries for justice?

None. "But they are blacks!" True, and they are also men; and, moreover, they are Americans by birth.

If it be said (which assertion is false) that the present race are beyond recovery; then I reply, in the language of a warm-hearted philanthropist, "Let us make no more slaves. Let us shiver to atoms those galling fetters, under the pressure of which so many hearts have bursted. Let us not shackle the limbs of the future workmanship of God. Let us pour into their minds the fertilizing streams of piety and knowledge; imbue their hearts with gratitude for extending to them this heaven's best boon; and suffer their souls to walk abroad in their majesty."

I come to my second proposition, the right of the free states to remonstrate against the continuance, and to assist in the overthrow of slavery.

This, I am aware, is a delicate subject, surrounded with many formidable difficulties. But if delay adds to its intricacy, wherefore shun an immediate investigation? I know that we of the North affectedly believe that we have no local interest in the removal of this great evil; that the slave states can take care of themselves, and that any proffered assistance, on our part, would be rejected as impertinent, dictatorial, or meddlesome; and that we have no right to lift up even a note of remonstrance. But I believe that these opinions are crude, preposterous, dishonorable, unjust. Sirs, this is a business in which, as members of one great family, we have a common interest; but we take no responsibility, either individually or collectively. Our hearts are cold, our blood stagnates in our veins. We act, in relation to the slaves, as if they were something lower than the brutes that perish.

On this question, I ask no support from the injunction of Holy Writ, which says, "therefore all things whatsoever ye would that men should do unto you, do ye even so to them: for this is the law and the prophets." I throw aside the common dictates of humanity. I assert the right of the free states to demand a gradual abolition of slavery, because, by its continuance, they participate in the guilt thereof, and are threatened with ultimate destruction; because they are bound to watch over the interests of the whole country without reference to territorial divisions; because their white population is nearly double that of the slave states, and the voice of this overwhelming majority should be potential; because they are now deprived of their just influence in the councils of the nation; because it is absurd and anti-republican to suffer property to be represented as men, and *vice versa;* because it gives the South an unjust ascendancy over other portions of territory, and a power that may be perverted on every occasion.

Now I say that, on the broad system of equal rights, this monstrous inequality should no longer be tolerated. If it cannot be speedily put down, not by force, but by fair persuasion; if we are always to remain shackled by unjust constitutional provisions, when the emergency that imposed them has long since passed away; if we must share in the guilt and danger of destroying the bodies and souls of men, *as the price of our Union;* if the slave states will haughtily spurn our assistance, and refuse to consult in the general welfare, then the fault is not ours if a separation eventually takes place.

It may be objected, that the laws of the slave states form insurmountable barriers to any interference on our part.

Answer. I grant that we have not the right, and I trust not the disposition, to use coercive measures. But do these laws hinder our prayers, or obstruct the flow of our sympathies? Cannot our charities alleviate the condition of the slave, and perhaps break his fetters? Can we not operate upon public sentiment (the lever that can move the moral world) by way of remonstrance, advice, or entreaty? Is Christianity so powerful, that she can tame the red men of our forests, and abolish the Burman caste, and overthrow the gods of Paganism, and liberate lands over which the darkness of superstition has lain for ages; and yet so weak, in her own dwelling-place, that she can make no impression upon her civil code? Can she contend successfully with cannibals, and yet be conquered by her own children?

Suppose that, by a miracle, the slaves should suddenly become white. Would you shut your eyes upon their sufferings, and calmly talk of constitutional limitations? No; your voice would peal in the ears of the taskmasters like deep thunder; you would carry the Constitution by force, if it could not be taken by treaty; patriotic assemblies would congregate at the corner of every street; the old Cradle of Liberty would rock to a deeper tone than ever echoed therein at British aggression; the pulpit would acquire new and unusual eloquence from our holy religion. The argument, that these white slaves are degraded, would not then obtain. You would say, it is enough that they are white, and in bondage, and they ought immediately to be set free. You would multiply your schools of instruction, and your temples of worship, and rely upon them for security.

But the plea is prevalent, that any interference by the free states, however benevolent or cautious it might be, would only irritate and inflame the jealousies of the South, and retard the cause of emancipation.

If any man believes that slavery can be abolished without a struggle with the worst passions of human nature, quietly, harmoniously, he cherishes a delusion. It can never be done, unless the age of miracles return. No; we must expect a collision, full of sharp asperities and bitterness. We shall have to contend with the insolence, and pride, and selfishness, of many a heartless being. But these can be easily conquered by meekness, and perseverance, and prayer.

Sirs, the prejudices of the North are stronger than those of the South; they bristle, like so many bayonets, around the slaves; they forge and rivet the chains of the nation. Conquer them, and the victory is won. The enemies of emancipation take courage from our criminal timidity. They have justly stigmatized us, even on the floor of Congress, with the most contemptuous epithets. We are—they say—their "white slaves," afraid of our own shadows, who have been driven back to the wall again and again; who stand trembling under their whips; who turn pale, retreat, and surrender, at a talismanic threat to dissolve the Union.

It is often despondingly said, that the evil of slavery is beyond our control. Dreadful conclusion, that puts the seal of death upon our country's existence! If we cannot conquer the monster in his infancy, while his cartilages are tender and his limbs powerless, how shall we escape his wrath when he goes forth a gigantic cannibal, seeking whom he may devour? If we cannot safely unloose two millions of slaves now, how shall we bind upwards of *twenty millions* at the close of the present century? But there is no cause for despair. We have seen how readily, and with what ease, that horrid gorgon, Intemperance, has been checked in its ravages. Let us take courage. Moral influence, when in vigorous exercise, is irresistible. It has an immortal essence. It can no more be trod out of existence by the iron foot of time, or by the ponderous march of iniquity, than matter can be annihilated. It may disappear for a time; but it lives in some shape or other, in some place or other, and will rise with renovated strength. Let us, then, be up and doing. In the simple and stirring language of the stout-hearted Lundy, "all the friends of the cause must go to work, keep to work, hold on, and never give up."

If it be still objected that it would be dangerous to liberate the present race of blacks,

I answer, that the emancipation of all the slaves of this generation is most assuredly out of the question. The fabric, which now towers above the Alps, must be taken away brick by brick, and foot by foot, till it is reduced so low that it may be overturned without burying the nation in its ruins. Years may elapse before the completion of the achievement; generations of blacks may go down to the grave, manacled and lacerated, without a hope for their children; the philanthropists, who are now pleading in behalf of the oppressed, may not live to witness the dawn which will precede the glorious day of universal emancipation; but the work will go on—laborers in the cause will multiply—new resources will be discovered—the victory will be obtained, worth the desperate struggle of a thousand years. Or, if defeat follow, woe to the safety of this people! The nation will be shaken as if by a mighty earthquake. A cry of horror, a cry of revenge, will go up to heaven in the darkness of midnight, and re-echo from every cloud. Blood will flow like water—the blood of guilty men, and of innocent women and children. Then will be heard lamentations and weeping, such as will blot out the remembrance of the horrors of St. Domingo. The terrible judgments of an incensed God will complete the catastrophe of republican America.

And since so much is to be done for our country; since so many prejudices are to be dispelled, obstacles vanquished, interests secured, blessings obtained; since the cause of emancipation must progress heavily, and meet with much unhallowed opposition, why delay the work? There must be a beginning, and now is a propitious time—perhaps the last opportunity that will be granted us by a long-suffering God. No temporizing, lukewarm measures will avail aught. We must put our shoulder to the wheel, and heave with our united strength. Let us not look coldly on, and see our Southern brethren contending single-handed against an all-powerful foe—faint, weary, borne down to the earth. We are all alike guilty. Slavery is strictly a national sin. New-England money has been expended in buying human flesh; New-England ships have been freighted with sable victims; New-England men have assisted in forging the fetters of those who groan in bondage.

I call upon the ambassadors of Christ everywhere to make known this proclamation: "Thus saith the Lord God of the Africans, Let this people go, that they may serve me." I ask them to "proclaim liberty to the captives, and the opening of the prison to them that are bound"—to light up a flame of philanthropy, that shall burn till all Africa be redeemed from the night of moral death, and the song of deliverance be heard throughout her borders.

I call upon the churches of the living God to lead in this great enterprise. If the soul be immortal, priceless, save it from redeemless woe. Let them combine their energies, and systematize their plans, for the rescue of suffering humanity. Let them pour out their supplications to heaven in behalf of the slave. Prayer is omnipotent: its breath can melt adamantine rocks—its touch can break the stoutest chains. Let anti-slavery charity-boxes stand uppermost among those for missionary, tract and educational purposes. On this subject, Christians have been asleep; let them shake off their slumbers, and arm for the holy contest.

I call upon our New-England women to form charitable associations to relieve the degraded of their sex. As yet, an appeal to their sympathies was never made in vain. They outstrip us in every benevolent race. Females are doing much for the cause at the South; let their example be imitated, and their exertions surpassed, at the North.

I call upon the great body of newspaper editors to keep this subject constantly before their readers; to sound the trumpet of alarm, and to plead eloquently for the rights of man. They must give the tone to public sentiment. One press may ignite twenty; a city may warm a state; a state may impart a generous heat to a whole country.

I call upon the American people to enfranchise a spot, over which they hold complete sovereignty; to cleanse that worse than Augean stable, the District of Columbia, from its foul impurities. I conjure them to select those as Representatives, who are not too ignorant to know, too blind to see, nor too timid to perform their duty.

I will say, finally, that I tremble for the republic while slavery exists therein. If I look up to God for success, no smile of mercy or forgiveness dispels the gloom of futurity; if to our resources, they are daily diminishing; if to all history, our destruction is not only possible, but almost certain. Why should we slumber at this momentous crisis? If our hearts were dead to every throb of humanity; if it were lawful to oppress, where power is ample; still, if we had any regard for our safety and happiness, we should strive to crush the vampire which is feeding upon our life-blood. All the selfishness of our nature cries aloud for a better security. Our own vices are too strong for us, and keep us in perpetual alarm; how, in addition to these, shall we be able to contend successfully with millions of armed and desperate men, as we must eventually, if slavery do not cease?

MESSAGE TO THE LEGISLATURE OF SOUTH CAROLINA, 1835.

BY GEORGE McDUFFIE

Introduction

Governor George McDuffie's message to the Legislature of South Carolina in 1835 fired the opening gun in the South's counterattack against militant abolitionism. It marked the development of a new approach by Southern spokesmen to the rationalization and justification of the South's peculiar institution. It indicated the transition in Southern thought from what has been termed the "necessary evil" to the "positive good" defense of slavery. In one form or another the arguments set forth were to be echoed again and again, and to be carefully elaborated, in the ideological battle over slavery that continued right up to and through the Civil War.

At the time of the Revolution and the triumph of natural rights philosophy as expressed in the Declaration of Independence, no clear and resolute defense of slavery as a national institution existed. There was, indeed, at the time great uncertainty with respect to its future. In the North by 1790 slavery was everywhere in course of extinction. In the

South continuing and severe economic crises in the field of tobacco production gave ground for the belief that here, too, the final abolition of the system could not be long delayed.

But decisive events occurred which operated, over the course of several decades, to produce a fundamental change in the Southern attitude.

In the first place, the economic crisis was solved by a market revolution, which in the first two decades of the nineteenth century substituted cotton for tobacco as the principal Southern crop. The mounting and apparently insatiable demand of both British and Yankee factories for this raw material provided a new and tragically fertile field for the employment of slaves. As early as the 1780's, the cotton crop began to produce a harvest of gold for its producers. It was hardly to be expected that so profitable a turn of events would be accompanied indefinitely with a defensive, hangdog approach to the employment of slaves.

In the second place, the rapid extension of cotton cultivation throughout the South, and the consequent rise of a new slave empire, produced a strong reaction among antislavery spokesmen, both North and South. Garrison's leadership was important because it signaled the birth of a new mood among Americans. It raised a cry of alarm at the extension of an iniquitous system of exploitation. It warned of a mortal danger to republican democracy and to Christian morals. It called for an immediate end to slaveholding, and was determined that neither the Federal government nor public opinion should truckle to it. This new antislavery mood was generating a social movement, and was marshaling an array of articulate and many-sided criticisms against the system. This, thought the Southerners, must be answered—before the world, the South, the slaves themselves, and before the American people without whose at least passive cooperation slavery could not for a single day continue to exist and to develop.

Thus it came about that proslavery spokesmen abandoned their traditional defensive and apologetic attitude. Slavery, they said, must be defended because it was good. It could be defended effectively in no other way.

For this purpose Southerners mustered many of the old arguments in favor of slavery that had been advanced at an earlier time, and gave them a new emphasis and an elaborate development. One aspect of this new approach was a stress upon the social benefits of the slave system. Did it not take the Negro—an inferior being, doomed in Africa to a life of degradation and inferiority—and subject him to the beneficent guidance of a Christian civilization? Did it not protect him from the horrors of exploitation to which the greedy capitalist subjected factory operatives, Irish paupers and continental peasantry? Did it not guarantee him a respectable old age relieved of cares and passed in the bosom of his family? Slavery, concluded McDuffie, far from being an evil, was in very truth the cornerstone of the republican edifice.

George McDuffie (1790-1851) was born in Georgia to a family in poor and humble circumstances. He became a lawyer and served in Congress as a representative from South Carolina from 1821 to 1834. In the latter year he was elected governor of the state. As a young man his convictions, like his contemporary Calhoun's, were strongly nationalist. During the 1820's he adopted a passionate states-rights, anti-tariff position, and became the acknowledged leader of the diehard states' sovereignty and nullification group known to history as the "fire-eaters." McDuffie was one of the South Carolina politicians instrumental in winning Calhoun over to a states-rights position during Jackson's first administration—ironically enough, since Calhoun thereafter rapidly supplanted him as the South's leading spokesman for both slavery and states rights.

GOVERNOR MCDUFFIE'S MESSAGE
ON THE SLAVERY QUESTION*

Since your last adjournment, the public mind, throughout the slaveholding states, has been intensely, indignantly, and justly excited by the wanton, officious, and incendiary proceedings of certain societies and persons in some of the non-slaveholding states, who have been actively employed in attempting to circulate among us, pamphlets, papers, and pictorial representations of the most offensive and inflam-

* The document reproduced here is that portion of the governor's message to the Legislature of South Carolina dealing with the slavery question. It is taken from the *Journal of the General Assembly of the State of South Carolina* for the year 1835, pages 4-10.

matory character, and eminently calculated to seduce our slaves from their fidelity, and excite them to insurrection and massacre. These wicked monsters and deluded fanatics, overlooking the numerous objects in their own vicinity, who have a moral, if not a legal claim upon their charitable regard, run abroad, in the expansion of their hypocritical benevolence, muffled up in the saintly mantle of Christian meekness, to fulfil the fiend-like errand of mingling the blood of the master and the slave, to whose fate they are equally indifferent, with the smouldering ruins of our peaceful dwellings. No principle of human action so utterly baffles all human calculation as that species of fanatical enthusiasm, which is made of envy and ambition, assuming the guise of religious zeal, and acting upon the known prejudices, religious or political, of an ignorant multitude. Under the influence of this species of voluntary madness, nothing is sacred that stands in the way of its purposes. Like all other religious impostures, it has power to consecrate every act, however atrocious, and every person, however covered with "multiplying villanies," that may promote its diabolical ends, or worship at its infernal altars. By its unholy creed, murder itself becomes a labor of love and charity, and the felon renegado, who flies from the justice of his country, finds not only a refuge, but becomes a sainted minister, in the sanctuary of its temple.

No error can be more mischievous, than to underrate the danger of such a principle, and no policy can be more fatal than to neglect it, from a contempt for the supposed insignificance of its agents. The experience of both France and Great Britain fearfully instruct us, from what small and contemptible beginnings, this *ami des noirs* philanthropy may rise to a gigantic power, too mighty to be resisted by all the influence and energy of the government; in the one case, shrouding a wealthy and flourishing island in the blood of its white inhabitants; in the other, literally driving the ministry, by means of an instructed Parliament, to perpetrate that act of suicidal legislation, and colonial oppression, the emancipation of slaves in the British West Indies. It may be not unaptly compared to the element of fire, of which, a neglected spark, amongst combustible materials, which a timely stamp of the foot might have extinguished forever, speedily swells into a sweeping torrent of fiery desolation, which no human power can arrest or control. In the opinion of intelligent West India planters, it is because the local authorities, from a sense of false security, neglected to hang up the first of these political missionaries that made their appearance on the British Islands, that they are doomed to barrenness and desertion, and to be the wretched abodes of indolent and profligate blacks, exhibiting, in their squalid poverty, gross immorality, and slavish subjection to an iron despotism of British bayonets, the fatal mockery of all the promised blessings of emancipation.

Under these circumstances, and in this critical conjuncture of our affairs, the solemn and responsible duty devolves on the legislature, of "taking care that the republic receive no detriment."

The crime which these foreign incendiaries have committed against the peace of the state, is one of the very highest grade known to human laws. It not only strikes at the very existence of society, but seeks to accomplish the catastrophe, by the most horrible means, celebrating the obsequies of the state in a saturnial carnival of blood and murder, and while brutally violating all the charities of life, and desecrating the very altars of religion, impiously calling upon Heaven to sanction these abominations. It is my deliberate opinion, that the laws of every community should punish this species of interference by death without benefit of clergy, regarding the authors of it as "enemies of the human race." Nothing could be more appropriate than for South Carolina to set this example in the present crisis, and I trust the Legislature will not adjourn till it discharges this high duty of patriotism.

It cannot be disguised, however, that any laws which may be enacted by the authority of this state, however adequate to punish and repress offences committed within its limits, will be wholly insufficient to meet the exigencies of the present conjuncture. If we go no farther than this, we had as well do nothing.

The outrages against the peace and safety of the state are perpetrated in other communities, which hold and exercise sovereign and exclusive jurisdiction over all persons and things within their territorial limits. It is within these limits, protected from responsibility to our laws by the sovereignty of the states in which they reside, that the authors of all this mischief, securely concoct their schemes, plant their batteries, and hurl their fiery missiles among us, aimed at that mighty magazine of combustible matter, the explosion of which would lay the state in ruins.

It will, therefore, become our imperious duty, recurring to those great principles of international law, which still exist in all their primitive force amongst the sovereign states of this confederacy, to demand of our sovereign associates the condign punishment of those enemies of our peace, who avail themselves of the sanctuaries of their respective jurisdictions, to carry on schemes of incendiary hostility against the institutions, the safety, and the existence of the state. In performing this high duty, to which we are constrained by the great law of self-preservation, let us approach to our co-states with all the fraternal mildness which becomes us as members of the same family of confederated republics, and at the same time with that firmness and decision, which becomes a sovereign state, while maintaining her dearest interests and most sacred rights.

For the institution of domestic slavery we hold ourselves responsible only to God, and it is utterly incompatible with the dignity and the safety of the state, to permit any foreign authority to question our right to maintain it. It may nevertheless be appropriate, as a voluntary token of our respect for the opinions of our confederate brethren, to present some views to their consideration on this subject, calculated to disabuse their minds of false opinions and pernicious prejudices.

No human institution, in my opinion, is more manifestly consistent with the will of God, than domestic slavery, and no one of his ordinances is written in more legible characters than that which consigns the African race to this condition, as more conducive to their own happiness, than any other of which they are susceptible. Whether we consult the sacred Scriptures, or the lights of nature and reason, we shall find these truths as abundantly apparent, as if written with a sunbeam in the heavens. Under both the Jewish and Christian dispensations of our religion, domestic slavery existed with the unequivocal sanction of its prophets, its apostles, and finally its great Author. The patriarchs themselves, those chosen instruments of God, were slave-holders. In fact the divine sanction of this institution is so plainly written that "he who runs may read" it, and those over-righteous pretenders and Pharisees, who affect to be scandalized by its existence among us, would do well to inquire how much more nearly they walk in the ways of godliness, than did Abraham, Isaac, and Jacob.

That the African Negro is destined by providence to occupy this condition of servile dependence, is not less manifest. It is marked on the face, stamped on the skin, and evinced by the intellectual inferiority and natural improvidence of this race. They have all the qualities that fit them for slaves, and not one of those that would fit them to be freemen. They are utterly unqualified not only for rational freedom, but for self-government of any kind. They are, in all respects, physical, moral, and political, inferior to millions of the human race, who have for consecutive ages dragged out a wretched existence under a grinding political despotism, and who are doomed to this hopeless condition by the very qualities which unfit them for a better. It is utterly astonishing that any enlightened American, after contemplating all the manifold forms in which even the white race of mankind are doomed to slavery and oppression, should suppose it possible to reclaim the African race from their destiny. The capacity to enjoy freedom is an attribute not to be communicated by human power. It is an endowment of God, and one of the rarest which it has pleased his inscrutable wisdom to bestow upon the nations of the earth. It is conferred as the reward of merit, and only upon those who are qualified to enjoy it. Until the "Ethiopian can change his skin," it will be in vain to attempt, by any human power, to make freemen of those whom God has doomed to be slaves by all their attributes.

Let not, therefore, the misguided and designing intermeddlers who seek to destroy our peace, imagine that they are serving the cause of God by practically arraigning the decrees of his providence. Indeed it would scarcely excite surprise, if with the impious audacity of those who projected the Tower of Babel, they should attempt to scale the battlements of Heaven, and remonstrate with the God of wisdom for having put the mark of Cain and the curse of Ham upon the African race, instead of the European.

If the benevolent friends of the black race would compare the condition of that portion of them which we hold in servitude, with that which still remains in Africa, totally unblessed by the lights of civilization or Christianity, and groaning under a savage despotism, as utterly destitute of hope as of happiness, they would be able to form some tolerable estimate, of what our blacks have lost by slavery in America, and what they have gained by freedom in Africa. Greatly as their condition has been improved by their subjection to an enlightened and Christian people—the only mode under heaven by which it could have been accomplished—they are yet wholly unprepared for anything like a rational system of self-government. Emancipation would be a positive curse, depriving them of a guardianship essential to their happiness, and they may well say in the language of the Spanish proverb, "Save us from our friends and we will take care of our enemies." If emancipated, where would they live and what would be their condition? The idea of their remaining among us is utterly visionary. Amalgamation is abhorrent to every sentiment of nature; and if they remain as a separate caste, whether endowed with equal privileges or not, they will become our masters or we must resume the mastery over them. This state of political amalgamation and conflict, which the abolitionists evidently aim to produce, would be the most horrible condition imaginable, and would furnish Dante or Milton with the type for another chapter illustrating the horrors of the infernal regions. The only disposition, therefore, that could be made of our emancipated slaves would be their transportation to Africa, to exterminate the natives or be exterminated by them; contingencies either of which may well serve to illustrate the wisdom, if not the philanthropy, of these superserviceable madmen who in the name of humanity would desolate the fairest region of the earth and destroy the most perfect system of social and political happiness, that ever has existed.

It is perfectly evident that the destiny of the Negro race is, either the worst possible form of political slavery, or else domestic servitude as it exists in the slaveholding states. The advantage of domestic slavery over the most favorable condition of political slavery, does not admit of a question. It is the obvious interest of the master, not less than his duty, to provide comfortable food and clothing for his slaves; and whatever false and exaggerated stories may be propagated by mercenary travellers, who make a trade of exchanging calumny for hospitality, the peasantry and operatives of no country in the world are better provided for, in these respects, than the slaves of our country. In the single empire of Great Britain, the most free and enlightened nation in Europe, there are more wretched paupers and half starving operatives, than there are Negro slaves in the United States. In all respects, the comforts of our slaves are greatly superior to those of the English operatives, or the Irish and continental peasantry, to say nothing of the millions of paupers crowded together in those loathsome receptacles of starving humanity, the public poor-houses. Besides the hardships of incessant toil, too much almost for human nature to endure, and the sufferings of actual want, driving them almost to despair, these miserable creatures are perpetually annoyed by the most distressing cares for the future condition of themselves and their children.

From this excess of labor, this actual want, and these distressing cares, our slaves are entirely exempted. They habitually labor from two to four hours a day less than the operatives in other countries, and it has been truly remarked, by some writer, that a Negro cannot be made to injure himself by excessive labor. It may be safely affirmed that they usually eat as much wholesome and substantial food in one day, as English operatives or Irish peasants eat in two. And as it regards concern for the future, their condition may well be envied even by their masters. There is not upon the face of the earth, any class of people, high or low, so perfectly free from care and anxiety. They know that their masters will provide for them, under all circumstances, and that in the extremity of old age, instead of being driven to beggary or to seek public charity in a poor-house, they will be comfortably accommodated and kindly treated among their relatives and associates. Cato the elder has been regarded as a model of Roman virtue, and yet he is said to have sold his superannuated slaves to avoid the expense of maintaining them. The citizens of this state may not aspire to rival the virtue of the Romans, but it may be safely affirmed, that they would doom to execration the master who should imitate the inhuman example of the Roman paragon. The government of our slaves is strictly patriarchal, and produces those mutual feelings of kindness which result from a constant interchange of good offices, and which can only exist in a system of domestic or patriarchial slavery. They are entirely unknown either in a state of political slavery, or in that form of domestic servitude which exists in all other communities.

In a word, our slaves are cheerful, contented, and happy, much beyond the general condition of the human race except where those foreign intruders and fatal ministers of mischief, the emancipationists, like their arch-prototype in the garden of Eden, and actuated by no less envy, have tempted them to aspire above the condition to which they have been assigned in the order of providence.

Nor can it be admitted, as some of our own statesmen have affirmed, in a mischievous and misguided spirit of sickly sentimentality, that our system of domestic slavery is a curse to the white population—a moral and political evil much to be deplored but incapable of being eradicated. Let the tree be judged by its fruit. More than half a century ago, one of the most enlightened statesmen who ever illustrated the parliamentary annals of Great Britain, looking into political causes, with an eye of profound philosophy, ascribed the high and indomitable spirit of liberty which distinguished the Southern colonies, to the existence of domestic slavery; referring to the example of the free states of antiquity as a confirmation of his theory. Since those colonies have become independent states, they have amply sustained the glory of their primitive character. There is no coloring of national vanity in the assertion, which impartial history will ratify, that the principles of rational liberty are not less thoroughly understood, and have been more vigilantly, resolutely, and effectively defended against all the encroachments of power, by the slaveholding states, than by any other members of the confederacy. In which of our great political conflicts is it, that they have not been found arrayed against every form of usurpation, and fighting under the flag of liberty? Indeed it is a fact of historical notoriety, that those great Whig principles of liberty, by which government is restrained within constitutional limits, have had their origin, and for a long time had their only abiding place, in the slaveholding states.

Reason and philosophy can easily explain what experience so clearly testifies. It we look into the elements of which all political communities are composed, it will be found that servitude, in some form, is one of the essential constituents. No community ever has existed without it, and we may confidently assert, none ever will. In the very nature of things there must be classes of persons to discharge all the different offices of society, from the highest to the lowest. Some of those offices are regarded as degrading, though they must and will be performed. Hence those manifold forms of dependent servitude which produces a sense of superiority in the masters or employers, and of inferiority on the part of the servants. Where these offices are performed by members of the political community, a dangerous element is introduced into the body politic. Hence the alarming tendency to violate the rights of property by agrarian legislation, which is beginning to be manifest in the older states, where universal suffrage prevails without domestic slavery, a tendency that will increase in the progress of society with the increasing inequality of wealth. No government is worthy of the name that does not protect the rights of property, and no enlightened people will long submit to such a mockery. Hence it is that in older countries, different political orders are established to effect this indispensable object, and it will be fortunate for the non-slaveholding states, if they are not, in less than a quarter of a century, driven to the adoption of a similar institution, or to take refuge from robbery and anarchy under a military despotism.

But where the menial offices and dependent employments of society are performed by domestic slaves, a class well defined by their color and entirely separated from the political body, the rights of property are perfectly secure, without the establishment of artificial barriers. In a word, the institution of domestic slavery supersedes the necessity of an order of nobility, and all the other appendages of a hereditary system of government. If our slaves were emancipated, and admitted, bleached or unbleached, to an equal participation in our political privileges, what a commentary should we furnish upon the doctrines of the emancipationists, and what a revolting spectacle of republican equality should we exhibit to the mockery of the world! No rational man would consent to live in such a state of society, if he could find a refuge in any other.

Domestic slavery, therefore, instead of being a political evil, is the cornerstone of our republican edifice. No patriot who justly estimates our privileges will tolerate the idea of emancipation, at any period, however remote, or on any conditions of pecuniary advantage, however favorable. I would as soon think of opening a negotiation for selling the liberty of the state at once, as for making any stipulations for the ultimate emancipation of our slaves. So deep is my conviction on this subject, that if I were doomed to die immediately after recording these sentiments, I could say in all sincerity and under all the sanctions of Christianity and patriotism, "God forbid that my descendants, in the remotest generations, should live in any other than a community having the institution of domestic slavery, as it existed among the patriarchs of the primitive Church and in all the free states of antiquity."

If the Legislature should concur in these general views of this important element of our political and social system, our confederates should be distinctly informed, in any communications we may have occasion to make to them, that in claiming to be exempted from all foreign interference, we can recognize no distinction between ultimate and immediate emancipation.

It becomes necessary, in order to ascertain the extent of our danger, and the measures of precaution necessary to guard against it, that we examine into the real motives and ultimate purposes of the abolition societies and their prominent agents. To justify their officious and gratuitous interference in our domestic affairs—the most insulting and insolent outrage which can be offered to a community—they profess to hold themselves responsible for the pretended sin of our domestic slavery, because, forsooth, *they* tolerate its existence among *us*. If they are at all responsible for the sin of slavery, whatever that may be, it is not because they tolerate it now, but because their ancestors were the agents and authors of its original introduction. These ancestors sold ours the slaves and warranted the title, and it would be a much more becoming labor of filial piety for their descendants to pray for their souls, if they are Protestants, and buy masses to redeem them from purgatory, if they are Catholics, than to assail their warranty and slander their memory by denouncing them as "man-stealers and murderers."

But this voluntary and gratuitous assumption of responsibility, in imitation of a recent and high example in our history, but imperfectly conceals a lurking principle of danger, which deserves to be examined and exposed. What is there to make the people of New York or Massachusetts responsible for slavery in South Carolina, any more than the people of Great Britain? To assume that the people of those states are responsible for the continuance of this institution, is distinctly to assume that they have a right to abolish it. And whatever enforced disclaimers they may make, their efforts would be worse than unprofitable on any other hypothesis. The folly of attempting to convert the slaveholders to voluntary emancipa-

tion, by a course of slander and denunciation, is too great to
be ascribed even to fanaticism itself. They do not, indeed, disguise the fact that their principal object is to operate on public opinion in the non-slaveholding states. And to what purpose? They cannot suppose that the opinion of those states,
however unanimous, can break the chains of slavery by some
moral magic. The whole tenor of their conduct and temper of
their discussions clearly demonstrate that their object is to
bring the slaveholding states into universal odium, and the
public opinion of the non-slaveholding to the point of emancipating our slaves by Federal legislation, without the consent
of their owners. Disguise it as they may, "to this complexion
it must come at last."

It is in this aspect of the subject, that it challenges our
grave and solemn consideration. It behooves us then, in my
opinion, to demand, respectfully, of each and every one of the
non-slaveholding states:

1. A formal and solemn disclaimer, by its Legislature, of
the existence of any rightful power, either in such state or the
United States, in Congress assembled, to interfere in any manner, whatever, with the institution of domestic slavery in South
Carolina.

2. The immediate passage of penal laws by such Legislature, denouncing against the incendiaries of whom we complain, such punishments as will speedily and forever suppress
their machinations against our peace and safety. Though the
right to emancipate our slaves, by coercive legislation, has
been very generally disclaimed by popular assemblages in the
non-slaveholding states, it is nevertheless important that each
of those states should give this disclaimer and the authentic
and authoritative form of a legislative declaration, to be preserved as a permanent record for our future security. Our
right to demand of those states the enactment of laws for the
punishment of those enemies of our peace, who avail themselves of the sanctuary of their sovereign jurisdiction to wage
a war of extermination against us, is founded on one of the
most salutary and conservative principles of international law.
Every state is under the most sacred obligations, not only to
abstain from all such interference with the institutions of another as is calculated to disturb its tranquillity or endanger its
safety; but to prevent its citizens or subjects from such interference, either by inflicting condign punishment itself, or by

delivering them up to the justice of the offending community. As between separate and independent nations, the refusal of a state to punish these offensive proceedings against another, by its citizens or subjects, makes the state so refusing an accomplice in the outrage, and furnishes a just cause of war.

These principles of international law are universally admitted, and none have been more sacredly observed by just and enlightened nations. The obligations of the non-slaveholding states to punish and repress the proceedings of their citizens against our domestic institutions and tranquillity are greatly increased, both by the nature of those proceedings, and the fraternal relation which subsists between the states of this confederacy. For no outrage against any community can be greater than to stir up the elements of servile insurrection, and no obligation to repress it can be more sacred than that which adds to the sanctions of international law, the solemn guarantee of a constitutional compact, which is at once the bond and the condition of our union. The liberal, enlightened and magnanimous conduct of the people in many portions of the non-slaveholding states forbids us to anticipate a refusal on the part of those states to fulfil these high obligations of national faith and duty.

And we have the less reason to look forward to this inauspicious result, from considering the necessary consequences which would follow, to the people of those states, and of the whole commercial world, from the general emancipation of our slaves. These consequences may be presented, as an irresistible appeal, to every rational philanthropist in Europe or America. It is clearly demonstrable that the production of cotton depends not so much on soil and climate, as on the existence of domestic slavery. In the relaxing latitudes where it grows, not one half the quantity would be produced, but for the existence of this institution, and every practical planter will concur in the opinion, that if all the slaves in these states were now emancipated, the American crop would be reduced the very next year from 1,200,000 to 600,000 bales. No great skill in political economy will be required to estimate how enormously the price of cotton would be increased by this change, and no one who will consider how largely this staple contributes to the wealth of manufacturing nations, and to the necessaries and comforts of the poorer classes all over the world, can fail to perceive the disastrous effects of so great a reduction in the quantity, and so great an enhancement in the price of it. In Great Britain, France, and the United States, the catastrophe would be overwhelming, and it is not extravagant to say, that for little more than two millions of Negro slaves, cut loose from their tranquil moorings, and set adrift upon the untried ocean of at least a doubtful experiment, ten millions of poor white people would be reduced to destitution, pauperism, and starvation. An anxious desire to avoid the last sad alternative of an injured community prompts this final appeal to the interests and enlightened philanthropy of our confederate states. And we cannot permit ourselves to believe, that our just demands, thus supported by every consideration of humanity and duty, will be rejected by states, who are united to us by so many social and political ties, and who have so deep an interest in the preservation of that union.

EXPLORING BUTLER ISLAND

BY FRANCES ANNE KEMBLE

Introduction

A unique contribution toward the understanding of American slavery, and to the history of the Negro people who endured it, was made by an Englishwoman, Frances Anne Kemble. She was born in 1809 into England's most famous family of actors. Her aunt Sarah was the incomparable Mrs. Siddons, who until her retirement in 1812 was the country's leading Shakespearian actress; her father, too, was a noted actor and producer, and manager of the important Covent Garden theater in London.

Though her parents were reluctant to put Fanny on the stage, a family financial crisis obliged her to make her début at Covent Garden in 1829. She appeared in the role of Juliet, and England found, to its delight, that it had a new and brilliant leading lady. When Fanny arrived in New York in 1832 for an American tour—organized for financial reasons, since success did not materially diminish the family's monetary difficulties—she came as England's foremost actress and as one of her most famous and talented women.

Touring the eastern seaboard with her father, Fanny attracted a host of admirers—in particular Pierce Mease Butler,

scion of a wealthy Philadelphia family. He wooed her ardent-
ly and married her in 1834. But their union was not destined
to be a success. Fanny came from a country which, during
her youth, was embracing antislavery convictions, putting an
end to the infamous slave traffic, and emancipating the slaves
themselves. She reflected her countrymen's convictions, and
scorned the idea that a self-respecting Englishwoman could
entertain anything but the deepest detestation for physical
bondage in its cruelty and immorality. Her husband, on the
other hand, came into possession, two years after his marriage,
of Georgia's largest rice and cotton plantation, boasting of upwards of seven hundred slaves. This property, located among
the Georgia sea islands, had made a princely fortune for the
Butlers since it was first established in the 1790's by Pierce
Butler, one of the founding fathers and grandfather of Fanny's
husband. No one in the Butler family, until Fanny's arrival,
questioned either the propriety of owning slaves or the enjoyment of the wealth and prestige that accrued from their labor.

When she first came to the United States, Fanny had made
the acquaintance of William Ellery Channing and had developed a close friendship with him; his teaching concerning
the Christian duty of social reform—and in particular the explicit condemnation of the institution of slavery which he
made in a little book published in 1835—reinforced her
convictions and her determination to act. In 1838 Pierce
Mease Butler gave in to her pleas that they should visit
Georgia together. Fanny thus accompanied her husband on
his first visit to the ancestral estate. She wished to see slavery
at first hand for herself, and do what she could to prepare
her chattels for emancipation.

The Butler plantations were located on two islands in the
estuary of the Altamaha River. One of these, St. Simons
Island, specialized in cotton production; the other, Butler
Island, in rice. Fanny spent a total of four months here, dividing her stay equally between the two islands. She found
that slavery in actuality was all that she had imagined it to be
—and more. The emotional shock of the experience, and the
weight of an anguish which she found unable to share with
her husband, drove her to confide her feelings and her observations to her journal. The rough record, set down amidst
constant interruptions and often in note form, was written
up and revised on her return to Philadelphia. It was given to

the world almost a quarter of a century later, in 1863, under the title of A Journal of a Residence on a Georgian Plantation in 1838-9.

The Journal is valuable to the historian because it is drawn almost completely from personal observation and personal experience. It achieves a minuteness of detail which enables us literally to see the Butler plantations through Fanny Kemble's eyes. With a true artist's sense, she presents her picture of the human tragedy in a vividly painted natural setting. She is a master of savage epigram, and also of lyrical prose. Slavery, in one instance, is neatly summarized as

> "the most disgusting struggle which is going on, all the time, on the one hand to inflict, and on the other to evade, oppression and injustice."

In another place she speaks of

> "the unspeakable glories of these Southern heavens, the saffron brightness of morning, the blue intense brilliance of noon, the golden splendor and the rosy softness of sunset."

For what it tells us about slaves, and as a mirror of the mind of its creator, the Journal is a doubly human document.

Mrs. Kemble had read George McDuffie's message to the South Carolina Legislature (pp. 325 ff.), and had been deeply shocked by it. We may regard her Journal in the most immediate sense as an answer to McDuffie's views on the nature of slavery and of slaves. We reproduce below the chapter in the Journal that was the fruit of the actress' first exploration of her new home. The "Elizabeth" to whom the Journal was addressed and dedicated was Elizabeth Dwight Sedgwick of Lenox, Massachusetts, a great-granddaughter of Jonathan Edwards and an intimate friend of Mrs. Kemble's.

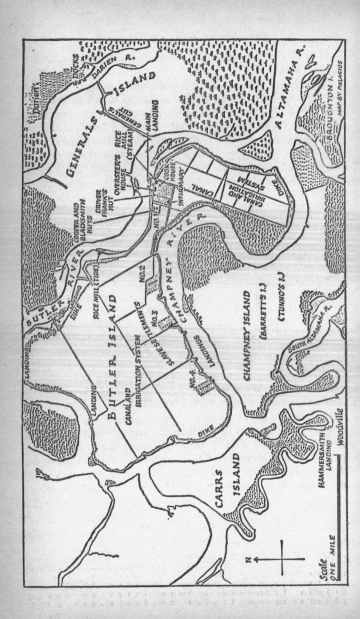

EXPLORING BUTLER ISLAND*

[Butler Island, January, 1839]

Dear E[lizabeth],

Minuteness of detail, and fidelity in the account of my daily doings, will hardly, I fear, render my letters very interesting to you now; but, cut off as I am here from all the usual resources and amusements of civilized existence, I shall find but little to communicate to you that is not furnished by my observations on the novel appearance of external nature, and the moral and physical condition of Mr. [Butler]'s people. The latter subject is, I know, one sufficiently interesting in itself to you, and I shall not scruple to impart all the reflections which may occur to me relative to their state during my stay here, where inquiry into their mode of existence will form my chief occupation, and, necessarily also, the staple commodity of my letters. I purpose, while I reside here, keeping a sort of journal, such as Monk Lewis[1] wrote during his visit to his West India plantations. I wish I had any prospect of rendering my diary as interesting and amusing to you as his was to me.

In taking my first walk on the island, I directed my steps toward the rice mill, a large building on the banks of the river, within a few yards of the house we occupy. Is it not rather curious that Miss Martineau[2] should have mentioned the erection of a steam mill for threshing rice somewhere in the vicinity of Charleston as a singular novelty, likely to form an era in Southern agriculture, and to produce the most desirable changes in the system of labor by which it is carried on? Now on this estate alone there are three threshing mills—one worked by steam, one by the tide, and one by horses; there are two private steam mills on plantations adjacent to ours, and a public one at Savannah, where the planters who have none on their own estates are in the habit of sending their rice to be threshed at a certain percentage; these have all been in operation for some years, and I therefore am at a loss to understand

*Source: *Journal of a Residence on a Georgian Plantation* in 1838-9 (New York, 1961), edited by John Anthony Scott. Reproduced by permission of Alfred A. Knopf, Inc. Copyright, 1961.

[1] Matthew Gregory Lewis was known as Monk Lewis, after the title of one of his novels. His *Journal of a West Indian Proprietor* was first published in London in 1834.

[2] Harriet Martineau visited the South in the winter of 1834-35. Despite the handicap of severe deafness she conversed with a great many people and published her impressions of the United States, *Society in America*, in 1837.

what made her hail the erection of the one at Charleston as likely to produce such immediate and happy results. By-the-by —of the misstatements, or rather mistakes, for they are such, in her books, with regard to certain facts—her only disadvantage in acquiring information was not by any means that natural infirmity on which the periodical press, both here and in England, has commented with so much brutality. She had the misfortune to possess, too, that unsuspecting reliance upon the truth of others which they are apt to feel who themselves hold truth most sacred; and this was a sore disadvantage to her in a country where I have heard it myself repeatedly asserted— and, what is more, much gloried in—that she was purposely misled by the persons to whom she addressed her inquiries, who did not scruple to disgrace themselves by imposing in the grossest manner upon her credulity and anxiety to obtain information. It is a knowledge of this very shameful proceeding which has made me most especially anxious to avoid *fact hunting*. I might fill my letters to you with accounts received from others, but, as I am aware of the risk which I run in so doing, I shall furnish you with no details but those which come under my own immediate observation.

To return to the rice mill: it is worked by a steam engine of thirty horsepower, and, besides threshing [a] great part of our own rice, is kept constantly employed by the neighboring planters, who send their grain to it in preference to the more distant mill at Savannah, paying, of course, the same percentage, which makes it a very profitable addition to the estate. Immediately opposite to this building is a small shed, which they call the cook's shop, and where the daily allowance of rice and corn grits of the people is boiled and distributed to them by an old woman, whose special business this is. There are four settlements or villages (or, as the Negroes call them, camps) on the island, consisting of from ten to twenty houses, and to each settlement is annexed a cook's shop with capacious caldrons, and the oldest wife of the settlement for officiating priestess. Pursuing my walk along the river's bank, upon an artificial dike, sufficiently high and broad to protect the fields from inundation by the ordinary rising of the tide—for the whole island is below high-water mark—I passed the blacksmith's and cooper's shops. At the first all the common iron implements of husbandry or household use for the estate are made, and at the latter all the rice barrels necessary for the crop, besides tubs and buckets, large and small, for the use of the people, and cedar tubs, of noble dimensions and exceedingly neat workmanship, for our own household purposes. The fragrance of these when they are first made, as well as their ample size, renders them preferable as dressing-room furniture, in my opinion, to all the china foot tubs that ever came out of Staffordshire. After this I got out of the vicinity of the settlement, and pursued my way along a narrow dike—the river on the one hand, and, on the other, a slimy, poisonous-looking swamp, all rattling with sedges of enormous height, in which one might lose one's way as effectually as in a forest of oaks. Beyond this, the low rice fields, all clothed in their rugged stubble, divided by dikes into monotonous squares, a species of prospect by no means beautiful to the mere lover of the picturesque. The only thing that I met with to attract my attention was a most beautiful species of ivy, the leaf longer and more graceful than that of the common English creeper, glittering with the highest varnish, delicately veined, and of a rich brown-green, growing in profuse garlands from branch to branch of some stunted evergreen bushes which border the dike, and which the people call salt-water bush. My walks are rather circumscribed, inasmuch as the dikes are the only promenades. On all sides of these lie either the marshy rice fields, the brimming river, or the swampy patches of yet unreclaimed forest, where the huge cypress trees and exquisite evergreen undergrowth spring up from a stagnant sweltering pool, that effectually forbids the foot of the explorer.

As I skirted one of these thickets today, I stood still to admire the beauty of the shrubbery. Every shade of green, every variety of form, every degree of varnish, and all in full leaf and beauty in the very depth of winter. The stunted dark-colored oak; the Magnolia bay (like our own culinary and fragrant bay), which grows to a very great size; the wild myrtle, a beautiful and profuse shrub, rising to a height of six, eight, and ten feet, and branching on all sides in luxuriant tufted fullness; most beautiful of all, that pride of the South, the Magnolia *grandiflora*, whose lustrous dark green perfect foliage would alone render it an object of admiration, without the queenly blossom whose color, size, and perfume are unrivaled in the whole vegetable kingdom. This last magnificent creature grows to the size of a forest tree in these swamps, but seldom adorns a high or dry soil, or suffers itself to be suc-

cessfully transplanted. Under all these the spiked palmetto
forms an impenetrable covert, and from glittering graceful
branch to branch hang garlands of evergreen creepers, on
which the mockingbirds are swinging and singing even now;
while I, bethinking me of the pinching cold that is at this hour
tyrannizing over your region, look round on this strange scene
—on these green woods, this unfettered river, and sunny sky
—and feel very much like one in another planet from yourself.

The profusion of birds here is one thing that strikes me as
curious, coming from the vicinity of Philadelphia, where even
the robin redbreast, held sacred by the humanity of all other
Christian people, is not safe from the *gunning* prowess of the
unlicensed sportsmen of your free country. The Negroes (of
course) are not allowed the use of firearms, and their very
simply constructed traps do not do much havoc among the
feathered hordes that haunt their rice fields. Their case is
rather a hard one, as partridges, snipes, and the most delicious
wild ducks abound here, and their allowance of rice and Indian
meal would not be the worse for such additions. No day passes
that I do not, in the course of my walk, put up a number of
land birds, and startle from among the gigantic sedges the
long-necked waterfowl by dozens. It arouses the killing propensity in me most dreadfully, and I really entertain serious
thoughts of learning to use a gun, for the mere pleasure of
destroying these pretty birds as they whirr from their secret
coverts close beside my path. How strong an instinct of animal
humanity this is, and how strange if one be more strange than
another. Reflection rebukes it almost instantaneously, and yet
for the life of me I cannot help wishing I had a fowling piece
whenever I put up a covey of these creatures; though I suppose, if one were brought bleeding and maimed to me, I
should begin to cry, and be very pathetic, after the fashion of
Jaques.[3] However, one must live, you know; and here our living consists very mainly of wild ducks, wild geese, wild
turkeys, and venison. Nor, perhaps, can one imagine the universal doom overtaking a creature with less misery than in the
case of the bird who, in the very moment of his triumphant
soaring, is brought dead to the ground. I should like to bargain
for such a finis myself amazingly, I know, and have always
thought that the death I should prefer would be to break my

---

[3] Jaques in *As You Like It* weeps over the plight of a wounded stag.
See Act II, scene 1.

neck off the back of my horse at a full gallop on a fine day. Of course a bad shot should be hung—a man who shatters his bird's wings and legs; if I undertook the trade, I would learn of some Southern duelist, and always shoot my bird through the head or heart—as an expert murderer knows how.

Besides these birds of which we make our prey, there are others that prey upon their own fraternity. Hawks of every sort and size wheel their steady rounds above the rice fields; and the great turkey buzzards—those most unsightly carrion birds—spread their broad black wings, and soar over the river like so many mock eagles. I do not know that I ever saw any winged creature of so forbidding an aspect as these same turkey buzzards; their heavy flight, their awkward gait, their bald-looking head and neck, and their devotion to every species of foul and detestable food, render them almost abhorrent to me. They abound in the South, and in Charleston are held in especial veneration for their scavenger-like propensities, killing one of them being, I believe, a finable offense by the city police regulations. Among the Brobdignagian sedges that in some parts of the island fringe the Altamaha, the nightshade (apparently the same as the European creeper) weaves a perfect matting of its poisonous garlands, and my remembrance of its prevalence in the woods and hedges of England did not reconcile me to its appearance here. How much of this is mere association I cannot tell; but, whether the wild duck makes its nest under its green arches, or the alligators and snakes of the Altamaha have their secret bowers there, it is an evil-looking weed, and I shall have every leaf of it cleared away.

I must inform you of a curious conversation which took place between my little girl and the woman who performs for us the offices of chambermaid here—of course one of Mr. [Butler]'s slaves. What suggested it to the child, or whence indeed she gathered her information, I know not; but children are made of eyes and ears, and nothing, however minute, escapes their microscopic observation. She suddenly began addressing this woman.

"Mary, some persons are free and some are not (the woman made no reply). I am a free person (of a little more than three years old). I say, I am a free person, Mary—do you know that?"

"Yes, missis."

"Some persons are free and some are not—do you know that, Mary?"

"Yes, missis, *here*," was the reply; "I know it is so here, in this world."

Here my child's white nurse, my dear Margery, who had hitherto been silent, interfered, saying: "Oh, then you think it will not always be so?"

"Me hope not, missis."

I am afraid, E[lizabeth], this woman actually imagines that there will be no slaves in heaven; isn't that preposterous, now, when, by the account of most of the Southerners, slavery itself must be heaven, or something uncommonly like it? Oh, if you could imagine how this title "Missis," addressed to me and to my children, shocks all my feelings! Several times I have exclaimed: "For God's sake do not call me that!" and only been awakened, by the stupid amazement of the poor creatures I was addressing, to the perfect uselessness of my thus expostulating with them; once or twice, indeed, I have done more— I have explained to them, and they appeared to comprehend me well, that I had no ownership over them, for that I held such ownership sinful, and that, though I was the wife of the man who pretends to own them, I was, in truth, no more their mistress than they were mine. Some of them, I know, understood me, more of them did not.

Our servants—those who have been selected to wait upon us in the house—consist of a man, who is quite a tolerable cook (I believe this is a natural gift with them, as with Frenchmen); a dairywoman, who churns for us; a laundrywoman; her daughter, our housemaid, the aforesaid Mary; and two young lads of from fifteen to twenty, who wait upon us in the capacity of footmen. As, however, the latter are perfectly filthy in their persons and clothes—their faces, hands, and naked feet being literally incrusted with dirt—their attendance at our meals is not, as you may suppose, particularly agreeable to me, and I dispense with it as often as possible. Mary, too, is so intolerably offensive in her person that it is impossible to endure her proximity, and the consequence is that, among Mr. [Butler]'s slaves, I wait upon myself more than I have ever done in my life before. About this same personal offensiveness, the Southerners, you know, insist that it is inherent with the race, and it is one of their most cogent reasons for keeping them as slaves. But, as this very disagreeable peculiarity does not prevent Southern women from hanging their infants at the breasts of Negresses, nor almost every planter's wife and daughter from having one or more little pet blacks sleeping like puppy dogs in their very bedchamber, nor almost every planter from admitting one or several of his female slaves to the still closer intimacy of his bed, it seems to me that this objection to doing them right is not very valid. I cannot imagine that they would smell much worse if they were free, or come in much closer contact with the delicate organs of their white fellow countrymen; indeed, inasmuch as good deeds are spoken of as having a sweet savor before God, it might be supposed that the freeing of the blacks might prove rather an odoriferous process than the contrary. However this may be, I must tell you that this potent reason for enslaving a whole race of people is no more potent with me than most of the others adduced to support the system, inasmuch as, from observation and some experience, I am strongly inclined to believe that peculiar ignorance of the laws of health and the habits of decent cleanliness are the real and only causes of this disagreeable characteristic of the race, thorough ablutions and change of linen, when tried, having been perfectly successful in removing all such objections; and if ever you have come into anything like neighborly proximity with a low Irishman or woman, I think you will allow that the same causes produce very nearly the same effects. The stench in an Irish, Scotch, Italian, or French hovel is quite as intolerable as any I ever found in our Negro houses, and the filth and vermin which abound about the clothes and persons of the lower peasantry of any of those countries as abominable as the same conditions in the black population of the United States. A total absence of self-respect begets these hateful physical results, and in proportion as moral influences are remote, physical evils will abound. Well-being, freedom, and industry induce self-respect, self-respect induces cleanliness and personal attention, so that slavery is answerable for all the evils that exhibit themselves where it exists—from lying, thieving, and adultery, to dirty houses, ragged clothes, and foul smells.

But to return to our Ganymedes.[4] One of them—the eldest son of our laundrywoman, and Mary's brother, a boy of the

---

[4] Ganymede in Greek mythology was a Trojan youth whom the gods had made immortal and taken up into heaven as their cupbearer. The use of the term in the present context is a shaft of sarcasm.

name of Aleck (Alexander)—is uncommonly bright and intelligent; he performs all the offices of a well-instructed waiter with great efficiency, and anywhere out of slaveland would be able to earn fourteen or fifteen dollars a month for himself; he is remarkably good tempered and well disposed. The other poor boy is so stupid that he appears sullen from absolute darkness of intellect; instead of being a little lower than the angels, he is scarcely a little higher than the brutes, and to this condition are reduced the majority of his kind by the institutions under which they live. I should tell you that Aleck's parents and kindred have always been about the house of the overseer, and in daily habits of intercourse with him and his wife; and wherever this is the case the effect of involuntary education is evident in the improved intelligence of the degraded race. In a conversation which Mr. [Butler] had this evening with Mr. O———, the overseer, the latter mentioned that two of our carpenters had in their leisure time made a boat, which they had disposed of to some neighboring planter for sixty dollars.

Now, E[lizabeth], I have no intention of telling you a one-sided story, or concealing from you what are cited as the advantages which these poor people possess; you, who know that no indulgence is worth simple justice, either to him who gives or him who receives, will not thence conclude that their situation thus mitigated is, therefore, what it should be. On this matter of the sixty dollars earned by Mr. [Butler]'s two men much stress was laid by him and his overseer. I look at it thus: if these men were industrious enough, out of their scanty leisure, to earn sixty dollars, how much more of remuneration, of comfort, of improvement might they not have achieved were the price of their daily labor duly paid them, instead of being unjustly withheld to support an idle young man and his idle family, i.e., myself and my children.

And here it may be well to inform you that the slaves on this plantation are divided into field hands and mechanics or artisans. The former, the great majority, are the more stupid and brutish of the tribe; the others, who are regularly taught their trades, are not only exceedingly expert at them, but exhibit a greater general activity of intellect, which must necessarily result from even a partial degree of cultivation. There are here a gang (for that is the honorable term) of coopers, of blacksmiths, of bricklayers, of carpenters, all well acquainted with their peculiar trades. The latter constructed the washhand stands, clothespresses, sofas, tables, etc., with which our house is furnished, and they are very neat pieces of workmanship—neither veneered or polished indeed, nor of very costly materials, but of the white pinewood planed as smooth as marble—a species of furniture not very luxurious perhaps, but all the better adapted therefore to the house itself, which is certainly rather more devoid of the conveniences and adornments of modern existence than anything I ever took up my abode in before. It consists of three small rooms, and three still smaller, which would be more appropriately designated as closets, a wooden recess by way of pantry, and a kitchen detached from the dwelling—a mere wooden outhouse, with no floor but the bare earth, and for furniture a congregation of filthy Negroes, who lounge in and out of it like hungry hounds at all hours of the day and night, picking up such scraps of food as they can find about, which they discuss squatting down upon their hams, in which interesting position and occupation I generally find a number of them whenever I have sufficient hardihood to venture within those precincts, the sight of which and its tenants is enough to slacken the appetite of the hungriest hunter that ever lost all nice regards in the mere animal desire for food. Of our three apartments, one is our sitting, eating, and *living* room, and is sixteen feet by fifteen. The walls are plastered indeed, but neither painted nor papered; it is divided from our bedroom (a similarly elegant and comfortable chamber) by a dingy wooden partition covered all over with hooks, pegs, and nails, to which hats, caps, keys, etc., etc., are suspended in graceful irregularity. The doors open by wooden latches, raised by means of small bits of packthread—I imagine, the same primitive order of fastening celebrated in the touching chronicle of Red Riding Hood; how they shut I will not attempt to describe, as the shutting of a door is a process of extremely rare occurrence throughout the whole Southern country. The third room, a chamber with sloping ceiling, immediately over our sitting room and under the roof, is appropriated to the nurse and my two babies. Of the closets, one is Mr. O———, the overseer's, bedroom, the other his office or place of business; and the third, adjoining our bedroom, and opening immediately out of doors, is Mr. [Butler]'s dressing room and *cabinet d'affaires,* where he gives audiences to the Negroes, redresses grievances, distributes red woolen caps (a singular gratification to a slave), shaves himself, and performs the other offices of his toilet. Such being our abode, I think you will allow there is little danger of my being dazzled by the luxurious splendors of a Southern slave residence. Our sole mode of summoning our attendants is by a packthread bell-rope suspended in the sitting room. From the bedrooms we have to raise the windows and our voices, and bring them by power of lungs, or help ourselves—which, I thank God, was never yet a hardship to me.

I mentioned to you just now that two of the carpenters had made a boat in their leisure time. I must explain this to you, and this will involve the mention of another of Miss Martineau's mistakes with regard to slave labor, at least in many parts of the Southern states. She mentions that on one estate of which she knew, the proprietor had made the experiment, and very successfully, of appointing to each of his slaves a certain task to be performed in the day, which once accomplished, no matter how early, the rest of the four-and-twenty hours were allowed to the laborer to employ as he pleased. She mentions this as a single experiment, and rejoices over it as a decided amelioration in the condition of the slave, and one deserving of general adoption. But in the part of Georgia where this estate is situated, the custom of task labor is universal, and it prevails, I believe, throughout Georgia, South Carolina, and parts of North Carolina; in other parts of the latter state, however—as I was informed by our overseer, who is a native of that state—the estates are small, rather deserving the name of farms, and the laborers are much upon the same footing as the laboring men at the North, working from sunrise to sunset in the fields with the farmer and his sons, and coming in with them to their meals, which they take immediately after the rest of the family. In Louisiana and the new Southwestern slave states, I believe, task labor does not prevail; but it is in those that the condition of the poor human cattle is most deplorable. As you know it was there that the humane calculation was not only made, but openly and unhesitatingly avowed, that the planters found it, upon the whole, their most profitable plan to work off (kill with labor) their whole number of slaves about once in seven years, and renew the whole stock. By-the-by, the Jewish institution of slavery is much insisted upon by the Southern upholders of the system; perhaps this is their notion of the Jewish jubilee, when the slaves were by Moses' strict enactment to be all set free.

Well, this task system is pursued on this estate; and thus it is that the two carpenters were enabled to make the boat they sold for sixty dollars. These tasks, of course, profess to be graduated according to the sex, age, and strength of the laborer; but in many instances this is not the case, as I think you will agree when I tell you that on Mr. [Butler]'s first visit to his estates he found that the men and the women who labored in the fields had the same task to perform. This was a noble admission of female equality, was it not?—and thus it had been on the estate for many years past. Mr. [Butler], of course, altered the distribution of the work, diminishing the quantity done by the women.

I had a most ludicrous visit this morning from the midwife of the estate—rather an important personage both to master and slave, as to her unassisted skill and science the ushering of all the young Negroes into their existence of bondage is entrusted. I heard a great deal of conversation in the dressing room adjoining mine while performing my own toilet, and presently Mr. [Butler] opened my room door, ushering in a dirty, fat, good-humored looking old Negress, saying: "The midwife, Rose, wants to make your acquaintance."

"Oh massa!" shrieked out the old creature, in a paroxysm of admiration, "where you get this lilly alabaster baby!"

For a moment I looked round to see if she was speaking of my baby; but no, my dear, this superlative apostrophe was elicited by the fairness of *my skin:* so much for degrees of comparison. Now I suppose that if I chose to walk arm in arm with the dingiest mulatto through the streets of Philadelphia, nobody could possibly tell by my complexion that I was not his sister, so that the mere quality of mistress must have had a most miraculous effect upon my skin in the eyes of poor Rose. But this species of outrageous flattery is as usual with these people as with the low Irish, and arises from the ignorant desire, common to both the races, of propitiating at all costs the fellow creature who is to them as a Providence—or rather, I should say, a fate—for 'tis a heathen and no Christian relationship.

Soon after this visit, I was summoned into the wooden porch or piazza of the house, to see a poor woman who desired to speak to me. This was none other than the tall, emaciated-looking Negress who, on the day of our arrival, had embraced me and my nurse with such irresistible zeal. She appeared very ill today, and presently unfolded to me a most distressing history of bodily afflictions. She was the mother of a very large family, and complained to me that, what with childbearing and hard field labor, her back was almost broken in two. With an almost savage vehemence of gesticulation, she suddenly tore up her scanty clothing, and exhibited a spectacle with which I was inconceivably shocked and sickened. The facts, without any of her corroborating statements, bore tolerable witness to the hardships of her existence. I promised to attend to her ailments and give her proper remedies; but these are natural results, inevitable and irremediable ones, of improper treatment of the female frame; and, though there may be alleviation, there cannot be any cure when once the beautiful and wonderful structure has been thus made the victim of ignorance, folly, and wickedness.

After the departure of this poor woman, I walked down the settlement toward the infirmary or hospital, calling in at one or two of the houses along the row. These cabins consist of one room, about twelve feet by fifteen, with a couple of closets smaller and closer than the staterooms of a ship, divided off from the main room and each other by rough wooden partitions, in which the inhabitants sleep. They have almost all of them a rude bedstead, with the gray moss of the forests for mattress, and filthy, pestilential-looking blankets for covering. Two families (sometimes eight and ten in number) reside in one of these huts, which are mere wooden frames pinned, as it were, to the earth by a brick chimney outside, whose enormous aperture within pours down a flood of air, but little counteracted by the miserable spark of fire, which hardly sends an attenuated thread of lingering smoke up its huge throat. A wide ditch runs immediately at the back of these dwellings, which is filled and emptied daily by the tide. Attached to each hovel is a small scrap of ground for a garden, which, however, is for the most part untended and uncultivated.

Such of these dwellings as I visited today were filthy and wretched in the extreme, and exhibited that most deplorable consequence of ignorance and an abject condition, the inability of the inhabitants to secure and improve even such pitiful comfort as might yet be achieved by them. Instead of the order, neatness, and ingenuity which might convert even these miserable hovels into tolerable residences, there was the careless, reckless, filthy indolence which even the brutes do not exhibit in their lairs and nests, and which seemed incapable of applying to the uses of existence the few miserable means of comfort yet within their reach. Firewood and shavings lay littered about the floors, while the half-naked children were cowering round two or three smouldering cinders. The moss with which the chinks and crannies of their ill-protecting dwellings might have been stuffed was trailing in dirt and dust about the ground, while the back door of the huts, opening upon a most unsightly ditch, was left wide open for the fowls and ducks, which they are allowed to raise, to travel in and out, increasing the filth of the cabin by what they brought and left in every direction.

In the midst of the floor, or squatting round the cold hearth, would be four or five children from four to ten years old, the latter all with babies in their arms, the care of the infants being taken from the mothers (who are driven afield as soon as they recover from child labor), and devolved upon these poor little nurses, as they are called, whose business it is to watch the infant, and carry it to its mother whenever it may require nourishment. To these hardly human little beings I addressed my remonstrances about the filth, cold, and unnecessary wretchedness of their room, bidding the older boys and girls kindle up the fire, sweep the floor, and expel the poultry. For a long time my very words seemed unintelligible to them, till, when I began to sweep and make up the fire, etc., they first fell to laughing, and then imitating me. The incrustations of dirt on their hands, feet, and faces were my next object of attack, and the stupid Negro practice (by-the-by, but a short time since nearly universal in enlightened Europe) of keeping the babies with their feet bare, and their heads, already well capped by nature with their woolly hair, wrapped in half a dozen hot, filthy coverings.

Thus I traveled down the "street," in every dwelling endeavoring to awaken a new perception, that of cleanliness, sighing, as I went, over the futility of my own exertions, for how can slaves be improved? Nathless, thought I, let what can be done; for it may be that, the two being incompatible, improvement may yet expel slavery; and so it might, and surely would, if, instead of beginning at the end, I could but begin at the beginning of my task. If the mind and soul were awakened, instead of mere physical good attempted, the physical good would result, and the great curse vanish away; but my hands are tied fast, and this corner of the work is all that I may do. Yet it cannot be but, from my words and actions, some revelations should reach these poor people; and going in and out among them perpetually, I shall teach, and they learn involuntarily a thousand things of deepest import. They must learn, and who can tell the fruit of that knowledge alone, that there are beings in the world, even with skins of a different color from their own, who have sympathy for their misfortunes, love for their virtues, and respect for their common nature—but oh! my heart is full almost to bursting as I walk among these most poor creatures.

The infirmary is a large two-story building, terminating the broad orange-planted space between the two rows of houses which form the first settlement; it is built of whitewashed wood, and contains four large-sized rooms. But how shall I describe to you the spectacle which was presented to me on entering the first of these? But half the casements, of which there were six, were glazed, and these were obscured with dirt, almost as much as the other windowless ones were darkened by the dingy shutters, which the shivering inmates had fastened to in order to protect themselves from the cold. In the enormous chimney glimmered the powerless embers of a few sticks of wood, round which, however, as many of the sick women as could approach were cowering, some on wooden settles, most of them on the ground, excluding those who were too ill to rise; and these last poor wretches lay prostrate on the floor, without bed, mattress, or pillow, buried in tattered and filthy blankets, which, huddled round them as they lay strewed about, left hardly space to move upon the floor. And here, in their hour of sickness and suffering, lay those whose health and strength are spent in unrequited labor for us— those who, perhaps even yesterday, were being urged on to their unpaid task—those whose husbands, fathers, brothers, and sons were even at that hour sweating over the earth, whose produce was to buy for us all the luxuries which health can revel in, all the comforts which can alleviate sickness. I stood in the midst of them, perfectly unable to speak, the tears pouring from my eyes at this sad spectacle of their misery, myself and my emotion alike strange and incomprehensible to them. Here lay women expecting every hour the terrors and agonies of childbirth, others who had just brought their doomed offspring into the world, others who were groaning over the anguish and bitter disappointment of miscarriages— here lay some burning with fever, others chilled with cold and aching with rheumatism, upon the hard cold ground, the draughts and dampness of the atmosphere increasing their sufferings, and dirt, noise, and stench, and every aggravation of which sickness is capable, combined in their condition— here they lay like brute beasts, absorbed in physical suffering; unvisited by any of those Divine influences which may ennoble the dispensations of pain and illness, forsaken, as it seemed to me, of all good; and yet, O God, Thou surely hadst not forsaken them! Now pray take notice that this is the hospital of an estate where the owners are supposed to be humane, the overseer efficient and kind, and the Negroes remarkably well cared for and comfortable.

As soon as I recovered from my dismay, I addressed old Rose the midwife, who had charge of this room, bidding her open the shutters of such windows as were glazed, and let in the light. I next proceeded to make up the fire; but, upon my lifting a log for that purpose, there was one universal outcry of horror, and old Rose, attempting to snatch it from me, exclaimed: "Let alone, missis—let be; what for you lift wood? you have nigger enough, missis, to do it!" I hereupon had to explain to them my view of the purposes for which hands and arms were appended to our bodies, and forthwith began making Rose tidy up the miserable apartment, removing all the filth and rubbish from the floor that could be removed, folding up in piles the blankets of the patients who were not using them, and placing, in rather more sheltered and comfortable positions, those who were unable to rise. It was all that I could do, and having enforced upon them all my earnest desire that they should keep their room swept, and as tidy as possible, I passed on to the other room on the ground floor, and to the two above, one of which is appropriated to the use of the men who are ill. They were all in the same deplorable condition, the upper rooms being rather the more miserable, inasmuch as none of the windows were glazed at all, and they had, therefore, only the alternative of utter darkness, or killing draughts of air from the unsheltered casements. In all, filth, disorder, and misery abounded; the floor was the only bed, and scanty begrimed rags of blankets the only covering. I left this refuge for Mr. [Butler]'s sick dependents with my clothes covered with dust, and full of vermin, and with a heart heavy enough, as you will well believe. My morning's work had fatigued me not a little, and I was glad to return to the house, where I gave vent to my indignation and regret at the scene I had just witnessed to Mr. [Butler] and his overseer, who, here, is a member of our family. The latter told me that the condition of the hospital had appeared to him, from his first entering upon his situation (only within the last year), to require a reform, and that he had proposed it to the former manager, Mr. K[ing], and Mr. [Butler]'s brother, who is part proprietor of the estate, but, receiving no encouragement from them, had supposed that it was a matter of indifference to the owners, and had left it in the condition in which he had found it, in which condition it has been for the last nineteen years and upward.

This new overseer of ours has lived fourteen years with an old Scotch gentleman, who owns an estate adjoining Mr. [Butler]'s, on the island of St. Simons, upon which estate, from everything I can gather, and from what I know of the proprietor's character, the slaves are probably treated with as much humanity as is consistent with slavery at all, and where the management and comfort of the hospital in particular had been most carefully and judiciously attended to. With regard to the indifference of our former manager upon the subject of the accommodation for the sick, he was an excellent overseer, *videlicet* the estate returned a full income under his management, and such men have nothing to do with sick slaves: they are tools, to be mended only if they can be made available again; if not, to be flung by as useless, without further expense of money, time, or trouble.

I am learning to row here, for circumscribed as my walks necessarily are, impossible as it is to resort to my favorite exercise on horseback upon these narrow dikes, I must do something to prevent my blood from stagnating; and this broad brimming river, and the beautiful light canoes which lie moored at the steps, are very inviting persuaders to this species of exercise. My first attempt was confined to pulling an oar across the stream, for which I rejoiced in sundry aches and pains altogether novel, letting alone a delightful row of blisters on each of my hands.

I forgot to tell you that in the hospital were several sick babies, whose mothers were permitted to suspend their field labor in order to nurse them. Upon addressing some remonstrances to one of these, who, besides having a sick child, was ill herself, about the horribly dirty condition of her baby, she assured me that it was impossible for them to keep their children clean; that they went out to work at daybreak, and did not get their tasks done till evening, and that then they were too tired and worn out to do anything but throw themselves down and sleep. This statement of hers I mentioned on my return from the hospital, and the overseer appeared extremely annoyed by it, and assured me repeatedly that it was not true.

In the evening Mr. [Butler], who had been over to Darien, mentioned that one of the storekeepers there had told him that, in the course of a few years, he had paid the Negroes of this estate several thousand dollars for moss, which is a very profitable article of traffic with them: they collect it from the trees, dry and pick it, and then sell it to the people in Darien for mattresses, sofas, and all sorts of stuffing purposes, which, in my opinion, it answers better than any other material whatever that I am acquainted with, being as light as horsehair, as springy and elastic, and a great deal less harsh and rigid. It is now bedtime, dear E[lizabeth], and I doubt not it has been sleepy time with you over this letter long ere you came thus far. There is a preliminary to my repose, however, in this agreeable residence, which I rather dread, namely, the hunting for, or discovering without hunting, in fine relief upon the white-washed walls of my bedroom, a most hideous and detestable species of *reptile* called centipedes, which come out of the cracks and crevices of the walls, and fill my very heart with dismay. They are from an inch to two inches long, and appear to have not a hundred, but a thousand legs. I cannot ascertain very certainly from the Negroes whether they sting or not, but they look exceedingly as if they might, and I visit my babies every night in fear and trembling, lest I should find one or more of these hateful creatures mounting guard over them. Good night; you are well to be free from centipedes—better to be free from slaves.

Negro Spirituals and
Slave Songs

Bound to Go
Poor Rosy
Go in the Wilderness
All the Pretty Little Horses
Lay this Body Down
O Freedom!

Introduction

From the tragic experience of the Negro people under slavery there came a music that immeasurably enriched American culture, and was also of world significance. Appropriating whatever materials were available—in the Bible, in white spirituals, hymns, and secular songs—the genius of a people enslaved fused these with musical elements of its own African tradition. In this way there came into being an incomparably profound and original expression of American reality.

The Negro people created during slavery days a vast repertoire of song. Much of their secular music, in the form in which it was originally played and sung, has been lost to us. The majority of the songs that have survived from that time, and that we have inherited, are spirituals. But the slave spirituals were far more than the name implies: that is, devotional songs to be sung in church or on other solemn occasions. Spirituals were put to the most varied uses: as laments, as work songs in the fields and mills, as rowing and hauling songs, as war songs, as lullabies, as the special form of sacred dance known as the "shout," and as funeral dirges.[1] It is important to know this; spirituals were sung with endless variations of style and tempo, depending upon the occasion. The

[1] "The same songs," wrote Lucy McKim Garrison in 1862, "are sung at every sort of work." *Dwight's Journal of Music* xxi–xxii (November 8, 1862), p. 255.

spiritual as it was actually sung had little or nothing in common with the stylized and harmonized versions that have graced the church services and concert halls of later days.

The development of the spiritual among the slaves was linked to one of their major social and religious achievements —Christianization. The movement to bring Christianity to the Negro people had begun in the eighteenth century, taking its first impulse from that same Great Awakening which has been discussed above. After the Revolution, the movement quickened pace, and in the ante-bellum period—particularly after 1820—it became a flood. Slaveholders were, for the most part, reluctant witnesses of this development, but they had to make the best of it. It is true that the Christian religion could be used, and indeed was, to inculcate acceptance of one's lot on earth, obedience to masters, and "pie in the sky by and by." But this is only one side of the matter. The "awakening" of the slaves to Protestantism—most of them became Baptists—served the same purpose among them as it did among whites. It endowed them with a sense of unity, an interpretation of history, and a readiness to accept sacrifice and struggle for what was right. The connection between the rise of Christianity among the slaves, the massive role played by the Negro in the Civil War, and the disintegration of chattel bondage is clear and demonstrable.

The role played by the spiritual in the education and Christianization of the slaves was a unique one. Focus and expression of the people's profoundest beliefs and aspirations, it bound the race together with a consciousness of its common oppression and of its common destiny. It gave strength to face the ordeals of a life of slavery: the monotony of unending toil, humiliation, pain and cold, flight and battle, disease and death. It made it possible for human beings to accept their fate when they could do nothing else; and it summoned them to a sustained protest against that same fate whenever the hour struck.

Our pioneer collectors of the songs of slavery were the fighters against slavery—Northern soldiers, ministers, scholars and teachers. This work owed its inception to the capture of Port Royal in 1861 by the Union forces, and the liberation of the slave population on the sea islands of that area. In 1862 Salmon Chase, Secretary of the Treasury, launched a plan for the education of the freed men and the social reorganization of the Port Royal islands. Northern soldiers and teachers hastened south to take part in the experiment. Among these were Lucy McKim Garrison, daughter-in-law of the celebrated abolitionist; William Francis Allen, one of America's foremost classical scholars and educators; and Colonel Thomas Wentworth Higginson, who was given the command of the First South Carolina Volunteers, a regiment of freed men who went into training near Beaufort, S.C., in October, 1862. These people found in the spirituals sung so freely by the ex-slaves an incredibly vital, moving and, to them, new form of music. They busied themselves in noting down as much of it as time and other duties permitted. A few of the many exquisite songs noted by these people— authentic slave songs, unmodified by time or latter-day arranging—are included in the selection given below.[2]

Bound to Go is not only a spiritual but a rousing boat song, with chorus and refrain collected by Superintendent Charles Pickard Ware and W. F. Allen at Coffin's Point and other plantations on St. Helena Island. It bears a marked resemblance to the beautiful sea shanty A Long Time Ago. There is an old minstrel tune of the same title, which leads one to suspect that spiritual and shanty alike are derived from some earlier Negro song.

Poor Rosy is a spiritual that was used for all kinds of work, including rowing. One ex-slave told Superintendent Ware that this song could not be sung "without a full heart and a troubled mind."

Go in the Wilderness is the theme of all seekers after God, who have gone out alone into the desert or the wilderness to seek Him and the certainty of His revelation. For the sea islanders "wilderness" meant the swamps surrounding the low-lying plantations on every side. This song gives

---

[2] Gilbert Chase charges [America's Music from the Pilgrims to the Present (New York, 1955), p. 257], that these early folksong collectors, whom he calls "educational uplifters," were "intent upon dignifying the Negro and emphasizing what they considered to be his higher, spiritual qualities"; and that therefore they stressed spirituals to the exclusion of secular songs.

Such is not the case. These people were much concerned with the rapid disappearance of secular songs, and the need to collect them before they vanished. W. F. Allen stated explicitly that it was "no easy matter to persuade them to sing their old songs, even as a curiosity, such is the sense of dignity that has come with freedom. It is earnestly to be desired that some person, who has the opportunity, should make a collection of these now, before it is too late." *Slave Songs of the United States* (New York, 1951), p. x.

a brilliant reflection of the religious awakening of the Negro masses and what this portended for the future of the institution of slavery. Lincoln used a variant of it as a campaign song in 1860 (Old Abe Lincoln Came Out of the Wilderness).

All the Pretty Little Horses: Alan Lomax, pioneer collector of Southern songs, learned this slave lullaby from his mother, who took it from North Carolina to Texas after the Civil War. It was sung by slave nurses looking after white children. "The second stanza," says Mr. Lomax, "reflects the slave mother's anxiety about her own neglected child." The song has been in oral tradition throughout the South ever since slavery days.

Lay This Body Down was sung by freed men in the First South Carolina Volunteers. Colonel T. W. Higginson, commanding, listened with rapt admiration to the endless singing of his soldiers, took down the words as best he could, writing furtively under the concealment of his coat. This spiritual, too, was used as a boat song and as a funeral chant. It may well have been the dirge whose "high wailing notes" Fanny Kemble heard as she stood by the graveside of Shadrach on Butler Island in 1839.[2] It is perhaps one of the most consummately simple and profound laments in the whole range of our music and literature.

O Freedom! was evidently composed in the last days of slavery—or the first of freedom. It ranks among the great freedom songs known to the modern world. Here the Negro people pronounces the final verdict upon slavery and all its works.

---

[2] *Journal of a Residence, op. cit.,* p. 147.

BOUND TO GO

I build my house up-on the rock,

O yes, Lord! No wind, no storm can

blow it down, O yes, Lord!

March on, mem-ber, bound to go;

Been to the fer-ry, bound to go;

Left St. He-len-a, bound to go;

Bro-ther, fare you well.

I build my house upon the rock,
   O yes, Lord!
No wind, no storm can blow it down,
   O yes, Lord!
      March on, member, bound to go;
      Been to the ferry, bound to go;
      Left St. Helena, bound to go;
      Brother, fare you well.

I build my house on shifting sand,
   O yes, Lord!
The first wind come he blow him down,
   O yes, Lord!
      March on, member, bound to go; etc.

I am not like the foolish man
   O yes, Lord!
He build his house upon the sand,
   O yes, Lord!
      March on, member, bound to go; etc.

One morning as I was walkin' along,
   O yes, Lord!
I saw the berries a-hanging down,
   O yes, Lord!
      March on, member, bound to go; etc.

I pick the berries and I suck the juice,
   O yes, Lord!
He sweeter than the honey comb,
   O yes, Lord!
      March on, member, bound to go; etc.

I took them, brother, two by two,
   O yes, Lord!
I took them, sister, three by three,
   O yes, Lord!
      March on, member, bound to go; etc.

POOR ROSY

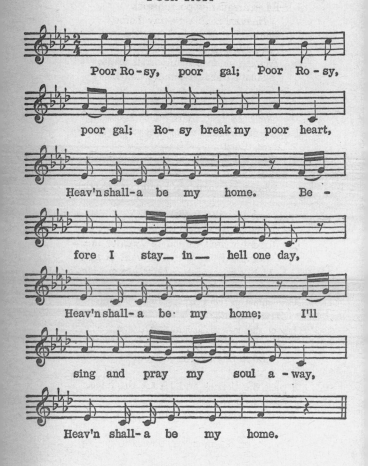

Poor Ro-sy, poor gal; Poor Ro-sy, poor gal; Ro-sy break my poor heart, Heav'n shall-a be my home. Be-fore I stay in hell one day, Heav'n shall-a be my home; I'll sing and pray my soul a-way, Heav'n shall-a be my home.

Poor Rosy, poor gal;
Poor Rosy, poor gal;
Rosy break my poor heart,
    Heaven shall-a be my home.
Before I stay in hell one day,
    Heaven shall-a be my home;
I'll sing and pray my soul away,
    Heaven shall-a be my home.

Got hard trial in my way;
Got hard trial in my way;
Got hard trial in my way,
    Heaven shall-a be my home.
O when I walk and talk with God,
    Heaven shall-a be my home
O when I walk and talk with God,
    Heaven shall-a be my home.

I dunno what de massa want of me;
I dunno what de massa want of me;
I dunno what de massa want of me,
    Heaven shall-a be my home.
Before I stay in hell one day,
    Heaven shall-a be my home.
I'll sing and pray my soul away,
    Heaven shall-a be my home.

GO IN THE WILDERNESS

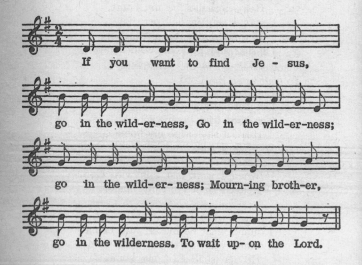

If you want to find Jesus, go in the wilderness, go in the wilderness, Go in the wilderness; go in the wilderness; Mourning brother, go in the wilderness. To wait upon the Lord.

If you want to find Jesus, go in the wilderness,
 Go in the wilderness, go in the wilderness,
Mourning brother, go in the wilderness,
 To wait upon the Lord.

Mourning brother, go in the wilderness,
 Go in the wilderness, go in the wilderness,
If you want to be a Christian, go in the wilderness,
 To wait upon the Lord.

If you want to be a Christian, go in the wilderness,
 Go in the wilderness, go in the wilderness,
If you want to get religion, go in the wilderness,
 To wait upon the Lord.

If you want to get religion, go in the wilderness,
 Go in the wilderness, go in the wilderness,
O weeping Mary, go in the wilderness,
 To wait upon the Lord.

O weeping Mary, go in the wilderness,
 Go in the wilderness, go in the wilderness,
Afflicted sister, go in the wilderness,
 To wait upon the Lord.

Afflicted sister, go in the wilderness,
 Go in the wilderness, go in the wilderness,
Jesus is waiting to meet you in the wilderness,
 To wait upon the Lord.

Jesus is waiting to meet you in the wilderness,
 Go in the wilderness, go in the wilderness,
Mourning brother, go in the wilderness,
 To wait upon the Lord.

ALL THE PRETTY LITTLE HORSES

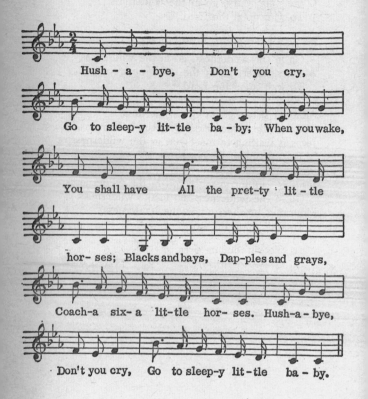

Hushabye,
Don't you cry,
Go to sleepy little baby;
When you wake,
You shall have
All the pretty little horses;
Blacks and bays,
Dapples and grays,
Coach-a six-a little horses.
Hushabye,
Don't you cry,
Go to sleepy little baby.

Hushabye,
Don't you cry,
Go to sleepy little baby;
Way down yonder,
In the meadow,
There's a poor little lambie,
The bees and the butterflies
Peckin' out its eyes,
The poor little thing cried, "Mammy!"
Hushabye,
Don't you cry,
Go to sleepy, little baby.

LAY DIS BODY DOWN

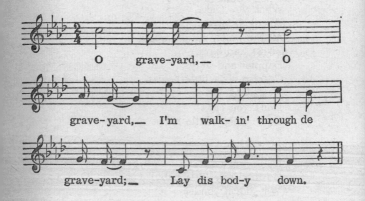

O graveyard, O graveyard,
I'm walkin' through de graveyard;
Lay dis body down.

O my soul! O my soul!
I'm goin' to de graveyard
To lay dis body down.

I know moonlight, I know starlight,
I'm walkin' through de starlight;
Lay dis body down.

I lay in the grave and stretch out my arms,
I'm goin' to de graveyard;
Lay dis body down.

I go to de judgment in the evenin' of the day,
I'm goin' to de graveyard;
Lay dis body down.

O graveyard, O graveyard,
I'm walkin' through de graveyard;
Lay dis body down.

OH, FREEDOM!

1. Oh, freedom! Oh, freedom!
   Oh, freedom over me;
   And before I'll be a slave,
   I'll lie buried in my grave,
   And go home to my Lord, and be free.

2. No more moaning, no more moaning,
   No more moaning over me;
   And before, etc.

3. No more mourning, no more mourning,
   No more mourning, over me;
   And before, etc.

4. No more weeping, no more weeping,
   No more weeping over me;
   And before, etc.

5. No more sighing, no more sighing,
   No more sighing over me;
   And before, etc.

6. O, what singing, oh what singing,
   Oh, what singing over me;
   And before, etc.

7. O, what shouting, oh what shouting,
   Oh, what shouting over me;
   And before, etc.

8. Oh, freedom! Oh, freedom!
   Oh, freedom over me;
   And before, etc.

Slavery and
═Civil Rights═════════

ARGUMENT BEFORE THE SUPREME COURT OF MASSA-
CHUSETTS, IN THE CASE OF SARAH C. ROBERTS v.
THE CITY OF BOSTON. DECEMBER 4, 1849

BY CHARLES SUMNER

Introduction

*The brief written by Charles Sumner in the case of Sarah
C. Roberts v. the City of Boston is considered to be a classic
contribution to the philosophy and law of interracial democracy.*[1] *It is offered in evidence to show that the great champions of the antislavery cause were not the bigoted and starry-
eyed fanatics they have so often been painted, but great,
courageous and wise pioneers in the continuing struggle for
the civil rights of all Americans, Negro as well as white.*

*The system of slavery that had existed in the North through-
out the colonial period had been buttressed by a series of laws
institutionalizing segregation, forbidding the social intermin-
gling of the races, and denying to Negroes the full and equal
rights of citizenship. Though slavery crumbled away everywhere in the North in the years following the Revolution, laws
discriminating against the Negro did not. In Massachusetts
the campaign to abolish such laws was fiercely fought by the
antislavery forces, and by 1846 had been largely crowned with
success, at least as far as Massachusetts itself was concerned.
By this date Negroes had won their constitutional right to
vote. The law prohibiting interracial marriage had been abolished. Jim Crow railroad coaches had been swept away. The
sole stronghold of segregation which remained was the Boston
school system. There Negro children were denied the right
to attend the common schools. They were segregated in the
Abiel Smith Grammar School in the basement of the African*

---

[1] It "deserves to be included in a volume of great documents on American
democracy, for its nobility of sentiment, literary excellence, and grasp of
principles which have been validated by modern sociology." Leonard W. Levy
and Harlan Phillips, "The Roberts Case: Source of the 'Separate but Equal'
Doctrine," *American Historical Review,* LVI (April, 1951), pp. 512–13.

Baptist Church on Belknap Street, or in one of the Jim Crow primary schools connected with this.

Sarah C. Roberts, through her father Benjamin, brought suit to recover damages for illegal exclusion from the public schools. Sarah, a five-year-old child, had been repeatedly refused permission to enter one of the all-white primary schools in the neighborhood of her home. She was obliged to walk almost half a mile to school every day, passing on her way five other primaries reserved exclusively for white students.

Charles Sumner was retained for the plaintiff, with a Negro lawyer, Robert Morris, as his assistant. Sumner (1811-74), Boston born, graduated from Harvard College in 1830. In the following fifteen years he gained a reputation as a brilliant lawyer, editor and lecturer. In 1845, when the war clouds were gathering over Mexico, he erupted into Massachusetts politics with a July 4th address boldly denouncing war as a means of settling international disputes. It became evident to the world that an American orator of the first rank had made his appearance. At the same time he championed the anti-slavery cause. When the Roberts case came to court at the end of 1849, Sumner had already resigned from the Whig party over the slavery issue, had taken an active part in organizing the Free Soil party, and had run for Congress on the Free Soil ticket. In 1851 he would be elected to the United States Senate by a Free Soil-Democratic coalition in the Massachusetts legislature, thereby beginning a senatorial career that was to last until the end of his life.

Boston's defense in the Roberts case, conducted by the city solicitor, was not recorded, but the line taken is clear enough from previous statements of the School Committee, of the solicitor himself, and from the context of Sumner's brief. Boston argued:

(a) That there was an ineradicable distinction between Negro and white in the physical, moral and mental nature of the two races, and specifically in their innate intelligence and ability to learn; and that therefore segregated education did not violate equality before the law, and was both just and expedient.

(b) That the School Committee was authorized by statute to make provision for the educational welfare of the students, and to classify them for this purpose according to age, sex and ability, according to the Committee's best judgment.

(c) That the education offered the Negro child in the segregated schools was equivalent to that offered the whites, and did not, therefore, violate constitutional provisions for equality of treatment of citizens. Equality of treatment was not violated if a school for Negro children was provided with competent instructors and with advantages equal to those offered to white children.

(d) Ill-clad Negro children would feel at a disadvantage in schools where "not only color, but dress and station, would be so strongly contrasted"; and this situation would result in "sneers, insults, assaults, jeers."

(e) Negro people associated together in their own churches, community organizations and clubs. Segregated schools had been in existence for many years. Why should Negroes object to them now?

Sumner based his plea, first and last, on the constitutional rights of Negro children to full equality before the law—under the Constitution of the United States, and under the Constitution and laws of Massachusetts.[2] His concluding remarks concerning the psychological damage inflicted upon both Negro and white by segregation were in the nature of argumenta ad hominem; but they foreshadowed with clarity the basis upon which the Supreme Court of the United States would act in its famous decision of May 17, 1954.

The Supreme Court of Massachusetts unanimously sustained the City of Boston's case. Thereby it placed the weight of its opinion behind the "separate but equal" doctrine that was, after the Civil War, to rationalize and sanction more than sixty years of school segregation throughout the South. But in Massachusetts itself the decision was reversed in 1855 by an act of the legislature which stated that

> "In determining the qualifications of scholars to be admitted into any Public School or District School in this Commonwealth, no distinction shall be made on account of the race, color, or religious opinions of the applicant or scholar."

[2] Sumner's most recent biographer, David Donald, argues that Sumner's arguments were based on "philosophical and psychological grounds rather than on common-law precedents." *Charles Sumner and the Coming of the Civil War* (New York, 1960).

In September of that year Negro students were integrated into the Boston schools without disturbance.

Sumner's brief, printed and circulated as a pamphlet in 1849, was designed for the education and enlightenment of the American people on the interracial issue as well as for the legal guidance of the Court. For this reason it is reproduced in full.

EQUALITY BEFORE THE LAW*

May It Please Your Honors:

Can any discrimination on account of race or color be made among children entitled to the benefit of our common schools under the constitution and laws of Massachusetts? This is the question which the Court is now to hear, to consider, and to decide.

Or, stating the question with more detail, and with more particular application to the facts of the present case, is the committee having superintendence of the common schools of Boston intrusted with *power*, under the constitution and laws of Massachusetts, to exclude colored children from the schools, and compel them to find education at separate schools, set apart for colored children only, at distances from their homes less convenient than schools open to white children?

This important question arises in an action by a colored child only five years old, who, *by her next friend*, sues the City of Boston for damages on account of a refusal to receive her into one of the common schools.

It would be difficult to imagine any case appealing more strongly to your best judgment, whether you regard the parties or the subject. On the one side is the City of Boston, strong in wealth, influence, character; on the other side is a little child, of degraded color, of humble parents, and still within the period of natural infancy, but strong from her very weakness, and from the irrepressible sympathies of good men, which, by a divine compensation, come to succor the weak. This little child asks at your hands her *personal rights*. So doing, she

---

*Source: *Charles Sumner: His Complete Works,* Statesman Edition (Boston, 1900), III, pp. 51–100. This version was edited by Sumner for publication and is far superior to the pamphlet version issued in Boston in 1849.

calls upon you to decide a question which concerns the personal rights of other colored children—which concerns the constitution and laws of the Commonwealth—which concerns that *peculiar institution* of New England, the common schools —which concerns the fundamental principles of human rights —which concerns the Christian character of this community. Such parties and such interests justly challenge your earnest attention.

Though this discussion is now for the first time brought before a judicial tribunal, it is no stranger to the public. In the School Committee of Boston for five years it has been the occasion of discord. No less than four different reports, two majority and two minority, forming pamphlets, of solid dimensions, devoted to this question, have been made to this committee, and afterwards published. The opinions of learned counsel have been enlisted. The controversy, leaving these regular channels, overflowed the newspaper press, and numerous articles appeared, espousing opposite sides. At last it has reached this tribunal. It is in your power to make it subside forever.

Forgetting many of the topics and all of the heats heretofore mingling with the controversy, I shall strive to present the question in its juridical light, as becomes the habits of this tribunal. It is a question of jurisprudence on which you are to give judgment. But I cannot forget that the principles of morals and of natural justice lie at the foundation of all jurisprudence. Nor can any reference to these be inappropriate in a discussion before this Court.

Of equality I shall speak, not only as a sentiment, but as a principle embodied in the constitution of Massachusetts, and obligatory upon court and citizen. It will be my duty to show that this principle, after finding its way into our state constitution, was recognized in legislation and judicial decisions. Considering next the circumstances of this case, it will be easy to show how completely they violate constitution, legislation, and judicial proceedings—*first*, by subjecting colored children to inconvenience inconsistent with the requirements of equality, and, *secondly*, by establishing a system of caste odious as that of the Hindus—leading to the conclusion that the School Committee have no such power as they have exercised, and that it is the duty of the Court to set aside their unjust by-laws. In the course of this discussion I shall exhibit the true idea of our common schools, and the fallacy of the pretension that any exclusion or discrimination founded on race or color can be consistent with equal rights.

In opening this argument, I begin naturally with the fundamental proposition which, when once established, renders the conclusion irresistible. According to the constitution of Massachusetts, *all men, without distinction of race or color, are equal before the law.* In the statement of this proposition I use language which, though new in our country, has the advantage of precision.

All Men, Without Distinction of Color or Race, Are Equal Before the Law.

I might, perhaps, leave this proposition without one word of comment. The equality of men will not be directly denied on this occasion; and yet it is so often assailed of late, that I shall not seem to occupy your time superfluously, I trust, while endeavoring to show what is understood by this term, when used in laws, constitutions, or other political instruments. Here I encounter a prevailing misapprehension. Lord Brougham, in his recent work on political philosophy, announces, with something of pungency, that "the notion of equality, or anything approaching to equality, among the different members of any community, is altogether wild and fantastic." Mr. Calhoun, in the Senate of the United States, assails both the principle and the form of its statement. He does not hesitate to say that the claim in the Declaration of Independence is "the most false and dangerous of all political errors"—that it "has done more to retard the cause of liberty and civilization, and is doing more at present, than all other causes combined"—that "for a long time it lay dormant, but in the process of time it began to germinate and produce its poisonous fruits." Had these two distinguished authorities chosen to comprehend the extent and application of the term thus employed, something, if not all, of their objection would have disappeared. That we may better appreciate its meaning and limitation, I am induced to exhibit the origin and growth of the sentiment, which, finally ripening into a formula of civil and political right, was embodied in the constitution of Massachusetts.

Equality as a sentiment was early cherished by generous

souls. It showed itself in dreams of ancient philosophy, and was declared by Seneca, when, in a letter of consolation on death, he said, *prima enim pars æquitatis est æqualitas:* "The chief part of equity is equality." But not till the truths of the Christian religion was it enunciated with persuasive force. Here we learn that God is no respecter of persons— that He is the Father of all—and that we are all His children, and brethren to each other. When the Saviour gave us the Lord's Prayer, He taught the sublime doctrine of human brotherhood, enfolding the equality of men.

Slowly did this sentiment enter the state. The whole constitution of government was inconsistent with it. An hereditary monarchy, an order of nobility, and the complex ranks of superior and inferior, established by the feudal system, all declare, not the equality, but the inequality of men, and all conspire to perpetuate this inequality. Every infant of royal blood, every noble, every vassal, is a present example, that, whatever may be the injunctions of religion or the sentiment of the heart, men under these institutions are not born equal.

The boldest political reformers of early times did not venture to proclaim this truth, nor did they truly perceive it. Cromwell beheaded his king, but secured the supreme power in hereditary succession to his eldest son. It was left to his loftier contemporary, John Milton, in poetic vision to be entranced

"With fair equality, fraternal state."

Sidney, who perished a martyr to the liberal cause, drew his inspiration from classic, and not from Christian foundations. The examples of Greece and Rome fed his soul. The English Revolution of 1688, partly by force and partly by the popular voice, changed the succession to the crown, and, if we may credit loyal Englishmen, secured the establishment of freedom throughout the land. But the Bill of Rights did not declare, nor did the genius of Somers or Maynard conceive the political axiom, that all men are born equal. It may find acceptance from Englishmen in our day, but it is disowned by English institutions.

I would not forget the early testimony of the "judicious" Hooker, who in his *Ecclesiastical Polity*, that masterly work, dwells on the equality of men by nature, or the subsequent testimony of Locke, in his *Two Treatises of Government*, who, quoting Hooker, asserts for himself that "creatures of the same species and rank, promiscuously born to all the same advantages of nature and the use of the same facilities, should also be *equal* one amongst another, without subordination or subjection." Hooker and Locke saw the equality of men in a state of nature; but their utterances found more acceptance across the Channel than in England.

It is to France that we must pass for the earliest development of this idea, its amplest illustration, and its most complete, accurate, and logical expression. In the middle of the last century appeared the renowned *Encyclopédie*, edited by Diderot and d'Alembert. This remarkable production, where science, religion, and government are discussed with revolutionary freedom, contains an article on equality, first published in 1755. Here we find the boldest expression of this sentiment down to that time.

> "Natural equality," says this authority, "is that which exists between all men by the constitution of their nature only. This equality is the principle and the foundation of liberty. Natural or moral equality is, then, founded upon the constitution of human nature common to all men, who are born, grow, subsist, and die in the same manner. Since human nature finds itself the same in all men, it is clear, that, according to Nature's law, each ought to esteem and treat the others as beings who are naturally equal to himself, that is to say, who are men as well as himself."

It is then remarked that political and civil slavery is in violation of this equality; and yet the inequalities of nobility in the state are allowed to pass without condemnation. Alluding to these, it is simply said that "they who are elevated above others ought to treat their inferiors as naturally their equals, shunning all outrage, exacting nothing beyond what is their due, and exacting with humanity what is incontestably their due."

Considering the period at which this article was written, we are astonished less by its vagueness and incompleteness than by its bravery and generosity. The dissolute despotism of Louis XV poisoned France. The antechambers of the king were thronged by selfish nobles and fawning courtiers. The councils of government were controlled by royal mistresses.

The king, only a few years before, in defiance of equality—but in entire harmony with the conduct of the School Committee in Boston—founded a military school *for nobles only,* carrying into education the distinction of caste. At such a period the *Encyclopédie* did well in uttering important and effective truth. The *sentiment* of equality was fully declared. Nor should we be disappointed that, at this early day, even the boldest philosophers did not adequately perceive, or, if they perceived, did not dare to utter, our axiom of liberty.

Thus it is with all moral and political ideas. First appearing as a sentiment, they awake a noble impulse, filling the soul with generous sympathy, and encouraging to congenial effort. Slowly recognized, they finally pass into a formula, to be acted upon, to be applied, to be defended in the concerns of life, as principles.

Almost contemporaneously with this article in the *Encyclopédie* our attention is arrested by a poor solitary, of humble extraction, born at Geneva, in Switzerland, of irregular education and life, a wanderer from his birthplace, enjoying a temporary home in France—Jean-Jacques Rousseau. Of audacious genius, setting at nought received opinions, he rushed into notoriety by an eccentric essay "On the Origin of the Inequality among Men," where he sustained the irrational paradox, that men are happier in a state of nature than under the laws of civilization. At a later day appeared his famous work on *The Social Contract.* In both the sentiment of equality is invoked against abuses of society, and language is employed tending far beyond equality in civil and political rights. The conspicuous position since awarded to the speculations of Rousseau, and their influence in diffusing this sentiment, would make this sketch imperfect without allusion to him; but he taught men to feel rather than to know, and his words have more of inspiration than of precision.

The French Revolution was at hand. That great outbreak for enfranchisement was the expression of this sentiment. Here it received distinct and authoritative enunciation. In the constitutions of government successively adopted, amid the throes of bloody struggle, the equality of men was constantly proclaimed. Kings, nobles, and all distinctions of birth, passed away before this mighty and triumphant truth.

These constitutions show the grandeur of the principle, and how it was explained and illustrated. The Constitution of

1791, in its first article, declares that "men are born and continue free and *equal in their rights.*" This great declaration was explained in the sixth article: "The law is the expression of the general will. . . . It ought to be the same for all, whether it protect or punish. All citizens, being equal in its eyes, are equally admissible to all dignities, places, and public employments, according to their capacity, and without other distinction than their virtues and talents." At the close of the Declaration of Rights there is this further explanation: "The National Assembly, wishing to establish the French Constitution on the principles which it has just acknowledged and declared, abolishes irrevocably the institutions which bounded liberty and equality of rights. There is no longer nobility, or peerage, or hereditary distinctions, or distinction of orders, or feudal rule, or patrimonial jurisdictions, or any titles, denominations, or prerogatives thence derived, or any orders of chivalry, or any corporations or decorations for which proofs of nobility were required, or which supposed distinctions of birth, or any other superiority than that of public functionaries in the exercise of their functions. . . . *There is no longer, for any part of the nation, or for any individual, any privilege or exception to the common right of all Frenchmen.*" These diffuse articles all begin and end in the equality of men.

In fitful mood, another Declaration of Rights was brought forward by Condorcet, February 15, 1793. Here are fresh inculcations of equality. Article I places equality among the natural, civil, and political rights of man. Article VII declares: "Equality consists in this, that each individual can enjoy the same rights." Article VIII: *"The law ought to be equal for all,* whether it recompense or punish, whether it protect or repress." Article IX: "All citizens are admissible to all public places, employments, and functions. Free people know no other motives of preference in their choice than talents and virtues." Article XXIII: "Instruction is the need of all, and society owes it equally to all its members." Article XXXII: "There is oppression, when a law violates the natural, civil, and political rights which it ought to guarantee. There is oppression, when the law is violated by the public functionaries in its application to individual cases."

Here again is the same constant testimony, reinforced by the accompanying report explaining the constitution, where it is said: "All hereditary political power is at the same time an evident violation of natural equality and an absurd institution, since it supposes the inheritance of qualities proper for the discharge of a public function. Every exception to the common law made in favor of an individual is a blow struck at the rights of all." And in another part of the same report, "the sovereignty of the people, *equality among men*, the unity of the Republic," are declared to have been "the guiding principles always present in the formation of the constitution."

Next came the Constitution of June, 1793, announcing, in its second article, that the natural and imprescriptible rights of men are "*equality*, liberty, security, property." In the next article we learn precisely what is meant by equality, when it says, "All men are equal by nature *and before the law*." So just and captivating was this definition, which we encounter here for the first time, that it held its place through all the political vicissitudes of France, under the Directory, the Consulate, the Empire, the Restoration, and the Constitutional Government of Louis Philippe. It was a conquest which, when achieved, was never abandoned. Every charter and constitution certified to it. The charter of Louis Philippe testifies as follows: "Frenchmen are *equal before the law*, whatever may be their titles and ranks." Nor was its use confined to France. It passed into other constitutions, and Napoleon, who so often trampled on the rights of equality, dictated to the Poles the declaration, that *all persons are equal before the law*. Thus the phrase is not only French, but continental, although never English.

While recognizing this particular form of speech as more specific and satisfactory than the statement that all men are born equal, it is impossible not to be reminded that it finds a prototype in the ancient Greek language, where, according to Herodotus, "the government of the many has the most beautiful name of all, ισονομια *isonomy*," which may be defined equality before the law. Thus, in an age when *equality before the law* was practically unknown, this remarkable language, by its comprehensiveness and flexibility, supplied a single word, not found in modern tongues, to express an idea practically recognized only in modern times. Such a word in our own language, as the substitute for equality, might have superseded criticism to which this declaration is exposed.

*Equality Under the Constitution of Massachusetts
and the Declaration of Independence*

The way is now prepared to consider the nature of equality, as secured by the constitution of Massachusetts. The Declaration of Independence, which followed the French *Encyclopédie* and the political writings of Rousseau, announces among self-evident truths, *"that all men are created equal;* that they are endowed by their Creator with certain unalienable rights; that among these are life, liberty, and the pursuit of happiness." The constitution of Massachusetts repeats the same truth in a different form, saying, in its first article: *"All men are born free and equal,* and have certain natural essential, and unalienable rights, among which may be reckoned the right of enjoying and defending their lives and liberties." Another article explains what is meant by equality, saying: "No man, nor corporation or association of men, have any other title to obtain advantages, or particular and exclusive privileges, distinct from those of the community, than what arises from the consideration of services rendered to the public; and this title being in nature neither hereditary, nor transmissible to children, or descendants, or relations by blood, the idea of a man being born a magistrate, lawgiver, or judge is absurd and unnatural." This language, in its natural signification, condemns every form of inequality in civil and political institutions.

These declarations, though in point of time before the ampler declarations of France, may be construed in the light of the latter. Evidently, they seek to declare the same principle. They are declarations of *rights;* and the language employed, though general in character, is obviously limited to those matters within the design of a declaration of *rights.* And permit me to say, it is a childish sophism to adduce any physical or mental inequality in argument against equality of rights.

Obviously, men are not born equal in physical strength or in mental capacity, in beauty of form or health of body. Diversity or inequality in these respects is the law of creation. From this difference springs divine harmony. But this inequality is in no particular inconsistent with complete civil and political equality.

The equality declared by our fathers in 1776, and made the

fundamental law of Massachusetts in 1780, was *equality before the law*. Its object was to efface all political or civil distinctions, and to abolish all institutions founded upon *birth*. "All men are *created* equal," says the Declaration of Independence. "All men are *born* free and equal," says the Massachusetts Bill of Rights. These are not vain words. Within the sphere of their influence, no person can be *created*, no person can be *born*, with civil or political privileges not enjoyed equally by all his fellow-citizens; nor can any institution be established, recognizing distinction of birth. Here is the Great Charter of every human being drawing vital breath upon this soil, whatever may be his condition and whoever may be his parents. He may be poor, weak, humble, or black—he may be of Caucasian, Jewish, Indian, or Ethiopian race—he may be of French, German, English, or Irish extraction; but before the constitution of Massachusetts all these distinctions disappear. He is not poor, weak, humble, or black; nor is he Caucasian, Jew, Indian, or Ethiopian; nor is he French, German, English, or Irish; he is a *man*, the equal of all his fellowmen. He is one of the children of the state, which, like an impartial parent, regards all its offspring with an equal care. To some it may justly allot higher duties, according to higher capacities; but it welcomes all to its equal hospitable board. The state, imitating the divine justice, is no respecter of persons.

Here nobility cannot exist, because it is a privilege from birth. But the same anathema which smites and banishes nobility must also smite and banish every form of discrimination founded on birth—*Quamvis ille niger, quamvis tu candidus esses*. [No matter how black one may be, no matter how white, another.]

The legislature of Massachusetts, in entire harmony with the constitution, has made no discrimination of race or color, in the establishment of common schools.

Any such discrimination by the laws would be unconstitutional and void. But the legislature has been too just and generous, too mindful of the Bill of Rights, to establish any such privilege of *birth*. The language of the statutes is general, and applies equally to all children, of whatever race or color.

The provisions of the law are entitled, *Of the Public Schools*, meaning our common schools. To these we must look to ascertain what constitutes a public school. Only those established in conformity with the law can be legally such. They may, in fact, be more or less public; yet, if they do not come within the terms of the law, they do not form part of the beautiful system of our public schools—they are not public schools, or, as I prefer to call them, common schools. The two terms are used as identical; but the latter is that by which they were earliest known, while it is most suggestive of their comprehensive character. A "common" in law is defined to be "open ground equally used by many persons"; and the same word, when used as an adjective, is defined by lexicographers as "belonging equally to many or to the public," thus asserting equality.

If we examine the text of this statute, we shall find nothing to sustain the rule of exclusion which has been set up. The first section provides that "in every town, containing fifty families or householders, there shall be kept in each year, at the charge of the town, by a teacher or teachers of competent ability and good morals, *one school* for the instruction of *children* in orthography, reading, writing, English grammar, geography, arithmetic, and good behavior, for the term of six months, or two or more such schools for terms of time that shall together be equivalent to six months." The second, third, and fourth sections provide for the number of such schools in towns having respectively one hundred, one hundred and fifty, and five hundred families or householders. There is no language recognizing any discrimination of race or color. Thus, in every town, the schools, whether one or more, are "for the instruction of *children*" generally—not children of any particular class or race or color, but children—meaning the children of the town where the schools are.

The fifth and sixth sections provide a school, in certain cases, where additional studies are to be pursued, which "shall be kept *for the benefit of all the inhabitants* of the town." The language here recognizes no discrimination among the children, but seems directly to exclude it.

In conformity with these sections is the peculiar phraseology of the memorable colonial law of 1647, founding common schools, "to the end that learning may not be buried in the graves of our forefathers." This law obliged townships having fifty householders to "forthwith appoint one within their towns to teach *all such children as shall resort to him* to write and read." Here again there is no discrimination among the children. All are to be taught.

On this legislation the common schools of Massachusetts have been reared. The section of the revised statutes, and the statute of 1838, appropriating small sums, in the nature of a contribution, from the school fund, for the support of common schools among the Indians, do not interfere with this system. These have the anomalous character of all the legislation concerning the Indians. It does not appear, however, that separate schools are established by law among the Indians, nor that the Indians are in any way excluded from the common schools in their neighborhood.

I conclude, on this head, that there is but one public school in Massachusetts. This is the common school, equally free to all the inhabitants. There is nothing establishing an exclusive or separate school for any particular class, rich or poor, Catholic or Protestant, white or black. In the eye of the law there is but *one class*, where all interests, opinions, conditions, and colors commingle in harmony—excluding none, therefore comprehending all.

Equality Under Judicial Decisions

The courts of Massachusetts, in harmony with the constitution and the laws, have never recognized any discrimination founded on race or color, in the administration of the common schools, but have constantly declared the equal rights of all the inhabitants.

There are only a few decisions bearing on this subject, but they breathe one spirit. The sentiment of equality animates them all. In the case of *The Commonwealth v. Dedham* (16 Mass. R., 146), while declaring the equal rights of all the inhabitants, in both grammar and district schools, the Court said:

"The schools required by the statute are to be maintained for the benefit of the whole town, *as it is the wise policy of the law to give all the inhabitants equal privileges for the education of their children in the public schools*. Nor is it in the power of the majority to deprive the minority of this *privilege*. . . . Every inhabitant of the town has a right to participate in the benefits of both descriptions of schools; and it is not competent for a town to establish a grammar school for the benefit of one part of the town to the exclusion of the other, although the money raised for the support of schools may be in other respects fairly apportioned."

Here is equality from beginning to end.

In the case of *Withington v. Eveleth* (7 Pick. R., 106), the Court said they "are all satisfied that the power given to towns to determine and define the limits of school districts can be executed only by a geographical division of the town for that purpose." A limitation of the district, merely *personal*, was held invalid. This same principle was again recognized in *Perry v. Dover* (12 Pick. R., 213), where the Court said, "towns, in executing the power to form school districts, are bound so to do it as to include *every inhabitant* in some of the districts. They cannot lawfully omit any, and thus deprive them *of the benefits of our invaluable system of free schools.*" Thus at every point the Court has guarded the equal rights of all.

The constitution, the legislation, and the judicial decisions of Massachusetts have now been passed in review. We have seen what is contemplated by the equality secured by the constitution—also what is contemplated by the system of common schools, as established by the laws of the Commonwealth and illustrated by decisions of the Supreme Court. The way is now prepared to consider the peculiarities in the present case, and to apply the principle thus recognized in the constitution, laws, and judicial decisions.

Separate Schools Are Inconsistent with Equality

It is easy to see that the exclusion of colored children from the public schools is a constant inconvenience to them and their parents, which white children and white parents are not obliged to bear. Here the facts are plain and unanswerable, showing a palpable violation of equality. *The black and white are not equal before the law.* I am at a loss to understand how anybody can assert that they are.

Among the regulations of the Primary School Committee is one to this effect: "Scholars to go to the school nearest their residences. Applicants for admission to our schools (with the exception and provision referred to in the preceding rule) are especially entitled to enter the schools nearest to their places of residence." The exception here is "of those for whom special provision has been made" in separate schools—that is, colored children.

In this rule—without the unfortunate exception—is part of the beauty so conspicuous in our common schools. It is the boast of England that, through the multitude of courts, justice is brought to every man's door. It may also be the boast of our common schools that through the multitude of schools, education in Boston is brought to every *white* man's door. But it is not brought to every *black* man's door. He is obliged to go for it, to travel for it, to walk for it—often a great distance. The facts in the present case are not so strong as those of other cases within my knowledge. But here the little child, only five years old, is compelled, if attending the nearest African school, to go a distance of two thousand one hundred feet from her home, while the nearest primary school is only nine hundred feet; and, in doing this, she passes by no less than five different primary schools, forming part of our common schools, and open to white children, all of which are closed to her. Surely this is not equality before the law.

Such a fact is sufficient to determine this case. If it be met by the suggestion that the inconvenience is trivial and such as the law will not notice, I reply that it is precisely such as to reveal an existing inequality, and therefore the law cannot fail to notice it. There is a maxim of the illustrious civilian, Dumoulin, a great jurist of France, which teaches that even a trivial fact may give occasion to an important application of the law. *Modica enim circumstantia facti inducit magnam juris diversitatem.* Also, from the best examples of our history, we learn that the insignificance of a fact cannot obscure the grandeur of the principle at stake. It was a paltry tax on tea, laid by a parliament where they were not represented, that aroused our fathers to the struggles of the Revolution. They did not feel the inconvenience of the tax, but they felt its oppression. They went to war for a principle. Let it not be said, then, that in the present case the inconvenience is too slight to justify the appeal I make in behalf of colored children for equality before the law.

Looking beyond the facts of this case, it is apparent that the inconvenience from the exclusion of colored children is such as to affect seriously the comfort and condition of the African race in Boston. The two primary schools open to them are in Belknap Street and Sun Court. I need not add that the whole city is dotted with schools open to white children. Colored parents, anxious for the education of their children, are compelled to live in the neighborhood of the schools, to gather about them, as in Eastern countries people gather near a fountain or a well. The liberty which belongs to the white man, of choosing his home, is not theirs. Inclination or business or economy may call them to another part of the city; but they are restrained for their children's sake. There is no such restraint upon the white man; for he knows that, wherever in the city inclination or business or economy may call him, there will be a school open to his children near his door. Surely this is not equality before the law.

If a colored person, yielding to the necessities of position, removes to a distant part of the city, his children may be compelled daily, at an inconvenience which will not be called trivial, to walk a long distance for the advantages of the school. In our severe winters this cannot be disregarded, in the case of children so tender in years as those of the primary schools. There is a peculiar instance of hardship which has come to my knowledge. A respectable colored parent became some time since a resident of East Boston, separated from the mainland by water. Of course there are common schools at East Boston, but none open to colored children. This parent was obliged to send his children, three in number, daily across the ferry to the distant African school. The tolls amounted to a sum which formed a severe tax upon a poor man, while the long way to travel was a daily tax upon the time and strength of his children. Every toll paid by this parent, as every step taken by the children, testifies to that inequality which I now arraign.

This is the conduct of a colored parent. He is well deserving of honor for his generous efforts to secure the education of his children. As they grow in knowledge they will rise and call him blessed; but at the same time they will brand as accursed that arbitrary discrimination of color in the common schools of Boston which rendered it necessary for their father, out of small means, to make such sacrifices for their education.

Here is a grievance which, independent of any stigma from color, calls for redress. It is an inequality which the constitution and the laws of Massachusetts repudiate. But it is not on the ground of inconvenience only that it is odious. And this brings me to the next head.

Separate Schools Are in the Nature of Caste

The separation of children in the schools, on account of race or color, is in the nature of *caste*, and, on this account, a violation of equality. The case shows expressly that the child was excluded from the school nearest to her dwelling—the number in the school at the time warranting her admission— "on the sole ground of color." The first majority report presented to the School Committee, and mentioned in the statement of facts, presents the ground of this discrimination with more fulness, saying, "It is one of *races*, not of *colors* merely. The distinction is one which the All-wise Creator has seen fit to establish; and it is founded deep in the physical, mental, and moral natures of the two races. No legislation, no social customs, can efface this distinction." Words cannot be chosen more apt than these to describe the heathenish relation of caste.

This term, which has its prototype in Spanish and French, finds its way into English from the Portuguese *casta*, which signifies family, breed, race; and is generally used to designate any hereditary distinction, particularly of race. It is most often employed in India, and it is there that we must go to understand its full force. A recent English writer says that it is "not only a distinction by birth, but is founded on the doctrine of an essentially distinct origin of the different races, which are thus unalterably separated." This is the very ground of the Boston School Committee.

This word is not now for the first time applied to the distinction between the white and black races. Alexander von Humboldt, speaking of the Negroes in Mexico, characterizes them as a caste. Following him, a recent political and juridical writer of France uses the same term to denote not only the distinctions in India, but those of our own country, especially referring to the exclusion of colored children from the common schools as among "the humiliating and brutal distinctions" by which their caste is characterized. It is, then, on authority and reason alike that we apply this term to the hereditary distinction on account of color now established in the schools of Boston.

Boston is set on a hill, and her schools have long been the subject of observation, even in this respect. As far back as the last century, the French consul here made a report on our "separate" school; and de Tocqueville, in his masterly work, testifies, with evident pain, that the same schools do not receive the children of the African and European. All this is only a reproduction of the *cagots* in France, who for generations were put under the ban, relegated to a corner of the church, as in a "Negro pew," and even in the last resting place, where all are equal, these wretched people were separated by a line of demarcation from the rest. The *cagots* are called an "accursed race," and this language may be applied to the African under our laws. Strange that here, under a state constitution declaring the equality of all men, we should follow the worst precedents and establish among us a caste.

Seeing the discrimination in this light, we learn to appreciate its true character. In India, Brahmins and Sudras, from generation to generation, were kept apart. If a Sudra presumed to sit upon a Brahmin's carpet, his punishment was banishment. With similar inhumanity here, the black child who goes to sit on the same benches with the white is banished, not indeed from the country, but from the school. In both cases it is the triumph of caste. But the offence is greater with us, because, unlike the Hindus, we acknowledge that men are born equal.

So strong is my desire that the Court should feel the enormity of this system, thus legalized, not by the legislature, but by an inferior local board, that I shall introduce an array of witnesses all testifying to the unchristian character of caste, as it appears in India, where it is most studied and discussed. As you join in detestation of this foul institution, you will learn to condemn its establishment among our children.

I take these authorities from the work of Mr. Roberts to which I have already referred, *Caste opposed to Christianity*, published in London in 1847. Time will not allow me to make comments. I can only quote the testimony and then pass on.

The eminent Bishop Heber, of Calcutta, characterizes caste in these forcible terms:

"It is a system which tends, more than any else the Devil has yet invented, to destroy the feelings of general benevolence, and to make nine-tenths of mankind the hopeless slaves of the remainder."

But this is the very system now in question here. Bishop Wilson, also of Calcutta, the successor of Heber, says:

"The Gospel recognizes no such distinction as those of castes, imposed by a heathen usage, bearing in some respects a supposed religious obligation, condemning those in the lower ranks to perpetual abasement, placing an immovable barrier against all general advance and improvement in society, cutting asunder the bonds of human fellowship on the one hand, and preventing those of Christian love on the other. Such distinctions, I say, the Gospel does not recognize. On the contrary, it teaches us that God 'hath made of one blood all the nations of men.'"

The same sentiment is echoed by Bishop Corrie, of Madras:

"Thus caste sets itself up as a judge of our Saviour himself. His command is, 'condescend to men of low estate. Esteem others better than yourself.' 'No,' says caste, 'do not commune with low men: consider yourself of high estimation. Touch not, taste not, handle not.' Thus caste condemns the Saviour."

Here is the testimony of Rev. Mr. Rhenius, a zealous and successful missionary:

"I have found caste, both in theory and practice, to be diametrically opposed to the Gospel, which inculcates love, humility, and union; whereas caste teaches the contrary. It is a fact, in those entire congregations where caste is allowed, the spirit of the Gospel does not enter; whereas in those from which it is excluded we see the fruits of the Gospel spirit."

Another missionary, Rev. C. Mault, follows in similar strain:

"Caste must be entirely renounced; for it is a noxious plant, by the side of which the graces cannot grow; for facts demonstrate, that, where it has been allowed, Christianity has never flourished."

So also does the Rev. John McKenny, a Wesleyan missionary:

"I have been upward of twelve years in India, and have directed much of my attention to the subject of caste, and am fully of opinion that it is altogether contrary to the nature and principles of the Gospel of Christ, and therefore ought not to be admitted into the Christian Church."

So also the Rev. R. S. Hardy, a Wesleyan missionary, and author of *Notices of the Holy Land:*

"The principle of caste I consider so much at variance with the spirit of the Gospel as to render impossible, where its authority is acknowledged, the exercise of many of the most beautiful virtues of our holy religion."

So also the Rev. D. J. Gorgerly, of the same Society:

"I regard the distinction of caste, both in its principles and operations, as directly opposed to vital godliness, and consequently inadmissible into the Church of Christ."

So also the Rev. W. Bridgnall, of the same Society:

"I perfectly agree with a writer of respectable authority, in considering the institution of caste as the most formidable engine that was ever invented for perpetuating the subjugation of men; so that, as a friend of humanity only, I should feel myself bound to protest against and oppose it; but in particular as a Christian, I deem it my obvious and imperative duty wholly to discountenance it, conceiving it to be utterly repugnant to all the principles and the whole spirit of Christianity. He who is prepared to support the system of caste is, in my judgment, neither a true friend of man nor a consistent follower of Christ."

So also the Rev. S. Allens, of the same Society:

"During a residence of more than nine years in Ceylon I have had many opportunities of witnessing the influence of caste on the minds of the natives, and I firmly believe it is altogether opposed to the spirit of Christianity; and it appears to me that its utter and speedy extinction cannot but be desired by every minister of Christ."

So also the Rev. R. Stoup, of the same Society:

"From my own personal observation, during a four years' residence in Ceylon, I am decidedly of opinion that caste is directly opposed to the spirit of Christianity, and consequently ought to be discouraged in every possible way."

I conclude these European authorities with the confirmation of Rev. Joseph Roberts, author of the work on caste:

"We must in every place witness against it, and show that even government itself is nurturing a tremendous evil, that through its heathen managers it is beguiled into a course which obstructs the progress of civilization, which keeps in repulsion our kindlier feelings, which creates and nurses distinctions the most alien to all the cordialities of life, and which, more than any other thing, makes the distance so immense betwixt the governed and governors."

There is also the testimony of native Hindus converted to Christianity, who denounce caste as Jefferson denounced the despotism of slavery. Listen to the voice of a Hindu:

"Caste is the stronghold of that principle of pride which makes a man think of himself more highly than he ought to think. Caste infuses itself into and forms the very essence of pride itself."

Another Hindu testifies as follows:

"I therefore regard caste as opposed to the main scope, principles, and doctrines of Christianity; for either caste must be admitted to be true and of divine authority, or Christianity must be so admitted. If you admit caste to be true, the whole fabric of Christianity must come down; for the nature of caste and its associations destroy the first principles of Christianity. Caste makes distinctions among creatures where God has made none."

Another native expresses himself thus:

"When God made man, his intention was, not that they should be divided, and hate one another, and show contempt, and think more highly of themselves than others. Caste makes a man think that he is holier than another, and that he has some inherent virtue which another has not. It makes him despise all those that are lower than himself in regard to caste, which is not the design of God."

Still another native uses this strong language:

"Yes, we regard caste as part and parcel of idolatry, and of all heathen abominations, because it is in many ways contrary to God's word, and directly contrary to God himself."

I hope that I have not occupied too much time with this testimony, which is strictly in point. There is not a word which is not plainly applicable to the present case. The witnesses are competent, and in their evidence, as in a mirror, may be seen the true character of the discrimination which I bring to judgment before this Court.

It will be vain to say that this distinction, though seeming to be founded on color, is in reality founded on natural and physical peculiarities independent of color. Whatever they may be, they are peculiarities of race; and any discrimination on this account constitutes the relation of caste, in the most restricted sense of this term. Disguise it as you will, it is nothing but this hateful, irreligious institution. But the words caste and equality are contradictory. They mutually exclude each other. Where caste is, there cannot be equality; where equality is, there cannot be caste.

Unquestionably there is a distinction between the Ethiopian and the Caucasian. Each received from the hand of God certain characteristics of color and form. The two may not readily intermingle, although we are told by Homer that Jupiter did not

> "disdain to grace
> The feasts of Ethiopia's blameless race."

One may be uninteresting or offensive to the other, precisely as individuals of the same race and color may be uninteresting or offensive to each other. But this distinction can furnish no ground for any discrimination before the law.

We abjure nobility of all kinds; but here is a nobility of the skin. We abjure all hereditary distinctions; but here is an hereditary distinction, founded not on the merit of the ancestor, but on his color. We abjure all privileges of birth; but here is a privilege which depends solely on the accident whether an ancestor is black or white. We abjure all inequality before the law; but here is an inequality which touches not an individual, but a race. We revolt at the relation of caste; but here is a caste which is established under a constitution declaring that all men are born equal.

Condemning caste and inequality before the law, the way is prepared to consider more particularly the powers of the School Committee. Here it will be necessary to enter into details.

The School Committee Has No Power to Discriminate on Account of Color

The committee charged with the superintendence of the common schools of Boston has no *power* to make any discrimination on account of race or color.

It has been seen already that this power is inconsistent with the Declaration of Independence, with the constitution and laws of Massachusetts, and with adjudications of the Supreme Court. The stream cannot rise higher than the fountainhead; and if there be nothing in these elevated sources from which this power can spring, it must be considered a nullity. Having seen that there is nothing, I might here stop; but I wish to show the shallow origin of this pretension.

Its advocates, unable to find it among express powers conferred upon the School Committee, and forgetful of the constitution, where "either it must live or bear no life," place it among implied or incidental powers. The Revised Statutes provide for a School Committee "who shall have *the general charge and superintendence* of all the public schools" in their respective towns. Another section provides that "the School Committee shall determine the number and qualifications of the scholars to be admitted into the school kept for the use of the whole town." These are all the clauses conferring powers on the committee.

From them no person will imply a power to defeat a cardinal principle of the constitution. It is absurd to suppose that the committee, in their general charge and superintendence of schools, and in determining the number and qualifications of scholars, may engraft upon the schools a principle of inequality, not only unknown to the constitution and laws, but in defiance of their letter and spirit. In the exercise of these powers they cannot put colored children to personal inconvenience greater than that of white children. Still further, they cannot brand a whole race with the stigma of inferiority and degradation, constituting them a caste. They cannot in any way violate that fundamental right of all citizens, equality before the law. To suppose that they can do this would place the committee above the constitution. It would enable them, in the exercise of a brief and local authority, to draw a fatal circle, within which the constitution cannot enter—nay, where the very Bill of Rights becomes a dead letter.

In entire harmony with the constitution, the law says expressly what the committee shall do. Besides the general charge and superintendence, they shall "determine the *number* and *qualifications* of the scholars to be admitted into the school"—thus, according to a familiar rule of interpretation, excluding other powers. *Mentio unius est exclusio alterius.*

The power to determine the *number* is easily executed, and admits of no question. The power to determine the *qualifications*, though less simple, must be restricted to age, sex, and fitness, moral and intellectual. The fact that a child is black, or that he is white, cannot of itself be a qualification or a disqualification. Not to the skin can we look for the criterion of fitness.

It is sometimes pretended that the committee, in the exercise of their power, are intrusted with a discretion, under which they may distribute, assign, and classify all children belonging to the schools *according to their best judgment*, making, if they think proper, a discrimination of race or color. Without questioning that they are intrusted with a discretion, it is outrageous to suppose that their discretion can go to this extent. The committee can have no discretion which is not in harmony with the constitution and laws. Surely they cannot, in any mere discretion, nullify a sacred and dear-bought principle of human rights expressly guaranteed by the constitution.

Still further—and here I approach a more technical view of the subject—it is an admitted principle that the regulations and by-laws of municipal corporations must be *reasonable*, or they are inoperative and void. This has been recognized by the Supreme Court in two different cases, *Commonwealth v. Worcester* (3 Pick. R., 462), and in Vandine's case (6 Pick. R., 187). In another case, *City of Boston v. Shaw* (1 Met. R., 130), it was decided that a by-law of Boston, prescribing a particular form of contribution toward the expenses of making the common sewers, was void for inequality and unreasonableness.

Assuming that this principle is applicable to the School Committee, their regulations and by-laws must be *reasonable*. Their discretion must be exercised in a reasonable manner. And this is not what the committee or any other body of men think reasonable, but what is reasonable in the eye of the law. It must be *legally reasonable*. It must be approved by the *reason* of the law.

Here we are brought once more, in another form, to the question of the discrimination on account of color. Is this *legally reasonable?* Is it reasonable, in the exercise of a just discretion, to separate descendants of the African race from white children merely in consequence of descent? Passing over those principles of the constitution and those provisions of law which of themselves decide the question, constituting as they do *the highest reason*, but which have been already amply considered, look for a moment at the educational system of Massachusetts, and it will be seen that practically no discrimination of color is made by law in any part of it. A descendant of the African race may be governor of the Commonwealth, and as such, with the advice and consent of the Council, may select the Board of Education. As lieutenant-governor, he may be *ex officio* a member of the Board. He may be secretary of the Board, with the duty imposed on him by law of seeing "that *all* children in this Commonwealth, who depend upon common schools for instruction, may have the best education which those schools can be made to impart." He may be member of any school committee or teacher in any common school of the state. As legal voter, he can vote in the selection of any school committee.

Thus, in every department connected with our common schools, throughout the whole hierarchy of their government, from the very head of the system down to the humblest usher in the humblest primary school, and to the humblest voter, there is no distinction of color known to the law. It is when we reach the last stage of all, the children themselves, that the beautiful character of the system is changed to the deformity of caste as, in the picture of the ancient poet, what above was a lovely woman terminated below in a vile, unsightly fish. And all this is done by the School Committee, with more than necromantic power, in the exercise of a mere discretion.

It is clear that the committee may classify scholars according to age and sex, for the obvious reasons that these distinctions are inoffensive and that they are especially recognized as *legal* in the law relating to schools. They may also classify scholars according to moral and intellectual qualifications because such a power is necessary to the government of schools. But the committee cannot assume, *a priori*, and without individual examination, that all of an *entire race* are so deficient in proper moral and intellectual qualifications as to justify their universal degradation to a class by themselves. Such an exercise of discretion must be unreasonable and therefore illegal.

Separate Schools Are Not an Equivalent for the Common School

But it is said that the School Committee, in thus classifying the children, has not violated any principle of equality, inasmuch as it provides a school with competent instructors for colored children, where they have advantages equal to those provided for white children. It is argued that in excluding colored children from common schools open to white children the committee furnishes an *equivalent*.

Here there are several answers. I shall touch them briefly, as they are included in what has been already said.

(1) The separate school for colored children is not one of the schools established by the law relating to public schools. It is not a common school. As such it has no legal existence and therefore cannot be a *legal equivalent*. In addition to what has been already said, bearing on this head, I call attention to one other aspect. It has been decided that a town can execute its power to form school districts only by geographical divisions of its territory, that there cannot be what I would call a *personal* limitation of a district, and that *certain individuals* cannot be selected and set off by *themselves* into a district. The admitted effect of this decision is to render a separate school for colored children illegal and impossible in towns divided into districts. They are so regarded in Salem, Nantucket, New Bedford, and in other towns of this Commonwealth. The careful opinion of a learned member of this Court[1] who is not sitting in this case, given while at the bar, and extensively published, is considered as practically settling this point.

But there cannot be one law for the country and another for Boston. It is true that Boston is not divided strictly into geographical districts. In this respect its position is anomalous. But if separate colored schools are illegal and impossible in the country, they must be illegal and impossible in Boston. It is absurd to suppose that this city, failing to establish school districts and treating all its territory as a single district, should be able to legalize a caste school, which otherwise

---

[1] Richard Fletcher of Vermont (1788–1869) began to practice law in Boston in 1820, at once taking a place with leading Massachusetts practitioners. His main triumph was in the Charles River Bridge Case. He became judge of the Massachusetts Supreme Court October, 1848, and served until 1853.

it could not do. Boston cannot do indirectly what other towns cannot do directly. This is the first answer to the allegation of equivalents.

(2) The second is that in point of fact the separate school is not an equivalent. We have already seen that it is the occasion of inconvenience to colored children, which would not arise if they had access to the nearest common school, besides compelling parents to pay an additional tax and inflicting upon child and parent the stigma of caste. Still further —and this consideration cannot be neglected—the matter taught in the two schools may be precisely the same, but a school exclusively devoted to one class must differ essentially in spirit and character from that common school known to the law where all classes meet together in equality. It is a mockery to call it an equivalent.

(3) But there is yet another answer. Admitting that it is an equivalent, still the colored children cannot be compelled to take it. Their rights are found in equality before the law; nor can they be called to renounce one jot of this. They have an equal right with white children to the common schools. A separate school, though well endowed, would not secure to them that precise equality which they would enjoy in the common schools. The Jews in Rome are confined to a particular district called the Ghetto and in Frankfort to a district known as the Jewish Quarter. It is possible that their accommodations are as good as they would be able to occupy, if left free to choose throughout Rome and Frankfort; but this compulsory segregation from the mass of citizens is of itself an *inequality* which we condemn. It is a vestige of ancient intolerance directed against a despised people. It is of the same character with the separate schools in Boston.

Thus much for the doctrine of equivalents as a substitute for equality.

In determining that the School Committee has no *power* to make this discrimination we are strengthened by another consideration. If the power exists in the present case, it cannot be restricted to this. The committee may distribute all the children into classes, according to mere discretion. It may establish a separate school for Irish or Germans, where each may nurse an exclusive nationality alien to our institutions. It may separate Catholics from Protestants, or, pursuing their discretion still further, may separate different sects of Protestants and establish one school for Unitarians, another for Presbyterians, another for Baptists, and another for Methodists. It may establish a separate school for the rich, that the delicate taste of this favored class may not be offended by the humble garments of the poor. It may exclude the children of mechanics and send them to separate schools. All this, and much more, can be done in the exercise of that high-handed power which makes a discrimination on account of race or color. The grand fabric of our common schools, the pride of Massachusetts—where, at the feet of the teacher, innocent childhood should come, unconscious of all distinctions of birth—where the equality of the constitution and of Christianity should be inculcated by constant precept and example, will be converted into a heathen system of proscription and caste. We shall then have many different schools, representatives of as many different classes, opinions, and prejudices; but we shall look in vain for the true common school of Massachusetts. Let it not be said that there is little danger that any committee will exercise a discretion to this extent. It must not be intrusted with the power. Here is the only safety worthy of a free people.

The By-Law of the School Committee Is Unconstitutional and Illegal

The Court will declare the by-law of the School Committee unconstitutional and illegal, although there are no express words of prohibition in the constitution and laws.

It is hardly necessary to say anything in support of this proposition. Slavery was abolished in Massachusetts, under the declaration of rights in our constitution, without any specific words of abolition in that instrument or in any subsequent legislation. The same words which are potent to destroy slavery must be equally potent against any institution founded on inequality or caste. The case of *Boston v. Shaw* (1 Metcalf, 130), to which reference has been already made, where a by-law of the city was set aside as unequal and unreasonable and therefore void, affords another example of the power which I here invoke. But authorities are not needed. The words of the constitution are plain, and it will be the duty of the Court to see that they are applied to the discrimination now waiting for judgment.

The Court might justly feel delicacy, if called to revise an act of the legislature. But it is simply the action of a local committee that they are to overrule. They may also be encouraged by the circumstance that it is only to the schools of Boston that their decision can be applicable. Already the other towns have voluntarily banished caste. Banishing it from the schools of Boston, the Court will bring them into much-desired harmony with the schools of other towns and with the whole system of common schools. I am unwilling to suppose that there can be any hesitation or doubt. If any should arise, there is a rule of interpretation which is plain. According to familiar practice, judicial interpretation is made always in favor of life or liberty. So here the Court should incline in favor of equality, that sacred right which is the companion of those other rights. In proportion to the importance of this right will the Court be solicitous to vindicate and uphold it. And in proportion to the opposition which it encounters from prejudices of society will the Court brace themselves to this task. It has been pointedly remarked by Rousseau that "it is precisely because the force of things tends always to destroy equality that the force of legislation should always tend to maintain it." In similar spirit, and for the same reason, the Court should always tend to maintain equality.

Concluding Remarks

In extenuation of the Boston system, it is sometimes said that the separation of white and black children was originally made at the request of colored parents. This is substantially true. It appears from the interesting letter of Dr. Belknap, in reply to Judge Tucker's queries respecting slavery in Massachusetts, at the close of the last century, that no discrimination on account of color existed then in the common schools of Boston. "The same provision," he says, "is made by the public for the education of the children of the blacks as for those of the whites. In this town the committee which superintends the free schools has given in charge to the schoolmasters to receive and instruct black children as well as white." Dr. Belknap had "not heard of more than three or four who had taken advantage of this privilege, though the number of blacks in Boston probably exceeded one thousand." Much I fear that the inhuman bigotry of caste—sad relic of the servitude from which they had just escaped—was at this time too strong to allow colored children kindly welcome in the free schools, and that, from timidity and ignorance, they hesitated to take a place on the same benches with the white children. Perhaps the prejudice was so inveterate that they could not venture to assert their rights. In 1800 a petition from sixty-six colored persons was presented to the School Committee, requesting the establishment of a school for their benefit. Some time later, private munificence came to the aid of this work, and the present system of separate schools was brought into being.

These are interesting incidents belonging to the history of the Boston schools, but they cannot in any way affect the rights of colored people or the powers of the School Committee. These rights and these powers stand on the constitution and laws. Without adopting the suggestion of Jefferson that one generation cannot by legislation bind its successors, all must agree that the assent of a few to an unconstitutional and illegal course nearly half a century ago, when their rights were imperfectly understood, cannot alter the constitution and the laws so as to bind their descendants forever in the thrall of caste. Nor can the committee derive from this assent, or from any lapse of time, powers in derogation of the constitution and the Rights of Man.

It is clear that the sentiments of the colored people have now changed. The present case, and the deep interest which they manifest in it, thronging the Court to watch this discussion, attest the change. With increasing knowledge they have learned to know their rights and feel the degradation to which they are doomed. In them revives the spirit of Paul, even as when he demanded, "Is it lawful for you to scourge a man that is a Roman, and uncondemned?" Their present effort is the token of a manly character, which this Court will respect and cherish.

But it is said that these separate schools are for the benefit of both colors and of the public schools. In similar spirit slavery is sometimes said to be for the benefit of master and slave and of the country where it exists. There is a mistake in the one case as great as in the other. This is clear. Nothing unjust, nothing ungenerous, can be for the benefit of any person or any thing. From some seeming selfish superiority, or from the gratified vanity of class, short-sighted mortals may hope to draw permanent good; but even-handed justice rebukes these efforts and redresses the wrong. The whites themselves are injured by the separation. Who can doubt this? With the law as their monitor, they are taught to regard a portion of the human family, children of God, created in His image, co-equals in His love, as a separate and degraded class; they are taught practically to deny that grand revelation of Christianity, the brotherhood of man. Hearts, while yet tender with childhood, are hardened, and ever afterward testify to this legalized uncharitableness. Nursed in the sentiments of caste, receiving it with the earliest food of knowledge, they are unable to eradicate it from their natures, and then weakly and impiously charge upon our Heavenly Father the prejudice derived from an unchristian school. Their characters are debased, and they become less fit for the duties of citizenship.

The helots of Sparta were obliged to intoxicate themselves, that by example they might teach the deformity of intemperance. Thus sacrificing one class to the other, both were injured—the imperious Spartan and the abased helot. The School Committee of Boston acts with similar double-edged injustice in sacrificing the colored children to the prejudice or fancied advantage of the white.

A child should be taught to shun wickedness and, as he is yet plastic under impressions, to shun wicked men. Horace was right when, speaking of a person morally wrong, false, and unjust, he calls him black and warns against him:

Hic niger est: hunc tu, Romane, cavete.
[This man is black; of this man, Roman, beware.]

The Boston Committee adopt the warning but apply it not to the black in heart but the black in skin. They forget the admonition addressed to the prophet: "The Lord said unto Samuel, *Look not on his countenance:* for the Lord seeth not as man seeth; for man looketh on the outward appearance, *but the Lord looketh on the heart.*" The committee looks on the outward appearance, without looking on the heart, and thus fancies that it is doing right!

Who can say that this does not injure the blacks? Theirs, in its best estate, is an unhappy lot. A despised class, blasted by prejudice and shut out from various opportunities, they feel this proscription from the common schools as a peculiar brand. Beyond this, it deprives them of those healthful, animating influences which would come from participation in the studies of their white brethren. It adds to their discouragements. It widens their separation from the community and postpones that great day of reconciliation which is yet to come.

The whole system of common schools suffers also. It is a narrow perception of their high aim which teaches that they are merely to furnish an equal amount of knowledge to all, and therefore, provided all be taught, it is of little consequence where and in what company. The law contemplates not only that all shall be taught, but that *all* shall be taught *together*. They are not only to receive equal quantities of knowledge, but all are to receive it in the same way. All are to approach the same common fountain together; nor can there be any exclusive source for individual or class. The school is the little world where the child is trained for the larger world of life. It is the microcosm preparatory to the macrocosm, and therefore it must cherish and develop the virtues and the sympathies needed in the larger world. And since, according to our institutions, all classes, without distinction of color, meet in the performance of civil duties, so should they all, without distinction of color, meet in the school, beginning there those relations of equality which the constitution and laws promise to all.

As the state derives strength from the unity and solidarity of its citizens without distinction of class, so the school derives strength from the unity and solidarity of all classes beneath its roof. In this way the poor, the humble, and the neglected not only share the companionship of the more favored, but enjoy also the protection of their presence, which draws toward the school a more watchful superintendence. A degraded or neglected class, if left to themselves, will become more degraded or neglected. "If any man have ears to hear, let him hear. . . . For he that hath, to him shall be given; and he that hath not, from him shall be taken even that which he hath." The world, perverting the true sense of these words, takes from the outcast that which God gave him capacity to enjoy. Happily, our education system, by the blending of all classes, draws upon the whole school that attention which is too generally accorded only to the favored few, and thus secures to the poor their portion of the fruitful sunshine. But the colored children, placed apart in separate schools, are deprived of this peculiar advantage. Nothing is more clear than that the welfare of classes, as well as of individuals, is promoted by mutual acquaintance. Prejudice is the child of ignorance. It is sure to prevail where people do not know each other. Society and intercourse are means established by providence for human improvement. They remove antipathies, promote mutual adaptation and conciliation, and establish relations of reciprocal regard. Whoso sets up barriers to these thwarts the ways of providence, crosses the tendencies of human nature, and directly interferes with the laws of God.

May it please your Honors: Such are some of the things which I feel it my duty to say in this important cause. I have occupied much time, but the topics are not yet exhausted. Still, which way soever we turn, we are brought back to one single proposition—*the equality of men before the law*. This stands as the mighty guardian of the colored children in this case. It is the constant, ever-present, tutelary genius of this Commonwealth, frowning upon every privilege of birth, every distinction of race, every institution of caste. You cannot slight it or avoid it. You cannot restrain it. God grant that you may welcome it! Do this, and your words will be a "charter and freehold of rejoicing" to a race which by much suffering has earned a title to much regard. Your judgment will become a sacred landmark, not in jurisprudence only, but in the history of freedom, giving precious encouragement to the weary and heavy-laden wayfarers in this great cause. Massachusetts, through you, will have fresh title to respect and be once more, as in times past, an example to the whole land.

Already you have banished slavery from this Commonwealth. I call upon you now to obliterate the last of its footprints and to banish the last of the hateful spirits in its train. The law interfering to prohibit marriage between blacks and whites has been abolished by the legislature. Railroads, which, imitating the Boston schools, placed colored people apart by themselves, are compelled, under the influence of an awakened public sentiment, to abandon this regulation and to allow them the privileges of other travellers. Only recently I have read that his Excellency, our present governor, took his seat in a train by the side of a Negro. In the caste schools of Boston the prejudice of color seeks its final refuge. It is for you to drive it forth. You do well when you rebuke and correct individual offences; but it is a higher office to rebuke and correct a vicious institution. Each individual is limited in influence; but an institution has the influence of numbers organized by law. The charity of one man may counteract or remedy the uncharitableness of another; but no individual can counteract or remedy the uncharitableness of an organized injury. Against it private benevolence is powerless. It is a monster to be hunted down by the public and the constituted authorities. And such is the institution of caste in the common schools of Boston, which now awaits a just condemnation from a just Court.

One of the most remarkable expositions of slavery is from the pen of Condorcet, in a note to the *Thoughts* of Pascal. Voltaire, in his later commentary on the same text, speaks of this "terrible" note and adopts its conclusion. In the course of this arraignment, the philosopher, painting the character of the slave-master, says, "such is the excess of his stupid contempt for this wretched race, that, returning to Europe, he is indignant to see them clothed as men and *placed by his side.*" Thus the repugnance of the slave-master to see the wretched race *placed by his side* is adduced as crowning evidence of the inhumanity of slavery. But this very repugnance has practical sanction among us, and you are to determine whether it shall be longer permitted. Slavery, in one of its enormities, is now before you for judgment. Hesitate not, I pray you, to strike it down. Let the blow fall which shall end its domination here in Massachusetts.

The civilization of the age joins in this appeal. I need not remind you that this prejudice of color is peculiar to our country. You may remember that two youths of African blood only recently gained the highest honors in a college at Paris and on the same day dined with the King of the French, the descendant of St. Louis, at the Palace of the Tuileries. And let me add, if I may refer to my own experience, that at the School of Law in Paris I have sat for weeks on the same benches with colored pupils, listening, like myself, to the learned lectures of Degerando and Rossi; nor do I remember, in the throng of sensitive young men, any feeling toward them except of companionship and respect. In Italy, at the Convent of Palazzuolo, on the shores of the Alban Lake, amidst a scene of natural beauty enhanced by historical association, where I was once a guest, I have, for days, seen a native of Abyssinia, recently from his torrid home, and ignorant of the language spoken about him, mingling, in delightful and affectionate familiarity, with the Franciscan friars, whose visitor and scholar he was. Do I err in saying that the Christian spirit shines in these examples?

The Christian spirit, then, I again invoke. Where this prevails, there is neither Jew nor Gentile, Greek nor Barbarian, bond nor free, but all are alike. From this we derive new and solemn assurance of the equality of men, as an ordinance of God. Human bodies may be unequal in beauty or strength; these mortal cloaks of flesh may differ, as do these wordly garments; these intellectual faculties may vary, as do opportunities of action and advantages of position; but amid all unessential differences there is essential agreement and equality. Dives and Lazarus are equal in the sight of God: they must be equal in the sight of all human institutions.

This is not all. The vaunted superiority of the white race imposes corresponding duties. The faculties with which they are endowed and the advantages they possess must be exercised for the good of all. If the colored people are ignorant, degraded, and unhappy, then should they be especial objects of care. From the abundance of our possessions must we seek to remedy their lot. And this Court, which is parent to all the unfortunate children of the Commonwealth, will show itself most truly parental when it reaches down, and, with the strong arm of law, elevates, encourages, and protects our colored fellow-citizens.

The
Nature of the
Union

ADDRESS TO THE PEOPLE OF THE UNITED
STATES. PREPARED FOR THE CONVENTION
OF THE PEOPLE OF SOUTH CAROLINA,
NOVEMBER, 1832

BY JOHN C. CALHOUN AND OTHERS

AND

PROCLAMATION TO THE PEOPLE OF THE
UNITED STATES. DECEMBER 10, 1832

BY ANDREW JACKSON AND EDWARD LIVINGSTON

Introduction

The tariff crisis of 1832 is a focus of extraordinary interest in the history of the United States prior to the Civil War. It produced a direct collision between South Carolina and the Federal government involving the immediate risk of an armed clash. It gave rise to important statements of both the national and states-rights theories of the Constitution. It proved a turning point in the career of John C. Calhoun. Study of this crisis sheds light on the evolution of the political parties, and in particular upon the emerging Southern concept of the Democratic party as an alliance of South and West, based upon states rights and white supremacy. Underlining the deep connection between Federal policies and the slavery question in the Jacksonian age, the crisis marked a first step in the successive lowering of tariff barriers that continued almost without interruption until the onset of the Civil War. This process was an index of the growing ascendancy in national affairs of Southern proslavery and antitariff interests.

411

Federal tariffs originated in an age when there was no income tax, when government had to place reliance upon other methods of collecting a revenue adequate to its needs. From the inception of government under the Constitution until the end of the War of 1812, Federal tariffs were levied primarily for the purpose of raising revenue. But the growing industrialization of the Northeast, particularly after the conclusion of the War of 1812, and the reality of stiff competition from imported British goods, brought rising pressure from business interests for the utilization of the tariff system as an instrument for the protection of American industry. The idea that tariffs should be thus used to protect infant industries from the competition of cheaply produced foreign goods had been originally popularized by Alexander Hamilton. With protective tariffs, of course, revenue did accrue to the government, but this was considered to be a by-product rather than the main objective of the system.

The Tariff of 1816 responded to these pressures and marked a new departure in national economic policy. Interests in every section of the country gained something from it. It provided protection for Northern textile manufacturers, but also for Western growers of flax and hemp. Southern sugar producers in Louisiana won a 3 cents per pound duty on imported brown sugar sufficient to launch them upon a period of highly profitable expansion.

Southern cotton growers opposed protective tariffs. They saw in them primarily an economic weapon that would benefit the North at the expense of the South—that would foster and accelerate the growth of industry and of population in the North, thus diminishing the relative economic power and political influence of the South. Such opposition, smoldering throughout the '20's, had solidified by 1828, due largely to the passage of the tariff act of that year. This peculiar law, the so-called "tariff of abominations," precipitated a sharp anti-tariff campaign in South Carolina headed by a group who came to be known as fire-eaters, and whose leading members included George McDuffie, Robert Y. Hayne, James Hamilton and James Hammond. Politically it was inexpedient for Calhoun, then Vice-President, to join this group, but he entertained close relations with them.

The fire-eaters advocated defiance by South Carolina of the tariff laws, the passage of constitutional amendments to nullify them, and, if all else failed, secession. But the crisis arising from Federal determination to enforce the law and South Carolina's determination to defy it, did not break out until 1832, four years after the passage of the "tariff of abominations." The main reason for this was that Calhoun, as Vice-President, confidently expected to succeed the ailing Andrew Jackson to the Presidency. In these circumstances he would be in a position to use his influence in the Federal government to initiate a downward trend in tariffs; and this would be part of a broader sectional program to create a Western-Southern alliance against the industrial and commercial interests of the Northeast.

But this expectation was defeated by accidental circumstances. Jackson was, in reality, physically much tougher than he appeared; his relationship with Calhoun rapidly deteriorated as a result of the Peggy Eaton affaire, and this rift was skillfully exploited by Martin Van Buren. The estrangement between President and Vice-President put an end, at least temporarily, to Calhoun's bid for the leadership of the Democratic party; and in 1832 he joined forces openly with the South Carolina fire-eaters. Andrew Jackson faced re-election in 1832, and was in no position to make substantial concessions to the South on tariff matters. The new tariff law passed in July, 1832, continued the protectionist principle of 1828 with certain modifications.

Under these circumstances the South Carolina leadership changed its tactics and produced a crisis around the issue of a direct defiance of Federal authority in the event that the objectionable measure was not withdrawn. In November, 1832, a specially convened state assembly met and passed an ordinance nullifying the Tariff Acts of 1828 and 1832, and ordering state officials not to comply with them. The ordinance raised the possibility of secession from the Union in the event that Federal action were taken to enforce the law.[1]

This ordinance was accompanied by an "Address to the People of the United States," which set forth in greater detail the basis of South Carolina's complaints and the theory of the Constitution upon which she acted. The product of the combined thinking of South Carolina's states-rights leadership, this address is the first of the two documents reproduced in

---

[1] The main points of this ordinance are summarized at the opening of Andrew Jackson's proclamation (p. 428–9).

full below. It was based upon an essay that Calhoun had written for the group secretly four years before—the "South Carolina Exposition" of 1828.

Andrew Jackson reacted swiftly to what he saw as a clear threat to the Federal Union and to national authority. He submitted to Congress a Force Bill authorizing the use of troops against South Carolina; and he had his Secretary of State, Edward Livingston, draw up a "Proclamation to the American People." This document, the second of the two reproduced below, ranks as one of the country's outstanding state papers and as a brilliant expression of national constitutional theory. Placing the issues in the crisis before the American people, it asked for their full support of the Federal government in its determination to enforce the law and to defend the supremacy of the Constitution.

Of Calhoun, principal author of the South Carolina "Address," more will be said later (p. 474-6). Jackson's proclamation came from the pen of one of America's ablest jurists, Edward Livingston (1764-1836), was a member of one of New York's most distinguished families. Admitted to the bar in 1785 he served three terms in Congress as a Clintonian Democrat. In 1804 he moved to New Orleans following a financial scandal that occurred while he was Mayor of New York City, and that left him saddled with heavy debts. During the defense of New Orleans against the British in 1814 he established close connections with Andrew Jackson, whose Secretary of State he became in 1831.

The crisis was resolved in 1833 short of war. The South failed to come to South Carolina's support. With the help of Henry Clay a compromise was worked out whereby South Carolina accepted a new and more moderate tariff bill. But the whole episode was instructive, for it sketched out sharply a strategy which the Southern slave oligarchy would follow in succeeding years until the outbreak of the Civil War: a strategy, either to rule the Union, using the Federal machinery for the advancement of proslavery interests, or to ruin it if a determined free-state majority should offer a decisive challenge either to the proslavery interests or to the Federal policies which they fostered and supported.

The formulation and development of the states-rights theory of the Constitution was linked closely with the effort to defend vested minority and sectional interests. For this purpose, and above all in the South, states-rights theory has shown an enduring vitality from that day to this. For this reason, too, Livingston's defense of the national sovereignty and the national Constitution is as apposite today as when it was first written.

ADDRESS TO THE PEOPLE OF THE UNITED STATES. PREPARED FOR THE CONVENTION OF THE PEOPLE OF SOUTH CAROLINA, NOVEMBER, 1832 [by John C. Calhoun] *

To the People of Maine, New Hampshire, Massachusetts, Rhode Island, Connecticut, Vermont, New York, New Jersey, Pennsylvania Delaware, Maryland, Virginia, North Carolina, Georgia, Kentucky, Tennessee, Ohio, Louisiana, Indiana, Mississippi, Illinois, Alabama and Missouri:

We, the people of South Carolina assembled in Convention in our sovereign capacity, as one of the parties to the compact, which formed the Constitution of the United States, have declared the act of Congress, approved the 14th of July, 1832, to alter and amend the several acts imposing duties on imports, and the acts, which it alters and amends, —to be unconstitutional, and therefore null and void; and have invested the Legislature of the State with power to adopt such measures, not repugnant to the Constitution of the United States, nor of this State,—as it may deem proper, to carry the same into effect. In taking this step, we feel it to be due to the intimate political relations existing between the States of the Union, to make known to them, distinctly, the principles on which we have acted, with the cause and motive by which we have been influenced;—to fulfil which is the object of the present communication.

For this purpose, it will be necessary to state, summarily, what we conceive to be the nature and character of the

Source: "Address to the People of the United States," *Works of John C. Calhoun,* edited by Richard K. Crallé (New York, 1856), II, pp. 193–209.

Constitution of the United States, with the rights and duties of the States,—so far as they relate to the subject,—in reference both to the Union and to their own citizens;—and also the character and effect, in a political point of view, of the system of protective duties, contained in the acts which we have declared to be unconstitutional, as far as it may be necessary, in reference to the same subject.

We, then, hold it as unquestionable, that, on the separation from the Crown of Great Britain, the people of the several colonies became free and independent States, possessed of the full right of self-government;—and that no power can be rightfully exercised over them, but by the consent and authority of their respective States, expressed or implied. We also hold it as equally unquestionable, that the Constitution of the United States is a compact between the people of the several States, constituting free, independent, and sovereign communities;—that the Government it created was formed and appointed to execute, according to the provisions of the instrument, the powers therein granted, as the joint agent of the several States; that all its acts, transcending these powers, are simply and of themselves, null and void, and that in case of such infractions, it is the right of the States, in their sovereign capacity, each acting for itself and its citizens, in like manner as they adopted the Constitution, to judge thereof in the last resort, and to adopt such measures—not inconsistent with the compact—as may be deemed fit, to arrest the execution of the act within their respective limits. Such we hold to be the right of the States, in reference to an unconstitutional act of the Government; nor do we deem their duty to exercise it on proper occasions, less certain and imperative, than the right itself is clear.

We hold it to be a very imperfect conception of the obligation, which each State contracted in ratifying the Constitution, and thereby becoming a member of the Union, to suppose that it would be fully and faithfully discharged, simply by abstaining, on its part, from exercising the powers delegated to the Government of the Union, or by sustaining it in the due execution of those powers. These are, undoubtedly, important federal duties, but there is another not less important,—to resist the Government, should it, under color of exercising the delegated, encroach on the reserved powers. The duty of the States is no less clear in the one case than in the other; and the obligation as binding in the one as in the other; and in like manner, the solemn obligation of an oath, imposed by the States through the Constitution, on all public functionaries, federal and State, to support that instrument, comprehends the one as well as the other duty;—as well that of maintaining the Government in the due exercise of its powers, as that of resisting it when it transcends them.

But the obligation of a State to resist the encroachments of the Government on the reserved powers, is not limited simply to the discharge of its federal duties. We hold that it embraces another, if possible, more sacred;—that of protecting its citizens, derived from their original sovereign character, viewed in their separate relations. There are none of the duties of a State of higher obligation. It is, indeed, the primitive duty,—preceding all others, and in its nature paramount to them all; and so essential to the existence of a State, that she cannot neglect or abandon it, without forfeiting all just claims to the allegiance of her citizens, and with it, her sovereignty itself. In entering into the Union, the States by no means exempted themselves from the obligation of this, the first and most sacred of their duties; nor, indeed, can they without sinking into subordinate and dependent corporations. It is true, that in ratifying the Constitution, they placed a large and important portion of the rights of their citizens, under the joint protection of all the States, with a view to their more effectual security; but it is not less so, that they reserved, at the same time, a portion still larger, and not less important, under their own immediate guardianship; and in relation to which, the original obligation, to protect the rights of their citizens, from whatever quarter assailed, remained unchanged and unimpaired. Nor is it less true, that the General Government, created in order to preserve the rights placed under the joint protection of the States, and which, when restricted to its proper sphere, is calculated to afford them the most perfect security, may become, when not so restricted, the most dangerous enemy to the rights of their citizens, including those reserved under the immediate guardianship of the States respectively, as well as those under their joint protection; and thus, the original and inherent obligation of the States to protect their citizens, is united with that which they have contracted to support the Constitution; thereby rendering it the most sacred of all their duties to watch over and resist the encroachments of the Government; —and on the faithful performance of which, we solemnly believe the duration of the Constitution and the liberty and happiness of the country depend.

But, while we hold the rights and duties of the States to be such as we have stated, we are deeply impressed with the conviction, that it is due to the relation existing between them, as members of a common Union, and the respect which they ought ever to entertain towards the Government ordained to carry into effect the important objects for which the Constitution was formed, that the occasion to justify a State in interposing its authority, ought to be one of necessity; where all other peaceful remedies have been unsuccessfully tried; and where the only alternative is, interposition on one side, or oppression of its citizens, and imminent danger to the Constitution and liberty of the country on the other; and such we hold to be the present.

That the prohibitory, or protective system, which, as has been stated, is embraced in the acts which we have declared to be unconstitutional, and therefore null and void, is, in fact, unconstitutional, unequal, and oppressive in its operation on this, and the other staple and exporting States, and dangerous to the Constitution and liberty of the country,— and that (all other peaceful remedies having been tried without success) an occasion has occurred, where it becomes the right and duty of the State to interpose its authority to arrest the evil within its limits, we hold to be certain; and it is under this deep and solemn conviction, that we have acted.

For more than ten years, the system has been the object of continued, united, and strenuous opposition on the part both of the Government of the State and its representatives in Congress; and, we may add, of the other staple and exporting States. During this long period, all the ordinary means of opposition—discussion, resolution, petition, remonstrance, and protest—have been tried and exhausted, without effect. We have, during the whole time, waited with patience under the unequal and oppressive action of the system, hoping that the final payment of the public debt, when there would be no longer a pretext for its continuance, would bring it to a termination. That period, for all practical purposes, is now passed. The small remnant of debt which now remains, is amply provided for by the revenue already accrued; but the system remains in full force;—its restrictive character established and openly avowed; the inequality of its action, between this and other sections, greatly increased; and the amount of its exertions vastly exceeding,—probably doubling, the just and constitutional wants of the Government. The event, which, it was hoped, would put an end to its duration, has thus but served to give it increased strength; and, instead of mitigating, has aggravated its most obnoxious features. Having stood this shock, it seems almost impossible that any other within the ordinary scope of events, can shake it. It now stands for the first time, exclusively on its own basis, as an independent system; having a self-existing power, with an unlimited capacity of increasing,—which, left unopposed, must continue to expand, till it controls the entire labor and capital of the staple and exporting States;—subjecting them completely, as tributaries, to the great dominant and sectional interest, which has grown up at their expense. With this prospect of the indefinite extent and duration of the system, we had thus presented the alternative of silently acquiescing in its oppression and danger, or of interposing as the last peaceful measure of redress, the authority of the State to arrest the evil within its limits. We did not hesitate.

When we reflect on the principle on which the system rests, and from which the Government claims the power to control the labor and capital of the country, and the bitter fruits it has already produced,—the decay and impoverishment of an entire section of the country;—and the wide spread of discord and corruption,—we cannot doubt, that there is involved in the issue, not only the prosperity of this and the other staple and exporting States, but also the Constitution and liberty of the country. In rearing up the system it was not pretended, nor is it now, that there is in the Constitution any positive grant of power to protect manufactures; nor can it be denied that frequent attempts were made in the Convention to obtain the power, and that they all failed: and yet, without any grant, and notwithstanding the failure to obtain one, it has become one of the leading powers of the Government,—influencing more extensively its movements, and affecting more deeply and permanently the relative interests and condition of the States, and the probable fate of the Government itself, than any, or all of the enumerated powers united.

From whatever source its advocates may derive this power, —whether from the right, "to lay and collect taxes, duties, imposts, and excises," or from that, "to regulate commerce," it plainly rests on the broad assumption, that the power to impose duties may be applied, not only to effect the original objects,—to raise revenue, or regulate commerce, but also to protect manufactures; and this, not as an incidental, but as a substantive and independent power,—without reference to revenue or commerce; and, in this character, it has been used in building up the present system.

That such a power, resting on such a principle, is unauthorized by the Constitution;—that it has become an instrument in the hands of the great dominant interests of the country, to oppress the weaker;—that it must, ultimately, concentrate the whole power of the community in the General Government, and abolish the sovereignty of the States;—and that discord, corruption, and, eventually, despotism must follow, if the system be not resisted,—we hold to be certain. Already we see the commencement of this disastrous train of consequences;— the oppression of the weaker;—the assumption by Government of the right to determine, finally and conclusively, the extent of its own powers;—the denial and denunciation of the right of the States to judge of their reserved powers, and to defend them against the encroachments of the Government;— followed by discord, corruption, and the steady advance of despotic power.

That something is wrong, all admit; and that the assumption, by Government, of a power so extensive and dangerous, and the control which it has thereby acquired, through its fiscal operations, over the wealth and labor of the country,— exacting, in the shape of high duties, a large portion of the annual income of our section, and bestowing it in the form of monopolies and appropriations on the other,—is the true cause of the existing disorder,—and the only adequate one that can be assigned,—we cannot entertain a doubt. To this unequal and excessive fiscal action of the Government, may be immediately and clearly traced the growing discontent and alienation on the part of the oppressed portion of the community, and the greedy pursuit of office;—and with it, the increasing spirit of servility, subserviency, and corruption on the other;—which all must see and acknowledge, and which every lover of the country, and its institutions must deplore. Nor is it less clear, that this dangerous assumption, by which the reserved powers of the States have been transferred to the General Government, is rapidly concentrating, by a necessary operation, the whole power of the Government, in the hands of the Executive. We must be blind to the lessons of reason and experience not to see, that, the more a government interferes with the labor and wealth of a community,—the more it exacts from one portion, and bestows on another,—just in the same proportion must the power of that department, which is vested with its patronage, be increased. It ought not, then, to be a subject of surprise, that, with this vast increase of the power and revenues of the Federal Government, and its unequal fiscal action, both in the collection and distribution of the latter, the power of the Executive, on whose will the disposition of the patronage of the Government mainly depends, and on which, in turn, depends that powerful, active and mercenary corps of expectants, created by the morbid moneyed action of the Government,—should be, of late, so greatly and dangerously increased. It is indeed not difficult to see that the present state of things, if continued, must end,—and that speedily,—in raising this department of the Government into an irresponsible and despotic power; with the capacity of perpetuating itself through its own influence;—first, virtually appointing its successor, or, by controlling the Presidential election, through the patronage of the Government; and, finally, —as the virtue and patriotism of the people decay, by the introduction and open establishment of the hereditary principle.

The Federal Government has, indeed, already passed through the first and most difficult part of this process,—which, if permitted to proceed, must terminate, as it ever has, in the absolute and unlimited power of a single despot.

We hold it as certain, that, wherever the majority of a people becomes the advocate of high taxes, and profuse appropriations and expenditures, there the despotic power is already, in fact, established, and liberty virtually lost,—be the form of government what it may; and experience has proved that the transition from this stage to the absolute power of a single individual, is certain and rapid;—and that it can only be arrested by the interposition of some high power out of the ordinary course. Our Government has already clearly reached the first stage; and will inevitably—unless the process be arrested by some such power—speedily terminate its career in the last. In the mean time, while this train of events is consummating itself in the loss of the liberty of all, the oppression and impoverishment of this and the other staple and exporting States will necessarily advance with equal steps. The very root of the system,—that from which it derives its existence and sprouts forth all its evils, is its unjust and unequal action;—giving to one portion what it takes from another,—and thus creating that powerful and irresistible interest in favor of high taxes and profuse expenditures, which are fast sweeping away, at the same time, the foundation of our liberty, and exhausting and reducing to poverty a large portion of the community. That such is, in truth, the real state of things, the extraordinary spectacle, which our Government now exhibits to the world, affords the most conclusive proof. On what other principle can it be explained, that a popular government, with all the forms of freedom, after having discharged a long standing and heavy public debt, should resist every effort to make a corresponding reduction of the public burden? What other cause can be assigned for a fact so remarkable, as that of a free community refusing to repeal this tax, when the proceeds are, confessedly, no longer wanted,—and when the embarrassment of the Government is,—not to find the revenue, but the objects on which to expend it?

Such is the nature of the disorder which the system has engendered. Of all the diseases which can afflict the body politic, we hold it to be the most inveterate and difficult to remedy. Others, originating in ignorance, delusion, or some sudden popular impulse,—yield to the influence of time and reflection; and we may, accordingly, look in such cases, with confidence, for relief, to the returning good sense and feelings of the community. Not so in this. Having its source in the most powerful passions of the human heart,—the love of gain and power,—neither time, reflection, reason, discussion, entreaty, nor remonstrance can arrest or impede its course: nor, if left to itself, will it stop while there is a cent to be exacted, or a particle of power to be acquired. With us, the disease must assume the most aggravated character. There is no country in which so many and such powerful causes exist to give to the unequal fiscal action of the government, in which it originates, so powerful an impetus, and an operation so oppressive and dangerous. When we reflect on the extent of our country, and the diversity of its interests;—on the peculiar nature of the labor and production of this, and the other suffering States;—with how much facility they may be made subservient to the power and wealth of the other sections,—as experience has shown,—and how deep, radical, and disastrous must be the change in the social and political condition of this and the other States similarly situated in reference to pursuits and population, when the increasing pressure shall reach the point at which the exactions of the Government shall not leave a sufficient amount of the proceeds of labor to remunerate the expense of maintenance and supervision;—we cannot but foresee, if the system be not arrested, calamity awaiting us and our posterity, greater than ever befell a free and enlightened people. Already we perceive indications of its approach, that cannot be mistaken. It appears in that quarter, to which, from the nature of the disease, we would naturally look for it; that quarter where labor is the least productive, and is least capable of bearing the pressure of the system.

Such, we hold to be the general character of the system, viewed in its political connections, and its certain effects, if left to its natural operations;—to arrest the evils of which, within our limits, we have interposed the authority of the State as the only peaceful remedy that remains of defending the Constitution against its encroachments,—the citizens of the State against its oppression,—and the liberty of the country against its corrupting influence and danger.

In performing this high and sacred duty, our anxious desire has been to embarrass the action of the Government in the smallest degree possible, consistent with the object we have in view; and had it been possible to separate the portion of duties necessary for revenue, from that imposed for the purpose of protection, the action of the State would have been limited exclusively to the latter. But we could have no right to discriminate when the Government had made no discrimination; and if we had, it would have been impossible; as revenue and protection are so blended throughout,—and the duties, as well those included in the act of July last, as those contained in the acts it alters and amends, comprehending the unprotected and the protected articles,—are adjusted so obviously with the design to form one entire system of protection,—as much so, as if the whole had been incorporated in a single act, passed expressly with that intention, and without regard to revenue, except as a mere incident. The whole, thus forming one system, equally contaminated throughout by the same unconstitutional principle,—no alternative was left, but to declare the entire system unconstitutional; and as such, null and void. Anxious however, while thus compelled to arrest an unconstitutional act, to continue in the discharge of all our constitutional obligations, and to bear our just and full share of the public burdens, we have, with a view to effect these objects, pledged the State to make good her proportional part of the revenue that would have accrued on the imports into the State, which may be exempted from duties, by the interposition of the State;—calculated according to the rate per centum on the general imports which may, on a fair estimate, be considered requisite to meet the just and constitutional wants of the Government; and have, accordingly, authorized the Government of the State, to adopt the necessary measures on its part to adjust the same, on the termination of the present unhappy controversy.

That so desirable an event may be speedily brought about to the satisfaction of all, is our sincere desire. In taking the stand which she has, the State has been solely influenced by a conscientious sense of duty to her citizens, and to the Constitution, without the slightest feeling of hostility towards the interests of any section of the country, or the remotest view to revolution,—or wish to terminate her connection with the Union;—to which she is now, as she ever has been, devotedly attached. Her object is, not to destroy, but to restore and preserve: and, in asserting her right to defend her reserved powers, she disclaims all pretension to control or interfere with the action of the Government within its proper sphere,—or to resume any powers that she has delegated to the Government, or conceded to the confederated States. She simply claims the right of exercising the powers which, in adopting the Constitution, she reserved to herself;—and among them,—the most important and essential of all,—the right to judge, in the last resort, of the extent of her reserved powers,—a right never delegated nor surrendered,—nor, indeed, could be, while the State retains her sovereignty. That it has not been, we appeal with confidence to the Constitution itself, which contains not a single grant that, on a fair construction, can be held to comprehend the power. If to this we add the fact, which the Journals of the Convention abundantly establish, that reiterated, but unsuccessful attempts were made, in every stage of its proceedings, to divest the States of the power in question, by conferring on the General Government the right to annul such acts of the States, as it might deem to be repugnant to the Constitution, and the corresponding right to coerce their obedience,—we have the highest proof of which the subject is susceptible, that the power in question was not delegated, but reserved to the States. To suppose that a State, in exercising a power so unquestionable, resists the Union, would be a fundamental and dangerous error,—originating in a radical misconception of the nature of our political institutions. The Government is neither the Union, nor its representative, except as an agent to execute its powers. The States themselves, in their confederated character, represent the authority of the Union; and, acting in the manner prescribed by the Constitution, through the concurring voice of three fourths of their number, have the right to enlarge or diminish, at pleasure, the powers of the Government,—and to amend, alter, or even abolish the Constitution, and, with it, the Government itself. Correctly understood, it is not the State that interposes to arrest an unconstitutional act,—but the Government that passed it, which resists the authority of the Union. The Government has not the right to add a particle to its powers; and to assume, on its part, the exercise of a power not granted, is plainly to oppose the confederated authority of the States, to which the right of granting powers exclusively belongs;—and, in so doing, the Union itself, which they represent. On the contrary, a State, as a member of the body in which the authority of the Union resides,—in arresting an unconstitutional act of the Government, within its limits,—so far from opposing, in reality supports the Union, and that in the only effectual mode in which it can be done in such cases. To divest the States of this right, would be, in effect, to give to the Government that authority over the Constitution, which belongs to them exclusively; and which can only be preserved to them, by leaving to each State, —as the Constitution has done,—to watch over and defend its reserved powers against the encroachments of the Government,—and in performing which, it acts, at the same time, as a faithful and vigilant sentinel over the confederate powers of the States. It was doubtless with these views, that the Convention which framed the Constitution, steadily resisted, as has been observed, the many attempts which were made, under the specious but fallacious argument of preserving the peace and harmony of the Union, to divest the States of this important right,—which is not less essential to the defence of their joint confederate powers, than to the preservation of their separate sovereignty, and the protection of their citizens.

With these views,—views on which the Convention acted in refusing to divest the States of this right,—has this State acted, in asserting it on the present occasion;—and this with a full understanding of all the responsibilities attached to the position she has assumed, and with a determination as fixed as her conception of her right and duty is clear, to maintain it under every circumstance, and at every hazard. She has weighed all the consequences, and can see, in no possible result, greater disasters than those which must certainly follow a surrender of the right, and an abandonment of her duty.

Having thus taken, immovably, her stand, there remain,—to bring the controversy to a happy termination, but two possible courses. It may be effected, by the Government ceasing to exercise the unconstitutional power, through which, under the name of duties, it has assumed the control over the labor and wealth of the country, and substituting, for the present high rates, an average ad valorem duty,—or some other system of revenue equally just and fair;—or by obtaining a positive grant of the power, in the manner prescribed by the Constitution.

But, when we consider the great interests at stake, and the number and magnitude of the questions involved in the issue, directly and indirectly; and the necessity of a full understanding on all the points, in order to a satisfactory and permanent adjustment of the controversy; we hold it difficult, if not impracticable, to bring it to a final and satisfactory close, short of convening again, the body, to whose authority and wisdom we are indebted for the Constitution: and under this conviction we have made it the duty of the Legislature of the State to apply, in the manner prescribed by the Constitution, for a general convention of the States, as the most certain, prompt, and effectual, if not the only practicable mode of terminating the conflict, and restoring harmony and confidence to the country. If the other States of the Union be actuated by the same feelings which govern us;—if their desire to maintain the Constitution,—to preserve the Union,—and to transmit to posterity the blessings of liberty,—be as strong as ours (and we doubt not that it is), this most august of all assemblies,—provided by the Constitution to meet this and similar emergencies,—as a great moral substitute for revolution and force,—may be convened in a few months; when the present, and every other constitutional question, endangering the peace and harmony of the Union,—may be satisfactorily adjusted.

If there be any conceivable occasion that can justify the call of a Convention of the States, we hold the present to be that occasion; and surely the framers of the Constitution, in providing a mode for calling one, contemplated that great emergencies would arise in the course of events, in which it ought to be convened. They were not so vain as to suppose that their work was so perfect, as to be too clear to admit of diversity of opinion,—or too strong for passion or interest to derange. They accordingly, in their wisdom, provided a double remedy to meet the contingencies, which, if not provided for, might endanger our political system:—one, to meet ordinary and less pressing occurrences,—by vesting in two thirds of Congress the power to propose amendments to the Constitution, to be ratified by three fourths of the States;—the other, for those of a more urgent character, when some deep derangement of the system,—or some great and dangerous conflict of interests or opinion, might threaten, with a catastrophe, the institutions of the country. That such a remedy is provided, is proof of the profound wisdom of the great men who formed our Constitution; and entitles them to the lasting gratitude of the country. But it will be in vain that their wisdom devised a remedy so admirable, —a substitute so infinitely superior to the old and irrational mode of terminating such controversies as are of too high a nature to be adjusted by the force of reason, or through the ordinary tribunals,—if their descendants be so blind as not to perceive its efficacy,—or so intently bent on schemes of ambition and avarice, as to prefer to this constitutional, peaceful, and safe remedy, the wanton, hazardous, and, we may add, immoral arbitrament of force. We hold that our country has arrived at the very point of difficulty and danger, contemplated by the framers of the Constitution, in providing for a General Convention of the States of the Union;

and that, of course, the question now remaining to be tested, is,—whether there be sufficient moral elevation, patriotism, and intelligence in the country, to adjust, through the interposition of this highest of tribunals, whose right none can question, the conflicts which now threaten the very existence of our institutions, and liberty itself,—and which, as experience has proved, there is no other body belonging to the system, having sufficient weight of authority to terminate.

Such, at least, is our conviction; and we have acted accordingly. It now rests with the other States to determine whether a General Convention shall be called or not;—and on that determination hangs, we solemnly believe, the future fate of the country. If it should be in favor of a call, we may, with almost perfect certainty, entertain the prospect of a speedy and happy termination of all our difficulties,—followed by peace, prosperity, and lengthened political existence: but if not, we shall, by rejecting the remedy provided by the wisdom of our ancestors, prove that we deserve the fate, which, in that event, will, in all probability, await the country.

PROCLAMATION TO THE PEOPLE OF THE UNITED STATES. DECEMBER 10, 1832. [BY ANDREW JACKSON, PRESIDENT OF THE UNITED STATES] *

I

Whereas a convention assembled in the State of South Carolina have passed an ordinance by which they declare "that the several acts and parts of acts of the Congress of the United States purporting to be laws for the imposing of duties and imposts on the importation of foreign commodities, and now having actual operation and effect within the United States, and more especially" two acts for the same purposes passed on the 29th of May, 1828, and on the 14th of July, 1832, "are unauthorized by the Constitution of the United States, and violate the true meaning and intent thereof, and are null and void and no law," nor binding on the citizens of that State or its officers; and by the said ordinance it is

*Source: "Proclamation to the People of the United States," by Andrew Jackson, Messages and Papers of the Presidents, edited by James D. Richardson (New York, 1897), III, pp. 1203–19.

further declared to be unlawful for any of the constituted authorities of the State or of the United States to enforce the payment of the duties imposed by the said acts within the same State, and that it is the duty of the legislature to pass such laws as may be necessary to give full effect to the said ordinance; and

Whereas by the said ordinance it is further ordained that in no case of law or equity decided in the courts of said State wherein shall be drawn in question the validity of the said ordinance, or of the acts of the legislature that may be passed to give it effect, or of the said laws of the United States, no appeal shall be allowed to the Supreme Court of the United States, nor shall any copy of the record be permitted or allowed for that purpose, and that any person attempting to take such appeal shall be punished as for contempt of court; and, finally, the said ordinance declares that the people of South Carolina will maintain the said ordinance at every hazard, and that they will consider the passage of any act by Congress abolishing or closing the ports of the said State or otherwise obstructing the free ingress or egress of vessels to and from the said ports, or any other act of the Federal Government to coerce the State, shut up her ports, destroy or harass her commerce, or to enforce the said acts otherwise than through the civil tribunals of the country, as inconsistent with the longer continuance of South Carolina in the Union, and that the people of the said State will thenceforth hold themselves absolved from all further obligation to maintain or preserve their political connection with the people of the other States, and will forthwith proceed to organize a separate government and do all other acts and things which sovereign and independent states may of right do; and

Whereas the said ordinance prescribes to the people of South Carolina a course of conduct in direct violation of their duty as citizens of the United States, contrary to the laws of their country, subversive of its Constitution, and having for its object the destruction of the Union—that Union which, coeval with our political existence, led our fathers, without any other ties to unite them than those of patriotism and a common cause, through a sanguinary struggle to a glorious independence; that sacred Union, hitherto inviolate, which, perfected by our happy Constitution, has brought us, by the favor of Heaven, to a state of prosperity at home and high consideration abroad rarely, if ever, equaled in the history of nations:

To preserve this bond of our political existence from destruction, to maintain inviolate this state of national honor and prosperity, and to justify the confidence my fellow-citizens have reposed in me, I, Andrew Jackson, President of the United States, have thought proper to issue this my proclamation, stating my views of the Constitution and laws applicable to the measures adopted by the convention of South Carolina and to the reasons they have put forth to sustain them, declaring the course which duty will require me to pursue, and, appealing to the understanding and patriotism of the people, warn them of the consequences that must inevitably result from an observance of the dictates of the convention.

II

Strict duty would require of me nothing more than the exercise of those powers with which I am now or may be hereafter invested for preserving the peace of the Union and for the execution of the laws; but the imposing aspect which opposition has assumed in this case, by clothing itself with State authority, and the deep interest which the people of the United States must all feel in preventing a resort to stronger measures while there is a hope that anything will be yielded to reasoning and remonstrance, perhaps demand, and will certainly justify, a full exposition to South Carolina and the nation of the views I entertain of this important question, as well as a distinct enunciation of the course which my sense of duty will require me to pursue.

The ordinance is founded, not on the indefeasible right of resisting acts which are plainly unconstitutional and too oppressive to be endured, but on the strange position that any one State may not only declare an act of Congress void, but prohibit its execution; that they may do this consistently with the Constitution; that the true construction of that instrument permits a State to retain its place in the Union and yet be bound by no other of its laws than those it may choose to consider as constitutional. It is true, they add, that to justify this abrogation of a law it must be palpably contrary to the Constitution; but it is evident that to give the right of resisting laws of that description, coupled with the uncontrolled right to decide what laws deserve that character, is to give the power of resisting all laws; for as by the theory there is no appeal, the reasons alleged by the State, good or bad, must prevail. If it should be said that public opinion is a sufficient check against the abuse of this power, it may be asked why it is not deemed a sufficient guard against the passage of an unconstitutional act by Congress?

There is, however, a restraint in this last case which makes the assumed power of a State more indefensible, and which does not exist in the other. There are two appeals from an unconstitutional act passed by Congress—one to the judiciary, the other to the people and the States. There is no appeal from the State decision in theory, and the practical illustration shows that the courts are closed against an application to review it, both judges and jurors being sworn to decide in its favor. But reasoning on this subject is superfluous when our social compact, in express terms, declares that the laws of the United States, its Constitution, and treaties made under it are the supreme law of the land, and, for greater caution, adds "that the judges in every State shall be bound thereby, anything in the constitution or laws of any State to the contrary notwithstanding." And it may be asserted without fear of refutation that no federative government could exist without a similar provision. Look for a moment to the consequence. If South Carolina considers the revenue laws unconstitutional and has a right to prevent their execution in the port of Charleston, there would be a clear constitutional objection to their collection in every other port; and no revenue could be collected anywhere, for all imposts must be equal. It is no answer to repeat that an unconstitutional law is no law so long as the question of its legality is to be decided by the State itself, for every law operating injuriously upon any local interest will be perhaps thought, and certainly represented, as unconstitutional, and, as has been shown, there is no appeal.

If this doctrine had been established at an earlier day, the Union would have been dissolved in its infancy. The excise law in Pennsylvania, the embargo and nonintercourse law in the Eastern States, the carriage tax in Virginia, were all deemed unconstitutional, and were more unequal in their operation than any of the laws now complained of; but, fortunately, none of those States discovered that they had the right now claimed by South Carolina. The war into which we were forced to support the dignity of the nation and the rights of our citizens might have ended in defeat and disgrace, instead of victory and honor, if the States who supposed it a ruinous and unconstitutional measure had thought they possessed the right of nullifying the act by which it was declared and denying supplies for its prosecution. Hardly and unequally as those measures bore upon several members of the Union, to the legislatures of none did this efficient and peaceable remedy, as it is called, suggest itself. The discovery of this important feature in our Constitution was reserved to the present day. To the statesmen of South Carolina belongs the invention, and upon the citizens of the State will unfortunately fall the evils of reducing it to practice.

If the doctrine of a State veto upon the laws of the Union carries with it internal evidence of its impracticable absurdity, our constitutional history will also afford abundant proof that it would have been repudiated with indignation had it been proposed to form a feature in our Government.

In our colonial state, although dependent on another power, we very early considered ourselves as connected by common interest with each other. Leagues were formed for common defense, and before the declaration of independence we were known in our aggregate character as *the United Colonies of America*. That decisive and important step was taken jointly. We declared ourselves a nation by a joint, not by several acts, and when the terms of our Confederation were reduced to form, it was in that of a solemn league of several States, by which they agreed that they would collectively form one nation for the purpose of conducting some certain domestic concerns and all foreign relations. In the instrument forming that Union is found an article which declares that "every State shall abide by the determinations of Congress on all questions which by that Confederation should be submitted to them."

Under the Confederation, then, no State could legally annul a decision of the Congress or refuse to submit to its execution; but no provision was made to enforce these decisions, Congress made requisitions, but they were not complied with. The Government could not operate on individuals. They had no judiciary, no means of collecting revenue.

But the defects of the Confederation need not be detailed. Under its operation we could scarcely be called a nation. We had neither prosperity at home nor consideration abroad. This state of things could not be endured, and our present happy Constitution was formed, but formed in vain if this fatal doctrine prevails. It was formed for important objects that are announced in the preamble, made in the name and by the authority of the people of the United States, whose delegates framed and whose conventions approved it. The most important among these objects—that which is placed first in rank, on which all the others rest—is *"to form a more perfect union."* Now, is it possible that even if there were no express provision giving supremacy to the Constitution and laws of the United States over those of the States, can it be conceived that an instrument made for the purpose of *"forming a more perfect union"* than that of the Confederation could be so constructed by the assembled wisdom of our country as to substitute for that Confederation a form of government dependent for its existence on the local interest, the party spirit, of a State, or of a prevailing faction in a State? Every man of plain, unsophisticated understanding who hears the question will give such an answer as will preserve the Union. Metaphysical subtlety, in pursuit of an impracticable theory, could alone have devised one that is calculated to destroy it.

I consider, then, the power to annul a law of the United States, assumed by one State, *incompatible with the existence of the Union, contradicted expressly by the letter of the Constitution, unauthorized by its spirit, inconsistent with every principle on which it was founded, and destructive of the great object for which it was formed.*

After this general view of the leading principle, we must examine the particular application of it which is made in the ordinance.

III

The preamble rests its justification on these grounds: It assumes as a fact that the obnoxious laws, although they purport to be laws for raising revenue, were in reality intended for the protection of manufactures, which purpose it asserts to be unconstitutional; that the operation of these laws is unequal; that the amount raised by them is greater than is required by the wants of the Government; and, finally, that the proceeds are to be applied to objects unauthorized by the Constitution. These are the only causes alleged to justify an open opposition to the laws of the country and a threat of seceding from the Union if any attempt should be made to enforce them. The first virtually acknowledges that the law in question was passed under a power expressly given by the Constitution to lay and collect imposts; but its constitutionality is drawn in question from the *motives* of those who passed it. However apparent this purpose may be in the present case, nothing can be more dangerous than to admit the position that an unconstitutional purpose entertained by the members who assent to a law enacted under a constitutional power shall make that law void. For how is that purpose to be ascertained? Who is to make the scrutiny? How often may bad purposes be falsely imputed, in how many cases are they concealed by false professions, in how many is no declaration of motive made? Admit this doctrine, and you give to the States an uncontrolled right to decide, and every law may be annulled under this pretext. If, therefore, the absurd and dangerous doctrine should be admitted that a State may annul an unconstitutional law, or one that it deems such, it will not apply to the present case.

The next objection is that the laws in question operate unequally. This objection may be made with truth to every law that has been or can be passed. The wisdom of man never yet contrived a system of taxation that would operate with perfect equality. If the unequal operation of a law makes it unconstitutional, and if all laws of that description may be abrogated by any State for that cause, then, indeed, is the Federal Constitution unworthy of the slightest effort for its preservation. We have hitherto relied on it as the perpetual bond of our Union; we have received it as the work of the assembled wisdom of the nation; we have trusted to it as to the sheet anchor of our safety in the stormy times of conflict with a foreign or domestic foe; we have looked to it with sacred awe as the palladium of our liberties, and with all the solemnities of religion have pledged to each other our lives and fortunes here and our hopes of happiness hereafter in its defense and support. Were we mistaken, my countrymen, in attaching this importance to the Constitution of our country? Was our devotion paid to the wretched, inefficient, clumsy contrivance which this new doctrine would make it? Did we pledge ourselves to the support of an airy nothing— a bubble that must be blown away by the first breath of disaffection? Was this self-destroying, visionary theory the work of the profound statesmen, the exalted patriots, to whom the task of constitutional reform was intrusted? Did the name of Washington sanction, did the States deliberately ratify, such an anomaly in the history of fundamental legislation? No; we were not mistaken. The letter of this great instrument is free from this radical fault. Its language directly contradicts the imputation; its spirit, its evident intent, contradicts it. No; we did not err. Our Constitution does not contain the absurdity of giving power to make laws and another to resist them. The sages whose memory will always be reverenced have given us a practical and, as they hoped, a permanent constitutional compact. The father of his country did not affix his revered name to so palpable an absurdity. Nor did the States, when they severally ratified it, do so under the impression that a veto on the laws of the United States was reserved to them or that they could exercise it by implication. Search the debates in all their conventions, examine the speeches of the most zealous opposers of Federal authority, look at the amendments that were proposed; they are all silent—not a syllable uttered, not a vote given, not a motion made to correct the explicit supremacy given to the laws of the Union over those of the States, or to show that implication, as is now contended, could defeat it. No; we have not erred. The Constitution is still the object of our reverence, the bond of our Union, our defense in danger, the source of our prosperity in peace. It shall descend, as we have received it, uncorrupted by sophistical construction, to our posterity; and the sacrifices of local interest, of State prejudices, of personal animosities, that were made to bring it into existence, will again be patriotically offered for its support.

The two remaining objections made by the ordinance to these laws are that the sums intended to be raised by them are greater than are required and that the proceeds will be unconstitutionally employed.

The Constitution has given, expressly, to Congress the right of raising revenue and of determining the sum the public exigencies will require. The States have no control over the exercise of this right other than that which results from the power of changing the representatives who abuse it, and thus procure redress. Congress may undoubtedly abuse this discretionary power; but the same may be said of others with which they are vested. Yet the discretion must exist somewhere. The Constitution has given it to the representatives of all the people, checked by the representatives of the States and by the Executive power. The South Carolina construction gives it to the legislature or the convention of a single State, where neither the people of the different States, nor the States in their separate capacity, nor the Chief Magistrate elected by the people have any representation. Which is the most discreet disposition of the power? I do not ask you, fellow-citizens, which is the constitutional disposition; that instrument speaks a language not to be misunderstood. But if you were assembled in general convention, which would you think the safest depository of this discretionary power in the last resort? Would you add a clause giving it to each of the States, or would you sanction the wise provisions already made by your Constitution? If this should be the result of your deliberations when providing for the future, are you, can you, be ready to risk all that we hold dear, to establish for a temporary and a local purpose, that which you must acknowledge to be destructive, and even absurd, as a general provision? Carry out the consequences of this right vested in the different States, and you must perceive that the crisis your conduct presents at this day would recur whenever any law of the United States displeased any of the States, and that we should soon cease to be a nation.

The ordinance, with the same knowledge of the future that characterizes a former objection, tells you that the proceeds of the tax will be unconstitutionally applied. If this could be ascertained with certainty, the objection would with more propriety be reserved for the law so applying the proceeds, but surely cannot be urged against the laws levying the duty.

These are the allegations contained in the ordinance. Examine them seriously, my fellow-citizens; judge for yourselves. I appeal to you to determine whether they are so clear, so convincing, as to leave no doubt of their correctness; and even if you should come to this conclusion, how far they justify the reckless, destructive course which you are directed to pursue. Review these objections and the conclusions drawn from them once more. What are they? Every law, then, for raising revenue according to the South Carolina ordinance, may be rightfully annulled, unless it be so framed as no law ever will or can be framed. Congress have a right to pass laws for raising revenue and each State have a right to oppose their execution—two rights directly opposed to each other; and yet is this absurdity supposed to be contained in an instrument drawn for the express purpose of avoiding collisions between the States and the General Government by an assembly of the most enlightened statesmen and purest patriots ever embodied for a similar purpose.

In vain have these sages declared that Congress shall have power to lay and collect taxes, duties, imposts, and excises; in vain have they provided that they shall have power to pass laws which shall be necessary and proper to carry those powers into execution, that those laws and that Constitution shall be the "supreme law of the land, and that the judges in every State shall be bound thereby, anything in the constitution or laws of any State to the contrary notwithstanding"; in vain have the people of the several States solemnly sanctioned these provisions, made them their paramount law, and individually sworn to support them whenever they were called on to execute any office. Vain provisions! ineffectual restrictions! vile profanation of oaths! miserable mockery of legislation! if a bare majority of the voters in any one State may, on a real or supposed knowledge of the intent with which a law has been passed, declare themselves free from its operation; say, here it gives too little, there, too much, and operates unequally; here it suffers articles to be free that ought to be taxed; there it taxes those that ought to be free; in this case the proceeds are intended to be applied to purposes which we do not approve; in that, the amount raised is more than is wanted. Congress, it is true, are invested by the Constitution with the right of deciding these questions according to their sound discretion. Congress is composed of the representatives of all the States and of all the people of all the States. But *we*, part of the people of one State, to whom the Constitution has given no power on the subject, from whom it has expressly taken it away; *we*, who have solemnly agreed that this Constitution shall be our law; *we*, most of whom have sworn to support it—*we* now abrogate this law and swear, and force others to swear, that it shall not be obeyed; and we do this not because Congress have no right to pass such laws—this we do not allege—but because they have passed them with improper views. They are unconstitutional from the motives of those who passed them, which we can never with certainty know; from their unequal operation, although it is impossible, from the nature of things, that they should be equal; and from the disposition which we presume may be made of their proceeds, although that disposition has not been declared. This is the plain meaning of the ordinance in relation to laws which it abrogates for alleged unconstitutionality. But it does not stop there. It repeals in express terms an important part of the Constitution itself and of laws passed to give it effect, which have never been alleged to be unconstitutional.

The Constitution declares that the judicial powers of the United States extend to cases arising under the laws of the United States, and that such laws, the Constitution, and treaties shall be paramount to the State constitutions and laws. The judiciary act prescribes the mode by which the case may be brought before a court of the United States by appeal when a State tribunal shall decide against this provision of the Constitution. The ordinance declares there shall be no appeal—makes the State law paramount to the Constitution and laws of the United States, forces judges and jurors to swear that they will disregard their provisions, and even makes it penal in a suitor to attempt relief by appeal. It further declares that it shall not be lawful for the authorities of the United States or of that State to enforce the payment of duties imposed by the revenue laws within its limits.

Here is a law of the United States, not even pretended to be unconstitutional, repealed by the authority of a small majority of the voters of a single State. Here is a provision of the Constitution which is solemnly abrogated by the same authority.

On such expositions and reasonings the ordinance grounds not only an assertion of the right to annul the laws of which it complains, but to enforce it by a threat of seceding from the Union if any attempt is made to execute them.

This right to secede is deduced from the nature of the Constitution, which, they say, is a compact between sovereign States who have preserved their whole sovereignty and therefore are subject to no superior; that because they made the compact they can break it when in their opinion it has been departed from by the other States. Fallacious as this course of reasoning is, it enlists State pride and finds advocates in the honest prejudices of those who have not studied the nature of our Government sufficiently to see the radical error on which it rests.

The people of the United States formed the Constitution, acting through the State legislatures in making the compact, to meet and discuss its provisions, and acting in separate conventions when they ratified those provisions; but the terms used in its construction show it to be a Government in which the people of all the States, collectively, are represented. We are *one people* in the choice of President and Vice-President. Here the States have no other agency than to direct the mode in which the votes shall be given. The candidates having the majority of all the votes are chosen. The electors of a majority of States may have given their votes for one candidate, and yet another may be chosen. The people, then, and not the States, are represented in the executive branch.

In the House of Representatives there is this difference, that the people of one State do not, as in the case of President and Vice-President, all vote for the same officers. The people of all the States do not vote for all the members, each State electing only its own representatives. But this creates no material distinction. When chosen, they are all representatives of the United States, not representatives of the particular State from which they come. They are paid by the United States, not by the State; nor are they accountable to it for any act done in the performance of their legislative functions; and however they may in practice, as it is their duty to do, consult and prefer the interests of their particular constituents when they come in conflict with any other partial or local interest, yet it is their first and highest duty, as representatives of the United States, to promote the general good.

The Constitution of the United States, then, forms a *government,* not a league; and whether it be formed by compact between the States or in any other manner, its character is the same. It is a Government in which all the people are represented, which operates directly on the people individually, not upon the States; they retained all the power they did not grant. But each State, having expressly parted with so many powers as to constitute, jointly with the other States, a single nation, cannot, from that period, possess any right to secede, because such secession does not break a league, but destroys the unity of a nation; and any injury to that unity is not only a breach which would result from the contravention of a compact, but it is an offense against the whole Union. To say that any State may at pleasure secede from the Union is to say that the United States are not a nation, because it would be a solecism to contend that any part of a nation might dissolve its connection with the other parts, to their injury or ruin, without committing any offense. Secession, like any other revolutionary act, may be morally justified by the extremity of oppression; but to call it a constitutional right is confounding the meaning of terms, and can only be done through gross error or to deceive those who are willing to assert a right, but would pause before they made a revolution or incur the penalties consequent on a failure.

Because the Union was formed by a compact, it is said the parties to that compact may, when they feel themselves aggrieved, depart from it; but it is precisely because it is a compact that they cannot. A compact is an agreement or binding obligation. It may by its terms have a sanction or penalty for its breach, or it may not. If it contains no sanction, it may be broken with no other consequence than moral guilt; if it have a sanction, then the breach incurs the designated or implied penalty. A league between independent nations generally has no sanction other than a moral one; or if it should contain a penalty, as there is no common superior it cannot be enforced. A government, on the contrary, always has a sanction, express or implied; and in our case it is both necessarily implied and expressly given. An attempt, by force of arms, to destroy a government is an offense, by whatever means the constitutional compact may have been formed; and such government has the right by the law of self-defense to pass acts for punishing the offender, unless that right is modified, restrained, or resumed by the constitutional act. In our system, although it is modified in the case of treason, yet authority is expressly given to pass all laws necessary to carry its powers into effect, and under this grant provision has been made for punishing acts which obstruct the due administration of the laws.

It would seem superfluous to add anything to show the nature of that union which connects us, but as erroneous opinions on this subject are the foundation of doctrines the most destructive to our peace, I must give some further development to my views on this subject. No one, fellow-citizens, has a higher reverence for the reserved rights of the States than the Magistrate who now addresses you. No one would make greater personal sacrifices or official exertions to defend them from violation; but equal care must be taken to prevent, on their part, an improper interference with or resumption of the rights they have vested in the nation. The line has not been so distinctly drawn as to avoid doubts in some cases of the exercise of power. Men of the best intentions and soundest views may differ in their construction of some parts of the Constitution; but there are others on which dispassionate reflection can leave no doubt. Of this nature appears to be the assumed right of secession. It rests, as we have seen, on the alleged undivided sovereignty of the States and on their having formed in this sovereign capacity a compact which is called the Constitution, from which, because they made it, they have the right to secede. Both of these positions are erroneous, and some of the arguments to prove them have been anticipated.

The States severally have not retained their entire sovereignty. It has been shown that in becoming parts of a nation, not members of a league, they surrendered many of their essential parts of sovereignty. The right to make treaties, declare war, levy taxes, exercise exclusive judicial and legislative powers, were all of them functions of sovereign power. The States, then, for all these important purposes were no longer sovereign. The allegiance of their citizens was transferred, in the first instance, to the Government of the United States; they became American citizens and owed obedience to the Constitution of the United States and to laws made in conformity with the powers it vested in Congress. This last position has not been and cannot be denied. How, then, can that State be said to be sovereign and independent whose citizens owe obedience to laws not made by it and whose magistrates are sworn to disregard those laws when they come in conflict with those passed by another? What shows conclusively that the States cannot be said to have reserved an undivided sovereignty is that they expressly ceded the right to punish treason—not treason against their separate power, but treason against the United States. Treason is an offense against *sovereignty,* and sovereignty must reside with the power to punish it. But the reserved rights of the States are not less sacred because they have, for their common interest, made the General Government the depository of these powers. The unity of our political character (as has been shown for another purpose) commenced with its very existence. Under the royal Government we had no separate character; our opposition to its oppressions began as *united colonies*. We were the *United States* under the Confederation, and the name was perpetuated and the Union rendered more perfect by the Federal Constitution. In none of these stages did we consider ourselves in any other light as forming one nation. Treaties and alliances were made in the name of all. Troops were raised for the joint defense. How, then, with all these proofs that under all changes of our position we had, for designated purposes and with defined powers, created national governments, how is it that the most perfect of those several modes of union should now be considered as a mere league that may be dissolved at pleasure? It is from an abuse of terms. Compact is used as synonymous with league, although the true term is not employed, because it would at once show the fallacy of the reasoning. It would not do to say that our Constitution was only a league, but it is labored to prove it a compact (which in one sense it is) and then to argue that as a league is a compact every compact between nations must of course be a league, and that from such an engagement every sovereign power has a right to secede. But it has been shown that in this sense the States are not sovereign, and that even if they were, and the national Constitution had been formed by compact, there would be no right in any one State to exonerate itself from its obligations.

So obvious are the reasons which forbid this secession that it is necessary only to allude to them. The Union was formed for the benefit of all. It was produced by mutual sacrifices of interests and opinions. Can those sacrifices be recalled? Can the States who magnanimously surrendered their title to the territories of the West recall the grant? Will the inhabitants of the inland States agree to pay the duties that may be imposed without their assent by those on the Atlantic or the Gulf for their own benefit? Shall there be a free port in one State and onerous duties in another? No one believes that any right exists in a single State to involve all the others in these and countless other evils contrary to engagements solemnly made. Everyone must see that the other States, in self-defense, must oppose it at all hazards.

These are the alternatives that are presented by the convention—a repeal of all the acts for raising revenue, leaving the Government without the means of support, or an acquiescence in the dissolution of our Union by the secession of one of its members. When the first was proposed, it was known that it could not be listened to for a moment. It was known, if force was applied to oppose the execution of the laws, that it must be repelled by force; that Congress could not, without involving itself in disgrace and the country in ruin, accede to the proposition; and yet if this is not done in a given day, or if any attempt is made to execute the laws, the State is by the ordinance declared to be out of the Union. The majority of a convention assembled for the purpose have dictated these terms, or rather this rejection of all terms, in the name of the people of South Carolina. It is true that the governor of the State speaks of the submission of their grievances to a convention of all the States, which, he says, they "sincerely and anxiously seek and desire." Yet this obvious and constitutional mode of obtaining the sense of the other States on the construction of the federal compact, and amending it if necessary, has never been attempted by those who have urged the State on to this destructive measure. The State might have proposed the call for a general convention to the other States, and Congress, if a sufficient number of them concurred, must have called it. But the first magistrate of South Carolina, when he expressed a hope that "on a review by Congress and the functionaries of the General Government of the merits of the controversy" such a convention will be accorded to them, must have known that neither Congress nor any functionary of the General Government has authority to call such a convention unless it be demanded by two-thirds of the States. This suggestion, then, is another instance of the reckless inattention to the provisions of the Constitution with which this crisis has been madly hurried on, or of the attempt to persuade the people that a constitutional remedy had been sought and refused. If the legislature of South Carolina "anxiously desire" a general convention to consider their complaints, why have they not made application for it in the way the Constitution points out? The assertion that they "earnestly seek" it is completely negatived by the omission.

This, then, is the position in which we stand: A small majority of the citizens of one State in the Union have elected delegates to a State convention; that convention has ordained that all the revenue laws of the United States must be repealed, or that they are no longer a member of the Union. The governor of that State has recommended to the legislature the raising of an army to carry the secession into effect, and that he may be empowered to give clearances to vessels in the name of the State. No act of violent opposition to the laws has yet been committed, but such a state of things is hourly apprehended. And it is the intent of this instrument to *proclaim*, not only that the duty imposed on me by the Constitution "to take care that the laws be faithfully executed" shall be performed to the extent of the powers already vested in me by law, or of such others as the wisdom of Congress shall devise and intrust to me for that purpose, but to warn the citizens of South Carolina who have been deluded into an opposition to the laws of the danger they will incur by obedience to the illegal and disorganizing ordinance of the convention; to exhort those who have refused to support it to persevere in their determination to uphold the Constitution and laws of their country; and to point out to all the perilous situation into which the good people of that State have been led, and that the course they are urged to pursue is one of ruin and disgrace to the very State whose rights they affect to support.

IV

Fellow-citizens of my native State, let me not only admonish you, as the First Magistrate of our common country, not to incur the penalty of its laws, but use the influence that a father would over his children whom he saw rushing to certain ruin. In that paternal language, with that paternal feeling, let me tell you, my countrymen, that you are deluded by men who are either deceived themselves or wish to deceive you. Mark under what pretenses you have been led on to the brink of insurrection and treason on which you stand. First, a diminution of the value of your staple commodity, lowered by overproduction in other quarters, and the consequent diminution in the value of your lands were the sole effect of the tariff laws. The effect of those laws was confessedly injurious, but the evil was greatly exaggerated by the unfounded theory you were taught to believe—that its burthens were in proportion to your exports, not to your consumption of imported articles. Your pride was roused by the assertion that a submission to those laws was a state of vassalage and that resistance to them was equal in patriotic merit to the opposition our fathers offered to the oppressive laws of Great Britain. You were told that this opposition might be peaceably, might be constitutionally, made; that you might enjoy all the advantages of the Union and bear none of its burthens. Eloquent appeals to your passions, to your State pride, to your native courage, to your sense of real injury, were used to prepare you for the period when the mask which concealed the hideous features of *disunion* should be taken off. It fell, and you were made to look with complacency on objects which not long since you would have regarded with horror. Look back to the arts which have brought you to this state; look forward to the consequences to which it must inevitably lead! Look back to what was first told you as an inducement to enter into this dangerous course. The great political truth was repeated to you that you had the revolutionary right of resisting all laws that were palpably unconstitutional and intolerably oppressive. It was added that the right to nullify a law rested on the same principle, but that it was a peaceable remedy. This character which was given to it made you receive with too much confidence the assertions that were made of the unconstitutionality of the law and its oppressive effects. Mark, my fellow-citizens, that by the admission of your leaders the unconstitutionality must be *palpable*, or it will not justify either resistance or nullification. What is the meaning of the word *palpable* in the sense in which it is here used? That which is apparent to everyone; that which no man or ordinary intellect will fail to perceive. Is the unconstitutionality of these laws of that description? Let those among your leaders who once approved and advocated the principle of protective duties answer the question; and let them choose whether they will be considered as incapable then of perceiving that which must have been apparent to every man of common understanding, or as imposing upon your confidence and endeavoring to mislead you now. In either case they are unsafe guides in the perilous path they urge you to tread.

Ponder well on this circumstance, and you will know how

to appreciate the exaggerated language they address to you. They are not champions of liberty, emulating the fame of our Revolutionary fathers, nor are you an oppressed people, contending, as they repeat to you, against worse than colonial vassalage. You are free members of a flourishing and happy Union. There is no settled design to oppress you. You have indeed felt the unequal operation of laws which may have been unwisely, not unconstitutionally, passed; but that inequality must necessarily be removed. At the very moment when you were madly urged on to the unfortunate course you have begun, a change in public opinion had commenced. The nearly approaching payment of the public debt and the consequent necessity of a diminution of duties had already produced a considerable reduction, and that, too, on some articles of general consumption in your State. The importance of this change was underrated, and you were authoritatively told that no further alleviation of your burthens was to be expected at the very time when the condition of the country imperiously demanded such a modification of the duties as should reduce them to a just and equitable scale. But, as if apprehensive of the effect of this change in allaying your discontents, you were precipitated into the fearful state in which you now find yourselves.

I have urged you to look back to the means that were used to hurry you on to the position you have now assumed and forward to the consequences it will produce. Something more is necessary. Contemplate the condition of that country of which you still form an important part. Consider its Government, uniting in one bond of common interest and general protection so many different States, giving to all their inhabitants the proud title of *American citizen*, protecting their commerce, securing their literature and their arts, facilitating their intercommunication, defending their frontiers, and making their name respected in the remotest parts of the earth. Consider the extent of its territory, its increasing and happy population, its advance in arts which render life agreeable, and the sciences which elevate the mind! See education spreading the lights of religion, morality, and general information into every cottage in this wide extent of our Territories and States. Behold it as the asylum where the wretched and the oppressed find a refuge and support. Look on this picture of happiness and honor and say, *We too are citizens* of America. Carolina is one of these proud States; her arms have defended, her best blood has cemented, this happy Union. And then add, if you can, without horror and remorse, *This happy Union we will dissolve; this picture of peace and prosperity we will deface; this free intercourse we will interrupt; these fertile fields we will deluge with blood; the protection of that glorious flag we renounce; the very name of Americans we discard.*

And for what, mistaken men? For what do you throw away these inestimable blessings? For what would you exchange your share in the advantages and honor of the Union? For the dream of a separate independence—a dream interrupted by bloody conflicts with your neighbors and a vile dependence on a foreign power? If your leaders could succeed in establishing a separation, what would be your situation? Are you united at home? Are you free from the apprehension of civil discord, with all its fearful consequences? Do our neighboring republics, every day suffering some new revolution or contending with some new insurrection, do they excite your envy? But the dictates of a high duty oblige me solemnly to announce that you can not succeed. The laws of the United States must be executed. I have no discretionary power on the subject; my duty is emphatically pronounced in the Constitution. Those who told you that you might peaceably prevent their execution deceived you; they could not have been deceived themselves. They know that a forcible opposition could alone prevent the execution of the laws, and they know that such opposition must be repelled. Their object is disunion. But be not deceived by names. Disunion by armed force is *treason*. Are you really ready to incur its guilt? If you are, on the heads of the instigators of the act be the dreadful consequences; on their heads be the dishonor, but on yours may fall the punishment. On your unhappy State will inevitably fall all the evils of the conflict you force upon the Government of your country. It can not accede to the mad project of disunion, of which you would be the first victims. Its First Magistrate can not, if he would, avoid the performance of his duty.

The consequence must be fearful for you, distressing to your fellow-citizens here and to the friends of good government throughout the world. Its enemies have beheld our prosperity with a vexation they could not conceal; it was a standing refutation of their slavish doctrines, and they will point to our discord with the triumph of malignant joy. It is yet in your power to disappoint them. There is yet time to show that the descendants of the Pinckneys, the Sumpters, the Rutledges, and of the thousand other names which adorn the pages of your Revolutionary history will not abandon that Union to support which so many of them fought and bled and died. I adjure you, as you honor their memory, as you love the cause of freedom, to which they dedicated their lives, as you prize the peace of your country, the lives of its best citizens, and your own fair name, to retrace your steps. Snatch from the archives of your State the disorganizing edict of its convention; bid its members to reassemble and promulgate the decided expressions of your will to remain in the path which alone can conduct you to safety, prosperity, and honor. Tell them that compared to disunion all other evils are light, because that brings with it an accumulation of all. Declare that you will never take the field unless the star-spangled banner of your country shall float over you; that you will not be stigmatized when dead, and dishonored and scorned while you live, as the authors of the first attack on the Constitution of your country. Its destroyers you cannot be. You may disturb its peace, you may interrupt the course of its prosperity, you may cloud its reputation for stability; but its tranquillity will be restored, its prosperity will return, and the stain upon its national character will be transferred and remain an eternal blot on the memory of those who caused the disorder.

Fellow-citizens of the United States, the threat of unhallowed disunion, the names of those once respected by whom it is uttered, the array of military force to support it, denote the approach of a crisis in our affairs on which the continuance of our unexampled prosperity, our political existence, and perhaps that of all free governments may depend. The conjuncture demanded a free, a full, and explicit enunciation, not only of my intentions, but of my principles of action; and as the claim was asserted of a right by a State to annul the laws of the Union, and even to secede from it at pleasure, a frank exposition of my opinions in relation to the origin and form of our Government and the construction I give to the instrument by which it was created seemed to be proper. Having the fullest confidence in the justness of the legal and constitutional opinion of my duties which has been expressed, I rely with equal confidence on your undivided support in my determination to execute the laws, to preserve the Union by all constitutional means, to arrest, if possible, by moderate and firm measures the necessity of a recourse to force; and if it be the will of Heaven that the recurrence of its primeval curse on man for the shedding of a brother's blood should fall upon our land, that it be not called down by any offensive act on the part of the United States.

Fellow-citizens, the momentous case is before you. On your undivided support of your Government depends the decision of the great question it involves—whether your sacred Union will be preserved and the blessing it secures to us as one people shall be perpetuated. No one can doubt that the unanimity with which that decision will be expressed will be such as to inspire new confidence in republican institutions, and that the prudence, the wisdom, and the courage which it will bring to their defense will transmit them unimpaired and invigorated to our children.

May the Great Ruler of Nations grant that the signal blessings with which He has favored ours may not, by the madness of party or personal ambition, be disregarded and lost; and may His wise providence bring those who have produced this crisis to see the folly before they feel the misery of civil strife, and inspire a returning veneration for that Union which, if we may dare to penetrate His designs, He has chosen as the only means of attaining the high destinies to which we may reasonably aspire.

In testimony whereof I have caused the seal of the United States to be hereunto affixed, having signed the same with my hand.

[SEAL.] Done at the city of Washington, this 10th day of December, A. D. 1832, and of the Independence of the United States the fifty-seventh.

ANDREW JACKSON.

By the President:
EDWARD LIVINGSTON,
Secretary of State.

Westward
by
Land
and
by
Sea

THE GREENLAND WHALE FISHERY
ACROSS THE WESTERN OCEAN
LOW BRIDGE, EVERYBODY DOWN
PADDY WORKS ON THE RAILROAD
SANTY ANNO

Introduction

The economic development of the United States between 1814 and the end of the war with Mexico in 1848 was swift, dramatic and colorful. This was the heroic age of American seafaring, when whaling became one of the country's greatest industries, and American sailing ships won the title of the fastest and the loveliest on earth. This was the age when hundreds of thousands of European immigrants, urged on by hunger and the lure of jobs and land, swarmed across the Atlantic in one of the vastest and most rapid migrations known to history. This time witnessed the birth of the modern industrial system and the first utilization in America of steam power to turn factory wheels and to run the great cotton gins of the South. It saw a fever of canal and railroad building and the launching of a communications network that would shortly span the continent and convert it into a single economic entity. In this age huge land areas were added to the country by conquest or purchase; a whole epoch of territorial expansion was brought virtually to a close.

All this activity found a manifold expression and reflection in song.

450

The Greenland Whale Fishery achieves a rapid condensation of the events of a three- or four-year whaling voyage into the framework of a single eight-verse ballad. Of English origin, it became popular with American whalermen in the early nineteenth century.

Across the Western Ocean originated as a sea shanty, or work song, but in the form given here it was sung by Irish immigrants who, driven by famine and oppression, abandoned their native land by the hundreds of thousands in the 1830's and '40's. As might be expected, there was often a close connection between sea songs and immigrant songs. The sailors borrowed from the immigrants, and vice versa.

One of the most notable events of the Jacksonian era was the engineering feat involved in digging the Erie Canal connecting Lake Erie and the Hudson river. The canal, which was completed in 1825, affected a revolution in American commerce and settlement: it provided the Midwest with an outlet to the Atlantic and made possible, for westward-moving settlers, rapid penetration of the continent along the strategic Hudson-Mohawk route. The canal was rightly celebrated in song, of which Low Bridge, Everybody Down is one of the most effective. Songs such as these were sung by muledrivers walking the towpaths and urging on the beasts that hauled the heavy barges.

The railroad era followed hard on the heels of the canals. By 1850 over 8,000 miles of rail had been laid, the most complete network being in New England. The sinews for the heavy work of both canal digging and railroad building were provided primarily by the Irish immigrants. The exquisite songs that this great people brought with them from the Old World constituted a notable addition to America's musical heritage; henceforth Irish melodies would be a basic component of American folksong. Paddy Works on the Railroad arose from a new and bitter experience. It is one of the few railroad songs that have survived from these early days of industrialization.

Westward expansion, in the Jacksonian era, was climaxed by the war of 1846-48, which wrested millions of acres from Mexican possession and brought the rich lands of California to the Union. The value of this act of conquest became immediately apparent when gold was discovered at Sutter's Mill in January, 1848. This was four months after Santa Anna's surrender at Mexico City, and a few days before the treaty of peace was signed at Guadalupe Hidalgo which formally ceded California to the United States.

The discovery of gold touched off a wild race for the Far West—overland along the California trail, through the fever-ridden swamps of Panama, by boat around Cape Horn. The last was seemingly the longest route, but it was the wisest, and it is celebrated in the beautiful Santy Anno, by all odds one of the greatest and most revealing of the numerous gold rush songs that have been left to us. Originating as a pump shanty sung by British sailors, the American version reproduced here gloats over the United States victory over Santa Anna "on the plains of Mexico"—a victory that opened California to the Yankees and brought gold within their grasp. As the last verse suggests, some of the sailors who sung this song were making their last voyage before the mast. Many ships made the race around the Horn with their cargo of California goods and immigrants only once. Captain and crew alike abandoned their vessels and went to look for gold, and the hulks rotted on the beach.

THE GREENLAND WHALE FISHERY

1. It was eighteen hundred and forty-four,
   Of June the seventh day,
   That we hoisted our colors to the top of the mast,
   For Greenland bound away, brave boys,
   For Greenland bound away.

2. The lookout in the cross-trees stood,
   With his spyglass in his hand,
   "There's a whale, there's a whale, there's a whalefish," he
        cried,
   "She blows on every strand, brave boys,
   She blows on every strand."

3. Now the captain stood on the quarter deck,
   And the ice was in his eye,
 "Overhaul, overhaul, elt your davy tackles fall,
   Till you land your boats in the sea, brave boys,
   Till you land your boats in the sea."

4. Now the boats got down and the men aboard,
   And the whale was full in view,
 Resolved, resolved was each whalerman bold
   To steer where the whalefish blew, brave boys,
   To steer where the whalefish blew.

5. Now the harpoon was struck and the line run out,
   But he gave such a florish with his tail,
 That the boat capsized and four men were drowned,
   And we never caught that whale, brave boys,
   And we never caught that whale.

6. "O to lose those men," the captain said,
   "It grieves my heart full sore,
 But to lose a hundred barrel whale,
   It grieves me ten times more, brave boys,
   It grieves me ten times more."

7. "Up anchor, now," the captain cried,
   "There is the winter star,
 It's time to leave this dreadful place,
   And for New England steer, brave boys,
   And for New England steer."

8. O, Greenland is a hellish place,
   A land that's never green,
 Where there's ice and snow, and the whalefishes blow,
   And daylight's seldom seen, brave boys,
   And daylight's seldom seen.

ACROSS THE WESTERN OCEAN

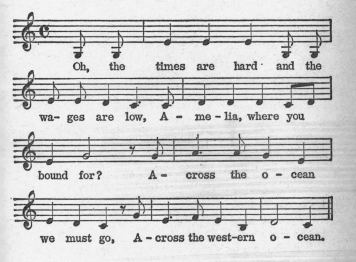

Oh, the times are hard and the wages are low,
Amelia, where you bound for?
Across the ocean we must go,
Across the western ocean.

Beware these packet ships, I say,
Amelia, where you bound for?
They'll steal your stores and clothes away,
Across the western ocean.

Father and mother, say goodbye,
    Across the western ocean,
Brother and sister, don't you cry,
    Across the western ocean.

She would not wear and she would not stay,
    Amelia, where you bound for?
She shipped great seas both night and day,
    Across the western ocean.

It was rotten meat and weevily bread,
    Amelia, where you bound for?
Eat it or starve, the captain said,
    Across the western ocean.

Oh, the winds were foul and the times were hard,
    Amelia, where you bound for?
From Liverpool Dock to the Brooklyn yard,
    Across the western ocean.

LOW BRIDGE

I've got a mule and her name is Sal,

Fif - teen years on the E-rie Ca-nal, She's a

good old work-er and a good old pal,

Fif - teen years on the E-rie Ca-nal. We have

hauled some barges in our day, Filled with lumber,

coal, and hay; And ev - ery inch of the

way I know from Al-ban-y to Buf-fal-o.—

Low bridge, ev - ery-bo - dy down, for it's

Low bridge, and we're coming to a town; You can

al - ways tell   your neigh-bor, you   can

al - ways tell   your pal,   If   you've

ev - er nav- i-gat- ed on the Er - ie Canal.

I've got a mule and her name is Sal,
Fifteen years on the Erie Canal,
She's a good old worker and a good old pal,
Fifteen years on the Erie Canal.
We have hauled some barges in our day,
Filled with lumber, coal, and hay;
And every inch of the way I know
From Albany to Buffalo.

    Low bridge, everybody down, for it's
    Low bridge, and we're coming to a town;
    You can always tell your neighbor, you can always tell
       your pal,
    If you're ever navigated on the Erie Canal.

We'd better get along on our way, old pal,
Fifteen years on the Erie Canal,
You can bet your life I'd never part with Sal,
Fifteen years on the Erie Canal.
Look out there, mule, here comes a lock,
We'll make Rome 'bout six o'clock,
One more trip and then we'll go
Right back home to Buffalo.

    Low bridge, everybody down, etc.

Paddy Works on the Railway

In eight-een hun-dred and for-ty one, I put my cor-du-roy breech-es on, I put my cor-du-roy breech-es on To work up-on the rail-way. Fi-li-me oo-ri-oo-ri-ay, fi-li-me oo-ri-oo-ri-ay, fi-li-me oo-ri-oo-ri ay, To work up-on the rail-way.

1. In eighteen hundred and forty-one,
   I put my corduroy breeches on,
   I put my corduroy breeches on
   To work upon the railway.
   > Fili-me oori-oori-ay
   > Fili-me oori-oori-ay
   > Fili-me oori-oori-ay
   > To work upon the railway.

2. In eighteen hundred and forty-two,
   I left the Old World for the New.
   Bad cess to the luck that brought me through
   To work upon the railway!
   > Fili-me oori-oori-ay, etc.

3. In eighteen hundred and forty-three,
   'Twas then I married sweet Billie McGee,
   And an elegant wife she's proved to me
   For working on the railway.
   > Fili-me oori-oori-ay, etc.

4. In eighteen hundred and forty-four,
   I landed on Columbia's shore,
   I landed on Columbia's shore
   To work upon the railway.
   > Fili-me oori-oori-ay, etc.

5. In eighteen hundred and forty-five,
   I found myself more dead than alive,
   I found myself more dead than alive
   From working on the railway.
   > Fili-me oori-oori-ay, etc.

6. In eighteen hundred and forty-six,
   The gang pelted me with stones and sticks,
   And then I was in a hell of a fix
   To work upon the railway.
   > Fili-me oori-oori-ay, etc.

7. In eighteen hundred and forty-seven,
   Sweet Billie McGee she went to heaven.
   If she left one child she left eleven
   To work upon the railway.
       Fili-me oori-oori-ay, etc.

8. In eighteen hundred and forty-eight,
   I learned to take my whisky straight.
   Its an elegant drink and can't be beat
   For working on the railway.
       Fili-me oori-oori-ay, etc.

SANTY ANNO

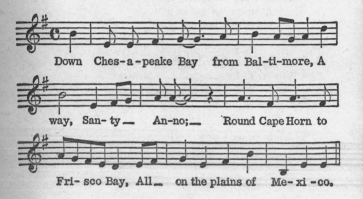

Down Ches-a-peake Bay from Bal-ti-more, A

way, San-ty— An-no;— Round Cape Horn to

Fri-sco Bay, All— on the plains of Me-xi-co.

1. Down Chesapeake Bay from Baltimore,
     Away, Santy Anno!
   Round Cape Horn to Frisco Bay,
     All on the plains of Mexico.
   Chorus: (repeats melody)
       Heave her up, and away we'll go,
         Away, Santy Anno!
       Heave her up, and away we'll go
         All on the plains of Mexico.

2. She's a fast clipper ship and a bully crew,
     Away, Santy Anno!
   A down-east Yankee for her captain too
     All on the plains of Mexico.
         Heave her up, etc.

3. There's plenty of gold so I've been told,
     Away, Santy Anno!
   There's plenty of gold so I've been told
     Way out in Californio.
         Heave her up, etc.

4. Back in the days of Forty-nine,
    Away, Santy Anno!
Those were the days of the good old times
    All on the plains of Mexico.
        Heave her up, etc.

5. When Zach Taylor gained the day,
    Away, Santy Anno!
He made poor Santy run away,
    All on the plains of Mexico.
        Heave her up, etc.

6. Santy Anno was a good old man,
    Away, Santy Anno!
'Til he went to war with Uncle Sam
    All on the plains of Mexico.
        Heave her up, etc.

7. When I leave this ship I'll settle down,
    Away, Santy Anno!
Marry a girl named Sally Brown
    All on the plains of Mexico.
        Heave her up, etc.

Union
and
Secession
1849-1863

At the conclusion of the war against Mexico in 1848, the American people were faced with a fundamental political decision in regard to slavery. The alternatives confronting them were set forth in the decade from 1850 to 1860, and were throughout this period widely canvassed and critically debated. These years witnessed the most important political dialogue conducted in the United States since the constitutional crisis of the 1780's.

The Southern proslavery position in its most extreme form received a classic formulation in 1850 in the famous last speech of John C. Calhoun; and this is the first of the documents relating to the slavery debate reproduced in full below. Reiterated and further elaborated as a Supreme Court decision in the Dred Scott case, Calhoun's position was adopted by the South's proslavery leadership in 1860–61 following the election of Abraham Lincoln to the Presidency. The essence of this view was that the South was entitled to take slaves into any Federal territories, and from these they might not lawfully be excluded under the terms of the Constitution. The implications of this position, as Northerners were not slow to see, were far-reaching. If the Constitution upheld the right to property in man in the territories, then such property surely could not rightfully be excluded from the free states themselves. Furthermore, the denial of these alleged rights involved a clear risk of war: rather, said Calhoun, than submit to a Congressional decision limiting the expansion of slavery, the South should secede and draw the sword in defense of its basic interests.

In 1850 Democrats, both Northern and Southern, recoiled from so sweeping a position. Their efforts to find a basis upon which the sections might continue to live together in the Union were smiled upon by the unexpected death, in July, 1850, of President Zachary Taylor, who had opposed any compromise which would permit the further extension of what he termed the "exciting topic" of slavery to the lands won from Mexico. In the weeks that followed Taylor's death, Stephen Douglas, Democratic Senator from Illinois, emerged as the party leader who successfully engineered the Congressional enactment of the Compromise of 1850.

This compromise was one of the most important agreements reached during the course of the nineteenth century between North and South. Its central principle was embodied in a formula which, it was hoped, would reconcile conflicting sectional interests. The New Mexico and Utah territories, recently won from Mexico, were to be admitted to the Union with or without slavery, at the discretion of the local inhabitants; but the introduction of slaves would be permitted during the territorial phase of their existence.

This formula, which remained thereafter linked with the name of Senator Douglas, became known as popular, or "squatter," sovereignty. At first sight it seemed to have much to commend it as a solution of conflicts between pro- and antislavery interests. It removed an embarrassing question from the Federal jurisdiction and placed the responsibility for voting slavery up or down upon the shoulders of the local inhabitants of a territory. Such a move might be calculated to appeal to deep-rooted democratic instincts. Was not slavery a controversial question? And should not the people themselves, in their sovereign power, have the right to decide whether or not they would admit it to their state?

The trouble with this formula was its lack of stability. Some Northerners in 1850 approved of it in good faith as a way of putting to rest the troublesome but quite specific question of the status of slavery in the territories won from Mexico by the war of 1846-48; the South saw in it a precedent of great value, not only for settling the status of territory that might be acquired by the Union in the future, but for reversing the status of slavery in territories where this question had already, in the past, been settled by congressional action. This is precisely what happened in 1854 when, again under the leadership of Senator Douglas, yet another bill was thrust through Congress that embodied the popular sovereignty principle, and that became law as the Kansas-Nebraska Act. This measure opened up Kansas to the advance of the slaveowner. Kansas was a territory where slavery had been long since banned under the Missouri Compromise of 1820; from a wider point of view it served notice upon the nation that the slaveowners were bent on reversing congressional decisions made years before with respect to the territories and which had, up to that time, been regarded by Northerners as irreversible.

The attempt to apply popular sovereignty in Kansas precipitated a new national crisis. The Republican party came into being on the simple program of putting a stop to the expansion of proslavery interests into the national territories. By 1856 popular sovereignty and the Republican program were the alternatives before the Northern electorate; in 1858 these conflicting positions received definition in a classic debate between their respective protagonists in the Illinois elections—Stephen Douglas and Abraham Lincoln. But the very form of the discussion, its terms of reference, was dictated by the Supreme Court's decision in the Dred Scott case, which had been handed down in March, 1857. An understanding of this decision is necessary if we wish to grasp, not only the extreme Southern position, but the Lincoln and Douglas positions which were to a greater or lesser degree in conflict with it.

Dred Scott was one of many slaves who were taken by their masters during the ante-bellum period into the free states or territories in the course of their pursuit of business or pleasure. The significance of the case lay in the sweeping issues which it raised. Did residence by a slave in a free state or territory, where slavery was banned either by Federal law or the state constitution, render such a man free? And, if he was thus liberated, but still wrongfully held as a slave, did he have the right to sue, as an American citizen, in the state and Federal courts?

The decision of the Court was written by Chief Justice Roger Taney, with the concurrence of a majority of the justices. It stated and elaborated the following propositions: Proposition I: A Negro cannot be a citizen of a state, within the meaning of the Federal Constitution, and cannot sue in the courts. Neither slaves nor their descendants are, nor can they ever be, members of the political community known as the United States. They do not, nor can they ever, enjoy those rights extended by the Declaration of Independence to the white man. They do not, therefore, come under the protection of the Constitution, nor was there, from the very start, any expectation that they should.

Elaboration: The framers of the Declaration of Independence, said Taney, fully realized that the language which they used "would not in any part of the civilized world be supposed to embrace the Negro race, which, by common consent, had been excluded from the civilized Governments and the family of nations, and doomed to slavery." This point was buttressed by an erudite survey of the Negro's legal status in colonial times and after. Taney had little difficulty in showing that the law held the Negro to be an inferior class from whom any or all rights might be withheld at the pleasure of the dominant white race; and this situation, he showed, prevailed not only in the slave states but in those also from which slavery had been excluded. The United States government, under the Constitution, had no right to interfere with this state of affairs except to protect the right of an owner to his property, and his general security. It was left completely to the states "to deal with this race, whether emancipated or not, as each state may think justice, humanity, and the interest and safety of society require. The states evidently intended to reserve this power exclusively to themselves."

Proposition II: Residence of a Negro slave in a territory of the United States declared closed to slavery by congressional law does not confer freedom upon such a person. This is so, because Congress has no authority, under the Constitution, to pass laws banning slavery from the territories, nor to prohibit a citizen from taking his lawful property into such territories.

Elaboration: Whatever territory the United States acquires, said Taney, is acquired for the joint benefit of the people of the several states composing the Union. But the right of property in slaves, he continued, is distinctly and expressly affirmed in the Constitution; the right to traffic in slaves, as an ordinary article of merchandize, was expressly guaranteed to the citizens under the constitutional compact until the year 1808; and in the same instrument the government was pledged to protect, for all future time, the owner's right to the recovery of runaway slave property. All of this was recorded in language too plain to be misunderstood. The government, furthermore, was enjoined, under the Fifth Amendment to the Constitution, from depriving the people of their property without due process of law, and this prohibition, he maintained, extended not merely to the states but to the entire area over which the Constitution gave Congress power to legislate. Hence, concluded Taney, to ban slavery in any Federal territory was a violation of the Constitution. The Missouri Compromise, which excluded slavery from the Kansas-Nebraska territories, must be reversed.

Democrats hailed the Dred Scott decision gleefully, for

they considered that it would settle the slavery question once and for all; but their calculations were wrong, for in actuality this decision precipitated a political storm that led directly to the election of a Republican candidate as president and to the secession of the Southern states from the Union. The Dred Scott decision defined the proslavery position in extreme and unequivocal terms, and its implications were even more sweeping than what was said explicitly. Clearly, if Congress could not constitutionally bar slavery from the territories because this would violate the Fifth Amendment, then neither could the states bar it from the lands over which they exercised authority, and for the same reason. The decision, if accepted by the nation, would open the door to the introduction of slavery everywhere throughout the Union.

Such was the political situation when the Illinois elections were held in 1858; and such was the Supreme Court view of the slavery question in relation to which both Stephen Douglas and Abraham Lincoln, as their parties' respective candidates for election to the United States Senate, were called upon to define their own positions. This they did together, by mutual agreement, in a series of seven debates between August 21 and October 15. The fifth of these, held at Galesburg on October 7, is reproduced in full below.

In these debates Douglas confined himself to a restatement of his popular sovereignty formula: slavery, he said, might go anywhere that the local inhabitants wanted it, and where they did not want it they could exclude it by local regulations. Lincoln took advantage of the national audience following the debates to hammer home the clear contradiction between the popular sovereignty and Dred Scott positions;[1] and then set forth the Republican position, that while slavery was not to be interfered with in the South, where it existed by virtue of the original constitutional compact, Congress had full authority to control it in the territories. This authority must be used, he said, to put a stop to the spread of the institution, since it was clearly wrong and incompatible with the funda-

---

[1] The effect of this was not to make Douglas *persona non grata* with the Southern Democrats—his earlier opposition to the Administration's English Bill (see pp. 507 ff.) had been more than enough to accomplish that. The main impact of Lincoln's words was made on the *Northern* audience which hitherto had had illusions about popular sovereignty. See D. E. Fehrenbacher, "Lincoln, Douglas, and the 'Freeport Question,'" *American Historical Review* LXVI (April, 1961), pp. 599–617.

mental philosophy of the Republic as expressed in the Declaration of Independence.

Lincoln's position, further refined, elaborated and documented, was set forth in far greater detail in the Cooper Institute address in New York City on February 27, 1860. This is the third of the documents reproduced in full below.

So far we have discussed the debate around the second proposition set forth by the Supreme Court—the question of the constitutionality of slavery in the territories. But debate also took place on the first question raised by the Court —the rights of the Negro people under the Declaration of Independence.

On this question Douglas agreed with Taney: that the Negro was not intended to be, and could never be, an American citizen under the protection of the Federal Constitution; that he was forever excluded from the rights, including the right to freedom, guaranteed by the Constitution to the white man. The Negro, Douglas thought, might enjoy certain rights, but only those which the individual states might concede to him on a purely pragmatic basis. Slavery was not wrong, and it certainly was not condemned by the Declaration of Independence. The Negro, he concluded, might be slave, or he might be free—it was a matter of indifference. But if free, the Negro would occupy an inferior role as hewer of wood and drawer of water for the white man. His would be, for all time, a status of helotry.

In this matter Abraham Lincoln differed radically from Stephen Douglas. Lincoln believed that the Declaration of Independence was intended to apply to all men, and that under it the Negro people had the same rights as anybody else. Slavery was wrong, and the founding fathers understood it to be so; freedom was the original breath and inspiration of the American Republic. But the Negro's rights were to be enjoyed, not in the United States, but under an African sun.[2] In 1858 Lincoln was very far from being a man of radical antislavery convictions. He was poles apart from Charles Sumner, W. L. Garrison, Frederick Douglass and other such champions of interracial equality. He adhered, on the con-

[2] This position is completely substantiated by an examination of Lincoln's pronouncements in the debates with Douglas and in the Cooper Institute address. And it is also diametrically opposed to the interpretation of the matter given by Dwight L. Dumond, who argues that "in proposing compensated emancipation and colonization he [Lincoln] was proposing something

trary, to the old colonization idea; the slave question must be eliminated by eliminating the Negro and by shipping him back to Africa. Lincoln thought of the Negro as an alien in America and of his sojourn in this country as something temporary; during his debates with Douglas he stated in no uncertain terms that so long as these people were in America, he was in favor of assigning them a legal and social status inferior to that of the white man. Both Southern servitude and Northern helotry, he thought, must be tolerated, but only as temporary evils to be liquidated by colonization as rapidly as was expedient.

Dred Scott, popular sovereignty, and the Republican position—such were the main choices confronting the American people in the election of 1860. As is known, the Democratic voters divided themselves along sectional lines between Dred Scott and popular sovereignty. The balance of the electorate, with the exception of voters in certain of the border states, cast their ballots for the Republican candidate. This choice was confirmed by the test of war. The Emancipation Proclamation of January 1, 1863, swept slavery into the discard; and the 13th and 14th Amendments to the Constitution confirmed this measure by banning slavery and by decreeing full citizenship rights, under Federal law, for the Negro people. These amendments committed the country to the radical antislavery position, that the physical emancipation of the slave was the first step upon a new path. Full freedom for the Negro people, under the Constitution, required the eradication of all the badges, marks and insignia of slavery and racism. It required the extension of full and complete civil rights to the entire colored population.

This vision of interracial equality so ably propounded by Charles Sumner and the small band of antislavery propagandists found its sublimest expression during the war years not in writing, but in deeds. Colonel Robert Gould Shaw gave in his life and death an imperishable expression to the interracial vision which it still remains for the American people

he must have known was not acceptable to the Northern people. He was paving the way for—easing the shock of—his Emancipation Proclamation. . . ." *Antislavery Origins of the Civil War in the United States* (Ann Arbor paperback: 1960), p. 112. Dumond errs in his belief—stated in the same writing, page 107—that Lincoln was an abolitionist. Lincoln came to abolitionism painfully, slowly, and out of the compulsions of war. In fact he had abolitionism thrust upon him by the war crisis itself.

to achieve as a reality. An account of Shaw's life made up from his own correspondence, together with a few of the great songs produced by the Civil War, terminate our story.

═On Slavery═

THE SPEECH OF MARCH 4, 1850

BY JOHN C. CALHOUN

Introduction

John Caldwell Calhoun (1782-1850) was born at Abbeville, South Carolina, the son of a Scots-Irish frontiersman and petty slaveowner. He persuaded his family to send him to college and chose Yale, from which he graduated with high honors in 1804. He remained in Connecticut two years longer, studying the law, and returned home to enter the South Carolina Assembly as its Abbeville representative—a position held for many years previously by his father. In 1811 he married Floride Colhoun, an heiress from the rich plantation lands around Charleston. Later that same year he went to Washington as a representative from the Abbeville district. The remainder of his life was spent in the capital as a leading figure in national politics—either in the House of Representatives or in the Senate (to which he was elected in 1832) or as Secretary of State.

From the War of 1812 until the years of the nullification crisis, 1828-32, Calhoun was identified with the cause of Federal Union and even of extreme nationalism. On tariffs, taxation, national defense, internal improvements and administrative "consolidation," or centralization, he took in these years a position, broadly speaking, closely similar to that advocated by Alexander Hamilton. He followed Marshall in open advocacy of the doctrine that the ultimate power to interpret the Constitution was vested, by that very document, in the Supreme Court, and that all governments in the country were legally subordinate to this sovereign.

The rise of powerful sectional interests, and in particular of militant slavocracy both in South Carolina and throughout the South, exposed Calhoun to bitter attack and to heavy pressure, either to change his position or face political destruction. By 1832 this shift had taken place; Calhoun had become identified with the states-rights wing of South Carolina politics, and, what was more significant, he placed his unrivaled intellectual abilities at the disposal of these interests. Thus Southern sectionalism and the slaveowners acquired a theoretical spokesman of the first rank.

Calhoun opposed the Mexican War—he foresaw, correctly, that the acquisition of new lands, vast acreages of which were unsuited to the use of the slaveowner, would intensify and precipitate the sectional crisis which was actually thrust upon the country at the conclusion of peace with Mexico. By the Treaty of Guadalupe Hidalgo the United States won not only Mexican recognition of the annexation of Texas (that had actually been carried out by joint resolution of both Houses of Congress in 1845) but also the rich lands of California and the vast desert zone of Nuevo Mexico that lay between. During the war itself Northern opinion, as Calhoun feared, hardened against the admission of any new slave states into the Union. The presidential elections of 1848 witnessed the emergence of the Free Soil party which played a major role in the campaign and exerted enormous pressure upon both Whigs and Democrats. Zachary Taylor, the new President, expressed himself in favor of a plan—termed by Calhoun "the executive proviso"—to admit both California and New Mexico to the Union as free states. This provision Southern leaders declared that they would never accept.

Thus there opened in December, 1849, a critical debate upon the future of the Union. In general, three alternatives were presented to Congress: the executive proviso, a compromise plan outlined by Henry Clay with the support of Daniel Webster, and the extreme Southern position as presented by Calhoun. Clay's plan would, in essence, be adopted by Congress in September, 1850, and would go down in history as the Compromise of 1850. Calhoun's thinking alone is presented below. It is, to be sure, an excellent introduction to the great debate of this year, but its significance goes far beyond that. For, looking at the situation with a cold, unblinking realism, Calhoun explained in his speech precisely why the interests of the Southern slaveholders required that they should secede at once from the Union and unsheath the sword in defense of their "peculiar institution." Ten years later they would follow Calhoun's advice and do exactly that. Perhaps there is, in all the history of American thought, no more brilliantly clear-sighted exposition of the factors leading the slaveowners to make the sane, clear and deliberate calculation to stake their fate, and the country's fate, upon secession and war.

In the early months of 1850 Calhoun was bedridden and dying. He dictated his speech to his secretary, Joseph Scoville, and made numerous and careful corrections in his own hand. On March 4, a bright spring day, Senator James A. Mason read the crabbed manuscript, not without difficulty, to a hushed and crowded chamber. Its author, white and emaciated, sat in his place listening. Death followed within the month.

ON SLAVERY, MARCH 4, 1850*

I have, Senators, believed from the first that the agitation of the subject of slavery would, if not prevented by some timely and effective measure, end in disunion. I have, on all proper occasions, endeavored to call the attention of both the two great parties which divide the country to adopt some measure to prevent so great a disaster, but without success. The agitation has been permitted to proceed, with almost no attempt to resist it, until it has reached a period when it can no longer be disguised or denied, that the Union is in danger. You have thus had forced upon you the greatest and the gravest question that can ever come under your consideration: how can the Union be preserved?

To give a satisfactory answer to this mighty question, it is indispensable to have an accurate and thorough knowledge of the nature and the character of the cause, by which the Union is endangered. Without such knowledge it is impossible to pronounce, with any certainty, by what measure it can be saved; just as it would be impossible for a physician to pronounce in the case of some dangerous disease, with any certainty, by what remedy the patient could be saved,

*Source: The edition of the speech reproduced below has been prepared from Calhoun's own manuscript, now in the Library of Congress. It supersedes all the earlier printed versions—in the Congressional *Globe*, in Calhoun's *Works*, and in pamphlet form—all of which contain numerous inaccuracies.

without similar knowledge of the nature and character of the cause of the disease.

The first question, then, presented for consideration, in the investigation I propose, in order to obtain such knowledge, is: what is it that has endangered the Union?

To this question there can be but one answer, that the immediate cause is the almost universal discontent which pervades all the states composing the Southern section of the Union. This widely extended discontent is not of recent origin. It commenced with the agitation of the slavery question, and has been increasing ever since.

The next question is: what has caused this widely diffused and almost universal discontent?

It is a great mistake to suppose, as is by some, that it originated with demagogues, who excited the discontent with the intention of aiding their personal advancement, or with disappointed ambitious individuals, who resorted to it as the means of raising their fallen fortunes. There is no foundation for this opinion. On the contrary, all the great political influences of the section were arrayed against excitement, and exerted to the utmost to keep the people quiet. The great mass of the people of the South were divided, as in the other section, into Whigs and Democrats. The leaders and the presses of both parties in the South were very solicitous to prevent excitement and to preserve quiet; because it was seen that the effects of the former would necessarily tend to weaken, if not destroy, the political ties which united them with their respective parties in the other section. Those who know the strength of party ties will readily appreciate the immense force which this cause exerted against agitation, and in favor of preserving quiet. But, as great as it was, it was not sufficient to prevent the widespread discontent which now pervades the section. No; some cause far deeper and more powerful must exist to produce a discontent so wide and deep, than the one inferred.

The question then recurs: what is the cause of this discontent? It will be found in the belief of the people of the Southern states, as prevalent as the discontent itself, that they cannot remain, as things now are, consistently with honor and safety, in the Union.

The next question to be considered, is: what has caused this belief?

One of the causes is, undoubtedly, to be traced to the long continued agitation of the slave question on the part of the North, and the many aggressions which they have made on the rights of the South during the time. I will not enumerate them at present, as it will be done hereafter in its proper place.

There is another lying back of it but with which this is intimately connected, that may be regarded as the great and primary cause. It is to be found in the fact that the equilibrium between the two sections in the government as it stood when the Constitution was ratified, and the government put into action, has been destroyed. At that time there was nearly a perfect equilibrium between the two, which afforded ample means to each to protect itself against the aggression of the other; but, as it now stands, one section has exclusive power of controlling the government, which leaves the other without any adequate means of protecting itself against its encroachment and oppression.

To place this subject distinctly before you, I have, Senators, prepared a brief statistical statement, showing the relative weight of the two sections in the government under the first census of 1790 and the last census of 1840.

According to the former, the population of the United States, including Vermont, Kentucky, and Tennessee, which then were in their incipient condition of becoming states, but were not actually admitted, amounted to 3,929,827. Of this number the Northern states had 1,977,899, and the Southern 1,952,072, making a difference of only 25,827 in favor of the former states. The number of states, including Vermont, Kentucky, and Tennessee, was sixteen; of which eight, including Vermont, belonged to the Northern section, and eight, including Kentucky and Tennessee, to the Southern, making an equal division of the states between the two sections under the first census. There was a small preponderance in the House of Representatives, and in the electoral college, in favor of the Northern, owing to the fact that, according to the provisions of the Constitution, in estimating Federal numbers, five slaves count but three; but it was too small to affect sensibly the perfect equilibrium of numbers, a true, perfect equilibrium which, with that exception, existed at the time.

Such was the equality of the two sections when the states composing them agreed to enter into a Federal Union.

Since then the equilibrium between them has been greatly disturbed. According to the last census the aggregate population of the United States amounted to 17,063,357, of which the Northern section contained 9,728,920, and the Southern 7,334,437, making a difference, in round numbers, of 2,400,000. The number of states had increased from sixteen to twenty-six, making an addition of ten states. In the meantime the position of Delaware had become doubtful, as to which section she properly belonged. Considering her neutral, the Northern states will have thirteen and the Southern states twelve, making a difference in the Senate of two Senators in favor of the former. According to the apportionment under the census of 1840, there were two hundred and twenty-three members of the House of Representatives, of which the Northern states had one hundred and thirty-five, and the Southern states (considering Delaware as neutral) eighty-seven, making a difference in favor of the former in the House of Representatives of forty-eight. The difference in the Senate of two members, added to this, gives to the North in the electoral college a majority of fifty. Since the census of 1840, four states have been added to the Union: Iowa, Wisconsin, Florida, and Texas. They leave the difference in the Senate as it stood when the census was taken; but add two to the side of the North in the House, making the present majority in the House in its favor fifty, and in the electoral college fifty-two.

The result of the whole is to give the Northern section a predominance in every department of the government, and thus concentrate in it the two elements which constitute the Federal government—majority of states, and a majority of their population, estimated in Federal numbers. Whatever section concentrates the two in itself, possesses the control of the entire government.

But we are just at the close of the sixth decade, and the commencement of the seventh. The census is to be taken this year, which must add greatly to the decided preponderance of the North in the House of Representatives and in the electoral college. The prospect is also that a great increase will be added to its present preponderance, during the period of the decade, by the addition of new states. Two territories, Oregon and Minnesota, are already in progress, and strenuous efforts are being made to bring in three additional states from the territory recently conquered from Mexico; which, if successful, will add three other states in a short time to the Northern section, making five states and increasing its present number of states from fifteen to twenty, and of its Senators from thirty to forty. On the contrary, there is not a single territory in progress in the Southern section, and no certainty that any additional state will be added to it during the decade.

The prospect then is, that the two sections in the Senate, should the efforts now made to exclude the South from the newly conquered territories succeed, will stand before the end of the decade twenty Northern states to fourteen Southern (considering Delaware as neutral), and forty Northern Senators to twenty-four Southern. This great increase of Senators, added to the great increase of members of the House of Representatives and electoral college on the part of the North, which must take place over the next decade, will effectually and eventually destroy the equilibrium which existed when the government commenced.

Had this destruction been the operation of time, without the interference of government, the South would have had no reason to complain; but such was not the fact. It was caused by the legislation of this government, which was appointed as the common agent of all, and charged with the protection of the interests and security of all. The legislation by which it has been effected may be classed under three heads. The first is that series of acts by which the South has been excluded from the common territory belonging to all of the states as the members of the Federal Union, which had the effect of extending vastly the portion allotted to the Northern section, and restricting within narrow limits the portion left to the South. The next consists in adopting a system of revenue and disbursements, by which an undue proportion of the burden of taxation has been imposed upon the South, and an undue proportion of its proceeds appropriated to the North; and the last is a system of political measures, by which the original character of the government has been radically changed.

I propose to bestow upon each of these, in the order they stand, a few remarks, with the view of showing that it is owing to the action of this government, that the equilibrium between the two sections has been destroyed, and the whole powers of the system centered in a sectional majority.

The first of the series of acts by which the South was deprived of its due share of the territories, originated with the confederacy which preceded the existence of this government. It is to be found in the provision of the Ordinance of 1787.[1] Its effect was to exclude the South entirely from that vast and fertile region which lies between the Ohio and the Mississippi, now embracing five states and one territory. The next of the series is the Missouri Compromise, which excluded the South from that large portion of Louisiana which lies north of 36° 30', excepting what is included in the state of Missouri. The last of the series excluded the South from the whole of the Oregon Territory. All these, in the slang of the day, were what are called slave territory, and not free soil; that is, territories belonging to slaveholding powers and open to the emigration of masters with their slaves. By these several acts, the South was excluded from 1,238,025 square miles, an extent of country considerably exceeding the entire valley of the Mississippi.

To the South was left the portion of the territory of Louisiana lying south of 36° 30', and the portion north of it included in the state of Missouri. The portion lying south of 36° 30' includes the states of Louisiana and Arkansas, and the territory lying west of the latter and south of 36° 30', called the Indian Country. These, with the Territory of Florida, now the state, make, in the whole, 283,503 square miles. To this must be added the territory acquired with Texas. If the whole should be added to the Southern section, it would make an increase of 325,520, which would make the whole left to the South, 609,023. But a large part of Texas is still in contest between the two sections, which leaves it uncertain what will be the real extent of the portion of her territory that may be left to the South.

I have not included the territory recently acquired by the treaty with Mexico. The North is making the most strenuous efforts to appropriate the whole to herself, by excluding the South from every foot of it. If she should succeed, it will add to that from which the South has already been excluded 526,078 square miles, and would increase the whole the North

---

[1] See Appendix, p. 615.

has appropriated to herself to 1,764,023, not including the portion that she may succeed in excluding us from in Texas. To sum up the whole, the United States, since they declared their independence, have acquired 2,373,046 square miles of territory, from which the North will have excluded the South, if she should succeed in monopolizing the newly acquired territories, about three-fourths of the whole, leaving to the South but about one-fourth.

Such is the first and great cause that has destroyed the equilibrium between the two sections in the government.

The next is the system of revenue and disbursements which has been adopted by the government. It is well known that the main source from which the government has derived its revenue is the duties on imports. I shall not undertake to show that all such duties must necessarily fall mainly on the exporting states, and that the South, as the great exporting portion of the Union, has in reality paid vastly more than her due proportion of the revenue; because I deem it unnecessary, as the subject has on so many occasions been fully discussed. Nor shall I, for the same reason, undertake to show that a far greater portion of the revenue has been disbursed at the North, than its due share; and that the joint effect of these causes has been, to transfer a vast amount from South to North which, under an equal system of revenue and disbursements, would not have been lost to her. If to this be added, that many of the duties were imposed, not for revenue, but for protection; that is, intended to put money, not in the Treasury, but directly into the pocket of the manufacturers, some conception may be formed of the immense amount which, in the long course of so many years, has been transferred from South to North. There are no data by which it can be estimated with any certainty; but it is safe to say, that it amounts to hundreds of millions of dollars. Under the most moderate estimate, it would be sufficient to add greatly to the wealth of the North, and by that greatly increase her population by attracting emigration from all quarters in that direction.

These two causes combined amply explain why the North has acquired a preponderance in every department of the government by its disproportionate increase of population and states. The former, as has been shown, has increased, in fifty years, 2,400,000 over that of the South. This increase of population, during so long a period, is satisfactorily accounted for, by the number of emigrants, and the increase of their descendants, which have been attracted to the Northern section from Europe and the Southern section, in consequence of the advantages derived from the causes assigned. If they had not existed, if the South had retained all the capital which has been extracted from her by the fiscal action of the government; and, if they had not been excluded by the Ordinance of 1787 and the Missouri Compromise from the region lying between the Ohio and the Mississippi, and between the Mississippi and the Rocky Mountains north of 36° 30′, it scarcely admits of a doubt, that she would have divided the immigration with the North, and by retaining her own people, would have at least equalled the North in population under the census of 1840, and probably under that about to be taken. She would also, if she had retained her equal rights in those territories, have maintained an equality in the number of states with the North, and have preserved the equilibrium between the two sections that existed at the commencement of the government. The loss, then, of the equilibrium is to be attributed to the action of this government.

But while these measures were destroying the equilibrium between the two sections, the action of the government was leading to a radical change in its character, by concentrating all the power of the system in itself. The occasion will not permit me to trace the measures by which this great change has been consummated. If it did, it would not be difficult to show that the process commenced at an early period of the government; that it proceeded almost without interruption, step by step, until it absorbed virtually its entire powers. Without, however, going through the whole process to establish the fact, it may be done satisfactorily by a very short statement.

That this government claims, and practically maintains, the right to decide in the last resort, as to the extent of its powers, will scarcely be denied by anyone conversant with the political history of the country. That it also claims the right to resort to force to maintain whatever power it claims, against all opposition, is equally certain. Indeed it is apparent, from what we daily hear, that this has become the prevailing and fixed opinion of a great majority of the community. Now I ask, what limitation can possibly be placed upon the powers of a government claiming and exercising such rights? And, if none can be, how can the separate government of the states maintain and protect the powers reserved to them by the Constitution, or the people of the several states maintain those which are reserved to them, and among them their sovereign powers by which they ordained and established, not only their separate state constitutions and governments, but also the Constitution and government of the United States? But, if they have no constitutional means of maintaining them against the right claimed by this government, it necessarily follows that they hold them at its pleasure and discretion, and that all the powers of the system are in reality concentrated in it. It also follows that the character of the government has been changed in consequence, from a Federal Republic, as it originally came from the hands of its framers, and that it has been changed into a great national consolidated democracy. It has indeed at present all the characteristics of the latter, and not one of the former, although it still retains its outward form.

The result of the whole of these causes combined is that the North has acquired a decided ascendancy over every department of this government, and through it a control over all the powers of the system. A single section governed by the will of the numerical majority has now in fact the control of the government and the entire powers of the system. What was once a constitutional Federal Republic is now converted, in reality, into one as absolute as that of the Autocrat of Russia, and as despotic in its tendency as any absolute government that ever existed.

As, then, the North has the absolute control over the government, it is manifest that on all questions between it and the South, where there is a diversity of interests, the interest of the latter will be sacrificed to the former, however oppressive the effects may be; as the South possesses no means by which it can resist through the action of the government. But if there was no question of vital importance to the South, in reference to which there was a diversity of views between the two sections, this state of things might be endured, without the hazard of destruction to the South. But such is not the fact. There is a question of vital importance to the Southern section, in reference to which the views and feelings of the two sections are opposite and hostile as they can possibly be.

I refer to the relation between the two races in the Southern section, which constitutes a vital portion of her social organization. Every portion of the North entertains views and feelings more or less hostile to it. Those most opposed and hostile regard it as a sin, and consider themselves under the most sacred obligation to use every effort to destroy it. Indeed, to the extent that they conceive that they have power, they regard themselves as implicated in the sin, and responsible for suppressing it by the use of all and every means. Those less opposed and hostile regard it as a crime—an offense against humanity, as they call it—and although not so fanatical, feel themselves bound to use all efforts to effect the same object; while those who are least opposed and hostile, regard it as a blot and a stain on the character of what they call the nation, and feel themselves, accordingly, bound to give it no countenance or support. On the contrary, the Southern section regards the relation as one which cannot be destroyed without subjecting the two races to the greatest calamity, and the section to poverty, desolation, and wretchedness; and accordingly feel bound by every consideration of interest, safety, and duty, to defend it.

This hostile feeling on the part of the North towards the social organization of the South, long lay dormant, but it only required some cause, which would make the impression on those, who felt it most intensely, that they were responsible for its continuance, to call it into action. The increasing power of this government, and of the control of the Northern section over all its departments, furnished the cause. It was they made an impression on the minds of many, that there was little or no restraint to prevent the government to do whatever it might choose to do. This was sufficient of itself to put the most fanatical portion of the North in action, for the purpose of destroying the existing relation between the two races in the South.

The first organized movement towards it commenced in 1835. Then, for the first time, societies were organized, presses established, lecturers sent forth to excite the people of the North, and incendiary publications scattered over the whole South through the mail. The South was thoroughly aroused. Meetings were held everywhere, and resolutions adopted, calling upon the North to apply a remedy to arrest the threatened evil, and pledging themselves to adopt measures for their own protection if it was not arrested. At the meeting of Congress, petitions poured in from the North, calling upon Congress to abolish slavery in the District of Columbia, and to prohibit what they called the internal slave trade between the states—announcing at the same time, that their ultimate object was to abolish slavery not only in the District but in the states and throughout the Union.

At this period, the number engaged in the agitation was small, and possessed little or no personal influence. Neither party in Congress had at that time any sympathy with them or their cause. The members of each party presented their petitions with great reluctance. Nevertheless, as small and as contemptible as the party then was, both of the great parties of the North dreaded them. They felt that, though small, they were organized in reference to a subject which had a great and a commanding influence over the Northern mind. Each party, on that account, feared to oppose their petitions, lest the opposite party should take advantage of the one who opposed by favoring them. The effect was, that both united in insisting that the petitions should be received, and that Congress take jurisdiction over the subject for which they prayed; and to justify their course they took the extraordinary ground, that Congress was bound to receive petitions on every subject, however objectionable it might be, and whether they had or had not jurisdiction over the subject.

These views prevailed in the House of Representatives, and partially in the Senate; and thus the party succeeded, in their first movement, in gaining what they proposed—a position in Congress from which agitation could be extended over the whole Union. This was the commencement of the agitation, which has ever since continued, and which, as is now acknowledged, has endangered the Union itself.

As to myself, I believed at that early period, that if the party who got up the petitions should succeed in getting Congress to take jurisdiction, that agitation would follow, and that it would in the end, if not arrested, destroy the Union. I then so expressed myself in debate, and called upon both parties to take grounds against taking jurisdiction; but in vain. Had my voice been heeded, and Congress refused to take jurisdiction by the united votes of all parties, the agitation which followed would have been prevented, and the fanatical movements accompanying the agitation, which have brought us to our present perilous condition, would have become extinct from the want of something to feed the flame. *That* was the time for the North to have shown her devotion to the Union; but, unfortunately, both of the great parties of that section were so intent on obtaining or retaining party ascendancy, that all other considerations were overlooked or forgotten.

What has since followed are but natural consequences. With the success of their first movement, this small fanatical party began to acquire strength; and with that, to become an object of courtship of both of the great parties. The necessary consequence was, a further increase of power, and a gradual tainting of the opinion of both of the other parties with their doctrines, until the infection has extended over both, and the great mass of the population of the North who, whatever may be their opinion of the original abolition party which still keeps up its distinctive organization, hardly ever fail, when it comes to acting, to cooperate in carrying out their measures.

With the increase of their influence, they extend the sphere of their action. In a short period after they had commenced their first movement, they had acquired sufficient influence to induce the legislatures of most of the Northern states to pass acts, which in effect abrogated the clause of the Constitution that provides for the delivering up of fugitive slaves. Not long after, petitions followed to abolish slavery in forts, magazines, and dockyards, and all other places where Congress had exclusive power of legislation. This was followed by petitions and resolutions of legislatures of the Northern states, and popular meetings, to exclude the Southern states from all territories acquired, or to be acquired, and to prevent the admission of any state hereafter into the Union, which by its Constitution does not prohibit slavery. And Congress is invoked to do all this, expressly with the view to the final abolition of slavery in the states. *That* has been avowed to be the ultimate object from the beginning of the agitation until the present time; and yet the great body of both parties of the North, with the full knowledge of the fact, although disowning the abolitionists, have cooperated with them in almost all their measures.

Such is a brief history of the agitation as far as it has yet advanced. Now I ask, Senators, what is there to prevent its further progress, until it fulfils the ultimate end proposed, unless some decisive measure should be adopted to prevent it? Has any one of the causes, which has added to its increase from its original small and contemptible beginning, until it has attained its present magnitude, diminished in force? Is the original cause of the movement—that slavery is a sin and ought to be suppressed—weaker now than at the commencement? Or is the abolition party less numerous or influential? Or have they less influence over elections? Or less control over the two great parties of the North in elections? Or has the South greater means of influencing or controlling the movements of this government now, than it had when the agitation commenced? To all these questions but one answer can be given. No. No. No. The very reverse is true. Instead of weaker, all the elements in favor of agitation are stronger now than they were in 1835, when first commenced, while all the elements of influence on the part of the South are weaker. I again ask, what is to stop this agitation, unless something decisive is done, before the great and final object at which it aims—the abolition of slavery in the South— is consummated? Is it, then, not certain that if something decisive is not now done to arrest it, the South will be forced to choose between abolition and secession?

Indeed, as events are now moving, it will not require the South to secede, to dissolve the Union. Agitation will of itself effect it, of which past history furnishes abundant proof, as I shall next proceed to show.

It is a great mistake to suppose that disunion can be effected by a single blow. The cords which bind these states together in one common Union are far too numerous and powerful for that. Disunion must be the work of time. It is only through a long process, and successively, that the cords can be snapped, until the whole fabric falls asunder. Already the agitation of the slavery question has snapped some of the most important, and has greatly weakened all the others, as I shall proceed to show.

The cords which bind the states together are not only many, but various in character. Among them, some are spiritual or ecclesiastical; some political; others social. Others pertain to the benefit conferred by the Union, and others to the feelings of duty and obligation.

The strongest of those of a spiritual and ecclesiastical nature consisted in the unity of the great religious denominations, all of which originally embraced the Union. All these denominations, with the exception perhaps of the Catholics, were organized very much upon the principle of our political institutions. Beginning with smaller meetings, corresponding with the political divisions of the country, their organization terminated in one great central assemblage, corresponding very much with the character of Congress. At these meetings the principal clergymen and lay members of the respective denominations from all parts of the Union, met to transact business relating to their common concerns. It was not confined to what appertained to the doctrines and discipline of the respective denominations, but extended to plans for disseminating the Bible, establishing missionaries, distributing tracts, and of establishing presses for the publication of tracts, newspapers, and periodicals, with a view of diffusing religious information and for the support of the doctrines and creeds of the denomination.

All this combined contributed greatly to strengthen the bonds of the Union. The ties which held each denomination together formed a strong cord to hold the whole Union together. But, powerful as they were, they have not been able to resist the explosive effect of slavery agitation.

The first of these cords which snapped, under its explosive force, was that of the powerful Methodist Episcopal Church. The numerous and strong ties which held it together, are all broken, and its unity gone. They now form separate churches; and instead of that feeling of attachment and devotion to the interests of the whole church which was formerly felt, they are now arrayed into two hostile bodies, engaged in litigation about what was formerly their common property.

The next cord that snapped was that of the Baptists—one of the largest and most respectable of the denominations. That of the Presbyterian is not entirely snapped, but some of its strands have given way. That of the Episcopal Church is the only one of the four great Protestant denominations which remains unbroken and entire.

The strongest cord of a political character consists of the many and powerful ties that have held together the two great parties which have, with some modifications, existed from the beginning of the government. They both extended to every portion of the Union, and strongly contributed to hold all its parts together. But this powerful cord has fared no better than the spiritual. It resisted for a long time the explosive tendency of the agitation, but has finally snapped under its force—if not entirely, nearly so. Nor is there one of the remaining cords which has not been greatly weakened. To this extent the Union has already been destroyed by agitation, in the only way it can be, by snapping asunder and weakening the cords which bind it together.

If the agitation goes on, the same force acting with increased intensity, as has been shown, will snap the cords, when nothing will be left to hold the states together except force. But surely that can with no propriety of language be called a Union, when the only means by which the weaker is held connected with the stronger portion is by *force*. It may, indeed, keep them connected; but the connection will partake more of the character of subjugation on the part of the weaker to the stronger, than the union of free, independent, and sovereign states in one Federal Union, as they stood in the early stages of the government, and which only is worthy of the sacred name of Union.

Having now, Senators, explained what it is that endangers the Union, and traced it to its cause, and explained its nature and character, the question again recurs: how can the Union be saved? To this I answer, there is but one way by which it can be; and that is, by adopting such measures as will satisfy the states belonging to the Southern section, that they can remain in the Union consistently with their honor and their safety. There is, again, only one way by which this can be effected, and that is, by removing the causes by which this belief has been produced. Do that, and discontent will cease, harmony and kind feelings between the sections be restored, and every apprehension of danger to the Union removed.

The question, then, is: by what can this be done? But before I undertake to answer this question, I propose to show by what it cannot be done.

It cannot, then, be done by eulogies on the Union, however splendid or numerous. The cry of "Union, Union, the glorious Union!" can no more prevent disunion than the cry of "health, health, glorious health!" on the part of the physician, can save a patient lying dangerously ill. So long as the Union, instead of being regarded as a protector, is regarded in the opposite character, by not much less than a majority of the states, it will be in vain to attempt to conciliate them by pronouncing eulogies on it.

Besides, this cry of Union comes commonly from those whom we cannot believe to be sincere. It usually comes from our assailants. But we cannot believe them to be sincere; for, if they loved the Union, they would necessarily be devoted to the Constitution. It made the Union—and to destroy the Constitution would be to destroy the Union. But the only reliable and certain evidence of devotion to the Constitution is, to abstain on the one hand from violating it, and to repel on the other all attempts to violate it. It is only by faithfully performing these high duties that the Constitution can be preserved, and with it the Union.

But how then stands the profession of devotion to the Union by our assailants, when brought to this test? Have they abstained from violating the Constitution? Let the many acts passed by the Northern states to set aside and annul the clause of the Constitution providing for the delivering up of fugitive slaves answer. I cite this, not that it is the only instance (for there are many others), but because the violation in this particular is too notorious and palpable to be denied.

Again: have they stood forth faithfully to repel violations of the Constitution? Let their course in reference to the agitation of the slavery question, which was commenced and has been carried on for fifteen years, avowedly for the purpose of abolishing slavery in the states—an object all acknowledged to be unconstitutional—answer. Let them show a single instance during this long period, in which they have denounced the agitators or their many attempts to effect what is admitted to be unconstitutional, or a single measure which they have brought forward for that purpose.

How can we, with all these facts before us, believe that they are sincere in their profession of devotion to the Union, or avoid believing that, by assuming the cloak of patriotism, their profession is but intended to increase the vigor of their assaults and to weaken the force of our resistance?

Nor can we regard the profession of devotion to the Union, on the part of those who are not our assailants, as sincere, when they pronounce eulogies upon the Union, evidently with the intent of charging us with disunion, without uttering one word of denunciation against our assailants. If friends of the Union, their course should be to unite with us in repelling these assaults, and denouncing the authors as enemies of the Union. Why they avoid this, and pursue the obvious course they do, it is for them to explain.

Nor can the Union be saved by invoking the name of the illustrious Southerner whose mortal remains repose on the western bank of the Potomac. He was one of us—a slaveholder and a planter. We have studied his history, and find nothing in it to justify submission to wrong. On the contrary, his great fame rests on the solid foundation that, while he was careful to avoid doing wrong to others, he was prompt and decided in repelling wrong. I trust that, in this respect, we profited by his example.

Nor can we find anything in his history to deter us from seceding from the Union, should it fail to fulfil the objects for which it was instituted, by being permanently and hopelessly converted into the means of oppression instead of protection. On the contrary, we find much in his example to encourage us, should we be forced to the extremity of deciding between submission and disunion.

There existed then, as well as now, a Union—that between the parent country and her then colonies. It was a Union that had much to endear it to the people of the colonies. Under its protecting and superintending care, the colonies were planted and grew up and prospered through a long course of years, until they became populous and wealthy. Its benefits were not limited to them. Their extensive agricultural and other productions gave birth to a flourishing commerce, which richly rewarded the parent country for the trouble and expense of establishing and protecting them. Washington was born and grew up to manhood under that Union. He acquired his early distinction in its service, and there is every reason to believe that he was devotedly attached to it. But his devotion was a rational one. He was attached to it, not as an end, but as a means to an end. When it failed to fulfil its end and, instead of affording protection, was converted into the means of oppressing the colonies, he did not hesitate to draw his sword, and head the great movement by which that Union was forever severed, and the independence of these states established. This was the great and crowning glory of his life, which has spread his fame over the whole globe, and will transmit it to the latest posterity.

Nor can the plan proposed by the distinguished Senator from Kentucky, nor that of the administration, save the Union. I shall pass by without remark the plan proposed by the Senator, and proceed directly to the consideration of that of the administration. I however assure the distinguished and able Senator, that, in taking this course, I intend no disrespect whatever to him or his plan. I have adopted it, because so many Senators of distinguished abilities, who were present when he delivered his speech, and explained his plan, and who were fully capable to do justice to the side they support, have replied to him.

The plan of the administration cannot save the Union, because it can have no effect towards satisfying the states composing the Southern section of the Union, that they can consistently with safety and honor remain in the Union. It is, in fact, but a modification of the Wilmot Proviso. It proposes to effect the same object—to exclude the South from all territory acquired by the Mexican treaty. It is well known that the South is united against the Wilmot Proviso, and has committed itself by solemn resolutions to resist, should it be adopted. Its opposition *is not to the name*, but that which *it proposes to effect*. [It is well known] that the Southern states hold it to be unconstitutional, unjust, inconsistent with their equality as members of the common Union, and calculated to destroy irretrievably the equilibrium between the two sections.

These objections equally apply to what, for brevity, I will call the Executive Proviso. There is no difference between it and the Wilmot, except in the mode of effecting the object; and in that respect, I must say that the latter is much the least objectionable. It goes to its object openly, boldly, and directly. It claims for Congress unlimited power over the territories, and proposes to assert it over the territories acquired from Mexico, by a positive prohibition of slavery. Not so the Executive Proviso. It takes an indirect course, and in order to elude the Wilmot Proviso, and thereby avoid encountering the united and determined resistance of the South, it denies, by implication, the authority of Congress to legislate for the territories, and claims the right as belonging exclusively to the inhabitants of the territories. But to effect the object of excluding the South, it takes care, in the meantime, to let in emigrants freely from the Northern states and other quarters except emigrants from the South, which it takes special care to exclude by holding up to them the danger of having their slaves liberated under the Mexican laws. The necessary consequence is to exclude the South from the territory just as effectually as would the Wilmot Proviso. The only difference in this respect is, that what one proposes to effect directly and openly, the other proposes to effect indirectly and covertly.

But the Executive Proviso is more objectionable still than the Wilmot, in another and important particular. The latter, to effect its object, inflicts a dangerous wound upon the Constitution by depriving the Southern states, as joint partners and owners of the territories, of their rights in them; but it inflicts no greater wound than is absolutely necessary to effect its object. The former, on the contrary, while it inflicts the same wound, inflicts others equally great and, if possible greater, as I shall next proceed to explain.

In claiming the right for the inhabitants, instead of Congress, to legislate over the territories, in the Executive Proviso, it assumes that the sovereignty over the territories is vested in the former; or to express it in the language used in a resolution offered by one of the Senators from Texas (Gen. Houston, now absent), they "have the same inherent right of self-government as the people in the states." The assumption is utterly unfounded, unconstitutional, without example, and contrary to the entire practice of the government from its commencement to the present time, as I shall proceed to show.

The recent movement of individuals in California to form a constitution and a state government, and to appoint Senators and representatives, is the first fruit of this monstrous assumption. If the individuals who have made this movement had gone into California as adventurers, and if, as such, they had conquered the territory and established their independence, the sovereignty of the country would have been vested in them, as a separate and independent community. In that case they would have had the right to form a constitution, and to establish a government for themselves; and, if after that they thought proper to apply to Congress for admission into the Union as a sovereign and independent state, all this would have been regular, and according to established principles. But such is not the case. It was the United States who conquered California and finally acquired it by treaty. The sovereignty, of course, is vested in them, and not in the individuals who have attempted to form a constitution as a state without their consent. All this is clear beyond controversy, except it can be shown that they have since lost or been divested of their sovereignty.

Nor is it less clear that the power of legislating over the acquired territory is vested in Congress and not, as is assumed, in the inhabitants of the territories. None can deny that the government of the United States have the power to acquire territories, either by war or by treaty; but if the power to acquire exists, it belongs to Congress to carry it into execution. On this point there can be no doubt, for the Constitution expressly provides that Congress shall have power "to make all laws which shall be necessary and proper to carry into execution the foregoing powers"—those vested in Congress—"and all other powers vested by this Constitution *in the government* of the United States, or in *any department* or *officer* thereof."[1]

It matters not, then, where the power is vested; for, if vested at all in the government of the United States, or any of its departments or officers, this power of carrying it into execution is clearly vested in Congress. But this important provision, while it gives to Congress the power of legislating over territories, imposes important restrictions on its exercise, by restricting Congress to passing laws necessary and proper for carrying the power into execution. The prohibition extends not only to all laws not suitable or appropriate to the object of the power, but also to all that are unjust, unequal, or unfair; for all such laws would be unnecessary and improper and, therefore, unconstitutional.

Having now established beyond controversy that the sovereignty over the territories is vested in the United States—that is, in the several states composing the Union—and that the power of legislating over them is expressly vested in Congress, it follows that the individuals in California who have undertaken to form a constitution and a state, and to exercise the power of legislation without the consent of Congress, have usurped the sovereignty of the states and the authority of Congress, and have acted in open defiance of them both. In other words, what they have done is revolutionary and rebellious in its character, anarchal in its tendency, and calculated to lead

---

[1] The emphasis is Calhoun's.

to the most dangerous consequences. Had they acted from premeditation and design it would have been in fact actual rebellion; but such is not the case. The blame lies much less upon them than upon those who have induced them to take a course so unconstitutional and dangerous. They have been led into it by language held here, and the course pursued by the Executive branch of the government.

I have not seen the answer of the Executive to the calls made by the two houses of Congress for information as to the course which it took, or the part which it acted, in reference to what was done in California. I understand the answers have not yet been printed. But there is enough known to justify the assertion that those who profess to represent and act under the authority of the Executive have advised, aided, and encouraged the movement which terminated in forming what they call a constitution and a state. Gen. Riley, who professed to act as civil governor, called the convention, determined the number and distribution of the delegates, appointed the time and place of its meeting, was present during the session, and gave its proceedings his approbation and sanction. If he acted without authority he ought to have been tried, or at least reprimanded and disavowed. Neither having been done, the presumption is that his course has been approved. This of itself is sufficient to identify the Executive with his acts, and to make it responsible for them. I touch not the question whether Gen. Riley was appointed or received the instructions under which he professed to act from the present Executive or its predecessor. If from the former, it would implicate the preceding as well as the present administration. If not, the responsibility rests exclusively on the present.

It is manifest from this statement that the Executive department has undertaken to perform acts preparatory to the meeting of the individuals to form their so-called constitution and state government, which appertain exclusively to Congress. Indeed, they are identical in many respects with the provision adopted by Congress, when it gives permission to a new territory to form a constitution and government in order to be admitted as a state into the Union.

Having now shown that the assumption upon which the Executive and the individuals in California acted throughout this whole affair is unfounded, unconstitutional, and dangerous, it remains to make a few remarks, in order to show that what has been done is contrary to the entire practice of the government from its commencement to the present time.

From its commencement until the time that Michigan was admitted, the practice was uniform. Territorial governments were first organized by Congress. The government of the United States appointed the governors, judges, secretaries, marshalls, and other officers, and the inhabitants of the territory were represented by legislative bodies, whose acts were subject to the revision of Congress. This state of things continued until the government of a territory applied to Congress to permit its inhabitants to form a constitution and government, preparatory to admission into the Union. The preliminary act to giving permission was to ascertain whether the inhabitants were sufficiently numerous to authorize them to be formed into a state. This was done by taking a census. That being done, and the number proving sufficient, permission was granted. The act granting it fixed all the preliminaries—the time and place of holding the convention; the qualification of the voters; establishment of its boundaries, and all other measures necessary to be settled previous to admission. The act giving permission necessarily withdraws the sovereignty of the United States, and leaves the inhabitants of the incipient state as free to form their constitution and government as were the original states of the Union after they had declared their independence. At this stage, the inhabitants of the territory became for the first time a people, in legal and constitutional language. Prior to this they were, by the old acts of Congress, called inhabitants and not people. All this is perfectly consistent with the sovereignty of the United States, with the powers of Congress, and with the right of a people to self-government.

Michigan was the first case in which there was any departure from this uniform rule of acting. Hers was a very slight departure from established usage. The Ordinance of 1787 secured to her the right of becoming a state when she should have 60,000 inhabitants. Owing to some neglect, Congress delayed taking the census. In the meantime her population increased until it clearly exceeded more than twice the number which entitled her to admission. At this stage she formed a constitution and government without the census being taken by the United States, and Congress received the admission without going through the formality of taking it, as there was no doubt she had more than a sufficient number to entitle her to admission. She was not admitted at the first session she applied owing to some difficulty respecting the boundary between her and Ohio. The great irregularity, as to her admission, took place at the next session, but on a point which can have no possible connection with the case of California.

The irregularity in all other cases that have since occurred is of a similar character. In all there existed territorial governments established by Congress, with officers appointed by the United States. In all the territorial government took the lead in calling conventions and fixing preliminaries preparatory to the formation of a constitution and admission into the Union. They all recognized the sovereignty of the United States and the authority of Congress over the territories; and wherever there was any departure from established usage, it was done on the presumed consent of Congress, and not in defiance of its authority, or the sovereignty of the United States over the territories. In this respect California stands alone, without usage or a single example to cover her case.

It belongs now, Senators, for you to decide what part you will act in reference to this unprecedented transaction. The Executive has laid the paper purporting to be the constitution of California before you, and asks you to admit her into the Union as a state; and the question is, will you or will you not admit her? It is a grave question, and there rests upon you a heavy responsibility. Much, very much, will depend upon your decision. If you admit her, you endorse and give your sanction to all that has been done. Are you prepared to do so? Are you prepared to surrender your power of legislation for the territories—a power expressly vested in Congress by the Constitution, as has been fully established? Can you, consistently with your oath to support the Constitution, surrender it? Are you prepared to admit that the inhabitants of the territories possess the sovereignty over them, and that any number, more or less, may claim any extent of territory they please, may form a constitution and government, and erect it into a state, without asking your permission? Are you prepared to surrender the sovereignty of the United States over whatever territory may hereafter be acquired to the first adventurers which may rush into it? Are you prepared to surrender virtually to the Executive department all the powers which you have heretofore exercised over the territories? If not, how can you, consistently with your duty and your oaths to support the Constitution, give your assent to the admission of California as a state under a pretended constitution and government?

Can you believe that the project of a constitution which they have adopted has the least validity? Can you believe that there is such a state in reality as the state of California? No; there is no such state. It has no legal or constitutional existence. It has no validity, and can have none without your sanction. How then can you admit it as a state when, according to the provision of the Constitution, your power is limited to admitting new *states*? That is, they must be states, existing states, independent of your sanction, before you can admit them. When you give your permission to the inhabitants of a territory to form a constitution and a state, the constitution and the state they form derive their authority from the people, not from you. The state before admitted is actually a state, and does not become so by the act of admission, as would be the case with California should you admit her contrary to constitutional provision and established usage heretofore.

The Senators on the other side of the chamber must permit me to make a few remarks in this connection particularly applicable to them, with the exception of a few Senators from the South sitting on that side of the chamber. When the Oregon question was before this body not two years since, you took (if I mistake not) universally the ground that Congress had the sole and absolute power of legislating for the territories. How then can you now, after the short interval which has elapsed, abandon the ground which you took, and thereby virtually admit that the power of legislating, instead of being in Congress, is in the inhabitants of the territories? How can you justify and sanction by your votes the acts of the Executive, which are in direct derogation of what you then contended for?

But to approach still nearer to the present time how can you, after condemning a little more than a year since the grounds taken by the party which you defeated at the last election, wheel around and support by your votes the grounds which, as explained recently on this floor by the candidate of the party at the last election, are identical with those on which the Executive has acted in reference to California? What are we to understand by all this? Must we conclude that there is no sincerity, no faith, in the acts and declarations of public men, and that all is mere acting or hollow profession? Or are we to conclude that the exclusion of the South from the territory acquired from Mexico is an object of so paramount a character in your estimation that right, justice, Constitution, and consistency must all yield when they stand in the way of our exclusion?

But it may be asked, what is to be done with California should she not be admitted? I answer, remand her back to the territorial condition, as was done in the case of Tennessee, in the early stage of the government. Congress, in her case, had established a territorial government in the usual form, with a governor, judges, and other officers appointed by the United States. She was entitled under the deed of cession to be admitted into the Union as a state as soon as she had sixty thousand inhabitants. The territorial government, believing it had that number, took a census, by which it appeared it exceeded it. She then formed a constitution as a state and applied for admission. Congress refused to admit her, on the ground that the census should be taken by the United States, and that Congress had not determined whether the territory should be formed into one or two states, as it was authorized to do, under the cession. She returned quietly to her territorial condition. An act was passed to take a census by the United States, providing that the territory should form one state. All afterwards was regularly conducted, and the territory admitted as a state in due form.

The irregularities in the case of California are immeasurably greater, and afford a much stronger reason for pursuing the same course. But it may be said, California may not submit. That is not probable; but if she should not, when she refuses it will then be the time for us to decide what is to be done.

Having now shown what cannot save the Union, I return to the question with which I commenced: how can the Union be saved? There is but one way by which it can with any certainty be saved, and that is a full and final settlement, on the principle of justice, of all the questions at issue between the two sections. The South asks for justice, simple justice, and less she ought not to take. She has no compromise to offer, but the Constitution; and no concession or surrender to make. She has already surrendered so much that she has little left to surrender. Such a settlement would go to the root of the evil, and remove all cause of discontent, and satisfy the South that she could remain honorably and safely in the Union; and thereby restore the harmony and fraternal feelings between the sections, which existed anterior to the Missouri agitation. Nothing else can, with any certainty, finally and forever settle the questions at issue, terminate agitation, and save the Union.

But can this be done? Yes, easily; not by the weaker party, for it can of itself do nothing—not even protect itself—but by the stronger. The North has only to will it, to do justice and perform her duty, in order to accomplish it: to do justice by conceding to the South an equal right in the acquired territory, and to do her duty by causing the stipulations relative to fugitive slaves to be faithfully fulfilled: to cease the agitation of the slave question, and to provide for the insertion of a provision in the Constitution, by an amendment, which will restore to the South in substance the power she possessed of protecting herself, before the equilibrium between the sections was destroyed by the action of this government. There will be no difficulty in devising such a provision. One that will protect the South, and which, at the same time, will improve and strengthen the government, instead of impairing or weakening it.

But will the North agree to do this? It is for her to answer the question. But I will say, she cannot refuse, if she has half the love of the Union which she professes to have, or without justly exposing herself to the charge that her love of power and aggrandizement is far greater than her love of the Union. At all events, the responsibility of saving the Union is on the North and not the South. The South cannot save it by any act of hers, and the North may save it without any sacrifice whatever, unless to do justice and to perform her duties under the Constitution be regarded by her as a sacrifice.

It is time, Senators, that there should be an open and manly avowal on all sides, as to what is intended to be done. If the question is not now settled, it is uncertain whether it ever can hereafter be; and we, as the representatives of the states of this Union, regarded as governments, should come to a distinct understanding as to our respective views, in order to ascertain whether the great questions at issue between the two sections can be settled or not. If you, who represent the stronger portion, cannot agree to settle them on the broad principles of justice and duty, say so; and let the states we both represent agree to separate and part in peace. If you are unwilling we should part in peace, tell us so; and we shall know what to do, when you reduce the question to submission or resistance. If you remain silent, you then compel us to infer what you intend. In that case, California will become the test question. If you admit her, under all the difficulties that oppose her admission, you compel us to infer that you intend to exclude us from the whole of the acquired territories, with the intention of destroying irretrievably the equilibrium between the two sections. We would be blind not to perceive in that case that your real objects are power and aggrandizement, and infatuated not to act accordingly.

[Such are my opinions. It will be for the state I represent, and the other Southern states, to determine what will be their course. One thing they may be assured of, that they must all share a common fate, and that their security depends upon common and united action in the contingency presented.][2]

I have now, Senators, done my duty in expressing my opinions fully, freely, and candidly, on this solemn occasion. In doing so, I have been governed by the motives which have governed me in all the stages of the agitation of the slavery question since its commencement; and exerted myself to arrest it, with the intention of saving the Union, if it could be done; and, if it cannot, to save the section where it has pleased Providence to cast my lot, and which I sincerely believe has justice and the Constitution on its side. Having faithfully done my duty to the best of my ability, both to the Union and my section, throughout the whole of this agitation, I shall have the consolation, let what will come, that I am free from all responsibility.

---

[2] This passage was deleted in Calhoun's manuscript, and appears here in print for the first time.

Abraham
Lincoln
and
Stephen
═Douglas═══════════════════

THE DEBATE AT GALESBURG
OCTOBER 7, 1858

Introduction

The Lincoln-Douglas Debates of 1858 are American classics in the field of public oratory and ideological battle. They constituted a turning point in the advance of national concern over the slavery crisis. The debates both reflected this concern and contributed materially to focusing and deepening it. Lincoln, indeed, keenly realized the critical value of a public forum in an election campaign for the education of the Northern masses on the slavery issue. The people of this country would owe him, even if he had never become President, an everlasting debt of gratitude for the tremendous effort that he made on their behalf during the debates.

In Illinois before the Civil War, U.S. Senators were elected by vote of the entire legislature in joint session. Stephen Douglas had been elected to the Senate for his first term in 1847, and was consequently in 1858 a candidate for a third term. He had been for many years a dominant figure in Illinois politics, and, since 1850, a national figure in the Democratic party. His presidential ambitions were great. One might even say that they were the motivating force in his life.

For such a man the development of the slavery crisis presented many difficulties, since it began to drive a wedge between the Northern and Southern wings of the Democratic party and to destroy the unity which Douglas relied upon to put him into the White House. In 1854 he had fathered the

Kansas-Nebraska Act through Congress as a compromise measure that would, it was hoped, confer equal benefits on both Northern and Southern interests in the party.

But the Kansas-Nebraska Act achieved precisely opposite results. It aroused a storm of opposition in the North, heightened the slavery crisis, and precipitated the very dissolution of the Democratic party that Douglas feared. He himself was accused of being a "doughface"—a man from the North who served Southern interests and, worse, held Southern principles. His political position in Illinois itself was menaced by the rapid growth of the Republican party which created a coalition with anti-Nebraska or bolting Democrats.

This new coalition showed its strength in the fall of 1854 by electing a majority of anti-Nebraska men to the Illinois legislature. The latter, in turn, elected an anti-Nebraska Democrat, Judge Trumbull, to be Douglas' partner as junior Senator to the United States Senate.

Abraham Lincoln was among the prominent leaders of the new Republican party in Illinois, and in 1854 had been his party's preferred candidate for the United States Senate. He and Douglas had known each other since youth; but Lincoln as a Whig was on the opposite side of the political fence and had, for the most part, lived his life in obscurity and very much in the shadow of his famous opponent. They met for the first time in public debate during the election campaign of 1854.

The debates of 1858 took place at a time of mounting excitement and sectional tension brought about by the struggles in Kansas and by the Supreme Court decision in the Dred Scott case. The Republican party had put forward its antislavery program in the national elections of 1856 and conducted a vigorous campaign that drew a million votes for Frémont. Douglas in 1858 was fighting for his political life against a formidable antislavery coalition that threatened totally to disrupt the Democratic party.

The joint debates resulted from a challenge which Lincoln, as his party's senatorial candidate, addressed to Douglas on July 24, 1858, in an effort to raise the campaign from the ordinary low level of personal recrimination to a discussion of fundamental political issues. The two men met seven times, speaking from platforms in widely separated parts of the state at Ottawa, Freeport, Jonesboro, Charleston, Galesburg, Quincy, and Alton.

It is doubtful whether in the whole history of American political campaigns public discussion has ever, before or since, been conducted upon so high an intellectual level. The discussions took place before huge audiences, as many as 12,000 people at one time and place. Verbatim reports carried the words of the speakers to vast numbers of readers throughout the country.

In the debates three speeches were made at each place, with Lincoln and Douglas alternately opening and closing, for a total of one and one-half hours for each man. The Galesburg encounter, which is reproduced below, was the fifth in the series of debates, and took place on October 7, 1858. It is noteworthy as underlining the rift between Douglas and the administration over the admission of Kansas to the Union; for a full exposition of the famous Popular Sovereignty doctrine; and for Lincoln's merciless exposition of the logical contradictions in his opponent's position.

The 1858 debates placed antagonistic and competing policies before the Northern section of the country. Was it necessary to call a halt to the further extension of slavery; or was slavery's continued expansion still compatible with the survival of the Union and the security of the non-slave section of the nation? This was the issue which the voters of Illinois, and, beyond them, the people of the North, were called upon to decide.

We should note that Lincoln adroitly side-stepped all issues save the central one of checking the advance of slavery. He employed extreme caution in discussing the question of civil rights and the assimilation of the free Negro into American society. This was a matter on which Northern opinion was confused and divided, and which it would take more time to settle. By concentrating on the question of checking the advance of slavery into the territories, Lincoln differentiated himself from the abolitionists and the radical wing of his own party.

THE DEBATE AT GALESBURG*

Mr. Douglas's Speech

Ladies and Gentlemen: Four years ago I appeared before the people of Knox County for the purpose of defending my political action upon the compromise measure of 1850 and the passage of the Kansas-Nebraska Bill. Those of you before me who were present then, will remember that I vindicated myself for supporting those two measures by the fact that they rested upon the great fundamental principle that the people of each state and each territory of this Union have the right, and ought to be permitted to exercise the right, of regulating their own domestic concerns in their own way, subject to no other limitation or restriction than that which the Constitution of the United States imposes upon them. I then called upon the people of Illinois to decide whether that principle of self-government was right or wrong. If it was and is right, then the compromise measures of 1850 were right, and consequently, the Kansas and Nebraska Bill, based upon the same principle, must necessarily have been right.

The Kansas and Nebraska Bill declared, in so many words, that it was the true intent and meaning of the act not to legislate slavery into any state or territory, nor to exclude it therefrom, but to leave the people thereof perfectly free to form and regulate their domestic institutions in their own way, subject only to the Constitution of the United States. For the last

---

*Source: Lincoln's speeches in the debates were reported by Robert Hitt, a shorthand stenographer, on behalf of the Chicago *Press and Tribune*. The rival Chicago *Times* retained the services of Henry Binmore to report the speeches of Douglas. Lincoln carefully gathered together his own and his opponent's remarks as printed in these two papers, and pasted them into a scrapbook. This compilation, with Lincoln's own editorial corrections, constituted the manuscript for the first edition of the debates. Published by Follett, Foster and Co., of Columbus, Ohio, in 1860, it provided the Republican presidential nominee with a campaign weapon of major significance.

The version of the Galesburg debate reproduced below is based upon the Lincoln scrapbook, now in the Library of Congress. Lincoln's directions for the deletion of all audience reaction and comment as reported by the press have been scrupulously followed, except where such audience comment resulted in an interchange with the speaker himself.

four years I have devoted all my energies, in private and public, to commend that principle to the American people. Whatever else may be said in condemnation or support of my political course, I apprehend that no honest man will doubt the fidelity with which, under all circumstances, I have stood by it.

During the last year a question arose in the Congress of the United States whether or not that principle would be violated by the admission of Kansas into the Union under the Lecompton constitution. In my opinion, the attempt to force Kansas in under that constitution was a gross violation of the principle enunciated in the compromise measures of 1850, and Kansas and Nebraska Bill of 1854, and therefore I led off in the fight against the Lecompton constitution, and conducted it until the effort to carry that constitution through Congress was abandoned. And I can appeal to all men, friends and foes, Democrats and Republicans, Northern men and Southern men, that during the whole of that fight I carried the banner of Popular Sovereignty aloft, and never allowed it to trail in the dust, or lowered my flag until victory perched upon our arms.

When the Lecompton constitution was defeated, the question arose in the minds of those who had advocated it, what they should next resort to in order to carry out their views. They devised a measure known as the English bill, and granted a general amnesty and political pardon to all men who had fought against the Lecompton constitution, provided they would support that bill. I for one did not choose to accept the pardon, or to avail myself of the amnesty granted on that condition. The fact that the supporters of Lecompton were willing to forgive all differences of opinion at that time in the event those who opposed it favored the English bill, was an admission they did not think that opposition to Lecompton impaired a man's standing in the Democratic party.

Now, the question arises, what was the English bill which certain men are now attempting to make a test of political orthodoxy in this country? It provided, in substance, that the Lecompton constitution should be sent back to the people of Kansas for their adoption or rejection, at an election which was held in August last, and in case they refused admission under it, that Kansas should be kept out of the Union until she had 93,420 inhabitants. I was in favor of sending the constitution back in order to enable the people to say whether or not it was their act and deed, and embodied their will; but the other proposition, that if they refused to come into the Union under it, they should be kept out until they had double or treble the population they then had, I never would sanction by my vote. The reason why I could not sanction it is to be found in the fact that by the English bill, if the people of Kansas had only agreed to become a slaveholding state under the Lecompton constitution, they could have done so with 35,000 people, but if they insisted on being a free state, as they had a right to do, then they were to be punished by being kept out of the Union until they had nearly three times that population. I then said in my place in the Senate, as I now say to you, that whenever Kansas has population enough for a slave state, she has population enough for a free state. I have never yet given a vote, and I never intend to record one, making an odious and unjust distinction between the different states of this Union. I hold it to be a fundamental principle in our republican form of government that all the states of this Union, old and new, free and slave, stand on an exact equality.

Equality among the different states is a cardinal principle on which all our institutions rest. Wherever, therefore, you make a discrimination saying to a slave state that it will be admitted with 35,000 inhabitants, and to a free state that it shall not be admitted until it has 93,000 or 100,000 inhabitants, you are throwing the whole weight of the Federal government into the scale in favor of one class of states against the other. Nor would I, on the other hand, any sooner sanction the doctrine that a free state could be admitted into the Union with 35,000 people, while a slave state was kept out until it had 93,000. I have always declared in the Senate my willingness, and I am willing now to adopt the rule, that no territory shall ever become a state until it has the requisite population for a member of Congress, according to the then existing ratio. But while I have always been, and am now, willing to adopt that general rule, I was not willing and would not consent to make an exception of Kansas, as a punishment for her obstinacy, in demanding the right to do as she pleased in the formation of her constitution. It is proper that I should remark here, that my opposition to the Lecompton constitution did not rest upon the peculiar position taken by Kansas on the subject of slavery. I held then, and hold now, that if the people of Kansas want a slave state, it is their right to make one, and be received into the Union under it; if, on the contrary, they want a free state, it is their right to have it, and no man should ever oppose their admission because they ask it under the one or the other. I hold to that great principle of self-government which asserts the right of every people to decide for themselves the nature and character of the domestic institutions and fundamental law under which they are to live.

The effort has been and is now being made in this state by certain postmasters and other Federal office-holders to make a test of faith on the support of the English bill. These men are now making speeches all over the state against me and in favor of Lincoln, either directly or indirectly, because I would not sanction a discrimination between slave and free states by voting for the English bill. But while that bill is made a test in Illinois for the purpose of breaking up the Democratic organization in this state, how is it in the other states? Go to Indiana, and there you find English himself, the author of the English bill, who is a candidate for re-election to Congress, has been forced by public opinion to abandon his own darling project, and to give a promise that he will vote for the admission of Kansas at once, whenever she forms a constitution in pursuance of law, and ratifies it by a majority vote of her people. Not only is this the case with English himself, but I am informed that every Democratic candidate for Congress in Indiana takes the same ground. Pass to Ohio, and there you find that Groesbeck, and Pendleton, and Cox, and all the other anti-Lecompton men who stood shoulder to shoulder with me against the Lecompton constitution, but voted for the English bill, now repudiate it and take the same ground that I do on that question. So it is with the Joneses and others of Pennsylvania, and so it is with every other Lecompton Democrat in the free states. They now abandon even the English bill, and come back to the true platform which I proclaimed at the time in the Senate, and upon which the democracy of Illinois now stands.

And yet, notwithstanding the fact that every Lecompton and anti-Lecompton Democrat in the free states has abandoned the English bill, you are told that it is to be made a test upon me, while the power and patronage of the government are all exerted to elect men to Congress in the other states who occupy the same position with reference to it that I do. It seems that my political offense consists in the fact that I first did not vote for the English bill, and thus pledge myself to keep Kansas out of the Union until she has a population of 93,420, and then return home, violate that pledge, repudiate the bill, and take the opposite ground. If I had done this, perhaps the administration would now be advocating my re-election, as it is that of the others who have pursued this course. I did not choose to give that pledge, for the reason that I did not intend to carry out that principle. I never will consent, for the sake of conciliating the frowns of power, to pledge myself to do that which I do not intend to perform. I now submit the question to you, as my constituency, whether I was not right, first, in resisting the adoption of the Lecompton constitution, and secondly, in resisting the English bill. I repeat that I opposed the Lecompton constitution because it was not the act and deed of the people of Kansas, and did not embody their will. I denied the right of any power on earth, under our system of government, to force a constitution on an unwilling people. There was a time when some men could pretend to believe that the Lecompton constitution embodied the will of the people of Kansas; but that time has passed. The question was referred to the people of Kansas under the English bill last August, and then, at a fair election, they rejected the Lecompton constitution by a vote of from eight to ten against it to one in its favor. Since it has been voted down by so overwhelming a majority no man can pretend that it was the act and deed of that people.

I submit the question to you whether or not, if it had not been for me, that constitution would have been crammed down the throats of the people of Kansas against their consent. While at least ninety-nine out of every hundred people here present agree that I was right in defeating that project, yet my enemies use the fact that I did defeat it by doing right, to break me down and put another man in the United States Senate in my place. The very men who acknowledge that I was right in defeating Lecompton, now form an alliance with Federal office-holders, professed Lecompton men, to defeat me, because I did right. My political opponent, Mr. Lincoln, has no hope on earth, and has never dreamed that he had a chance of success, were it not for the aid that he is receiving from Federal office-holders, who are using their influence and the patronage of the government against me in revenge for my having defeated the Lecompton constitution.

What do you Republicans think of a political organization that will try to make an unholy and unnatural combination with its professed foes to beat a man merely because he has done right? You know that such is the fact with regard to your own party. You know that the axe of decapitation is suspended over every man in office in Illinois, and the terror of proscription is threatened every Democrat by the present administration, unless he supports the Republican ticket in preference to my Democratic associates and myself. I could find an instance in the postmaster of the city of Galesburg, and in every other postmaster in this vicinity, all of whom have been stricken down simply because they discharged the duties of their offices honestly, and supported the regular Democratic ticket in this state in the right. The Republican party is availing itself of every unworthy means in the present contest to carry the election, because its leaders know that if they let this chance slip they will never have another, and their hopes of making this a Republican state will be blasted forever.

Now, let me ask you whether the country has any interest in sustaining this organization known as the Republican party? That party is unlike all other political organizations in this country. All other parties have been national in their character—have avowed their principles alike in the slave and free states, in Kentucky, as well as Illinois, in Louisiana as well as in Massachusetts. Such was the case with the old Whig party, and such was and is the case with the Democratic party. Whigs and Democrats could proclaim their principles boldly and fearlessly in the North and in the South, in the East and in the West, wherever the Constitution ruled, and the American flag waved over American soil.

But now you have a sectional organization, a party which appeals to the Northern section of the Union against the Southern, a party which appeals to Northern passion, Northern pride, Northern ambition, Northern prejudices, against Southern people, the Southern states, and Southern institutions. The leaders of that party hope that they will be able to unite the Northern states in one great sectional party; and inasmuch as the North is the strongest section, that they will thus be enabled to out-vote, conquer, govern and control the South. Hence you find that they now make speeches advocating principles and measures which cannot be defended in any slaveholding state of this Union. Is there a Republican residing in Galesburg who can travel into Kentucky and carry his principles with him across the Ohio? What Republican from Massachusetts can visit the Old Dominion without leaving his principles behind him when he crosses Mason and Dixon's line? Permit me to say to you in perfect good humor, but in all sincerity, that no political creed is sound which cannot be proclaimed fearlessly in every state of this Union where the Federal Constitution is the supreme law of the land.

Not only is this Republican party unable to proclaim its principles alike in the North and in the South, in the free states and in the slave states, but it cannot even proclaim them in the same forms and give them the same strength and meaning in all parts of the same state. My friend Lincoln finds it extremely difficult to manage a debate in the center part of the state, where there is a mixture of men from the North and the South. In the extreme northern part of Illinois he can proclaim as bold and radical abolitionism as ever Giddings, Lovejoy, or Garrison enunciated; but when he gets down a little farther south he claims that he is an old line Whig, a disciple of Henry Clay, and declares that he still adheres to the old line Whig creed, and has nothing whatever to do with abolitionism, or Negro equality, or Negro citizenship. I once before hinted this of Mr. Lincoln in a public speech, and at Charleston he defied me to show that there was any difference between his speeches in the North and in the South, and that they were not in strict harmony. I will now call your attention to two of them, and you can then say whether you would be apt to believe that the same man ever uttered both. In a speech in reply to me at Chicago in July last, Mr. Lincoln, in speaking of the equality of the Negro with the white man used the following language:

> "I should like to know if, taking this old Declaration of Independence, which declares that all men are equal upon principle, and making exceptions to it, where will it stop? If one man says it does not mean a Negro, why may not another man say it does not mean another man? If the Declaration is not the truth, let us get the statute book in which we find it, and tear it out. Who is so bold as to do it? If it is not true, let us tear it out."

You find that Mr. Lincoln there proposed that if the doctrine of the Declaration of Independence, declaring all men to be born equal, did not include the Negro and put him on an equality with the white man, that we should take the statute book and tear it out. He there took the ground that the Negro race is included in the Declaration of Independence as the equal of the white race, and that there could be no such thing as a distinction in the races, making one superior and the other inferior. I read now from the same speech:

> "My friends," he says, "I have detained you about as long as I desire to do, and I have only to say, let us discard all this quibbling about this man and the other man, this race and that race and the other race being inferior, and therefore they must be placed in an inferior position, discarding our standard that we have left us. Let us discard all these things, and unite as one people throughout this land, until we shall once more stand up declaring that all men are created equal." [*Cries of "that's right," etc., from the audience*]

Yes, I have no doubt that you think it is right; but the Lincoln men down in Coles, Tazewell, and Sangamon counties *do not* think it is right. In the conclusion of the same speech, talking to the Chicago abolitionists, he said: "I leave you, hoping that the lamp of liberty will burn in your bosoms until there shall no longer be a doubt that all men are created free and equal." Well, you say good to that, and you are going to vote for Lincoln because he holds that doctrine. I will not blame you for supporting him on that ground; but I will show you, in immediate contrast with that doctrine, what Mr. Lincoln said down in Egypt in order to get votes in that locality, where they do not hold to such a doctrine. In a joint discussion between Mr. Lincoln and myself, at Charleston, I think, on the 18th of last month, Mr. Lincoln, referring to this subject, used the following language:

> "I will say, then, that I am not, nor ever have been, in favor of bringing about in any way the social and political equality of the white and black races; that I am not, nor ever have been, in favor of making voters of the free Negroes, or jurors, or qualifying them to hold office, or having them to marry with white people. I will say, in addition, that there is a physical difference between the white and black races which, I suppose, will forever forbid the two races living together

upon terms of social and political equality; and inasmuch as they cannot so live, that while they do remain together there must be the position of superior and inferior, that I, as much as any other man, am in favor of the superior position being assigned to the white man."

Fellow-citizens, here you find men hurrahing for Lincoln, and saying that he did right, when in one part of the state he stood up for Negro equality; and in another part, for political effect, discarded the doctrine, and declared that there always must be a superior and inferior race. Abolitionists up North are expected and required to vote for Lincoln because he goes for the equality of the races, holding that by the Declaration of Independence the white man and the Negro were created equal, and endowed by the divine law with that equality; and down South he tells the Old Whigs, the Kentuckians, Virginians, and Tennesseeans, that there is a physical difference in the races, making one superior and the other inferior, and that he is in favor of maintaining the superiority of the white race over the Negro.

Now, how can you reconcile those two positions of Mr. Lincoln? He is to be voted for in the South as a proslavery man, and he is to be voted for in the North as an abolitionist. Up here he thinks it is all nonsense to talk about a difference between the races, and says, that we must "discard all quibbling about this race and that race and the other race being inferior, and therefore they must be placed in an inferior position." Down South he makes this "quibble" about this race and that race and the other race being inferior as the creed of his party, and declares that the Negro can never be elevated to the position of the white man. You find that his political meetings are called by different names in different counties in the state. Here they are called Republican meetings; but in old Tazewell, where Lincoln made a speech last Tuesday, he did not address a *Republican* meeting, but "a grand rally of the *Lincoln men*." There are very few Republicans there, because Tazewell County is filled with old Virginians and Kentuckians, all of whom are Whigs or Democrats; and if Mr. Lincoln had called an abolition or Republican meeting there, he would not get many votes.

Go down into Egypt, and you find that he and his party are operating under an alias there, which his friend Trumbull has given them in order that they may cheat the people. When I was down in Monroe County a few weeks ago, addressing the people, I saw handbills posted announcing that Mr. Trumbull was going to speak in behalf of Lincoln and what do you think the name of his party was there? Why the *"Free Democracy."* Mr. Trumbull and Mr. Jehu Baker were announced to address the Free Democracy of Monroe County, and the bill was signed, "Many Free Democrats." The reason that Lincoln and his party adopted the name of "Free Democracy" down there was because Monroe County has always been an old-fashioned Democratic county, and hence it was necessary to make the people believe that they were Democrats, sympathized with them, and were fighting for Lincoln as Democrats.

Come up to Springfield, where Lincoln now lives and always has lived, and you find that the Convention of his party which assembled to nominate candidates for legislature, who are expected to vote for him if elected, dare not adopt the name of Republican, but assembled under the title of "all opposed to the Democracy." Thus you find that Mr. Lincoln's creed cannot travel through even one half of the counties of this state, but that it changes its hues and becomes lighter and lighter as it travels from the extreme north, until it is nearly white when it reaches the extreme south end of the state.

I ask you, my friends, why cannot Republicans avow their principles alike everywhere? I would despise myself if I thought that I was procuring your votes by concealing my opinions, and by avowing one set of principles in one part of the state, and a different set in another part. If I do not truly and honorably represent your feelings and principles, then I ought not to be your Senator; and I will never conceal my opinions, or modify or change them a hair's breadth, in order to get votes. I will tell you that this Chicago doctrine of Lincoln's—declaring that the Negro and the white man are made equal by the Declaration of Independence and by Divine Providence—is a monstrous heresy. The signers of the Declaration of Independence never dreamed of the Negro when they were writing that document. They referred to white men, to men of European birth and European descent, when they declared the equality of all men. I see a gentleman there in the crowd shaking his head. Let me remind him that when Thomas Jefferson wrote that document, he was the owner, and so continued until his death, of a large number of slaves. Did he intend to say in that Declaration that his Negro slaves, which he held and treated as property, were created his equals by divine law, and that he was violating the law of God every day of his life by holding them as slaves? It must be borne in mind that when that Declaration was put forth, every one of the thirteen colonies were slaveholding colonies, and every man who signed that instrument represented a slaveholding constituency. Recollect, also, that no one of them emancipated his slaves, much less put them on an equality with himself, after he signed the Declaration. On the contrary, they all continued to hold their Negroes as slaves during the Revolutionary War. Now, do you believe—are you willing to have it said— that every man who signed the Declaration of Independence declared the Negro his equal, and then was hypocrite enough to continue to hold him as a slave, in violation of what he believed to be the divine law? And yet when you say that the Declaration of Independence includes the Negro you charge the signers of it with hypocrisy.

I say to you frankly, that in my opinion this government was made by our fathers on the white basis. It was made by white men for the benefit of white men and their posterity forever, and was intended to be administered by white men in all time to come. But while I hold that under our Constitution and political system the Negro is not a citizen, cannot be a citizen, and ought not to be a citizen, it does not follow by any means that he should be a slave. On the contrary, it does follow that the Negro, as an inferior race, ought to possess every right, every privilege, every immunity, which he can safely exercise, consistent with the safety of the society in which he lives. Humanity requires, and Christianity commands, that you shall extend to every inferior being, and every dependent being, all the privileges, immunities, and advantages which can be granted to them, consistent with the safety of society. If you ask me the nature and extent of these privileges, I answer that that is a question which the people of each state must decide for themselves. Illinois has decided that question for herself. We have said that in this state the Negro shall not be a slave, nor shall he be a citizen. Kentucky holds a different doctrine. New York holds one different from either, and Maine one different from all. Virginia, in her policy on this question, differs in many respects from the others, and so on, until there are hardly two states whose policy is exactly alike in regard to the relation of the white man and the Negro. Nor can you reconcile them and make them alike. Each state must do as it pleases. Illinois had as much right to adopt the policy which we have on that subject as Kentucky had to adopt a different policy. The great principle of this government is, that each state has the right to do as it pleases on all these questions, and no other state or power on earth has the right to interfere with us, or complain of us merely because our system differs from theirs. In the compromise measures of 1850, Mr. Clay declared that this great principle ought to exist in the territories as well as in the states, and I reasserted his doctrine in the Kansas and Nebraska Bill in 1854.

But Mr. Lincoln cannot be made to understand, and those who are determined to vote for him, no matter whether he is a proslavery man in the south and a Negro equality advocate in the north, cannot be made to understand how it is that in a territory the people can do as they please on the slavery question under the Dred Scott decision. Let us see whether I cannot explain it to the satisfaction of all impartial men. Chief Justice Taney has said, in his opinion in the Dred Scott case, that a Negro slave, being property, stands on an equal footing with other property, and that the owner may carry them into United States territory the same as he does other property. Suppose any two of you, neighbors, should conclude to go to Kansas, one carrying $100,000 worth of Negro slaves, and the other $100,000 worth of mixed merchandise, including quantities of liquors. You both agree that under that decision you may carry your property to Kansas; but when you get it there, the merchant who is possessed of the liquors is met by the Maine liquor law, which prohibits the sale or use of his property, and the owner of the slaves is met by equally unfriendly legislation, which makes his property worthless after he gets it there. What is the right to carry your property into the territory worth to either, when unfriendly legislation in the territory renders it worthless after you get it there? The slaveholder when he gets his slaves there finds that there is no local law to protect him in holding them, no slave code, no police regulation maintaining and supporting him in his right, and he discovers at once that the absence of such friendly legislation excludes his property from the territory just as irresistibly as if there was a positive constitutional prohibition excluding it.

Thus you find it is with any kind of property in a territory:

it depends for its protection on the local and municipal law. If the people of a territory want slavery, they make friendly legislation to introduce it; but if they do not want it, they withhold all protection from it, and then it cannot exist there. Such was the view taken on the subject by different Southern men when the Kansas and Nebraska Bill passed. See the speech of Mr. Orr, of South Carolina, the present speaker of the House of Representatives of Congress, made at that time, and there you will find this whole doctrine argued out at full length. Read the speeches of other Southern Congressmen, Senators and Representatives, made in 1854, and you will find that they took the same view of the subject as Mr. Orr—that slavery could never be forced on a people who did not want it. I hold that in this country there is no power on the face of the globe that can force any institution on an unwilling people. The great fundamental principle of our government is that the people of each state and each territory shall be left perfectly free to decide for themselves what shall be the nature and character of their institutions.

When this government was made, it was based on that principle. At the time of its formation there were twelve slaveholding states and one free state in this Union. Suppose this doctrine of Mr. Lincoln and the Republicans, of uniformity of laws of all the states on the subject of slavery, had prevailed; suppose Mr. Lincoln himself had been a member of the Convention which framed the Constitution; and that he had risen in that august body, and, addressing the father of his country, had said as he did at Springfield:

"A house divided against itself cannot stand. I believe this government cannot endure permanently, half slave and half free. I do not expect the Union to be dissolved; I do not expect the house to fall; but I do expect it will cease to be divided. It will become all one thing or all the other."

What do you think would have been the result? Suppose he had made that Convention believe that doctrine, and they had acted upon it, what do you think would have been the result? Do you believe that the one free state would have outvoted the twelve slaveholding states, and thus abolished slavery? On the contrary, would not the twelve slaveholding states have outvoted the one free state, and under his doctrine have fastened slavery by an irrevocable constitutional provision upon every inch of American Republic?

Thus you see that the doctrine he now advocates, if proclaimed at the beginning of the government, would have established slavery everywhere throughout the American continent; and are you willing, now that we have the majority section, to exercise a power which we never would have submitted to when we were in the minority? If the Southern states had attempted to control our institutions, and make the states all slave, when they had the power, I ask, would you have submitted to it? If you would not, are you willing, now that we have become the strongest under that great principle of self-government that allows each state to do as it pleases, to attempt to control the Southern institutions? Then, my friends, I say to you that there is but one path of peace in this Republic, and that is to administer this government as our fathers made it, divided into free and slave states, allowing each state to decide for itself whether it wants slavery or not. If Illinois will settle the slavery question for herself, mind her own business and let her neighbors alone, we will be at peace with Kentucky and every other Southern state. If every other state in the Union will do the same, there will be peace between the North and the South, and in the whole Union.

I am told that my time has expired.

Mr. Lincoln's Reply

My Fellow-Citizens: A very large portion of the speech which Judge Douglas has addressed to you has previously been delivered and put in print [*laughter*]. I do not mean that for a hit upon the Judge at all [*renewed laughter*]. If I had not been interrupted, I was going to say that such an answer as I was able to make to a very large portion of it, had already been more than once made and published. There has been an opportunity afforded to the public to see our respective views upon the topics discussed in a large portion of the speech which he has just delivered. I make these remarks for the purpose of excusing myself for not passing over the entire ground that the Judge has traversed. I however desire to take up some of the points that he has attended to, and ask your attention to them, and I shall follow him backwards upon some notes which I have taken, reversing the order, by beginning where he concluded.

The Judge has alluded to the Declaration of Independence, and insisted that Negroes are not included in that Declaration; and that it is a slander upon the framers of that instrument to suppose that Negroes were meant therein; and he asks you: is it possible to believe that Mr. Jefferson, who penned the immortal paper, could have supposed himself applying the language of that instrument to the Negro race, and yet held a portion of that race in slavery? Would he not at once have freed them?

I only have to remark upon this part of the Judge's speech (and that too, very briefly, for I shall not detain myself, or you, upon that point for any great length of time), that I believe the entire records of the world, from the date of the Declaration of Independence up to within three years ago, may be searched in vain for one single affirmation, from one single man, that the Negro was not included in the Declaration of Independence. I think I may defy Judge Douglas to show that he ever said so, that Washington ever said so, that any President ever said so, that any member of Congress ever said so, or that any living man upon the whole earth ever said so, until the necessities of the present policy of the Democratic party, in regard to slavery, had to invent that affirmation. And I will remind Judge Douglas and this audience that while Mr. Jefferson was the owner of slaves, as undoubtedly he was, in speaking upon this very subject, he used the strong language that "he trembled for his country when he remembered that God was just"; and I will offer the highest premium in my power to Judge Douglas if he will show that he, in all his life, ever uttered a sentiment at all akin to that of Jefferson.

The next thing to which I will ask your attention is the Judge's comments upon the fact, as he assumes it to be, that we cannot call our public meetings as Republican meetings; and he instances Tazewell County as one of the places where the friends of Lincoln have called a public meeting and have not dared to name it a Republican meeting. He instances Monroe County as another, where Judge Trumbull and Jehu Baker addressed the persons whom the Judge assumes to be the friends of Lincoln, calling them the "Free Democracy." I have the honor to inform Judge Douglas that he spoke in

that very County of Tazewell last Saturday, and I was there
on Tuesday last; and when he spoke there, he spoke under a
call not venturing to use the word "Democrat." [*Turning to
Judge Douglas*] What do you think of this?

So, again, there is another thing to which I would ask the
Judge's attention upon this subject. In the contest of 1856 his
party delighted to call themselves together as the "National
Democracy"; but now, if there should be a notice put up
anywhere for a meeting of the "National Democracy," Judge
Douglas and his friends would not come. They would not
suppose themselves invited. They would understand that it
was a call for those hateful postmasters whom he talks about.

Now a few words in regard to these extracts from speeches
of mine which Judge Douglas has read to you, and which he
supposes are in very great contrast to each other. Those
speeches have been before the public for a considerable time,
and if they have any inconsistency in them, if there is any
conflict in them, the public have been able to detect it. When
the Judge says, in speaking on this subject, that I make
speeches of one sort for the people of the Northern end of
the state, and a different sort for the Southern people, he
assumes that I do not understand that my speeches will be
put in print and read North and South. I knew all the while
that the speech that I made at Chicago, and the one I made
at Jonesboro, and the one at Charleston, would all be put in
print, and all the reading and intelligent men in the community would see them and know all about my opinions. And I
have not supposed, and do not now suppose, that there is any
conflict whatever between them.

But the Judge will have it that if we do not confess that
there is a sort of inequality between the white and the black
races which justifies us in making them slaves, we must then
insist that there is a degree of equality that requires us to
make them our wives. Now, I have all the while taken a broad
distinction in regard to that matter; and that is all there is in
these different speeches which he arrays here; and the entire
reading of either of the speeches will show that that distinction was made. Perhaps by taking two parts of the same
speech he could have got up as much of a conflict as the one
he has found. I have all the while maintained, that in so far
as it should be insisted that there was an equality between
the white and black races that should produce a perfect

social and political equality, it was an impossibility. This you have seen in my printed speeches, and with it I have said that in their right to "life, liberty, and the pursuit of happiness," as proclaimed in that old Declaration, the inferior races are our equals. And these declarations I have constantly made in reference to the abstract moral question, to contemplate and consider when we are legislating about any new country which is not already cursed with the actual presence of the evil—slavery.

I have never manifested any impatience with the necessities that spring from the actual presence of black people amongst us, and the actual existence of slavery amongst us where it does already exist; but I have insisted that, in legislating for new countries where it does not exist, there is no just rule other than of moral and abstract right! With reference to those new countries, those maxims as to the right of people to "life, liberty, and the pursuit of happiness," were the just rules to be constantly referred to. There is no misunderstanding this, except by men interested to misunderstand it. I take it that I have to address an intelligent and reading community, who will pursue what I say, weigh it, and then judge whether I advance improper or unsound views, or whether I advance hypocritical, and deceptive, and contrary views in different portions of the country. I believe myself to be guilty of no such thing as the latter, though, of course, I cannot claim that I am entirely free from all error in the opinions I advance.

The Judge has also detained us a while in regard to the distinction between his party and our party. His he assumes to be a national party—ours a sectional one. He does this in asking the question whether this country has any interest in the maintenance of the Republican party? He assumes that our party is altogether sectional—that the party to which he adheres is national; and the argument is, that no party can be a rightful party—can be based upon rightful principles—unless it can announce its principles everywhere. I presume that Judge Douglas could not go into Russia and announce the doctrine of our national democracy; he could not denounce the doctrine of kings and emperors and monarchies in Russia; and it may be true of this country that in some places we may not be able to proclaim a doctrine as clearly true as the truth of democracy, because there is a section so directly opposed to it that they will not tolerate us in doing so. Is it the true test of the soundness of a doctrine that in some places people won't let you proclaim it? Is that the way to test the truth of any doctrine? Why, I understood that at one time the people of Chicago would not let Judge Douglas preach a certain favorite doctrine of his. I commend to his consideration the question, whether he takes that as a test of the unsoundness of what he wanted to preach?

There is another thing to which I wish to ask attention for a little while on this occasion. What has always been the evidence brought forward to prove that the Republican party is a sectional party? The main one was that in the Southern portion of the Union the people did not let the Republicans proclaim their doctrine amongst them. That has been the main evidence brought forward—that they had no supporters, or substantially none, in the slave states. The South have not taken hold of our principles as we announce them; nor does Judge Douglas now grapple with those principles.

We have a Republican state platform, laid down in Springfield in June last, stating our position all the way through the questions before the country. We are now far advanced in this canvass. Judge Douglas and I have made perhaps forty speeches apiece, and we have now for the fifth time met face to face in debate, and up to this day I have not found either Judge Douglas or any friend of his taking hold of the Republican platform, or laying his finger upon anything in it that is wrong. I ask you to recollect that Judge Douglas turns away from the platform of principles to the fact that he can find people somewhere who will not allow us to announce those principles. If he had great confidence that our principles were wrong, he would take hold of them and demonstrate them to be wrong. But he does not do so. The only evidence he has of their being wrong is in the fact that there are people who won't allow us to preach them. I ask again, is that the way to test the soundness of a doctrine?

I ask his attention also to the fact that by the rule of nationality he is himself fast becoming sectional. I ask his attention to the fact that his speeches would not go as current now south of the Ohio River as they have formerly gone there. I ask his attention to the fact that he felicitates himself today that all the Democrats of the free states are agreeing with him, while he omits to tell us that the Democrats of any slave state agree with him. If he has not thought of this, I commend to his consideration the evidence in his own declaration, on this day, of his becoming sectional too. I see it rapidly approaching. Whatever may be the result of this ephemeral contest between Judge Douglas and myself, I see the day rapidly approaching when his pill of sectionalism, which he has been thrusting down the throats of Republicans for years past, will be crowded down his own throat.

Now, in regard to what Judge Douglas said (in the beginning of his speech) about the Compromise of 1850 containing the principle of the Nebraska Bill, although I have often presented my views upon that subject, yet as I have not done so in this canvass, I will, if you please, detain you a little with them. I have always maintained, so far as I was able, that there was nothing of the principle of the Nebraska Bill in the Compromise of 1850 at all—nothing whatever. Where can you find the principle of the Nebraska Bill in that compromise? If anywhere, in the two pieces of the compromise organizing the territories of New Mexico and Utah. It was expressly provided in these two acts that when they came to be admitted into the Union, they should be admitted with or without slavery, as they should choose, by their own constitutions. Nothing was said in either of these acts as to what was to be done in relation to slavery during the territorial existence of those territories, while Henry Clay constantly made the declaration (Judge Douglas recognizing him as a leader) that, in his opinion, the old Mexican laws would control that question during the territorial existence, and that these old Mexican laws excluded slavery.

How can that be used as a principle for declaring that during the territorial existence as well as at the time of framing the constitution, the people, if you please, might have slaves if they wanted them? I am not discussing the question whether it is right or wrong; but how are the New Mexican and Utah laws patterns for the Nebraska Bill? I maintain that the organization of Utah and New Mexico *did not* establish a general principle at all. It had no feature of establishing a general principle. The Acts to which I have referred were a part of a general system of compromises. They did not lay down what was proposed as a regular policy for the territories, only an agreement in this particular case to do in that way, because other things were done that were to be a compensation for it. They were allowed to come in in that shape, because in another way it was paid for—considering that as a part of that system of measures called the Compromise of 1850, which finally included half-a-dozen acts. It included the admission of California as a free state, which was kept out of the Union for half a year because it had formed a free constitution. It included the settlement of the boundary of Texas, which had been undefined before, which was in itself a slavery question; for if you pushed the line farther west, you made Texas larger, and made more slave territory; while, if you drew the line toward the east, you narrowed the boundary and diminished the domain of slavery, and by so much increased free territory. It included the abolition of the slave trade in the District of Columbia. It included the passage of a new fugitive slave law.

All these things were put together, and though passed in separate acts, were, nevertheless, in legislation (as the speeches of the time will show) made to depend upon each other. Each got votes, with the understanding that the other measures were to pass, and by this system of compromise, in that series of measures, those two bills—the New Mexico and Utah bills—were passed: and I say for that reason they could not be taken as models, framed upon their own intrinsic principle, for all future territories. And I have the evidence of this in the fact that Judge Douglas, a year afterward, or more than a year afterward, perhaps, when he first introduced bills for the purpose of framing new territories, did not attempt to follow these bills of New Mexico and Utah; and even when he introduced this Nebraska Bill I think you will discover that he did not exactly follow them. But I do not wish to dwell at great length upon this branch of the discussion. My own opinion is, that a thorough investigation will show most plainly that the New Mexico and Utah bills were part of a system of compromise, and not designed as patterns for future territorial legislation; and that this Nebraska Bill did not follow them as a pattern at all.

The Judge tells, in proceeding, that he is opposed to making any odious distinction between free and slave states. I am altogether unaware that the Republicans are in favor of making any odious distinctions between the free and slave states. But there is still a difference, I think, between Judge Douglas and the Republicans in this. I suppose that the real difference between Judge Douglas and his friends, and the

Republicans on the contrary is, that the Judge is not in favor of making any difference between slavery and liberty, that he is in favor of eradicating, of pressing out of view, the questions of preference in this country for free or slave institutions; and consequently every sentiment he utters discards the idea that there is any wrong in slavery. Everything that emanates from him or his coadjutors in their course of policy carefully excludes the thought that there is anything wrong in slavery. All their arguments, if you will consider them, will be seen to exclude the thought that there is anything whatever wrong in slavery. If you will take the Judge's speeches, and select the short and pointed sentences expressed by him—as his declaration that he "don't care whether slavery is voted up or down," you will see at once that this is perfectly logical, if you do not admit that slavery is wrong. If you do admit that it is wrong, Judge Douglas cannot logically say he don't care whether a wrong is voted up or down.

Judge Douglas declares that if any community want slavery, they have a right to it. He can say that logically, if he says that there is no wrong in slavery; but if you admit that there is a wrong in it, he cannot logically say that anybody has a right to do wrong. He insists that, upon the score of equality, the owners of slaves and owners of property—of horses and every other sort of property—should be alike, and hold them alike in a new territory. That is perfectly logical if the two species of property are alike and are equally founded in right. But if you admit that one of them is wrong, you cannot institute any equality between right and wrong. And from this difference of sentiment—the belief on the part of one that the institution is wrong, and a policy springing from that belief which looks to the arrest of the enlargement of that wrong; and this other sentiment, that it is no wrong, and a policy sprung from that sentiment, which will tolerate no idea of preventing that wrong from growing larger, and looks to there never being an end of it through all the existence of things—arises the real difference between Judge Douglas and his friends on the one hand, and the Republicans on the other.

Now, I confess myself as belonging to that class in the country who contemplate slavery as moral, social, and political evil, having due regard for its actual existence amongst us and the difficulties of getting rid of it in any satisfactory way, and to all the constitutional obligations which have been thrown about it; but, nevertheless, desire a policy that looks to the prevention of it as a wrong, and looks hopefully to the time when as a wrong it may come to an end.

Judge Douglas has again, for I believe the fifth time, if not the seventh, in my presence, reiterated his charge of a conspiracy or combination between the National Democrats and Republicans. What evidence Judge Douglas has upon this subject I know not, inasmuch as he never favors us with any.

I have said upon a former occasion, and I do not choose to suppress it now, that I have no objection to the division in the Judge's party. He got it up himself. It was all his and their work. He had, I think, a great deal more to do with the steps that led to the Lecompton constitution than Mr. Buchanan had; though at last, when they reached it, they quarreled over it, and their friends divided upon it. I am very free to confess to Judge Douglas that I have no objection to the division; but I defy the Judge to show any evidence that I have in any way promoted that division, unless he insists on being a witness himself in merely saying so. I can give all fair friends of Judge Douglas here to understand exactly the view that Republicans take in regard to that division. Don't you remember how two years ago the opponents of the Democratic party were divided between Frémont and Fillmore? I guess you do. Any Democrat who remembers that division will remember also that he was at the time very glad of it, and then he will be able to see all there is between the National Democrats and the Republicans. What we now think of the two divisions of Democrats, you then thought of the Frémont and Fillmore divisions. That is all there is of it.

But if the Judge continues to put forward the declaration that there is an unholy and unnatural alliance between the Republican and the National Democrats, I now want to enter my protest against receiving him as an entirely competent witness upon that subject. I want to call to the Judge's attention an attack he made upon me in the first one of these debates, at Ottawa, on the 21st of August. In order to fix extreme abolitionism upon me, Judge Douglas read a set of resolutions which he declared had been passed by a Republican state convention, in October, 1854, at Springfield, Illinois, and he declared I had taken part in that convention. It turned out that although a few men calling themselves an anti-Nebraska state convention had sat at Springfield about that time, yet neither did I take any part in it, nor did it pass the resolutions or any such resolutions as Judge Douglas read. So apparent had it become that the resolutions which he read had not been passed at Springfield at all, nor by a state convention in which I had taken part, that seven days afterward, at Freeport, Judge Douglas declared that he had been misled by Charles H. Lanphier, editor of the *State Register*, and Thomas L. Harris, member of Congress in that district, and he promised in that speech that when he went to Springfield he would investigate the matter. Since then Judge Douglas has been to Springfield, and I presume has made the investigation; but a month has passed since he has been there, and, so far as I know, he has made no report of the result of his investigation. I have waited, as I think, a sufficient time for the report of that investigation, and I have some curiosity to see and hear it. A fraud, an absolute forgery was committed, and the perpetuation of it was traced to the three—Lanphier, Harris, and Douglas. Whether it can be narrowed in any way so as to exonerate any one of them, is what Judge Douglas's report would probably show.

It is true that the set of resolutions read by Judge Douglas were published in the *Illinois State Register* on the 16th of October, 1854, as being the resolutions of an anti-Nebraska convention which had sat in that same month of October, at Springfield. But it is also true that the publication in the *Register* was a forgery then, and the question is still behind, which of the three, if not all of them, committed that forgery? The idea that it was done by mistake, is absurd. The article in the *Illinois State Register* contains part of the real proceedings of the Springfield convention, showing that the writer of the article had the real proceedings before him, and purposely threw out the genuine resolutions passed by the convention, and fraudulently substituted the others. Lanphier then, as now, was the editor of the *Register*, so that there seems to be but little room for his escape. But then it is to be borne in mind that Lanphier had less interest in the object of that forgery than either of the other two. The main object of that forgery at that time was to beat Yates and elect Harris to Congress, and that object was known to be exceedingly dear to Judge Douglas at that time. Harris and Douglas were both in Springfield when the convention was in session, and although they both left before the fraud appeared in the

Register, subsequent events show that they have both had their eyes fixed upon that convention.

The fraud having been apparently successful upon the occasion, both Harris and Douglas have more than once since then been attempting to put it to new uses. As the fisherman's wife, whose drowned husband was brought home with his body full of eels, said when she was asked, "What was to be done with him?" *"Take the eels out and set him again,"* so Harris and Douglas have shown a disposition to take the eels out of that fraud by which they gained Harris's election, and set the fraud again more than once. On the 9th of July, 1856, Douglas attempted a repetition of it upon Trumbull on the floor of the Senate of the United States, as will appear from the appendix to the *Congressional Globe* of that date.

On the 9th of August, Harris attempted it again upon Norton in the House of Representatives, as will appear by the same document—the appendix to the *Congressional Globe* of that date. On the 21st of August last, all three—Lanphier, Douglas and Harris—reattempted it upon me at Ottawa. It has been clung to and played out again and again as an exceedingly high trump by this blessed trio. And now that it has been discovered publicly to be a fraud, we find that Judge Douglas manifests no surprise at it at all. He makes no complaint of Lanphier, who must have known it to be a fraud from the beginning. He, Lanphier, and Harris are just as cozy now, and just as active in the concoction of new schemes as they were before the general discovery of this fraud. Now, all this is very natural if they are all alike guilty in that fraud, and it is very unnnatural if any one of them is innocent. Lanphier perhaps insists that the rule of honor among thieves does not quite require him to take all upon himself, and consequently my friend Judge Douglas finds it difficult to make a satisfactory report upon his investigation. But meanwhile the three are agreed that each is *"a most honorable man."*

Judge Douglas requires an indorsement of his truth and honor by a re-election to the United States Senate, and he makes and reports against me and against Judge Trumbull, day after day, charges which we know to be utterly untrue, without for a moment seeming to think that this one unexplained fraud, which he promised to investigate, will be the least drawback to his claim to belief. Harris ditto. He asks a re-election to the lower house of Congress without seeming to remember at all that he is involved in this dishonorable fraud! The *Illinois State Register*, edited by Lanphier, then, as now, the central organ of both Harris and Douglas, continues to din the public ear with these assertions, without seeming to suspect that these assertions are at all lacking in title to belief.

After all, the question still recurs upon us, how did that fraud originally get into the *State Register*? Lanphier, then, as now, was the editor of that paper. Lanphier knows. Lanphier cannot be ignorant of how and by whom it was originally concocted. Can he be induced to tell, or, if he has told, can Judge Douglas be induced to tell how it originally was concocted? It may be true that Lanphier insists that the two men for whose benefit it was originally devised, shall at least bear their share of it! How that is, I do not know, and while it remains unexplained, I hope to be pardoned if I insist that the mere fact of Judge Douglas making charges against Trumbull and myself is not quite sufficient evidence to establish them!

While we were at Freeport, in one of these joint discussions, I answered certain interrogatories which Judge Douglas had propounded to me, and then in turn propounded some to him, which he in a sort of way answered. The third one of these interrogatories I have with me and wish now to make some comments upon it. It was in these words:

"If the Supreme Court of the United States shall decide that the states cannot exclude slavery from their limits, are you in favor of acquiescing in, adhering to, and following such decision as a rule of political action?"

To this interrogatory Judge Douglas made no answer in any just sense of the word. He contented himself with sneering at the thought that it was possible for the Supreme Court ever to make such a decision. He sneered at me for propounding the interrogatory. I had not propounded it without some reflection, and I wish now to address to this audience some remarks upon it.

In the second clause of the sixth article, I believe it is, of the Constitution of the United States, we find the following language:

"This Constitution and the laws of the United States which shall be made in pursuance thereof; and all treaties made, or which shall be made, under the authority of the United States, shall be the supreme law of the land; and the judges in every state shall be bound thereby, anything in the Constitution or laws of any state to the contrary, notwithstanding."

The essence of the Dred Scott case is compressed into the sentence which I will now read: "Now, as we have already said in an earlier part of this opinion, upon a different point, the right of property in a slave is distinctly and expressly affirmed in the Constitution." I repeat it, *"the right of property in a slave is distinctly and expressly affirmed in the Constitution."*

What is it to be *"affirmed"* in the Constitution? Made firm in the Constitution—so made that it cannot be separated from the Constitution without breaking the Constitution; durable as the Constitution, and part of the Constitution. Now, remembering the provision of the Constitution which I have read; affirming that that instrument is the supreme law of the land; that the judges of every state shall be bound by it, any law or constitution of any state to the contrary notwithstanding; that the right of property in a slave is affirmed in that Constitution, is made, formed into, and cannot be separated from it without breaking it; durable as the instrument; part of the instrument—what follows as a short and even syllogistic argument from it? I think it follows, and I submit to the consideration of men capable of arguing, whether as I state it, in syllogistic form, the argument has any fault in it:

Nothing in the constitution or laws of any state can destroy a right distinctly and expressly affirmed in the Constitution of the United States.

The right of property in a slave is distinctly and expressly affirmed in the Constitution of the United States.

Therefore, nothing in the constitution or laws of any state can destroy the right of property in a slave.

I believe that no fault can be pointed out in that argument; assuming the truth of the premises, the conclusion, so far as I have capacity at all to understand it, follows inevitably. There is a fault in it I think, but the fault is not in the reasoning: the falsehood in fact is a fault of the premises.

I believe that the right of property in a slave *is not* distinctly and expressly affirmed in the Constitution, and Judge Douglas thinks it *is*. I believe that the Supreme Court and the advocates of that decision may search in vain for the place in the Constitution where the right of property in a slave is distinctly and expressly affirmed. I say, therefore, that I think one of the premises is not true in fact. But it is true with Judge Douglas. It is true with the Supreme Court who pronounced it. They are estopped from denying it, and being estopped from denying it, the conclusion follows that the Constitution of the United States being the supreme law, no constitution or law can interfere with it. It being affirmed in the decision that the right of property in a slave is distinctly and expressly affirmed in the Constitution, the conclusion inevitably follows that no state law or constitution can destroy that right.

I then say to Judge Douglas and to all others, that I think it will take a better answer than a sneer to show that those who have said that the right of property in a slave is distinctly and expressly affirmed in the Constitution, are not prepared to show that no constitution or law can destroy that right. I say I believe it will take a far better argument than a mere sneer to show to the minds of intelligent men that whoever has so said, is not prepared, whenever public sentiment is so far advanced as to justify it, to say the other. This is but an opinion, and the opinion of one very humble man; but it is my opinion that the Dred Scott decision, as it is, never would have been made in its present form if the party that made it had not been sustained previously by the elections. My own opinion is, that the new Dred Scott decision, deciding against the right of the people of the states to exclude slavery, will never be made, if that party is not sustained by the elections. I believe, further, that it is just as sure to be made as to-morrow is to come, if that party shall be sustained.

I have said, upon a former occasion, and I repeat it now, that the course of argument that Judge Douglas makes use of upon this subject (I charge not his motives in this), is preparing the public mind for that new Dred Scott decision. I have asked him again to point out to me the reasons for his firm adherence to the Dred Scott decision as it is. I have turned his attention to the fact that General Jackson differed with him in regard to the political obligation of a Supreme Court decision. I have asked his attention to the fact that Jefferson differed with him in regard to the political obligation of a Supreme Court decision. Jefferson said that "judges are as honest as other men, and not more so." And he said, substantially, that "whenever a free people should give up in absolute submission to any department of government, retaining for themselves no appeal from it, their liberties were gone." I have asked his attention to the fact that the Cincinnati platform upon which he says he stands, disregards a time-honored decision of the Supreme Court, in denying the power of Congress to establish a National Bank. I have asked his attention to the fact that he himself was one of the most active instruments at one time in breaking down the Supreme Court of the State of Illinois, because it had made a decision distasteful to him—a struggle ending in the remarkable circumstance of his sitting down as one of the new judges who were to overslaugh that decision—getting his title of judge in that very way.

So far in this controversy I can get no answer at all from Judge Douglas upon these subjects. Not one can I get from him, except that he swells himself up and says, "All of us who stand by the decision of the Supreme Court are the friends of the Constitution; all you fellows that dare question it in any way, are the enemies of the Constitution." Now, in this very devoted adherence to this decision, in opposition to all the great political leaders whom he has recognized as leaders, in opposition to his former self and history, there is something very marked. And the manner in which he adheres to it—not as being right upon the merits, as he conceives (because he did not discuss that at all), but as being absolutely obligatory upon every one, simply because of the source from whence it comes—as that which no man can gainsay, whatever it may be; this is another marked feature of his adherence to that decision. It marks it in this respect, that it commits him to the next decision whenever it comes, as being as obligatory as this one, since he does not investigate it, and won't inquire whether this opinion is right or wrong. So he takes the next one without inquiring whether *it* is right or wrong. He teaches men this doctrine, and in so doing prepares the public mind to take the next decision when it comes, without any inquiry.

In this I think I argue fairly (without questioning motives at all) that Judge Douglas is most ingeniously and powerfully preparing the public mind to take that decision when it comes; and not only so, but he is doing it in various other ways. In these general maxims about liberty, in his assertions that he "don't care whether slavery is voted up or voted down"; that "whoever wants slavery has a right to have it"; that "upon principles of equality it should be allowed to go everywhere"; that "there is no inconsistency between free and slave institutions"—in this he is also preparing (whether purposely or not) the way for making the institution of slavery national! I repeat again, for I wish no misunderstanding, that I do not charge that he means it so; but I call upon your minds to inquire, if you were going to get the best instrument you could, and then set it to work in the most ingenious way, to prepare the public mind for this movement, operating in the free states, where there is now an abhorrence of the institution of slavery, could you find an instrument so capable of doing it as Judge Douglas, or one employed in so apt a way to do it?

I have said once before, and I will repeat it now, that Mr. Clay, when he was once answering an objection to the Colonization Society, that it had a tendency to the ultimate emancipation of the slaves, said that "those who would repress all tendencies to liberty and ultimate emancipation must do more than put down the benevolent efforts of the Colonization Society—they must go back to the era of our liberty and independence, and muzzle the cannon that thunders its annual joyous return; they must blot out the moral lights around us; they must penetrate the human soul, and eradicate the light of reason and the love of liberty!" And I do think—I repeat, though I said it on a former occasion—that Judge Douglas and whoever, like him, teaches that the Negro has no share, humble though it may be, in the Declaration of Independence, is going back to the era of our liberty and Independence, and, so far as in him lies, muzzling the cannon that thunders its annual joyous return; that he is blowing out the moral lights around us, when he contends that whoever wants slaves has a right to hold them; that he is penetrating, so far as lies in his power, the human soul, and eradicating the light of reason and the love of liberty, when he is in every possible way preparing the public mind, by his vast influence, for making the institution of slavery perpetual and national.

There is, my friends, only one other point to which I will call your attention for the remaining time that I have left me, and perhaps I shall not occupy the entire time that I have, as that one point may not take me clear through it.

Among the interrogatories that Judge Douglas propounded to me at Freeport, there was one in about this language: "Are you opposed to the acquisition of any further territory to the United States, unless slavery shall first be prohibited therein?" I answered, as I thought, in this way, that I am not generally opposed to the acquisition of additional territory, and that I would support a proposition for the acquisition of additional territory, according as my supporting it was or was not calculated to aggravate this slavery question amongst us. I then proposed to Judge Douglas another interrogatory, which was correlative to that: "Are you in favor of acquiring additional territory, in disregard of how it may affect us upon the slavery question?" Judge Douglas answered—that is, in his own way he answered it. I believe that, although he took a good many words to answer it, it was a little more fully answered than any other. The substance of his answer was, that this country would continue to expand; that it would need additional territory; that it was as absurd to suppose that we could continue upon our present territory, enlarging in population as we are, as it would be to hoop a boy twelve years of age, and expect him to grow to man's size without bursting the hoops. I believe it was something like that. Consequently, he was in favor of the acquisition of further territory as fast as we might need it, in disregard of how it might affect the slavery question.

I do not say this as giving his exact language, but he said so substantially; and he would leave the question of slavery where the territory was acquired, to be settled by the people of the acquired territory. [*"That's the doctrine."*] Maybe it is; let us consider that for a while. This will probably, in the run of things, become one of the concrete manifestations of this slavery question. If Judge Douglas's policy upon this question succeeds, and gets fairly settled down, until all opposition is crushed out, the next thing will be a grab for the territory of poor Mexico, an invasion of the rich lands of South America, then the adjoining islands will follow, each one of which promises additional slave-fields. And this question is to be left to the people of those countries for settlement. When we shall get Mexico, I don't know whether the Judge will be in favor of the Mexican people that we get with it settling that question for themselves and all others; because we know the Judge has a great horror for mongrels, and I understand that the people of Mexico are most decidedly a race of mongrels. I understand that there is not more than one person there out of eight who is pure white, and I suppose from the Judge's previous declaration that when we get Mexico or any considerable portion of it, he will be in favor of these mongrels settling the question, which would bring him somewhat into collision with his horror of an inferior race.

It is to be remembered, though, that this power of acquiring additional territory is a power confided to the President and Senate of the United States. It is a power not under the control of the representatives of the people any further than they, the President and the Senate, can be considered the representatives of the people. Let me illustrate that by a case we have in our history. When we acquired the territory from Mexico in the Mexican war, the House of Representatives, composed of the immediate representatives of the people, all the time insisted that the territory thus to be acquired should be brought in upon condition that slavery should be forever prohibited therein, upon the terms and in the language that slavery had been prohibited from coming into this country. That was insisted upon constantly and never failed to call forth an assurance that any territory thus acquired should have that prohibition in it, so far as the House of Representatives was concerned. But at last the President and Senate acquired the territory without asking the House of Representatives anything about it, and took it without that prohibition. They have the power of acquiring territory without the immediate representatives of the people being called upon to say anything about it, and thus furnishing a very apt and powerful means of bringing new territory into the Union, and when it is once brought into the country, involving us anew in this slavery agitation.

It is, therefore, as I think, a very important question for the consideration of the American people, whether the policy of bringing in additional territory, without considering at all how it will operate upon the safety of the Union in reference to this one great disturbing element in our national politics, shall be adopted as the policy of the country. You will bear in mind that it is to be acquired, according to the Judge's view, as fast as it is needed, and the indefinite part of this proposition is that we have only Judge Douglas and his class of men to decide how fast it is needed. We have no clear and certain way of determining or demonstrating how fast territory is needed by the necessities of the country. Whoever wants to go out filibustering, then, thinks that more territory is needed. Whoever wants wider slave-fields, feels sure that some additional territory is needed as slave territory. Then it is as easy to show the necessity of additional slave territory as it is to assert anything that is incapable of absolute demonstration. Whatever motive a man or a set of men have for making annexation of property or territory, it is very easy to assert, but much less easy to disprove, that it is necessary for the wants of the country.

And now it only remains for me to say that I think it is a very grave question for the people of this Union to consider, whether, in view of the fact that this slavery question has been the only one that has ever endangered our republican institutions, the only one that has ever threatened or menaced a dissolution of the Union, that has ever disturbed us in such a way as to make us fear for the perpetuity of our liberty—in view of these facts, I think it is an exceedingly interesting and important question for this people to consider, whether we shall engage in the policy of acquiring additional territory, discarding altogether from our consideration, while obtaining new territory, the question how it may affect us in regard to this, the only endangering element to our liberties and national greatness.

The Judge's view has been expressed. I, in my answer to his question, have expressed mine. I think it will become an important and practical question. Our views are before the public. I am willing and anxious that they should consider them fully; that they should turn it about and consider the importance of the question, and arrive at a just conclusion as to whether it is or is not wise in the people of this Union, in the acquisition of new territory, to consider whether it will add to the disturbance that is existing amongst us—whether it will add to the one only danger that has ever threatened the perpetuity of the Union or our own liberties. I think it is extremely important that they shall decide, and rightly decide, that question before entering upon that policy.

And now, my friends, having said the little I wish to say upon this head, whether I have occupied the whole of the remnant of my time or not, I believe I could not enter upon any new topic so as to treat it fully, without transcending my time, which I would not for a moment think of doing. I give way to Judge Douglas.

Mr. Douglas's Reply

Gentlemen: The highest compliment you can pay me during the brief half-hour that I have to conclude is by observing a strict silence. I desire to be heard rather than to be applauded.

The first criticism that Mr. Lincoln makes on my speech was that it was in substance what I have said everywhere else in the state where I have addressed the people. I wish I could only say the same of his speech. Why, the reason I complain of him is because he makes one speech North, and another South. Because he has one set of sentiments for the abolition counties, and another set for the counties opposed to abolitionism. My point of complaint against him is that I cannot induce him to hold up the same standard, to carry the same flag, in all parts of the state. He does not pretend, and no other man will, that I have one set of principles for Galesburg, and another for Charleston. He does not pretend that I hold one doctrine in Chicago, and an opposite one in Jonesboro. I have proved that he has a different set of principles for each of these localities. All I asked of him was that he should deliver the speech that he has made here today in Coles County instead of in old Knox. It would have settled the question between us in that doubtful county. Here I understand him to reaffirm the doctrine of Negro equality, and to assert that by the Declaration of Independence the Negro is declared equal to the white man. He tells you today that the Negro was included in the Declaration of Independence when it is asserted that all men were created equal. ["*We believe it.*"] Very well.

Mr. Lincoln asserts today, as he did at Chicago, that the Negro was included in that clause of the Declaration of Independence which says that all men were created equal, and endowed by the creator with certain inalienable rights, among which are life, liberty, and the pursuit of happiness. If the Negro was made his equal and mine, if that equality was established by divine law, and was the Negro's inalienable

right, how came he to say at Charleston to the Kentuckians
residing in that section of our state that the Negro was physically inferior to the white man, belonged to an inferior race,
and he was for keeping him always in that inferior condition?
I wish you to bear these things in mind. At Charleston he
said that the Negro belonged to an inferior race, and that he
was for keeping him in that inferior condition. There he gave
the people to understand that there was no moral question
involved, because, the inferiority being established, it was
only a question of degree, and not a question of right; here,
today, instead of making it a question of degree, he makes it
a moral question, says that it is a great crime to hold the
Negro in that inferior condition. Is he right now, or was he
right in Charleston? He is right, then, sir, in your estimation,
not because he is consistent, but because he can trim his
principles any way, in any section, so as to secure votes. All
I desire of him is that he will declare the same principles in
the South that he does in the North.

But did you notice how he answered my position that a
man should hold the same doctrines throughout the length
and breadth of this Republic? He said, "Would Judge Douglas
go to Russia and proclaim the same principles he does here?"
I would remind him that Russia is not under the American
Constitution. If Russia was a part of the American Republic,
under our Federal Constitution, and I was sworn to support
the Constitution, I would maintain the same doctrine in
Russia that I do in Illinois. The slaveholding states are governed by the same Federal Constitution as ourselves, and
hence a man's principles, in order to be in harmony with the
Constitution, must be the same in the South as they are in
the North, the same in the free states as they are in the slave
states. Whenever a man advocates one set of principles in
one section, and another set in another section, his opinions
are in violation of the spirit of the Constitution which he was
sworn to support. When Mr. Lincoln went to Congress in
1847, and, laying his hand upon the holy evangelists, made a
solemn vow, in the presence of high Heaven, that he would be
faithful to the Constitution, what did he mean—the Constitution as he expounds it in Galesburg, or the Constitution as
he expounds it in Charleston?

Mr. Lincoln has devoted considerable time to the circumstance that at Ottawa I read a series of resolutions as having

been adopted at Springfield, in this state, on the 4th or 5th of October, 1854, which happened not to have been adopted there. He has used hard names; has dared to talk about fraud, about forgery, and has insinuated that there was a conspiracy between Mr. Lanphier, Mr. Harris, and myself to perpetrate a forgery. Now, bear in mind that he does not deny that these resolutions were adopted in a majority of all the Republican counties of this state in that year; he does not deny that they were declared to be the platform of this Republican party in the first Congressional District, in the second, in the third, and in many counties of the fourth, and that they thus became the platform of his party in a majority of the counties upon which he now relies for support; he does not deny the truthfulness of the resolutions, but takes exception to the *spot* on which they were adopted. He takes to himself great merit because he thinks they were not adopted on the right spot for me to use them against him, just as he was very severe in Congress upon the government of his country when he thought that he had discovered that the Mexican war was not begun in the right *spot*, and was therefore unjust. He tries very hard to make out that there is something very extraordinary in the place where the thing was done, and not in the thing itself.

I never believed before that Abraham Lincoln would be guilty of what has been done this day in regard to those resolutions. In the first place, the moment it was intimated to me that they had been adopted at Aurora and Rockford instead of Springfield, I did not wait for him to call my attention to the fact, but led off, and explained in my first meeting after the Ottawa debate what the mistake was, and how it had been made. I supposed that for an honest man, conscious of his own rectitude, that explanation would be sufficient. I did not wait for him, after the mistake was made, to call my attention to it, but frankly explained it at once as an honest man would. I also gave the authority on which I had stated that these resolutions were adopted by the Springfield Republican convention; that I had seen them quoted by Major Harris in a debate in Congress, as having been adopted by the first Republican state convention in Illinois, and that I had written to him and asked him for the authority as to the time and place of their adoption; that, Major Harris being extremely ill, Charles H. Lanphier had written to me, for him, that they were adopted at Springfield on the 5th of October, 1854, and had sent me a copy of the Springfield paper containing them. I read them from the newspaper just as Mr. Lincoln reads the proceedings of meetings held years ago from the newspapers. After giving that explanation, I did not think there was an honest man in the state of Illinois who doubted that I had been led into the error, if it was such, innocently, in the way I detailed; and I will now say that I do not now believe that there is an honest man on the face of the globe who will not regard with abhorrence and disgust Mr. Lincoln's insinuations of my complicity in that forgery, if it was a forgery. Does Mr. Lincoln wish to push these things to the point of personal difficulties here? I commenced this contest by treating him courteously and kindly; I always spoke of him in words of respect; and in return he has sought, and is now seeking to divert public attention from the enormity of his revolutionary principles by impeaching men's sincerity and integrity, and inviting personal quarrels.

I desire to conduct this contest with him like a gentleman; but I spurn the insinuation of complicity and fraud made upon the simple circumstance of an editor of a newspaper having made a mistake as to the place where a thing was done, but not as to the thing itself. These resolutions were the platform of this Republican party of Mr. Lincoln's of that year. They were adopted in a majority of the Republican counties in the state, and when I asked him at Ottawa whether they formed the platform upon which he stood, he did not answer, and I could not get an answer out of him. He then thought, as I thought, that those resolutions were adopted at the Springfield convention, but excused himself by saying that he was not there when they were adopted, but had gone to Tazewell court in order to avoid being present at the convention. He saw them published as having been adopted at Springfield, and so did I, and he knew that if there was a mistake in regard to them, that I had nothing under heaven to do with it. Besides, you find that in all these northern counties where the Republican candidates are running pledged to him, that the conventions which nominated them adopted that identical platform.

One cardinal point in that platform which he shrinks from is this: that there shall be no more slave states admitted into the Union, even if the people want them. Lovejoy stands pledged against the admission of any more slave states. So do you, you say. Farnsworth stands pledged against the admission of any more slave states. Washburne stands pledged the same way. The candidate for the legislature who is running on Lincoln's ticket in Henderson and Warren, stands committed by his vote in the legislature to the same thing; and I am informed, but do not know of the fact, that your candidate here is also so pledged.

Now, you Republicans all hurrah for him, and for the doctrine of "no more slave states," and yet Lincoln tells you that his conscience will not permit him to sanction that doctrine, and complains because the resolutions I read at Ottawa made him, as a member of the party, responsible for sanctioning the doctrine of no more slave states. You are one way, you confess, and he is, or pretends to be, the other; and yet you are both governed by *principle* in supporting one another. If it be true, as I have shown it is, that the whole Republican party in the northern part of the state stands committed to the doctrine of no more slave states, and that this same doctrine is repudiated by the Republicans in the other part of the state, I wonder whether Mr. Lincoln and his party do not present the case which he cited from the Scriptures, of a house divided against itself which cannot stand!

I desire to know what are Mr. Lincoln's principles and the principles of his party? I hold, and the party with which I am identified holds, that the people of each state, old and new, have the right to decide the slavery question for themselves; and when I used the remark that I did not care whether slavery was voted up or down, I used it in the connection that I was for allowing Kansas to do just as she pleased on the slavery question. I said that I did not care whether they voted slavery up or down because they had the right to do as they pleased on the question, and therefore my action would not be controlled by any such consideration. Why cannot Abraham Lincoln, and the party with which he acts, speak out their principles so that they may be understood? Why do they claim to be one thing in one part of the state, and another in the other part? Whenever I allude to the abolition doctrines, which he considers a slander to be charged with being in favor of, you all endorse them, and hurrah for them, not knowing that your candidate is ashamed to acknowledge them.

I have a few words to say upon the Dred Scott decision, which has troubled the brain of Mr. Lincoln so much. He insists that that decision would carry slavery into the free states, notwithstanding that that decision says directly the opposite, and goes into a long argument to make you believe that I am in favor of and would sanction, the doctrine that would allow slaves to be brought here and held as slaves contrary to our Constitution and laws. Mr. Lincoln knew better when he asserted this; he knew that one newspaper, and, so far as is within my knowledge, but one, ever asserted that doctrine, and that I was the first man in either House of Congress that read that article in debate, and denounced it on the floor of the Senate as revolutionary. When the *Washington Union*, on the 17th of last November, published an article to that effect, I branded it at once, and denounced it; and hence the *Union* has been pursuing me ever since. Mr. Toombs, of Georgia, replied to me, and said that there was not a man in any of the slave states south of the Potomac River that held any such doctrine.

Mr. Lincoln knows that there is not a member of the Supreme Court who holds that doctrine; he knows that every one of them, as shown by their opinions, holds the reverse. Why this attempt then to bring the Supreme Court into disrepute among the people? It looks as if there was an effort being made to destroy public confidence in the highest judicial tribunal on earth. Suppose he succeeds in destroying public confidence in the court, so that the people will not respect its decisions, but will feel at liberty to disregard them and resist the laws of the land, what will he have gained? He will have changed the government from one of laws into that of a mob, in which the strong arm of violence will be substituted for the decisions of the courts of justice. He complains because I did not go into an argument reviewing Chief Justice Taney's opinion, and the other opinions of the different judges, to determine whether their reasoning is right or wrong on the questions of law. What use would that be?

He wants to take an appeal from the Supreme Court to this meeting, to determine whether the questions of law were decided properly. He is going to appeal from the Supreme Court of the United States to every town meeting, in the hope that he can excite a prejudice against that court, and on the wave of that prejudice ride into the Senate of the United States, when he could not get there on his own principles or his own merits. Suppose he should succeed in getting into the Senate of the United States, what then will he have to do with the decision of the Supreme Court in the Dred Scott case? Can he reverse that decision when he gets there? Can he act upon it? Has the Senate any right to reverse it or revise it? He will not pretend that it has. Then why drag the matter into this contest, unless for the purpose of making a false issue, by which he can direct public attention from the real issue.

He has cited General Jackson in justification of the war he is making on the decision of the court. Mr. Lincoln misunderstands the history of the country if he believes there is any parallel in the two cases. It is true that the Supreme Court once decided that if a Bank of the United States was a necessary fiscal agent of the government, it was constitutional, and if not, that it was unconstitutional, and also, that whether or not it was necessary for that purpose, was a political question for Congress, and not a judicial one for the courts to determine. Hence the court would not determine the bank unconstitutional. Jackson respected the decision, obeyed the law, executed it, and carried it into effect during its existence; but after the charter of the bank expired and a proposition was made to create a new bank, General Jackson said, "It is unnecessary and improper, and therefore I am against it on constitutional grounds as well as those of expediency." Is Congress bound to pass every act that is constitutional? Why, there are a thousand things that are constitutional, but yet are inexpedient and unnecessary, and you surely would not vote for them merely because you had the right to? And because General Jackson would not do a thing which he had a right to do, but did not deem expedient or proper, Mr. Lincoln is going to justify himself in doing that which he has no right to do.

I ask him, whether he is not bound to respect and obey the decisions of the Supreme Court as well as me? The Constitution has created that court to decide all constitutional questions in the last resort; and when such decisions have been made, they become the law of the land, and you, and he, and myself, and every other good citizen, are bound by them.

Yet he argues that I am bound by their decisions, and he is not. He says that their decisions are binding on Democrats, but not on Republicans. Are not Republicans bound by the laws of the land as well as Democrats? And when the court has fixed the construction of the Constitution on the validity of a given law, is not their decision binding upon Republicans as well as upon Democrats? Is it possible that you Republicans have the right to raise your mobs and oppose the laws of the land and the constituted authorities, and yet hold us Democrats bound to obey them?

My time is within half a minute of expiring, and all I have to say is, that I stand by the laws of the land. I stand by the Constitution as our fathers made it, by the laws as they are enacted, and by the decisions of the courts, upon all points within their jurisdiction as they are pronounced by the highest tribunal on earth; and any man who resists these must resort to mob law and violence to overturn the government of laws.

══Cooper Institute══

THE ADDRESS OF FEBRUARY 27, 1860

BY ABRAHAM LINCOLN

Introduction

Abraham Lincoln first rose to national prominence in his debates with Stephen Douglas during the summer of 1858. His first appearance before an Eastern audience was made at Cooper Institute in New York City on February 27, 1860. It was four months since John Brown had electrified the country at Harpers Ferry. It was less than three before the Republican party would select its presidential candidate at Chicago.

Cooper Institute (now Cooper Union) had been opened in 1859 at a building on Astor Place as a venture in adult education. On the evening of February 27 "a large assemblage of the intellect and mental culture of our city," as the Tribune put it, gathered there to hear the Republican prophet from the Midwest.

There was nothing outwardly remarkable about the man who rose to address this audience. One observer recalled that "his clothes hung awkwardly on his giant frame; his face was of a dark pallor without the slightest tinge of color; his seamed and rugged features bore the furrows of hardship and struggle; his deep-set eyes looked sad and anxious."

Abraham Lincoln delivered a speech there which has passed into American history as one of its most brilliant documents. The address, carefully reasoned and logically constructed, was barer than a New England meeting house in its absence of ornament, color and symbols. But it drew heavily upon historical fact to deliver a powerful answer to the extreme Southern position: the position that from John C. Calhoun to Roger B. Taney affirmed that the exportation of slavery to the territories was a Federal right protected by the Federal Constitution.

Slavery, argued Lincoln, had been considered from the very founding of the United States as a historical anomaly in a free country, a local institution that must be tolerated only to the extent that its actual presence in the country made this necessary. Adjudged by the founding fathers and the people to be morally wrong, the very word slavery was not to be found in the Constitution. Slaves were referred to, not as property, but as "persons": "This mode of alluding to slaves and slavery," said Lincoln, "instead of speaking of them, was employed on purpose to exclude from the Constitution the idea that there could be property in man." And it was further expected that slavery would, in the fullness of time, die out where it existed, in the North and the South alike.

Lincoln charged that the slaveholders wished, in 1860, to reverse and abolish this simple and fundamental truth. They wished, said he, to establish slavery on the same footing as freedom, and to give it the equal protection of the Federal Constitution. This must be considered the complete negation of the fundamental purpose and inspiration of a free Republic and of its laws. Lincoln, it should be noted, disclaimed any intention to interfere with slavery where it already existed with Federal sanction; only slavery's expansion into territories and states where it did not already have such sanction was debarred. This was the crucial issue upon which the Republicans would rally millions to the support of their cause. In this way they proposed to check the unbridled expansion of an immoral institution, and to place it, even as the founding fathers had intended, in course of extinction.

THE COOPER INSTITUTE ADDRESS*
FEBRUARY 27, 1860.

Mr. President and fellow-citizens of New York: The facts with which I shall deal this evening are mainly old and familiar; nor is there anything new in the general use I shall make of them. If there shall be any novelty, it will be in the mode of presenting the facts, and the inferences and observations following that presentation.

In his speech last autumn at Columbus, Ohio, as reported in the New York *Times,* Senator Douglas said:

> Our fathers, when they framed the government under which we live, understood this question just as well, and even better, than we do now.

I fully indorse this, and I adopt it as a text for this discourse. I so adopt it because it furnishes a precise and an agreed starting point for a discussion between Republicans and that wing of the Democracy headed by Senator Douglas. It simply leaves the inquiry: *what was the understanding those fathers had of the question mentioned?*

What is the frame of government under which we live?

The answer must be, the Constitution of the United States. That Constitution consists of the original, framed in 1787, and under which the present government first went into operation; and twelve subsequently framed amendments, the first ten of which were framed in 1789.

Who were our fathers that framed the Constitution? I suppose the "thirty-nine" who signed the original instrument may be fairly called our fathers who framed that part of the present government. It is almost exactly true to say they framed it, and it is altogether true to say they fairly represented the opinion and sentiment of the whole nation at that time. Their names, being familiar to nearly all, and accessible to quite all, need not now be repeated.

I take these "thirty-nine," for the present, as being "our fathers who framed the government under which we live." What is the question which, according to the text, those

*Source: The Address of the Hon. Abraham Lincoln delivered at Cooper Institute, February 27, 1860. Pamphlet issued by George N. Nesbitt and Co., New York, 1860.

fathers understood "just as well, and even better, than we do now"?

It is this: does the proper division of local from Federal authority, or anything in the Constitution, forbid *our Federal government* to control as to slavery in *our Federal territories?*

Upon this, Senator Douglas holds the affirmative, and Republicans the negative. This affirmation and denial form an issue; and this issue—this question—is precisely what the text declares our fathers understood "better than we."

Let us now inquire whether the "thirty-nine," or any of them, ever acted upon this question; and if they did, how they acted upon it—how they expressed that better understanding.

In 1784, three years before the Constitution, the United States then owning the Northwestern territory and no other, the Congress of the Confederation had before them the question of prohibiting slavery in that territory; and four of the "thirty-nine" who afterward framed the Constitution were in that Congress, and voted on that question. Of these, Roger Sherman, Thomas Mifflin, and Hugh Williamson voted for the prohibition, thus showing that, in their understanding, no line dividing local from Federal authority, nor anything else, properly forbade the Federal government to control as to slavery in Federal territory. The other of the four, James McHenry, voted against the prohibition, showing that for some cause he thought it improper to vote for it.

In 1787, still before the Constitution, but while the Convention was in session framing it, and while the Northwestern territory still was the only territory owned by the United States, the same question of prohibiting slavery in the territory again came before the Congress of the Confederation; and two more of the "thirty-nine" who afterward signed the Constitution were in that Congress, and voted on the question. They were William Blount and William Few; and they both voted for the prohibition—thus showing that in their understanding no line dividing local from Federal authority, nor anything else, properly forbade the Federal government to control as to slavery in Federal territory. This time the prohibition became a law, being part of what is now well known as the Ordinance of '87.

The question of Federal control of slavery in the territories seems not to have been directly before the Convention which framed the original Constitution; and hence it is not recorded that the "thirty-nine," or any of them, while engaged on that instrument, expressed any opinion of that precise question.

In 1789, by the first Congress which sat under the Constitution, an act was passed to enforce the Ordinance of '87, including the prohibition of slavery in the Northwestern territory. The bill for this act was reported by one of the "thirty-nine"—Thomas Fitzsimmons, then a member of the House of Representatives from Pennsylvania. It went through all its stages without a word of opposition, and finally passed both branches without ayes and nays, which is equivalent to a unanimous passage. In this Congress there were sixteen of the thirty-nine fathers who framed the original Constitution. They were John Langdon, Nicholas Gilman, William S. Johnson, Roger Sherman, Robert Morris, Thomas Fitzsimmons, William Few, Abraham Baldwin, Rufus King, William Paterson, George Clymer, Richard Bassett, George Read, Pierce Butler, Daniel Carroll, and James Madison.

This shows that, in their understanding, no line dividing local from Federal authority, nor anything in the Constitution, properly forbade Congress to prohibit slavery in the Federal territory; else both their fidelity to correct principle, and their oath to support the Constitution, would have constrained them to oppose the prohibition.

Again, George Washington, another of the "thirty-nine," was then President of the United States, and as such approved and signed the bill, thus completing its validity as a law, and thus showing that, in his understanding, no line dividing local from Federal authority, nor anything in the Constitution, forbade the Federal government to control as to slavery in Federal territory.

No great while after the adoption of the original Constitution, North Carolina ceded to the Federal government the country now constituting the state of Tennessee; and a few years later Georgia ceded that which now constitutes the states of Mississippi and Alabama. In both deeds of cession it was made a condition by the ceding states that the Federal government should not prohibit slavery in the ceded country. Besides this, slavery was then actually in the ceded country. Under these circumstances, Congress, on taking charge of these countries, did not absolutely prohibit slavery within them. But they did interfere with it—take control of it—

even there, to a certain extent. In 1798 Congress organized the territory of Mississippi. In the act of organization they prohibited the bringing of slaves into the territory from any place without the United States, by fine, and giving freedom to slaves so brought. This act passed both branches of Congress without yeas and nays. In that Congress were three of the "thirty-nine" who framed the original Constitution. They were John Langdon, George Read, and Abraham Baldwin. They all, probably, voted for it. Certainly they would have placed their opposition to it upon record if, in their understanding, any line dividing local from Federal authority, or anything in the Constitution, properly forbade the Federal government to control as to slavery in Federal territory.

In 1803 the Federal government purchased the Louisiana country. Our former territorial acquisitions came from certain of our own states; but this Louisiana country was acquired from a foreign nation. In 1804 Congress gave a territorial organization to that part of it which now constitutes the state of Louisiana. New Orleans, lying within that part, was an old and comparatively large city. There were other considerable towns and settlements, and slavery was extensively and thoroughly intermingled with the people. Congress did not, in the Territorial Act, prohibit slavery; but they did interfere with it—take control of it—in a more marked and extensive way than they did in the case of Mississippi. The substance of the provision therein made in relation to slaves was:

1. That no slave should be imported into the territory from foreign parts.

2. That no slave should be carried into it who had been imported into the United States since the first day of May, 1798.

3. That no slave should be carried into it, except by the owner, and for his own use as a settler; the penalty in all the cases being a fine upon the violator of the law, and freedom to the slave.

This act also was passed without ayes or nays. In the Congress which passed it there were two of the "thirty-nine." They were Abraham Baldwin and Jonathan Dayton. As stated in the case of Mississippi, it is probable they both voted for it. They would not have allowed it to pass without recording their opposition to it if, in their understanding, it violated either the line properly dividing local from Federal authority, or any provision of the Constitution.

In 1819-20 came and passed the Missouri question. Many votes were taken, by yeas and nays, in both branches of Congress, upon the various phases of the general question. Two of the "thirty-nine"—Rufus King and Charles Pinckney —were members of that Congress. Mr. King steadily voted for slavery prohibition and against all compromises, while Mr. Pinckney as steadily voted against slavery prohibition and against all compromises. By this, Mr. King showed that, in his understanding, no line dividing local from Federal authority, nor anything in the Constitution, was violated by Congress prohibiting slavery in Federal territory; while Mr. Pinckney, by his votes, showed that, in his understanding, there was some sufficient reason for opposing such prohibition in that case.

The cases I have mentioned are the only acts of the "thirty-nine," or of any of them, upon the direct issue, which I have been able to discover.

To enumerate the persons who thus acted as being four in 1784, two in 1787, seventeen in 1789, three in 1798, two in 1804, and two in 1819-20, there would be thirty of them. But this would be counting John Langdon, Roger Sherman, William Few, Rufus King, and George Read each twice, and Abraham Baldwin three times. The true number of those of the "thirty-nine" whom I have shown to have acted upon the question which, by the text, they understood better than we, is twenty-three, leaving sixteen not shown to have acted upon it in any way.

Here, then, we have twenty-three out of our thirty-nine fathers "who framed the government under which we live," who have, upon their official responsibility and their corporal oaths, acted upon the very question which the text affirms they "understood just as well, and even better, than we do now"; and twenty-one of them—a clear majority of the whole "thirty-nine"—so acting upon it as to make them guilty of gross political impropriety and wilful perjury if, in their understanding, any proper division between local and Federal authority, or anything in the Constitution they had made themselves, and sworn to support, forbade the Federal government to control as to slavery in the Federal territories. Thus the twenty-one acted; and, as actions speak louder than words, so actions under such responsibility speak still louder.

Two of the twenty-three voted against congressional prohibition of slavery in the Federal territories, in the instances in which they acted upon the question. But for what reasons they so voted is not known. They may have done so because they thought a proper division of local from Federal authority, or some provision or principle of the Constitution, stood in the way; or they may, without any such question, have voted against the prohibition on what appeared to them to be sufficient grounds of expediency. No one who has sworn to support the Constitution can conscientiously vote for what he understands to be an unconstitutional measure, however expedient he may think it; but one may and ought to vote against a measure which he deems constitutional if, at the same time, he deems it inexpedient. It, therefore, would be unsafe to set down even the two who voted against the prohibition as having done so because, in their understanding, any proper division of local from Federal authority, or anything in the Constitution, forbade the Federal government to control as to slavery in Federal territory.

The remaining sixteen of the "thirty-nine," so far as I have discovered, have left no record of their understanding upon the direct question of Federal control of slavery in the Federal territories. But there is much reason to believe that their understanding upon that question would not have appeared different from that of their twenty-three compeers, had it been manifested at all.

For the purpose of adhering rigidly to the text, I have purposely omitted whatever understanding may have been manifested by any person, however distinguished, other than the thirty-nine fathers who framed the original Constitution; and, for the same reason, I have also omitted whatever understanding may have been manifested by any of the "thirty-nine" even on any other phase of the general question of slavery. If we should look into their acts and declarations on those other phases, as the foreign slave trade, and the morality and policy of slavery generally, it would appear to us that on the direct question of Federal control of slavery in Federal territories, the sixteen, if they had acted at all, would probably have acted just as the twenty-three did. Among that sixteen were several of the most noted anti-slavery men of those times—as Benjamin Franklin, Alexander

Hamilton, and Gouverneur Morris—while there was not one now known to have been otherwise, unless it may be John Rutledge, of South Carolina.

The sum of the whole is, that of our thirty-nine fathers who framed the original Constitution, twenty-one—a clear majority of the whole—certainly understood that no proper division of local from Federal authority, nor any part of the Constitution, forbade the Federal government to control slavery in the Federal territories; while all the rest had probably the same understanding. Such, unquestionably, was the understanding of our fathers who framed the original Constitution; and the text affirms that they understood the question "better than we."

But, so far, I have been considering the understanding of the question manifested by the framers of the original Constitution. In and by the original instrument, a mode was provided for amending it; and, as I have already stated, the present frame of "the government under which we live" consists of that original, and twelve amendatory articles framed and adopted since. Those who now insist that Federal control of slavery in Federal territories violates the Constitution, point us to the provisions which they suppose it thus violates; and, as I understand, they all fix upon provisions in these amendatory articles, and not in the original instrument. The Supreme Court, in the Dred Scott case, plant themselves upon the fifth amendment, which provides that no person shall be deprived of "life, liberty, or property without due process of law"; while Senator Douglas and his peculiar adherents plant themselves upon the tenth amendment, providing that "the powers not delegated to the United States by the Constitution" "are reserved to the states respectively, or to the people."

Now, it so happens that these amendments were framed by the first Congress which sat under the Constitution—the identical Congress which passed the act, already mentioned, enforcing the prohibition of slavery in the Northwestern territory. Not only was it the same Congress, but they were the identical, same individual men who, at the same session, and at the same time within the session, had under consideration, and in progress toward maturity, these constitutional amendments, and this act prohibiting slavery in all the territory the nation then owned. The constitutional amendments were introduced before, and passed after, the act enforcing the Ordinance of '87; so that, during the whole pendency of the act to enforce the Ordinance, the constitutional amendments were also pending.

The seventy-six members of that Congress, including sixteen of the framers of the original Constitution, as before stated, were pre-eminently our fathers who framed that part of "the government under which we live," which is now claimed as forbidding the Federal government to control slavery in the Federal territories.

Is it not a little presumptuous in any one at this day to affirm that the two things which that Congress deliberately framed, and carried to maturity at the same time, are absolutely inconsistent with each other? And does not such affirmation become impudently absurd when coupled with the other affirmation, from the same mouth, that those who did the two things alleged to be inconsistent, understood whether they really were inconsistent better than we—better than he who affirms that they are inconsistent?

It is surely safe to assume that the thirty-nine framers of the original Constitution, and the seventy-six members of the Congress which framed the amendments thereto, taken together, do certainly include those who may be fairly called "our fathers who framed the government under which we live." And so assuming, I defy any man to show that any one of them ever, in his whole life, declared that, in his understanding, any proper division of local from Federal authority, or any part of the Constitution, forbade the Federal government to control as to slavery in the Federal territories. I go a step further. I defy any one to show that any living man in the whole world ever did, prior to the beginning of the present century (and I might almost say prior to the beginning of the last half of the present century), declare that, in his understanding, any proper division of local from Federal authority, or any part of the Constitution, forbade the Federal government to control as to slavery in the Federal territories. To those who now so declare I give not only "our fathers who framed the government under which we live," but with them all other living men within the century in which it was framed, among whom to search, and they shall not be able to find the evidence of a single man agreeing with them.

Now, and here, let me guard a little against being mis-understood. I do not mean to say we are bound to follow implicitly in whatever our fathers did. To do so would be to discard all the lights of current experience—to reject all progress, all improvement. What I do say is that, if we would supplant the opinions and policy of our fathers in any case, we should do so upon evidence so conclusive, and argument so clear, that even their great authority, fairly considered and weighed, cannot stand; and most surely not in a case whereof we ourselves declare they understood the question better than we.

If any man at this day sincerely believes that a proper division of local from Federal authority, or any part of the Constitution, forbids the Federal government to control as to slavery in the Federal territories, he is right to say so, and to enforce his position by all truthful evidence and fair argu-ment which he can. But he has no right to mislead others, who have less access to history, and less leisure to study it, into the false belief that "our fathers who framed the government under which we live" were of the same opinion —thus substituting falsehood and deception for truthful evi-dence and fair argument. If any man at this day sincerely believes "our fathers who framed the government under which we live" used and applied principles, in other cases, which ought to have led them to understand that a proper division of local from Federal authority, or some part of the Con-stitution, forbids the Federal government to control as to slavery in the Federal territories, he is right to say so. But he should, at the same time, brave the responsibility of de-claring that, in his opinion, he understands their principles better than they did themselves; and especially should he not shirk that responsibility by asserting that they "understood the question just as well, and even better, than we do now."

But enough! *Let all who believe that "our fathers who framed the government under which we live understood this question just as well, and even better, than we do now," speak as they spoke, and act as they acted upon it. This is all Republicans ask—all Republicans desire—in relation to slavery. As those fathers marked it, so let it be again marked, as an evil not to be extended, but to be tolerated and pro-tected only because of and so far as its actual presence among us makes that toleration and protection a necessity. Let all the guaranties those fathers gave it, be, not grudgingly, but fully and fairly, maintained.* For this Republicans contend, and with this, so far as I know or believe, they will be content.

And now, if they would listen—as I suppose they will not —I would address a few words to the Southern people.

I would say to them: you consider yourselves a reasonable and a just people; and I consider that in the general qualities of reason and justice you are not inferior to any other people. Still, when you speak of us Republicans, you do so only to denounce us as reptiles, or, at the best, as no better than outlaws. You will grant a hearing to pirates or murderers, but nothing like it to "Black Republicans." In all your contentions with one another, each of you deems an unconditional condemnation of "Black Republicanism" as the first thing to be attended to. Indeed, such condemnation of us seems to be an indispensable prerequisite—license, so to speak—among you to be admitted to speak at all. Now can you, or not, be prevailed upon to pause and to consider whether this is quite just to us, or even to yourselves? Bring forward your charges and specifications, and then be patient long enough to hear us deny or justify.

You say we are sectional. We deny it. That makes an issue; and the burden of proof is upon you. You produce your proof; and what is it? Why, that our party has no existence in your section—gets no votes in your section. The fact is substantially true; but does it prove the issue? If it does, then in case we should, without change of principle, begin to get votes in your section, we should thereby cease to be sectional. You cannot escape this conclusion; and yet are you willing to abide by it? If you are, you will probably soon find that we have ceased to be sectional, for we shall get votes in your section this very year. You will then begin to discover, as the truth plainly is, that your proof does not touch the issue. The fact that we get no votes in your section is a fact of your making, and not of ours. And if there be fault in that fact, that fault is primarily yours, and remains so until you show that we repel you by some wrong principle or practice. If we do repel you by any wrong principle or practice, the fault is ours; but this brings you to where you ought to have started—to a discussion of the right or wrong of our principle. If our principle, put in practice, would wrong your section for the benefit of ours, or for any other object, then our principle, and we with it, are sectional, and are justly opposed and denounced as such. Meet us, then, on the question of whether our principle, put in practice, would wrong your section; and so meet us as if it were possible that something may be said on our side. Do you accept the challenge? No! Then you really believe that the principle which "our fathers who framed the government under which we live" thought so clearly right as to adopt it, and indorse it again and again, upon their official oaths, is in fact so clearly wrong as to demand your condemnation without a moment's consideration.

Some of you delight to flaunt in our faces the warning against sectional parties given by Washington in his Farewell Address. Less than eight years before Washington gave that warning, he had, as President of the United States, approved and signed an act of Congress enforcing the prohibition of slavery in the Northwestern Territory, which act embodied the policy of the government upon that subject up to and at the very moment he penned that warning; and about one year after he penned it, he wrote Lafayette that he considered that prohibition a wise measure, expressing in the same connection his hope that we should at some time have a confederacy of free states.

Bearing this in mind, and seeing that sectionalism has since arisen upon this same subject, is that warning a weapon in your hands against us, or in our hands against you? Could Washington himself speak, would he cast the blame of that sectionalism upon us, who sustain his policy, or upon you, who repudiate it? We respect that warning of Washington, and we commend it to you, together with his example pointing to the right application of it.

But you say you are conservative—eminently conservative —while we are revolutionary, destructive, or something of the sort. What is conservatism? Is it not adherence to the old and tried, against the new and untried? We stick to, contend for, the identical old policy on the point in controversy which was adopted by "our fathers who framed the government under which we live"; while you with one accord reject, and scout, and spit upon that old policy, and insist upon substituting something new. True, you disagree among yourselves as to what that substitute shall be. You are divided on new propositions and plans, but you are unanimous in rejecting and denouncing the old policy of the fathers. Some of you are for reviving the foreign slave trade; some for a congressional slave code for the territories; some for Congress forbidding the territories to prohibit slavery within their limits; some for maintaining slavery in the territories through the judiciary; some for the "gur-reat pur-rinciple" that "if one man would enslave another, no third man should object," fantastically called "popular sovereignty"; but never a man among you is in favor of Federal prohibition of slavery in Federal territories, according to the practice of "our fathers who framed the government under which we live." Not one of all your various plans can show a precedent or an advocate in the century within which our government originated. Consider, then, whether your claim of conservatism for yourselves, and your charge of destructiveness against us, are based on the most clear and stable foundations.

Again, you say we have made the slavery question more prominent than it formerly was. We deny it. We admit that it is more prominent, but we deny that we made it so. It was not we, but you, who discarded the old policy of the fathers. We resisted, and still resist, your innovation; and thence comes the greater prominence of the question. Would you have that question reduced to its former proportions? Go back to that old policy. What has been will be again, under the same conditions. If you would have the peace of the old times, readopt the precepts and policy of the old times.

You charge that we stir up insurrections among your slaves. We deny it; and what is your proof? Harpers Ferry! John Brown!! John Brown was no Republican; and you have failed to implicate a single Republican in his Harpers Ferry enterprise. If any member of our party is guilty in that matter, you know it, or you do not know it. If you do know it, you are inexcusable for not designating the man and proving the fact. If you do not know it, you are inexcusable for asserting it, and especially for persisting in the assertion after you have tried and failed to make the proof. You need not be told that persisting in a charge which one does not know to be true, is simply malicious slander.

Some of you admit that no Republican designedly aided or encouraged the Harpers Ferry affair, but still insist that our doctrines and declarations necessarily lead to such results.

We do not believe it. We know we hold no doctrine, and make no declaration, which were not held to and made by "our fathers who framed the government under which we live." You never dealt fairly by us in relation to this affair. When it occurred, some important state elections were near at hand, and you were in evident glee with the belief that, by charging the blame upon us, you could get an advantage of us in those elections. The elections came, and your expectations were not quite fulfilled. Every Republican man knew that, as to himself at least, your charge was a slander, and he was not much inclined by it to cast his vote in your favor. Republican doctrines and declarations are accompanied with a continual protest against any interference whatever with your slaves, or with you about your slaves. Surely this does not encourage them to revolt. True, we do, in common with "our fathers who framed the government under which we live," declare our belief that slavery is wrong; but the slaves do not hear us declare even this. For anything we say or do, the slaves would scarcely know there is a Republican party. I believe they would not, in fact, generally know it but for your misrepresentations of us in their hearing. In your political contests among yourselves, each faction charges the other with sympathy with Black Republicanism; and then, to give point to the charge, defines Black Republicanism to simply be insurrection, blood and thunder among the slaves.

Slave insurrections are no more common now than they were before the Republican party was organized. What induced the Southampton insurrection, twenty-eight years ago, in which at least three times as many lives were lost as at Harpers Ferry? You can scarcely stretch your very elastic fancy to the conclusion that Southampton was "got up by Black Republicanism." In the present state of things in the United States, I do not think a general, or even a very extensive, slave insurrection is possible. The indispensable concert of action cannot be attained. The slaves have no means of rapid communication; nor can incendiary freemen, black or white, supply it. The explosive materials are everywhere in parcels, but there neither are, nor can be supplied, the indispensable connecting trains.

Much is said by Southern people about the affection of slaves for their masters and mistresses; and a part of it, at least, is true. A plot for an uprising could scarcely be devised and communicated to twenty individuals before some one of them, to save the life of a favorite master or mistress, would divulge it. This is the rule; and the slave revolution in Haiti was not an exception to it, but a case occurring under peculiar circumstances. The gunpowder plot of British history, though not connected with slaves, was more in point. In that case only about twenty were admitted to the secret; and yet one of them, in his anxiety to save a friend, betrayed the plot to that friend, and, by consequence, averted the calamity. Occasional poisonings from the kitchen, and open or stealthy assassinations in the field, and local revolts extending to a score or so, will continue to occur as the natural results of slavery; but no general insurrection of slaves, as I think, can happen in this country for a long time. Whoever much fears, or much hopes for such an event, will be alike disappointed.

In the language of Mr. Jefferson, uttered many years ago, "It is still in our power to direct the process of emancipation and deportation peaceably, and in such slow degrees, as that the evil will wear off insensibly; and their places be, *pari passu*, filled up by free white laborers. If, on the contrary, it is left to force itself on, human nature must shudder at the prospect held up."

Mr. Jefferson did not mean to say, nor do I, that the power of emancipation is in the Federal government. He spoke of Virginia; and, as to the power of emancipation, I speak of the slaveholding states only. The Federal government, however, as we insist, has the power of restraining the extension of the institution—the power to insure that a slave insurrection shall never occur on any American soil which is now free from slavery.

John Brown's effort was peculiar. It was not a slave insurrection. It was an attempt by white men to get up a revolt among slaves, in which the slaves refused to participate. In fact it was so absurd that the slaves, with all their ignorance, saw plainly enough it could not succeed. That affair, in its philosophy, corresponds with the many attempts, related in history, at the assassination of kings and emperors. An enthusiast broods over the oppression of a people till he fancies himself commissioned by Heaven to liberate them. He ventures the attempt, which ends in little else than his own execution.

Orsini's attempt on Louis Napoleon and John Brown's attempt at Harpers Ferry were, in their philosophy, precisely the same. The eagerness to cast blame on old England in the one case and on New England in the other, does not disprove the sameness of the two things.

And how much would it avail you, if you could, by the use of John Brown, Helper's book, and the like, break up the Republican organization? Human action can be modified to some extent, but human nature cannot be changed. There is a judgment and a feeling against slavery in this nation which cast at least a million and a half of votes. You cannot destroy that judgment and feeling—that sentiment—by breaking up the political organization which rallies around it. You can scarcely scatter and disperse an army which has been formed into order in the face of your heaviest fire; but if you could, how much would you gain by forcing the sentiment which created it out of the peaceful channel of the ballot-box into some other channel? What would that other channel probably be? Would the number of John Browns be lessened or enlarged by the operation?

But you will break up the Union rather than submit to a denial of your constitutional rights.

That has a somewhat reckless sound; but it would be palliated, if not fully justified, were we proposing, by the mere force of numbers, to deprive you of some right plainly written down in the Constitution. But we are proposing no such thing.

When you make these declarations, you have a specific and well-understood allusion to an assumed constitutional right of yours to take slaves into the Federal territories, and to hold them there as property. But no such right is specifically written in the Constitution. That instrument is literally silent about any such right. We, on the contrary, deny that such a right has any existence in the Constitution, even by implication.

Your purpose, then, plainly stated, is that you will destroy the government, unless you be allowed to construe and force the Constitution as you please, on all points in dispute between you and us. You will rule or ruin in all events.

This, plainly stated, is your language. Perhaps you will say the Supreme Court has decided the disputed constitutional question in your favor. Not quite so. But waiving the lawyer's distinction between dictum and decision, the court has decided the question for you in a sort of way. The court has substantially said, it is your constitutional right to take slaves into the Federal territories, and to hold them there as property. When I say the decision was made in a sort of way, I mean it was made in a divided court, by a bare majority of the judges, and they not quite agreeing with one another in the reasons for making it; that it is so made as that its avowed supporters disagree with one another about its meaning, and that it was mainly based upon a mistaken statement of fact—the statement in the opinion that "the right of property in a slave is distinctly and expressly affirmed in the Constitution."

An inspection of the Constitution will show that the right of property in a slave is not "*distinctly* and *expressly* affirmed" in it. Bear in mind, the judges do not pledge their judicial opinion that such right is *impliedly* affirmed in the Constitution; but they pledge their veracity that it is "*distinctly* and *expressly*" affirmed there—"distinctly," that is, not mingled with anything else—"expressly," that is, in words meaning just that, without the aid of any inference, and susceptible of no other meaning.

If they had only pledged their judicial opinion that such right is affirmed in the instrument by implication, it would be open to others to show that neither the word "slave" nor "slavery" is to be found in the Constitution, nor the word "property" even, in any connection with language alluding to the things slave, or slavery; and that wherever in that instrument the slave is alluded to, he is called a "person"; and wherever his master's legal right in relation to him is alluded to, it is spoken of as "service or labor which may be due"—as a debt payable in service or labor. Also it would be open to show, by contemporaneous history, that this mode of alluding to slaves and slavery, instead of speaking of them, was employed on purpose to exclude from the Constitution the idea that there could be property in man.

To show all this is easy and certain.

When this obvious mistake of the judges shall be brought to their notice, is it not reasonable to expect that they will withdraw the mistaken statement, and reconsider the conclusion based upon it?

And then it is to be remembered that "our fathers who framed the government under which we live"—the men who made the Constitution—decided this same constitutional question in our favor long ago: decided it without division among themselves when making the decision; without division among themselves about the meaning of it after it was made, and, so far as any evidence is left, without basing it upon any mistaken statement of facts.

Under all these circumstances, do you really feel yourselves justified to break up this government unless such a court decision as yours is shall be at once submitted to as a conclusive and final rule of political action? But you will not abide the election of a Republican President! In that supposed event, you say, you will destroy the Union; and then, you say, the great crime of having destroyed it will be upon us! That is cool. A highwayman holds a pistol to my ear, and mutters through his teeth, "Stand and deliver, or I shall kill you, and then you will be a murderer!"

To be sure, what the robber demanded of me—my money —was my own; and I had a clear right to keep it; but it was no more my own than my vote is my own; and the threat of death to me to extort my money and the threat of destruction to the Union, to extort my vote, can scarcely be distinguished in principle.

A few words now to Republicans. *It is exceedingly desirable that all parts of this great Confederacy shall be at peace and in harmony one with another. Let us Republicans do our part to have it so. Even though much provoked, let us do nothing through passion and ill temper. Even though the Southern people will not so much as listen to us, let us calmly consider their demands, and yield to them if, in our deliberate view of our duty, we possibly can.* Judging by all they say and do, and by the subject and nature of their controversy with us, let us determine, if we can, what will satisfy them.

Will they be satisfied if the territories be unconditionally surrendered to them? We know they will not. In all their present complaints against us, the territories are scarcely mentioned. Invasions and insurrections are the rage now. Will it satisfy them if, in the future, we have nothing to do with invasions and insurrections? We know it will not. We so know, because we know we never had anything to do with invasions and insurrections; and yet this total abstaining does not exempt us from the charge and the denunciation.

The question recurs, what will satisfy them? Simply this:

we must not only let them alone, but we must somehow convince them that we do let them alone. This, we know by experience, is no easy task. We have been so trying to convince them from the very beginning of our organization, but with no success. In all our platforms and speeches we have constantly protested our purpose to let them alone; but this has had no tendency to convince them. Alike unavailing to convince them is the fact that they have never detected a man of us in any attempt to disturb them.

These natural and apparently adequate means all failing, what will convince them? This, and this only: cease to call slavery *wrong*, and join them in calling it *right*. And this must be done thoroughly—done in *acts* as well as in *words*. Silence will not be tolerated—we must place ourselves avowedly with them. Senator Douglas's new sedition law must be enacted and enforced, suppressing all declarations that slavery is wrong, whether made in politics, in presses, in pulpits, or in private. We must arrest and return their fugitive slaves with greedy pleasure. We must pull down our free-state constitutions. The whole atmosphere must be disinfected from all taint of opposition to slavery, before they will cease to believe that all their troubles proceed from us.

I am quite aware they do not state their case precisely in this way. Most of them would probably say to us, "Let us alone; *do* nothing to us, and *say* what you please about slavery." But we do let them alone,—have never disturbed them,—so that, after all, it is what we say which dissatisfies them. They will continue to accuse us of doing, until we cease saying.

I am also aware they have not as yet, in terms, demanded the overthrow of our free-state constitutions. Yet those constitutions declare the wrong of slavery with more solemn emphasis than do all other sayings against it; and when all these other sayings shall have been silenced, the overthrow of these constitutions will be demanded, and nothing be left to resist the demand. It is nothing to the contrary that they do not demand the whole of this just now. Demanding what they do, and for the reason they do, they can voluntarily stop nowhere short of this consummation. Holding, as they do, that slavery is morally right and socially elevating, they cannot cease to demand a full national recognition of it as a legal right and a social blessing.

Nor can we justifiably withhold this on any ground save our conviction that slavery is wrong. If slavery is right, all words, acts, laws, and constitutions against it are themselves wrong, and should be silenced and swept away. If it is right, we cannot justly object to its nationality—its universality; if it is wrong, they cannot justly insist upon its extension—its enlargement. All they ask we could readily grant, if we thought slavery right; all we ask they could as readily grant, if they thought it wrong. Their thinking it right and our thinking it wrong is the precise fact upon which depends the whole controversy. Thinking it right, as they do, they are not to blame for desiring its full recognition as being right; but thinking it wrong, as we do, can we yield to them? Can we cast our votes with their view, and against our own? In view of our moral, social, and political responsibilities, can we do this?

Wrong as we think slavery is, we can yet afford to let it alone where it is, because that much is due to the necessity arising from its actual presence in the nation; but can we, while our votes will prevent it, allow it to spread into the national territories, and to overrun us here in these free states? If our sense of duty forbids this, then let us stand by our duty fearlessly and effectively. Let us be diverted by none of those sophistical contrivances wherewith we are so industriously plied and belabored—contrivances such as groping for some middle ground between the right and the wrong, vain as the search for a man who should be neither a living man nor a dead man; such as a policy of "don't care" on a question about which all true men do care; such as Union appeals beseeching true Union men to yield to disunionists, reversing the divine rule, and calling, not the sinners, but the righteous, to repentance; such as invocations to Washington, imploring men to unsay what Washington said and undo what Washington did.

Neither let us be slandered from our duty by false accusations against us, nor frightened from it by menaces of destruction to the government, nor of dungeons to ourselves. *Let us have faith that right makes might, and in that faith let us, to the end, dare to do our duty as we understand it.*

=In Memoriam=

ROBERT GOULD SHAW 1837-63

Robert Gould Shaw led one of the first Negro regiments to be sent into battle by the Union during the Civil War; and he was killed leading his men into action. A young white officer, he gave his life for the Negro people and for Negro soldiers in their struggle for freedom and equality and against slavery.

It is fitting that in 1963, one hundred years after his death, the American people should commemorate his sacrifice and rededicate themselves to winning the ideal for which he died.

Robert Gould Shaw was born in Boston, Massachusetts, in October, 1837, the second child of Francis George Shaw and Sarah Blake Sturgis. His mother was the daughter of a wealthy Boston merchant, and his father was the son of a veritable merchant prince. Shaw money came from overseas trade, from banking and investments, from railroads, real estate and from textiles. Francis George Shaw inherited wealth, and he also married wealth; but these were people who took their social obligations very seriously. Throughout their lives they gave generous support to worthy causes.

When Robert Gould Shaw was born, the Shaws were living in Roxbury; and when he was a little boy his parents found themselves next door neighbors to Brook Farm. They were friends of George Ripley, the founder of that project; they contributed generously to its support and were constant visitors at the Farm. As the times changed and the slavery issue rose to be the predominant one in the nation, the Shaws embraced the antislavery cause. By the mid-'40's they were leaders of Boston's progressive aristocracy, with linkages by marriage and political association to New England's liberal avant-garde. They were among those influential New England intellectuals —Theodore Parker, Lydia Maria Child, the Sedgwicks of Stockbridge, Edmund Quincy, Charles Sumner, Wendell Phillips, English-born actress Fanny Kemble and many more— who wrote and agitated against slavery.

Robert Shaw's secondary education was completed in Europe, in Swiss and German schools. He entered Harvard College in 1856 with the class of 1860. When the Civil War broke out the Shaws were living on Staten Island, where they had come some years before because of Sarah Blake Shaw's health. Robert left Harvard in 1859 to go into business, and in 1860 he enlisted in New York's Seventh Regiment—the pride of its militia. On April 19, 1861, one week after the bombardment of Fort Sumter, he left with his regiment for Washington, to help defend that city. He was quartered in the House of Representatives and found time, along with a friend, to pay a call on the President. Presidents, in those days, were more accessible to the citizenry, even in wartime, than they are today; and his impressions of Lincoln, as written to his mother, are not without interest:

"We were shown into a room," he wrote, "where Mr. Lincoln was sitting at a desk. . . . He got up and shook hands with us both, in the most cordial way, asked us to be seated, and seemed glad to have us come. It is really too bad to call him one of the ugliest men in the country, for I have seldom seen a pleasanter or more kind-hearted looking one, and he certainly has a very striking face."

Shortly afterwards, Robert Shaw received notice that he had been commissioned a second lieutenant in the Second Regiment of the Massachusetts Volunteer Infantry, and he was soon in training at Camp Andrew, on the very site of Brook Farm where he had once played. He stayed with this regiment for eighteen months, until the end of 1862, took part in campaigns in Virginia and Maryland, and became a battle-hardened veteran.

During these months Shaw developed strong convictions about the use of Negro troops. During the spring and summer of 1862 he was stationed at Harpers Ferry and also at Charlestown, Virginia, where John Brown had been tried and hanged. His headquarters were located in the offices of Andrew Hunter, who had been the prosecuting attorney in Brown's case. In the idle hours that are inseparable from a soldier's life he made a careful study of the many documents that he found in Hunter's files. We know that Shaw pondered long the meaning of Brown's life and sacrifice. By August of 1862 he had reached the firm conclusion that the Negro ought to be armed. A very interesting letter, written to Sidney Howard Gay, one of his family's closest friends and neighbors and a famous antislavery editor, has survived:

"Isn't it extraordinary," wrote Shaw, "that the Government won't make use of the instrument that would finish the war sooner than anything else—that is, the slaves? . . . They would probably make a fine army after a little drill, and could certainly be kept under better discipline than our independent Yankees. . . ."

In his letters to his father, Shaw coupled complaints about the dullness of his military assignment and expressions of his desire for active service, with commentary upon the Negro. The first suggestion that he should have something to do, personally, with arming and leading the Negro had been given him by one of his colleagues, a Major Copeland:

"He [Major Copeland] says," wrote Shaw, "that it would be much wiser to enlist men in the North, who have had the courage to run away and have already suffered for their freedom than to take them all from the contrabands at Port Royal and other places. Copeland thinks," he continued, "that the raising of black regiments will be an era in our history and the greatest thing that has ever been done for the Negro race."

Such thoughts were set aside for a while in the stress of battle. On May 24, 1862, the Second Massachusetts clashed with the enemy in the neighborhood of Winchester, Virginia, and was driven back. In August the regiment was again engaged near Culpepper in the battle of Cedar Mountain. On September 17th it was involved in the battle of Antietam Creek in Maryland. In these months Shaw had his first battlefield experience and was, for the first time, under fire.

In these months he not only gained invaluable military experience but found himself as a soldier. Earlier he had chafed at the idleness that accompanies military life and had discussed with his father the possibility of transfer to a regiment where he would see more active service. But the campaigning of the summer of 1862 resolved Shaw's doubts about staying with the Second Massachusetts. He had gained battle experience, was very popular with his men, and was conscious of his own usefulness as an officer in a regiment which had lost many of its leaders in action. "A man," he wrote to his father, "should be very loath to leave a regiment in which he has gone through as much as we have in this. . . ."

On January 1, 1863, came the long-awaited Proclamation giving freedom to the slaves. Antislavery leaders accepted this event with jubilation; this Proclamation converted the war into a crusade and gave not only the slave but the Northern Negro something to fight for. It thus at once strengthened the hand of those who believed that freedom would be of little value to the Negro if he himself did not fight for it. Foremost among these champions of Negro enlistment were the supporters of the antislavery cause in New England and their leader, John Andrew.

John Andrew, governor of Massachusetts, was forty years old when the Civil War broke out. A leading member of the antislavery group that included Francis George Shaw, Charles Sumner and the rest of that brilliant galaxy that we mentioned earlier, he was also one of the architects of the Free Soil and Republican parties in New England. He was a spokesman for the antislavery cause in his fearless defense and vindication of John Brown in 1859. He and his most active assistant, John Forbes Murray, held to the view as passionately as Brown himself that the Negro would only win his freedom arms in hand. Upon his shoulders fell John Brown's mantle and the cause for which Brown had given his life. By 1860 Andrew had become the most popular man in Massachusetts, and was virtually drafted by the people of that state to govern them for the duration of the war emergency.

After the Emancipation Proclamation, Andrew moved swiftly to initiate the enlistment and organization of the Union's first Negro regiment. He understood that mobilization of the Negro on a massive scale faced heartbreaking delays, hostility, scepticism and sheer indifference. The way to shatter this roadblock was to get a regiment into action and to prove from its example for all the world to see that Negroes could fight.

It is hard for us today to understand the urgency and the importance of this task as it faced Andrew. We know from the experience of all too many subsequent wars that the American Negro fights with magnificent courage. But the years between the Revolution and the Civil War had seen a tragic advance of racist attitudes and practices throughout the North. In most of the free states the feeling that the Negro was and should be treated as a second-class citizen, that he was an inferior being, lacking in courage, intelligence and ability, was widespread. In most free states he was denied the right to vote, the right to integrated schooling and the right to equal job consideration. He had been pressed down into the role of a helot, whom the mass of whites regarded at best with contempt, whom too often they treated with violence and with scorn. This was the situation which Andrew wished to remedy. A fighting Negro, he thought, would not only help to end slavery, but he would contribute toward the creation of a true interracial democracy in the North.

On January 30, 1863, John Andrew turned to his dearest friend for advice and help in getting his project under way. He wrote to Francis George Shaw, asking for his only son, Robert:

> "It will be," he said, "the first Colored Regiment to be raised in the free states, and . . . its success or failure will go far to elevate or to depress the estimation in which the character of the colored Americans will be held throughout the world." To command this Regiment, he was looking, he said, "for young men of military experience, of firm antislavery principles, ambitious, superior to a vulgar contempt for color, and having faith in the capacity of colored men for military service. It occurs to me," he concluded, "to offer the colonelcy of such a Regiment to your son."

The elder Shaw hastened down to Virginia to bring Governor Andrew's invitation to Robert. One may guess the conflicts that arose in the young man's mind. He was now a captain in the regiment to which he was bound by ties of loyalty and long, honorable service. Not only was he asked to abandon his own regiment, but to assume a command that entailed great risks—risks of failure, ostracism, derision and contempt. We do know that Shaw rejected Andrew's invitation and sent his father home in great sadness and disappointment—and that overnight he changed his mind and wired his acceptance. And to Annie Haggerty, the Lenox girl to whom he was engaged, he wrote, "You know how many eminent men consider a Negro army of the greatest importance to our country at this time."

In February, 1863, the 54th Massachusetts Infantry (colored) was commissioned. Recruiting started and training got under way. On May 25th, the regiment marched through Boston amid an immense concourse of people and embarked on a transport headed for Port Royal in South Carolina.

After a short stay at Port Royal the regiment was landed on St. Simons Island in Georgia and went into camp hardly more than a stone's throw from Pierce Butler's cotton plantation. The place had a special interest for Robert—its mistress had been Fanny Kemble, whom he had known since he was a little boy and who had recounted to him in Italy the story of her plantation experience. But Shaw, when he rode over to visit the large and beautiful estate, did not find the hundreds of slaves about which Fanny had told him. All that was left of Georgia's greatest plantation was a small band of ancient and decrepit slaves bemoaning the loss of their families.

In the last week of June, 1863, the regiment made ready to take part in an attack upon Charleston, and on June 26th it had moved up to St. Helena's Island. Shaw's main concern here was the matter of his soldiers' pay. Word had reached him of a decision announced in Washington that colored soldiers were to receive $10.00 instead of the statutory $13.00 a month accorded to white troops. He wrote in hot indignation to his father and to Governor Andrew that if his regiment was included in this piece of discrimination it should "be mustered out of the service, as they were enlisted on the understanding that they were to be on the same footing as other Massachusetts volunteers."

Early in July the 54th Massachusetts moved up to the islands skirting Charleston harbor. On July 18th, after some preliminary skirmishing, Shaw reported to General Strong, commander of the assault operations, and was offered the post of honor in the first assault upon Fort Wagner, on Morris Island, commanding the entrance to Charleston harbor.

The rest is history. The 54th was the first to attack the fort, and they were repulsed with heavy losses. Shaw, with sword held high, was the first to climb upon the ramparts—and the first to die. The rebels buried his body, stripped of its uniform, in a common grave with dozens more of his Negro comrades.

In the course of time Shaw's own generation paid due honor to his memory, and a beautiful monument created by St. Gaudens was erected on Boston Common. But in succeeding years—up to our own time—Shaw's name has fallen into something very close to oblivion. Very many of our history books do not mention him. There is no biography of Shaw. And as for that circle of generous souls, headed by John Andrew and his own father, of whose ideals he was the supreme embodiment, they have been of little concern to historians. The very waters of the Atlantic have closed over the ruins of the fort and the anonymous grave at its foot.

A recent and authoritative writer about the Civil War speaks of Robert Gould Shaw as a "minor figure." Perhaps the time has come to revise this judgment. Perhaps we should say that Shaw's sacrifice and the lesson of his life epitomize the essence of the Civil War and do not merely decorate its fringes: epitomize the essence of its bloody lesson—that white and black men can and must live together in this country in freedom and in equality.

Songs
of
the
Soldiers

THE MISSISSIPPI VOLUNTEERS
JOHN BROWN OF MASSACHUSETTS
GENERAL LEE'S WOOING
MANY THOUSAND GONE
THE FIRST OF ARKANSAS
ROLL, ALABAMA, ROLL

Introduction

The people who fought the Civil War created and sang many thousands of songs and verses to tell of their experience. The best of these have value for us today. They illuminate a chapter in the struggle for human freedom. They are worthy to be cherished as an enduring part of our heritage.

The soldiers themselves wrote many songs, and these were often sung to traditional ballad tunes. Numbers of these songs were printed as broadsides and circulated in factory, field and camp by tens of thousands. The Civil War continued and enriched the broadside ballad tradition of colonial and early national times. Hundreds of these broadside ballads have survived; many have found their way into the soldiers' songbooks, or songsters, that came off the presses during the war in enormous numbers.

Professional songwriters turned to writing war songs and their products circulated as sheet music. Some of these people achieved wide popularity, notably the gifted composer George F. Root. Much of what they wrote has been preserved.

Frank Moore (1828-1904), America's pioneer collector of historical song, ranks as a source of Civil War music in his own right. During the conflict he began to collect soldiers'

573

songs, verses and stories; these he published in a series of works that constitute a monument to the common soldier.

The above, along with what has survived in oral tradition, are the main sources for the study of Civil War song. The examples reproduced below represent a tiny fraction of a heritage that, for the most part, still awaits discovery.

Song of the Mississippi Volunteers, with its sense of loneliness underlying a pose of bravado and its haunting refrain, has been widely found throughout the South. The melody is a favorite with children.

John Brown of Massachusetts is a stirring version of John Brown's Body, much sung by the soldiers of Brown's native state. It underlines the fact—too easily forgotten, perhaps—that Brown's Northern contemporaries thought of him as a hero whose sacrifice in the struggle against slavery and treason pointed the road which his own countrymen were soon to follow.

General Lee's Wooing is a soldier's poem which illuminates in a single flash the bloody struggle at Antietam Creek in Maryland where, on September 17, 1862, General Lee's forces were checked in their first major invasion of the North. This battle proved to be one of the great turning points in the war; for following it Lincoln issued his first emancipation proclamation of September 22 announcing that slaves in states still in rebellion would be freed on January 1, 1863. These commemorative verses, written by a Northern soldier and set to the tune of Tannenbaum, are amongst the finest lyrics the war produced.

Many Thousand Gone is the slaves' own unforgettable reaction to the news of emancipation that came on January 1, 1863.

The First of Arkansas was originally sung by the First Arkansas Regiment (Colored), but it became generally popular with Negro troops who flocked to the colors in 1863 and 1864. Its author, Captain Lindley Miller was, when the war began, a member of New York's elite Seventh Regiment, who elected later to lead Negro troops. He recalled that the song was sung with enthusiasm on dress parade and that it was also "a good song to fight with."

Roll, Alabama, Roll is a Civil War version of a sea shanty that probably originated with Negro roustabouts in New Orleans. With impressive conciseness it tells the story of the Confederate raider Alabama from its construction in 1861 to its sinking by the U.S. man-o'-war Kearsarge off Cherbourg, June 19, 1864. Such British-built raiders took a formidable toll of Northern shipping.

Song of the Mississippi Volunteers

O, I would not marry a con-script, a-
hid-ing in the woods, I'd ra-ther marry a
vol-unt-eer and do my coun-try good.
Sol-dier boy, o sol-dier boy, a
sol-dier boy for me, If ev-er I get
mar-ried, a sol-dier's wife I'll be.
We go walk-ing on the green grass,
thus, thus, thus. Come all ye fair and

prett - y maids, come walk - a - long with

us. So prett - y and so fair as you

take your-selves to be, I'll choose you for a

part - ner, Come walk a - long with me.

O, I would not marry a conscript a-hidin' in the wood,
I'd rather marry a volunteer and do my country good,
Soldier boy, o soldier boy, a soldier boy for me,
If ever I get married, a soldier's wife I'll be.

    We go walking on the green grass thus, thus, thus.
    Come all ye fair and pretty maids and walk along with us.
    So pretty and so fair as you take yourselves to be
    I'll choose you for a partner, come walk along with me.

O, I would not marry a lawyer who's pleading at the bar,
I'd rather marry a soldier boy who wears a Southern star.
Soldier boy, etc.
    We go walking on the green grass, etc.

O, I would not be a lady that Southrons call a belle,
I'd rather be a soldier boy and hear the Yankees yell,
Soldier boy, etc.
    We go walking on the green grass, etc.

O, I would not be a nursemaid and hear the children squall,
I'd rather be a volunteer and face a cannon ball.
Soldier boy, etc.
    We go walking on the green grass, etc.

O, I would not be a farmer who's toiling in the sun,
I'd rather be a soldier boy and see the Yankees run.
Soldier boy, etc.
    We go walking on the green grass, etc.

O, I would not be a miller who grinds the people's grain,
I'd rather be a soldier boy who walks through wind and rain.
Soldier boy, etc.
    We go walking on the green grass, etc.

JOHN BROWN OF MASSACHUSETTS

tune: *John Brown's Body*

Old John Brown's body is a-mouldering in the dust,
Old John Brown's rifle's red with blood spots turned to rust,
Old John Brown's pike has made its last, unflinching thrust,
His soul is marching on!
　　　Glory, glory hallelujah,
　　　"Forward," calls the Lord, our Captain,
　　　Glory, glory hallelujah,
　　　With him we're marching on.

For treason hung because he struck at treason's root,
When soon palmetto tree had ripened treason's fruit,
His dust, disquieted, stirred at Sumter's last salute,
His soul is marching on!
　　　Glory, glory hallelujah, etc.

Who rides before the army of martyrs to the Word?
The heavens grow bright as He makes bare his flaming sword,
The glory fills the earth of the coming of the Lord,
His soul is marching on!
　　　Glory, glory hallelujah, etc.

His sacrifice we share! Our sword shall victory crown!
For God and country strike the fiend rebellion down!
For freedom and the right remember old John Brown!
His soul is marching on!
　　　Glory, glory hallelujah, etc.

GENERAL LEE'S WOOING

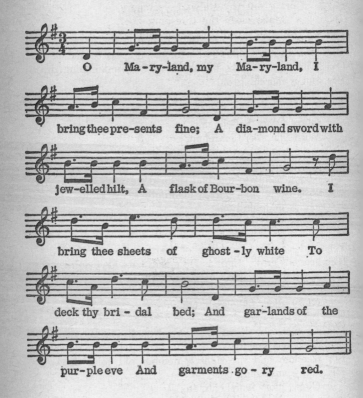

O Maryland, my Maryland,
    I bring thee presents fine;
A diamond sword with jewelled hilt,
    A flask of Bourbon wine.
I bring thee sheets of ghostly white
    To deck thy bridal bed;
And garlands of the purple eve
    And garments gory red.

O Maryland, my Maryland,
   Sweet land upon the shore,
Bring out thy stalwart yeomanry,
   Make clean the threshing floor.
My ready wains lie stretching far
   Across the fertile plain,
And I among the reapers stand
   To gather in the grain.

O Maryland, my Maryland,
   I fondly wait to see,
Thy banners flaunting in the breeze
   Beneath the trysting tree.
While all my gallant chivalry,
   Proud gentlemen with spurs,
Come tramping, tramping o'er the hills
   And tramping through the furze.

O Maryland, my Maryland,
   I feel the leaden rain,
I see the winged messenger
   Come hurling to my brain.
I feathered with thy golden hair,
   'Tis feathered now in vain,
I spurn the hand that loosed the shaft,
   And curse thee in my pain.

O Maryland, my Maryland,
   Alas the ruthless day,
That sees my gallant buttonwoods
   Ride galloping away.
And ruthless for my chivalry,
   Proud gentlemen with spurs,
Whose bones lie stark upon the hills,
   And stark among the furze.

Many Thousand Gone

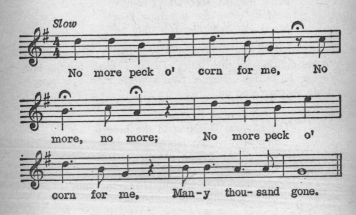

No more peck o' corn for me, No more, no more; No more peck o' corn for me, Man-y thou-sand gone.

No more peck o' corn for me,
No more, no more;
No more peck o' corn for me,
Many thousand gone.

No more driver's lash for me,
No more, no more;
No more driver's lash for me,
Many thousand gone.

No more pint o' salt for me,
No more, no more;
No more pint o' salt for me,
Many thousand gone.

No more mistress call for me,
No more, no more;
No more mistress call for me,
Many thousand gone.

MARCHING SONG OF THE FIRST ARKANSAS (COLORED) REGIMENT

tune: *John Brown's Body*

Oh, we're the bully soldiers of the "First of Arkansas,"
We are fighting for the Union, we are fighting for the law,
We can hit a Rebel further than a white man ever saw,
As we go marching on.

    Glory, glory hallelujah,
    Glory, glory hallelujah,
    Glory, glory hallelujah,
    As we go marching on.

See, there above the center, where the flag is waving bright,
We are going out of slavery; we're bound for freedom's light;
We mean to show Jeff Davis how the Africans can fight,
As we go marching on!
    Glory, glory hallelujah, etc.

We have done with hoeing cotton, we have done with hoeing
    corn,
We are colored Yankee soldiers, now, as sure as you are born;
When the masters hear us yelling, they'll think it's Gabriel's
    horn,
As we go marching on.
    Glory, glory hallelujah, etc.

They will have to pay us wages, the wages of their sin,
They will have to bow their foreheads to their colored kith
    and kin,
They will have to give us house-room, or the roof shall tumble
    in!
As we go marching on.
    Glory, glory hallelujah, etc.

They said, "Now colored brethren, you shall be forever free,
From the first of January, Eighteen hundred sixty-three."
We heard it in the river going rushing to the sea,
As it went sounding on.
    Glory, glory hallelujah, etc.

Father Abraham has spoken and the message has been sent,
The prison doors he opened, and out the prisoners went,
To join the sable army of the "African descent,"
As we go marching on.
    Glory, glory hallelujah, etc.

Then fall in, colored brethren, you'd better do it soon,
Don't you hear the drum a-beating the Yankee Doodle tune?
We are with you now this morning, we'll be far away at noon,
As we go marching on.
    Glory, glory hallelujah, etc.

ROLL, ALABAMA, ROLL

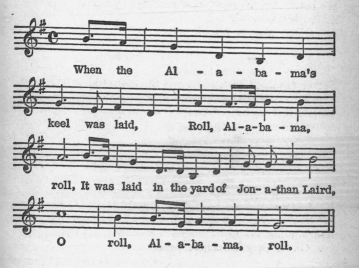

When the Al - a - ba - ma's
keel was laid, Roll, Al-a-ba - ma,
roll, It was laid in the yard of Jon- a-than Laird,
O roll, Al - a-ba - ma, roll.

1. When the Alabama's keel was laid,
   Roll, Alabama, roll,
   'Twas laid in the yard of Jonathan Laird,
   O, roll, Alabama, roll.

2. 'Twas laid in the yard of Jonathan Laird,
   Roll, Alabama, roll,
   'Twas laid in the town of Birkenhead,
   O, roll, Alabama, roll.

3. Down the Mersey ways she rolled then,
      Roll, Alabama, roll,
   Liverpool fitted her with guns and men,
      O, roll, Alabama, roll.

4. From the western isles she sailed forth,
      Roll, Alabama, roll,
   To destroy the commerce of the North,
      O, roll, Alabama, roll.

5. To Cherbourg Port she sailed one day,
      Roll, Alabama, roll,
   To take her count of prize monnay,
      O, roll, Alabama, roll.

6. Many a sailor he saw his doom,
      Roll, Alabama, roll,
   When the Kearsarge hove in view,
      O, roll, Alabama, roll.

7. Till a ball from the forward pivot that day
      Roll, Alabama, roll,
   Shot the Alabama's stern away,
      O, roll, Alabama, roll.

8. Off the three-mile limit in '64,
      Roll, Alabama, roll,
   The Alabama sank to the ocean floor,
      O, roll, Alabama, roll.

Appendix

THE MAYFLOWER COMPACT
NOVEMBER 11, 1620

In the name of God, amen. We, whose names are underwritten, the loyal subjects of our dread sovereign lord King James, by the grace of God, of Great Britain, France, and Ireland, King, Defender of the Faith, etc. Having undertaken for the glory of God, and advancement of the Christian faith, and honor of our King and Country, a voyage to plant the first colony in the northern parts of Virginia, do by these presents, solemnly and mutually in the presence of God and of one another, covenant and combine ourselves together into a civil body politic, for our better ordering and preservation, and furtherance of the ends aforesaid; and by virtue hereof do enact, constitute, and frame, such just and equal laws, ordinances, acts, constitutions, and offices, from time to time, as shall be thought most meet and convenient for the general good of the colony; unto which we promise all due submission and obedience. In witness whereof we have hereunto subscribed our names at Cape Cod the eleventh of November, in the reign of our sovereign lord King James of England, France, and Ireland, the eighteenth, and of Scotland, the fifty-fourth. Anno Domini, 1620.

Mr. John Carver
Mr. William Bradford
Mr. Edward Winslow
Mr. William Brewster
Isaac Allerton
Miles Standish
John Alden
John Turner
Francis Eaton
James Chilton
John Craxton
John Billington
Joses Fletcher
John Goodman
Mr. Samuel Fuller
Mr. Christopher Martin
Mr. William Mullins

Mr. William White
Mr. Richard Warren
John Howland
Mr. Stephen Hopkins
Digery Priest
Thomas Williams
Gilbert Winslow
Edmund Margesson
Peter Brown
Richard Bitteridge
George Soule
Edward Tilly
John Tilly
Francis Cooke
Thomas Rogers
Thomas Tinker
John Ridgate

Edward Fuller   Thomas English
Richard Clark   Edward Doten
Richard Gardiner   Edward Liester
Mr. John Allerton

THE BODY OF LIBERTIES
1641

The Liberties of the Massachusetts Colony in
New England, 1641

The free fruition of such liberties immunities and privileges
as humanity, civility, and Christianity call for as due to every
man in his place and proportion without impeachment and
infringement, hath ever been and ever will be the tranquillity
and stability of churches and commonwealths. And the denial
or deprival thereof, the disturbance if not the ruin of both.

We hold it therefore our duty and safety, whilst we are
about the further establishing of this government, to collect
and express all such freedoms as for present we foresee may
concern us, and our posterity after us, and to ratify them with
our solemn consent.

We do therefore this day religiously and unanimously decree and confirm these following rights, liberties, and privileges concerning our churches and civil state, to be respectively impartially and inviolably enjoyed and observed throughout
our jurisdiction for ever.

1. No man's life shall be taken away, no man's honor or
good name shall be stained, no man's person shall be arrested,
restrained, banished, dismembered, nor any ways punished,
no man shall be deprived of his wife and children, no man's
goods or estate shall be taken away from him, nor any way
endamaged under color of law or countenance of authority,
unless it be by virtue or equity of some express law of the
country warranting the same, established by a General Court
and sufficiently published, or in case of the defect of a law in
any particular case, by the word of God. And in capital cases,
or in cases concerning dismembering or banishment, according
to that word to be judged by the General Court.

2. Every person within this jurisdiction, whether inhabitant

or foreigner, shall enjoy the same justice and law, that is general for the plantation, which we constitute and execute one toward another without partiality or delay.

3. No man shall be urged to take any oath or subscribe any articles, covenants, or remonstrance, of a public and civil nature, but such as the General Court hath considered, allowed and required.

4. No man shall be punished for not appearing at or before any civil assembly, court, council, magistrate, or officer, nor for the omission of any office or service, if he shall be necessarily hindered by any apparent act or providence of God, which he could neither foresee nor avoid. Provided that this law shall not prejudice any person of his just cost and damage, in any civil action.

5. No man shall be compelled to any public work or service unless the press be grounded upon some act of the General Court, and have reasonable allowance therefor.

6. No man shall be pressed in person to any office, work, wars or other public service, that is necessarily and sufficiently exempted by any natural or personal impediment, as by want of years, greatness of age, defect of mind, failing of senses, or impotency of limbs.

7. No man shall be compelled to go out of the limits of this plantation upon any offensive wars which this Commonwealth or any of our friends or confederates shall voluntarily undertake. But only upon such vindictive and defensive wars in our own behalf or the behalf of our friends and confederates as shall be enterprized by the counsel and consent of a Court General, or by authority derived from the same.

8. No man's cattle or goods of what kind soever shall be pressed or taken for any public use or service, unless it be by warrant grounded upon some act of the General Court, nor without such reasonable prices and hire as the ordinary rates of the country do afford. And if his cattle and goods shall perish or suffer damage in such service, the owners shall be sufficiently recompensed.

9. No monopolies shall be granted or allowed amongst us, but of such new inventions that are profitable to the country, and that for a short time.

10. All our lands and heritages shall be free from all fines and license upon alienations, and from all hariots, wardships, liveries, primer-seizins, year day and waste, escheats, and for-

feitures, upon the deaths of parents or ancestors, be they natural, casual, or judicial.

11. All persons which are of the age of 21 years, and of right understanding and memories, whether excommunicate or condemned, shall have full power and liberty to make their wills and testaments, and other lawful alienations of their lands and estates.

12. Every man whether inhabitant or foreigner, free or not free, shall have liberty to come to any public court, council, or town meeting, and either by speech or writing to move any lawful, seasonable, and material question, or to present any necessary motion, complaint, petition, bill or information, whereof that meeting hath proper cognizance, so it be done in convenient time, due order, and respective manner.

13. No man shall be rated here for any estate or revenue he hath in England, or in any foreign parts til it be transported hither.

14. Any conveyance or alienation of land or other estate whatsoever, made by any woman that is married, any child under age, idiot or distracted person, shall be good if it be passed and ratified by the consent of a General Court.

15. All covenous or fraudulent alienations or conveyances of lands, tenements, or any hereditaments, shall be of no validity to defeat any man from due debts or legacies, or from any just title, claim or possession, of that which is so fraudulently conveyed.

16. Every inhabitant that is a householder shall have free fishing and fowling in any great ponds and bays, coves and rivers, so far as the sea ebbs and flows within the precincts of the town where they dwell, unless the free men of the same town or the General Court have otherwise appropriated them, provided that this shall not be extended to give leave to any man to come upon others property without their leave.

17. Every man of or with this jurisdiction shall have free liberty, notwithstanding any civil power, to remove both himself, and his family at their pleasure out of the same, provided there be no legal impediment to the contrary.

*Rights, Rules and Liberties concerning Judicial
Proceedings*

18. No man's person shall be restrained or imprisoned by
any authority whatsoever, before the law hath sentenced him
thereto, if he can put in sufficient security, bail or mainprise
for his appearance and good behavior in the meantime, unless
it be in crimes capital, and contempts in open Court, and in
such cases where some express act of Court doth allow it.

19. If in a General Court any miscarriage shall be amongst
the assistants when they are by themselves that may deserve
an admonition or fine under 20/–, it shall be examined and
sentenced by themselves. If amongst the deputies when they
are by themselves, it shall be examined and sentenced amongst
themselves. If it be when the whole Court is together, it shall
be judged by the whole Court, and not severally as before.

20. If any which are to sit as judges in any other Court
shall demean themselves offensively in the Court, the rest of
the judges present shall have power to censure him for it; if
the cause be of a high nature it shall be presented to and cen-
sured at the next superior Court.

21. In all cases where the first summons are not served six
days before the Court, and the cause briefly specified in the
warrant, where appearance is to be made by the party summoned, it shall be at his liberty whether he will appear or no,
except all cases that are to be handled in courts suddenly
called, upon extraordinary occasions. In all cases where there
appears present and urgent cause any assistant or officer appointed shall have power to make out attachments for the first
summons.

22. No man in any suit or action against another shall falsely pretend great debts or damages to vex his adversary; if it
shall appear he doth so, the Court shall have power to set a
reasonable fine on his head.

23. No man shall be adjudged to pay for detaining any
debt from any creditor above eight pounds in the hundred for
one year, and not above that rate proportionable for all sums
whatsoever, neither shall this be a color or countenance to allow any usury amongst us contrary to the law of God.

24. In all trespasses or damages done to any man or men,
if it can be proved to be done by the mere default of him or

them to whom the trespass is done, it shall be judged no trespass, nor any damage given for it.

25. No summons pleading judgment, or any kind of proceeding in Court or course of justice shall be abated, arrested or reversed upon any kind of circumstantial errors or mistakes, if the person and cause be rightly understood and intended by the Court.

26. Every man that findeth himself unfit to plead his own cause in any Court shall have liberty to employ any man against whom the Court doth not except, to help him, provided he give him no fee or reward for his pains. This shall not exempt the party himself from answering such questions in person as the Court shall think meet to demand of him.

27. If any plaintiff shall give into any Court a declaration of his cause in writing, the defendant shall also have liberty and time to give in his answer in writing, and so in all further proceedings between party and party, so it does not further hinder the dispatch of justice than the Court shall be willing unto.

28. The plaintiff in all actions brought in any Court shall have liberty to withdraw his action, or to be nonsuited before the jury hath given in their verdict, in which case he shall always pay full cost and charges to the defendant, and may afterwards renew his suit at another Court if he please.

29. In all actions at law it shall be the liberty of the plaintiff and defendant by mutual consent to choose whether they will be tried by the bench or by a jury, unless it be where the law upon just reason hath otherwise determined. The like liberty shall be granted to all persons in criminal cases.

30. It shall be in the liberty of plaintiff and defendant, and likewise every delinquent (to be judged by a jury) to challenge any of the jurors. And if his challenge be found just and reasonable by the bench, or the rest of the jury, as the challenger shall choose it shall be allowed him, and *tales de circumstantibus* impanelled in their room.

31. In all cases where evidence is so obscure or defective that the jury cannot clearly and safely give a positive verdict, whether it be a grand or petit jury, it shall have liberty to give a *non liquit*, or a special verdict, in which last—that is, in a special verdict—the judgment of the case shall be left to the Court. And all jurors shall have liberty in matters of fact, if they cannot find the main issue, yet to find and present in their

verdict so much as they can. If the bench and jurors shall so suffer at any time about their verdict that either of them cannot proceed with peace of conscience, the case shall be referred to the General Court, who shall take the question from both and determine it.

32. Every man shall have liberty to replevy his cattle or goods impounded, distrained, seized, or extended, unless it be upon execution after judgment, and in payment of fines. Provided he puts in good security to prosecute his replevin, and to satisfy such demands as his adversary shall recover against him in law.

33. No man's person shall be arrested, or imprisoned upon execution of judgment for any debt or fine, if the law can find competent means of satisfaction otherwise from his estate, and if not, his person may be arrested and imprisoned where he shall be kept at his own charge, not the plaintiff's, till satisfaction be made, unless the Court shall otherwise provide.

34. If any man shall be proved and judged a common barrator vexing others with unjust, frequent, and endless suits, it shall be in the power of courts both to deny him the benefit of the law, and to punish him for his barratry.

35. No man's corn nor hay that is in the field or upon the cart, nor his garden stuff, nor anything subject to present decay, shall be taken in any distress, unless he that takes it doth presently bestow it where it may not be embezzled nor suffer spoil or decay, or give security to satisfy the worth whereof if it comes to any harm.

36. It shall be in the liberty of every man cast, condemned or sentenced in any cause in any inferior Court, to make their appeal to the Court of Assistants, provided they tender their appeal and put in security to prosecute it before the Court be ended wherein they were condemned, and within six days next ensuing put in good security before some assistant to satisfy what his adversary shall recover against him; and if the cause be of a criminal nature, for his good behavior and appearance. And every man shall have liberty to complain to the General Court of any injustice done him in any Court of Assistants or other.

37. In all cases where it appears to the Court that the plaintiff hath willingly and wittingly done wrong to the defendant in commencing and prosecuting an action or complaint against him, they shall have power to impose upon him a proportion-

able fine to the use of the defendant or accused person, for his false complaint or clamor.

38. Every man shall have liberty to record in the public rolls of any Court any testimony given upon oath in the same Court, or before two assistants, or any deed or evidence legally confirmed, there to remain *in perpetuam rei memoriam,* that is, for perpetual memorial or evidence upon occasion.

39. In all actions both real and personal between party and party, the Court shall have power to respite execution for a convenient time, when in their prudence they see just cause so to do.

40. No conveyance, deed, or promise whatsoever shall be of validity, if it be gotten by illegal violence, imprisonment, threatening, or any kind of forcible compulsion called duress.

41. Every man that is to answer for any criminal cause, whether he be in prison or under bail, his cause shall be heard and determined at the next Court that hath proper cognizance thereof; and may be done without prejudice of justice.

42. No man shall be twice sentenced by civil justice for one and the same crime, offence, or trespass.

43. No man shall be beaten with above 40 stripes, nor shall any true gentleman, nor any man equal to a gentleman, be punished with whipping, unless his crime be very shameful and his course of life vicious and profligate.

44. No man condemned to die shall be put to death within four days next after his condemnation, unless the Court see special cause to the contrary, or in case of martial law; nor shall the body of any man so put to death be unburied 12 hours unless it be in case of anatomy.

45. No man shall be forced by torture to confess any crime against himself nor any other unless it be in some capital case, where he is first fully convicted by clear and sufficient evidence to be guilty, after which, if the cause be of that nature, that it is very apparent there be other conspirators or confederates with him, then he may be tortured, yet not with such tortures as be barbarous and inhumane.

46. For bodily punishments we allow amongst us none that are inhumane, barbarous, or cruel.

47. No man shall be put to death without the testimony of two or three witnesses or that which is equivalent thereunto.

48. Every inhabitant of the country shall have free liberty to search and view any rules, records, or registers of any Court

or office except the Council; and to have a transcript of exemplification thereof, written, examined, and signed by the hand of the officer of the office, paying the appointed fees therefor.

49. No free man shall be compelled to serve upon juries above two courts a year, except grand jurymen, who shall hold two courts together at the least.

50. All jurors shall be chosen continually by the freemen of the town where they dwell.

51. All associates selected at any time to assist the assistants in inferior courts, shall be nominated by the towns belonging to that court, by orderly agreement among themselves.

52. Children, idiots, distracted persons, and all that are strangers, or newcomers to our plantation, shall have such allowances and dispensations in any cause whether criminal or other as religion and reason require.

53. The age of discretion for passing away of lands or such kind of hereditaments, or for giving of votes, verdicts, or sentence in any civil courts or causes, shall be one and twenty years.

54. Whensoever anything is to be put to vote, any sentence to be pronounced, or any other matter to be proposed, or read in any court or assembly, if the president or moderator thereof shall refuse to perform it, the major part of the members of that court or assembly shall have power to appoint any other meet man of them to do it. And if there be just cause, to punish him that should and would not.

55. In all suits or actions, in any court, the plaintiff shall have liberty to make all the titles, and claims to that he sues for, he can. And the defendant shall have liberty to plead all the pleas he can in answer to them, and the court shall judge according to the entire evidence of all.

56. If any man shall behave himself offensively at any town meeting, the rest of the freemen then present shall have power to sentence him for his offence. So be it the fine or penalty exceed not twenty shillings.

57. Whensoever any person shall come to any very sudden, untimely, and unnatural death, some assistant, or the constables of that town, shall forthwith summon a jury of twelve freemen to inquire of the cause and manner of their death, and shall present a true verdict thereof to some near assistant, or the next court to be held for that town upon their oath.

Liberties more peculiarly concerning the Freemen.

58. Civil authority hath power and liberty to see the peace, ordinances and rules of Christ observed in every church according to his word, so it be done in a civil and not an ecclesiastical way.

59. Civil authority hath power and liberty to deal with any church member in a way of civil justice, notwithstanding any church relation, office, or interest.

60. No church censure shall degrade or depose any man from any civil dignity, office, or authority he shall have in the Commonwealth.

61. No magistrate, juror, officer, or other man shall be bound to inform present or reveal any private crime or offense, wherein there is no peril or danger to this plantation or any member thereof, when any necessary tie of conscience binds him to secrecy grounded upon the word of God, unless it be in case of testimony lawfully required.

62. Any shire or town shall have liberty to choose their deputies whom and where they please for the General Court. So be it they be freemen, and have taken their oath of fealty, and inhabiting in this jurisdiction.

63. No governor, deputy governor, assistant, associate, or grand juryman at any court, nor any deputy for the General Court, shall at any time bear his own charges at any court, but their necessary expenses shall be defrayed either by the town or shire in whose service they are, or by the country in general.

64. Every action between party and party, and proceedings against delinquents in criminal causes, shall be briefly and distinctly entered on the rolls of every court by the recorder thereof. That such actions be not afterwards brought again to the vexation of any man.

65. No custom or prescription shall ever prevail amongst us in any moral cause; our meaning is to maintain anything that can be proved to be morally sinful by the word of God.

66. The freemen of every township shall have power to make such by-laws and constitutions as may concern the welfare of their town, provided they be not of a criminal, but only of a prudential nature, and that their penalties exceed not 20/— for one offence, and that they be not repugnant to the

public laws and orders of the country. And if any inhabitant shall neglect or refuse to observe them, they shall have power to levy the appointed penalties by distress.

67. It is the constant liberty of the freemen of this plantation to choose yearly at the court of election out of the freemen all the general officers of this jurisdiction. If they please to discharge them at the day of election by way of vote, they may do it without showing cause; but if at any other General Court, we hold it due justice, that the reasons thereof be alleged and proved. By general officers we mean, our governor, deputy governor, assistants, treasurer, general of our wars, and our admiral at sea, and such as are or hereafter may be of the like general nature.

68. It is the liberty of the freemen to choose such deputies for the General Court out of themselves, either in their own towns or elsewhere, as they judge fittest. And because we cannot foresee what variety and weight of occasions may fall into future consideration, and what counsels we may stand in need of, we decree: that the deputies (to attend the General Court in the behalf of the country) shall not at any time be stated or enacted, but from Court to Court, or at the most but for one year, that the country may have an annual liberty to do in that case what is most behooveful for the best welfare thereof.

69. No General Court shall be dissolved or adjourned without the consent of the major part thereof.

70. All freemen called to give any advice, vote, verdict, or sentence in any court, council, or civil assembly, shall have full freedom to do it according to their true judgments and consciences, so it be done orderly and inoffensively for the manner.

71. The governor shall have a casting voice whensoever an equivote shall fall out in the Court of Assistants or general assembly. So shall the president or moderator have in all civil courts or assemblies.

72. The governor and deputy governor jointly consenting, or any three assistants concurring in consent, shall have power out of court to reprieve a condemned malefactor til the next quarter or General Court. The General Court only shall have power to pardon a condemned malefactor.

73. The General Court hath liberty and authority to send out any member of this Commonwealth of what quality, condition, or office whatsoever into foreign parts about any public

message or negotiation. Provided the party sent be acquainted with the affair he goeth about, and be willing to undertake the service.

74. The freemen of every town or township shall have full power to choose yearly or for less time out of themselves a convenient number of fit men to order the planting or prudential occasions of that town, according to instructions given them in writing; provided nothing be done by them contrary to the public laws and orders of the country, provided also the number of such select persons be not above nine.

75. It is and shall be the liberty of any member or members of any court, council, or civil assembly in cases of making or executing any order or law, that properly concern religion, or any cause capital, or wars, or subscription to any public articles or remonstrance, in case they cannot in judgment and conscience consent to that way the major vote or suffrage goes, to make their contra-remonstrance or protestation in speech or writing, and upon request to have their dissent recorded in the rolls of that court. So it be done christianly and respectfully for the manner. And their dissent only be entered without the reasons thereof, for the avoiding of tediousness.

76. Whensoever any jury of trials or jurors are not clear in their judgments or consciences concerning any cause wherein they are to give their verdict, they shall have liberty in open court to advise with any man they think fit to resolve or direct them, before they give in their verdict.

77. In all cases wherein any freeman is to give his vote, be it in point of election, making constitutions and orders, or passing sentence in any case of judicature or the like, if he cannot see reason to give it positively one way or another, he shall have liberty to be silent, and not pressed to a determined vote.

78. The general or public treasure or any part thereof shall never be expended but by the appointment of a General Court, nor any shire treasure, but by the appointment of the freemen thereof, nor any town treasure but by the freemen of that township.

Liberties of Women

79. If any man at his death shall not leave his wife a competent portion of his estate, upon just complaint made to the General Court she shall be relieved.

80. Every married woman shall be free from bodily correction or stripes by her husband, unless it be in his own defence upon her assault. If there be any just cause of correction, complaint shall be made to authority assembled in some court, from which only she shall receive it.

Liberties of Children

81. When parents die intestate, the elder son shall have a double portion of his whole estate real and personal, unless the General Court upon just cause alleged shall judge otherwise.

82. When parents die intestate having no [male] heir of their bodies, their daughters shall inherit as co-partners, unless the General Court upon just reason shall judge otherwise.

83. If any parents shall willfully and unreasonably deny any child timely or convenient marriage, or shall exercise any unnatural severity towards them, such children shall have free liberty to complain to authority for redress.

84. No orphan during their minority which was not committed to tuition or service by the parents in their lifetime, shall afterwards be absolutely disposed of by any kindred, friend, executor, township, or church, nor by themselves, without the consent of some court wherein two assistants at least shall be present.

Liberties of Servants

85. If any servants shall flee from the tyranny and cruelty of their masters to the house of any freeman of the same town, they shall be there protected and sustained till due order be taken for their relief. Provided due notice thereof be speedily given to their masters from whom they fled, and [to] the next assistant or constable where the party flying is harbored.

86. No servant shall be put off for above a year to any other neither in the lifetime of their master nor after their death by their executors or administrators, unless it be by consent of authority assembled in some court or two assistants.

87. If any man smite out the eye or tooth of his man-servant, or maid-servant, or otherwise maim or much disfigure him, unless it be by mere casualty, he shall let them go free

from his service. And shall have such further recompense as the court shall allow him.

88. Servants that have served diligently and faithfully to the benefit of their masters seven years, shall not be sent away empty. And if any have been unfaithful, negligent, or unprofitable in their service, notwithstanding the good usage of their masters, they shall not be dismissed till they have made satisfaction according to the judgment of authority.

Liberties of Foreigners and Strangers

89. If any people of other nations professing the true Christian religion shall flee to us from the tyranny or oppression of their persecutors, or from famine, wars, or the like necessary and compulsory cause, they shall be entertained and succored amongst us, according to that power and prudence God shall give us.

90. If any ships or other vessels, be it friend or enemy, shall suffer shipwreck upon our coast, there shall be no violence or wrong offered to their persons or goods. But their persons shall be harbored, and relieved, and their goods preserved in safety till authority may be certified thereof, and shall take further order therein.

91. There shall never be any bond slavery, villeinage or captivity amongst us unless it be lawful captives taken in just wars, and such strangers as willingly sell themselves or are sold to us. And these shall have all the liberties and Christian usages which the law of God established in Israel concerning such persons doth morally require. This exempts none from servitude who shall be judged thereto by authority.

Of the Brute Creature

92. No man shall exercise any tyranny or cruelty towards any brute creature which are usually kept for man's use.

93. If any man shall have occasion to lead or drive cattle from place to place that is far off, so that they be weary, or hungry, or all sick, or lame, it shall be lawful to rest or refresh them, for competent time, in any open place that is not corn, meadow, or enclosed for some peculiar use.

94. CAPITAL LAWS

I

If any man after legal conviction shall have or worship any other God, but the lord God, he shall be put to death (Deut. 13: 6, 10; Deut. 17: 2, 6; Ex. 22: 20).

II

If any man or woman be a witch (that is, hath or consulteth with a familiar spirit), they shall be put to death (Ex. 22: 18; Lev. 20: 27; Deut. 18: 10).

III

If any person shall blaspheme the name of God, the Father, Son, or Holy Ghost, with direct, express, presumptuous or high-handed blasphemy, or shall curse God in the like manner, he shall be put to death (Lev. 24: 15, 16).

IV

If any person commit any wilful murder, which is man-slaughter, committed upon premeditated malice, hatred, or cruelty, not in a man's necessary and just defence, nor by mere casualty against his will, he shall be put to death (Ex. 21: 12; Numb. 35: 13, 14, 30, 31).

V

If any person slayeth another suddenly in his anger or cruelty of passion, he shall be put to death (Numb. 25: 20, 21; Lev. 24: 17).

VI

If any person shall slay another through guile, either by poisoning or other such devilish practice, he shall be put to death (Ex. 21: 14).

VII

If any man or woman shall lie with any beast or brute creature by carnal copulation, they shall surely be put to death. And the beast shall be slain, and buried and not eaten (Lev. 20: 15, 16).

VIII

If any man lieth with mankind as he lieth with a woman, both of them have committed abomination, they both shall surely be put to death (Lev. 20: 13).

IX

If any person committeth adultery with a married or espoused wife, the adulterer and adulteress shall surely be put to death (Lev: 20: 19 and 18: 20; Deut. 22: 23, 24).

X

If any man stealeth a man or mankind, he shall surely be put to death (Ex. 21: 16).

XI

If any man rise up by false witness, wittingly and of purpose to take away any man's life, he shall be put to death (Deut. 19: 16, 18, 19).

XII

If any man shall conspire and attempt any invasion, insurrection, or public rebellion against our commonwealth, or shall endeavor to surprise any town or towns, fort or forts therein, or shall treacherously and perfidiously attempt the alteration and subversion of our frame of polity or government fundamentally, he shall be put to death.

95. A DECLARATION OF THE LIBERTIES THE LORD JESUS HATH GIVEN TO THE CHURCHES.

I

All the people of God within this jurisdiction who are not in a church way, and be orthodox in judgment, and not scandalous in life, shall have full liberty to gather themselves into a church estate; provided they do it in a Christian way, with due observation of the rules of Christ revealed in his word.

II

Every church hath full liberty to exercise all the ordinances of God, according to the rules of scripture.

III

Every church hath free liberty of election and ordination of all their officers from time to time, provided they be able, pious and orthodox.

IV

Every church hath free liberty of admission, recommendation, dismission, and expulsion or deposal of their officers and members, upon due cause, with free exercise of the discipline and censures of Christ according to the rules of his word.

V

No injunctions are to be put upon any church, church officers or member in point of doctrine, worship or discipline, whether for substance or circumstance besides the institutions of the Lord.

VI

Every church of Christ hath freedom to celebrate days of

fasting and prayer, and of thanksgiving according to the word of God.

VII

The elders of churches have free liberty to meet monthly, quarterly, or otherwise, in convenient numbers and places, for conferences and consultations about Christians and church questions and occasions.

VIII

All churches have liberty to deal with any of their members in a church way that are in the hand of justice. So it be not to retard or hinder the course thereof.

IX

Every church hath liberty to deal with any magistrate, deputy of court, or other officer whatsoever that is a member in a church way in case of apparent and just offence given in their places, so it be done with due observance and respect.

X

We allow private meetings for edification in religion amongst Christians of all sorts of people. So it be without just offence for number, time, place, and other circumstances.

XI

For the preventing and removing of error and offence that may grow and spread in any of the churches in this jurisdiction, and for the preserving of truth and peace in the several churches within themselves, and for the maintenance and exercise of brotherly communion amongst all the churches in the country, it is allowed and ratified, by the authority of this General Court as a lawful liberty of the churches of Christ: that once in every month of the year (when the season will bear it) it shall be lawful for the ministers and elders of the churches near adjoining together, with any other of the brethren, with the consent of the churches, to assemble by course in each several church one after another. To the intent, after the preaching of the word by such a minister as shall be requested thereto by the elders of the church where the assembly is held, the rest of the day may be spent in public Christian conference about the discussing and resolving of any such doubts and cases of conscience concerning matter of doctrine or worship or government of the church as shall be propounded by any of the brethren of that church, will leave also to any other brother to propound his objections or answers for further satisfaction according to the word of God. Provided that the whole action be guided and moderated by the elders of the church where the assembly is held, or by such others as they shall appoint. And that nothing be concluded and imposed by way of authority from one or more churches upon another, but only by way of brotherly conference and consultations. That the truth may be searched out to the satisfying of every man's conscience in the sight of God according to his word. And because such an assembly and the work thereof cannot be duly attended to if other lectures be held in the same week, it is therefore agreed with the consent of the churches, that in that week when such an assembly is held, all the lectures in all the neighboring churches for that week shall be forborne. That so the public service of Christ in this more solemn assembly may be transacted with greater diligence and attention.

96. Howsoever these above specified rites, freedoms, immunities, authorities and privileges, both civil and ecclesiastical, are expressed only under the name and title of liberties, and not in the exact form of laws or statutes, yet we do with one consent fully authorize, and earnestly entreat all that are and shall be in authority, to consider them as laws, and not to fail to inflict condign and proportionable punishments upon every man impartially, that shall infringe or violate any of them.

97. We likewise give full power and liberty to any person that shall at any time be denied or deprived of any of them, to commence and prosecute their suit, complaint or action against any man that shall so do in any court that hath proper cognizance or judicature thereof.

98. Lastly, because our duty and desire is to do nothing suddenly which fundamentally concerns us, we decree that these rights and liberties shall be audibly read and deliberately weighed at every General Court that shall be held within three years next ensuing. And such of them as shall not be altered or repealed, they shall stand so ratified, that no man shall infringe them without due punishment.

And if any General Court within these next three years shall fail or forget to read and consider them as above said, the governor and deputy governor for the time being, and every assistant present at such courts, shall forfeit 20/– a man, and every deputy 10/– a man for each neglect, which shall be paid out of their proper estate, and not by the country or the towns which choose them; and whensoever there shall arise any question in any court among the assistants and associates thereof about the explanation of these rights and liberties, the General Court only shall have power to interpret them.

THE ARTICLES OF CONFEDERATION
MARCH 1, 1781

To all to whom these presents shall come, we the undersigned delegates of the states affixed to our names send greeting. Whereas the delegates of the United States of America in Congress assembled did on the fifteenth day of November in the year of our Lord one thousand seven hundred and seventy-seven, and in the second year of the independence of America agree to certain Articles of Confederation and Perpetual Union between the states of New Hampshire, Massachusetts Bay, Rhode Island and Providence plantations, Connecticut, New York, New Jersey, Pennsylvania, Delaware, Maryland, Virginia, North Carolina, South Carolina and Georgia in the words following, viz.: Articles of Confederation and Perpetual Union between the states [as aforesaid].

ARTICLE I. The stile of this confederacy shall be "The United States of America."

ARTICLE II. Each state retains its sovereignty, freedom and independence, and every power, jurisdiction and right, which is not by this confederation expressly delegated to the United States, in Congress assembled.

ARTICLE III. The said states hereby severally enter into a firm league of friendship with each other, for their common defence, the security of their liberties, and their mutual and general welfare, binding themselves to assist each other, against all force offered to, or attacks made upon them, or any of them, on account of religion, sovereignty, trade, or any other pretence whatever.

ARTICLE IV. The better to secure and perpetuate mutual friendship and intercourse among the people of the different states in this Union, the free inhabitants of each of these states, paupers, vagabonds and fugitives from justice excepted, shall be entitled to all privileges and immunities of free citizens in the several states; and the people of each state shall have free ingress and regress to and from any other state, and shall enjoy therein all the privileges of trade and commerce, subject to the same duties, impositions and restrictions as the inhabitants thereof respectively, provided that such restrictions shall not extend so far as to prevent the removal of property imported into any state, to any other state of which the owner is an inhabitant; provided also that no imposition, duties or restriction shall be laid by any state, on the property of the United States, or either of them.

If any person guilty of, or charged with treason, felony, or other high misdemeanor in any state, shall flee from justice, and be found in any of the United States, he shall upon demand of the governor of executive power, of the state from which he fled, be delivered to the state having jurisdiction of his offence.

Full faith and credit shall be given in each of these states to the records, acts and judicial proceedings of the courts and magistrates of every other state.

ARTICLE V. For the more convenient management of the general interests of the United States, delegates shall be annually appointed in such manner as the legislature of each state shall direct, to meet in Congress on the first Monday in November, in every year, with a power reserved to each state, to recall its delegates, or any of them, at any time within the year, and to send others in their stead, for the remainder of the year.

No state shall be represented in Congress by less than two, nor by more than seven members; and no person shall be capable of being a delegate for more than three years in any term of six years; nor shall any person, being a delegate, be capable of holding any office under the United States, for which he, or another for his benefit receives any salary, fees, or emolument of any kind.

Each state shall maintain its own delegates in a meeting of the states, and while they act as members of the committee of the states.

In determining questions in the United States, in Congress assembled, each state shall have one vote.

Freedom of speech and debate in Congress shall not be impeached or questioned in any court, or place out of Congress, and the members of Congress shall be protected in their persons from arrests and imprisonments, during the time of their going to and from, and attendance on Congress, except for treason, felony, or breach of the peace.

ARTICLE VI. No state without the consent of the United States in Congress assembled, shall send any embassy to, or receive any embassy from, or enter into any conference, agreement, alliance or treaty with any king, prince or state; nor shall any person holding any office or profit or trust under the United States, or any of them, accept of any present, emolument, office or title of any kind whatever from any king, prince or foreign state; nor shall the United States in Congress assembled, or any of them, grant any title of nobility.

No two or more states shall enter into any treaty, confederation or alliance whatever between them, without the consent of the United States in Congress assembled, specifying accurately the purposes for which the same is to be entered into, and how long it shall continue.

No state shall lay any imposts or duties, which may interfere with any stipulations in treaties, entered into by the United States in Congress assembled, with any king, prince or state, in pursuance of any treaties already proposed by Congress, to the courts of France and Spain.

No vessels of war shall be kept up in time of peace by any state, except such number only, as shall be deemed necessary by the United States in Congress assembled, for the defence of such state, or its trade; nor shall any body of forces be kept up by any state, in time of peace, except such number only, as in the judgment of the United States, in Congress assembled, shall be deemed requisite to garrison the forts necesssary for the defence of such state; but every state shall always keep up a well regulated and disciplined militia, sufficiently armed and accoutred, and shall provide and constantly have ready for use, in public stores, a due number of field pieces and tents, and a proper quantity of arms, ammunition and camp equipage.

No state shall engage in any war without the consent of the United States in Congress assembled, unless such state be actually invaded by enemies, or shall have received certain advice of a resolution being formed by some nation of Indians to invade such state, and the danger is so imminent as not to admit of a delay, till the United States in Congress assembled can be consulted: nor shall any state grant commissions to any ships or vessels of war, nor letters of marque or reprisal, except it be after a declaration of war by the United States in Congress assembled, and then only against the kingdom or state and the subjects thereof, against which war has been so declared, and under such regulations as shall be established by the United States in Congress assembled, unless such state be infested by pirates, in which case vessels of war may be fitted out for that occasion, and kept so long as the danger shall continue, or until the United States in Congress assembled shall determine otherwise.

ARTICLE VII. When land-forces are raised by any state for the common defence, all officers of or under the rank of colonel, shall be appointed by the legislature of each state respectively by whom such forces shall be raised, or in such manner as such state shall direct, and all vacancies shall be filled up by the state which first made the appointment.

ARTICLE VIII. All charges of war, and all other expenses that shall be incurred for the common defence or general welfare, and allowed by the United States in Congress assembled, shall be defrayed out of a common treasury, which shall be supplied by the several states, in proportion to the value of all land within each state, granted to or surveyed for any person, as such land and the buildings and improvements thereon shall be estimated according to such mode as the United States in Congress assembled, shall from time to time direct and appoint.

The taxes for paying that proportion shall be laid and levied by the authority and direction of the legislatures of the several states within the time agreed upon by the United States in Congress assembled.

ARTICLE IX. The United States in Congress assembled, shall have the sole and exclusive right and power of determining on peace and war, except in the cases mentioned in the sixth article—of sending and receiving ambassadors—entering into treaties and alliances, provided that no treaty of commerce shall be made whereby the legislative power of the respective states shall be restrained from imposing such imposts and duties on foreigners, as their own people are subjected to, or from prohibiting the exportation or importation of any species of good or commodities whatsoever—of establishing rules for deciding in all cases, what captures on land or water shall be legal, and in what manner prizes taken by land or naval forces in the service of the United States shall be divided or appropriated—of granting letters of marque and reprisal in times of peace—appointing courts for the trial of piracies and felonies committed on the high seas and establishing courts for receiving and determining finally appeals in all cases of captures, provided that no member of Congress shall be appointed a judge of any of the said courts.

The United States in Congress assembled shall also be the last resort on appeal in all disputes and differences now subsisting or that hereafter may arise between two or more states concerning boundary, jurisdiction or any other cause whatever; which authority shall always be exercised in the manner following. Whenever the legislative or executive authority or lawful agent of any state in controversy with another shall present a petition to Congress, stating the matter in question and praying for a hearing, notice thereof shall be given by order of Congress to the legislative or executive authority of the other state in controversy, and a day assigned for the appearance of the parties by their lawful agents, who shall then be directed to appoint by joint consent, commissioners or judges to constitute a court for hearing and determining the matter in question: but if they cannot agree, Congress shall name three persons out of each of the United States, and from the list of such persons each party shall alternately strike out one, the petitioners beginning, until the number shall be reduced to thirteen; and from that number not less than seven, nor more than nine names as Congress shall direct, shall in the presence of Congress be drawn out by lot, and the persons whose names shall be so drawn or any five of them, shall be commissioners or judges, to hear and finally determine the controversy, so always as a major part of the judges who shall hear the cause shall agree in the determination: and if either party shall neglect to attend at the day appointed, without showing reasons, which Congress shall judge sufficient, or being present shall refuse to strike, the

Congress shall proceed to nominate three persons out of each state, and the Secretary of Congress shall strike in behalf of such party absent or refusing; and the judgment and sentence of the court to be appointed, in the manner before prescribed, shall be final and conclusive; and if any of the parties shall refuse to submit to the authority of such court, or to appear or defend their claim or cause, the court shall nevertheless proceed to pronounce sentence, or judgment, which shall in like manner be final and decisive, the judgment or sentence and other proceedings being in either case transmitted to Congress, and lodged among the acts of Congress for the security of the parties concerned: provided that every commissioner, before he sits in judgment, shall take an oath to be administered by one of the judges of the supreme or superior court of the state where the cause shall be tried, "well and truly to hear and determine the matter in question, according to the best of his judgment, without favour, affection or hope of reward": provided also that no state shall be deprived of territory for the benefit of the United States.

All controversies concerning the private right of soil, claimed under different grants of two or more states, whose jurisdictions as they may respect such lands, and the states which passed such grants, are adjusted, the said grants or either of them being at the same time claimed to have originated antecedent to such settlement of jurisdiction, shall on the petition of either party to the Congress of the United States, be finally determined as near as may be in the same manner as is before prescribed for deciding disputes respecting territorial jurisdiction between different states.

The United States in Congress assembled shall also have the sole and exclusive right and power of regulating the alloy and value of coin struck by their own authority, or by that of the respective states—fixing the standard of weights and measures throughout the United States—regulating the trade and managing all affairs with the Indians, not members of any of the states, provided that the legislative right of any state within its own limits be not infringed or violated—establishing and regulating post-offices from one state to another, throughout all the United States, and exacting such postage on the papers passing thro' the same as may be requisite to defray the expenses of the said office—appointing all officers of the land forces in the service of the United

States, excepting regimental officers—appointing all the officers of the naval forces, and commissioning all officers whatever in the service of the United States—making rules for the government and regulation of the said land and naval forces, and directing their operations.

The United States in Congress assembled shall have authority to appoint a committee, to sit in the recess of Congress, to be denominated "a committee of the states," and to consist of one delegate from each state; and to appoint such other committees and civil officers as may be necessary for managing the general affairs of the United States under their direction—to appoint one of their number to preside, provided that no person be allowed to serve in the office of President more than one year in any term of three years; to ascertain the necessary sums of money to be raised for the service of the United States, and to appropriate and apply the same for defraying the public expenses—to borrow money, or emit bills on the credit of the United States, transmitting every half year to the respective states an account of the sums of money so borrowed or emitted—to build and equip a navy—to agree upon the number of land forces, and to make requisitions from each state for its quota, in proportion to the number of white inhabitants in such state; which requisitions shall be binding, and thereupon the legislature of each state shall appoint the regimental officers, raise the men and clothe, arm and equip them in a soldier-like manner, at the expense of the United States; and the officers and men so clothed, armed and equipped shall march to the place appointed, and within the time agreed on by the United States in Congress assembled: but if the United States in Congress assembled shall, on consideration of circumstances, judge proper that any state should not raise men, or should raise a smaller number of men than its quota, and that any other state should raise a greater number of men than the quota thereof, such extra number shall be raised, officered, clothed, armed and equipped in the same manner as the quota of such state, unless the legislature of such state shall judge that such extra number cannot be safely spared out of the same, in which case they shall raise, officer, clothe, arm and equip as many of such extra number as they judge can be safely spared. And the officers and men so clothed, armed and equipped, shall march to the place appointed, and within the time agreed on by the United States in Congress assembled.

The United States in Congress assembled shall never engage in a war, nor grant letters of marque and reprisal in time of peace, nor enter into any treaties or alliances, nor coin money, nor regulate the value thereof, nor ascertain the sums and expenses necessary for the defence and welfare of the United States, or any of them, nor emit bills, nor borrow money on the credit of the United States, nor appropriate money, nor agree upon the number of vessels of war to be built or purchased, or the number of land or sea forces to be raised, nor appoint a commander in chief of the army or navy, unless nine states assent to the same: nor shall a question on any other point, except for adjourning from day to day be determined, unless by the votes of a majority of the United States in Congress assembled.

The Congress of the United States shall have power to adjourn to any time within the year, and to any place within the United States, so that no period of adjournment be for a longer duration than the space of six months, and shall publish the journal of their proceedings monthly, except such parts thereof relating to treaties, alliances or military operations, as in their judgment require secrecy; and the yeas and nays of the delegates of each state on any question shall be entered on the journal, when it is desired by any delegate; and the delegates of a state, or any of them, at his or their request shall be furnished with a transcript of the said journal, except such parts as are above excepted, to lay before the legislatures of the several states.

ARTICLE X. The committee of the states, or any nine of them, shall be authorized to execute, in the recess of Congress, such of the powers of Congress as the United States in Congress assembled, by the consent of nine states, shall from time to time think expedient to vest them with; provided that no power be delegated to the said committee, for the exercise of which, by the Articles of Confederation, the voice of nine states in the Congress of the United States assembled is requisite.

ARTICLE XI. Canada acceding to this confederation, and joining in the measures of the United States, shall be admitted into, and entitled to all the advantages of this Union: but no other colony shall be admitted into the same, unless such admission be agreed to by nine states.

ARTICLE XII. All bills of credit emitted, monies borrowed and debts contracted by, or under the authority of Congress, before the assembling of the United States, in pursuance of the present confederation, shall be deemed and considered as a charge against the United States, for payment and satisfaction whereof the said United States, and the public faith are hereby solemnly pledged.

ARTICLE XIII. Every state shall abide by the determinations of the United States in Congress assembled, on all questions which by this confederation are submitted to them. And the articles of this confederation shall be inviolably observed by every state, and the Union shall be perpetual; nor shall any alteration at any time hereafter be made in any of them; unless such alteration be agreed to in a Congress of the United States, and be afterwards confirmed by the legislatures of every state.

And whereas it has pleased the Great Governor of the world to incline the hearts of the legislatures we respectively represent in Congress, to approve of, and to authorize us to ratify the said Articles of Confederation and Perpetual Union. Know ye that we the undersigned delegates, by virtue of the power and authority to us given for that purpose, do by these presents, in the name and in behalf of our respective constituents, fully and entirely ratify and confirm each and every of the said Articles of Confederation and Perpetual Union, and all and singular the matters and things therein contained: and we do further solemnly plight and engage the faith of our respective constituents, that they shall abide by the determinations of the United States in Congress assembled, on all questions, which by the said Confederation are submitted to them. And that the articles thereof shall be inviolably observed by the states we respectively represent, and that the Union shall be perpetual.

THE NORTHWEST ORDINANCE
JULY 13, 1787

I

An Ordinance for the government of the territory
of the United States northwest of the river Ohio

Be it ordained by the United States in Congress assembled, that the said territory, for the purposes of temporary government, be one district, subject, however, to be divided into two districts, as future circumstances may, in the opinion of Congress, make it expedient.

Be it ordained by the authority aforesaid, that the estates, both of resident and non-resident proprietors in the said territory, dying intestate, shall descend to, and be distributed among their children, and the descendants of a deceased child, in equal parts; the descendants of a deceased child or grandchild to take the share of their deceased parent in equal parts among them: And where there shall be no children or descendants, then in equal parts to the next of kin in equal degree; and among collaterals, the children of a deceased brother or sister of the intestate shall have, in equal parts among them, their deceased parents' share; and there shall in no case be a distinction between kindred of the whole and half-blood; saving, in all cases, to the widow of the intestate her third part of the real estate for life, and one-third part of the personal estate; and this law relative to descents and dower, shall remain in full force until altered by the legislature of the district. And until the governor and judges shall adopt laws as hereinafter mentioned, estates in the said territory may be devised or bequeathed by wills in writing, signed and sealed by him or her in whom the estate may be (being of full age), and attested by three witnesses; and real estates may be conveyed by lease and release, or bargain and sale, signed sealed and delivered by the person, being of full age, in whom the estate may be, and attested by two witnesses, provided such wills be duly proved, and such conveyances be acknowledged, or the execution thereof duly proved, and be recorded within one year after proper magistrates, courts, and registers shall be appointed for that purpose; and personal property may be transferred by delivery; saving, however to the French and Canadian inhabitants and other settlers of the Kaskaskies, St. Vincents and the neighboring villages, who have heretofore professed themselves citizens of Virginia, their laws and customs now in force among them relative to the descent and conveyance of property.

Be it ordained by the authority aforesaid, that there shall be appointed from time to time by Congress, a governor, whose commission shall continue in force for the term of three years, unless sooner revoked by Congress; he shall reside in the district, and have a freehold estate therein in 1,000 acres of land, while in the exercise of his office.

There shall be appointed from time to time by Congress, a secretary, whose commission shall continue in force for four years unless sooner revoked; he shall reside in the district, and have a freehold estate therein in 500 acres of land, while in the exercise of his office. It shall be his duty to keep and preserve the acts and laws passed by the legislature, and the public records of the district, and the proceedings of the governor in his executive department, and transmit authentic copies of such acts and proceedings, every six months, to the secretary of Congress: there shall also be appointed a court to consist of three judges, any two of whom to form a court, who shall have a common law jurisdiction, and reside in the district, and have each therein a freehold estate in 500 acres of land while in the exercise of their offices; and their commissions shall continue in force during good behavior.

The governor and judges, or a majority of them, shall adopt and publish in the district such laws of the original states, criminal and civil, as may be necessary and best suited to the circumstances of the district, and report them to Congress from time to time: which laws shall be in force in the district until the organization of the general assembly therein, unless disapproved of by Congress; but afterwards the legislature shall have authority to alter them as they shall think fit.

The governor, for the time being, shall be commander-in-chief of the militia, appoint and commission all officers in the same below the rank of general officers; all general officers shall be appointed and commissioned by Congress.

Previous to the organization of the general assembly, the governor shall appoint such magistrates and other civil officers in each county or township, as he shall find necessary for the preservation of the peace and good order in the same: after the general assembly shall be organized, the powers and duties of the magistrates and other civil officers shall be regulated and defined by the said assembly; but all magistrates and other civil officers not herein otherwise directed, shall, during the continuance of this temporary government, be appointed by the governor.

For the prevention of crimes and injuries, the laws to be adopted or made shall have force in all parts of the district, and for the execution of process, criminal and civil, the governor shall make divisions thereof; and he shall proceed from time to time as circumstances may require, to lay out the parts of the district in which the Indian titles shall have been extinguished, into counties and townships, subject however to such alterations as may thereafter be made by the legislature.

So soon as there shall be five thousand free male inhabitants of full age in the district, upon giving proof thereof to the governor, they shall receive authority, with time and place, to elect representatives from their counties or townships to represent them in the general assembly: provided, that, for every five hundred free male inhabitants, there shall be one representative, and so on progressively with the number of free male inhabitants shall the right of representation increase, until the number of representatives shall amount to twenty-five; after which, the number and proportion of representatives shall be regulated by legislature: provided, that no person be eligible or qualified to act as a representative unless he shall have been a citizen of one of the United States three years, and be a resident in the district, or unless he shall have resided in the district three years; and, in either case, shall likewise hold in his own right, in fee simple, two hundred acres of land within the same: provided, also, that a freehold in fifty acres of land in the district, having been a citizen of one of the states, and being resident in the district, or the like freehold and two years residence in the district, shall be necessary to qualify a man as an elector of a representative.

The representatives thus elected, shall serve for the term of two years; and, in case of death of a representative, or removal from office, the governor shall issue a writ to the county or township for which he was a member, to elect another in his stead, to serve for the residue of the term.

The general assembly or legislature shall consist of the governor, legislative council, and a house of representatives.

The legislative council shall consist of five members, to continue in office five years, unless sooner removed by Congress; any three of whom to be a quorum: and the members of the council shall be nominated and appointed in the following manner, to wit: as soon as representatives shall be elected, the governor shall appoint a time and place for them to meet together; and, when met, they shall nominate ten persons, residents in the district, and each possessed of a freehold in five hundred acres of land, and return their names to Congress; five of whom Congress shall appoint and commission to serve as aforesaid; and, whenever a vacancy shall happen in the council, by death or removal from office, the house of representatives shall nominate two persons, qualified as aforesaid, for each vacancy, and return their names to Congress; one of whom Congress shall appoint and commission for the residue of the term. And every five years, four months at least before the expiration of the time of service of the members of the council, the said house shall nominate ten persons, qualified as aforesaid, and return their names to Congress; five of whom Congress shall appoint and commission to serve as members of the council five years, unless soon removed. And the governor, legislative council, and house of representatives, shall have authority to make laws in all cases, for the good government of the district, not repugnant to the principles and articles in this ordinance established and declared. And all bills, having passed by a majority in the house, and by a majority in the council, shall be referred to the governor for his assent; but no bill, or legislative act whatever, shall be of any force without his assent. The governor shall have power to convene, prorogue, and dissolve the general assembly, when, in his opinion, it shall be expedient.

The governor, judges, legislative council, secretary, and such other officers as Congress shall appoint in the district, shall take an oath or affirmation of fidelity and of office; the governor before the president of congress, and all other officers before the governor. As soon as a legislature shall be formed in the district, the council and house assembled in one room, shall have authority by joint ballot, to elect a delegate to Congress, who shall have a seat in Congress, with a right of debating but not of voting during this temporary government.

II

And, for extending the fundamental principles of civil and religious liberty, which form the basis whereon these republics, their laws and constitutions are erected; to fix and establish those principles as the basis of all laws, constitutions, and governments, which forever hereafter shall be formed in the said territory: to provide also for the establishment of states, and permanent government therein, and for their admission to a share in the federal councils on an equal footing with the original states, at as early periods as may be consistent with the general interest:

It is hereby ordained and declared by the authority aforesaid, that the following articles shall be considered as articles of compact between the original states and the people and states in the said territory and forever remain unalterable, unless by common consent, to wit:

ARTICLE 1. No person, demeaning himself in a peaceable and orderly manner, shall ever be molested on account of his mode of worship or religious sentiments, in the said territory.

ARTICLE 2. The inhabitants of the said territory shall always be entitled to the benefits of the writ of habeas corpus, and of the trial by jury; of a proportionate representation of the people in the legislature; and of judicial proceedings according to the course of the common law. All persons shall be bailable, unless for capital offences, where the proof shall be evident or the presumption great. All fines shall be moderate; and no cruel or unusual punishments shall be inflicted. No man shall be deprived of his liberty or property, but by the judgment of his peers or the law of the land; and, should the public exigencies make it necessary, for the common preservation, to take any person's property, or to demand his particular services, full compensation shall be made for the same. And, in the just preservation of rights and property, it is understood and declared, that no law ought ever to be made, or have force in the said territory, that shall, in any manner whatever, interfere with or affect private contracts or engagements, bona fide, and without fraud, previously formed.

ARTICLE 3. Religion, morality, and knowledge, being necessary to good government and the happiness of mankind, schools and the means of education shall forever be encouraged. The utmost good faith shall always be observed towards the Indians; their lands and property shall never be taken from them without their consent; and, in their property, rights, and liberty, they shall never be invaded or disturbed, unless in just and lawful wars authorized by Congress; but laws founded in justice and humanity, shall from time to time be made for preventing wrongs being done to them, and for preserving peace and friendship with them.

ARTICLE 4. The said territory, and the states which may be formed therein, shall forever remain a part of this Confederacy of the United States of America, subject to the Articles of Confederation, and to such alterations therein as shall be constitutionally made; and to all the acts and ordinances of the United States in Congress assembled, conformable thereto. The inhabitants and settlers in the said territory shall be subject to pay a part of the federal debts contracted or to be contracted, and a proportional part of the expenses of government, to be apportioned on them by Congress according to the same common rule and measure by which apportionments thereof shall be made on the other states; and the taxes for paying their proportion shall be laid and levied by the authority and direction of the legislatures of the district or districts, or new states, as in the original states, within the time agreed upon by the United States in Congress assembled. The legislatures of those districts or new states, shall never interfere with the primary disposal of the soil by the United States in Congress assembled, nor with any regulations Congress may find necessary for securing the title in such soil to the bona fide purchasers. No tax shall be imposed on lands the property of the United States; and, in no case, shall non-resident proprietors be taxed higher than residents. The navigable waters leading into the Mississippi and St. Lawrence, and the carrying places between the same, shall be common highways and forever free, as well to the inhabitants of the said territory as to the citizens of the United States, and those of any other states that may be admitted into the Confederacy, without any tax, impost, or duty therefor.

ARTICLE 5. There shall be formed in the said territory, not less than three nor more than five states; and the boundaries of the states, as soon as Virginia shall after her act of cession, and consent to the same, shall become fixed and established as follows, to wit: the western state in the said territory, shall be bounded by the Mississippi, the Ohio, and Wabash Rivers; a direct line drawn from the Wabash and Post Vincents, due north, to the territorial line between the United States and Canada; and, by the said territorial line, to the Lake of the Woods and Mississippi. The middle state shall be bounded by the said direct line, the Wabash from Post Vincents to the Ohio, by the Ohio, by a direct line, drawn due north from the mouth of the Great Miami, to the said territorial line, and by the said territorial line. The eastern state shall be bounded by the last mentioned direct line, the Ohio, Pennsylvania, and the said territorial line: provided, however, and it is further understood and declared, that the boundaries of these three states shall be subject so far to be altered, that, if Congress shall hereafter find it expedient, they shall have authority to form one or two states in that part of the said territory which lies north of an east and west line drawn through the southerly bend or extreme of Lake Michigan. And, whenever any of the said states shall have sixty thousand free inhabitants therein, such state shall be admitted, by its delegates, into the Congress of the United States, on an equal footing with the original states in all respects whatever, and shall be at liberty to form a permanent constitution and state government: provided, the constitution and government so to be formed, shall be republican, and in conformity to the principles contained in these articles; and, so far as it can be consistent with the general interest of the Confederacy, such admission shall be allowed at an earlier period, and when there may be a less number of free inhabitants in the state than sixty thousand.

ARTICLE 6. There shall be neither slavery nor involuntary servitude in the said territory, otherwise than in the punishment of crimes whereof the party shall have been duly convicted: provided, always, that any person escaping into the same, from whom labor or service is lawfully claimed in any one of the original states, such fugitive may be lawfully reclaimed and conveyed to the person claiming his or her labor or service as aforesaid.

Be it ordained by the authority aforesaid, that the resolutions of the 23rd of April 1784, relative to the subject of this ordinance, be, and the same are hereby repealed and declared null and void.

THE CONSTITUTION OF THE UNITED STATES

Adopted September 17, 1787
Effective March 4, 1789

We the People of the United States, in order to form a more perfect Union, establish Justice, ensure domestic Tranquillity, provide for the common defence, promote the general Welfare, and secure the Blessings of Liberty to ourselves and our Posterity, do ordain and establish this Constitution for the United States of America.

ARTICLE I

Section 1. All legislative powers herein granted shall be vested in a Congress of the United States, which shall consist of a Senate and House of Representatives.

Section 2. The House of Representatives shall be composed of members chosen every second year by the people of the several states, and the electors in each state shall have the qualifications requisite for electors of the most numerous branch of the state legislature.

No person shall be a representative who shall not have attained to the age of twenty-five years, and been seven years a citizen of the United States, and who shall not, when elected, be an inhabitant of that state in which he shall be chosen.

Representatives and direct taxes shall be apportioned among the several states which may be included within this union, according to their respective numbers, which shall be determined by adding to the whole number of free persons, including those bound to service for a term of years, and excluding Indians not taxed, three-fifths of all other persons. The actual enumeration shall be made within three years after the first meeting of the Congress of the United States, and within every subsequent term of ten years, in such manner as they shall by law direct. The number of representatives shall not exceed one for every 30,000, but each state shall have at least one representative; and until such enumeration shall be made, the state of New Hampshire shall be entitled to choose three, Massachusetts eight, Rhode Island and Providence Plantations one, Connecticut five, New York six, New Jersey four, Pennsylvania eight, Delaware one, Maryland six, Virginia ten, North Carolina five, South Carolina five, and Georgia three.

When vacancies happen in the representation from any state, the executive authority thereof shall issue writs of election to fill such vacancies.

The House of Representatives shall choose their speaker and other officers; and shall have the sole power of impeachment.

Section 3. The Senate of the United States shall be composed of two senators from each state, chosen by the legislature thereof, for six years, and each senator shall have one vote.

Immediately after they shall be assembled in consequence of the first election, they shall be divided as equally as may be into three classes. The seats of the senators of the first class shall be vacated at the expiration of the second year, of the second class at the expiration of the fourth year, and of the third class at the expiration of the sixth year, so that one-third may be chosen every second year; and if vacancies happen by resignation, or otherwise, during the recess of the legislature of any state, the executive thereof may make temporary appointments until the next meeting of the legislature, which shall then fill such vacancies.

No person shall be a senator who shall not have attained to the age of 30 years, and been nine years a citizen of the United States, and who shall not, when elected, be an inhabitant of that state for which he shall be chosen.

The Vice-President of the United States shall be president of the Senate, but shall have no vote, unless they be equally divided.

The Senate shall choose their other officers, and also a president *pro tempore*, in the absence of the Vice-President, or when he shall exercise the office of President of the United States.

The Senate shall have the sole power to try all impeachments. When sitting for that purpose, they shall be on oath or affirmation. When the President of the United States is tried, the chief justice shall preside: And no person shall be convicted without the concurrence of two-thirds of the members present.

Judgment in cases of impeachment shall not extend further than to removal from office, and disqualification to hold and enjoy any office of honor, trust or profit under the United States; but the party convicted shall nevertheless be liable and subject to indictment, trial, judgment and punishment, according to law.

Section 4. The times, places and manner of holding elections for senators and representatives, shall be prescribed in each state by the legislature thereof: but the Congress may at any time by law make or alter such regulations, except as to the places of choosing senators.

The Congress shall assemble at least once in every year, and such meeting shall be on the first Monday in December, unless they shall by law appoint a different day.

Section 5. Each house shall be the judge of the elections, returns and qualifications of its own members, and a majority of each shall constitute a quorum to do business; but a smaller number may adjourn from day to day, and may be authorized to compel the attendance of absent members, in such manner, and under such penalties as each house may provide.

Each house may determine the rules of its proceedings, punish its members for disorderly behaviour, and, with the concurrence of two-thirds, expel a member.

Each house shall keep a journal of its proceedings, and from time to time publish the same, excepting such parts as may, in their judgment, require secrecy; and the yeas and nays of the members of either house on any question shall, at the desire of one-fifth of those present, be entered on the journal.

Neither house, during the session of Congress, shall, without the consent of the other, adjourn for more than three days, nor to any other place than that in which the two houses shall be sitting.

Section 6. The senators and representatives shall receive a compensation for their services, to be ascertained by law, and paid out of the Treasury of the United States. They shall in all cases, except treason, felony and breach of the peace, be privileged from arrest during their attendance at the session of their respective houses, and in going to and returning from the same; and for any speech or debate in either house, they shall not be questioned in any other place.

No senator or representative shall, during the time for which he was elected, be appointed to any civil office under the authority of the United States, which shall have been created, or the emoluments whereof shall have been increased during such time; and no person holding any office under the United States, shall be a member of either house during his continuance in office.

Section 7. All bills for raising revenue shall originate in the House of Representatives; but the Senate may propose or concur with amendments as on other bills.

Every bill which shall have passed the House of Representatives and the Senate, shall, before it become a law, be presented to the President of the United States; if he approve, he shall sign it, but if not, he shall return it, with his objections, to that house in which it shall have originated, who shall enter the objections at large on their journal, and proceed to reconsider it. If after such reconsideration, two-thirds of that house shall agree to pass the bill, it shall be sent, together with the objections, to the other house, by which it shall likewise be reconsidered, and if approved by two-thirds of that house, it shall become a law. But in all such cases the votes of both houses shall be determined by yeas and nays, and the names of the persons voting for and against the bill shall be entered on the journal of each house respectively. If any bill shall not be returned by the president within ten days (Sundays excepted), after it shall have been presented to him, the same shall be a law, in like manner as if he had signed it, unless the Congress by their adjournment prevent its return, in which case it shall not be a law.

Every order, resolution, or vote to which the concurrence of the Senate and House of Representatives may be necessary (except on a question of adjournment), shall be presented to the President of the United States; and before the same shall take effect, shall be approved by him, or, being disapproved by him, shall be re-passed by two-thirds of the Senate and

House of Representatives, according to the rules and limitations prescribed in the case of a bill.

Section 8. The Congress shall have power:

To lay and collect taxes, duties, imposts and excises, to pay the debts and provide for the common defence and general welfare of the United States; but all duties, imposts and excises shall be uniform throughout the United States:

To borrow money on the credit of the United States:

To regulate commerce with foreign nations, and among the several states, and with the Indian tribes:

To establish an uniform rule of naturalization, and uniform laws on the subject of bankruptcies throughout the United States:

To coin money, regulate the value thereof, and of foreign coin, and fix the standard of weights and measures:

To provide for the punishment of counterfeiting the securities and current coin of the United States:

To establish post-offices and post-roads:

To promote the progress of science and useful arts, by securing for limited times to authors and inventors the exclusive right to their respective writings and discoveries:

To constitute tribunals inferior to the Supreme Court:

To define and punish piracies and felonies committed on the high seas, and offences against the law of nations:

To declare war, grant letters of marque and reprisal, and make rules concerning captures on land and water:

To raise and support armies, but no appropriation of money to that use shall be for a longer term than two years:

To provide and maintain a navy:

To make rules for the government and regulation of the land and naval forces:

To provide for calling forth the militia to execute the laws of the Union, suppress insurrections and repel invasions:

To provide for organizing, arming and disciplining the militia, and for governing such part of them as may be employed in the service of the United States, reserving to the states respectively, the appointment of the officers, and the authority of training the militia according to the discipline prescribed by Congress:

To exercise exclusive legislation in all cases whatsoever, over such district (not exceeding ten miles square) as may, by cession of particular states, and the acceptance of Congress, became the seat of the government of the United States, and to exercise like authority over all places purchased by the consent of the legislature of the state in which the same shall be, for the erection of forts, magazines, arsenals, dockyards, and other needful buildings: and,

To make all laws which shall be necessary and proper for carrying into execution the foregoing powers, and all other powers vested by this constitution in the government of the United States, or in any department or officer thereof.

Section 9. The migration or importation of such persons as any of the states now existing shall think proper to admit, shall not be prohibited by the Congress prior to the year 1808, but a tax or duty may be imposed on such importations, not exceeding ten dollars for each person.

The privilege of the writ of *habeas corpus* shall not be suspended, unless when in cases of rebellion or invasion the public safety may require it.

No bill of attainder or *ex post facto* law shall be passed.

No capitation, or other direct tax shall be laid unless in proportion to the *census* or enumeration herein before directed to be taken.

No tax or duty shall be laid on articles exported from any state.

No preference shall be given by any regulation of commerce or revenue to the ports of one state over those of another: nor shall vessels bound to, or from one state, be obliged to enter, clear, or pay duties in another.

No money shall be drawn from the Treasury but in consequence of appropriations made by law; and a regular statement and account of the receipts and expenditures of all public money shall be published from time to time.

No title of nobility shall be granted by the United States: and no person holding any office of profit or trust under them, shall, without the consent of the Congress, accept of any present, emolument, office, or title, of any kind whatever, from any king, prince or foreign state.

Section 10. No state shall enter into any treaty, alliance, or confederation; grant letters of marque and reprisal; coin money; emit bills of credit; make any thing but gold and silver coin a tender in payment of debts; pass any bill of attainder, *ex post facto* law, or law impairing the obligation of contracts, or grant any title of nobility.

No state shall, without the consent of the Congress, lay any imposts or duties on imports or exports, except what may be absolutely necessary for executing its inspection laws; and the net produce of all duties and imposts, laid by any state on imports and exports, shall be for the use of the Treasury of the United States; and all such laws shall be subject to the revision and control of the Congress.

No state shall, without the consent of Congress, lay any duty of tonnage, keep troops, or ships of war in time of peace, enter into any agreement or compact with another state, or with a foreign power, or engage in war, unless actually invaded, or in such imminent danger as will not admit of delay.

ARTICLE II

Section 1. The executive power shall be vested in a President of the United States of America. He shall hold his office during the term of four years, and, together with the Vice-President, chosen for the same term, be elected as follows:

Each state shall appoint, in such manner as the legislature thereof may direct, a number of electors, equal to the whole number of senators and representatives to which the state may be entitled in the Congress; but no senator or representative, or person holding an office of trust or profit under the United States, shall be appointed an elector.

The electors shall meet in their respective states, and vote by ballot for two persons, of whom one at least shall not be an inhabitant of the same state with themselves. And they shall make a list of all the persons voted for, and of the number of votes for each; which list they shall sign and certify, and transmit sealed to the seat of the government of the United States, directed to the president of the Senate. The president of the Senate shall, in the presence of the Senate and House of Representatives, open all the certificates and the votes shall then be counted. The person having the greatest number of votes shall be the President, if such number be a majority of the whole number of electors appointed; and if there be more than one who have such majority, and have an equal number of votes, then the House of Representatives shall immediately choose by ballot one of them for President; and if no person have a majority, then from the five highest on the list, the said House shall, in like manner, choose the President. But in choosing the President, the votes shall be taken by states, the representation from each state having one vote; a quorum for this purpose shall consist of a member or members from two-thirds of the states, and a majority of all the states shall be necessary to a choice. In every case, after the choice of the President, the person having the greatest number of votes of the electors shall be the Vice-President. But if there should remain two or more who have equal votes, the Senate shall choose from them by ballot the Vice-President.

The Congress may determine the time of choosing the electors, and the day on which they shall give their votes; which day shall be the same throughout the United States.

No person except a natural born citizen, or a citizen of the United States, at the time of the adoption of this constitution, shall be eligible to the office of President; neither shall any person be eligible to that office, who shall not have attained to the age of thirty-five years, and been fourteen years a resident within the United States.

In case of the removal of the President from office, or of his death, resignation, or inability to discharge the powers and duties of the said office, the same shall devolve on the Vice-President, and the Congress may by law provide for the case of removal, death, resignation, or inability, both of the President and Vice-President, declaring what officer shall then act as President, and such officer shall act accordingly, until the disability be removed, or a President shall be elected.

The President shall, at stated times, receive for his services, a compensation, which shall neither be increased nor diminished during the period for which he shall have been elected, and he shall not receive within that period any other emolument from the United States, or any of them.

Before he enter on the execution of his office, he shall take the following oath or affirmation:

"I do solemnly swear (or affirm) that I will faithfully execute the office of President of the United States, and will to the best of my ability, preserve, protect and defend the Constitution of the United States."

Section 2. The President shall be commander-in-chief of the army and navy of the United States, and of the militia of the several states, when called into the actual service of the United States; he may require the opinion, in writing, of the principal officer in each of the executive departments, upon any subject relating to the duties of their respective offices, and he shall have power to grant reprieves and pardons for offences against the United States, except in cases of impeachment.

He shall have power, by and with the advice and consent of the Senate, to make treaties, provided two-thirds of the senators present concur; and he shall nominate, and by and with the advice and consent of the Senate, shall appoint ambassadors, other public ministers and consuls, judges of the Supreme Court, and all other officers of the United States, whose appointments are not herein otherwise provided for, and which shall be established by law. But the Congress may by law vest the appointment of such inferior officers, as they think proper in the President alone, in the courts of law, or in the heads of departments.

The President shall have power to fill up all vacancies that may happen during the recess of the Senate, by granting commissions, which shall expire at the end of their next session.

Section 3. He shall, from time to time, give to the Congress information of the state of the Union, and recommend to their consideration, such measures as he shall judge necessary and expedient; he may, on extraordinary occasions, convene both houses, or either of them, and in case of disagreement between them, with respect to the time of adjournment, he may adjourn them to such time as he shall think proper; he shall receive ambassadors and other public ministers; he shall take care that the laws be faithfully executed, and shall commission all the officers of the United States.

Section 4. The President, Vice-President, and all civil officers of the United States shall be removed from office on impeachment for, and conviction of, treason, bribery, or other high crimes and misdemeanors.

ARTICLE III

Section 1. The judicial power of the United States, shall be vested in one Supreme Court, and in such inferior courts as the Congress may, from time to time, ordain and establish. The judges, both of the Supreme and inferior courts, shall hold their offices during good behavior, and shall, at stated times, receive for their services a compensation, which shall not be diminished during their continuance in office.

Section 2. The judicial power shall extend to all cases, in law and equity, arising under this Constitution, the laws of the United States, and treaties made, or which shall be made under their authority; to all cases affecting ambassadors, other public ministers and consuls; to all cases of admiralty and maritime jurisdiction; to controversies to which the United States shall be a party: to controversies between two or more states, between a state and citizens of another state, between citizens of different states, between citizens of the same state, claiming lands under grants of different states, and between a state, or the citizens thereof, and foreign states, citizens or subjects.

In all cases affecting ambassadors, other public ministers and consuls, and those in which a state shall be party, the Supreme Court shall have original jurisdiction. In all the other cases before-mentioned, the Supreme Court shall have appellate jurisdiction, both as to law and fact, with such exceptions, and under such regulations as the Congress shall make.

The trial of all crimes, except in cases of impeachment, shall be by jury; and such trial shall be held in the state where the said crimes shall have been committed; but when not committed within any state, the trial shall be at such place or places as the Congress may by law have directed.

Section 3. Treason against the United States shall consist only in levying war against them, or in adhering to their enemies, giving them aid and comfort. No person shall be convicted of treason unless on the testimony of two witnesses to the same overt act, or on confession in open court.

The Congress shall have power to declare the punishment of treason, but no attainder of treason shall work corruption of blood, or forfeiture, except during the life of the person attainted.

ARTICLE IV

Section 1. Full faith and credit shall be given in each state to the public acts, records and judicial proceedings of every other state. And the Congress may by general laws prescribe the manner in which such acts, records and proceedings shall be proved, and the effect thereof.

Section 2. The citizens of each state shall be entitled to all privileges and immunities of citizens in the several states.

A person charged in any state with treason, felony, or other crime, who shall flee from justice, and be found in another state, shall, on demand of the executive authority of the state from which he fled, be delivered up, to be removed to the state having jurisdiction of the crime.

No person held to service or labor in one state, under the laws thereof, escaping into another, shall, in consequence of any law or regulation therein, be discharged from such service or labour, but shall be delivered up on claim of the party to whom such service or labor may be due.

Section 3. New states may be admitted by the Congress into this Union; but no new state shall be formed or erected within the jurisdiction of any other state, nor any state be formed by the junction of two or more states, or parts of states, without the consent of the legislatures of the states concerned, as well as of the Congress.

The Congress shall have power to dispose of and make all needful rules and regulations respecting the territory or other property belonging to the United States; and nothing in this Constitution shall be so construed as to prejudice any claims of the United States, or of any particular state.

Section 4. The United States shall guarantee to every state in this Union, a republican form of government, and shall protect each of them against invasion; and on application of the legislature, or of the executive (when the legislature cannot be convened), against domestic violence.

ARTICLE V

The Congress, whenever two-thirds of both houses shall deem it necessary, shall propose amendments to this Constitution, or on the application of the legislatures of two-thirds of the several states, shall call a convention for proposing amendments, which, in either case, shall be valid to all intents and purposes, as part of this Constitution, when ratified by the legislatures of three-fourths of the several states, or by conventions in three-fourths thereof, as the one or the other mode of ratification may be proposed by the Congress: Provided, that no amendment which may be made prior to the year 1808, shall in any manner affect the first and fourth clauses in the ninth section of the first article; and that no state, without its consent, shall be deprived of its equal suffrage in the Senate.

ARTICLE VI

All debts contracted and engagements entered into, before the adoption of this Constitution, shall be as valid against the United States under this Constitution, as under the Confederation.

This Constitution, and the laws of the United States which shall be made in pursuance thereof; and all treaties made, or which shall be made, under the authority of the United States, shall be the supreme law of the land; and the judges in every state shall be bound thereby, any thing in the constitution or laws of any state to the contrary notwithstanding.

The senators and representatives before-mentioned, and the members of the several state legislatures, and all executive and judicial officers, both of the United States and of the several states, shall be bound by oath or affirmation, to support this Constitution; but no religious test shall ever be required as a qualification to any office or public trust under the United States.

ARTICLE VII

The ratification of the conventions of nine states, shall be sufficient for the establishment of this Constitution between the states so ratifying the same.

Done in convention, by the unanimous consent of the states present, the 17th day of September, in the year of our Lord 1787, and of the independence of the United States of America the 12th. In witness whereof we have hereunto subscribed our names.

George Washington, President,
And Deputy from Virginia.

New Hampshire	John Langdon, Nicholas Gilman.
Massachusetts	Nathaniel Gorham, Rufus King.
Connecticut	William Samuel Johnson, Roger Sherman.
New York	Alexander Hamilton.
New Jersey	William Livingston, David Brearly, William Paterson, Jonathan Dayton.
Pennsylvania	Benjamin Franklin, Thomas Mifflin, Robert Morris, George Clymer, Thomas Fitzsimmons, Jared Ingersoll, James Wilson, Gouveneur Morris.
Delaware	George Read, Gunning Bedford, jun., John Dickinson, Richard Bassett, Jacob Broom.
Maryland	James McHenry, Daniel of St .Thomas Jenifer, Daniel Carroll.

Virginia	John Blair, James Madison, jun.
North Carolina	William Blount, Richard Dodds Spaight, Hugh Williamson.
South Carolina	John Rutledge, Charles Cotesworth Pinckney, Charles Pinckney, Pierce Butler.
Georgia	William Few, Abraham Baldwin.
Attest:	William Jackson, Secretary.

AMENDMENTS TO THE CONSTITUTION

ARTICLE I

Congress shall make no law respecting an establishment of religion, or prohibiting the free exercise thereof; or abridging the freedom of speech or of the press; or the right of the people peaceably to assembly, and to petition the government for a redress of grievances.

ARTICLE II

A well-regulated militia being necessary to the security of a free state, the right of the people to keep and bear arms shall not be infringed.

ARTICLE III

No soldier shall, in time of peace, be quartered in any house without the consent of the owner, nor in time of war but in a manner to be prescribed by law.

ARTICLE IV

The right of the people to be secure in their persons, houses, papers, and effects, against unreasonable searches and seizures, shall not be violated, and no warrants shall issue but upon probable cause, supported by oath or affirmation, and particularly describing the place to be searched, and the persons or things to be seized.

ARTICLE V

No person shall be held to answer for a capital or otherwise infamous crime unless on a presentment or indictment of a grand jury, except in cases arising in the land or naval forces, or in the militia, when in actual service, in time of war or public danger; nor shall any person be subject for the same offence to be twice put in jeopardy of life or limb; nor shall be compelled in any criminal case to be a witness against himself, nor be deprived of life, liberty, or property, without due process of law; nor shall private property be taken for public use without just compensation.

ARTICLE VI

In all criminal prosecutions, the accused shall enjoy the right to a speedy and public trial, by an impartial jury of the state and district wherein the crime shall have been committed, which district shall have been previously ascertained by law, and to be informed of the nature and cause of the accusation; to be confronted with the witnesses against him; to have compulsory process for obtaining witnesses in his favor, and to have the assistance of counsel for his defence.

ARTICLE VII

In suits at common law, where the value in controversy shall exceed twenty dollars, the right of trial by jury shall be preserved, and no fact tried by a jury shall be otherwise re-examined in any court of the United States than according to the rules of the common law.

ARTICLE VIII

Excessive bail shall not be required, nor excessive fines imposed, nor cruel and unusual punishments inflicted.

ARTICLE IX

The enumeration in the Constitution of certain rights shall not be construed to deny or disparage others retained by the people.

ARTICLE X

The powers not delegated to the United States by the Constitution, nor prohibited by it to the states, are reserved to the states respectively, or to the people.

[The foregoing ten amendments were adopted at the first session of Congress, and were declared to be in force, December 15, 1791.]

ARTICLE XI

The judicial power of the United States shall not be construed to extend to any suit in law or equity, commenced or prosecuted against one of the United States, by citizens of another state, or by citizens or subjects of any foreign state.

[Declared in force, January 8, 1798.]

ARTICLE XII

The electors shall meet in their respective states, and vote by ballot for President and Vice-President, one of whom at least shall not be an inhabitant of the same state with themselves; they shall name in their ballots the person voted for as President, and in distinct ballots the person voted for as Vice-President; and they shall make distinct lists of all persons voted for as President, and of all persons voted for as Vice-President, and of the number of votes for each, which lists they shall sign and certify, and transmit, sealed, to the seat of the government of the United States directed to the president of the Senate; the president of the Senate shall, in the presence of the Senate and House of Representatives, open all the certificates, and the votes shall then be counted; the person having the greatest number of votes for President shall be the President, if such number be a majority of the whole number of electors appointed; and if no person have such majority, then from the persons having the highest numbers not exceeding three, on the list of those voted for as President, the House of Representatives shall choose immediately, by ballot, the President. But in choosing the President, the votes shall be taken by states, the representation from each state having one vote; a quorum for this purpose shall consist of a member or members from two-thirds of the states, and a majority of all the states shall be necessary to a choice. And if the House of Representatives shall not choose a President, whenever the right of choice shall devolve upon them, before the fourth day of March next following, then the Vice-President shall act as President, as in the case of the death or other constitutional disability of the President. The person having the greatest number of votes as Vice-President shall be the Vice-President, if such number be a majority of the whole number of electors appointed, and if no person have a majority, then from the two highest numbers on the list the Senate shall choose the Vice-President; a quorum for the purpose shall consist of two-thirds of the whole number of senators, and a majority of the whole number shall be necessary to a choice. But no person constitutionally ineligible to the office of President shall be eligible to that of Vice-President of the United States.

[Declared in force, September 25, 1804.]

ARTICLE XIII

Section 1. Neither slavery nor involuntary servitude, except as a punishment for crime whereof the party shall have been duly convicted, shall exist within the United States, or any place subject to their jurisdiction.

Section 2. Congress shall have power to enforce this article by appropriate legislation.

[Declared in force, December 18, 1865.]

ARTICLE XIV

Section 1. All persons born or naturalized in the United States, and subject to the jurisdiction thereof, are citizens of the United States and of the state wherein they reside. No state shall make or enforce any law which shall abridge the privileges or immunities of citizens of the United States; nor shall any state deprive any person of life, liberty, or property without due process of law; nor deny to any person within its jurisdiction the equal protection of the laws.

Section 2. Representatives shall be apportioned among the several states according to their respective numbers, counting the whole number of persons in each state, excluding Indians not taxed. But when the right to vote at any election for the choice of electors for President and Vice-President of the United States, representatives in Congress, the executive and judicial officers of a state, or the members of the legislature thereof, is denied to any of the male members of such state being of twenty-one years of age, and citizens of the United States or in any way abridged, except for participation in rebellion or other crime, the basis of representation therein shall be reduced in the proportion which the number of such male citizens shall bear to the whole number of male citizens twenty-one years of age in such state.

Section 3. No person shall be a senator or representative in Congress, or elector of President and Vice-President, or hold any office, civil or military, under the United States, or under any state, who, having previously taken an oath, as a member of Congress, or as an officer of the United States, or as a member of any state legislature, or as an executive or judicial officer of any state, to support the Constitution of the United States, shall have engaged in insurrection or rebellion against the same, or given aid and comfort to the enemies thereof. But Congress may, by a vote of two-thirds of each House, remove such disability.

Section 4. The validity of the public debt of the United States, authorized by law, including debts incurred for payment of pensions and bounties for services in suppressing insurrection or rebellion, shall not be questioned. But neither the United States nor any state shall assume or pay any debt or obligation incurred in aid of insurrection or rebellion against the United States, or any claim for the loss or emancipation of any slave; but all such debts, obligations, and claims shall be held illegal and void.

Section 5. The Congress shall have power to enforce, by appropriate legislation, the provisions of this article.

[Declared in force, July 23, 1868.]

ARTICLE XV

Section 1. The right of the citizens of the United States to vote shall not be denied or abridged by the United States or by any state, on account of race, color, or previous condition of servitude.

Section 2. The Congress shall have power to enforce this article by appropriate legislation.

[Declared in force, March 30, 1870.]

ARTICLE XVI

The Congress shall have power to lay and collect taxes on incomes, from whatever source derived, without apportionment among the several states, and without regard to any census or enumeration.

[Declared in force, February 25, 1913.]

ARTICLE XVII

The Senate of the United States shall be composed of two senators from each state, elected by the people thereof for six years; and each senator shall have one vote. The electors in each state shall have the qualifications requisite for electors of the most numerous branch of the state legislatures.

When vacancies happen in the representation of any state in the senate, the executive authority of such state shall issue writs of election to fill such vacancies; provided, that the legislature of any state may empower the executive thereof to make temporary appointments until the people fill the vacancies by election as the legislature may direct.

This amendment shall not be so construed as to affect the election or term of any senator chosen before it becomes valid as part of the Constitution.

[Declared in force, May 31, 1913.]

ARTICLE XVIII

Section 1. After one year from the ratification of this article the manufacture, sale, or transportation of intoxicating liquors within, the importation thereof into, or exportation thereof from the United States and all territory subject to the jurisdiction thereof, for beverage purposes is hereby prohibited.

Section 2. The Congress and the several states shall have concurrent power to enforce this article by appropriate legislation.

Section 3. This article shall be inoperative unless it shall have been ratified as an amendment to the Constitution by the legislatures of the several states, as provided in the Constitution, within seven years from the date of submission hereof to the states by the Congress.

[Declared in force, January 29, 1919; repealed by Twenty-first Amendment.]

ARTICLE XIX

The right of the citizens of the United States to vote shall not be denied or abridged by the United States or by any state on account of sex.

Congress shall have power to enforce this article by appropriate legislation.

[Declared in force, August 26, 1920.]

ARTICLE XX

Section 1. The terms of the President and Vice-President shall end at noon on the 20th day of January, and the terms of senators and representatives at noon on the 3rd day of January, of the years in which such terms would have ended if this article had not been ratified; and the terms of their successors shall then begin.

Section 2. The Congress shall assemble at least once in every year, and such meeting shall begin at noon on the 3rd day of January, unless they shall by law appoint a different day.

Section 3. If, at the time fixed for the beginning of the term of President, the President elect shall have died, the

Vice-President elect shall become President. If a President shall not have been chosen before the time fixed for the beginning of his term, or if the President elect shall have failed to qualify, then the Vice-President elect shall act as President until a President shall have qualified; and the Congress may by law provide for the case wherein neither a President elect nor a Vice-President elect shall have qualified, declaring who shall then act as President, or the manner in which one who is to act shall be selected, and such person shall act accordingly until a President or Vice-President shall have qualified.

Section 4. The Congress may by law provide for the case of the death of any of the persons from whom the House of Representatives may choose a President, wherever the right of choice shall have devolved upon them, and for the case of the death of any of the persons from whom the Senate may choose a Vice-President, whenever the right of choice shall have devolved upon them.

Section 5. Sections 1 and 2 shall take effect on the 15th day of October following the ratification of this article.

Section 6. This article shall be inoperative unless it shall have been ratified as an amendment to the Constitution by the legislatures of three-fourths of the several states within seven years from the date of its submission.

[Declared in force, February 6, 1933.]

ARTICLE XXI

Section 1. The eighteenth article of amendment to the Constitution of the United States is hereby repealed.

Section 2. The transportation or importation into any state, territory, or possession of the United States, for delivery or use therein of intoxicating liquors, in violation of the laws thereof, is hereby prohibited.

Section 3. This article shall be inoperative unless it shall have been ratified as an amendment to the Constitution by conventions in the several states, as provided in the Constitution, within seven years from the date of the submission hereof to the states by the Congress.

[Declared in force, December 5, 1933.]

ARTICLE XXII

No person shall be elected to the office of the President more than twice, and no person who has held the office of President, or acted as President, for more than two years of a term to which some other person was elected President shall be elected to the office of the President more than once. But this article shall not apply to any person holding the office of President when this article was proposed by the Congress, and shall not prevent any person who may be holding the office of President, or acting as President, during the term within which this article becomes operative from holding the office of President or acting as President during the remainder of such term.

[Declared in force, February 26, 1951.]

ARTICLE XXIII

Section 1. The District constituting the seat of government of the United States shall appoint in such manner as the Congress may direct: A number of electors of President and Vice-President equal to the whole number of senators and representatives in Congress to which the District would be entitled if it were a state, but in no event more than the least populous state; they shall be in addition to those appointed by the states, but they shall be considered, for the purposes of the election of President and Vice-President, to be electors appointed by a state; and they shall meet in the District and perform such duties as provided by the twelfth article of amendment.

Section 2. The Congress shall have power to enforce this article by appropriate legislation.

[Declared in force, April 3, 1961.]

THE EMANCIPATION PROCLAMATION
JANUARY 1, 1863

[ABRAHAM LINCOLN]

By The President of The United States of America: A Proclamation

Whereas, on the twenty-second day of September, in the year of our Lord one thousand eight hundred and sixty-two, a proclamation was issued by the President of the United States, containing, among other things, the following, to wit:

"That on the first day of January, in the year of our Lord one thousand eight hundred and sixty-three, all persons held as slaves within any state, or designated part of a state, the people whereof shall then be in rebellion against the United States, shall be then, thenceforward, and forever free; and the Executive government of the United States, including the military and naval authority thereof, will recognize and maintain the freedom of such persons, and will do no act or acts to repress such persons, or any of them, in any efforts they may make for their actual freedom.

"That the Executive will, on the first day of January aforesaid, by proclamation, designate the states and parts of states, if any, in which the people thereof respectively shall then be in rebellion against the United States; and the fact that any state, or the people thereof, shall on that day be in good faith represented in the Congress of the United States by members chosen thereto at elections wherein a majority of the qualified voters of such state shall have participated, shall in the absence of strong countervailing testimony be deemed conclusive evidence that such state and the people thereof are not then in rebellion against the United States."

Now, therefore, I, Abraham Lincoln, President of the United States, by virtue of the power in me vested as commander-in-chief of the army and navy of the United States, in time of actual armed rebellion against the authority and government of the United States, and as a fit and necessary war measure for suppressing said rebellion, do, on this first day of January, in the year of our Lord one thousand eight hundred and sixty-three, and in accordance with my purpose so to do, publicly proclaim for the full period of 100 days from the day first above mentioned, order and designate as the states and parts of states wherein the people thereof, respectively, are this day in rebellion against the United States, the following, to wit:

Arkansas, Texas, Louisiana (except the parishes of St. Bernard, Plaquemines, Jefferson, St. John, St. Charles, St. James, Ascension, Assumption, Terre Bonne, Lafourche, St. Mary, St. Martin, and Orleans, including the city of New Orleans), Mississippi, Alabama, Florida, Georgia, South Carolina, North Carolina, and Virginia (except the forty-eight counties designated as West Virginia, and also the counties of Berkeley, Accomac, Northampton, Elizabeth City, York, Princess Ann, and Norfolk, including the cities of Norfolk and Portsmouth), and which excepted parts are for the present left precisely as if this proclamation were not issued.

And by virtue of the power and for the purpose aforesaid, I do order and declare that all persons held as slaves within said designated states and parts of states are, and henceforward shall be, free; and that the Executive government of the United States, including the military and naval authorities thereof, will recognize and maintain the freedom of said persons.

And I hereby enjoin upon the people so declared to be free to abstain from all violence, unless in necessary self-defense; and I recommend to them that, in all cases when allowed, they labor faithfully for reasonable wages.

And I further declare and make known that such persons of suitable condition will be received into the armed service of the United States to garrison forts, positions, stations, and other places, and to man vessels of all sorts in said service. And upon this act, sincerely believed to be an act of justice, warranted by the Constitution upon military necessity, I invoke the considerate judgment of mankind and the gracious favor of Almighty God.

THE GETTYSBURG ADDRESS
NOVEMBER 19, 1863

[ABRAHAM LINCOLN]

Four score and seven years ago our fathers brought forth on this continent, a new nation, conceived in Liberty, and dedicated to the proposition that all men are created equal.

Now we are engaged in a great civil war, testing whether that nation or any nation so conceived and so dedicated, can long endure. We are met on a great battlefield of that war. We have come to dedicate a portion of that field, as a final resting place for those who here gave their lives that that nation might live. It is altogether fitting and proper that we should do this.

But, in a larger sense, we can not dedicate—we can not consecrate—we can not hallow—this ground. The brave men, living and dead, who struggled here, have consecrated it, far above our poor power to add or detract. The world will little note, nor long remember what we say here, but it can never forget what they did here. It is for us the living, rather, to be dedicated here to the unfinished work which they who fought here have thus far so nobly advanced. It is rather for us to be here dedicated to the great task remaining before us—that from these honored dead we take increased devotion to that cause for which they gave the last full measure of devotion—that we here highly resolve that these dead shall not have died in vain—that this nation, under God, shall have a new birth of freedom—and that government of the people, by the people, for the people, shall not perish from the earth.

═══Bibliography═══

Note. This is a highly selective list of suggestions for further exploration of the topics dealt with in this book. In compiling this list a stress has been laid upon works that have been published recently and that are at the time of writing available to the general reader, especially in paperbacks.

Pre-Columbian

Paul Weatherwax, *Indian Corn in America* (New York, 1954) is a botanical study that demonstrates the Indian's major scientific achievement in the hybridization of corn, and that provides indispensable background for the understanding of cultures based upon corn production. "Moved," says the author, "by the beneficent qualities of the plant and by its beauty of color and form, the Indian . . . found time to develop around it a great culture of art, science, literature, and religion." Frank H. Cushing's own story of his Zuñi experiences is told in *My Adventures in Zuñi* (Santa Fe, N.M., 1941). A readable introduction to Cushing and the Zuñis will be found in Edmund Wilson, *Red, Black, Blonde and Olive* (New York, 1956).

First Settlements

One of the most able surveys of early colonization—though biased against the Puritans—is Charles M. Andrews, *Our Earliest Colonial Settlements* (Great Seal paperback: Ithaca, New York, 1959). For Massachusetts and Puritanism in the seventeenth century, the following are indispensable: William Haller, *The Rise of Puritanism* (Harper Torchbooks: New York, 1957); Perry Miller, *The New England Mind—The Seventeenth Century* (Beacon Press paperback: Boston, 1954); and George Lee Haskins, *Law and Authority in Early Massachusetts* (New York, 1960).

White Servants and Negro Slaves

Abbot Emerson Smith, *Colonists in Bondage: White Servitude and Convict Labor in America, 1607–1776* (Raleigh, N. C., 1947), is a comprehensive study of great value with respect to white servants in colonial times. Basil Davidson, *Black Mother: the Years of the African Slave Trade* (Boston, 1961), is invaluable, for it sets the slave trade in its place as part of African history, and not merely as an event in the American past. Another recent work on the same subject, Daniel P. Mannix and Malcolm Cowley, *Black Cargoes* (New York, 1962), concentrates on the Atlantic traffic itself. Operating on a purely descriptive level, these authors do not treat the forces that brought about the rise of the trade and also made for its decline. But theirs is a pioneer work in that it supplies in abundant detail those elementary facts about this traffic which have hitherto been unavailable to the general reader.

The Great Awakening

This subject is a somewhat neglected aspect of the American past that awaits the pen of the historian. Jonathan Edwards' essay on *The Nature of True Virtue*, composed in 1755, is available as an Ann Arbor paperback (Ann Arbor, Michigan, 1960). His life and thought is treated in Ola Elizabeth Winslow, *Jonathan Edwards 1703–1758* (Collier Books paperback: New York, 1961), and in Perry Miller, *Jonathan Edwards* (Meridian paperback: New York, 1961). Edwin Scott Gaustad, *The Great Awakening in New England* (New York, 1957), is a helpful survey. An extremely detailed and important work on the same subject is C. C. Goen, *Revivalism and Separatism in New England, 1740–1800* (New Haven, 1962). Still valuable but older studies for other colonies are: Charles H. Maxson, *The Great Awakening in the Middle Colonies* (Gloucester, Mass., 1958), and Wesley Gewehr, *The Great Awakening in Virginia* (Durham, N. C., 1930). For Charles Chauncy and the Arminian revolt against orthodox Calvinist doctrine in the eighteenth century, Conrad Wright, *The Beginnings of Unitarianism in America* (Boston, 1955), is to be highly recommended.

The French and Indian Wars

Edward P. Hamilton, *The French and Indian Wars: the story of battles and forts in the wilderness* (New York, 1962), is a one volume treatment of value for those without time for the voluminous older works. Consult also Howard H. Peckham, *Pontiac and the Indian Uprising* (Phoenix Books: Chicago, 1961).

The American Revolution

Recent years have seen the publication, or re-issuing, of a number of excellent works dealing with the origins of the Revolution in colonial times; unhappily only a few of these have as yet been issued in paperback, notably Charles M. Andrews, *The Colonial Background of the American Revolution* (Yale paperback: New Haven, 1961) and Bernhard Knollenberg, *Origin of the American Revolution 1759–1766* (Macmillan paperback: New York, 1961). Among the hardcover books Lawrence Henry Gipson, *The Coming of the Revolution 1763–1775* (New York, 1954), is a useful narrative of the unfolding of events in the period indicated; and O. M. Dickerson, *The Navigation Acts and the American Revolution* (Philadelphia, 1951), puts to rest the old thesis that the Acts of Navigation as such were the main factor responsible for the disruption of the British Empire.

Thomas Paine's *Common Sense* is available in a Doubleday Dolphin paperback (New York, n.d.). Provocative commentary on the Declaration of Independence will be found in Carl Becker's study of that title (Vintage paperback: New York, 1958). A most stimulating essay on the wider significance of the revolutionary struggle is J. Franklin Jameson, *The American Revolution considered as a Social Movement* (Beacon paperback: Boston, 1962); however this work should not have been re-issued without incorporating into it a critique of its thesis in the light of the historical research undertaken since it was first propounded in 1925.

The Revolutionary War has given rise to a number of good popular treatments. Probably the best of these, in terms of clarity of writing, competence of treatment and excellence of sketch maps, is Lynn Montross, *Rag, Tag, and Bobtail—the Story of the Continental Army, 1775–83* (New York, 1952).

Another good brief treatment is John Richard Alden, *The American Revolution, 1775–83* (New York, 1954). As for a full scale documentary history of the Revolution, it is sad to record that there is none available: Frank Moore's pioneer *Diary of the Revolution* has been out of print now for nearly one hundred years. George F. Scheer and Hugh F. Rankin, *Rebels and Redcoats* (Mentor Books: New York, 1959), provides a miscellany of quotations from participants in the military struggle, but it ignores the social and political life of the period. Much better as an introduction to the period is Richard M. Dorson, ed., *America Rebels* (Pantheon Books: New York, 1953), and Thomas Dring, *Recollections of the Jersey Prison Ship* (Corinth Books: New York, 1961).

There are many studies of Jefferson, but two only will be mentioned here: Daniel J. Boorstin's excellent study of the Jeffersonian mind, *The Lost World of Thomas Jefferson* (Beacon paperback: Boston, 1960); and Nathan Schachner, *Thomas Jefferson* (New York, 1957), useful for its detailed factual reference (shortly promised in paperback).

Federalists and Anti-Federalists

There is an excellent paperback edition of the *Federalist Papers* edited by Clinton Rossiter (Mentor Books: New York, 1961). Unfortunately no one has yet edited an edition of anti-Federalist writings, and this is far more necessary than the proliferation of editions of the *Federalist* with which we are currently being deluged. There is a scholarly but dull analysis by Jackson Turner Main: *The Anti-Federalists* (Raleigh, N. C., 1961).

The most interesting discussion of early American foreign policy will be found in a recent monograph by Felix Gilbert: *To the Farewell Address* (Princeton, N. J., 1961). The diplomacy of the period is discussed with a maximum of factual detail and a minimum of theory in two books by Samuel Flagg Bemis: *The Diplomacy of the American Revolution* (Midland Books paperback: Bloomington, Indiana, 1960), and *Pinckney's Treaty: America's Advantage from Europe's Distress 1783–1800* (Yale paperback: New Haven, 1960).

Three invaluable recent monographs cover a great deal of the history of Federalist and Jeffersonian political organization: Noble E. Cunningham, *The Jeffersonian Republicans*

(Raleigh, N. C., 1957); Stephen G. Kurtz, *The Presidency of John Adams* (Philadelphia, 1957); and Shaw Livermore, Jr., *The Twilight of Federalism* (Princeton, N.J., 1962). A useful biography of Alexander Hamilton is available in paperback by Nathan Schachner (A. P. Barnes paperback: New York, 1961). Charles Beard's interpretation of the Federalists is available in two paperbacks: *An Economic Interpretation of the Constitution of the United States* (Macmillan paperbacks: New York, 1961), and *The Supreme Court and the Constitution* (Spectrum Books: Englewood Cliffs, N.J., 1962).

The Industrial Revolution

Paul Mantoux' classic study of the revolutionary social, economic, and technological changes in eighteenth-century England, and the beginning of the modern factory system, *The Industrial Revolution in the Eighteenth Century*, is available in an English edition (Jonathan Cape: London, 1961). A number of excellent paperbacks illuminate the impact of these changes upon the American scene: Jeanette Mirsky and Allan Nevins, *The World of Eli Whitney: a full-scale portrait of the father of mass production* (Collier Books: New York, 1962); Ivor B. Hart, *James Watt and the History of Steam Power* (Collier Books: New York, 1961); Roger Burlingame, *March of the Iron Men: a social history of union through invention* (Universal Library: New York, 1938); James Thomas Flexner, *Inventors in Action: the story of the steamboat* (Collier Books: New York, 1962); Dirk J. Struik, *Yankee Science in the Making* (Collier Books: New York, 1962); and John F. Stover, *American Railroads* (Chicago, 1961).

Immigration (1814–60)

A standard work, Marcus Lee Hansen, *The Atlantic Migration of 1670-1860* is available in paperback (Harper Torchbooks: New York, 1961). It provides much valuable information, but is not an adequate treatment of the forces that drove people to emigrate. For the background of Irish immigration, see Edmund Curtis' superb *History of Ireland* (University paperback: New York, 1961). Much fascinating and useful information may be found in George W. Potter, *To the*

Golden Door: the story of the Irish in Ireland and America (Boston, 1960). The famine itself has been the subject of a recent full-scale study: Cecil Woodham-Smith, *The Great Hunger* (New York, 1963). British immigration in this period is treated in some detail in Rowland T. Berthoff, *British Immigrants in Industrial America 1790-1950* (Cambridge, Mass., 1953).

The Transcendental Revolt

Invaluable for a general picture of the Jacksonian reform movement is Alice Felt Tyler, *Freedom's Ferment* (Harper Torchbooks: New York, 1962). The background and the origins of Unitarianism are dealt with very effectively in Conrad Wright, *Unitarianism in America* previously cited. *Three Prophets of Religious Liberalism: Channing, Emerson, Parker* (Beacon paperback: Boston, 1961), edited by the same author, makes cheaply available to the modern reader three classic sermons of the religious liberals. There are a number of useful biographies of William Ellery Channing, but Arthur W. Brown's *William Ellery Channing* (College and University Press paperback: New Haven, 1961) is the only one that need be mentioned here. On the wider question of the Transcendental Movement, Octavius Brooks Frothingham, *Transcendentalism in New England: a History* (Harper Torchbooks: New York, 1959), and F. O. Matthiessen, *American Renaissance: Art and Expression in the Age of Emerson and Whitman* (New York. 1954), are still perhaps the best introductions. Works of Whitman, Melville, Hawthorne, Thoreau and others are abundantly available in cheap editions. The writings of Ripley, brilliant essayist and author, still await an editor.

Slavery and Civil Rights

The best, most dispassionate survey of the institution of slavery is Kenneth Stampp, *The Peculiar Institution* (New York, 1956), and it may be supplemented with the following modern editions of contemporary accounts: Frederick Law Olmsted, *The Cotton Kingdom* ed. Arthur M. Schlesinger (New York, 1953); Frances Anne Kemble, *Journal of a Residence on a Georgian Plantation in 1838-9*, ed. John Anthony

Scott (New York, 1961); and *The Life and Times of Frederick Douglass* (Collier Books: New York, 1962). William Sumner Jenkins, *Pro-Slavery Thought in the Old South* (Chapel Hill, N.C., 1935), is a first-rate introduction to the literature and ideology of the South in the ante-bellum period.

There is no single work that encompasses even the most general introduction to the antislavery movement, 1830-60, with the possible exception of two books: Dwight Lowell Dumond, *Antislavery: the Crusade for Freedom in America* (Ann Arbor, Michigan, 1961), and Louis Filler, *The Crusade against Slavery 1830-60* (New York, 1960). The former of these has factual and descriptive material of value, but it is an enormously expensive work, and so biased against the New England contribution that it is of minimal value as a contribution to the theory and philosophy of the antislavery movement. Filler's book is a mine of information about people, but again, attempts no theoretical analysis. The selected bibliography omits even the most important of the modern monographs.

There is a superb study of the problems confronting the free Negro in Leon F. Litwack, *North of Slavery—the Negro in the Free States 1790-1860* (Chicago, 1961). Russel Nye has a useful brief biography of William Lloyd Garrison (New York, 1955), and Lawrence Lader, *The Bold Brahmins* (New York, 1961), gives a rapid survey of antislavery struggles, primarily in Boston, in the period 1831-63. The work of making the great writings of antislavery leaders once more available to the public still remains to be done. A fine contribution to this task are Louis Ruchames' documentary collections, *A John Brown Reader*, and *The Abolitionists* (New York, 1959 and 1963 respectively).

Union and Secession, 1849–63

John Caldwell Calhoun, a major figure in American history, has not been accorded by biographers the attention that he deserves. By far the best introduction to him as a political thinker is Gerald M. Capers, *John C. Calhoun: a Reappraisal* (Gainesville, Florida, 1960).

As for the Compromise of 1850, the best place to study it is still in the Congressional debates from January to September, 1850. Helpful background is provided by Holman Hamilton, *Zachary Taylor: Soldier in the White House* (New York, 1951). The national reaction to the Fugitive Slave Law of 1850—part of the Compromise of that year—is best studied in Harriet Beecher Stowe, *Uncle Tom's Cabin* (Washington Square Press paperback: New York, 1963). Russel Nye's estimate of Mrs. Stowe's novel (Introduction, p. xvii) as "not a major novel on the level of *Moby Dick* or *The Scarlet Letter* or *Huck Finn*" is an estimate with which one may disagree. Neither Nye nor Kenneth S. Lynn in the Harvard University Press edition of the *Cabin* (1962) attempts a fundamental reappraisal of the novel in the context of the times that produced it. This is to be regretted, for anyone who wishes to comprehend the decade of the 1850's must read and reread Mrs. Stowe's work. It is not only an excellent novel— with occasional lapses into maudlin sentimentality—but it gives us the literal truth about slavery as the American people came to understand it in the immediate years before the Civil War.

The story of Kansas and its relationship to the developing battle between Democrats and Republicans is effectively handled—from different points of view—in Samuel A. Johnson, *The Battle Cry of Freedom* (Lawrence, Kansas, 1954), and Alice Nichols, *Bleeding Kansas* (New York, 1954). As for the Lincoln-Douglas debates of 1858, no definitive modern edition with adequate historical commentary exists. Paul M. Angle ed. *Created Equal? The Complete Lincoln-Douglas Debates of 1858* (Chicago, 1958), fills the gap for the time being. There is no life of Douglas in print.

No attempt can be made to review the literature on Lincoln that is presently available to the public. Probably the best one-volume biography is Benjamin P. Thomas, *Abraham Lincoln* (New York, 1952). For the rest, little written about Lincoln compares in vitality to what he wrote himself. A complete modern edition of his speeches and writings is available, edited by Roy P. Basler and others, *The Collected Works of Abraham Lincoln* (Rutgers, N.J., 1953-5), 9 vols. This ought to be in all public and school libraries. Also useful is a three-volume condensation of Carl Sandburg's multivolume work: *Abraham Lincoln, The Prairie Years and the War Years* (Laurel paperback: New York, 1960).

On the battles of the Civil War, Fletcher Pratt, *A Short History of the Civil War* (Pocket Books: New York, 1956), is a classic. But both it and the more detailed Harry Hansen, *The Civil War* (Mentor paperbacks: New York, 1961), are handicapped by lack of adequate maps. Among the hardcover books there is nothing better, as an introduction, than Bruce Catton, *This Hallowed Ground* (New York, 1956); the sketch maps are excellent, but too few. The Southern story during the war may be followed in Clement Eaton, *A History of the Southern Confederacy* (Collier Books: New York, 1961), though the total absence of maps is here deplorable. Henry Steele Commager gives a valuable documentary introduction to the war in *The Blue and the Gray* (New York, 1950). The human side of the struggle is movingly conveyed in *Walt Whitman's Civil War,* edited by Walter Lowenfels (New York, 1960).

On the Negro soldier's contribution to the struggle for freedom, see Dudley Taylor Cornish, *The Sable Arm: Negro Troops in the Union Army* (New York, 1956), and Benjamin Quarles, *The Negro in the Civil War* (Boston, 1953). Thomas Wentworth Higginson, *Army Life in a Black Regiment* (East Lansing, Michigan, 1960), is a modern edition of a Civil War classic written by the colonel in charge of the First South Carolina Volunteers. Robert Gould Shaw is mentioned in these writings. There is as yet no work devoted specially to his role in the war, but one is promised from the pen of Peter Burchard.

Songs

Recordings of a number of the songs reproduced in this book are available.

Scarborough Fair	Ewan McColl, *Matching Songs of the British Isles and America.* Riverside Folklore Series, 12-637
The Two Sisters	Cynthia Gooding, *The Queen of Hearts.* Elektra 131
The Cherry Tree Carol	Cynthia Gooding, *Faithful Lovers.* Elektra 107

Old Hundred	Margaret Dodd Singers *Early American Psalmody*. New Records Inc., 2007
Déirin Dé	Gráinne Ní Eigeartaigh, *Irish Folk Songs*. Spoken Arts 206.
Katie Cruel	Bill and Gene Bonyun, *Yankee Legend*. Heirloom 500
Sinner Man	The Weavers, *Travelling on with the Weavers*. Vanguard, 9043 (variant). The Harvesters on *Pastures of Plenty* (Folkways Record 2406) sing this song in the same way.
Springfield Mountain	The old, serious version of the song reproduced in this book has not been recorded. A version of the song offered by *Life* as "an early example of an original American ballad" *(The New World*. Record I) is a Boston stage version that did not make an appearance until the 1830's.
Montcalm and Wolfe	The version reproduced here has not been recorded. Another version is given by: Frank Warner, *Songs and Ballads of America's Wars*. Elektra 13
Young Ladies in Town *The Rich Lady over the Sea* *The Folks on t'Other Side the Wave* *British Lamentation*	Bill and Gene Bonyun, John Anthony Scott, *The American Revolution through its Songs and Ballads*. Heirloom 502

Jefferson and Liberty	Ed McCurdy, *American History in Ballad and Song.* Folkways Records 5801
Constitution and Guerrière *The Hunters of Kentucky*	Wallace House, *The War of 1812.* Folkways Records 5002
Johnny Bull my jo John	*John Anderson My jo*—the original Scots version of this song— is sung by: Betty Sanders, *Songs of Robert Burns.* Riverside Specialty Series 12-823
All the Pretty Little Horses	Alan Lomax, *Texas Folksongs.* Tradition Records 1029
Freedom, oh Freedom	Odetta, *Ballads and Blues.* Tradition Records 1010 (an original version of a great song by a truly great singer). Recordings of the other slave songs and spirituals reproduced in this book either have not been made or are unobtainable.
The Greenland Whale *Fishery*	Bill Bonyun, *Songs of Yankee Whaling.* Heirloom (an outstanding record by an authority on songs of the sea).
Across the Western Ocean *(Leave her, Johnny)*	Paul Clayton, *Fo'c'sle Songs and Shanties.* Folkways Records 2429
Low Bridge, Everybody *Down*	Clarence Cooper, *American Folksongs.* Elektra 27

Paddy Works on the Railroad	Fieldston School Assembly,
Deirin Dé	*Irish Immigration through its Songs and Ballads.* Heirloom Ed. 2
Santy Anno	Odetta, *Ballads and Blues.* Tradition 1010.
Song of the Mississippi Volunteers	All these songs are given on: Frank Warner, Bill Bonyun and others,
John Brown of Massachusetts	
General Lee's Wooing	*The Civil War through its Songs and Ballads.* Heirloom 503.
Many Thousand Gone (Auction Block)	
The First of Arkansas	
Roll, Alabama Roll	

ERRATA

Psalm 100 (p. 66). Read G for F, last note, stave 2.

Low Bridge (pp. 457-8). Read D for C, first note, fifth bar of chorus.

Greenland Whale Fisheries (p. 453). Read E for F, first note of penultimate bar.